Lecture Notes in Computer Science 16610

The series Lecture Notes in Computer Science (LNCS), including its subseries Lecture Notes in Artificial Intelligence (LNAI) and Lecture Notes in Bioinformatics (LNBI), has established itself as a medium for the publication of new developments in computer science and information technology research, teaching, and education.

LNCS enjoys close cooperation with the computer science R & D community, the series counts many renowned academics among its volume editors and paper authors, and collaborates with prestigious societies. Its mission is to serve this international community by providing an invaluable service, mainly focused on the publication of conference and workshop proceedings and postproceedings. LNCS commenced publication in 1973.

Zhaoyu Liu · Vishal Misra
Editors

Sports Analytics

Third International Conference, ISACE 2026
Vancouver, BC, Canada, June 1–2, 2026
Proceedings

Springer

Editors
Zhaoyu Liu
National University of Singapore
Singapore, Singapore

Vishal Misra
Columbia University
New York, NY, USA

ISSN 0302-9743 ISSN 1611-3349 (electronic)
Lecture Notes in Computer Science
ISBN 978-3-032-27271-3 ISBN 978-3-032-27272-0 (eBook)
https://doi.org/10.1007/978-3-032-27272-0

This Springer imprint is published by the registered company Springer Nature Switzerland AG
The registered company address is: Gewerbestrasse 11, 6330 Cham, Switzerland

Preface

Sports analytics is the application of AI, data science, psychology, and smart devices to improve sports performance, strategy, and decision-making. It involves collecting, processing, and interpreting data from various sources such as video footage, performance metrics, wearable sensors, and scouting reports, and using this information to gain insights into player and team performance, prevent injury, and help coaches and team managers make more informed decisions and optimize their resources to achieve better results.

The vision of the International Sports Analytics Conference and Exhibition (ISACE) series is to bring leading academics, researchers, coaches, psychologists, managers, and technologists together to advance the state of the art of sports analytics.

ISACE 2026 – the 3rd edition of ISACE – was hosted in Vancouver, Canada, on June 1–2, 2026, ahead of the 2026 FIFA World Cup. ISACE 2026 received 74 submissions covering both theory and applications in sports analytics. Papers were reviewed based on originality, technical quality, relevance to the conference, methodological soundness, significance, and clarity. Most papers received three single-blind reviews, while a small fraction received two reviews. Acceptance decisions were made based on the review scores and reviewer comments; only papers with at least one positive recommendation and an overall positive evaluation were accepted. The committee selected 29 contributed papers for inclusion in the proceedings. In addition, 2 invited papers are included in the volume. These invited papers were reviewed by the volume editors, and external expert review was sought where needed to ensure that they satisfied the quality standards of the proceedings.

This edition of ISACE was honoured to have two distinguished keynote speakers. Jin-Song Dong spoke on *Reasoning Beyond LLMs and a Vision for Life After Superintelligence: The Player Era*, where he discussed the limitations of large language models in reliable sports analytics, introduced recent work integrating probabilistic model checking, LLMs, and computer vision for principled and explainable sports analysis, and presented a broader vision of human society in the post-superintelligence era. Oliver Schulte delivered a keynote on *Ranking and Representing Hockey Players with Deep Reinforcement Learning*, in which he showed how reinforcement learning can be used to model success probabilities from sports data and support the ranking of player performance in the National Hockey League. These two keynotes covered both visionary and technical aspects of sports analytics and revealed many promising future directions.

ISACE 2026's success was due to the contribution and involvement of the program committee members, reviewers, organizers, and volunteers around the globe who supported the organization, review process, and selection of the best contributions. This event would not have been possible without the authors and invited contributors who submitted their work. We express our sincere thanks to every reviewer, author, program committee member, and organizing committee member involved in the success of ISACE 2026.

The EasyChair system was set up for the management of ISACE 2026, supporting the submission, review, and volume preparation processes. It once again proved to be a powerful and reliable tool.

Springer kindly accepted our proposal to publish the proceedings in its prestigious LNCS series. We are grateful for this continued collaboration and hope to maintain a fruitful long-term relationship in future editions of ISACE. We also thank all organizers, collaborators, and supporters whose efforts helped the conference run smoothly.

Looking into the future, we hope that ISACE will continue to grow as a premier international venue for sports analytics and will further strengthen the global community spanning academia, industry, and professional sport. We look forward to seeing everybody at future ISACE events.

June 2026

Zhaoyu Liu
Vishal Misra

Organization

General Co-chairs

Zhe Hou	Griffith University, Australia
Vishal Misra	Columbia University, USA

Program Chair

Zhaoyu Liu	National University of Singapore, Singapore

Publicity Co-chairs

Mark Huasong Meng	University College Dublin, Ireland
Henry (Yuanheng) Wang	AWS Generative AI Innovation Center, USA

Program Committee

Bimlesh Wadhwa	National University of Singapore, Singapore
Chunyang Chen	Technical University of Munich, Germany
David Saxby	Griffith Centre of Biomedical and Rehabilitation Engineering, Griffith University, Australia
Elizabeth Bradshaw	Deakin University, Australia
Hadrien Bride	Dependable Intelligence, France
Jin Song Dong	National University of Singapore, Singapore
John Komar	National Institute of Education, Nanyang Technological University, Singapore
Kan Jiang	National University of Singapore, Singapore
Lijun Guo	Ningbo University, China
Luke Wildman	RGB Assurance, Australia
Masoumeh Izadi	Television Content Analytics Pte. Ltd, Singapore
Oliver Schulte	Simon Fraser University, Canada
Sebastian Binnewies	Griffith University, Australia
Seungbok Lee	Yonsei University, South Korea
Teck Khim Ng	National University of Singapore, Singapore
Wei-Yao Wang	National Yang Ming Chiao Tung University, Taiwan

Yamine Ait Ameur	IRIT - National Polytechnic Institute of Toulouse, France
Yun Lin	Shanghai Jiao Tong University, China
Zhaoyu Liu	National University of Singapore, Singapore
Dr Zhe Hou	Griffith University, Australia
Zhiyong Huang	National University of Singapore, Singapore
Xiaofei Xie	Singapore Management University, Singapore
Mehul Raval	Ahmedabad University, India
Srikrishnan Divakaran	Krea University, India
Tolga Kaya	Sacred Heart University, USA
Daniel Bolarinwa	Accenture, UK
Rajdeep Singh Hundal	National University of Singapore, Singapore
Dileepa Fernando	Singapore University of Technology and Design, Singapore
Isuru Supasan	SLTC Research University, Sri Lanka
Karan Gupta	SunPower, USA
Raveendran Paramesran	Monash University, Malaysia
Bessam Abdulrazak	University of Sherbrooke, Canada
Steven Lin	Azra Games, USA
Tao Lin	Ethiqly, USA
Robert Moskovitch	Ben-Gurion University of the Negev, Israel
David Clausi	University of Waterloo, Canada
Ruchir Pandya	ex-Disruptive, ex-Meta, ex-NBA, USA
Siqi Hao	Huawei, Finland
Willie Harrison	Brigham Young University, USA
Matthew Caron	VfL Wolfsburg, Germany
Leili Javadpour	University of the Pacific, USA
Jacomine Grobler	Stellenbosch University, South Africa
Charles Danoff	Mr. Danoff's Teaching Laboratory, USA
Klaus Müller	Wictory.ai, Austria
Markus Unterweger	Wictory.ai, Austria
Chean Khim Toa	Xiamen University Malaysia, Malaysia
Divya Mehta	Queensland University of Technology, Australia
Haresh Suppiah	La Trobe University, Australia
Xian Song	Zhejiang University, China
Yu Xin	Ningbo University, China
Ruchika Malhotra	Delhi Technological University, India
Shaobo Cai	Shanghai Jiao Tong University, China
Roland Janos Nemes	Hosei University, Japan
Guoqing Luo	University of Alberta, Canada
Yutao Yue	Hong Kong University of Science and Technology (Guangzhou), China

Contents

Short Papers

Invited Papers

Reasoning Beyond LLMs and a Vision for Life After Superintelligence: The Player Era

Jin Song Dong[1(✉)], Zhaoyu Liu[1], Zhe Hou[2], Kan Jiang[1], and Yun Lin[3]

[1] National University of Singapore, Singapore, Singapore
{dcsdjs,liuzy,jiangkan}@nus.edu.sg
[2] Griffith University, Brisbane, Australia
z.hou@griffith.edu.au
[3] Shanghai Jiao Tong University, Shanghai, China
lin_yun@sjtu.edu.cn

Abstract. Large Language Models (LLMs) are increasingly used in sports analytics for tasks such as coaching recommendations, video analysis, and automated commentary generation. However, their outputs are not inherently reliable due to well-known hallucination issues. Probabilistic Model Checking (PMC), by contrast, has long been employed for rigorous reliability analysis in safety-critical systems. For example, the reliability of an aircraft can be systematically derived from the reliability of its constituent components, such as engines, wings, and sensors. We extend PMC to a new domain: sports analytics. Specifically, we model a player's overall performance (e.g., winning probability) as a function of the success rates of individual sub-skills, such as serve, forehand, and backhand in tennis. The first part of the talk highlights the limitations of LLMs in complex decision-making and video analytics, and presents our recent work integrating PMC, LLMs, and computer vision to enable principled and explainable sports analysis. The second part introduces a forward-looking vision for life after superintelligence, termed the Player Era. In this vision, human society evolves into four interconnected roles: Player, Explorer, Co-Creator, and Gatekeeper, forming the foundation of a civilization centered on meaning, creativity, and responsibility.

Keywords: Sports Analytics · Probabilistic Model Checking · Computer Vision · Large Language Models · Superintelligence

1 Introduction

The application of artificial intelligence in sports analytics has fundamentally shifted how athletic performance is quantified. Recently, Large Language Models (LLMs) have demonstrated significant utility in synthesizing sports narratives and providing generalized tactical advice. Nevertheless, LLMs operate primarily on statistical language patterns rather than formal logic. Consequently, they

Z. Liu and V. Misra (Eds.): ISACE 2026, LNCS 16610, pp. 3–14, 2026.
https://doi.org/10.1007/978-3-032-27272-0_1

frequently generate plausible but tactically unsound recommendations, a phenomenon known as hallucination, which precludes their use in rigorous, reliable strategy optimization (as shown in Fig. 1).

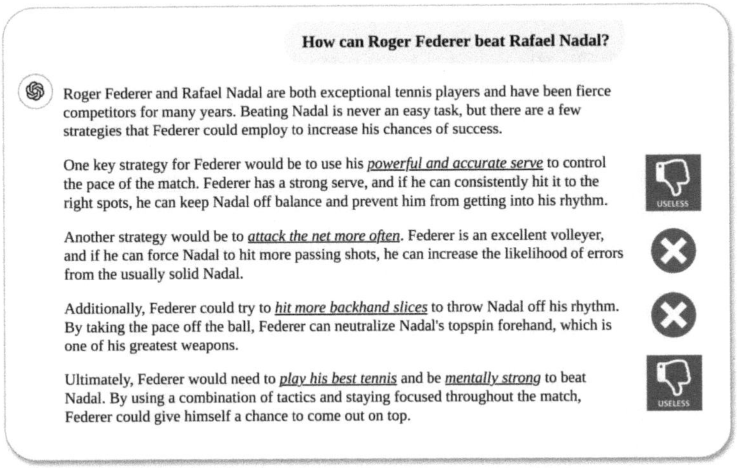

Fig. 1. Example response from GPT to a sports strategy-related question.

To overcome these limitations, we present a synthesis of our recent advancements in formal sports strategy analytics. Specifically, we adapt Probabilistic Model Checking (PMC), a formal verification method traditionally reserved for safety-critical engineering, to the domain of sports. By modeling games as Markov Decision Processes (MDPs), we calculate a player's holistic reliability (winning percentage) derived directly from the empirical reliability (success rates) of their specific sub-skills.

Because PMC necessitates highly accurate empirical distributions, we champion an **inter-disciplinary research** paradigm that bridges formal methods and deep learning. We deploy advanced computer vision architectures to autonomously extract fast, frequent, and fine-grained action sequences directly from standard broadcast footage, closing the data-reasoning loop.

The successful automation of both raw data perception and complex strategic reasoning signals a broader paradigm shift. As superintelligent systems increasingly master specialized cognitive and physical labor, the core objective of human existence will fundamentally transform. We conclude by articulating a realistic, grounded vision for this impending societal evolution: The Player Era.

2 The Technical Foundation: Reasoning Beyond LLMs

While LLMs excel at processing textual data and historical sports narratives, they lack the inherent mathematical rigor required for precise tactical optimization. For instance, when tasked with formulating a winning strategy for an elite

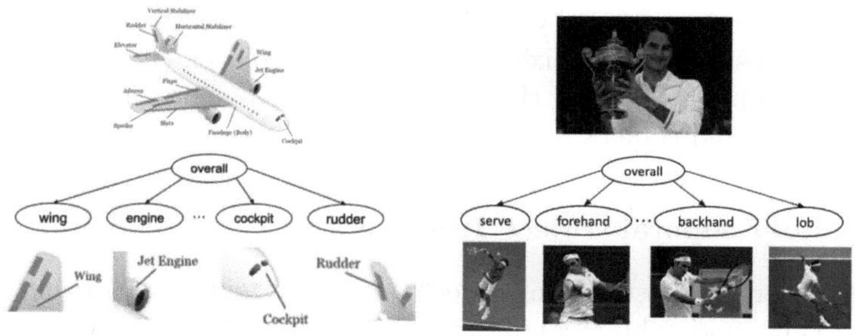

Fig. 2. Probabilistic model checking in sports (tennis).

tennis match (e.g., Federer vs. Nadal), an LLM might give suggestions that are overly generic or tactically inaccurate as shown in Fig. 1. However, it fails to quantify exactly *how much* a player should alter their serve distribution to maximize the overall probability of winning a match, nor can it provide a mathematically sound sensitivity analysis. This lack of rigorous grounding necessitates a paradigm shift towards formal methods.

Probabilistic reasoning refers to the use of probability theory to model and manage uncertainty in decision-making processes. Probabilistic Model Checking (PMC) is a formal technique traditionally used to evaluate system reliability, where overall performance is derived from component-level reliability (e.g., aircraft subsystems). Dong et al. [9] first extended this idea to sports analytics (Fig. 2). In tennis, a player's performance is modeled based on the success rates of sub-skills (e.g., forehand or backhand), estimated from historical data. These components define a probabilistic player profile, which is used to construct a Markov model capturing interactions between players.

By applying PMC to the constructed Markov model, we can calculate a player's probability of winning against a specific opponent through reachability analysis. Furthermore, by modifying the probability distributions within the model, the effects of different strategic adjustments on match outcomes can be systematically explored through sensitivity analysis [22].

3 Integrating Computer Vision for Actionable Data

The effectiveness of PMC depends on the availability of fine-grained and accurate probabilistic data. However, manual annotation is not scalable, and proprietary tracking systems are often cost-prohibitive. To address this, we adopt an interdisciplinary approach that integrates multimodal deep learning and computer vision to automatically extract precise action sequences from broadcast videos.

3.1 Robust Court Detection via Perspective Fields

Court detection maps 2D image coordinates to standardized court coordinates. Traditional homography-based methods are sensitive to noise and occlusion.

Jiang et al. [20] address this by predicting dense Perspective Fields (PF) using a CNN, which estimates per-pixel x- and y-axis displacements. This produces a robust point-to-point mapping that generalizes across sports and remains stable under occlusion and camera motion.

3.2 Spatio-Temporal Object Tracking

Tracking players and fast-moving objects, such as a tennis ball or shuttlecock, is complicated by motion blur, complex backgrounds, and frequent occlusion. Jiang et al. [21] addressed this by fusing CNN-based spatial detection with Bayesian temporal estimation. The CNN extracts spatial features to locate objects within individual frames. Simultaneously, the Bayesian estimator leverages temporal priors, utilizing the high correlation between an object's trajectory in preceding frames and its current state. This dual-stream approach effectively filters out spatial false positives and interpolates missing detections during frames with heavy occlusion or extreme velocity.

3.3 Fast, Frequent, and Fine-Grained Event Detection

To capture the exact mechanics of a game, we must precisely spot rapid actions, such as the exact frame of a racket strike and the specific stroke classification. Liu et al. [23] formalize this challenge as Fast, Frequent, and Fine-grained (F^3) event detection (Fig. 3). To overcome severe motion blur and subtle visual discrepancies, Liu et al. [24] propose an advanced architecture, the Unified Multi-Entity Graph Network (UMEG-Net). Going beyond standard spatial-temporal graph convolutions, UMEG-Net integrates human skeletal joints and sport-specific object keypoints into a unified graph. By employing multimodal distillation and correlating these enriched kinematic features with synchronized auditory impact signals, our framework achieves robust, few-shot precise event spotting. These high-fidelity outputs provide the empirical parameters required for our MDPs, completing the automated reasoning loop.

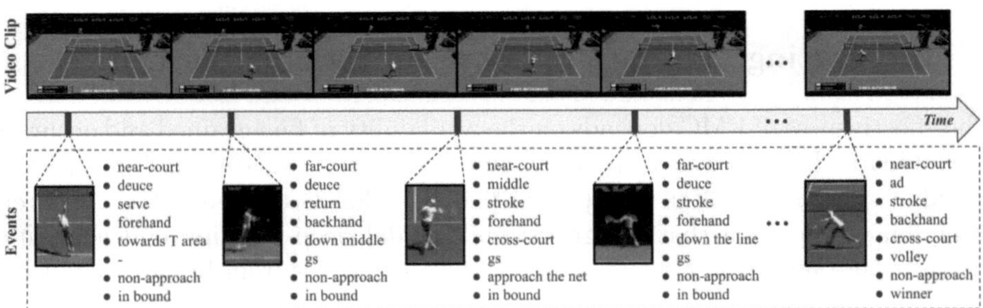

Fig. 3. Detecting fast, frequent, and fine-grained events with precise moments.

3.4 Expert-Level Multimodal Understanding and Commentary

Extracting fine-grained events is only the foundational step. Translating these raw tactical parameters into human-understandable insights bridges the critical gap between formal reasoning and practical athletic application. As a culmination of our inter-disciplinary research, Liu et al. [25] introduced TennisVL, a comprehensive multimodal framework designed for analytical sports video understanding. Unlike traditional generative systems that merely provide descriptive, play-by-play narration, TennisVL emphasizes tactical, expert-level commentary.

By fine-tuning advanced Multimodal Large Language Models (i.e., Qwen3-VL), the framework successfully synthesizes the mathematically rigorous outputs and the fine-grained visual tracking data into actionable narrative advice. This approach not only democratizes elite sports analytics but also provides transparent, expert-level analysis for athletes and coaches.

4 Life Beyond Superintelligence: The Player Era

As superintelligence surpasses human capabilities across professional domains, the central question shifts from job preservation to the redefinition of human purpose. Similar to the Industrial Revolution, this transition is not expected to eliminate human relevance, but to expand human agency by freeing individuals from routine labor and enabling new forms of creativity, exploration, and social organization. In this context, we define a new epoch: the *Player Era*, where human roles evolve from production to participation, specifically as the **Player**, **Explorer**, **Co-Creator**, and **Gate-Keeper**. Freed from survival-driven work, individuals can focus on activities that bring fulfillment, including play, discovery, and collaboration with AI systems.

This transition is already underway, with early signals evident in sports. In soccer, there are about 128,700 registered players worldwide, with 20,000–30,000 able to sustain a living [12]. In professional tennis, players ranked within the top 150 can typically break even, while golf shows similar patterns, with secondary tours averaging $112,560 [19,27]. Beyond elite athletes, participation is expanding: NCAA athletes receive scholarships [2,29], and amateur players increasingly gain support from sponsors and local organizations [13]. Similar trends appear in e-sports, where participants earn income through competitions and digital platforms [14,18]. As AI reduces the cost of basic necessities [5], the threshold for sustaining participation is expected to decline, enabling broader engagement beyond elite tiers.

A parallel can be observed in internet platforms, where barriers to entry have been lowered and participation has scaled dramatically. While only a few become global superstars, many individuals sustain modest yet viable incomes through platform-mediated ecosystems. In such an environment, individuals are no longer merely spectators but active participants across competitive and creative domains. Beyond the Player role, new identities are emerging. Explorers pursue continuous discovery, such as FIRE communities and long-term travel [32]. Co-Creators collaborate with AI to design and innovate, while Gate-Keepers ensure the safety, alignment, and fairness of increasingly powerful systems. Together, these roles provide a framework for understanding how human purpose evolves in a post-labor world, where meaning is derived not from necessity, but from participation, exploration, and creation.

4.1 The Four Roles of the New Era

As superintelligence assumes tasks required for human survival, individuals engage with life beyond traditional occupations. Human activity can be characterized by four core roles—the Player, the Explorer, the Co-Creator, and the Gate-Keeper—which are fluid and complementary. Together, these roles define how humans participate, create, and sustain purpose in the Player Era (Fig. 4).

The Player: The Foundation. At the foundation of this new era is the **Player** identity, where individuals engage in physical, digital, and social forms of play. In the Player Era, play becomes a primary mode of learning, connection, and self-discovery. Advances in automation and digital infrastructure lower the barrier to participation, enabling large-scale engagement beyond elite levels. As a result, play becomes inclusive rather than exclusive, supporting diverse levels of skill and commitment while still rewarding mastery and innovation. The Player serves as the entry point for broader human engagement in an AI-supported world.

The Explorer: Beyond Boundaries. Emerging from play, the **Explorer** is driven by curiosity and experimentation. Exploration involves engaging with

Fig. 4. Illustration of a continuous iterative cycle comprised of 3 stages: "Play", "Explore", and "Co-create". The "Gatekeeper" ensures the AI system remains aligned with humanity through rigorous verification (generated by Gemini Nano Banana).

uncertainty, where individuals seek unfamiliar environments, activities, and ideas. This behavior aligns with established theories of curiosity-driven learning [4]. With AI reducing logistical and cognitive barriers [3], exploration becomes widely accessible. Technologies such as VR enable immersive experiences [31], while emerging domains like commercial space exploration expand the frontier of human activity [28]. In this context, exploration cultivates adaptability and cross-domain understanding, forming a critical step toward creation.

The Co-Creator: Collaborating with AI. From exploration arises the **Co-Creator**, who collaborates with AI to design systems, environments, and experiences. This reflects a shift from tool usage to interactive human–AI co-creation [26,30]. AI provides scalable infrastructure through advances such as procedural content generation [17], while humans contribute intent, creativity, and judgment. Creation becomes a dynamic process of iterative interaction, where individuals shape not only artefacts but also the rules and systems that enable large-scale participation. Foundational knowledge in areas such as mathematics and probability further enhances this capability [11,15,16].

The Gate-Keeper: The Guardian of Purpose. Finally, the **Gate-Keeper** ensures the safety, reliability, and alignment of AI systems. This role is grounded in the integration of Formal Methods and Large Language Models (FM+LLM), where formal verification constrains AI behavior while LLMs improve accessibility and scalability of verification processes. Prior work demonstrates this synergy through applications such as correctness-guaranteed code generation [6] and automated model checking workflows [36], as well as broader frameworks for trustworthy AI systems [35]. By enforcing formal guarantees on safety, fairness, and correctness, the Gate-Keeper establishes principled boundaries for AI systems, enabling scalable governance while preserving human control and creativity.

4.2 Sports as the New Infrastructure of Society

Sports become a cornerstone of daily life, not merely as hobbies but as avenues for skill development, community engagement, and personal growth. Urban spaces are repurposed accordingly: streets become cycling paths, office buildings turn into gyms, and rooftops transform into small soccer fields. Beyond infrastructure, this shift also reshapes social and institutional structures.

The growing importance of sports is reflected in the rise of major conferences such as the *MIT Sloan Sports Analytics Conference* [1] and the *International Sports Analytics Conference and Exhibition (ISACE)* [7,8,10], highlighting the expanding role of sports in society.

The Expansion of Collegiate Sports. Colleges and universities, freed from preparing students for obsolete jobs, will evolve into multigenerational athletic and exploratory hubs. The NCAA (or its future equivalents) will expand into a vast, multi-tiered system:

- **Traditional Student Leagues**: College teams persist but with expanded scope and flexibility. Universities host diverse sport types beyond traditional varsity offerings, while AI-managed scheduling allows students to move across sports, skill tiers, and formats. Performance analytics provide personalized feedback, positioning sport as both training and exploratory learning.
- **Alumni Leagues (Ages 25–80)**: Alumni participation becomes central, with graduates returning for sustained athletic engagement under age- and health-adjusted conditions. Off-season scheduling keeps facilities active year-round, while AI-driven monitoring, adaptive scoring, and injury prevention support inclusive, lifelong participation.
- **Community-Integrated Divisions**: Universities act as civic sport hubs, opening facilities to local residents. Mixed-age participation becomes common, supported by AI systems that balance pace, difficulty, and competition. These divisions strengthen intergenerational connections while ensuring safety and fairness.
- **Off-Season Innovation Games**: Universities host events to prototype new sport formats, such as *Symphony Sprint*, where running pacing must synchronize with collaboratively co-created music, or *Mixed-Reality Obstacle Courses* that blend physical parkour with AR-based logic puzzles.

E-Sports: From Pastime to Universe. In this new era, e-sports will evolve beyond pre-built games into persistent universes:

- **Real-Time World Editing**: Competitive matches will take place in mutable environments. Teams might reshape terrain to block sightlines or construct defensive structures during play, with AI continuously evaluating balance and safety constraints.
- **Hybrid E-sports**: Virtual matches will blend with real-world athletic components. An avatar might gain enhanced mobility only if the player completes a real-world sprint, or a team's collective stamina pool could be dynamically tied to real-time physiological signals like heart-rate variability.
- **Persistent Team Universes**: E-sports teams will inhabit evolving worlds that persist across seasons, blending competition, world-building, and cultural identity into a single continuous experience.

Sports and E-Sports Rebuild Connection. The significance of the *Player Era* lies not only in play itself, but in its ability to rebuild human connection beyond work. In both physical and virtual settings, individuals from different ages, cultures, and backgrounds engage through shared effort rather than professions. For example, a 70-year-old professor may play table tennis with a 16-year-old prodigy, bonding despite language barriers. In virtual worlds inspired by platforms such as *Fortnite*, players from different cities collaborate to build and defend environments. Similarly, alumni leagues enable mixed-age participation, where experienced athletes and younger players compete and learn together.

Across these settings, sports and e-sports dissolve boundaries between age, profession, and geography, fostering connection through participation, collaboration, and shared experience.

4.3 Purpose After Work

Critics may question whether play alone provides meaning. However, similar concerns arise in early retirement and among professional athletes, who often retire young yet retain purpose through training, coaching, and new pursuits. Purpose does not vanish with the end of formal work.

In the Player Era, purpose is closely tied to progress, such as improving in a sport, teaching others, or creating experiences for a community. Existing systems such as the USTA rating [33] and Universal Tennis Rating (UTR) [34] already provide structured pathways for skill development. Similar progression systems extend across domains, where individuals pursue growth through participation, competition, and community engagement.

Beyond sports, a similar shift occurs in entertainment. As AI absorbs much of the technical labor of production, creative activities become increasingly participatory. Individuals move from passive consumption to active involvement, creating, remixing, and collaborating within shared environments. Platforms such as TikTok and RedNote already illustrate this transition, where the boundary between creator and audience becomes blurred.

In this setting, purpose emerges from continuous improvement, contribution, and recognition within communities. Structured systems, such as rankings, leagues, and showcases, provide guidance without restricting participation. More broadly, superintelligence does not eliminate human purpose, but enables it by removing constraints and expanding opportunities for meaningful engagement. *Superintelligence does not replace human purpose. It clears the way for it.*

4.4 Challenges Remain

The *Player Era* introduces new challenges: (1) How do we ensure equal access to facilities? (2) How do we prevent competition from becoming an obsession? (3) How do we design safe, inclusive systems for all ages?

While superintelligence can assist, it cannot determine human values. AI may support resource allocation, monitor participation, and promote fairness, but decisions about purpose and societal direction remain human responsibilities. Ultimately, the Player Era requires not only technological advances, but also new norms and policies to ensure benefits are shared and aligned with values.

5 Conclusion

This paper bridges technical challenges in AI reliability with a profound vision for human society. By integrating PMC and multimodal computer vision, we establish a mathematically rigorous sports analytics framework that overcomes LLM hallucinations. Extrapolating from this automation of complex reasoning, we introduce the *Player Era*, a post-labor epoch where superintelligence assumes our survival necessities. This liberation allows humanity to redefine its purpose through four interconnected roles: Player, Explorer, Co-Creator, and Gate-Keeper. Ultimately, superintelligence does not render us obsolete; it clears the path for a civilization centered on intrinsic progress, collaborative creation, and community, all secured by formal safeguards aligned with human values.

References

1. MIT Sloan sports analytics conference. https://www.sloansportsconference.com/
2. Akarapanagiotis: Athletic scholarships: Definition, types, tuition coverage, and key differences (2025). https://www.unicaf.org/athletic-scholarships/. Accessed 12 Dec 2025
3. Amershi, S., et al.: Guidelines for human-AI interaction. In: CHI (2019)
4. Berlyne, D.E.: Conflict, Arousal, and Curiosity. McGraw-Hill (1960)
5. Brynjolfsson, E., McAfee, A.: The Second Machine Age: Work, Progress, and Prosperity in a Time of Brilliant Technologies. W. W. Norton & Company (2014)
6. Cai, Y., et al.: Automated program refinement: guide and verify code large language model with refinement calculus. In: ACM Principles of Programming Languages (PoPL) (2025)
7. Dong, J.S., Hou, Z., Liu, Z.: Sports Analytics: Third International Conference, ISACE 2026, Vancouver, Canada, 1–2 June 2026. Springer (2026)
8. Dong, J.S., Izadi, M., Hou, Z.: Sports Analytics: First International Conference, ISACE 2024, Paris, France, 12–13 July 2024, Proceedings, vol. 14794. Springer (2024)
9. Dong, J.S., Shi, L., Jiang, K., Sun, J.: Sports strategy analytics using probabilistic reasoning. In: 20th International Conference on Engineering of Complex Computer Systems (ICECCS), pp. 182–185. IEEE (2015)
10. Dong, J.S., Sun, J., Xie, X., Jiang, K.: Sports Analytics: Second International Conference, ISACE 2025, Shanghai, China, 26–27 September 2025, Proceedings. LNCS. Springer, Cham (2025). https://books.google.com.sg/books?id=PvqN0QEACAAJ
11. Ferrini-Mundy, J.: Principles and standards for school mathematics: a guide for mathematicians. Not. Am. Math. Soc. **47**(8) (2000)
12. FIFA: FIFA professional football report 2023. Technical report (2024). https://digitalhub.fifa.com/m/2a5dc95026d9cf8a/original/FIFA-Professional-Football-Report-2023.pdf
13. Fundraising.com: Leveraging local businesses for sports team sponsorship (2023). https://fundraising.com/blog/leveraging-local-businesses-for-sports-team-sponsorship. Accessed 19 Dec 2025
14. Gevme: Esports events: How gaming tournaments are redefining the industry (2024). https://www.gevme.com/en/blog/esports-events-how-gaming-tournaments-are-redefining-the-industry/. Accessed 12 Dec 2025

15. Gigerenzer, G.: Reckoning with Risk: Learning to Live with Uncertainty. Penguin (2002)
16. Haase, J., Pokutta, S.: Human-AI co-creativity: exploring synergies across levels of creative collaboration. arXiv preprint arXiv:2411.12527 (2024)
17. Hendrikx, M., et al.: Procedural content generation for games. ACM Comput. Surv. (2013)
18. Icon-Era: Global esports revenue projections for 2025 (2025). https://icon-era.com/blog/global-esports-revenue-projections-for-2025.212/. Accessed 12 Dec 2025
19. Inspired, G.: The financial journey of Korn ferry tour players (2025). https://golfinspired.com/korn-ferry-tour-financial-journey/
20. Jiang, K., Li, J., Liu, Z., Dong, C.: Court detection using masked perspective fields network. In: 2023 IEEE 28th Pacific Rim International Symposium on Dependable Computing (PRDC), pp. 342–345. IEEE (2023)
21. Jiang, K., Liu, Z., Wu, Q., Ma, M., Dong, J.S.: Tracking small and fast moving ball in broadcast videos using transfer learning and the enhanced interactive multi-motion model. In: International Sports Analytics Conference and Exhibition, pp. 81–96. Springer (2024)
22. Liu, Z., Jiang, K., Hou, Z., Lin, Y., Dong, J.S.: Insight analysis for tennis strategy and tactics. In: 2023 IEEE International Conference on Data Mining (ICDM), pp. 1169–1174. IEEE (2023)
23. Liu, Z., Jiang, K., Ma, M., Hou, Z., Lin, Y., Dong, J.S.: F^3set: towards analyzing fast, frequent, and fine-grained events from videos. In: The Thirteenth International Conference on Learning Representations (ICLR) (2025)
24. Liu, Z., Jiang, K., Ma, M., Hou, Z., Lin, Y., Dong, J.S.: Few-shot precise event spotting via unified multi-entity graph and distillation. In: The 40th Annual AAAI Conference on Artificial Intelligence (AAAI) (2026)
25. Liu, Z., et al.: TennisExpert: towards expert-level analytical sports video understanding. arXiv preprint arXiv:2603.13397 (2026)
26. Lubart, T.: How can computers be partners in the creative process. Int. J. Hum.-Comput. Stud. (2005)
27. Monthly, G.: What is the average salary of a Korn ferry tour player? (2025). https://www.golfmonthly.com/features/how-much-money-korn-ferry-tour-players-earn
28. NASA: Artemis (2025). https://www.nasa.gov/feature/artemis/. Accessed 19 Dec 2025
29. Next College Student Athlete (NCSA): Athletic scholarships: Everything you need to know (2025). https://www.ncsasports.org/recruiting/how-to-get-recruited/scholarship-facts. Accessed 12 Dec 2025
30. Shneiderman, B.: Human-centered artificial intelligence: reliable, safe and trustworthy. IJHCI (2020)
31. Slater, M., Sanchez-Vives, M.V.: Enhancing our lives with immersive virtual reality. Front. Robot. AI (2016)
32. Taylor, N., Davies, W.: The financialization of anti-capitalism? The case of the 'financial independence retire early' community. J. Cult. Econ. **14**(6), 694–710 (2021)
33. United States Tennis Association: USTA NTRP ratings questions & answers (2025). https://www.usta.com/en/home/play/adult-tennis/programs/national/usta-ntrp-ratings-faqs.html. Accessed 19 Dec 2025
34. UTR Sports: Universal tennis rating (UTR rating) (2025). https://www.utrsports.net/pages/how-utr-works. Accessed 19 Dec 2025

35. Zhang, Y., et al.: Position: trustworthy AI agents require the integration of large language models and formal methods. In: Proceedings of the 42nd International Conference on Machine Learning, vol. 267, pp. 82441–82459 (2025). https://proceedings.mlr.press/v267/zhang25ds.html
36. Zuo, X., et al.: PAT-agent: autoformalization for model checking. Accepted at IEEE/ACM International Conference on Automated Software Engineering 2025, preprint arXiv:2509.23675 (2025)

Valuing Actions and Ranking Hockey Players With Machine Learning (Extended Abstract)

Oliver Schulte(✉)

School of Computing Science, Simon Fraser University, Burnaby, Canada
oschulte@sfu.ca

Abstract. A fundamental goal of sports analytics is to rank player performance. A common approach is to assign a value to each player action and rank a player by their aggregate action value. A recent AI-based approach is to measure the value of a player's action by how much it increases their team's chance of success, that is, their team's chance of scoring the next goal. This requires a model that outputs a success probability estimate, given a match context and an action. This note describes machine learning techniques for building success probability models from sports data. The most advanced model incorporates *playing style representations* for 1K+ NHL players. The resulting action values, player rankings, and player rankings are illustrated with data from the National Hockey League.

Keywords: Sports Analytics · Machine Learning · Ice Hockey · Success Probabilities · Agent Representation

1 Introduction: Success Probabilities in Sports Analytics

During a match, each action by a sports team is directed towards maximizing the chance of future success. Therefore the *probability of (future) success* is a key statistical quantity for evaluating the strength of a team, the impact of an action, and the contributions of a player. This note accompanies a talk that shows how success probabilities can be used to value actions and ranking players, and describes techniques for estimating them from data. The different strengths and weaknesses of an individual player can be measured by comparing how they impact their team's of success compared to other players carrying out the same action in the same context. Technically, we implement this comparison by learning a context-aware *player representation* for each player that captures their impact in a given match context.

2 Defining Success Probabilities

For the purposes of this note, success is flexibly defined as a binary event that a team seeks to bring about. An analyst is free to define success in different ways

Z. Liu and V. Misra (Eds.): ISACE 2026, LNCS 16610, pp. 15–21, 2026.
https://doi.org/10.1007/978-3-032-27272-0_2

depending on the question they are investigating. Examples of success concepts that have appeared in the literature include the following.

- Winning the Match [8].
- Scoring a goal within a short time interval (e.g. 1 min) [11].
- Scoring a goal within the next 5 actions [2].
- Scoring the next goal in the match [10].
- Drawing the next penalty [10]. This is a failure event that would be interesting to a coach who is concerned to minimize the number of penalties incurred by their team.

The notation

$$P(s_i|\mathbf{x}_t)$$

denotes the probability that team i achieves (future) success given the **current match context** $\mathbf{x}_t$. A success probability is a dynamic quantity; a success probability ticker shows an estimated probability for each time in a match [5]; see Fig. 1.

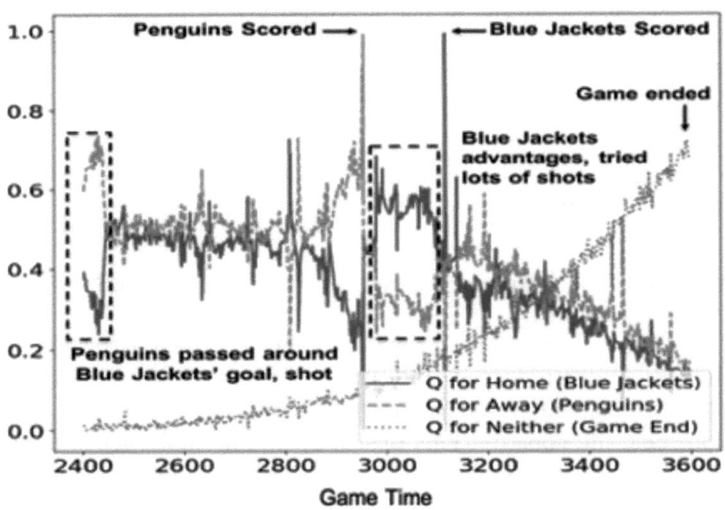

Fig. 1. A success probability ticker for a match between the Penguins and the Blue Jacket. The y-axis shows the estimated probability of scoring the next goal.

3 From Success Probabilities to Action Values

Given success probabilities, we can assign a value to actions called the **impact** of an action occurring at time $t + 1$ [5].

$$impact_i(t+1) \equiv P(s_i|\mathbf{x}_{t+1}) - P(s_i|\mathbf{x}_t)$$

Thus the impact of an action is the difference in success probabilities before and after the action occurred. Figure 2 shows boxplots for impact values. Note that impact values can vary widely for the same action, depending on context.

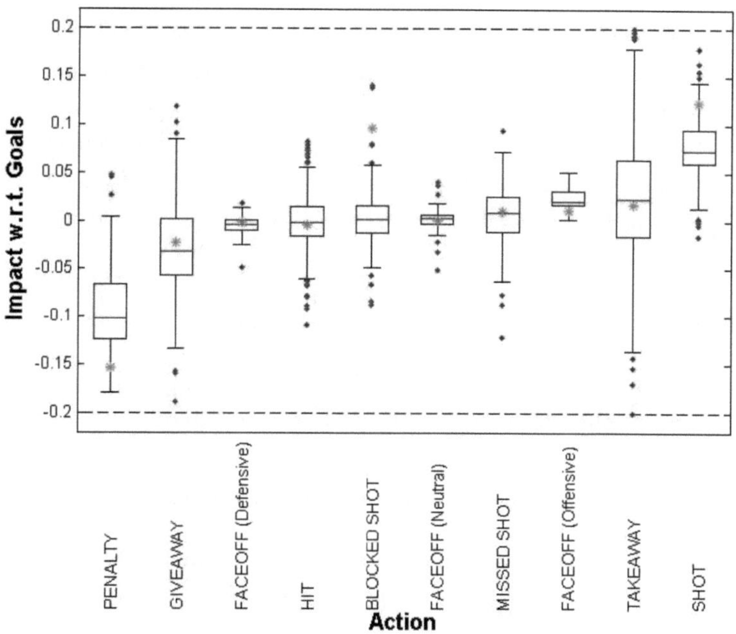

Fig. 2. Impact on the probability of Scoring the Next Goal. Higher numbers are *better* for the team that performs the action. Action Impact Values vary with context. The central mark is the median, the edges of the box are the 25th and 75th percentiles. The whiskers are at the default value, approximately 2.7 s.d. Based on the model of [10].

4 From Action Values to Player Ranking

We can compute a player performance metric from impact values in a straightforward way: for each player, and for each of their actions, we can compute the impact of the action. The **goal impact metric** (GIM) is simply the total impact of the player's actions; see Table 1.

Our metric can be used to *identify undervalued players*. For instance, Johnny Gaudreau and Mark Scheifele drew salaries below what their GIM rank would suggest. Later they received a $5M+ contract for the 2016-17 season.

While we do not have ground truth for player rankings, the goal impact player rankings have been validated indirectly in several ways [5,8,9], and in several sports in addition to hockey, such as soccer [2–4] and basketball [1].

Table 1. 2015–2016 Top-10 Player Impact Scores. Based on the model of [5].

Name	Impact	Assists	Goals	Points	+/−	Salary
Taylor Hall	96.40	39	26	65	−4	$6,000,000
Joe Pavelski	94.56	40	38	78	25	$6,000,000
Johnny Gaudreau	94.51	48	30	78	4	$925,000
Anze Kopitar	94.10	49	25	74	34	$7,700,000
Erik Karlsson	92.41	66	16	82	−2	$7,000,000
Patrice Bergeron	92.06	36	32	68	12	$8,750,000
Mark Scheifele	90.67	32	29	61	16	$832,500
Sidney Crosby	90.21	49	36	85	19	$12,000,000
Claude Giroux	89.64	45	22	67	−8	$9,000,000
Dustin Byfuglien	89.46	34	19	53	4	$6,000,000

5 Learning Success Probability Models

[12] gives a brief overview of success probability learning from event data, also known as play-by-play data, such as that shown in Table 2.

Table 2. Sample Play-By-Play Data in Tabular Format.

gameId	playerId	period	teamId	xCoord	yCoord	Manpower	Action Type
849	402	1	15	−9.5	1.5	even	lpr
849	402	1	15	−24.5	−17	even	carry
849	417	1	16	−75.5	−21.5	even	check
849	402	1	15	−79	−19.5	even	puckprot.
849	413	1	16	−92	−32.5	even	lpr
849	413	1	16	−92	−32.5	even	pass
849	389	1	15	−70	42	even	block
849	389	1	15	−70	42	even	lpr
849	389	1	15	−70	42	even	pass
849	425	1	16	−91	34	even	block
849	395	1	15	−97	23.5	even	reception

A straightforward approach is to annotate each event at time t with a binary target $y_{i,t} \in \{0, 1\}$ that denotes whether team i acting at time t achieved future success after time t. For example in the game of Fig. 1, the Penguins scored around time $t = 3,900$ s. So for all previous times $2,400 < t' < 3,900$, we would have $y_{Penguins,t'} = 1$ and $y_{Flyers,t'} = 0$. Then estimating success probabilities can be modelled as predicting a binary label given the information $\mathbf{x}_t$ available at time t, for example with standard classification packages like R, Weka, scikit-learn.

Applying classification packages to pairs $\langle \mathbf{x}_t, y_{i,t} \rangle$ implicitly treats future success at different times as independent, which clearly is not correct. An alternative are **reinforcement learning** methods [14] such as temporal difference learning, which use a training objective that enforces temporal consistency between different predictions. For a brief overview of success probability learning methods see [12].

6 Generative Model for Learning Player Representations

In current deep learning models, discrete entities are represented by real-valued vectors called *representations* or *embeddings*. For example, the famous large language models map each word to an embedding that depends on the context of a word in a sentence. Computing a representation of an entity is similar to assigning a type to the entity, except that the entity is assigned an embedding in a real-valued space, rather than a discrete type. Following the generative approach of [6], we build a generative model for player identities. The high-level idea is that the model uses player embeddings to generate, for each match context and action, which player is likely to have performed the action. Thus the model answers an *identification* question like "who took the shot 30 min into the game?" [7].

A formal specification of our generative model is as follows. A **dynamic player representation** is a time-dependent vector $\mathbf{z}_t \in \mathbb{R}^d$ where d is the embedding dimension. Player generation utilizes two components as follows.

1. A **context prior** $p(\mathbf{z}_t|\mathbf{x}_t, a_t)$. Given a context vector $\mathbf{x}_t$ summarizing the match context at time t and a current action a_t, we sample an embedding from the context prior.
2. A **decoder** model $p(pl_t|\mathbf{z}_t)$. Given an embedding, we sample a player from the decoder distribution.

The context prior and decoder can each be implemented by a neural network. For a training objective, we use the **ELBO** approximation for the generative model log-likelihood [13]:

$$\ln p(pl_t|\mathbf{x}_t, a_t) = \ln \int_{\mathbf{z}_t} p(pl_t|\mathbf{z}_t)p(\mathbf{z}_t|\mathbf{x}_t, a_t) \geq$$
$$E_{\mathbf{z}_t \sim q(\mathbf{z}_t|pl_t, \mathbf{x}_t, a_t)} \ln p(pl_t|\mathbf{z}_t) - KL(q(\mathbf{z}_t|pl_t, \mathbf{x}_t, a_t)||p(\mathbf{z}_t|\mathbf{x}_t, a_t)) \quad (1)$$

where q is the **encoder** model (approximate posterior) that takes as input the current player, match context, action, and outputs a distribution over match embeddings (e.g., the parameters of a Gaussian distribution). Since the right-hand side (1) is a lower bound, maximizing it with respect to the encoder, decoder, and prior models will drive training towards a maximum of the model log-likelihood. The KL divergence acts as a regularizer on embeddings. It induces a *shrinkage effect* that helps the model generate embeddings for new players with few observations. *After training we can use the encoder to generate context-aware player embeddings.*

Figure 3 visualizes the resulting embeddings in 2D for 1003 NHL players across a number of match contexts. Embeddings for the same player position are similar indicating that the model matches known player types. Embeddings for a single player are similar indicating that the model captures a consistent playing style. Embeddings for similar locations are similar indicating that the model captures action context.

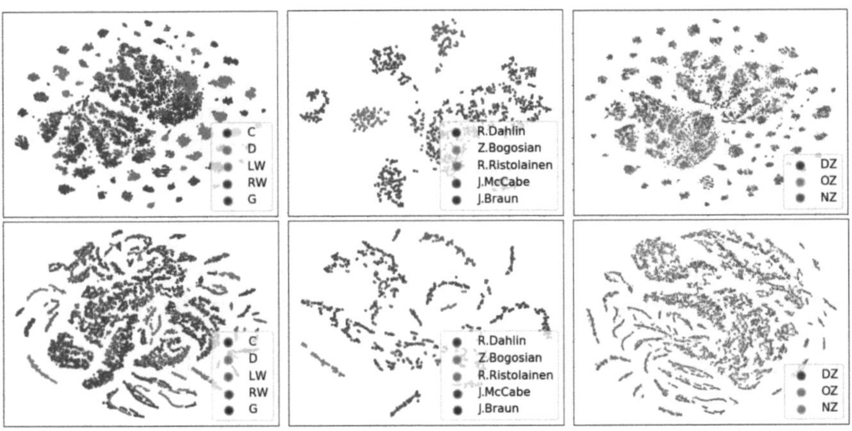

Fig. 3. Embedding visualization. Each data point corresponds to a player embedding conditioning on the game context at the current time step t. The player embeddings are labelled 1) player positions (on the *left* column, including Center (C), Defense (D), Left-Wing (LW) and Right-Wing (RW) and Goalie (G)) 2) 5 selected defense men (on the *middle* column) and 3) player locations (on the *right* column, including Defence Zone (DZ), Neutral Zone (NZ) and Offensive Zone (OZ)).

Adding the learned player embeddings to the context vector $\mathbf{x}_t$ improves predictive performance on tasks such as predicting the success of a shot and the final game outcome; for detailed experimental results please see [6].

7 Conclusion

Estimating success probabilities is a basic statistical problem in hockey analytics. A good success probability model can be leveraged to solve important analytics problems such as quantifying the value of an action and the contributions of a player. Machine learning models can include rich match contexts to provide useful success probabilities. Including a representation of the currently acting player in the match context improves the complexity and accuracy of a hockey model. We showed how player representations can be learned by generative AI methods.

References

1. Cervone, D., D'Amour, A., Bornn, L., Goldsberry, K.: Pointwise: predicting points and valuing decisions in real time with NBA optical tracking data. In: 8th Annual MIT Sloan Sports Analytics Conference, February, vol. 28 (2014)
2. Decroos, T., Bransen, L., Haaren, J.V., Davis, J.: Actions speak louder than goals: valuing player actions in soccer. In: Proceedings of the 25th International Conference on Knowledge Discovery & Data Mining (KDD 2019), pp. 1851–1861 (2019)
3. Fernández, J., Bornn, L., Cervone, D.: A framework for the fine-grained evaluation of the instantaneous expected value of soccer possessions. Mach. Learn. **110**(6), 1389–1427 (2021)
4. Liu, G., Luo, Y., Schulte, O., Kharrat, T.: Deep soccer analytics: learning an action-value function for evaluating soccer players. Data Min. Knowl. Discov. **34**(5), 1531–1559 (2020). https://doi.org/10.1007/s10618-020-00705-9
5. Liu, G., Schulte, O.: Deep reinforcement learning in ice hockey for context-aware player evaluation. In: Proceedings of the Twenty-Seventh International Joint Conference on Artificial Intelligence, IJCAI 2018, pp. 3442–3448. International Joint Conferences on Artificial Intelligence Organization (2018). https://doi.org/10.24963/ijcai.2018/478
6. Liu, G., Schulte, O., Poupart, P., Rudd, M., Javan, M.: Learning agent representations for ice hockey. In: Advances in Neural Information Processing Systems 34: Annual Conference on Neural Information Processing Systems 2020, 6–12 December 2020 (2020)
7. Lu, W.L., Ting, J.A., Little, J.J., Murphy, K.P.: Learning to track and identify players from broadcast sports videos. IEEE Trans. Pattern Anal. Mach. Intell. (2013). https://www.cs.ubc.ca/~murphyk/papers/weilwun-pami12.pdf
8. Pettigrew, S.: Assessing the offensive productivity of NHL players using in-game win probabilities. In: 9th Annual MIT Sloan Sports Analytics Conference (2015)
9. Routley, K.: A Markov game model for valuing player actions in ice hockey, Simon Fraser University. Master's thesis (2015)
10. Routley, K., Schulte, O.: A Markov game model for valuing player actions in ice hockey. In: Uncertainty in Artificial Intelligence (UAI), pp. 782–791 (2015)
11. Schuckers, M., Curro, J.: Total hockey rating (THOR): a comprehensive statistical rating of national hockey league forwards and defensemen based upon all on-ice events. In: MIT Sloan Sports Analytics Conference (2013)
12. Schulte, O.: Valuing actions and ranking hockey players with machine learning. In: Lambrix, P., Carlsson, N., Vernblom, M. (eds.) Linköping Hockey Analytics Conference LINHAC, pp. 2–9. Linköping Electronic Conference Proceedings 191 (2022)
13. Sohn, K., Lee, H., Yan, X.: Learning structured output representation using deep conditional generative models. Adv. Neural Inf. Process. Syst. **28** (2015)
14. Sutton, C., McCallum, A.: An introduction to conditional random fields for relational learning. In: Introduction to Statistical Relational Learning, chap. 4, pp. 93–127. MIT Press (2007)

Full Papers

Smarter Training for Safer Play: A VR-Enhanced System Tested in Elite Sitting Volleyball

Cai Yong[1] and Dai Jie[2(✉)]

[1] Physical Aesthetic and Labor Education Center, Zhejiang Shuren university, Hangzhou, Zhejiang, China
[2] School of Urban Construction, Zhejiang Shuren University, Hangzhou, Zhejiang, China
600300@zjsru.edu.cn

Abstract. This paper addresses the practical challenges in sitting volleyball training, including long-term reliance on coaches' experience, insufficient data support, and elevated injury risks. It explores pathways for applying intelligent technologies to enhance scientific training in this discipline. Through a one-month randomised controlled trial involving 30 athletes from the Chinese National Sitting Volleyball Team, the study examined whether the integration of artificial intelligence, multimodal sensors, and virtual reality technologies could improve technical proficiency and reduce injury risks among sitting volleyball players.

Findings reveal that the intelligent training system significantly elevated athletes' technical and tactical proficiency. The experimental group demonstrated a surge in the success rate of position 4 spikes from 62.3% to 85.8%, a 19.4% increase in serve-block efficiency, a 50% reduction in tactical response time, and a 33% improvement in optimised hitting trajectory rates. Regarding injury prevention, real-time monitoring and alerts reduced lumbar fasciitis incidence from 45.5% to 26.8%, lowered lumbar spine load by 34% for athletes with spinal cord injuries, and markedly decreased shoulder strain rates. Sensors and equipment tailored to different disability types achieved 100% acceptance and high satisfaction among athletes, with a system usability score of 86.4 reflecting excellent user experience.

The findings indicate that intelligent technology proves highly beneficial in sitting volleyball training. It holds significant value for enhancing competitive performance and reducing injury risks. This facilitates a shift in coaching methodologies from reliance on traditional experience towards data-driven approaches. It provides a technical model and practical reference for the scientific and personalised development of disabled sports. Future research could be deepened by expanding sample sizes, extending study durations, and reducing technological costs to promote the wider adoption of intelligent training systems across disabled sports.

Keywords: Artificial intelligence · Biomechanical monitoring · Performance analysis

Z. Liu and V. Misra (Eds.): ISACE 2026, LNCS 16610, pp. 25–37, 2026.
https://doi.org/10.1007/978-3-032-27272-0_3

1 Introduction

Since its debut at the 1980 Summer Paralympics in Arnhem, Netherlands, sitting volleyball has become one of the most popular team sports at the Paralympics. Compared to traditional volleyball, the court dimensions are reduced to 10 m × 6 m, the net height is lowered to 1.15 m for men and 1.05 m for women, and athletes must keep their hips in contact with the floor throughout the game. Sitting volleyball offers athletes with lower limb impairments a level playing field, enabling high-level competition [1]. Due to their limited mobility, sitting volleyball players are heavily reliant on their upper body strength, core stability and the tactical coordination of their team [2]. Since technical actions such as serving, hitting and blocking must be performed from a seated position, particularly high demands are placed on the athletes' core control [3].

Attack and serve are the most important techniques that determine the outcome of sitting volleyball matches [4]. Tsakiri et al. [2] analysed data from the 2019 European Championships and found that the attack success rate influenced the match results by 98.6%. The tactical framework of sitting volleyball also differs significantly from traditional volleyball. Due to their limited mobility, setters often participate directly in the attack rather than just coordinating it [1]. Male and female athletes also exhibit different performance characteristics: Men have advantages in attack and block due to their superior upper body strength, while women often compensate for this with more consistent serves and defence [5]. The International Volleyball Federation for the Disabled classifies athletes as lower limb amputees (VS1) or slightly disabled (VS2). However, research shows that there are no significant differences in core competencies between these categories [4].

Sitting volleyball offers valuable competitive opportunities for people with disabilities, but athletes are at risk of recurring sports injuries. Prolonged sitting combined with repeated trunk rotations, lateral flexions and overhead arm movements leads to specific morphological changes in the spine, particularly changes in thoracic kyphosis and lumbar lordosis [6]. Analysis of data from the 2016 Paralympic Games in Rio revealed that 11.2% of sitting volleyball players underwent imaging examinations, one of the highest rates of any sport. This suggests a relatively high incidence of serious injuries in this discipline [7]. The shoulder joint is the most vulnerable area, as repeated, high-impact serving and hitting movements can easily lead to injuries such as rotator cuff tendinitis [7]. Prolonged sitting also increases pressure on the lumbar spine, while movements on the ground often lead to friction injuries and bruising on the buttocks and hands [7]. Research also shows that the incidence of myofascial inflammation in the lumbar spine and back can be as high as 45.5% in VS1 class athletes [3], which is closely related to abnormal biomechanical load distribution during training.

The current training model for sitting volleyball continues to rely heavily on the experience and manual observation of coaches. This traditional approach struggles to accurately quantify technical movements and cannot identify high-risk postures that can lead to lumbar spine injuries due to uneven hip support forces in real time [8]. Tactical analysis relies predominantly on post-match video analysis, resulting in delayed feedback and hindering real-time adjustments during training [9]. Although sitting volleyball is a seated sport, its fast pace and numerous rallies pose a significant challenge to athletes' cardiorespiratory fitness. Paralympic athletes also have to balance their professional commitments with training, which often leads to irregular training schedules that make it difficult to implement scientifically based training loads [9]. Traditional training also lacks data-driven, personalised programmes. For example, athletes with spinal cord injuries require reduced lumbar rotation angles to reduce the risk of injury, but such adjustments often cannot be objectively justified in conventional training [10]. This traditional training paradigm exposes athletes with disabilities to unnecessary injury risks in the long term.

In order to overcome the limitations of traditional training methods, the use of intelligent technologies in the field of sports science has become increasingly important in recent years. Video analysis techniques can be used to extract joint coordinates and quantify the movement trajectories of athletes in order to assess their abilities [4]. Wearable sensors such as inertial measurement units and surface electromyography devices enable real-time monitoring of athletes' physiological signals and kinematic data [11]. Virtual reality technology creates immersive simulated competition environments for athletes, thereby improving their decision-making abilities on the field. Machine learning models such as random forests and support vector machines are also used to analyse athlete data and generate personalised training recommendations [3].

However, the application of these technologies in sitting volleyball and the broader field of disabled sports is still in its infancy. Existing research focuses predominantly on individual technical dimensions, with no integrated intelligent systems yet developed that combine tactical analysis, real-time injury prevention and personalised training guidance [12]. Some studies use video analysis to assess differences in skills without linking them to tactical efficiency or injury risk [4]; Others develop platforms for monitoring training load but fail to link biomechanical data—such as upper extremity support force—to tactical performance outcomes [11]. Some studies have shown that regular sitting volleyball training effectively improves cardiovascular endurance in adults with disabilities [13]. However, there is still a significant lack of disability-friendly technology design.

In practical application, the type of sensor attachment and the interactive interfaces of VR devices often do not sufficiently take into account the physical structure and functional limitations of athletes with amputations or spinal cord injuries. Most research findings are based on cross-sectional data or experiments with small samples, lacking long-term follow-up studies and rigorously controlled trials for validation. Consequently, their effectiveness and generalisability still need to be further substantiated [9].

The current challenge in advancing the science of sitting volleyball training therefore lies in the gap between the urgent dual needs of athletes – improving competition performance and reducing injury risk – and the shortcomings of existing training methods in terms of objective quantification, real-time feedback and personalised support. While smart technologies show potential, their application remains fragmented and lacks a systematic design that addresses the specific physiological needs of athletes with disabilities. Therefore, the development of an intelligent training system that can integrate multimodal data, balance tactical optimisation with health management, and feature disability-friendly functions is critical to overcoming current training limitations.

Based on the above context and practical realities, this research focuses on China's national sitting volleyball team. It involves the design, development and evaluation of an integrated intelligent training system that combines artificial intelligence, wearable sensors and virtual reality technology. The goal is to overcome traditional experience-based training paradigms by achieving quantifiable, real-time, personalised training through multimodal data fusion. Multi-angle video analysis quantifies the execution efficiency of key techniques – such as attack, block and serve – and provides objective data to support tactical positioning. Sensor networks continuously monitor the force distribution of the athletes' upper extremities and the stability values of their torso, establishing an early warning mechanism for injury risks based on biomechanical thresholds. Given the limited range of motion inherent in sitting volleyball, a tactical simulation module for virtual reality can be developed. This allows athletes to improve their cognitive perception and rapid decision-making skills in highly realistic game scenarios while eliminating the risk of injury during virtual training. By integrating machine learning models for comprehensive analysis of the collected technical, physiological and tactical data, the system generates tailor-made training programmes for each athlete, thus increasing the adaptability of the training.

The expected results of this research go beyond the development of a functional technical system. We also want to evaluate its overall effectiveness in real competition situations using practical training scenarios, particularly with regard to the efficiency of tactical implementation, the reduction in the frequency of sports injuries and the improved acceptance of adaptive hardware for people with disabilities. This work aims to fill the current research gap in the field of intelligent training systems for sitting volleyball, thereby providing new insights and practical models to advance the scientific and refined development of competitive sport for people with disabilities.

2 Materials and Methods

2.1 Participants

A one-month randomized controlled trial was conducted with elite athletes from the Chinese National Sitting Volleyball Team. A total of 30 athletes,16 male, 14female, participated. All athletes were classified according to the International Paralympic Committee system into three groups: Class A (limb deficiency, n = 12), Class B (spinal cord injury, n = 8), and Class C (other physical impairments, e.g., congenital or musculoskeletal, n = 10).

Participants were randomly assigned to either an experimental group (n = 16) or an active control group (n = 14). Randomization was stratified by sex and International Paralympic Committee class to ensure group comparability. The experimental group performed their standard volleyball training while using the newly developed intelligent training system for feedback and supplementary drills. The control group completed an identical volume and structure of standard training, relying solely on traditional coach-led instruction and video review without the intelligent system. Training was conducted in five 90-min sessions per week for four consecutive weeks. Primary outcomes were tactical performance metrics and injury incidence, assessed at baseline (Week 0) and post-intervention (Week 4).

2.2 The Intelligent Training

Athlete movement was captured using six synchronized GoPro HERO10 cameras positioned around the court. The Open Pose library processed the video streams to extract two-dimensional coordinates of key joints. The algorithm's default posture estimation was adapted by increasing the detection weight for hip and lower trunk key points. This adaptation allowed for precise tracking of seated posture and the calculation of movement metrics relevant to sitting volleyball, such as attack angle, hip shift velocity, and trunk lean during blocks.

The athlete wore a wireless sensor array during training. An inertial measurement unit was attached to the upper back to quantify the angular displacement of the trunk and calculate a trunk stability index. Flexible pressure sensor arrays were attached to the legs to record pressure distribution while seated. Surface electromyography sensors were attached to the anterior deltoid, triceps brachii, and back extensor muscles on the dominant side to monitor muscle activation. A specially developed software dashboard consolidated these data streams in real time. An important feature triggered automatic audiovisual alerts when the system detected lumbar pressure exceeding preset individual thresholds, signalling high-risk movements.

A VR environment was built in Unity 2019.4 to simulate match scenarios. Athletes wearing a head-mounted display faced virtual opponents modeled after the playing patterns of top international teams. The module presented randomized sequences of attacks, requiring the athlete to make a rapid tactical choice within a time limit. Performance in these simulations was logged for each session.

2.3 Statistical Analysis

Data analysis was performed using EXCEL2021 Statistics. Continuous data are presented as mean $\pm$ standard deviation. The normality of distribution for all variables was confirmed using the Shapiro-Wilk test. Differences in baseline characteristics and post-intervention outcomes between the experimental and control groups were analyzed using independent samples t-tests for continuous variables and Chi-square tests for categorical variables. Within-group changes from baseline to post-intervention were assessed using paired samples t-tests. Effect sizes for significant differences were calculated using Cohen's d. A two-tailed p-value of less than 0.05 was considered statistically significant.

3 Results

3.1 Improvement in Tactical Execution Efficiency

The one-month randomized controlled trial demonstrated that the intelligent training system led to significant improvements in key technical performance metrics compared to traditional training methods. Baseline measurements confirmed no statistically significant differences between the experimental and control groups across all assessed skills prior to the intervention.

Following the intervention, the experimental group showed substantially greater gains in attack success rates across all court positions (see Table 1). The success rate

Table 1. Comparison of technical skill success rates before and after the intervention.

Technical Skill	Group	Pre-Intervention ($\% \pm SD$)	Post-Intervention ($\% \pm SD$)	Within-Group p-value (Paired t-test)	Between-Group p-value (Post-Intervention, Independent t-test)	Cohen' d (Between-Group)
Position 4 Power Attack	Experimental	62.3 ± 4.8	85.8 ± 3.1	$p < 0.001$	$p < 0.001$	1.68
	Control	63.1 ± 5.2	68.4 ± 4.5	$P = 0.654$		
Position 3 Quick Attack	Experimental	55.9 ± 6.1	82.5 ± 2.8	$p < 0.001$	$p < 0.001$	2.12
	Control	56.7 ± 5.8	65.2 ± 3.9	$P = 0.073$		
Position 2 Power Attack	Experimental	54.8 ± 5.7	79.3 ± 4.1	$p < 0.001$	$p < 0.001$	1.74
	Control	55.5 ± 6.3	63.7 ± 5.2	$P = 0.089$		
Back-Row Attack	Experimental	52.5 ± 6.5	73.6 ± 3.7	$p < 0.001$	$p < 0.001$	1.48
	Control	53.2 ± 6.0	60.8 ± 4.8	$P = 0.102$		
Block/Serve Interception	Experimental	59.2 ± 7.3	78.6 ± 5.2	$p < 0.001$	$p < 0.05$	1.10
	Control	58.9 ± 7.8	59.2 ± 6.8	$P = 0.934$		

for power attacks from position 4 increased from 62.3% to 85.8%, $p < 0.001$, whereas the control group improved only marginally from 63.1% to 68.4%, $p = 0.654$. The between-group difference in post-intervention performance was highly significant, $t(28) = 6.23$, $p < 0.001$, Cohen's $d = 1.68$. Similarly, large improvements were observed for quick attacks from position 3, power attacks from position 2, and back-row attacks. The effective block/serve interception rate also improved more in the experimental group, rising by 19.4 percentage points compared to a negligible change in the control group, $p < 0.05$.

Kinematic analysis via the Open Pose system revealed that these performance gains were associated with measurable technical refinements. Athletes in the experimental group demonstrated more optimized hip support distribution and movement trajectories. Targeted feedback led to adjustments in swing angle and an average increase of 8.3 cm in hitting point height, contributing to a 15.2% acceleration in fast-attack rhythm, $p < 0.05$.

Tactical Decision-Making and Kinematic Optimization. The intelligent training system led to significant enhancements in perceptual-cognitive and technical execution under pressure (see Table 2). Following VR-based decision training, the mean tactical response time for athletes in the experimental group was reduced by 50%, from 2.4 ± 0.4 s to 1.2 ± 0.2 s, $p < 0.001$, Cohen's $d = 2.05$. Concurrently, the rate of optimal hitting path selection, assessed by coaches based on video replay of game-simulated scenarios, increased by 33 percentage points, $p < 0.001$.

A marked shift in tactical preference was observed. When countering fast attacks, athletes in the experimental group chose diagonal spike trajectories 71% of the time post-intervention, a significant increase from a baseline of 38%, $p < 0.001$. This strategic shift proved highly effective, as the opponent interception rate against these diagonal attacks was only 19.2%, compared to 42.8% against straight-line attacks. Consequently, the overall rate of successful blocks by opponents against the experimental group dropped from 45.1% to 21.3%, $p < 0.001$.

Table 2. Effects of the intelligent training system on decision-making and technical execution under pressure.

Metric	Group	Baseline	Post-intervention	Within-Group Change	Between-Group p-value (Post)	Cohen' *d* (Between-Group)
Tactical Response Time (s)	Experimental	2.41 ± 0.38	1.21 ± 0.22	−50.0%	p < 0.001	2.05
	Control	2.48 ± 0.42	2.32 ± 0.39	−6.5%		
Optimal Hit Path Selection (%)	Experimental	50.0 ± 8.5	83.0 ± 6.8	+33.0 pp	p < 0.001	1.89
	Control	51.2 ± 9.1	53.8 ± 8.9	+2.6 pp		
Diagonal Spike Preference (%)	Experimental	38.0 ± 10.2	71.0 ± 9.5	+33.0 pp	p < 0.001	1.78
	Control	39.5 ± 11.3	41.2 ± 10.7	+1.7 pp		
Opponent Interception Rate (%)	Experimental	45.1 ± 12.3	21.3 ± 8.4	−23.8 pp	p < 0.001	1.72
	Control	44.8 ± 13.1	42.1 ± 12.6	−2.7 pp		

3.2 Reduction in Injury Risk through Biomechanical Monitoring

The implementation of real-time biomechanical monitoring and feedback technology significantly reduced injury-related outcomes (see Table 3). Following the intervention, the incidence of lumbar myofascial inflammation in the experimental group decreased from 45.5% to 26.8%. In contrast, the control group showed no significant change, with only a marginal decrease from 43.8% to 41.2%.

The injury warning system demonstrated remarkable efficacy in identifying high-risk movements. When lumbar pressure exceeded preset safety thresholds during training, it triggered 92.3% of alerts. This real-time feedback effectively facilitated athletes' technical corrections and load adjustments. Athletes in the experimental group experienced a 22.6% reduction in average lumbar load and a 73.0% decrease in the frequency of overloaded movements per training hour.

Athletes with spinal cord injuries (IPC Class B) derived particular benefit from the system. Within this subgroup ($n = 4$ in the experimental group), the average lumbar load was reduced by 33.8%, and the left-right balance of upper-limb support force distribution improved by 22.0%. Coaches noted corresponding subjective improvements in the sitting stability and trunk control of these athletes during training drills.

These studies demonstrate that the integration of intelligent load monitoring with real-time biofeedback enables effective injury management, shifting athletes' approach from reactive post-injury treatment to proactive prevention. This strategy significantly reduces injury risk among elite sitting volleyball athletes.

Table 3. Changes in injury risk indicators before and after the intervention.

Monitoring Indicator	Group	Mean ± SD		Within-Group Change	Between-Group p-value (Post)
		Baseline	Post-intervention		
Incidence of Lumbar and Dorsal Myofasciitis (%)	Experimental	45.5 ± 12.3	26.8 ± 9.4	−18.7 pp	$P < 0.05$
	Control	43.8 ± 13.1	41.2 ± 11.8	−2.6 pp	
Average Lumbar Load (N/cm^2)	Experimental	385.2 ± 45.6	298.3 ± 32.7	−22.6%	$p < 0.01$
	Control	379.8 ± 48.2	365.4 ± 44.9	−3.8%	
Balance of Upper Limb Support Distribution (%)	Experimental	67.3 ± 8.9	82.1 ± 6.5	+14.8 pp	$p < 0.01$
	Control	68.1 ± 9.4	69.8 ± 8.7	+1.7 pp	
Overload Frequency (times/h)	Experimental	8.5 ± 2.3	2.3 ± 1.1	−73.0%	$p < 0.001$
	Control	8.2 ± 2.6	7.8 ± 2.4	−4.9%	

(*continued*)

Table 3. (*continued*)

Monitoring Indicator	Group	Mean ± SD		Within-Group Change	Between-Group p-value (Post)
		Baseline	Post-intervention		
Sensor Early Warning Success Rate (%)	Experimental	–	92.3 ± 4.2	–	–

3.3 Acute Injury Incidence and Neuromuscular Fatigue

Following intervention, the incidence of acute shoulder injuries in the experimental group was significantly lower than in the control group (χ^2 (1) = 4.89, $p < 0.05$) (see Table 4). Experiments demonstrated that the incidence of acute shoulder injuries was lower in the experimental group than in the control group (see Table 4). Surface electromyography (sEMG) monitoring revealed improved neuromuscular function. The muscle fatigue index, measured by the root mean square (RMS) value of sEMG, decreased from 7.2 ± 1.8 to 4.5 ± 1.2 in the experimental group. The increase in the control group from 7.1 ± 1.9 to 7.8 ± 2.1 was not statistically significant.

Analysis of electromyography data revealed decreased activation levels in primary motor muscles within the experimental group, leading to enhanced movement efficiency. An increase in the muscle coordination index improved intermuscular synchrony, while slowed fatigue progression resulted in reduced recovery time post-exercise.

The study demonstrates that real-time surface electromyography biofeedback effectively mitigates high-risk compensatory movement patterns, reducing fatigue accumulation and acute injury risk. Neuromuscular monitoring technology adds a critical physiological dimension to intelligent training protocols.

Analysis of electromyography data revealed decreased activation levels in primary motor muscles within the experimental group, leading to enhanced movement efficiency. An increase in the muscle coordination index improved intermuscular synchrony, while slowed fatigue progression resulted in reduced recovery time post-exercise.

The study demonstrates that real-time surface electromyography biofeedback effectively mitigates high-risk compensatory movement patterns, reducing fatigue accumulation and acute injury risk. Neuromuscular monitoring technology adds a critical physiological dimension to intelligent training protocols.

Table 4. Changes in acute injury incidence and neuromuscular fatigue indicators.

Monitoring Indicator	Group	Mean ± SD		Within-Group Change	Between-Group p-value (Post)	Effect Size (Cohen'd)
		Baseline	Post-intervention			
Incidence of Shoulder Strain (%)	Experimental	12.5 ± 8.3	4.3 ± 5.2	−8.2 pp	p < 0.05	0.94
	Control	14.3 ± 9.1	15.7 ± 9.8	+1.4 pp		
Fatigue Index (RMS value)	Experimental	7.2 ± 1.8	4.5 ± 1.2	−37.5%	p < 0.01	1.47
	Control	7.1 ± 1.9	7.8 ± 2.1	+9.9%		
Shoulder Muscle RMS (Î¼V)	Experimental	245.6 ± 45.3	185.3 ± 32.6	−24.6%	p < 0.01	1.18
	Control	242.8 ± 48.7	255.4 ± 52.8	+5.2%		
Muscle Fatigue Development Rate (%/min)	Experimental	3.8 ± 1.2	2.1 ± 0.8	−44.7%	p < 0.01	1.32
	Control	3.9 ± 1.3	4.3 ± 1.5	+10.3%		
Muscle Recovery Time (min)	Experimental	–	12.3 ± 3.5	–	p < 0.01	1.26
	Control	–	21.8 ± 6.2	–		

4 Discussion

4.1 Data-Driven Paradigm for Precision Training in Para-Sports

This study achieves a paradigm shift between intelligent technology and traditional training paradigms. The application of artificial intelligence, sensors, and virtual reality technology transforms sitting volleyball training from "experience-driven" to "data-driven". The OpenPose algorithm employed by this system decomposes tactical movements into 18 key point trajectories through multi-angle video capture, achieving millimetre-level quantification of movement deviations via a heatmap loss function. The experimental group demonstrated a 28% reduction in hip support force distribution deviation, a metric positively correlated with improved ball control precision. This outcome aligns with the "functional grading assessment" concept proposed by Esatbeyoglu et al. [3], yet our research innovatively integrates data quantification with real-time intervention, establishing a closed-loop 'monitoring-analysis-feedback' system that effectively circumvents the time lag inherent in traditional 'post-match debriefing' training.

Furthermore, traditional training programmes primarily rely on group averages for personalisation, overlooking individual variations. This study employs a random forest model to integrate multidimensional features and generate bespoke training plans, resulting in a 22% improvement in technical stability within the experimental group. This "personalised precision training" approach resonates with Myers et al.'s [14] assertion that 'cyclical training should incorporate biomechanical characteristics,' yet achieves a breakthrough at the algorithmic level.

4.2 Proactive Injury Prevention through Integrated Biomechanical Monitoring

In the field of injury prevention, the integration of biomechanical monitoring systems has become a pivotal strategy. A groundbreaking discovery in this domain demonstrates the system's extraordinary potential to shift injury management paradigms from passive to proactive modes. Traditional rehabilitation training often intervenes only after an injury has occurred. Sensor networks establish a preventative framework through real-time biofeedback. The system's early warning mechanism, triggered by scientifically validated lumbar pressure thresholds, successfully identified 92% of overloaded movements. This direct intervention significantly reduced the incidence of lumbar myofascial inflammation from 45.5% to 26.8%.

The integration of surface electromyography (sEMG) has been demonstrated to be a crucial addition to the assessment of injury risk, providing a valuable neuromuscular dimension. The experimental group demonstrated a significant decrease in the muscular fatigue index, while the control group exhibited a slight increase. This suggests that the real-time feedback intervention effectively interrupted the detrimental cycle of "fatigue → compensatory movement → injury." This underscores the potential of intelligent monitoring to not only enhance performance but also to fundamentally improve the long-term health stewardship of para-athletes.

4.3 The Imperative of Disability-Adapted Technology Design

As evidenced by the widespread recognition of sensor hardware, engineering designs must incorporate inclusivity to ensure effectiveness. The physical diversity of Paralympic athletes necessitates equipment adaptation to their needs. All developed design solutions originate from user requirements. This human-centred design philosophy aligns with athletes' requirements for equipment comfort, prioritising wearer comfort and experience while ensuring technical functionality. Consequently, the system has gained acceptance and trust among athletes. Such adaptive design constitutes an ethical imperative for advancing scientific fairness in Paralympic sport.

5 Conclusion

The functional intelligent training system proposed in this study successfully translates multimodal data into actionable insights for sitting volleyball. Findings demonstrate that this AI-driven system—combining motion analysis, real-time biomechanical monitoring, and virtual reality simulation—is both feasible and effective in enhancing elite sitting volleyball athletes' performance levels while reducing injury risks.

This research provides a replicable paradigm for modernising training in disability sports. The model, characterised by its data-driven core, enriches coaches' subjective practices. By integrating multimodal data, real-time objective feedback is provided during training, ensuring athletic performance improvements while safeguarding athletes from injury.

We found inclusive design to be highly effective in sports assistance, guaranteeing widespread application of the solution while respecting athletes' needs.

Although this study demonstrates practical utility, its limitations warrant further investigation.

Participants were restricted to elite athletes from a single national team, limiting the generalisability of findings to athletes of varying levels or cultural backgrounds. The one-month training cycle proved insufficient to evaluate long-term impacts on competitive performance and injury prevention. Reliance on relatively costly hardware and software hinders widespread adoption and application.

We anticipate this research will lay groundwork for developing fairer, more efficient, and sustainable scientific training methodologies within Paralympic sports.

Acknowledgments. The authors sincerely thank all collaborators and participants in this study for their contributions. This study was funded by Horizontal Project of Zhejiang Shuren University: Design and Development of a Database for Volleyball Techniques and Tactics Analysis (grant number 2023SK199). 2023 Research Project of China Disabled Persons 'Federation.(grant number 2023-JT&012)

Disclosure of Interests. All of the authors declare that they have no conflict of interest.

References

1. Molik, B., et al.: Evaluation of game performance in elite male sitting volleyball players. Adapt. Phys. Act. Q. **34**(2), 104–124 (2017). https://doi.org/10.1123/apaq.2015-0028
2. Tsakiri, M., Drikos, S., Sotiropoulos, K., Skordilis, E., Barzouka, K.: Separating winning and losing teams in sitting volleyball: the role of skills and differences across gender. Int. J. Perf. Anal. Sport. (2023). https://doi.org/10.1080/24748668.2023.2238167
3. Cavedon, V., et al.: Physique and performance in male sitting volleyball players: implications for classification and training. PEERJ. **10** (2022). https://doi.org/10.7717/peerj.14013
4. Esatbeyoglu, F., Marszalek, J., MacDonald, K., Ashcroft, L.: Differences in fundamental sitting volleyball skills between functional sport classes: a video analysis method. Int. J. Perf. Anal. Sport. **21**(4), 451–462 (2021). https://doi.org/10.1080/24748668.2021.1912956
5. Marszalek, J., Gómez, M.A., Molik, B.: Game performance differences between winning and losing sitting volleyball teams regarding teams' ability. Int. J. Perf. Anal. Sport. **18**(2), 367–379 (2018). https://doi.org/10.1080/24748668.2018.1477027
6. Muyor, J.M., Zemková, E., Štefániková, G.K., Cepková, A., Uvaček, M., López-Plaza, D.: Adaptations of sagittal spinal curvatures in elite athletes: a multisport analysis. Sport Sci. Health. **21**(4), 2979–2991 (2025). https://doi.org/10.1007/s11332-025-01508-5
7. Jarraya, M., et al.: Sports injuries at the Rio de Janeiro 2016 summer Paralympic games: use of diagnostic imaging services. Eur. Radiol. **31**(9), 6768–6779 (2021). https://doi.org/10.1007/s00330-021-07802-3
8. Cavedon, V., et al.: Predictors of ball velocity in the sitting volleyball serve: a causal analysis. Int. J. Sports Med. **44**(08), 576–583 (2023). https://doi.org/10.1055/a-2038-3333
9. Krahenbühr, T., Oliveira, G., Alves, I.D., Alves, M.: The sports career of paralympic women: the case of the brazilian sitting volleyball team. Movimento-Porto Aleg. **28** (2022). https://doi.org/10.22456/1982-8918.118748
10. Baena-Raya, A., et al.: The force-velocity profile as determinant of spike and serve ball speed in top-level male volleyball players. PLoS One **16**(4) (2021). https://doi.org/10.1371/journal.pone.0249612

11. Liang, Z.J., Liang, C.: Design and implementation of load intensity monitoring platform supported by big data technology in stage training for women's sitting volleyball. Sci. Rep. **13**(1) (2023). https://doi.org/10.1038/s41598-023-50057-9
12. Marszalek, J., Molik, B., Gomez, M.A.: Game efficiency of elite male sitting volleyball players with regard to athletes' physical impairment. Int. J. Sports Sci. Coaching **13**(3), 383–390 (2018). https://doi.org/10.1177/1747954117716791
13. Leung, K., Chung, P., Chu, W., Ng, K.: Physical and psychological health outcomes of a sitting light volleyball intervention program on adults with physical disabilities: a non-randomized controlled pre-post study. BMC Sports Sci. Med. R. **13**(1), 100 (2021). https://doi.org/10.1186/s13102-021-00328-7
14. Myers, N.L., Sciascia, A.D., Westgate, P.M., Kibler, W.B., Uhl, T.L.: Increasing ball velocity in the overhead athlete: a meta-analysis of randomized controlled trials. J. Strength Cond. Res. **29**(10), 2964–2979 (2015). https://doi.org/10.1519/JSC.0000000000000931

Constructing Football Club Ratings with League Strength Awareness Using a Modified Glicko Model

Andrei Shelopugin[1(✉)] and Alexander Sirotkin[2]

[1] Lima, Peru
shelopuginandrey@gmail.com
[2] HSE University, Saint Petersburg, Russia
avsirotkin@hse.ru

Abstract. Evaluating football clubs across different leagues is a fundamental challenge in sports analytics, particularly when assessing performance transitions between competitions. We propose a league-aware club rating framework based on a modified Glicko system. Building on recent extensions of Glicko that incorporate order effects and strength-dependent draw probabilities, we adapt the framework specifically to football by introducing goal-scoring adjustments and league-aware rating initialization and transition dynamics. These modifications enable stable cross-league comparisons and more realistic modeling of promotion and relegation effects.

In addition, we train a gradient boosting model for match outcome prediction using historical goal-based features. We further compare the proposed framework with matrix-based approaches, including the Dixon–Coles and Markov chain models. Experimental results demonstrate that the modified Glicko-based framework achieves higher predictive accuracy than competing methods while maintaining a transparent probabilistic structure and clear interpretability. The resulting ratings can be applied to player evaluation, transfer analysis, and match outcome forecasting across leagues.

Keywords: glicko · rating systems · sports analytics · football match outcome prediction · machine learning

1 Introduction

One of the key challenges for football managers, scouts, and analysts is accurately evaluating player abilities. This can be achieved through video analysis of player performance or by examining performance metrics [1]. In the latter case, it is crucial for analysts to understand the competitive level of different leagues in order to make informed decisions about player recruitment. For example, a player

A. Shelopugin—Independent Researcher.

Z. Liu and V. Misra (Eds.): ISACE 2026, LNCS 16610, pp. 38–61, 2026.
https://doi.org/10.1007/978-3-032-27272-0_4

who is the top goal scorer in a lower-tier league may fail to replicate the same performance level after transferring to a more competitive league.

Another important task in soccer analytics is predicting match outcomes [3]. To improve the accuracy of match outcome predictions, a ranking model needs to be developed. This model enables the simulation of future match results, helping football managers make strategic decisions, particularly regarding player transfers. Additionally, the ranking model can be used to set constraints in draw simulators for final tournaments, ensuring balanced groups and enhancing overall fan engagement.

The UEFA rating system[1]. is widely regarded in soccer, but it has several weaknesses. Firstly, it does not account for the strength of opponents, treating victories over both top teams and weaker opponents equally. Secondly, it relies heavily on past performances, which can distort a team's current ranking and influence tournament draw outcomes. If a team's performance declines, they may still face stronger opponents, making it difficult to accumulate points. Additionally, the system applies the same weight to matches regardless of the season or year, failing to accurately reflect the current strength of teams.

In addition to these major issues, the UEFA rating system has several minor limitations. For instance, the rating points are not based on a solid mathematical foundation, making the system difficult to interpret. Furthermore, it does not effectively assess the strength of a national league, as it primarily focuses on the performance of top teams, which are typically the ones participating in international competitions. This approach provides little to no information about the performance of weaker teams in the first division or those in lower leagues.

This paper aims to address these limitations. We propose an alternative football club rating system based on the Glicko model, with several modifications.

2 Experimental Setup

2.1 Data

The data were collected from Flashscore[2] and consist of matches from the first and second divisions of nearly all countries, as well as national cup competitions and international tournaments such as the UEFA Champions League and Copa Libertadores. Matches involving teams from lower-ranked leagues (third division and below) were deliberately excluded, including national cup matches featuring third-tier teams. In addition, matches decided by forfeit were removed from the dataset.

The final dataset contains approximately 1,120,000 matches played between 2000 and 2025, involving 8,196 unique clubs across 257 leagues.

We train the model using match data from the 2000/2001 through the 2020/2021 seasons. Matches from the 2021/2022 to the 2025/2026 seasons are reserved for out-of-sample evaluation.

---

[1] https://www.uefa.com/nationalassociations/uefarankings/country, accessed February 13, 2026.

[2] https://www.flashscore.com, accessed February 13, 2026.

2.2 Approaches

There are two effective approaches to predicting soccer match outcomes. The first approach is based on predicting the number of goals each team will score and translating these goal expectations into probabilities of a win, draw, or loss. The second approach relies on rating systems to quantify team strength, in which the probabilistic nature is embedded in the model formulation. Consequently, probabilities of a win, draw, or loss arise directly from the rating dynamics. We discuss both approaches in Sects. 3 and 4, respectively.

3 Approach 1: Match Outcome Prediction via Goal Expectations

3.1 Idea

This approach leverages a widely recognized concept for forecasting football match results, focusing on predicting the number of goals each team will score against its respective opponent. We assume that the number of goals in football *approximately* follows a Poisson distribution [3]. We then translate these goal expectations into outcome probabilities.

3.2 Implementation

Gradient boosting models have demonstrated impressive performance when applied to tabular data [9]. Consequently, we constructed a machine learning model utilizing the LightGBM [11] framework to predict the goal count for both competing teams. We also experimented with the CatBoost [12] model; however, it yielded inferior results. Since the goals in football approximately follow a Poisson distribution, we set the LightGBM parameter `objective` to `poisson`. We note, however, that empirical goal distributions deviate from the strict Poisson assumption. This limitation is addressed later through model refinements.

The algorithm was trained using the following features, with each row in the dataset corresponding to a participant in a match:

- a team plays at home (true/false);
- a match is played at a neutral venue (true/false);
- a match takes place during the pandemic period (true/false);
- the number of days since the previous match (numeric);
- the number of games played in the current season (numeric);
- the average number of goals scored in the last 5, 10, 20, and 30 matches (numeric);
- the average number of goals conceded in the last 5, 10, 20, and 30 matches (numeric);
- the average number of goals scored by the opponent in the last 5, 10, 20, and 30 matches (numeric);
- the average number of goals conceded by the opponent in the last 5, 10, 20, and 30 matches (numeric);

- the mean and median number of goals scored at the current location (home or away) in the last 5, 10, 20, and 30 matches (numeric);
- the mean number of goals conceded at the current location in the last 5, 10, 20, and 30 matches (numeric);
- the median number of goals conceded at the current location in the last 10 matches (numeric);
- the maximum number of goals scored at the current location in the last 10 matches (numeric);
- the team's league and the opponent's league (categorical);
- the tournament and the tournament type (categorical).

3.3 Outcome Probabilities via the Skellam Distribution

The Poisson assumption, together with the assumption of independence between the goal-scoring processes of the two teams, allows us to use the probability mass function associated with the Skellam distribution:

$$p(k, \mu_1, \mu_2) = exp(-(\mu_1 + \mu_2))(\frac{\mu_1}{\mu_2})^{\frac{k}{2}} I_k(2\sqrt{\mu_1 \mu_2}) \quad (1)$$

In Eq. (1), I_k is the modified Bessel function, and k represents the score difference in a football match. If $k > 0$, the value of the probability mass function corresponds to the probability of the first team winning; for $k = 0$, it gives the draw probability; and if $k < 0$, it provides the probability of the second team winning. The parameters μ_1 and μ_2 are the means of two Poisson-distributed random variables. In our case, we use the predicted goals as μ_1 and μ_2.

3.4 Score Matrix Models

While the Skellam distribution provides a direct way to compute win, draw, and loss probabilities from goal expectations, it does not explicitly represent the full joint distribution of possible scorelines. To obtain a more detailed description of match outcomes, we construct a score probability matrix.

Let $p(i, j)$ denote the probability that the home team scores i goals and the away team scores j goals. The collection of probabilities $\{p(i, j)\}$ forms a two-dimensional matrix representing the joint distribution of match scores. In practice, the infinite support of goal counts must be truncated for computational purposes. We approximate the joint distribution by constructing a 15×15 score matrix corresponding to goal counts from 0 to 14 for each team. For typical goal expectations observed in professional football, the probability of exceeding this range is negligible; the matrix is subsequently renormalized so that the total probability mass equals one.

Outcome probabilities are then computed by summing over appropriate regions of this matrix:

$$\begin{aligned} p_H &= \sum_{i>j} p(i,j), \\ p_D &= \sum_{i=j} p(i,j), \\ p_A &= \sum_{i<j} p(i,j). \end{aligned} \tag{2}$$

This matrix-based formulation offers several advantages. First, it provides the complete distribution over scorelines rather than only the score difference. Second, it allows flexible modeling of dependence structures between the two teams' goal processes. Third, it serves as a unifying framework within which different probabilistic models can be implemented.

In the following subsections, we describe three alternative constructions of the score matrix.

3.5 Score Matrix Under Independent Poisson Assumption

The simplest approach assumes that the number of goals scored by the home and away teams follows independent Poisson distributions with means μ_1 and μ_2, respectively.

Let $x_i = p(G_{\text{home}} = i)$ and $y_j = p(G_{\text{away}} = j)$ denote the corresponding Poisson probabilities. Under the independence assumption, the joint score probability is given by

$$p(i,j) = x_i y_j. \tag{3}$$

3.6 Dixon–Coles Score Matrix

Although the independent Poisson model provides a convenient baseline, empirical football data reveal dependence between the goal-scoring processes of the two teams, particularly in low-scoring matches. The independent model tends to overestimate the probabilities of certain outcomes such as $(0,0)$ and $(1,1)$.

To account for this, we adopt the Dixon–Coles adjustment [3]. Starting from the independent Poisson construction given in Eq. (3), the probabilities of specific low-score outcomes are modified.

The Dixon–Coles model introduces a dependence parameter ρ that adjusts the probabilities as follows:

$$\begin{aligned} p(0,0) &\leftarrow p(0,0)\,(1 - \mu_1\mu_2\rho), \\ p(0,1) &\leftarrow p(0,1)\,(1 + \mu_1\rho), \\ p(1,0) &\leftarrow p(1,0)\,(1 + \mu_2\rho), \\ p(1,1) &\leftarrow p(1,1)\,(1 - \rho). \end{aligned} \tag{4}$$

All other scoreline probabilities remain unchanged. After applying the correction factors, the score matrix is renormalized to ensure that the total probability sums to one.

When $\rho = 0$, the model reduces to the independent Poisson formulation.

3.7 Markov Approach to Score Matrix Construction

Markov processes are frequently used in sports modeling to describe the dynamic evolution of game states. Goldner [8] applied a Markov model to American football drives, while Dixon and Robinson [2] modeled goal arrivals in soccer as a continuous-time birth process. In contrast to static score prediction, these approaches treat a match as a sequence of state transitions over time.

We model the match as a continuous-time Markov process on the state space of scorelines (i, j), where i and j denote the number of goals scored by the home and away teams. The match starts in state $(0, 0)$ at time $t = 0$ and evolves until the final time T.

Goal arrivals are governed by scoring intensities λ_1 and λ_2 for the home and away teams. In the simplest setting, these intensities are constant and equal to the expected goals μ_1 and μ_2. The only possible transitions are increases in the home or away score:

$$q_{(i,j)\to(i+1,j)} = \lambda_1, \quad q_{(i,j)\to(i,j+1)} = \lambda_2, \tag{5}$$

with diagonal elements ensuring that transition probabilities sum to one.

Let $\mathbf{p}(t)$ denote the probability distribution over scoreline states at time t. Its evolution is described by the Kolmogorov forward equation:

$$\frac{d\mathbf{p}(t)}{dt} = \mathbf{Q}^\top \mathbf{p}(t), \tag{6}$$

whose solution yields the score distribution at the end of the match:

$$\mathbf{p}(T) = \exp(\mathbf{Q}^\top T)\mathbf{p}(0), \tag{7}$$

with initial condition $\mathbf{p}(0) = [1, 0, 0, \ldots]^\top$.

A key advantage of the Markov formulation is that scoring intensities can depend on the current score. We therefore allow

$$\lambda_1(i, j) = \mu_1 \cdot \alpha(i - j), \quad \lambda_2(i, j) = \mu_2 \cdot \beta(j - i), \tag{8}$$

where $\alpha(\cdot)$ and $\beta(\cdot)$ capture score-dependent behavior. For example, a leading team may adopt a more defensive strategy, while a trailing team increases attacking intensity, creating a comeback effect.

Dixon-Coles-style adjustments are incorporated by modifying the transition rates for low-scoring states, with adjustment factors analogous to those in Eq. (4).

4 Approach 2: Match Outcome Prediction Using Modified Glicko

4.1 Rating Systems

Rating systems such as Elo [4], Glicko [5], and TrueSkill [10] have been widely applied to measure competitor strength in head-to-head games and sports. These systems were originally designed for competitions with binary outcomes (win or loss). Most implementations treat ties as equivalent to half a win and half a loss, ignoring the fact that draw probabilities may depend not only on the difference in competitor strengths but also on their absolute strength levels. However, their direct application to team sports such as football presents significant challenges, as standard rating models do not account for crucial sport-specific factors, including home-field advantage, roster changes due to player transfers, and strength-dependent draw probabilities.

In football, the occurrence of draws introduces additional complexity that classical rating systems cannot naturally accommodate. Empirical evidence suggests that draw probabilities depend not only on the relative strength difference between teams, but also on their absolute strength levels and goal-scoring tendencies. Recently, Glickman [6,7] extended the Glicko framework to incorporate strength-dependent tie probabilities in chess, recognizing that draws become more likely when competitors are closely matched in skill, and that stronger players are more likely to draw than weaker players. This development provides a principled foundation for adapting rating systems to football, where draws are similarly common and influenced by both team strengths.

In our previous work [13], we adapted the Glicko-2 model to football by incorporating draw probabilities, home-field advantage, and rating adjustments for league transitions. Building on these developments and Glickman's recent advances, we now adopt the strength-dependent draw framework from [6,7], extending it to account for goal-scoring tendencies—a football-specific factor where high-scoring teams produce fewer draws than low-scoring teams. This relationship is consistent with the nature of goal-scoring in football: teams with lower expected goal rates are more likely to remain at 0-0, thereby increasing the overall probability of a draw, while high-scoring teams generate more total goals, reducing the likelihood that both teams finish with identical scores. Furthermore, we incorporate league-specific characteristics and dynamic rating adjustments following promotion or relegation. Our approach enables cross-league comparisons and provides interpretable ratings that can be applied to player evaluation, transfer analysis, and match outcome prediction across diverse competitive environments.

Although some models calculate ratings for football leagues, such as Club Elo[3] and the UEFA coefficient system, existing approaches suffer from serious drawbacks including failure to account for opponent strength and lack of mathematical interpretability.

[3] http://clubelo.com, accessed February 13, 2026.

4.2 Glicko with Strength-Dependent Draws

The Glicko model represents competitor strength as a probability distribution. Each team is initially associated with a normal prior distribution characterized by a mean rating μ and uncertainty (rating deviation) ϕ. As match outcomes accumulate, ratings are updated via Bayesian inference toward a posterior distribution. When a team wins, its rating increases; the magnitude of this increase is primarily determined by two factors: the difference in ratings (larger upsets produce larger adjustments) and rating uncertainty (teams with limited match history experience larger changes).

Recent work by Glickman [6, 7] extends the Glicko framework to address two critical limitations of classical rating systems. First, order effects such as home-field advantage (analogous to the white piece advantage in chess) systematically favor one competitor. Second, the probability of a draw depends not only on the strength difference between competitors, but also on their absolute strength levels—stronger pairs are more likely to draw.

The original formulas are given below:

$$P(Y_{ij} = 1) = \frac{\exp\left(\theta_i + \frac{1}{4}x_{ij}\left(\alpha_0 + \alpha_1 \cdot \frac{\theta_i+\theta_j}{2}\right)\right)}{D_{ij}} \tag{9}$$

$$P(Y_{ij} = 0) = \frac{\exp\left(\theta_j - \frac{1}{4}x_{ij}\left(\alpha_0 + \alpha_1 \cdot \frac{\theta_i+\theta_j}{2}\right)\right)}{D_{ij}} \tag{10}$$

$$P(Y_{ij} = \tfrac{1}{2}) = \frac{\exp\left(\beta_0 + (1 + \beta_1) \cdot \frac{\theta_i+\theta_j}{2}\right)}{D_{ij}} \tag{11}$$

where:

- θ_i, θ_j are the ratings of team i (home) and team j (away)
- $x_{ij} \in \{-1, 0, 1\}$ indicates venue: $+1$ if team i plays at home, 0 for neutral venue, -1 if away
- α_0 captures baseline home-field advantage
- α_1 models strength-dependent order effects: home advantage may be stronger for high-rated teams
- β_0 sets the baseline draw probability
- β_1 captures strength-dependent draw probability: stronger pairs (large $\frac{\theta_i+\theta_j}{2}$) have different draw tendencies
- $D_{ij} = \exp(\cdots) + \exp(\cdots) + \exp(\cdots)$ is the normalization constant ensuring probabilities sum to one

The term $\frac{\theta_i+\theta_j}{2}$ represents the average strength of both teams. In Eqs. (9)–(10), this term modulates the home-field advantage: the parameter α_1 allows the advantage to vary with team quality. In Eq. (11), the coefficient $(1 + \beta_1)$ determines how draw probability changes with absolute team strength.

4.3 Custom Extensions of Glicko-2

Modified Outcome Probability Function. We modify the original probability specification by (i) incorporating expected goals into both the order effect and the draw component, and (ii) decomposing the baseline order effect into a crowd-related term and a logistic (travel) term. Let g_{ij} denote the expected goals associated with the match, obtained from the goal-based model.

The match outcome probabilities are defined as:

$$P(Y_{ij}=1)=\frac{\exp\left(\theta_i+x_{ij}\left(\alpha_{\text{crowd}}+\alpha_{\text{logistic}}+\alpha_1\frac{\theta_i+\theta_j}{2}+\alpha_2 g_{ij}\right)\right)}{D_{ij}}, \tag{12}$$

$$P(Y_{ij}=0)=\frac{\exp\left(\theta_j-x_{ij}\left(\alpha_{\text{crowd}}+\alpha_{\text{logistic}}+\alpha_1\frac{\theta_i+\theta_j}{2}+\alpha_2 g_{ij}\right)\right)}{D_{ij}}, \tag{13}$$

$$P(Y_{ij}=\tfrac{1}{2})=\frac{\exp\left(\beta_0+\beta_1\frac{\theta_i+\theta_j}{2}+\beta_2 g_{ij}\right)}{D_{ij}}. \tag{14}$$

Here, x_{ij} indicates venue, α_{crowd} and α_{logistic} jointly determine the baseline home advantage, α_1 captures strength-dependent order effects, and α_2 introduces a scoring-intensity adjustment. The draw component is governed by β_0 (baseline draw frequency), β_1 (strength dependence), and β_2 (scoring dependence).

The separation between α_{crowd} and α_{logistic} is identifiable due to the COVID-19 period, during which matches were played without spectators. While the crowd-related component was effectively removed, travel-related disadvantages remained, providing natural variation that allows the two effects to be estimated separately. Beyond the pandemic period, match-level annotations from Flashscore—such as "Limited number of spectators" or "Playing home matches at a different stadium"—enable further fine-tuning of these parameters. For instance, when a limited audience is reported, we reduce the crowd effect accordingly.

Rating Initialization. The Glicko model depends only on rating differences; adding a constant to all ratings does not affect predicted match outcomes. To enable cross-league comparability, we introduce an additional parameter referred to as the *initial league rating*, which represents the average strength level of a league. While this parameter does not affect predictions within a single national championship, it plays a crucial role when comparing teams across different leagues, particularly in international competitions.

However, naive initialization at the league average may lead to rating inflation. Since the initial league rating approximates the mean strength of the division, teams entering the dataset without recent match history may be assigned an unrealistically high starting value. For example, consider a team whose first recorded match in our dataset appears in 2015 in the second division. If the team previously competed in lower divisions not included in the dataset, its true strength is likely below the average level of the second league.

To address this issue, we adjust the initial rating for teams promoted from lower-ranked leagues by introducing a downward correction. Furthermore, if a team has no match history in the immediately preceding season, its rating is reinitialized even if earlier historical data exist. For instance, if a team competed in the second division during the 2013–2014 season, was relegated to the third division (excluded from the dataset), and later returned to the second division in 2015–2016, its rating is reinitialized prior to the 2015–2016 season.

Formally, the initialization rule is defined as:

$$r(\mu, \phi) = \begin{cases} r(\mu_{\text{init}} + \mu_{\text{new}}, \phi) & \text{if the team was promoted from a lower division,} \\ r(\mu_{\text{init}}, \phi) & \text{otherwise.} \end{cases} \tag{15}$$

The parameter μ_{new} is negative and represents the downward adjustment applied to teams entering from lower-ranked leagues.

Mid-Season. The fact that team rosters can change during the transfer window cannot be overlooked. To address this, we leverage the rating deviation parameter from the Glicko model. At the beginning of a tournament, ratings are significantly influenced by each win or loss; however, as more data accumulates, these ratings stabilize and experience fewer deviations. We update this parameter at the start of every season.

Additionally, we introduce a parameter that accounts for the tendency of teams to either strengthen or weaken during transitions between leagues. For instance, when a team is promoted to the Premier League or relegated to the Second League, its rating undergoes slight adjustments. This parameter enables us to capture the tendency of teams in different national leagues to engage in active transfer campaigns following a league change.

Consequently, we update team ratings at the beginning of each season using the following equation:

$$r(\mu, \phi) = \begin{cases} r(\mu + \mu_l, \phi + \phi_s) & \text{if team changed league,} \\ r(\mu, \phi + \phi_s) & \text{otherwise.} \end{cases} \tag{16}$$

The parameter ϕ_s should be positive to introduce a degree of uncertainty. The parameter μ_l should be positive for promoted teams and negative for relegated teams because the club budget typically increases after promotion and decreases after relegation.

Another factor that can lead to rating inflation is the change in the number of teams due to alterations in league rules, among other reasons. To prevent this inflation, we normalize all ratings after each season. Consequently, the average rating of all teams should remain constant.

4.4 Parameter Estimation

All model parameters are estimated separately for each league. For every league, we jointly estimate the initialization parameters μ_{init} and μ_{new}, the league-transition adjustment μ_l, the seasonal uncertainty parameter ϕ_s, and the outcome probability parameters α_{crowd}, α_{logistic}, α_1, α_2, β_0, β_1, and β_2.

Parameter estimation is performed by minimizing the log-loss function computed on historical match outcomes.

Although it may be theoretically appealing to assign team-specific parameters—incorporating factors such as stadium capacity, geographic distance between cities, or other determinants of home advantage—such an approach substantially increases model complexity and typically results in overfitting.

The complete estimation pipeline is illustrated in Fig. 1 in the Appendix.

5 Experimental Results

Model performance is evaluated on a held-out test set consisting of 251,738 matches. We report outcome-based log-loss (win/draw/loss probabilities).

5.1 Comparison of Score Distribution Models

We compare alternative constructions of the score distribution derived from identical goal expectations. The expected goals for both teams are obtained from the LightGBM-based goal model described in Sect. 3. These expectations are held fixed across all specifications. Differences therefore arise solely from the assumed probabilistic structure of the score distribution.

In particular, we evaluate:

(i) the direct Skellam formulation, (ii) the independent Poisson score matrix, (iii) the Dixon–Coles adjusted matrix, and (iv) the Markov score matrix (Table 1).

Table 1. Comparison of score distribution models

Model	Outcome Log Loss
Skellam (direct)	0.584307
Poisson matrix	0.584305
Dixon–Coles	0.584278
Markov	0.584240

The direct Skellam computation produces virtually identical outcome log-loss to the independent Poisson matrix formulation, confirming the internal consistency of the implementation.

The Dixon–Coles and Markov models achieve slightly lower loss values. Although the numerical improvements are modest, they are consistent across specifications. This suggests that incorporating dependence corrections and state-dependent dynamics yields incremental predictive gains relative to the independent Poisson assumption.

5.2 Comparison of Rating Models

We compare the original Glicko model with the proposed modified Glicko framework using outcome-based log-loss. The results are summarized in Table 2.

The modified Glicko model achieves lower log-loss than the original formulation. Although the absolute difference appears small, in the context of large-scale probabilistic forecasting this improvement is meaningful and consistent across the evaluation sample.

Notably, the gain relative to the classical Glicko model is an order of magnitude larger than the improvements observed among alternative score-distribution specifications, highlighting the importance of structural modifications to the rating framework.

For benchmarking purposes, we also evaluated matrix-based score distribution models. While these approaches provide flexible probabilistic representations of match outcomes, they lack interpretability compared to rating systems. In particular, matrix models do not produce stable, comparable strength parameters that can be directly used for cross-league analysis, player evaluation, or transfer assessment. In contrast, the Glicko framework yields structured and interpretable ratings that retain predictive power while offering broader analytical utility.

Importantly, evaluation is performed on the most recent seasons, where many teams already possess extensive match histories. Despite this, parameters designed to capture faster dynamics—such as mid-season and transition adjustments—continue to improve predictive performance, indicating that temporal responsiveness remains valuable even in mature rating trajectories.

Table 2. Comparison of rating models

Method	Log Loss
Original Glicko	0.579213
Modified Glicko	0.578241

5.3 Example of Application League Ratings in the Task of Players Metrics Prediction

Consider, for instance, our objective to predict various player metrics for the upcoming season, such as the number of goals a specific player will score. To make accurate predictions, we can take into account factors like player age, position, previous performance, and the number of goals scored in the previous season, along with other relevant features. However, a significant challenge arises when a player undergoes transfers, moving to a different club or league during their career. How can we effectively inform the model about such transitions?

One possible solution involves introducing a categorical feature, such as "player transfers from the Denmark Superliga to France Ligue 1." Nonetheless, this approach encounters the curse of dimensionality—there are relatively few transfers between these two leagues, making it challenging for the model to train effectively. A more viable approach, which aligns with our method, is to generate numeric features. For example, we can create a feature that quantifies the difference in ratings between the Denmark Superliga and France Ligue 1. This enables the model to account for league transitions more effectively.

Additionally, we can enhance the precision of player performance analysis, particularly within the context of a single team. For instance, we can calculate the average rating of the opposing teams faced by each player. This fine-grained analysis helps differentiate player performances, as several players may exhibit similar statistics, but the strength of the opponent teams they encounter can vary significantly.

6 Discussion

The primary limitation of the proposed framework is its reliance exclusively on match outcomes. As a result, the model implicitly assumes that team strength evolves smoothly over time. In practice, however, roster composition can change substantially during the season, particularly in second-tier leagues where transfers and financial instability are more common. Such structural breaks are only partially captured through seasonal and mid-season adjustments.

The dataset spans six confederations, providing broad global coverage. However, direct intercontinental competition remains relatively rare. Matches between clubs from different confederations are largely restricted to tournaments such as the FIFA Club World Cup, where the number of games is limited. This sparse cross-confederation interaction reduces the amount of information available to anchor ratings across regions and may introduce additional uncertainty when comparing clubs from different continents.

Despite these constraints, the proposed framework remains computationally efficient and relies solely on publicly available data. While alternative probabilistic score-distribution models yield only marginal performance differences, the modified Glicko framework consistently improves predictive accuracy and provides interpretable ratings that can be directly applied to downstream analytical tasks.

Acknowledgments. Andrei Shelopugin is thankful to Nikita Kozodoi and Viktoria Lokteva for their valuable feedback on this paper and for contributions to the earlier stages of this research.

A The Diagram of the Proposed Rating Estimation Algorithm

See Tables 3 and 4.

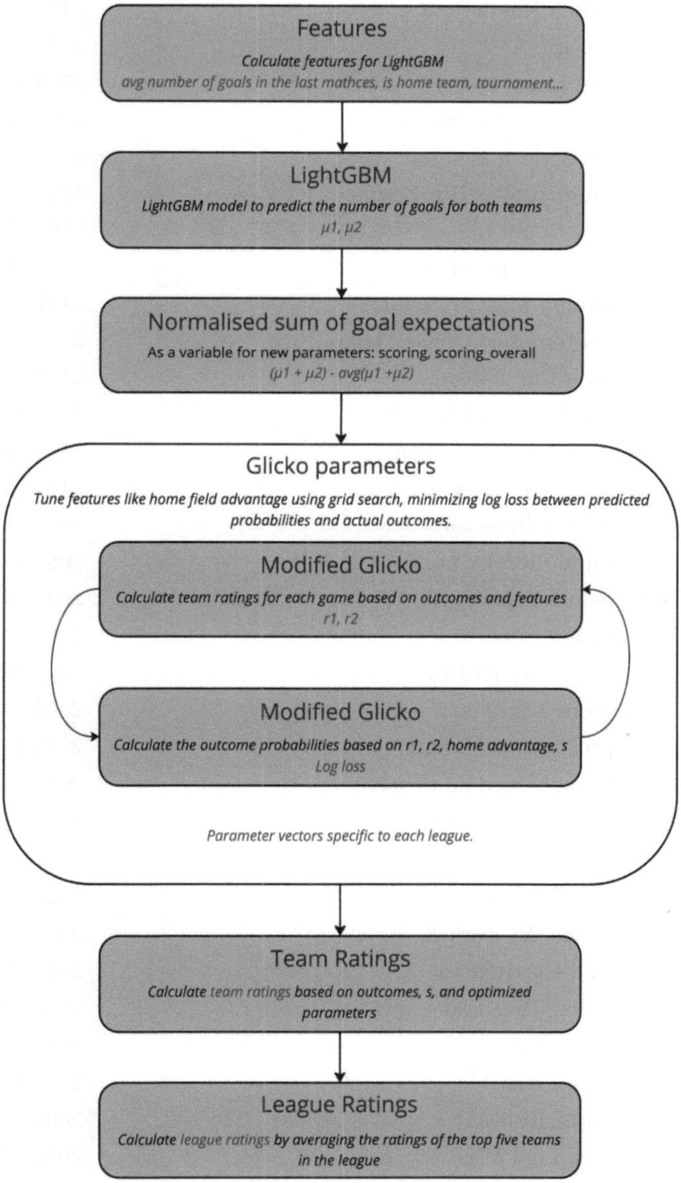

Fig. 1. The diagram of the proposed rating estimation algorithm. The outputs of each block are shown in italic red. (Color figure online)

Table 3. League Ratings Across All Competitions (average rating of top-7 teams)

#	League	Rating
1	Spain LaLiga	2513.55
2	England Premier League	2511.64
3	Germany Bundesliga	2471.33
4	Italy Serie A	2425.45
5	France Ligue 1	2359.32
6	Portugal Liga Portugal	2265.77
7	Brazil Serie A Betano	2237.02
8	Belgium Jupiler Pro League	2218.99
9	Turkey Super Lig	2204.77
10	Netherlands Eredivisie	2189.79
11	Argentina Liga Profesional	2147.46
12	Czech Republic Chance Liga	2138.67
13	Austria Bundesliga	2133.31
14	Russia Premier League*	2125.40
15	Germany 2. Bundesliga	2120.34
16	Greece Super League	2113.70
17	Norway Eliteserien	2090.31
18	Ukraine Premier League	2088.19
19	Romania Superliga	2087.93
20	Denmark Superliga	2065.03
21	Morocco Botola Pro	2058.27
22	Ecuador Liga Pro	2052.69
23	Cyprus Cyprus League	2052.29
24	Paraguay Copa de Primera	2051.25
25	Switzerland Super League	2047.16
26	England Championship	2042.17
27	Scotland Premiership	2027.61
28	Colombia Primera A	2023.66
29	Poland Ekstraklasa	2019.45
30	Sweden Allsvenskan	2018.42
31	Croatia HNL	2017.70
32	Algeria Ligue 1	2012.95
33	Israel Ligat ha'Al	2006.86
34	Mexico Liga MX	2002.97
35	Uruguay Liga AUF Uruguaya	1989.18

(*continued*)

Table 3. (*continued*)

#	League	Rating
36	Brazil Serie B Superbet	1982.86
37	Chile Liga de Primera	1970.91
38	Argentina Primera Nacional	1966.58
39	Slovenia Prva liga	1948.51
40	Belarus Vysshaya Liga	1944.18
41	Turkey 1. Lig	1933.36
42	Peru Liga 1	1931.11
43	Slovakia Nike liga	1930.64
44	Iran Persian Gulf Pro League	1930.27
45	Moldova Super Liga	1930.18
46	Egypt Premier League	1917.90
47	Bulgaria efbet League	1914.48
48	Finland Veikkausliiga	1912.78
49	Gambia GFA League	1912.26
50	Usa MLS	1909.45
51	France Ligue 2	1895.11
52	Serbia Mozzart Bet Super Liga	1891.89
53	Japan J1 League	1883.88
54	Tunisia Ligue Professionnelle 1	1882.06
55	Hungary NB I.	1866.22
56	North Macedonia 1. MFL	1861.59
57	South Africa Betway Premiership	1858.60
58	South Korea K League 1	1855.02
59	Iceland Besta deild karla	1853.30
60	China Super League	1848.46
61	Azerbaijan Premier League	1846.13
62	Nigeria NPFL	1842.72
63	Kazakhstan Premier League	1842.57
64	Romania Liga 2	1840.40
65	Paraguay Division Intermedia	1833.01
66	Algeria Ligue 2	1831.37
67	Ghana Premier League	1830.15
68	Venezuela Liga FUTVE	1826.97
69	Saudi Arabia Saudi Professional League	1821.62
70	Georgia Crystalbet Erovnuli Liga	1820.75

(*continued*)

Table 3. (*continued*)

#	League	Rating
71	Lithuania A Lyga	1812.98
72	Zambia Super League	1809.58
73	Bosnia And Herzegovina WWIN Liga BiH	1801.27
74	Libya Premier League	1800.26
75	Russia FNL*	1788.21
76	Norway OBOS-ligaen	1787.86
77	Mexico Liga de Expansion MX	1786.61
78	Albania Abissnet Superiore	1785.69
79	Uganda Premier League	1785.08
80	United Arab Emirates UAE League	1785.04
81	Dr Congo Ligue 1	1784.84
82	Bolivia Division Profesional	1781.15
83	Togo Championnat National	1779.53
84	Morocco Botola 2	1777.13
85	Poland Division 1	1767.45
86	Guinea Ligue 1	1766.13
87	Senegal Ligue 1	1766.08
88	Angola Girabola	1764.89
89	Switzerland Challenge League	1762.59
90	Barbados Premier League	1760.30
91	Mauritania Ligue 1	1758.79
92	Syria Premier League	1756.76
93	Mali Premiere Division	1754.26
94	Latvia Virsliga	1753.29
95	Israel Leumit League	1752.72
96	Armenia Premier League	1750.88
97	Iraq Stars League	1741.19
98	Kosovo Superliga	1736.98
99	Australia A-League	1735.69
100	Malawi Super League	1734.97
101	Bahrain Premier League	1731.21
102	Chile Liga de Ascenso	1722.06
103	Qatar QSL	1717.43
104	Malta Premier League	1715.59
105	Benin Ligue 1	1712.71

(*continued*)

Table 3. (*continued*)

#	League	Rating
106	Burundi Primus League	1712.64
107	Thailand Thai League 1	1709.58
108	Burkina Faso Premier League	1699.20
109	Cameroon Elite One	1697.27
110	Northern Ireland NIFL Premiership	1691.89
111	Niger Super Ligue	1686.58
112	Macao Elite League	1684.88
113	Ivory Coast Ligue 1	1684.80
114	Slovenia 2. SNL	1682.60
115	Ireland Premier Division	1676.49
116	Faroe Islands Premier League	1672.01
117	Tanzania Ligi Kuu Bara	1664.03
118	Costa Rica Primera Division	1662.35
119	Sweden Superettan	1662.27
120	Scotland Championship	1660.56
121	Liberia LFA First Division	1654.77
122	Rwanda Premier League	1647.44
123	Japan J2 League	1646.40
124	Montenegro Prva Crnogorska Liga	1643.82
125	Kuwait Premier League	1642.79
126	Dominican Republic LDF	1638.60
127	Eswatini Swazi MTN Premier League	1636.30
128	Slovakia 2. liga	1635.00
129	Ethiopia Premier League	1624.48
130	Luxembourg BGL Ligue	1622.82
131	Republic Of The Congo Ligue 1	1621.34
132	Gabon Championnat D1	1609.37
133	Kenya Premier League	1607.82
134	Sri Lanka Super League	1604.95
135	Sudan Premier League	1601.40
136	Lebanon Premier League	1601.15
137	Venezuela Liga FUTVE 2	1600.88
138	South Korea K League 2	1600.45
139	Suriname SML	1592.86
140	Iceland Division 1	1588.84

(*continued*)

Table 3. (*continued*)

#	League	Rating
141	Estonia Meistriliiga	1588.35
142	Nigeria NNL	1584.67
143	Canada Canadian Premier League	1567.05
144	South Africa Motsepe Foundation Championship	1562.45
145	Uzbekistan Super League	1551.44
146	Wales Cymru Premier	1550.23
147	Guatemala Liga Nacional	1547.83
148	Indonesia Super League	1545.08
149	Cameroon Elite Two	1539.44
150	Bhutan Premier League	1538.95
151	Honduras Liga Nacional	1535.51
152	Zimbabwe Premier Soccer League	1533.62
153	Jordan Premier League	1527.28
154	Malaysia Super League	1519.45
155	Haiti Championnat National	1518.98
156	India ISL	1514.52
157	El Salvador Primera Division	1513.93
158	Mozambique Mocambola	1508.38
159	Fiji Premier League	1507.85
160	Botswana Premier League	1507.16
161	Palestine West Bank League	1492.85
162	Oman Professional League	1464.15
163	Lesotho Premier League	1449.83
164	Vietnam V.League 1	1448.54
165	Chad Premiere Division	1445.40
166	Turkmenistan Yokary Liga	1444.69
167	Panama LPF	1432.68
168	Antigua & Barbuda ABFA Premier League	1431.43
169	Saudi Arabia Division 1	1424.72
170	India I-League	1411.38
171	Gibraltar National League	1401.82
172	Andorra Primera Divisió	1401.43
173	New Zealand National League	1388.85
174	Singapore Premier League	1383.79
175	Sierra Leone Premier League	1377.42

(*continued*)

Table 3. (*continued*)

#	League	Rating
176	Bermuda Premier League	1371.12
177	Trinidad And Tobago TT Premier League	1352.58
178	Mongolia Premier League	1344.09
179	Hong Kong Premier League	1343.61
180	Nicaragua Liga Primera	1336.70
181	Cambodia CPL	1310.84
182	Jamaica Premier League	1309.16
183	Taiwan Premier League	1308.86
184	Mauritius Super League	1279.30
185	Philippines PFL	1256.59
186	Tajikistan Vysshaya Liga	1239.66
187	Somalia National league	1211.42
188	Kyrgyzstan Premier Liga	1194.81
189	Bangladesh BFL	1191.75
190	Seychelles Premier League	1166.48
191	Vietnam V.League 2	1148.69
192	San Marino Campionato Sammarinese	1119.95
193	Yemen Division 1	1119.74
194	Laos Lao League	980.98
195	Myanmar National League	978.32

Table 4. Top 100 Clubs by Rating

Rank	Team	Rating	League
1	Real Madrid Spain	2681.44	Spain LaLiga
2	Barcelona Spain	2677.18	Spain LaLiga
3	PSG	2660.02	France Ligue 1
4	Bayern Munich	2645.91	Germany Bundesliga
5	Liverpool	2626.67	England Premier League
6	Inter Italy	2612.25	Italy Serie A
7	Manchester City	2582.54	England Premier League
8	Arsenal England	2580.66	England Premier League
9	Bayer Leverkusen	2579.09	Germany Bundesliga
10	Atl. Madrid	2558.40	Spain LaLiga
11	Dortmund	2492.73	Germany Bundesliga
12	Villarreal Spain	2483.08	Spain LaLiga
13	Newcastle England	2473.77	England Premier League

(*continued*)

Table 4. (*continued*)

Rank	Team	Rating	League
14	Ath Bilbao	2471.91	Spain LaLiga
15	Chelsea	2469.47	England Premier League
16	Sporting CP	2464.83	Portugal Liga Portugal
17	Benfica Portugal	2451.34	Portugal Liga Portugal
18	PSV	2446.32	Netherlands Eredivisie
19	Aston Villa England	2444.21	England Premier League
20	Napoli	2431.29	Italy Serie A
21	RB Leipzig	2409.33	Germany Bundesliga
22	Juventus Italy	2405.34	Italy Serie A
23	Crystal Palace England	2404.20	England Premier League
24	Eintracht Frankfurt	2402.77	Germany Bundesliga
25	Stuttgart	2399.53	Germany Bundesliga
26	Manchester Utd	2394.30	England Premier League
27	AC Milan	2393.56	Italy Serie A
28	Atalanta	2391.39	Italy Serie A
29	Galatasaray	2382.91	Turkey Super Lig
30	AS Roma	2381.95	Italy Serie A
31	Betis	2377.76	Spain LaLiga
32	Freiburg	2369.94	Germany Bundesliga
33	Brighton	2367.10	England Premier League
34	Club Brugge KV	2364.03	Belgium Jupiler Pro League
35	Lille	2362.69	France Ligue 1
36	Lazio	2362.39	Italy Serie A
37	Fenerbahce	2361.72	Turkey Super Lig
38	FC Porto	2358.09	Portugal Liga Portugal
39	Royale Union SG	2357.55	Belgium Jupiler Pro League
40	Olympiacos Piraeus	2355.77	Greece Super League
41	Osasuna	2345.06	Spain LaLiga
42	Monaco	2343.30	France Ligue 1
43	Slavia Prague	2340.86	Czech Republic Chance Liga
44	Palmeiras	2338.79	Brazil Serie A Betano
45	Real Sociedad Spain	2337.55	Spain LaLiga
46	Flamengo RJ	2336.41	Brazil Serie A Betano
47	Celta Vigo	2336.06	Spain LaLiga
48	Celtic Scotland	2329.49	Scotland Premiership

(*continued*)

Table 4. (*continued*)

Rank	Team	Rating	League
49	Bologna	2328.08	Italy Serie A
50	Marseille	2323.79	France Ligue 1
51	Mainz	2323.56	Germany Bundesliga
52	Werder Bremen	2321.33	Germany Bundesliga
53	Tottenham	2319.97	England Premier League
54	Lyon	2312.34	France Ligue 1
55	Valencia	2301.10	Spain LaLiga
56	Crvena zvezda	2298.89	Serbia Mozzart Bet Super Liga
57	Rayo Vallecano	2298.85	Spain LaLiga
58	Bournemouth	2293.65	England Premier League
59	Braga	2291.70	Portugal Liga Portugal
60	Nottingham	2286.10	England Premier League
61	Wolfsburg	2285.52	Germany Bundesliga
62	Mallorca	2284.60	Spain LaLiga
63	Brentford	2280.48	England Premier League
64	Fulham	2279.86	England Premier League
65	Shakhtar Donetsk	2278.17	Ukraine Premier League
66	Fiorentina	2277.51	Italy Serie A
67	Everton England	2275.34	England Premier League
68	Feyenoord	2275.33	Netherlands Eredivisie
69	West Ham	2274.12	England Premier League
70	Union Berlin	2272.69	Germany Bundesliga
71	Plzen	2270.69	Czech Republic Chance Liga
72	Nice	2266.87	France Ligue 1
73	Bodo/Glimt	2264.99	Norway Eliteserien
74	B. Monchengladbach	2263.93	Germany Bundesliga
75	Alaves	2262.13	Spain LaLiga
76	Augsburg	2260.03	Germany Bundesliga
77	Wolves England	2254.55	England Premier League
78	Girona	2246.30	Spain LaLiga
79	Lens	2246.23	France Ligue 1
80	Genk	2245.69	Belgium Jupiler Pro League
81	Salzburg	2245.31	Austria Bundesliga
82	Sevilla	2244.83	Spain LaLiga
83	FCSB	2241.26	Romania Superliga

(*continued*)

Table 4. (*continued*)

Rank	Team	Rating	League
84	Espanyol	2238.70	Spain LaLiga
85	Sturm Graz	2237.86	Austria Bundesliga
86	Getafe	2235.44	Spain LaLiga
87	Levante	2234.24	Spain LaLiga
88	Dyn. Kyiv	2231.55	Ukraine Premier League
89	Brest	2229.63	France Ligue 1
90	Ajax	2229.26	Netherlands Eredivisie
91	Sparta Prague	2225.63	Czech Republic Chance Liga
92	Viking Norway	2224.62	Norway Eliteserien
93	Botafogo RJ	2222.04	Brazil Serie A Betano
94	Hoffenheim	2219.19	Germany Bundesliga
95	Oviedo	2211.52	Spain LaLiga
96	Fluminense	2210.87	Brazil Serie A Betano
97	FC Copenhagen	2210.56	Denmark Superliga
98	Leganes	2208.57	Spain LaLiga
99	Anderlecht	2207.96	Belgium Jupiler Pro League
100	Strasbourg	2207.58	France Ligue 1

References

1. Bergkamp, T.L., Frencken, W.G., Niessen, A.S.M., Meijer, R.R., den Hartigh, R.J.: How soccer scouts identify talented players. Eur. J. Sport Sci. **22**(7), 994–1004 (2022)
2. Dixon, M., Robinson, M.: A birth process model for association football matches. J. Royal Stat. Soc. Ser. D (Stat.) **47**(3), 523–538 (1998)
3. Dixon, M.J., Coles, S.G.: Modelling association football scores and inefficiencies in the football betting market. J. Roy. Stat. Soc.: Ser. C (Appl. Stat.) **46**(2), 265–280 (1997)
4. Elo, A.E.: The proposed USCF rating system, its development, theory, and applications. Chess Life **22**(8), 242–247 (1967)
5. Glickman, M.E.: Example of the Glicko-2 System, vol. 28. Boston University (2012)
6. Glickman, M.E.: Paired comparison models with strength-dependent ties and order effects. Statistical Modelling p. 1471082X251400474 (2025)
7. Glickman, M.E.: Rating competitors in games with strength-dependent tie probabilities arXiv preprint arXiv:2506.11354 (2025)
8. Goldner, K.: A Markov model of football: using stochastic processes to model a football drive. J. Quant. Anal. Sports **8**(1) (2012)
9. Grinsztajn, L., Oyallon, E., Varoquaux, G.: Why do tree-based models still outperform deep learning on typical tabular data? Adv. Neural. Inf. Process. Syst. **35**, 507–520 (2022)
10. Herbrich, R., Minka, T., Graepel, T.: Trueskill^{TM}: a Bayesian skill rating system. Adv. Neural Inf. Process. Syst. **19** (2006)

11. Ke, G., et al.: LightGBM: a highly efficient gradient boosting decision tree. Adv. Neural Inf. Process. Syst., **30** (2017)
12. Prokhorenkova, L., Gusev, G., Vorobev, A., Dorogush, A.V., Gulin, A.: Catboost: unbiased boosting with categorical features. Adv. Neural Inf. Process. Syst. **31** (2018)
13. Shelopugin, A., Sirotkin, A.: Ratings of European and south American football leagues based on Glicko-2 with modifications. arXiv preprint arXiv:2310.11459 (2023)

A Multi-dimensional Spatial Similarity Framework for Football Player Comparison: Extending Positional Analysis with Tactical Context

Amr Safwat[1(✉)], Shehap Elhadary[1], Bassel Ahmed[1], Mohamed Hafez[2], and Tamer Basha[1]

[1] Cairo University, Faculty of Engineering, Giza, Egypt
{amrou.abdelmawla03,shehap.elhadary03,bassel.shahat03}@eng-st.cu.edu.eg, tamer.basha@eng1.cu.edu.eg
[2] Ontario Tech University, Oshawa, Canada
mohamed.hafez1@ontariotechu.net

Abstract. Traditional football player similarity methods often rely on collapsed positional heatmaps or aggregate statistics, conflating spatial occupation with functional behavior. As a result, players operating in similar zones of the pitch may be incorrectly identified as similar despite performing fundamentally different actions.

We propose an action-aware spatial similarity framework that models player behavior as a third-order spatial-action tensor, separating spatial distributions by action type. Channel-wise spatial association is computed using a bivariate spatial statistic, and similarities are aggregated through a profile-weighted fusion scheme. This design preserves functional context while incorporating spatial dependence.

The framework is evaluated using cross-match self-retrieval on two independent datasets: the Impect Bundesliga 2023/24 season and the FIFA World Cup 2022. Results demonstrate consistent improvements over a collapsed baseline across event budgets, with performance gains increasing as event volume grows. Qualitative case studies further illustrate that the proposed method retrieves functionally aligned players rather than those sharing only positional overlap.

These findings highlight the importance of action-specific spatial decomposition for robust and interpretable player similarity analysis in football analytics.

Keywords: Football Analytics · Player Similarity · Spatial Modeling · Action-Aware Representation · Event Data Analysis · Spatial Autocorrelation

1 Introduction

Modern football teams increasingly operate as complex system entities, each embodying a unique tactical identity derived from coaching methodology, player

Z. Liu and V. Misra (Eds.): ISACE 2026, LNCS 16610, pp. 62–72, 2026.
https://doi.org/10.1007/978-3-032-27272-0_5

attributes, and collective playing patterns [9]. This has created a growing need to identify players who can seamlessly fit into an existing system based on their spatial distributions, movement styles, or event profiles [8,10]. Consequently, precise player similarity assessment has become essential for scouting, squad construction, injury replacement, and preserving tactical cohesion [7].

Traditional scouting and evaluation methods heavily rely on aggregate statistics such as shots, passes, assists, or challenges [3]. While these metrics provide a high-level summary of a player's on-ball involvement, they fail to capture how and where actions are performed. Such metrics overlook spatial context, temporal dynamics, and interactions within the team structure. As a result, players with distinct playing styles operating in different tactical systems may appear similar, while players with comparable roles and behaviors may be incorrectly characterized as dissimilar.

A player's on-pitch identity should be defined not only by the actions taken, but also by when these actions occur, how they are executed, and the contextual conditions under which they take place. Tactical responsibilities are reflected in the types of actions a player repeatedly takes, while the spatial distributions of these actions capture role-specific patterns. Furthermore, how actions are performed under defensive pressure or within particular spatial patterns reveals decision-making processes. Moreover, temporal context shapes a player's identity by capturing how behavior changes throughout different phases of a match. Together, these spatiotemporal and behavioral dimensions provide a more comprehensive representation of player style than aggregate statistics alone [1].

Recent reviews of scouting talents in football show an increasing trend towards the use of data-driven frameworks that integrate match statistics, physical performance metrics, and different machine learning models. This shift stems from the need to standardize player evaluation and reduce subjectivity in scouting decisions. Such approaches mainly focus on aggregate event statistics and workload indicators. Although beneficial for predicting performance and supporting recruitment decisions, these frameworks provide limited information on the spatiotemporal profile of a player [11]. Moreover, many of the approaches involving machine learning models act as black-box systems [6], with limited interpretability and difficulty in understanding which aspects of the player's behavior drive similarity with other players. As a result, interpreting these model outputs into actionable football insights remains challenging.

More recent approaches in football data analytics started to address the gap between raw statistics and spatial information. One of the developments in this domain is the work of Gómez-Rubio et al. [2], which introduced a spatial similarity index based on spatial similarity [5]. In this work, a football field is discretized into a regular grid, and player activity within each spatial cell is aggregated to produce individual spatial density maps, commonly represented as heatmaps. Then spatial autocorrelation is measured, effectively quantifying the similarity of "clustering patterns" between two players' heatmaps. This method provides a mathematical framework for determining if two players occupy the same zones on the pitch.

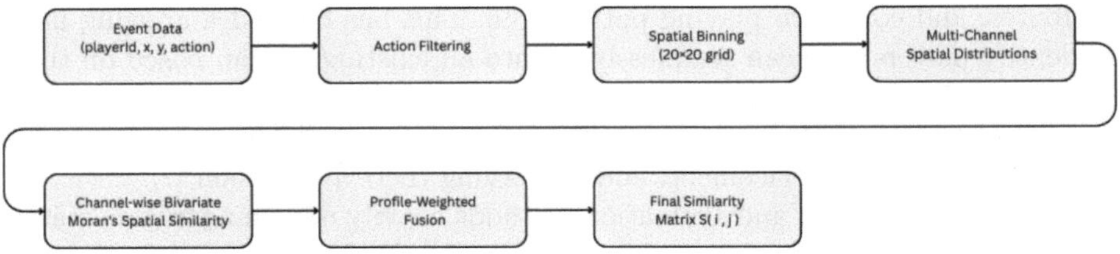

Fig. 1. Overview of the proposed action-aware spatial similarity framework. Event data are filtered into action channels and discretized into spatial grids to form a spatial-action tensor. Channel-wise spatial association is computed using bivariate Moran's statistic and aggregated via profile-weighted fusion to produce the final similarity matrix.

However, the separation between different action contexts remains a key limitation. The aggregation of all on-ball events into a single heatmap leads to the assumption that players operating in similar zones of the pitch exhibit similar playing styles. In practice, this assumption does not always hold. For example, if we observe two wingers who operate in wide areas, the framework will indicate similarity between both players. However, one mainly delivers crosses from the flank, while the other frequently dribbles into central zones. Players occupying the same positional role usually perform fundamentally different actions within the same spatial regions. Although their spatial heatmaps may appear similar, their functional role and style in contributions differ substantially. Collapsing these into a single spatial heatmap leads to a risk of masking real differences in playing style and tactical intent. As a result, using spatial similarity alone will fail to distinguish positional occupation with functional behavior, indicating higher similarity scores between players who share zones but have different tactical responsibilities.

To address this limitation, this study proposes a comprehensive action-aware framework. We build directly upon the framework based on Bivariate Moran's I statistic but expands the input from a single channel heatmap to a multi-channel heatmaps where each channel represents an action. Instead of analyzing only the player's location, we divide the events into distinct action types such as passing, shooting, defensive actions, and ball progressions. Then we compute spatial similarity using Bivariate Moran's I statistic. Using this approach ensures that a player's identity is defined not just by the regions they occupy, but by the specific actions they execute within that region, resolving the presence of ambiguity in aggregated spatial models.

2 Methodology

2.1 Overview

We propose an action-aware spatial similarity framework that models player behavior as a third-order spatial-action tensor. Unlike collapsed positional heatmaps, the proposed representation preserves functional context by separating actions into distinct spatial channels and incorporating spatial autocorrelation during similarity computation. An overview of the proposed framework is illustrated in Fig. 1.

2.2 Spatial-Action Tensor Representation

The pitch is standardized to 105×68 meters and discretized into a uniform $G \times G$ grid with $G = 20$, yielding G^2 spatial cells.

For player i and action type a, the spatial count in cell (x, y) is

$$C_{i,a}(x, y) = \text{count of action } a \text{ in cell } (x, y). \tag{1}$$

Counts are normalized to form spatial probability distributions:

$$H_{i,a}(x, y) = \frac{C_{i,a}(x, y)}{\sum_{x,y} C_{i,a}(x, y)}. \tag{2}$$

Each player is represented as a third-order tensor:

$$\mathcal{T}_i \in \mathbb{R}^{G \times G \times K}, \tag{3}$$

where K denotes the number of action channels and

$$\mathcal{T}_i(x, y, a) = H_{i,a}(x, y). \tag{4}$$

For comparison, a collapsed baseline is defined as

$$H_i^{\text{collapsed}}(x, y) = \frac{\sum_a C_{i,a}(x, y)}{\sum_{x,y,a} C_{i,a}(x, y)}. \tag{5}$$

2.3 Spatial Weights Matrix

To incorporate spatial dependence, we define a spatial weights matrix $W \in \mathbb{R}^{G^2 \times G^2}$ using queen contiguity (8-neighborhood).

$$W_{uv} = \begin{cases} 1 & \text{if cells } u \text{ and } v \text{ share a side or corner} \\ 0 & \text{otherwise.} \end{cases} \tag{6}$$

The matrix is row-standardized:

$$\tilde{W} = D^{-1} W, \tag{7}$$

where D is the diagonal matrix of row sums.

2.4 Channel-Wise Spatial Association (Bivariate Moran's I)

Let $\mathbf{x} = \mathrm{vec}(\mathcal{T}_i(:,:,a))$ and $\mathbf{y} = \mathrm{vec}(\mathcal{T}_j(:,:,a))$ denote the flattened spatial distributions $(G^2 \times 1)$ for players i and j in channel a.

Each vector is standardized:

$$\mathbf{x}_z = \frac{\mathbf{x} - \bar{x}\mathbf{1}}{\sigma_x}, \quad \mathbf{y}_z = \frac{\mathbf{y} - \bar{y}\mathbf{1}}{\sigma_y}. \tag{8}$$

The bivariate Moran (cross-Moran) statistic is computed as

$$I_{i,j,a} = \frac{n}{S^2} \mathbf{x}_z^\top \tilde{W} \mathbf{y}_z, \tag{9}$$

where $n = G^2$ is the number of spatial cells and $S = \sum_{u,v} W_{uv}$ is the total weight mass.

Following the asymptotic distribution of the statistic, we standardize it as

$$z_{i,j,a} = \frac{I_{i,j,a} - \mathbb{E}[I]}{\sqrt{\mathrm{Var}(I)}}. \tag{10}$$

The final channel-wise similarity score is defined as

$$S_a(i,j) = \Phi(z_{i,j,a}), \tag{11}$$

where $\Phi(\cdot)$ denotes the standard normal cumulative distribution function.

This transformation yields a significance-based spatial similarity measure in $(0,1)$, where larger values indicate stronger positive spatial association between players i and j in channel a.

2.5 Profile-Weighted Reliability Fusion

Channel-wise similarities are aggregated using a profile-weighted reliability scheme.

The relative importance of channel a for player i is defined as

$$w_{i,a} = \frac{V_{i,a}}{\sum_{b=1}^{K} V_{i,b}}, \tag{12}$$

where $V_{i,a}$ denotes the number of events of type a performed by player i.

To account for imbalance in channel volume between players, we define a reliability coefficient

$$\rho_{i,j,a} = \sqrt{\frac{m_{i,j,a}}{V_{i,a}}} \cdot \sqrt{\frac{m_{i,j,a}}{M_{i,j,a}}}, \tag{13}$$

where

$$m_{i,j,a} = \min(V_{i,a}, V_{j,a}), \quad M_{i,j,a} = \max(V_{i,a}, V_{j,a}).$$

The final similarity score is computed as

$$S(i,j) = \sum_{a=1}^{K} w_{i,a}\, \rho_{i,j,a}\, S_a(i,j). \tag{14}$$

This formulation emphasizes behaviorally dominant channels for player i while reducing the influence of channels with limited or imbalanced observations.

3 Experiments

3.1 Datasets

We evaluate the proposed framework on two independent event datasets.
FIFA World Cup 2022 (PFF FC). The first dataset consists of event-level data from all 64 matches of the FIFA World Cup 2022. The dataset provides on-ball event information including player identifiers, action types, and spatial coordinates.
Impect Bundesliga 2023/2024. The second dataset consists of 306 Bundesliga matches from the 2023/2024 season obtained from the Impect open-data repository. The data contains detailed event-level information including action type, start and end coordinates, player metadata, and contextual attributes such as pressure and phase of play [4].

Compared to the World Cup dataset, the Bundesliga dataset contains substantially more matches and event volume, enabling a more stable evaluation of the framework across different event budgets.

3.2 Preprocessing and Action Definitions

For both datasets, only on-ball actions were retained. Coordinates were normalized to a left-to-right attacking direction. For the FIFA World Cup dataset, spatial coordinates were explicitly normalized. For the Impect dataset, the provided adjusted coordinates (adjCoordinates) were used, which already standardize directionality [4].

The pitch was discretized into a 20×20 spatial grid.

Nine on-ball action types were used as separate spatial channels:

- PASS
- RECEPTION
- DRIBBLE
- SHOT
- INTERCEPTION
- BLOCK
- CLEARANCE
- GROUND_DUEL
- LOOSE_BALL_REGAIN

Each action type corresponds to one channel in the spatial-action tensor representation.

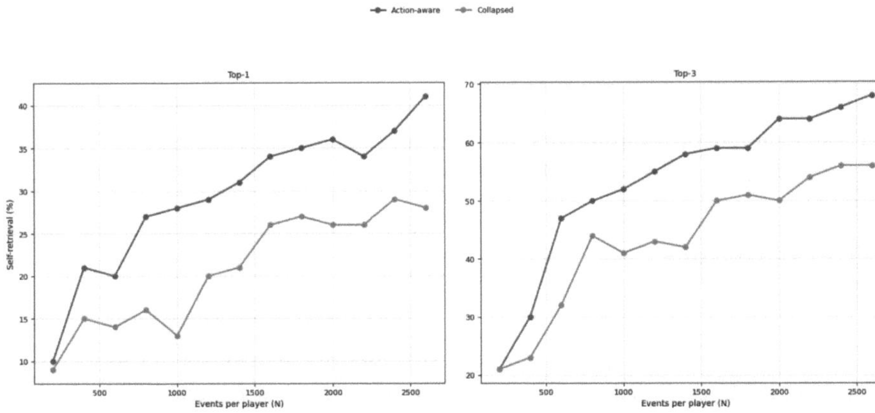

Fig. 2. Sample efficiency analysis on the Impect Bundesliga 2023/24 dataset ($m = 100$ players). Cross-match self-retrieval accuracy is reported as a function of the total number of events per player. The action-aware representation consistently outperforms the collapsed baseline across event budgets for both Top-1 (left) and Top-3 (right) retrieval.

3.3 Validation Protocol

We evaluate similarity quality using cross-match self-retrieval validation.

For each player, matches were split into two disjoint sets based on match index (odd vs. even matches). Heatmaps were constructed independently for each split. A player is considered correctly retrieved if their counterpart from the opposite split appears at rank k among all candidate players.

Bundesliga Event Budget Analysis. To analyze the effect of sample size, we selected a subset of 100 players with at least 2,700 events. Similarity was computed at the full budget (2,700 events), after which event counts were progressively downsampled (from 200 to 2,700 events) while keeping the player set fixed. Self-retrieval accuracy was evaluated at top-1 and top-3 ranks.

World Cup Evaluation. For the FIFA World Cup dataset, evaluation was conducted under the same oddeven cross-match split without event downsampling due to the limited number of matches.

4 Results

4.1 Sample Efficiency on Bundesliga

Figure 2 presents cross-match self-retrieval performance on the Impect Bundesliga 2023/24 dataset using a fixed cohort of $m = 100$ players. Performance is evaluated as a function of the total number of events per player.

Across all event budgets, the action-aware representation consistently outperforms the collapsed baseline. In Top-1 retrieval (Fig. 2 left), performance improves steadily as the event budget increases, reaching approximately 41% at $N = 2600$ events, compared to 28% for the collapsed model.

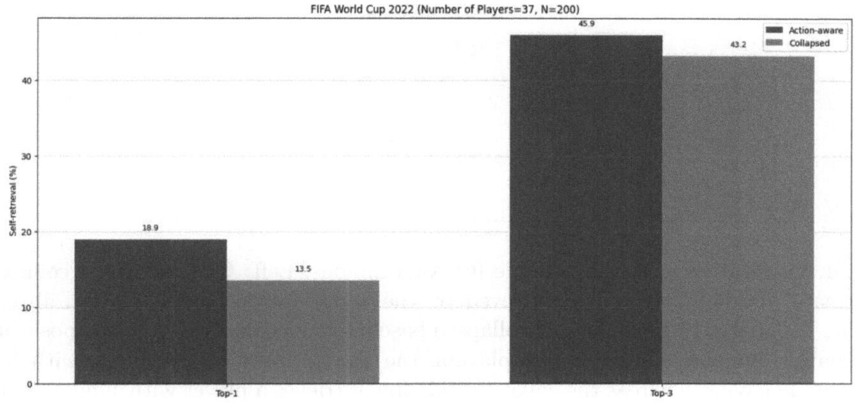

Fig. 3. Cross-match self-retrieval performance on the FIFA World Cup 2022 dataset ($m = 37$ eligible players, $N = 200$ events per player). Bars report Top-1 and Top-3 accuracy for the action-aware representation and the collapsed baseline.

A similar trend is observed for Top-3 retrieval (Fig. 2 right), where the action-aware model reaches nearly 68% accuracy at higher budgets, maintaining a clear margin over the collapsed baseline. The performance gap widens as more events become available, suggesting that preserving action-specific spatial structure yields increasing benefits with larger samples.

These results demonstrate both sample efficiency and scalability of the proposed action-aware similarity framework.

4.2 Evaluation on FIFA World Cup 2022

Figure 3 reports cross-match self-retrieval performance on the FIFA World Cup 2022 dataset. Due to limited match volume, evaluation was conducted on $m = 37$ eligible players using $N = 200$ events per player.

The action-aware representation achieves 18.9% Top-1 accuracy compared to 13.5% for the collapsed baseline. For Top-3 retrieval, action-aware reaches 45.9%, slightly outperforming the collapsed model at 43.2%.

Although the candidate set is smaller than in the Bundesliga experiment, the relative improvement of the action-aware model remains consistent. This indicates that the proposed framework generalizes across competitions and data regimes, even under lower event budgets and smaller player pools.

4.3 Qualitative Case Study

To illustrate the functional distinction captured by the proposed framework, we present a qualitative retrieval example for Xavi Simons (left winger).

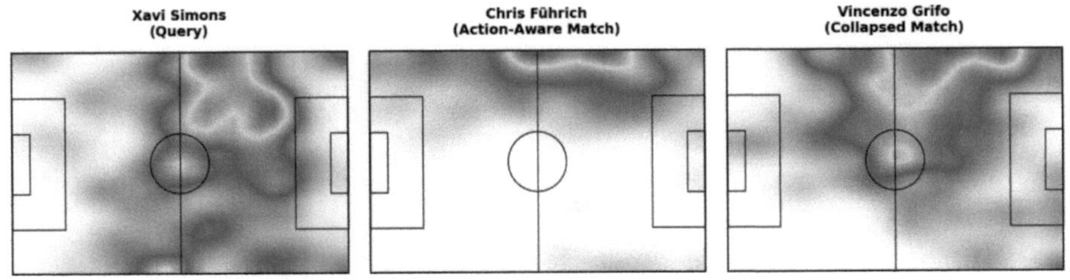

Fig. 4. Qualitative retrieval example for Xavi Simons. Left: Query player's collapsed heatmap. Middle: Top match retrieved by the action-aware model (Chris Führich). Right: Top match retrieved by the collapsed baseline (Vincenzo Grifo). While positional occupation appears similar across players, the action-aware model aligns with ball-carrying behavior, whereas the collapsed baseline retrieves a player with similar spatial coverage but different functional emphasis.

Figure 4 compares the query player with the top match retrieved by the action-aware model and the collapsed baseline.

Although the collapsed heatmaps exhibit similar positional occupation along the left attacking flank, they do not distinguish between the types of actions performed within those regions. Consequently, the collapsed model retrieves Vincenzo Grifo, whose spatial intensity overlaps with Simons in wide attacking zones. However, Grifo's contribution is primarily characterized by ball circulation and crossing patterns rather than frequent dribble progression.

In contrast, the action-aware model retrieves Chris Führich, whose spatial-action profile more closely aligns with Simons in ball-carrying and dribbling behavior. By separating action channels prior to similarity computation, the proposed framework differentiates between players who merely occupy similar spatial regions and those who perform similar functional roles within those regions.

This example demonstrates that incorporating action-specific spatial structure reduces the ambiguity inherent in collapsed positional representations and yields functionally meaningful similarity retrieval.

5 Discussion

The experimental results highlight the importance of separating positional occupation from functional behavior in player similarity modeling. While collapsed spatial heatmaps capture where a player operates on the pitch, they fail to distinguish how actions are performed within those regions. The consistent performance gap observed across event budgets indicates that incorporating action-specific spatial structure leads to more functionally meaningful similarity retrieval.

5.1 Functional Vs. Positional Similarity

The qualitative case study further illustrates this distinction. Players occupying similar spatial zones may exhibit fundamentally different behavioral profiles (e.g., ball circulation versus dribble progression). The action-aware framework reduces this ambiguity by modeling spatial distributions separately per action channel, allowing similarity to be driven by functional alignment rather than mere spatial overlap.

5.2 Effect of Event Volume

Performance improves steadily with increasing event budgets, suggesting that reliable spatial-action estimation requires sufficient sample size. At low event counts, channel-wise spatial distributions are sparse, leading to higher variance in similarity estimates. As more events are observed, spatial patterns stabilize and the advantage of the action-aware representation becomes more pronounced. This reflects a trade-off between representational expressiveness and sample efficiency: finer behavioral decomposition increases interpretability but requires adequate event volume to fully manifest its benefit.

5.3 Cross-Competition Generalization

Evaluation on both a domestic league dataset (Bundesliga) and an international tournament dataset (FIFA World Cup) demonstrates that the framework generalizes across competitions and data regimes. Despite differences in match volume and candidate set size, the action-aware model maintains a consistent relative improvement over the collapsed baseline, suggesting that the observed gains are not competition-specific.

5.4 Limitations

Several limitations should be noted. First, spatial representation relies on fixed grid discretization, which may introduce boundary artifacts. Second, similarity is computed solely from on-ball actions and does not incorporate contextual variables such as defensive pressure, team structure, or off-ball movement. Third, retrieval evaluation is limited to self-retrieval validation; future work could assess external scouting tasks or transfer learning scenarios. Finally, performance in low-event regimes remains sensitive to channel sparsity, particularly for infrequent action types.

These limitations provide natural directions for future extensions of the framework.

6 Conclusion

This paper introduced an action-aware spatial similarity framework for football player retrieval. By modeling player behavior as a third-order spatial-action tensor and computing channel-wise spatial association, the proposed method separates functional role from positional occupation. Unlike collapsed heatmap representations, the framework preserves action-specific structure and incorporates spatial dependence during similarity computation.

Empirical evaluation on two independent datasets—the Impect Bundesliga 2023/24 season and the FIFA World Cup 2022—demonstrates consistent improvements over a collapsed baseline. Sample-efficiency analysis shows that the advantage of the action-aware representation increases with event volume, while qualitative case studies illustrate its ability to distinguish players with similar spatial coverage but different behavioral profiles.

These findings suggest that incorporating action-specific spatial decomposition yields more functionally meaningful similarity retrieval in football analytics. Future work may extend the framework by incorporating contextual features such as defensive pressure and off-ball movement, exploring adaptive spatial discretization, and evaluating performance in external scouting and recruitment scenarios.

References

1. Decroos, T., Bransen, L., Van Haaren, J., Davis, J.: Actions speak louder than goals: valuing player actions in soccer. In: Proceedings of the 25th ACM SIGKDD International Conference on Knowledge Discovery and Data Mining, pp. 1851–1861. KDD '19, ACM (2019)
2. Gómez-Rubio, V., Lagos, J., Palmí-Perales, F.: Spatial similarity analysis of football players using heatmaps and spatial statistics. J. Sports Anal. **10**(9), 1–15 (2024)
3. Herold, M., Kempe, M., Bauer, P., Meyer, T.: Attacking key performance indicators in soccer: current practice and perceptions from the elite to youth academy level. J. Sports Sci. Med. **20**(1), 158–169 (2021)
4. Impect: Impect event data documentation. https://www.impect.com (2024). Accessed 16 Feb 2026
5. Lee, S.: A generalized significance testing method for global measures of spatial association: an extension of the mantel test. Environ Plan A **36**(9), 1687–1703 (2004)
6. Majumdar, A., Bakirov, R., Hodges, D., Scott, S., Rees, T.: Machine learning for understanding and predicting injuries in football. Sports Med. Open **8**(8), 73 (2022)
7. Pappalardo, L., Cintia, P., Ferragina, P., Massucco, E., Pedreschi, D., Giannotti, F.: PlayeRank: data-driven performance evaluation and player ranking in soccer via a machine learning approach. ACM Trans. Intell. Syst. Technol. **10**(5), 1–27 (2019)
8. Plakias, S., et al.: Identifying soccer players' playing styles: a systematic review. J. Funct. Morphol. Kinesiol. **8**(3), 104 (2023)
9. Santos, R., Ribeiro, J., Davids, K., Garganta, J.: Sports teams as collective homeostatic systems: exploiting self-organising tendencies in competition. New Ideas Psychol. **71**, 101048 (2023)
10. Silva, P., Vilar, L., Davids, K., Araújo, D., Garganta, J.: Sports teams as complex adaptive systems: manipulating player numbers shapes behaviours during football small-sided games. Springerplus **5**(1), 191 (2016)
11. Yunus, M., et al.: Talent scouting and standardizing fitness data in football club: systematic review. Retos **60**(7), 1382–1389 (2024)

Match Preparation in Professional Football: The Potential of Swarm Intelligence-Based Lineup Predictions

Marco Klaiber(✉) and Manfred Rössle

Aalen University of Applied Sciences, 73430 Aalen, Germany
marco.klaiber@hs-aalen.de

Abstract. Match preparation is an essential component for football (soccer) teams to be successful. Consequently, it is important to predict the opponent's possible lineup as accurately as possible to adjust tactics and increase the probability of success. Various providers offer their lineup predictions to clubs and fans at no cost. In addition to established expert-based predictions, providers relying on swarm intelligence can offer an effective alternative and potentially create different assessments. Therefore, we analyzed the prediction performance of three expert- and one swarm intelligence-based providers for teams during the 2024/25 German Bundesliga season. Our results show that swarm intelligence-based approaches can not only compete with established approaches but also outperform them for individual teams. The best provider achieved an overall accuracy of 84.32%, which underscores the potential for match preparation. Furthermore, we investigate the lineup stability and its impact on the predictions of the providers. All in all, our work provides the first insight into an underrepresented field of research on which future work can build.

Keywords: Lineup Prediction · Swarm Intelligence · Match Preparation

1 Introduction

Within football (soccer), data analysis is considered an emerging and elementary domain with significant benefits for teams, players and clubs [16]. Explicitly for analysis and performance prediction, many clubs integrate their own departments that focus on information from the teams and try to optimize preparation [16]. Within this preparation, a crucial question is: *"How to select an optimal team or lineup from the set of all candidates or applicants for a position in the team?"* [1]. This question is considered relevant because one of the biggest challenges for football coaches is choosing the lineup that promises the most success [4]. In addition to team strengths, the qualities and weaknesses of the opponent are usually taken into account when selecting the lineup, as this information can influence game performance [7]. Therefore, predicting the opponent's lineup is a

Z. Liu and V. Misra (Eds.): ISACE 2026, LNCS 16610, pp. 73–86, 2026.
https://doi.org/10.1007/978-3-032-27272-0_6

significant part of the game preparation, which can have a considerable influence on the game plan and the players selected [17].

However, lineup predictions are generally subjective, error-prone, and resource-intensive for a single club. As a result, publicly accessible providers are a popular way to obtain such information, which is usually provided by their internal insiders and experts. Besides for the clubs, public lineup predictions are also important for fans, e.g. to estimate whether their favorite players will play or not. In addition, Fantasy Football Manager (FFM) games are becoming increasingly popular, creating an ever-growing market where fans can lineup their favorite players and compete in rankings based on real-life performances. This development is further fueled by emerging Web3 [14] FFM games, such as Sorare [21], where real money or unique fan experiences can be won. Consequently, predicted lineups in this area are also relevant, as there is usually a fixed deadline for fantasy football lineups, although the official lineup cannot yet be viewed. Any missing player can be decisive, which is why an informative assessment in advance is crucial.

Consequently, lineup predictions are highly relevant for various stakeholders in football, with publicly available providers being popular worldwide. However, the question arises of whether lineup predictions based on expert knowledge or swarm intelligence (sometimes also described as crowd intelligence in prior work) can provide adequate preparation. The latter, in particular, is becoming increasingly popular, as swarm intelligence is used, for example, on Transfermarkt.com [23] to determine market values, a practice that is recognized worldwide [18]. An overall estimate is based on many judgments, in which many individual opinions are assumed to provide a better assessment than a single expert opinion [12]. Regarding lineup prediction, a popular example is SorareData [22], where users, i.e., football fans, can submit their lineup predictions for each match day, and a final lineup is derived from all submissions. This development raises the question of whether swarm-intelligence-based lineup predictions can bring added value and whether they can outperform expert-based predictions.

To the best of our knowledge, there is currently no work investigating lineup predictions, be it expert-based or based on swarm intelligence. Consequently, the research gap arises whether publicly accessible lineup predictions offer any added value for match preparation. Furthermore, whether there is a qualitative difference between expert-based and swarm intelligence-based predictions. In addition, we also examine to what extent the lineup stability – the consistency of the lineup to previous lineups – has an influence on the predictions.

Therefore, our work offers the following contributions:

- A seasonal analysis of publicly available lineup predictions in terms of their reliability.
- Assessing whether predictions based on swarm intelligence offer added value or outperform predictions based on expert opinion.
- An analysis of whether the stability of the lineup correlates with the probability of prediction.

2 Related Work

As described above, we present an initial study that analyzes the quality of lineup predictions made by football providers. The literature tends to focus on optimizing lineups from the perspective of clubs, which we consider related to our work. In the following, we present these approaches and distinguish our work from them.

Cao et al. [2] have proposed a method for visual analysis of formation selection in football. The focus is on the characterization of essential factors that play a role in the creation of the optimal lineup, as well as the support of the visual analysis of the lineup selection by the coach. In addition, they presented a web-based visual analysis system called Team-Builder, which allows coaches to interactively create, explain, and compare lineups created by an automatic model and integrate their own opinions into the lineup selection [2]. Furthermore, Salles et al. [19] presented a multi-criteria method with a genetic algorithm for the evaluation of football teams based on their formations using data from the Brazilian championship. The results showed that a 3–6-1 formation provides the best values for their case study, resulting in a value of 43.04% for team complementarity. Furthermore, it is underlined that it was possible to determine the most complementary team according to the desired tactical formation and the importance given to each criterion [19]. Another study was carried out by Cortez et al. [4], where physiological player variables were used to determine which players are best suited for the starting eleven. Data were collected using Global Positioning Systems (GPS), based on which relevant features were selected using recursive feature elimination followed by logistic regression. Finally, the so-called formation readiness index was presented, which provided satisfactory values for fullbacks, central midfielders, and wingers [4]. Carling [3], presented a similar study in which the influence of opponent team formation on the physical and skill-related performance of a professional football team was examined. Three seasons (2007/08 – 2009/10) from French League 1 were analyzed using multi-camera tracking. The results indicate that the physical performance of the reference team was not strongly influenced by the lineup of the opposing team and that the skill requirements differed significantly depending on the opposing lineup [3].

In contrast to the presented work, our study addresses the quality of the predicted lineups of public providers that clubs could use for match preparation. We do not refer to the physiological effects [3,4] of the selected lineups, but only to the quality of the prediction. Furthermore, we do not provide an application for optimal lineup selection [2,19], but rather examine the extent to which the stability of the lineups over different match days can influence the lineup predictions. All in all, we present a first study from a new perspective on match preparation, from which clubs and managers can benefit in the future.

3 Methodology

In this work, we analyze different lineup prediction providers. The aim is to examine whether swarm intelligence-based approaches can show competitive accuracy compared to established providers. Our approach is explained in detail below. First, we present the providers examined and their prediction process. We then discuss our approach to data collection and evaluation. In addition, we present a metric to calculate the lineup stability. An overview of the individual steps is presented in Fig. 1.

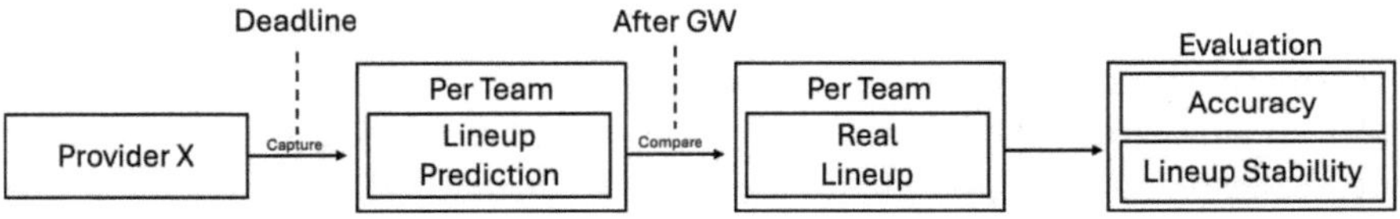

Fig. 1. Overview of the methodology for recording and evaluating lineups (Gameweek = GW).

3.1 Lineup Prediction Providers

In our work, we analyzed four providers for lineup predictions: two international providers with *SorareData* and *OneFootball*, as well as two providers with a focus on German football with *Kicker* and *Ligainsider*. The only swarm intelligence-based is *SorareData*.

SorareData. *SorareData.com* (SD) [22] is an analytics platform designed specifically for a fantasy football game that uses blockchain-based player cards called *Sorare* [21]. The provider collects comprehensive data on player performance, market trends, auction activity, and team statistics, providing actionable insights for users to make informed decisions. Within *Sorare*, it is of great importance to know the potential lineups of the teams in advance to be able to establish the best possible fantasy team consisting of 5 players for the upcoming gameweek (GW). Accordingly, SD offers swarm intelligence-based lineup predictions for almost all relevant professional leagues worldwide. SD users can submit their predicted lineups, with players marked as "starting player", "questionable", "substitute" or "not in team". As an incentive for the users and to ensure quality, all predictions are tracked and different rankings (e.g. a global ranking based on all predictions or a team ranking based on the predictions for a specific team, e.g. *Bayern Munich*) are created based on the accuracy of the predictions and the resulting points. Based on the rankings, the best users are then rewarded with collectibles, such as high-priced NFTs in Sorare or special badges on the manager gallery pages to display expertise.

Kicker. *Kicker.com* [11] is one of the most known sports publications in Germany, covering a wide range of football news, match reports, and analysis. Mostly the latest news on German football is published, but other relevant leagues, competitions, and sports are also covered. Accordingly, the provider also offers lineup predictions for upcoming matches, which is especially the case for the German league, and is usually published a few days before the match day. In general, *Kicker.com* does not provide a detailed technical breakdown of its internal methodology to the public, but individual details were revealed to us on request. The expected lineups are prepared by the respective club reporters, who have a high level of expertise due to their constant observation of the respective teams in matches and training. There is also additional information on player absences (injuries, suspensions) and tactical considerations, which can be derived partly from coach statements, partly from other information, or from their analyses (e.g., one or two strikers against a particular opponent). The first lineup prediction is published in print on Thursdays and is then continuously updated online until kick-off in the event of new information.

Ligainsider. *LigaInsider.de* [13] is an established platform that specializes in news, predicted lineups, and detailed statistics for the 1st German Bundesliga. The provider is aimed at football fans and explicitly at football fantasy managers who are not only interested in the latest news, but also want to get involved in match preparation. In addition, to match reports and player ratings, *LigaInsider* also offers special tools such as detailed scoring and ranking systems. Similarly to *Kicker*, not much is publicly known about the process of creating lineup predictions, but after contacting *LigaInsider.de*, we were provided with more details. On the one hand, a team of experts is responsible for the predictions, whereby, e.g. analysts are also consulted, who make a prediction according to the player types, player form, and other factors. On ther other hand, insider information also plays an increasing role, but this is only included in the forecasts as last-minute reports.

OneFootball. *OneFootball* [15] is a global football media platform that provides live scores, detailed statistics, breaking news, video content, and in-depth analysis of more than 100 international football leagues and competitions. *OneFootball* became popular primarily through its mobile app, which is available in several languages and serves a user base of over 100 million fans. Although *OneFootball* provides predicted lineups for a wide range of competitions, there is no official documentation regarding the underlying methodology and we have not received any further information. Given its structure as a media platform with a large editorial and publisher network, it is likely that lineup predictions are primarily based on expert-driven match previews and external content providers, potentially complemented by simple data-driven heuristics (e.g., recent lineups, player availability, and match context).

Based on the methodology of the providers presented, we define *Kicker*, *Ligainsider*, and *OneFootball* as expert-based. This is because their predictions are primarily based on expert knowledge. In contrast, we define *SorareData* as a swarm intelligence-based system, since its predictions are derived entirely based on assessments by community users. We refer to swarm intelligence as aggregated, collective decision-making, reflecting the concept of collective human judgment rather than bio-inspired optimization approaches.

3.2 Data Collection

For our study, we considered the 2024/2025 season of the highest division in Germany – the 1. Bundesliga –, whereby we select three diverse teams for our analysis. Our focus in the selection was on ensuring different levels of global recognition, playing different numbers of matches over a season, and assigning different levels of relevance to German football. Consequently, the following clubs were selected: (1) *FC Bayern Munich*, (2) *TSG 1899 Hoffenheim*, and (3) *Holstein Kiel*.

FC Bayern Munich is one of the biggest and best-known clubs worldwide, playing in the Champions League (CL) this season in addition to the cup and the league. A new coach, *Vincent Kompany*, was hired before the season. This combination of three competitions and new playing ideas could potentially make the lineup predictions more difficult. With its enormous fanbase and huge public interest, most of the information regarding players for *FC Bayern Munich*, for example, should be available.

The second club we consider is *TSG 1899 Hoffenheim*, which has been continuously playing in the Bundesliga since 2008. *TSG 1899 Hoffenheim* was able to qualify for the Europa League (EL) and also introduced a new coach in *Christian Ilzer*. On average, this club can be placed in the midfield of the Bundesliga, with deviations downward and upward over the years. In addition, public interest in the club is significantly lower than for *FC Bayern Munich*, for example.

The third club we selected is *Holstein Kiel*, who were promoted to the Bundesliga for the 2024/2025 season after a long absence. As a promoted team, *Holstein Kiel* enters the season as outsiders with the goal of staying in the league. This team can be regarded the smallest in our analysis, which attracts the least attention globally.

The primary aim of our study was to analyze the providers' predicted lineups, which should be carried out transparently and uniformly. It should be noted that the providers presented publish their forecasts at different times and occasionally update them. In general, press conferences for Bundesliga matches take place on Thursdays and Fridays, providing news about the players that could then be incorporated into the predictions. Such updates can lead to distortions in the data collection process as not all providers make adjustments at short notice. For this reason, a defined deadline has been set: Friday at 4 p.m. for each match day (except for the one-off midweek fixture, the deadline was set for Tuesday at 4 p.m.).

3.3 Evaluation Process

The described data collection steps were used to record the lineups predicted by each provider for the selected teams. After each match day, the official lineup was compared with the prediction and the differences were recorded. This can be described with the following; where $P_{p,j}$ is the set of players predicted by provider p for match j, A_j is the set of actual starting players on match day j, and $|\cdot|$ denotes the cardinality of a set:

$$\text{Acc}_{p,j} = \frac{|P_{p,j} \cap A_j|}{|A_j|} \tag{1}$$

It should be noted that only the players used were included in the analysis and not the tactical formation. This is due to the fact that, for example, *Kicker* does not provide any information on formations, while *SorareData* does provide this information, but the players are not assigned to positions. In addition to overall accuracy, we also record the accuracy per provider, as well as the overall and team-specific accuracy. In addition, contextual information is noted, taking into account whether the team had another match during the week, e.g., in the CL/EL or in the cup. Finally, the results of individual teams are also recorded to check for possible correlations with the lineups. In addition to analyzing how well the individual providers can predict the lineups, we also examine the effects of rotations on the prediction, as well as on the results of the teams. For this purpose, we introduce lineup stability, which indicates how many changes to the previous lineup are present in the current lineup. This metric is defined as follows:

$$\text{lineup Stability}_{\text{GW}} = \frac{|L_{\text{GW}} \cap L_{\text{GW-1}}|}{11} \times 100 \tag{2}$$

L_{GW}: set of players in the starting lineup for the current GW.
$L_{\text{GW-1}}$: set of players in the starting lineup for the previous GW.
$|L_{\text{GW}} \cap L_{\text{GW-1}}|$: number of players unchanged between the two GWs.

4 Results

In the following, we present our results regarding the individual accuracies per provider over the season, as well as the lineup stability of each team over the season. We also examine whether there is a correlation between the accuracies and the stabilities to analyze the extent to which rotation affects the prediction. In addition, we perform statistical significance tests on the results.

The main objective of our investigation was the research question of how well lineup providers can predict lineups and whether swarm intelligence-based lineup providers can compete with established expert-based ones. Table 1 shows that the overall accuracy of *Ligainsider* is the highest at 84.32%, with *SorareData* the second best at 83.51%. *Kicker* was able to achieve 82.71%, with *OneFootball* significantly less at 77.63%.

Table 1. Prediction Results.

	SorareData	Kicker	Ligainsider	OneFootball
FC Bayern Munich	**85.83**	83.69	85.56	77.54
TSG 1899 Hoffenheim	82.89	81.02	**84.49**	78.34
Holstein Kiel	81.82	**83.42**	82.89	77.01
Overall	83.51	82.71	**84.32**	77.63

Looking at individual teams, *SorareData* achieved the highest accuracy for *FC Bayern Munich* at 85.85%, which is potentially due to the large fan base and also defines the highest overall accuracy for all pair of team-providers. However, for *TSG 1899 Hoffenheim*, *Ligainsider* scored the highest with 84.49%. The smallest club, *Holstein Kiel*, was predicted the best by *Kicker* with 83.43%. Only *OneFootball* was significantly lower for all teams with values ranging from 77.01% to 78.34%.

In terms of lineup stability, the rotation of the individual teams was analyzed in relation to the previous game. The results per team over the entire season are shown in Table 2.

Table 2. Lineup Stability Results.

	FC Bayern	TSG Hoff.	H. Kiel
lineup Stab.	71.07	75.76	76.86

It can be seen that *Holstein Kiel* rotated the least with a stability of 76.86%, with *TSG 1899 Hoffenheim* just below that at 75.76%. *FC Bayern Munich*, on the other hand, rotated the most with 71.07% stability. Based on this, we present the results of the correlation between the lineup stability and the predictions of the individual providers in Table 3.

Table 3. Correlations results of lineup stability and the predictions of the individual providers.

	SorareData	Kicker	Ligainsider	OneFootball
FC Bayern Munich	0.3501	0.2364	0.3188	0.7255
TSG Hoffenheim	0.5127	0.6315	0.4821	0.7923
Holstein Kiel	0.8326	0.5465	0.8232	0.8019
Overall	0.5041	0.4233	0.5009	0.7448

In general, a positive correlation can be derived with respect to the predictions and stability. *OneFootball* (0.7448) has the highest overall correlation, which means that this provider copes better with stable lineups, but when the team rotates, the accuracy drops significantly. Accordingly, *OneFootball*'s predictions are particularly sensitive to stable lineups. *SorareData* (0.5041) and *Ligainsider* (0.5009) are almost identical at around 0.50, which we define as a moderate correlation. In contrast, the value for *Kicker* (0.4233) is slightly lower, suggesting that while stability helps *Kicker* predict lineups better, there remains unexplained variance.

In addition to seasonal correlation, we also calculate the rolling 5-game accuracy series of the individual providers for each team. To do this, we record the average of the 5-game rolling window accuracy values, as well as the standard deviation of these rolling 5-game accuracy values. The rolling min and max values are also calculated to show the worst and best consecutive 5-game period. In addition, we show the Pearson correlation between the provider's rolling 5-game accuracy and the team's rolling 5-game stability metric, which indicates how accurately the provider's predictions reflect the team's underlying lineup consistency. The results of this are shown in Fig. 2.

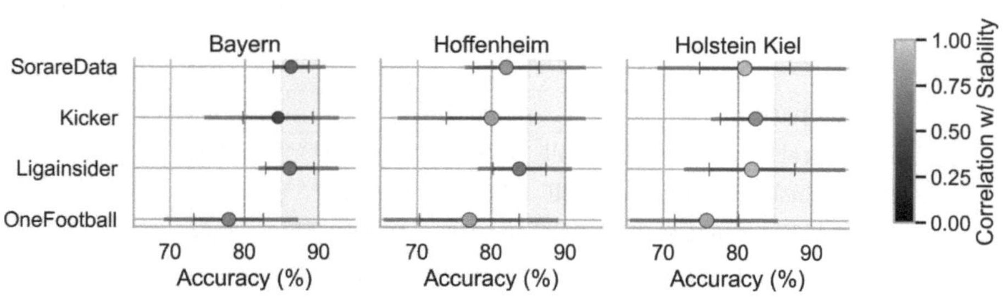

Fig. 2. 5-game rolling accuracy per provider and team. Point = mean value, bar = ±1 SD, line = observed range (minmax). Color scale codes the correlation with the lineup stability (01). Shaded band marks the 8590% range.

Figure 2 shows that in terms of overall predictive power with a moving average, *SorareData* has the highest value for *FC Bayern Munich* (86.24%), with *Ligainsider* has the highest result for *TSG 1899 Hoffenheim* (83.82%), and is almost on a par with *Kicker* for *Holstein Kiel* (81.94% compared to 82.43%), which means that, as in Table 1, it generally shows the best performance. Notable is that *OneFootball* has the lowest average accuracy for all three teams (≈76–78%).

In terms of volatility, *OneFootball* shows the highest (standard deviation up to 6.76% for *Hoffenheim*) and its minimum drops to as low as 65.46%, suggesting that it is sometimes well below the baseline. On the other hand, *SorareData* shows the narrowest distribution with a standard deviation $< 4.5\%$ for all teams and a minimum that never falls below 69%, indicating a more consistent performance. *Kicker* and *Ligainsider* are in the mid-range, with *Ligainsider's* standard deviation generally at 3–5% and *Kicker*'s at 4–6%. In line with this, SorareData is the most consistent, while OneFootball shows the most variation.

When looking at the correlation regarding lineup stability, *Holstein Kiel* shows the highest correlation across all providers (*SorareData* 0.93, *Ligainsider* 0.92, *OneFootball* 0.88). For *TSG Hoffenheim*, OneFootball (0.86) and *Kicker* (0.85) track stability better than *Ligainsider* (0.65). For *FC Bayern Munich*, the correlations are the lowest overall, with *OneFootball* still in the lead (0.72), followed by *Ligainsider* (0.65), *SorareData* (0.57) and *Kicker* (0.40).

To ensure further transparency of the results and to assess whether the observed differences in predictive accuracy between providers are statistically significant, a Friedman test [20] was conducted, taking into account the paired nature of the data (i.e., accuracy by match day and provider). The results indicate a statistically significant difference between providers ($\chi^2 = 29.50$, $p < 0.001$), suggesting that at least one provider differs significantly from the others. To further investigate these differences, pairwise comparisons were performed using the Wilcoxon test [5] with Bonferroni correction, which is summarized in Table 4.

Table 4. Pairwise comparison of prediction accuracy using the Wilcoxon signed-rank test with Bonferroni correction. Significance levels: *** $p_{adj} < 0.001$, ** $p_{adj} < 0.01$, * $p_{adj} < 0.05$.

Comparison	Mean Diff.	p_{adj}	Eff. Size (r)
SorareData vs OneFootball	0.0588	0.00003***	0.82
Ligainsider vs OneFootball	0.0668	0.00007***	0.78
Kicker vs OneFootball	0.0508	0.00194**	0.65
Kicker vs Ligainsider	-0.0160	0.583	0.31
SorareData vs Ligainsider	-0.0080	0.900	0.35
SorareData vs Kicker	0.0080	1.000	0.19

The results show that *OneFootball* performs significantly worse than all other providers. In particular, the differences between *OneFootball* and *SorareData*, *Kicker*, and *Ligainsider* are all statistically significant ($p_{adj} < 0.01$) and exhibit large effect sizes (r ranging from 0.65 to 0.82). The mean accuracy differences range from 5.1% to 6.7%, indicating not only statistical significance but also practical relevance. In contrast, no statistically significant differences were observed between *SorareData*, *Kicker*, and *Ligainsider* ($p_{adj} > 0.05$ in all cases), suggesting comparable predictive performance between these providers.

5 Discussion

In our work, we analyzed four providers and three teams, presenting the results of our investigation above. In the following, we discuss these results and their potential implications for the field of research.

As shown in Table 1, swarm intelligence-based lineup predictions can not only compete with established expert-based providers, but also surpass them in individual cases. The strength of swarm-based approaches is particularly evident for *FC Bayern Munich*, which has one of the largest fan bases in the world. Because a large number of *FC Bayern* fans can give their assessment, the estimate is increasing closer to the potential lineup. Explicitly, due to the wide availability of information on large clubs, e.g., through social media such as X or Instagram, where various insiders and experts post daily, the masses can reflect this more quickly than individual experts from traditional providers. But even for smaller teams, such as *Holstein Kiel* in our case, *SorareData* was able to make competitive predictions compared to *Kicker* or *Ligainsider*. Our study also shows that international providers such as *OneFootball* make significantly weaker predictions for a specific league, as their focus is not solely on one league, as is the case with *Ligainsider*, or on a few leagues, as is the case with *Kicker*.

However, while *Ligainsider* achieves the highest average accuracy, no statistically significant differences are observed between *Ligainsider*, *Kicker*, and *SorareData*. This suggests that these providers perform at a comparable level. From this, it can be deduced that experts who focus on one league may be closer to the actual lineup. Therefore, the provider's focus is fundamental and that the more leagues are covered, the weaker the individual predictions become. Statistical analysis also confirms that *OneFootball* performs significantly worse than all other providers. This suggests that the observed differences are not incidental but systematic, possibly due to the broader scope of *OneFootball*, which covers a wide range of leagues and may therefore lack depth in league-specific information. *SorareData* also covers a large number of leagues, but the respective fans of the teams are primarily responsible for the predictions, so the quality does not decline despite the broad coverage. This can be seen as an advantage of a swarm-based approach, but it is only valid as long as each team has enough users to make predictions, because with a small number of predictions, this approach moves away from swarm intelligence and toward expert assessment. This raises the question of how many lineup predictions are needed to define swarm intelligence or expert assessment. *SorareData* does not provide any information on the number of submissions for a lineup prediction.

Furthermore, there are unpredictable circumstances in sports that are difficult or impossible to take into account, such as last-minute absences due to illness or injuries during warm-ups before the game. In addition, coaches may deliberately spread false information to make it more difficult for their opponents to prepare. Under these circumstances, the probability of success in lineup prediction is generally higher for expert or insider-based providers, as they potentially receive this information firsthand. Swarm intelligence approaches, on the other hand, are largely based on public information. Nevertheless, it is likely that swarm-based predictions are inspired by public expert-based assessments and that the platforms also compare predictions with each other.

In addition to prediction performance, we also analyzed the lineup stability of three different teams and derived the effects of rotation on the predictions.

In general, teams that are represented in several competitions rotate more than teams that do not play internationally. This pattern is also confirmed by our results, in which *FC Bayern Munich* changes their lineup more often than the other two teams. The reasons for this are, for example, load management [8] or injuries [6], which can be more likely with more playing time. Although *TSG 1899 Hoffenheim* have also played internationally, their stability is higher and relatively close to that of newly promoted *Holstein Kiel*. This is partly due to the fact that *TSG 1899 Hoffenheim* was eliminated in the second half of the season and the new coach had found his regular lineup, which was hardly the case in the first half of the season, for example. A change of coach usually brings rotation, which in turn makes lineup prediction more difficult. Furthermore, it can be assumed that a top team such as *FC Bayern Munich* has a broader squad in terms of quality, which allows for rotations with smaller differences in performance.

Looking at the correlation of predictions and stability in Table 3 also shows that OneFootball does not only focus on the German Bundesliga, which is why this provider performs better with stable lineups. It can be deduced that this provider does not have the depth of information that others do and tends to assume that the team from the previous week will be back in action. This was evident on match day 2, for example, when *Vidovic* had already left *FC Bayern Munich* but was still included in *OneFootball*'s prediction. The same can be seen with obvious injuries to key players such as *Musiala* on match day 16. The other providers had moderate correlations with the stabilities, which could indicate that *Kicker* experts, for example, perceive minor injuries that lead to changes in the team lineup. It should also be noted that *FC Bayern Munich* in particular has relatively low correlations – with the exception of *OneFootball* – which may also be due to the fact that this club has the greatest media relevance. Ultimately, it can be said that there is a positive correlation between lineup stability and prediction accuracy for each provider-team pair. In particular, the lineup forecasts of *OneFootball* are strongly influenced by this, while other providers integrate additional information.

6 Limitations and Future Work

Within our work, we limited ourselves to four providers and three teams from the German Bundesliga. This can be seen as a limitation, as we focus on a selected amount of information, but nevertheless this selection reflects initial tendencies with 102 predicted lineups. However, it is possible to expand the selection of providers and teams. For this purpose, it is conceivable to analyze the top 5 leagues, as Gasparetto et al. [9] or Gyarmati et al. [10] in their study.

Another limitation is the definition of our deadline for collecting the predicted lineups, as this excludes potentially correct predictions after the deadline. This was necessary because not every provider took into account short-term changes. In the future, however, we could limit ourselves to providers who change their predictions shortly before the start of the game, whereby automated recording would be conceivable. However, it should be noted that teams often complete their preparations one day before the game, which is why last-minute changes are not particularly relevant.

Furthermore, the formation in which a team plays is considered relevant for match preparation, which we did not take into account in our predictions. This was because not every provider displayed a formation and we wanted to ensure comparability. In addition, experts can deduce the potential formation based on the selected players. However, it is conceivable that this information will be incorporated in future work.

7 Conclusion

In our work, we analyzed four different lineup prediction providers for the 1st German Bundesliga. During the 2024/25 season, we compared the prediction with actual lineups, investigating whether swarm intelligence-based approaches can compete with expert-based predictions. Our analysis shows that *SorareData*, a provider based on swarm intelligence, can not only compete with established expert-based approaches but also outperform them for individual teams. Nevertheless, no significant differences were found between *SorareData*, *Kicker*, and *Ligainsider*, which underscores their comparable predictive power. Furthermore, it could be shown that the focus of a provider has a significant influence on the prediction performance and therefore the local providers or swarm intelligence based providers should be preferred to obtain more accurate predictions. For future work, our study should be extended to multiple teams and/or leagues. In addition, further approaches based on swarm intelligence could be investigated. All in all, our work provides a first investigation in the field of lineup prediction, an area that can be of immense importance for match preparation.

Acknowledgment. Many thanks to Bennet Stark from *Ligainsider.de* and Sandra Löhlein from *Kicker.de* for the insights into the process for the lineup predictions on their websites.

References

1. Boon, B.H., Sierksma, G.: Team formation: matching quality supply and quality demand. Eur. J. Oper. Res. **148**(2), 277–292 (2003)
2. Cao, A., et al.: Team-builder: toward more effective lineup selection in soccer. IEEE Trans. Visual Comput. Graph. **29**(12), 5178–5193 (2023)
3. Carling, C.: Influence of opposition team formation on physical and skill-related performance in a professional soccer team. Eur. J. Sport Sci. **11**(3), 155–164 (2011)
4. Cortez, A., Trigo, A., Loureiro, N.: Football match line-up prediction based on physiological variables: a machine learning approach. Computers **11**(3), 1–14 (2022)
5. Divine, G., Norton, H.J., Hunt, R., Dienemann, J.: A review of analysis and sample size calculation considerations for Wilcoxon tests. Anesthesia Analgesia **117**(3), 699–710 (2013)

6. Enright, K., Green, M., Hay, G., Malone, J.J.: Workload and injury in professional soccer players: role of injury tissue type and injury severity. Int. J. Sports Med. **41**(02), 89–97 (2020)
7. Forcher, L., et al.: How coaches can improve their teams' match performance-the influence of in-game changes of tactical formation in professional soccer. Front. Psychol. **13**, 1–11 (2022)
8. Gardner, C., Navalta, J.W., Carrier, B., Aguilar, C., Perdomo Rodriguez, J.: Training impulse and its impact on load management in collegiate and professional soccer players. Technologies **11**(3), 1–15 (2023)
9. Gasparetto, T., Mishchenko, D., Zaitsev, E.: Factors influencing competitive balance across European football top tier leagues. Manag. Decis. Econ. **44**(4), 2068–2078 (2023)
10. Gyarmati, L., Orbán-Mihálykó, É., Mihálykó, C., Vathy-Fogarassy, Á.: Aggregated rankings of top leagues' football teams: application and comparison of different ranking methods. Appl. Sci. **13**(7), 1–24 (2023)
11. Kicker: Kicker.de. https://www.kicker.de/ (2025). Accessed 13 Nov 2025
12. Krause, S., James, R., Faria, J.J., Ruxton, G.D., Krause, J.: Swarm intelligence in humans: diversity can trump ability. Anim. Behav. **81**(5), 941–948 (2011)
13. LigaInsider: LigaInsider.de. https://www.ligainsider.de/ (2025). Accessed 13 Nov 2025
14. Liu, W., Cao, B., Peng, M.: Web3 technologies: challenges and opportunities. IEEE Netw. **38**(3), 187–193 (2024)
15. OneFootball: OneFootball. https://onefootball.com/de/home (2025). Accessed 13 Nov 2025
16. Papageorgiou, G., Sarlis, V., Tjortjis, C.: An innovative method for accurate NBA player performance forecasting and line-up optimization in daily fantasy sports. Int. J. Data Sci. Anal. , 1–24 (2024)
17. Plakias, S.: An integrative review of the game model in soccer: definition, misconceptions, and practical significance. Trends Sport Sci. **30**(3), 85–92 (2023)
18. Prockl, F., Frick, B.: Information precision in online communities: player valuations on www. transfermarkt. de. Int. J. Sport Financ. **13**(4), 319–335 (2018)
19. Salles, S.A.F., Da Hora, H.R.M., Erthal Júnior, M., Velasco, A.S., Croce, P.R.: Multiple choice method with genetic algorithm for the formation of soccer teams. Pesquisa Operacional **42**, 1–21 (2022)
20. Sheldon, M.R., Fillyaw, M.J., Thompson, W.D.: The use and interpretation of the Friedman test in the analysis of ordinal-scale data in repeated measures designs. Physiother. Res. Int. **1**(4), 221–228 (1996)
21. Sorare: Sorare, com. https://sorare.com/ (2025). Accessed 13 Nov 2025
22. SorareData: SorareData.com. https://soraredata.com/ (2025). Accessed 13 May 2025
23. TransferMarkt: transfermarkt.com. https://www.transfermarkt.de/ (2025). Accessed 13 Nov 2025

A Deep Learning Based Approach for Live Win Probability in NBA Games Using Play-by-Play Events and Compact Game State

Dogan C. Cicek(✉)

Bilkent University, Ankara, Turkey
cicek@ee.bilkent.edu.tr

Abstract. Estimating win probability during live basketball games requires integrating both the current game state and the sequential history of play-by-play events. We propose a neural architecture that learns dense embeddings from play-by-play event sequences and combines them with game state features to produce probability estimates. The model encodes each event using concatenated embeddings for event type, team attribution, and temporal dynamics, then applies a recency weighted pooling mechanism that emphasizes recent events while retaining information from the full sequence. A fusion layer combines the sequence representation with a game state embedding that encodes score differential, time remaining, and team strength priors. We evaluate our approach on 500 NBA games against the ESPN Analytics model, a widely deployed industry baseline. Our model improves log loss and Brier score under trajectory based evaluation, and it achieves lower expected calibration error under whole game evaluation across all events. The performance gap widens as games progress, indicating that accumulated event history provides increasingly valuable predictive signal over time. The results support the value of sequential modeling of play-by-play events beyond what instantaneous game state features express.

Keywords: Win Probability Estimation · Basketball Analytics · Sequence Modeling · Deep Learning

1 Introduction

Accurate estimation of win probability during live basketball games serves multiple stakeholders. Broadcasters use probability estimates to enhance viewer engagement by quantifying the significance of key moments. Coaches and analysts use these estimates to evaluate decision quality and inform strategic adjustments. Despite this broad interest, most existing approaches reduce the prediction task to a function of instantaneous game state variables such as score differential, time remaining, and possession indicator, discarding the rich sequential structure present in play-by-play event logs.[1]

[1] Source code is available at https://github.com/doganjr/LWPNBA.

Z. Liu and V. Misra (Eds.): ISACE 2026, LNCS 16610, pp. 87–102, 2026.
https://doi.org/10.1007/978-3-032-27272-0_7

Play-by-play data provide a detailed record of every event that occurs during a basketball game, including made and missed shots, rebounds, turnovers, fouls, and substitutions. This sequential information captures game dynamics that aggregate statistics cannot represent. Modeling this sequential structure through learned representations offers the potential to capture patterns that instantaneous game state features alone cannot express.

We propose a neural architecture that treats play-by-play events as a sequence and learns dense embeddings that capture event semantics, team attribution, and temporal dynamics. The model combines this learned sequence representation with a compact game state vector through a fusion mechanism that allows both information sources to contribute to the final probability estimate. A recency weighted pooling mechanism emphasizes recent events while retaining information from the full sequence history.

We evaluate our approach against the ESPN Analytics model, a widely deployed industry baseline that powers live win probability. Our model outperforms ESPN Analytics in log loss and Brier score on a test set of 500 NBA games under trajectory based evaluation. Under whole game evaluation across all events, our model also achieves lower expected calibration error. The performance gap widens as games progress, with our model achieving substantial improvements in later stages of games when accumulated event history provides the strongest predictive signal.

The contributions of this work are as follows.

- We propose a neural architecture that learns dense embeddings from play-by-play event sequences and combines them with game state features through a fusion mechanism to estimate win probability.
- We introduce a recency weighted temporal pooling mechanism that emphasizes recent events while retaining information from the full sequence and captures short term game dynamics.
- We demonstrate improved log loss and Brier score relative to ESPN Analytics under trajectory based evaluation and lower expected calibration error under whole game evaluation across all events.
- We provide empirical analysis showing that sequential event modeling contributes increasing predictive value as games progress, supporting the design choice of combining state and sequence representations.

2 Background and Related Work

2.1 Win Probability from Game State

Many studies of win probability in basketball start from a compact view of game state, typically score differential, time remaining, and possession context, and then model how outcomes evolve from these variables. Stylized score process models support this view because they treat score differences as stochastic over time and they use the game clock to quantify remaining uncertainty

[5,8,20]. Some approaches in this family incorporate differences in team strength when they explain score dynamics [8]. Bayesian formulations combine priors that depend on time and score with pregame expectations to estimate and predict win probability during the game [12]. Related work also applies score process models to betting markets and combines point spread and moneyline odds with stochastic score evolution to infer market implied uncertainty about the final result [15]. Public facing products popularize this state based framing and publish live win probability curves under ESPN Analytics, although the system does not disclose full methodological details [7]. Other work highlights the importance of late game states for decision making, and analysts use win probability based analysis to evaluate late game tactics such as shot selection and intentional fouling [13].

2.2 Play-by-Play and Sequential Modeling in Basketball

While game state models summarize the game into a small set of variables, a separate line of work treats basketball as an event driven process and uses play-by-play as a sequence [21,22]. Possession based Markov models simulate game progression using transition structure learned from NBA play-by-play, and some variants incorporate team level strength information [21]. Richer play-by-play models improve realism by allowing non homogeneous behavior across different segments of a game [22]. Complementary sequential views treat scoring as a stochastic counting process at game time resolution and produce in game outcome predictions from the evolution of scoring over time [19]. Extensions introduce latent structure to represent interactions among players and lineups. Continuous time network models treat games as dynamic transactional networks and infer latent player roles and clusters from interaction patterns [23]. Researchers also use play-by-play data to build stochastic generative models for lineup substitutions and lineup specific scoring dynamics [3]. Decision centric formulations frame basketball plays as Markov decision processes with time varying transition dynamics to analyze strategy, including shot clock dependent behavior and counterfactual policy changes [17]. Lineup focused MDP formulations combine traditional statistics with tracking information for lineup analysis [10]. In parallel, tracking based methods estimate fine grained possession value or expected points as a possession unfolds and enable evaluation of within possession actions beyond box score aggregates [4,18]. Representation learning approaches learn dense transferable player and lineup features directly from play outcomes or multi agent trajectories and provide embeddings for downstream prediction and analysis [1,9].

2.3 Related Approaches in Other Sports

Event stream modeling and continuously updated in play probabilities also appear outside basketball. In soccer, Bayesian in game win probability models estimate running win draw loss probabilities from contextual game state features and tailor the inference to low scoring dynamics [16]. Complementary football work applies deep latent structure methods such as deep embedded clustering to uncover team playing styles from large scale event data [6]. In cricket, dynamic logistic regression models provide in play win probabilities whose covariate effects evolve smoothly over match progression [2]. American football research also studies state based win probability. Researchers estimate pre play win probability by combining situational variables with pregame expectations such as the Vegas point spread and by using machine learning models such as random forests [11]. Other work proposes simpler interpretable in game probability models through logistic regression built from play-by-play derived features [14]. Taken together, these cross sport studies show that in play forecasting can rely on compact state variables or richer event histories depending on the sport and the available data [2,16].

3 Dataset

3.1 Data Collection

We collect play-by-play data from 4,920 regular season NBA games spanning four seasons from 2021–2022 through 2024–2025. Each game record provides a chronological sequence of events that describes all plays during the game, including made and missed shots, rebounds, turnovers, fouls, and substitutions. We exclude playoff games to maintain a consistent competitive environment, since playoff dynamics often differ from regular season play.

3.2 Event Representation

Each play-by-play event uses three features. **Event type** denotes the categorical type of play such as made three pointer, defensive rebound, turnover. The corpus contains 47 unique event types. **Team indicator** denotes whether the event is attributed to the home team, the away team, or neutral events such as jump balls. **Time elapsed** denotes the time in seconds since the previous event and captures pace of play.

3.3 Game State Features

At each prediction point, we extract a compact set of scalar game state features. The features include **time remaining** in regulation measured in seconds, **score differential** defined as home score minus away score, **period** indicating the current quarter or overtime period, and **team records** given by the pregame win and loss totals for both teams, which yield pregame win percentages.

3.4 Trajectory Sampling

In this work, a *trajectory* denotes the ordered sequence of play-by-play events observed from game start up to a selected time index. We adopt a trajectory based formulation in which each training example consists of such an event sequence up to a randomly sampled endpoint. For each game with N events, we uniformly sample 50 trajectory endpoints from indices 10 through N to enforce a minimum context length. Each sampled trajectory pairs with a binary label that indicates whether the home team wins the game. When a trajectory exceeds 600 events, we truncate it from the left and retain the most recent events.

3.5 Dataset Split

We simulate deployment by training on earlier games and evaluating on later games. We sort games chronologically by date and allocate the oldest games to training, followed by validation, and reserve the most recent games for testing. This temporal ordering prevents data leakage and provides a rigorous evaluation of the model's ability to generalize to unseen games.

4 Methodology

The proposed model factorizes the input into an event history stream and a structured state stream, and combines them to produce a single probability estimate. The remainder of this section specifies the input representation, the sequence encoder and pooling mechanism, the fusion architecture, and the training objective.

We model *home team win probability* from an in game trajectory consisting of a sequence of discrete play-by-play events and a compact vector of game state features. A *snapshot* i denotes a single prediction point during a game defined by the information available up to that time, including the current game state and the play-by-play event history. Given snapshot i, the model predicts $p_i \in (0, 1)$, the probability that the home team ultimately wins.

The architecture contains two parallel branches. The game state branch encodes a low dimensional summary of the current scoreboard and pregame context. The sequence branch encodes the recent play-by-play event history. A fusion module combines both representations and produces the final win probability estimate.

4.1 Game State Encoder

The state branch processes the game state vector into a dense representation that captures the current game context. While the sequence branch encodes the dynamic history of play-by-play events, the state branch summarizes the aggregate situation at the moment of prediction.

The input to the state branch is a 10 dimensional feature vector at snapshot i.

$$\mathbf{g}_i = [\tau_i, \delta_i, \pi_i, \delta_i^{\mathrm{w}}, a_i, \kappa_i, \rho_i^{\mathrm{away}}, \rho_i^{\mathrm{home}}, \Delta\rho_i, r_i] \in \mathbb{R}^{10}, \tag{1}$$

where i denotes the prediction point within the game, τ_i is normalized time remaining in the game, δ_i is normalized score differential computed as home score minus away score, π_i is normalized period, δ_i^{w} is time weighted score differential that amplifies the importance of leads as the game progresses, a_i is absolute score differential capturing margin magnitude regardless of direction, κ_i is a leverage term that increases for close games in late periods, ρ_i^{away} and ρ_i^{home} are pregame win percentages for the away and home teams computed from season records, $\Delta\rho_i$ is the win percentage difference between teams indicating relative strength, and r_i is a reliability term based on games played that down weights early season records.

These features capture three categories of information. The first category consists of scoreboard features that encode the current game situation. The second category consists of interaction features that capture nonlinear game dynamics. The time weighted score differential reflects that a large lead with two minutes remaining differs fundamentally from the same lead in the first quarter. The leverage term quantifies the pressure of close late game situations. The third category consists of team strength priors that incorporate pregame expectations based on season performance.

We transform the state vector through a two layer feedforward network.

$$\mathbf{z}_{\text{state},i} = \text{MLP}_{\text{state}}(\mathbf{g}_i) \in \mathbb{R}^d, \tag{2}$$

where $\text{MLP}_{\text{state}} : \mathbb{R}^{10} \to \mathbb{R}^d$ consists of an affine map from 10 dimensions to d dimensions followed by a nonlinearity and a second affine map that outputs a d dimensional vector, and $\mathbf{z}_{\text{state},i}$ is the resulting state embedding.

The state embedding provides a stable foundation for win probability estimation. Score differential and time remaining explain a substantial portion of win probability variance, as established by prior work on basketball win probability models. The state branch learns to combine these features with team strength priors and interaction terms to produce a context aware representation that the fusion layer combines with the sequence embedding.

4.2 Sequence Encoder

The sequence encoder maps an ordered event history to a sequence of latent vectors that capture both event semantics and temporal structure. Truncation enforces a bounded context window focused on the most recent events, while masking ensures that only real events contribute to the representation.

Let $(e_1, \ldots, e_L)$ denote the ordered sequence of play-by-play events for a snapshot, where e_1 is the oldest and e_L is the most recent. If a game contains more than $L_{\max}$ events, we retain only the most recent $L_{\max}$ events. Shorter sequences are left padded with a distinguished padding token, and a Boolean mask $m_t \in \{0, 1\}$ indicates valid positions.

For each event t, the model uses three aligned features. The event type is $e_t \in \{1, \ldots, V\}$ where V is the number of unique event types in the vocabulary such as made two pointer shot, block, substitution. The side indicator is $s_t \in \{0, 1, 2\}$ with values corresponding to neutral, home, and away. The inter event time gap is $\Delta t_t \geq 0$ in seconds.

An additive combination of the event type, side indicator, and time gap representations can induce interference among semantically distinct features. Accordingly, the three components are concatenated so that each signal is retained in a dedicated subspace.

$$\mathbf{c}_t = \left[\mathrm{Embed}_{\mathrm{event}}(e_t) \parallel \mathrm{Embed}_{\mathrm{side}}(s_t) \parallel \Delta t_t/T_0\right] \in \mathbb{R}^{57}, \tag{3}$$

where $\mathrm{Embed}_{\mathrm{event}} \in \mathbb{R}^{V\times 48}$ is the event embedding, $\mathrm{Embed}_{\mathrm{side}} \in \mathbb{R}^{3\times 8}$ is the side embedding, and $T_0 = 24$ seconds is a time scale that normalizes the time feature.

We then map the concatenated vector $\mathbf{c}_t$ to the model dimension d through a learned affine projection.

$$\mathbf{x}_t^{(0)} = \mathrm{MLP}_{\mathrm{proj}}(\mathbf{c}_t) \in \mathbb{R}^d, \tag{4}$$

where $\mathrm{MLP}_{\mathrm{proj}} : \mathbb{R}^{57} \to \mathbb{R}^d$ is a single layer feedforward network with learnable parameters that compresses the concatenated features into a dense representation, and $\mathbf{x}_t^{(0)}$ denotes the initial event embedding.

To encode event order within the retained window, we add a learnable positional embedding.

$$\mathbf{x}_t^{(1)} = \mathbf{x}_t^{(0)} + \mathrm{Embed}_{\mathrm{pos}}(p_t), \tag{5}$$

where p_t denotes the position of event t within the sequence and $\mathrm{Embed}_{\mathrm{pos}} \in \mathbb{R}^{L_{\max}\times d}$ maps each position to a d dimensional vector.

We process the embedded sequence $\{\mathbf{x}_t^{(1)}\}_{t=1}^{L}$ with a position wise feedforward network that applies the same transformation independently at each position.

$$\mathbf{h}_t = \mathrm{MLP}_{\mathrm{enc}}(\mathbf{x}_t^{(1)}) \in \mathbb{R}^d, \tag{6}$$

where $\mathrm{MLP}_{\mathrm{enc}} : \mathbb{R}^d \to \mathbb{R}^d$ is a feedforward network with a nonlinearity, and $\mathbf{h}_t$ denotes the hidden state for event t. Event order enters through positional embeddings and the recency weighted pooling defined below, while the encoder remains position wise to control model capacity and mitigate overfitting.

4.3 Temporal Pooling

Temporal pooling compresses the sequence of event level representations into a single fixed size vector. Win probability depends primarily on recent game dynamics. The last few possessions, scoring runs, and momentum shifts carry more predictive signal than events from earlier in the game. To capture this, we employ a recency weighted pooling operator that assigns exponentially increasing weights to more recent events.

Each position t in the sequence receives an unnormalized weight.

$$\tilde{w}_t = m_t \cdot \exp(\alpha\, p_t), \tag{7}$$

where $\tilde{w}_t$ denotes the unnormalized weight for position t, p_t denotes the position of event t within the sequence with larger values corresponding to more recent events, $m_t \in \{0,1\}$ is a binary mask that excludes padding positions from the computation, and $\alpha \in \mathbb{R}$ is a learned scalar parameter that controls the decay rate. A larger α causes the model to focus more sharply on recent events, while a smaller α distributes attention more evenly across the sequence.

We normalize these weights to sum to one.

$$w_t = \frac{\tilde{w}_t}{\sum_{j=1}^{L} \tilde{w}_j}, \tag{8}$$

where w_t denotes the normalized weight for position t and L denotes the sequence length.

The final sequence embedding is the weighted sum of all event level hidden states.

$$\mathbf{z}_{\text{seq}} = \sum_{t=1}^{L} w_t \, \mathbf{h}_t \in \mathbb{R}^d, \tag{9}$$

where $\mathbf{h}_t \in \mathbb{R}^d$ is the hidden state for event t produced by the sequence encoder, d is the model dimension, and $\mathbf{z}_{\text{seq}}$ is the resulting sequence embedding.

The learned weighting provides flexibility that fixed pooling strategies lack. Mean pooling treats all events equally regardless of temporal relevance, and max pooling selects only the most salient feature per dimension. Exponential recency weighting emphasizes recent events while retaining information from the full sequence and captures short term dynamics that matter for win probability estimation.

4.4 Fusion and Prediction Head

The fusion layer combines the sequence embedding with the state embedding to form a joint representation that captures both the dynamic event history and the static game context.

We concatenate the two embeddings.

$$\mathbf{z}_i = \left[\mathbf{z}_{\text{seq},i} \,\|\, \mathbf{z}_{\text{state},i}\right] \in \mathbb{R}^{2d}, \tag{10}$$

where $\mathbf{z}_{\text{seq},i} \in \mathbb{R}^d$ is the sequence embedding produced by temporal pooling, $\mathbf{z}_{\text{state},i} \in \mathbb{R}^d$ is the state embedding that encodes the current scoreboard and team strength, and $[\cdot \,\|\, \cdot]$ denotes concatenation along the feature dimension.

Concatenation preserves the full information from both branches and allows the prediction head to learn interactions between sequence derived features and state derived features. This design enables the model to weight the contributions of each branch differently depending on the game situation.

The prediction head processes the joint representation through a feedforward network.

$$\ell_i = \text{MLP}_{\text{head}}(\mathbf{z}_i), \tag{11}$$

where $\text{MLP}_{\text{head}} : \mathbb{R}^{2d} \to \mathbb{R}$ is a two layer feedforward network that reduces the dimension from $2d$ to d and then to a scalar, and $\ell_i \in \mathbb{R}$ is the unnormalized log odds score.

We convert this logit to a probability using the logistic sigmoid function.

$$p_i = \sigma(\ell_i) = \frac{1}{1 + \exp(-\ell_i)}, \quad (12)$$

where $p_i \in (0, 1)$ represents the predicted probability that the home team wins the game at snapshot i.

4.5 Training Objective and Optimization

We train the model by minimizing binary cross entropy between predicted probabilities and observed game outcomes.

Given a dataset of N snapshots where each snapshot i contains an event sequence $(e_1^{(i)}, \ldots, e_L^{(i)})$, a game state vector $\mathbf{g}^{(i)}$, and a label $y^{(i)} \in \{0, 1\}$ indicating whether the home team wins, the loss for a single example is

$$\mathcal{L}_{\mathrm{BCE}}(\ell, y) = -y \log \sigma(\ell) - (1 - y) \log(1 - \sigma(\ell)), \quad (13)$$

where $\ell \in \mathbb{R}$ is the predicted logit and $\sigma(\cdot)$ is the logistic sigmoid function.

The full training objective combines the cross entropy loss with ℓ_2 regularization.

$$\min_{\theta} \frac{1}{N} \sum_{i=1}^{N} \mathcal{L}_{\mathrm{BCE}}\big(\ell^{(i)}(\theta), y^{(i)}\big) + \frac{\lambda}{2} \|\theta\|_2^2, \quad (14)$$

where θ denotes the model parameters and λ controls the regularization strength.

We optimize using AdamW with decoupled weight decay and a cosine annealing learning rate schedule. We apply gradient clipping to stabilize training and employ early stopping based on validation loss to prevent overfitting.

4.6 Implementation Details

We set the maximum sequence length $L_{\max} = 600$ and the model dimension $d = 64$. The event embedding dimension is 48, the side embedding dimension is 8, and the time feature contributes 1 dimension after normalization, yielding a concatenated dimension of 57 before projection.

For the sequence encoder, we use a single layer position wise feedforward network. The temporal pooling initializes the recency parameter $\alpha = 0.01$. The state branch uses a two layer feedforward network mapping from 10 dimensions to d.

We train with batch size 256 and initial learning rate 10^{-4}. We use the AdamW optimizer with weight decay $\lambda = 10^{-4}$ and a cosine annealing schedule that decays the learning rate to 10^{-6} over the training period. We clip gradient norms to 1.0. Training proceeds for a maximum of 20 epochs with early stopping based on validation loss using a patience of 7 epochs.

We normalize the input features as follows. Time remaining is divided by total game duration, score differential is clipped to $[-30, 30]$ and divided by 30, period is divided by the maximum period, and inter event time gaps are divided by $T_0 = 24$ seconds. Team win percentages are computed from season records with a fallback to 0.5 for teams with no games played.

We split the games chronologically into training, validation, and test sets. The most recent 500 games form the test set, the preceding 500 games form the validation set, and the remaining games form the training set. We select the model checkpoint with the lowest validation loss for final evaluation.

5 Results

This section specifies the evaluation protocol used to assess predictive performance and calibration. It reports results on held out data and compares against a state only baseline.

5.1 Evaluation Metrics

We evaluate model performance using three complementary metrics that assess the quality of probabilistic predictions.

Log loss measures the quality of probabilistic predictions by assigning larger penalties to confident errors than to uncertain errors.

$$\mathcal{L}_{\text{log}} = -\frac{1}{N}\sum_{i=1}^{N}\Big(y_i \log p_i + (1 - y_i)\log(1 - p_i)\Big), \tag{15}$$

where N is the number of evaluated examples, $p_i \in (0, 1)$ is the predicted probability for example i, and $y_i \in \{0, 1\}$ is the corresponding binary outcome.

The Brier score measures the mean squared error between predicted probabilities and binary outcomes.

$$\mathcal{L}_{\text{Brier}} = \frac{1}{N}\sum_{i=1}^{N}(p_i - y_i)^2, \tag{16}$$

where p_i is the predicted probability and y_i is the true label for example i.

Expected calibration error quantifies calibration by comparing predicted probabilities with empirical outcome frequencies.

$$\text{ECE} = \sum_{m=1}^{M}\frac{|B_m|}{N}\big|\text{acc}(B_m) - \text{conf}(B_m)\big|, \tag{17}$$

where $\{B_m\}_{m=1}^{M}$ is a partition of the examples into M bins based on predicted probability, $|B_m|$ is the number of examples in bin m, $\text{acc}(B_m) = \frac{1}{|B_m|}\sum_{i \in B_m} y_i$ is the empirical accuracy in bin m, and $\text{conf}(B_m) = \frac{1}{|B_m|}\sum_{i \in B_m} p_i$ is the mean predicted probability in bin m.

Together, these three metrics capture both discriminative ability and calibration quality.

5.2 Logistic Regression Baseline

To contextualize the performance of our proposed model, we implement a logistic regression baseline that uses only the instantaneous game state features without access to the sequential event history.

The logistic regression model receives the same 10 dimensional game state vector $\mathbf{g}_i$ used by the state branch of our model. It includes normalized time remaining, normalized score differential, period indicator, time weighted score differential, absolute score differential, leverage term, pregame win percentages for both teams, win percentage difference, and record reliability. This baseline represents a simple approach to win probability estimation that relies solely on the current game situation.

We train the logistic regression model with ℓ_2 regularization on the same training set and evaluate on the same test set used for our model. Table 1 presents the results under trajectory based evaluation.

Our model achieves a log loss of 0.4374 compared to 0.4537 for the baseline and a Brier score of 0.1450 compared to 0.1511. The logistic regression baseline achieves an ECE of 0.0177 compared to 0.0181 for our model. The difference is small in practice and both models remain well calibrated under this evaluation protocol.

Table 1. Trajectory based comparison on sampled snapshots. The table compares logistic regression, ESPN Analytics, and our model on the test set.

Model	Log Loss	Brier Score	ECE
Logistic Regression	0.4537	0.1511	**0.0177**
ESPN Analytics	0.4482	0.1489	0.0182
Ours	**0.4374**	**0.1450**	0.0181

5.3 Trajectory Based Comparison

To benchmark our model against an established industry solution, we compare predicted probabilities with those produced by ESPN Analytics, which provides live win probability estimates for NBA games. The ESPN Analytics model is proprietary and does not disclose its full feature set or training procedure. We use the published event level probabilities as a reference for comparison.

Probability estimates from ESPN Analytics are available following each play during a game, producing a discrete time series of predictions that evolves as events occur. We collect these play-by-play probability estimates for all games in our test set via the ESPN public API. Each sample in our test dataset corresponds to a specific game state defined by the complete sequence of events from game start through event index k, where each event represents a discrete play such as a made field goal, defensive rebound, turnover, or foul. For the identical game state, a corresponding probability estimate from ESPN Analytics is available at event k. This correspondence enables direct comparison between both models on identical prediction tasks, since both use the same observed game history up to the same event index.

Table 1 summarizes the trajectory based comparison between ESPN Analytics and our model. Our model achieves lower log loss and Brier score while producing comparable calibration under this protocol.

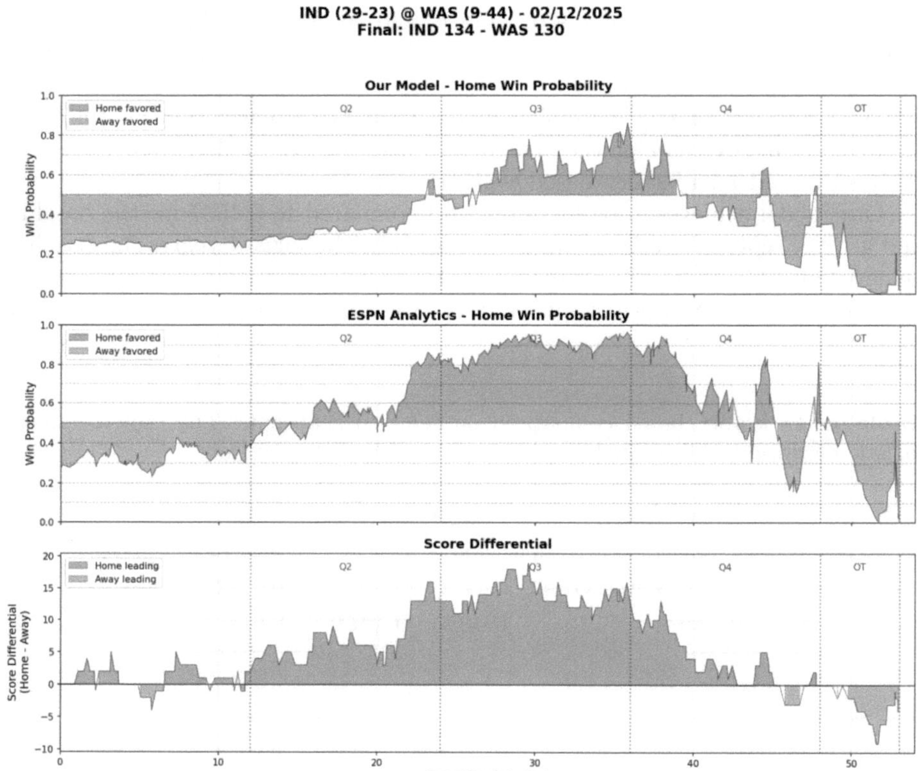

Fig. 1. Example game level win probability trajectories for our model and ESPN Analytics. The figure illustrates how the two models update predictions in response to play-by-play events over the course of a full game.

5.4 Evaluation on Complete Games

Trajectory based evaluation assesses model performance at sampled game states but it does not capture how predictions evolve continuously throughout a complete game. We therefore evaluate both models across all events within each game of the test set. During training, our model observes only 50 randomly sampled trajectory endpoints per game rather than predictions at every event. Evaluating on all events therefore tests generalization across diverse game states.

We process each game in its entirety and compute predictions at all event indices. This produces a complete probability curve for each game. We exclude the final two events of each game from this comparison, since these events often correspond to procedural end game updates where probabilities converge trivially to 1.0 or 0.0.

Table 2. Whole game comparison across all events in test set games.

Model	Log Loss	Brier Score	ECE
ESPN Analytics	0.4478	0.1482	0.0179
Ours	**0.4464**	**0.1481**	**0.0145**

Table 2 presents overall metrics across all events in the test set. Our model achieves a log loss of 0.4464 compared to 0.4478 for ESPN Analytics, a Brier score of 0.1481 compared to 0.1482, and an ECE of 0.0145 compared to 0.0179. These results indicate improved calibration under whole game evaluation.

To examine how performance varies throughout the course of a game, we partition events into three phases based on their relative position within the game. Table 3 presents the results for early, mid, and late phases. We also evaluate performance by quarter. Table 4 presents the results for each quarter.

The analysis reveals distinct performance characteristics between the two approaches. ESPN Analytics demonstrates stronger performance in the early portions of games, achieving a log loss of 0.5565 compared to 0.5722 for our model in the early phase and 0.5549 compared to 0.5769 in the first quarter.

Figure 1 compares our model with the ESPN Analytics model for one of the games that exhibits the largest prediction differences between the two approaches. The results indicate that the ESPN Analytics model produces more confident estimates and generates sharply polarized probabilities as early as the second quarter, largely driven by the score differential. In contrast, our model avoids making extreme predictions in the early stages of the game.

Our model exhibits progressively stronger performance as games advance. In the mid phase, our model achieves a log loss of 0.4889 compared to 0.5016 for ESPN Analytics. In the late phase, our model achieves a log loss of 0.2758 compared to 0.2829. The analysis by quarter confirms this pattern, with our model outperforming ESPN Analytics from the second quarter onward. The improvement is most pronounced in the fourth quarter, where our model achieves a log loss of 0.2633 compared to 0.2780 for ESPN Analytics.

These results suggest that sequential modeling captures evolving gameplay dynamics more effectively, allowing accumulated event information to increasingly inform predictions as the game progresses.

Table 3. Performance comparison by game phase.

Phase	Model	Log Loss	Brier Score	ECE
Early (0–33%)	ESPN Analytics	**0.5565**	**0.1888**	**0.0236**
	Ours	0.5722	0.1947	0.0337
Mid (33–67%)	ESPN Analytics	0.5016	0.1658	0.0379
	Ours	**0.4889**	**0.1621**	**0.0286**
Late (67–100%)	ESPN Analytics	0.2829	0.0891	**0.0086**
	Ours	**0.2758**	**0.0873**	0.0113

Table 4. Performance comparison by quarter.

Quarter	Model	Log Loss	Brier Score	ECE
Q1	ESPN Analytics	**0.5549**	**0.1880**	**0.0206**
	Ours	0.5769	0.1965	0.0405
Q2	ESPN Analytics	0.5264	0.1788	0.0428
	Ours	**0.5258**	**0.1770**	**0.0359**
Q3	ESPN Analytics	0.4422	0.1435	0.0297
	Ours	**0.4296**	**0.1405**	**0.0202**
Q4+	ESPN Analytics	0.2780	0.0861	**0.0102**
	Ours	**0.2633**	**0.0826**	0.0140

6 Discussion

The empirical results demonstrate that combining a compact game state vector with a learned representation of recent play-by-play events achieves competitive accuracy and improved calibration under whole game evaluation relative to a widely used industry baseline. The phase and quarter level analysis reveals a clear division of labor between the two information sources. Contextual information from before the game contributes most in early portions of games, while the incremental information contained in event sequences becomes increasingly predictive as the game evolves. This observation supports the modeling choice of retaining both a structured state stream and a sequential history stream rather than relying exclusively on either one.

Replacing the temporal pooling mechanism with transformer sequence encoders does not improve performance in our experiments. Transformers can learn long range dependencies and context dependent interactions between events. However, transformer variants overfit relative to the simpler temporal pooling approach. The higher effective capacity of self attention models and the limited amount of supervised signal per unique game context explain this behavior. Given the available data, a simpler encoder provides a more favorable bias variance trade off.

We do not incorporate player embeddings in the final model because each individual player appears in too few events to learn generalizable representations. The model architecture supports player embeddings by replacing the side indicator embeddings, but preliminary experiments indicate that this addition increases overfitting rather than improving predictive performance.

7 Conclusion

We present a neural architecture for estimating the probability that the home team wins an NBA game, given the play-by-play event history and current game state. The model combines a recency weighted sequence encoder with a state embedding branch and fuses both representations to produce probability estimates. Our approach improves log loss and Brier score under trajectory based evaluation and achieves lower expected calibration error under whole game evaluation across all events, relative to ESPN Analytics.

Future research can explore pretraining objectives that learn player representations from external data sources and enable robust player embeddings without overfitting. Explicit modeling of lineup compositions, substitution patterns, and possession boundaries offers further opportunities to capture structure specific to basketball.

The proposed architecture can adapt for richer decision support tasks. If player and lineup level representations can be learned robustly, the model can estimate interaction effects between players, evaluate counterfactual lineup arrangements, and recommend substitutions. Win probability estimation provides a natural foundation for these extensions because it quantifies downstream game impact and serves as an evaluation signal for comparing alternative lineup choices under realistic game contexts.

References

1. Alcorn, M.A., Nguyen, A.: baller2vec: A multi-entity transformer for multi-agent spatiotemporal modeling (2021). https://doi.org/10.48550/arXiv.2102.03291, https://arxiv.org/abs/2102.03291
2. Asif, M., McHale, I.G.: In-play forecasting of win probability in one-day international cricket: a dynamic logistic regression model. Int. J. Forecast. **32**(1), 34–43 (2016). https://doi.org/10.1016/j.ijforecast.2015.02.005
3. Bhat, H.S., Huang, L.H., Rodriguez, S.: Learning stochastic models for basketball substitutions from play-by-play data. In: Machine Learning and Data Mining for Sports Analytics (MLSA) Workshop (ECML/PKDD) (2015). https://dtai.cs.kuleuven.be/events/MLSA15/papers/mlsa15_submission_12.pdf
4. Cervone, D., D'Amour, A., Bornn, L., Goldsberry, K.: Pointwise: predicting points and valuing decisions in real time with NBA optical tracking data. In: MIT Sloan Sports Analytics Conference (2014)
5. Chen, T., Fan, Q.: A functional data approach to model score difference process in professional basketball games. J. Appl. Stat. **45**(1), 112–127 (2018). https://doi.org/10.1080/02664763.2016.1268106

6. Demir, E., Şahin, Y.H., Üre, N.K.: How do football teams play? A deep embedded clustering approach to reveal playing styles. In: Dong, J., Sun, J., Xie, X., Jiang, K. (eds.) ISACE 2025, vol. 15925, pp. 53–68. Springer, Cham (2026). https://doi.org/10.1007/978-3-032-06167-6_4
7. ESPN: ESPN analytics win probability (NBA gamecast). ESPN.com. Accessed 05 Feb 2026
8. Gabel, A., Redner, S.: Random walk picture of basketball scoring. J. Quant. Anal. Sports (2012)
9. Guan, W., Javed, N., Lu, P.: Nba2vec: dense feature representations of NBA players (2023). https://arxiv.org/abs/2302.13386
10. Liu, Z., Su, S.: Analyzing basketball lineups with MDP using NBA statistics and player tracking data. In: Dong, J., Sun, J., Xie, X., Jiang, K. (eds.) ISACE 2025, vol. 15925, pp. 142–154. Springer, Cham (2026). https://doi.org/10.1007/978-3-032-06167-6_11
11. Lock, D., Nettleton, D.: Using random forests to estimate win probability before each play of an NFL game. J. Quant. Anal. Sports **10** (2014). https://doi.org/10.1515/jqas-2013-0100
12. Maddox, J.T., Sides, R., Harvill, J.L.: Bayesian estimation of in-game home team win probability for NCAA division i men's college basketball games. J. Quant. Anal. Sports **18**(3), 233–245 (2022). https://doi.org/10.1515/jqas-2021-0086
13. McFarlane, P.: Evaluating NBA end-of-game decision-making. J. Sports Anal. **5**(1), 17–22 (2019). https://doi.org/10.3233/JSA-180231
14. Pelechrinis, K.: iWinRNFL: a simple and well-calibrated in-game NFL win probability model. arXiv preprint (2017). https://arxiv.org/abs/1704.00197
15. Polson, N.G., Stern, H.S.: The implied volatility of a sports game. J. Quant. Anal. Sports **11**(3), 149–165 (2015). https://doi.org/10.1515/jqas-2014-0095
16. Robberechts, P., Decroos, T., Davis, J.: A Bayesian approach to in-game win probability in soccer. In: Proceedings of the 27th ACM SIGKDD Conference on Knowledge Discovery and Data Mining (2021). https://doi.org/10.1145/3447548.3467194
17. Sandholtz, N., Bornn, L.: Markov decision processes with dynamic transition probabilities: an analysis of shooting strategies in basketball. Ann. Appl. Stat. **14**(3), 1122–1145 (2020). https://doi.org/10.1214/20-AOAS1348
18. Sicilia, A., Pelechrinis, K., Goldsberry, K.: Deephoops: evaluating micro-actions in basketball using deep feature representations of spatio-temporal data (2019). https://arxiv.org/abs/1902.08081
19. Song, K., Shi, J.: A gamma process based in-play prediction model for national basketball association games. Eur. J. Oper. Res. **283**(2), 706–713 (2020). https://doi.org/10.1016/j.ejor.2019.11.012
20. Stern, H.S.: A Brownian motion model for the progress of sports scores. J. Am. Stat. Assoc. **89**(428), 1128–1134 (1994). https://doi.org/10.1080/01621459.1994.10476851
21. Štrumbelj, E., Vračar, P.: Simulating a basketball match with a homogeneous Markov model and forecasting the outcome. Int. J. Forecast. **28**(2), 532–542 (2012). https://doi.org/10.1016/j.ijforecast.2011.01.004
22. Vračar, P., Štrumbelj, E., Kononenko, I.: Modeling basketball play-by-play data. Expert Syst. Appl. **44**, 58–66 (2016). https://doi.org/10.1016/j.eswa.2015.09.004
23. Xin, L., Zhu, M., Chipman, H.A.: A continuous-time stochastic block model for basketball networks. Ann. Appl. Stat. **11**(2), 553–597 (2017). https://doi.org/10.1214/16-AOAS993

Clustering Tactical Patterns in Football: Time Series Features from Tracking Data

James Anurathan, Philip Ritzer, Manuel Wengert, Christian Koot, Manfred Rössle, and Marco Klaiber(✉)

Aalen University of Applied Sciences, 73430 Aalen, Germany
marco.klaiber@hs-aalen.de

Abstract. Understanding and identifying tactical patterns in football is important for performance analysis and strategic decision making. This work presents a modular method that combines time series feature (TSF) extractors with clustering and cross-analysis to identify and evaluate offensive and defensive patterns. Using tracking and event data from professional games of the Deutsche Fußball Liga (DFL), we extract permutation-invariant spatial features from sequences that precede key situations. These sequences are processed with catch22 and QUANT TSF and clustered via k-means. By cross-analyzing offensive and defensive clusters, our approach estimates the probabilities of success and predicts outcomes in goal-related situations. The evaluation shows that catch22 with selected spatial features achieves strong predictive performance and produces interpretable patterns. Therefore, our paper offers a framework for tactical analysis and could help coaches and analysts identify effective or vulnerable matchups.

Keywords: Football · Tactical Patterns · Tracking Data · Time Series

1 Introduction

The Top 5 European football (soccer) leagues are among the most watched competitions worldwide [22]. The high level of performance exhibited by these teams attracts a global audience and generates significant revenues through broadcasting, making success on the pitch a priority for sporting and economic reasons. New technologies such as tracking systems or video-based motion analysis allow for detailed performance for data collection and analytics [14,19]. These data-driven analytics are particularly valuable in situations directly related to the match outcomes, such as scoring or preventing goals [23]. However, compared to other invasive team sports, such as basketball or ice-hockey, football is characterized by a low-scoring game [2,3]. Therefore, since match outcomes often depend on random factors, identifying offensive and defensive patterns emerges as a relevant area of research. This pattern identification is relevant, because coordinated player movements and spatial organization often precede critical game situations [25], and allows conclusions to be drawn about the tactics and strategies on which a team is based.

Z. Liu and V. Misra (Eds.): ISACE 2026, LNCS 16610, pp. 103–116, 2026.
https://doi.org/10.1007/978-3-032-27272-0_8

However, comparatively less attention has been paid to systematic analysis of tactical patterns that precede goals or big chances [3,14]. Typically, matches have been analyzed using notational analysis that statistically summarizes events and the actions of involved players to identify patterns that considerably influenced the outcome of the investigated situation. The identified patterns help teams improve their decision making and learn from matches more accurately, especially from goal-threatening offensive and defensive situations. However, such large amounts of data can hardly be handled by human recognition [27]. To exploit their full potential, recent studies in football analytics apply Machine Learning (ML) algorithms to extract meaningful insights [26]. ML is used mainly in supervised or unsupervised settings [14]. Although supervised approaches require labeled data and are limited to known patterns, unsupervised models operate solely on internal structures, and similarities, thus, have the potential to dynamically identify unknown patterns in football situations.

In order to use these models, complex temporal relationships within time series data must be represented in a format that is suitable for unsupervised learning. A common strategy for dealing with such data is to extract meaningful time series features (TSFs) that capture temporal and structural relations [6, 8]. These TSF extractors convert raw tracking data into feature vectors that describe the behavior of players and teams in short time windows.

Previous work by Decroos et al. [7] and Feuerhake [10] showed that clustering of event and tracking data can reveal tactical patterns but emphasized the need for situational analysis and cross-team generalization. This work builds on the work of Decroos et al. [7] and Feuerhake [10], investigating whether meaningful and generalizable offensive and defensive play patterns can be found within full tracking data. Furthermore, the study is extended by cross-analyzing identified patterns from different teams, searching for generalizable offensive and defensive patterns that are effective against specific opposed ones.

To the best of our knowledge, this is the first attempt to identify and cross-analyze offensive and defensive patterns with TSF extractors from different teams using full tracking data, leading to the following research questions:

1. How can offensive and defensive patterns be identified using tracking data?
2. Can the patterns found be matched via cross-analysis to identify information for teams to act and counteract when specific patterns occur within a game?

Consequently, this work makes the following contributions:

- A proof of concept to identify and cross-analyze offensive and defensive play patterns in football.
- Integration of TSF extractors to convert raw data into meaningful features to support unsupervised clustering of tactical patterns.
- Derivation of possible use cases for coaches and practitioners to further promote data-driven football analysis and tactical decision-making.

2 Related Work

Analyzing and understanding tactical behaviors in football has evolved significantly in the last decade, increasingly relying on advanced data-driven methodologies [20]. Recent studies highlight the increasing role of data-driven tactics, highlighting how ML and tracking data enable deeper analysis of player and team behavior [21].

Fernandez et al. [9] focus on quantifying the creation and occupation of space by modeling individual player influence and team-level pitch control. Akhanli and Hennig [1] cluster player performance data to study team composition and similarity. Van Haaren et al. [13] propose an inductive logic programming approach to identify recurring spatial and player interaction patterns that lead to goal attempts, aiming at interpretable tactical improvement.

In contrast to these studies, our research investigates typical offensive and defensive team behavior patterns specifically within goal-critical situations. Our aim is to evaluate which offensive patterns effectively counter particular defensive patterns and to identify generalizable tactical factors. Employing clustering techniques, we uncover tactical clusters of offensive and defensive behaviors to assess their effectiveness and derive generalizable actionable insights for tactical decision-making.

Furthermore, Goes et al. [12] contribute to the analysis of tactical behavior by examining spatiotemporal patterns of player subgroups (defenders, midfielders, and attackers) using position tracking data. They apply unsupervised clustering to dynamically identify these groups and analyze how well different parts of the team move together or in response to the opposing team during attacks. Their study focuses on movement coordination within single matches. We extend this by analyzing the full offensive and defensive sequences between teams to uncover which attacking patterns are effective against specific defensive ones.

Another relevant contribution comes from Knauf et al. [15], who introduce spatio-temporal convolution kernels to assess similarity between multi-player trajectories, primarily for clustering tasks. Although their approach is designed for broad applicability and emphasizes structural similarity, our work adds the focus to tactical evaluation by analyzing how specific offensive and defensive patterns interact and affect success in goal-critical situations.

3 Methodology

3.1 Data and Preprocessing

In our work, we utilized the *Integrated Dataset of Spatiotemporal and Event Data in Elite Football* (IDSSE), introduced by Bassek et al. [4]. The dataset is provided by the Deutsche Fußball Liga (DFL) and contains tracking and event data from seven professional football matches of the German Bundesliga and Bundesliga 2 during the 2022/23 season. In total, data from 10 teams are included, comprising 11 137 event annotations and 1 002 644 frames of positional data. The positional data includes the two-dimensional (x/y) coordinates of all players and the ball captured at 25 Hz.

As this work analyzes offensive and defensive play patterns, the respective sequences are extracted trigger-based as suggested by Feuerhake [10]. The sequences are multivariate time series that contain the x/y positions of the ball and all players of the last 10 s before a trigger event. For offensive patterns, the events "ChanceWithoutShot", "ShotAtGoal_OtherShot", "ShotAtGoal_SavedShot", "ShotAtGoal_ShotWoodWork", "ShotAtGoal_SuccessfulShot", "ShotAtGoal_ShotWide" were used as triggers to extract successful offensive situations. The events "GoalDisallowed", "PossessionLossBeforeGoal", "DefensiveClearance" and "ShotAtGoal_BlockedShot" are used as triggers for extracting successful defensive situations. After extraction, sequences that incorporate foul, set piece, or position data with less than 22 players on the field are excluded. The procedure yields an offensive dataset X_{off} that contains 69 successful and 92 unsuccessful offensive sequences and X_{def} that contains the corresponding 69 unsuccessful and 92 successful defensive sequences. Each sequence of X_{def} and X_{off} contains 24 x/y positions of the 11 players and the ball, measured over 10 s at 25 Hz, leading to 250 values per positional channel. In addition, each sequence has a label $y \in \{0, 1\}$ where 1 denotes an offensive and 0 a defensive success. The positions are flipped so that the attacked goal is always the same.

3.2 Feature Extraction

To analyze offensive and defensive patterns, TSF extractors combined with unsupervised clustering methods are utilized.

Spatial Features: The raw position time series cannot be meaningfully used as input for the TSF extractor since the channel identities are related to players and their order in the feature vector. If player indices are permuted or swapped, two scenes with exactly the same team shape produce different feature vectors, even though the underlying tactical configuration is identical as shown in Fig. 1.

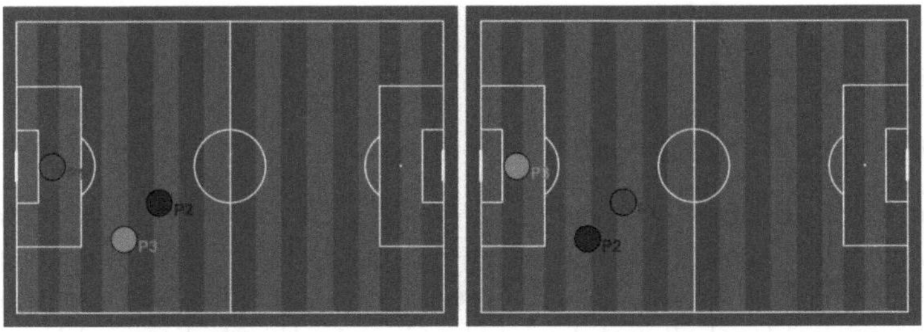

Fig. 1. Possible identical spatial features with permuting player identities.

In order to overcome this challenge, permutation-invariant spatial features have to be calculated from the teams' position data, except for the goalkeepers and the ball as they are unique entities with unique roles. In total, 34 spatial features as shown in the appendix (Table 1) are calculated from the field players position data and enriched with the ball position data for each timestep, leading to multivariate time series with 36 feature channels measured over 250 time steps. For defensive sequences, the x/y-positions of the goalkeeper are also included.

Time Series Features: To capture temporal information on spatial features within the sequence, the following TSF extractors are utilized:

catch22 computes 22 TSF selected from a set of 4 791 TSF and was introduced by Lubba et al. [17]. These features span diverse domains, including autocorrelation structure, value distribution, fluctuation scaling, outlier presence, and time-reversibility. Each feature is calculated in the z-normalized input time series to ensure invariance to mean and variance.

QUANT computes quantile-based features over dyadic subintervals of a time series and was introduced by Dempster et al. [8]. For each interval, a fixed number of equally spaced quantiles is computed, where every second interval is mean-normalized. The quantiles are extracted from different representations, including the original time series, its first and second derivatives, and the discrete fourier transform of the time series.

3.3 Evaluation Procedure

To identify and cross-analyze offensive and defensive play patterns within the IDSSE dataset $\mathcal{D}$, a systematic evaluation procedure is conducted as illustrated in Fig. 2.

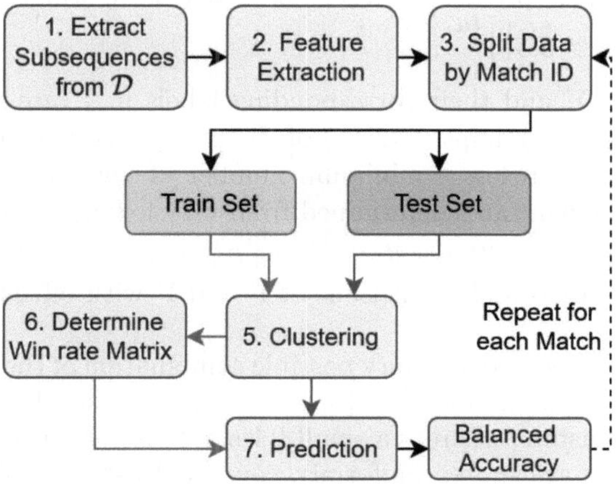

Fig. 2. Flowchart of the method with the applied evaluation procedure.

In the following, we describe the individual steps in more detail:

1. As described in Sect. 3.1, 161 offensive time series X_{off} and 161 defensive time series X_{def} are extracted with the corresponding labels Y.
2. Spatial features are calculated from the position data at each time step of each time series in X_{off} and X_{def} as described in Sect. 3.2, leading to the transformed datasets X'_{off} and X'_{def}. Subsequently, a TSF extractor $\mathcal{F}$ is applied to extract the normalized TSF vectors with z-score $\mathcal{F}(X'_{off})$ and $\mathcal{F}(X'_{def})$.
3. The datasets and labels are divided into a train split $\mathcal{F}(X'_{off})_{tr}$, $\mathcal{F}(X'_{def})_{tr}$ and Y_{tr}, as well as into a test split $\mathcal{F}(X'_{off})_{te}$, $\mathcal{F}(X'_{def})_{te}$ and Y_{te} such that the test split contains only instances and labels from a single match.
4. For clustering, k-means with Lloyd's algorithm is used [18] [16]. The clusterers M_{off} and M_{def} are fitted with k^{off} and k^{def} clusters on $\mathcal{F}(X'_{def})_{tr}$ and $\mathcal{F}(X'_{def})_{tr}$ respectively, assigning the cluster labels c^{off} and c^{def}.
5. Let $o \in C^{off}$ be the oth cluster, $d \in C^{def}$ be the dth defensive cluster and $\mathbb{I}$ be an indicator function that returns 1 if the condition is true otherwise 0. The number of offensive wins W^{off} is determined for any offensive-defensive cluster combination where c_i^{off} and c_i^{def} show the offensive and defensive clusters in a matchup, $W_{o,d}^{\text{off}} = \sum_{i=1}^{N} \mathbb{I}[c_i^{\text{off}} = o \wedge c_i^{\text{def}} = d] \cdot Y_i$. Afterwards, the number of cluster-pair matchups CMU is determined for all cluster combinations, $CMU_{o,d} = \sum_{i=1}^{N} \mathbb{I}[c_i^{\text{off}} = o \wedge c_i^{\text{def}} = d]$. Consequently, pairwise win rates are calculated by dividing the determined wins by the number of pairwise matchups $WR_{o,d}^{off} = \frac{W_{o,d}}{CMU_{o,d}}$ where the entirety of all calculated win rates displays the win rate matrix WR.
6. The clusters $\hat{c}^{off}$ for the TSF vectors in $\mathcal{F}(X'_{off})_{te}$ are determined by M^{off} and the clusters $\hat{c}^{def}$ for the TSF vectors in $\mathcal{F}(X'_{off})_{te}$ by M^{def}. Subsequently, predictions are made based on the win rates WR^{off} of the cluster pairs from the training data. If the win rate of the cluster pair is greater than 0.5, an offensive win is predicted, otherwise a defensive win is predicted, $\hat{Y} = \left\{\mathbb{I}\left[WR^{\text{off}}_{\hat{c}_i^{\text{off}}, \hat{c}_i^{\text{def}}} > 0.5\right]\right\}_{i=1}^{N_{\text{te}}}$.
7. Instances from $\hat{Y}$ and their corresponding labels in Y are removed if their numbers of total matchups $CMU_{o,d}$ of the predicting cluster pair o, d in the win rate matrix is below a minimum number of matchups per cluster pair CMU_{min} as the win rates determined from very few instances are unreliable. Afterwards, *balanced accuracy* $= \frac{1}{2}(\frac{TP}{TP+FN} + \frac{TN}{TN+FP})$ is calculated using the remaining labels and predictions of Y and $\hat{Y}$ with offensive wins treated as positives.
8. Steps 4 to 7 are repeated for every possible combination of the number clusters $k^{off} \in \{3, 4, \ldots, 20\}$ and $k^{def} \in \{3, 4, \ldots, 20\}$. In general, a high k leads to more specific clusters, whereas a small k leads to fewer but more generic clusters. The ranges are chosen uniformly, cover at least multiple cluster counts and are capped at 20, to ensure variation and inclusion of sequences from all matches for each k^{off} and k^{def} combination during evaluation.

9. Steps 3–8 are repeated so that all instances from $\mathcal{F}(X'_{off})$ and $\mathcal{F}(X'_{def})$ were assigned once to the test split. Subsequently, the resulting balanced accuracies were averaged to provide more robust results.

The procedure is repeated such that the data from each match was used once as test data and the results were averaged. We also report results for models using spatial features selected by balanced accuracy from 1000 runs with randomly chosen feature sets, employing catch22 as the TSF extractor. Except for the k-means clustering' numbers of clusters k^{off} and k^{def}, all hyperparameters for clusterers and TSF extractors are default as described in their original works.

4 Results and Discussion

The best balanced accuracies of the evaluated k^{off}-k^{def}-combinations are visualized alongside CMU_{min}. Since samples can be excluded for prediction, if the number of group matchups in the win rate matrix is below CMU_{min}, the proportion of predicted samples (PPS) is also visualized, i.e., the proportion of samples for all matches that were not excluded for the k^{off}-k^{def}-combination, which yielded the reported balanced accuracy. Additionally, the best balanced accuracies of the models are reported under the condition that only k^{off}-k^{def}-combinations are considered with a PPS of at least 50%.

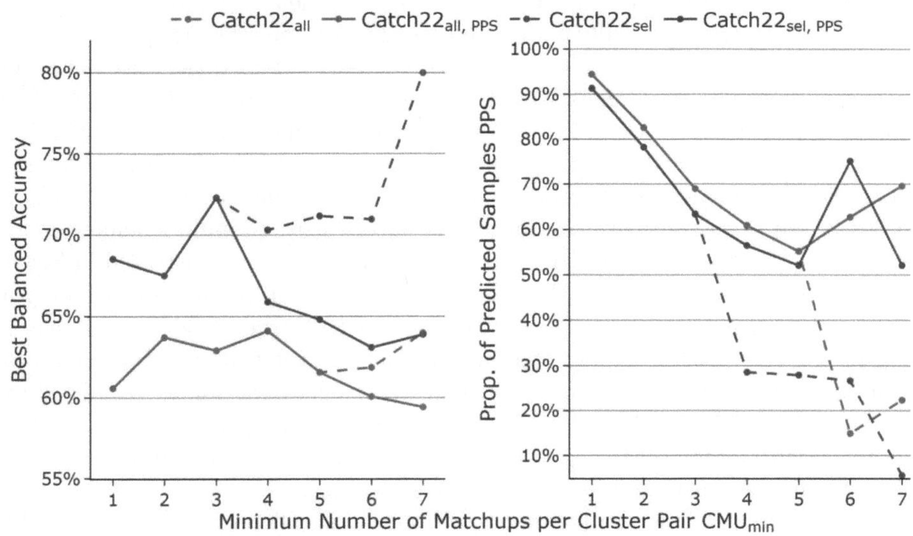

Fig. 3. Best Balanced Accuracies and PPS using catch22 across different CMU_{min}. Models with $PPS > 50\%$ are subscribed with PPS. Models that utilize the selected feature set are subscribed with sel.

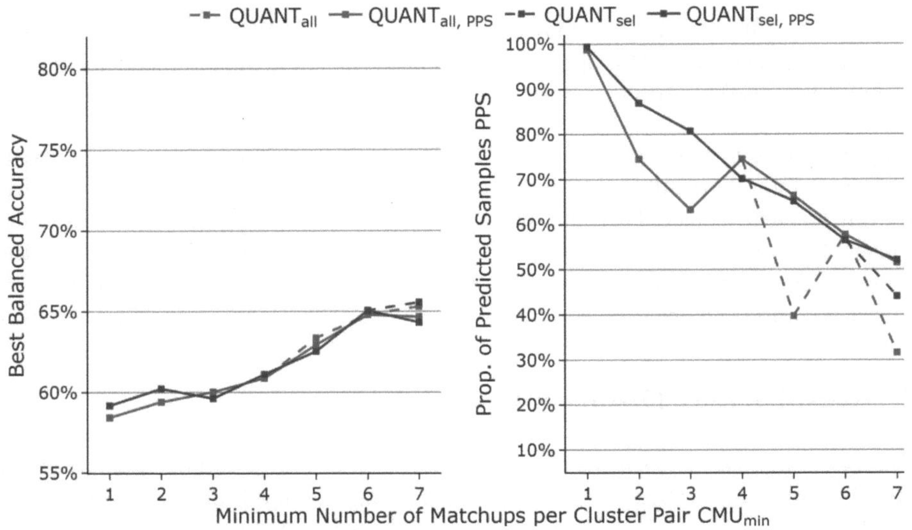

Fig. 4. Best Balanced Accuracies and PPS using QUANT across different CMU_{min}. Models with $PPS > 50\%$ are subscribed with PPS. Models that utilize the selected feature set are subscribed with sel.

The results for the TSF extractors catch22 and QUANT with and without spatial feature selection are shown in Figs. 3 and 4. The best balanced accuracies along CMU_{min} were generally higher for catch22 with the selected spatial feature set than for the entire feature set. In general, catch22 yielded the best balanced accuracy of 72.23% with the selected spatial feature set at $CMU_{min} = 3$. The models that utilized all spatial features performed similarly well, where QUANT was slightly better with a best balanced accuracy of 64.8%. The best balanced accuracies for both catch22 models with $PPS > 50\%$ increased until CMU_{min} equals 3 and 4, respectively, and decreased afterwards. A similar behavior can be observed for the QUANT models at a higher CMU_{min} as illustrated in Fig. 4.

The increase demonstrates the effectivity of excluding predictors with only a few matches, which comes at the cost of a smaller PPS when CMU_{min} increases. Except for the catch22 model that utilized all spatial features, the balanced accuracy could be further increased without the PPS restriction as visualized by the dashed lines in Fig. 3 and 4. The incline is caused by large k^{off} and k^{def} combined with a high CMU_{min} leading to few but more accurate and specialized cluster pairs, as illustrated by the heatmaps in Fig. 5.

The heatmaps show the balanced accuracies for different k^{off}-k^{def}- combinations at $CMU_{min} = 3$ and $CMU_{min} = 7$. In general, both heatmaps indicate a trend in which the model performs well in the area of $k^{off} > 13$ and $k^{def} > 9$. The trend also indicates that the investigated offensive patterns were more diverse than defensive, due to the larger k^{off}. For $CMU_{min} = 7$, cluster-pairs can be observed at the edges of this area with a small balanced accuracy, which are caused by sample removal leaving meaningless win rate cluster-pairs

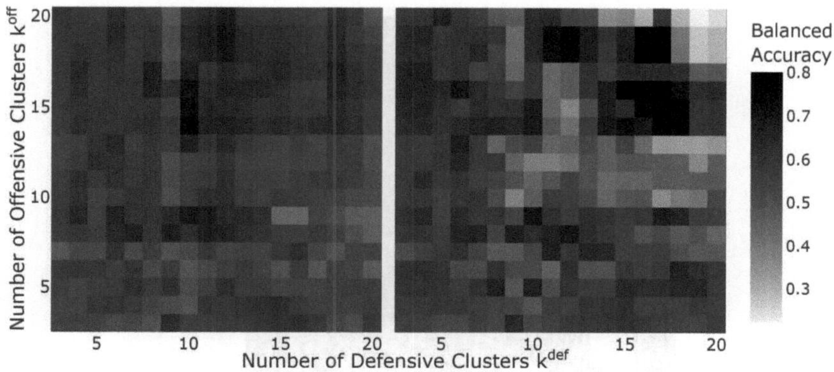

Fig. 5. Balanced accuracies for different k^{off}-k^{def} combinations with $CMU_{min} = 3$ (left) and $CMU_{min} = 7$ (right).

in the win rate matrix for prediction, especially for the area $k^{off} > 17$ and $k^{def} > 17$. The observations showed that the number of clusters k^{off} and k^{def} can influence the predictions in multiple ways. First, if the total number of clusters is large, the win rate matrix will be sparse, leading to many matrix elements with $CMU_{o,d} < CMU_{min}$, which will be excluded for prediction because they are considered unreliable predictors. However, increasing the number of clusters can lead to more specialized cluster matches, where $CMU_{o,d} > CMU_{min}$ and therefore can lead to better performance.

Models with a high CMU_{min} combined with the condition $PPS > 0.5$ exclude such specialized models, thus, the best balanced accuracies are reflected by models with smaller k^{off} and k^{def}, which performed less accurate as visualized in Figs. 3 and 4. The improvements due to larger CMU_{min}, k^{off} and k^{def} indicate that the models' utilities and performances can be further improved by more data. First, more data would lead to a less sparse win rate matrix enabling a larger diversity of cluster-pair matchups for prediction and a larger PPS. Second, more data would generally increase the number of cluster-pair matchups CMU, improving the reliability of the predictors.

In addition to predicting the outcome of an offensive situation, the proposed method can also be used in a more explorative way to find patterns that are effective against specific patterns. In this case, the method can be applied effectively to the investigated data to build and visualize the win rate matrix, as shown in Fig. 6.

The diagram shows the resulting win rate matrix for the selected feature set applied to the data from all matches with the best hyperparameters found, $CMU_{min} = 3$, $c^{off} = 14$ and $c^{def} = 10$. A practitioner may use the win rate matrix to identify tactical patterns that have weaknesses or strengths against other patterns. To provide an example using the illustrated heatmap, a practitioner may want to know how a team can improve its offensive chance to shoot at the goal against a team, which often uses defending patterns that correspond

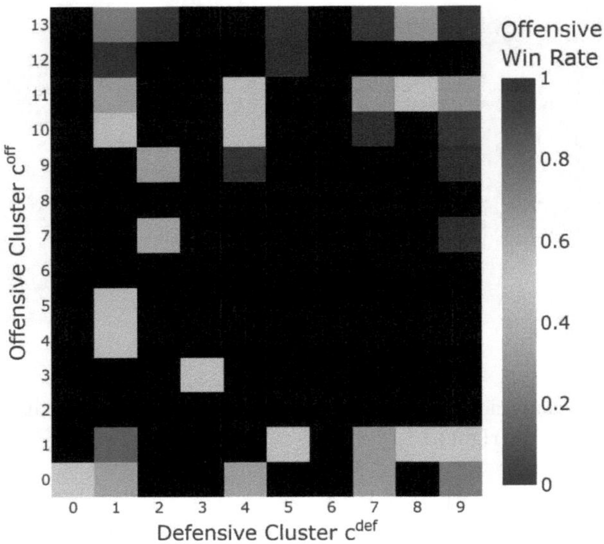

Fig. 6. Win rate matrix for catch22 with the selected feature set applied on the data of all matches using $CMU_{min} = 3$, $k^{off} = 14$ and $k^{def} = 10$.

to $c^{def} = 1$. The win rate matrix shows that the highest chances of overcoming such defense are in the offensive cluster patterns $c^{off} = 1$ and $c^{off} = 13$. Afterwards, tactical adaptations can be derived from these patterns.

The example utilized the selected spatial feature vectors of all matches. However, a practitioner can also use offensive or defensive sequences from a specific team to investigate its strengths and weaknesses. In a different setting, a practitioner may want to investigate the effectivity of different play characteristics such as a team's spread using a specific feature set. Therefore, the proposed method can not only be used to predict the outcome of an offensive matchup situation of two teams, it can also be exploratively used to find information on how a team should act or counteract in specific situations. For hyperparameter selection of the explorative approach, we suggest utilizing the hyperparameters that yield the best balanced accuracy of the predictive approach where the win rate matrix' elements are used as predictors. If the win-rate matrix is estimated poorly, the predictions for each element would be significantly more inaccurate, which would be reflected in low balanced accuracy.

5 Limitations and Future Work

Although this study presents a first proof of concept for unsupervised clustering of offensive and defensive football patterns using TSF extractors, it is subject to several limitations.

First, the dataset consists of only seven matches from the German Bundesliga and Bundesliga 2, which limits the generalizability of our results. Furthermore, position data is organized according to fixed player indices without a consistent assignment to tactical roles. As a result, temporal patterns extracted from the same input column can reflect different player behaviors depending on the team lineup.

To improve interpretability, this study focuses on a limited number of event triggers for pattern extraction. Although this targeted approach contributes to the understanding of the clusters, it may exclude important sequences related to the build-up of play or defensive transitions. Further, offensive and defensive clusters were extracted from overlapping time windows. This can lead to ambiguities in interpretation, especially when similar movement patterns occur in both contexts.

Although the TSF extractors used, catch22 and QUANT, showed promising results, their effectiveness varied depending on the set of features and the clustering setup. This suggests that combining different TSF extractors or integrating additional contextual features could improve clustering quality and prediction accuracy.

Future work could address these limitations by extending the dataset across multiple seasons and leagues, incorporating dynamic player role recognition to ensure consistent feature representation, and examining a wider range of events and time windows. Furthermore, the approach was developed from the perspective of ML practitioners. Hence, further analyses incorporating domain knowledge from experts have the potential to improve the method's predictive performance and interpretability.

6 Conclusion

This paper introduced an unsupervised ML approach to systematically identify and analyze tactical offensive and defensive patterns in football using TSF extractors based on detailed tracking and event data. Using catch22 and QUANT TSF extractors, the research successfully demonstrated that distinct tactical patterns can be identified and matched between different teams and game combinations.

Insights from the clustering of tactical behaviors highlighted the practical potential of our approach. In particular, the catch22 extractor with selected spatial features achieved the highest predictive accuracy, emphasizing its robustness in identifying meaningful tactical scenarios. The analysis also underscored the importance of a large dataset, as using more clusters improved prediction accuracy but also required enough examples to ensure reliable results.

Building on our results, future research should incorporate larger datasets spanning multiple leagues and seasons and utilize automated, role-specific player indexing to further refine tactical interpretations. Additionally, extending the analysis to include a more diverse set of event triggers and investigating sequences of different lengths or timing could reveal additional tactical insights and strengthen the generalizability and practical utility of unsupervised tactical pattern analysis in football.

A Appendix

Table 1. Selected Features are tagged with an asterisk

Feature	Description	Formula	Variables	Reference
		Team Tactical Shape Features		
Width / Height*	Team's horizontal / vertical spread	$\max(x_i) - \min(x_i)$, $\max(y_i) - \min(y_i)$	x_i, y_i: player coordinates	Frencken et al. [11]
Aspect Ratio*	Shape stretch across axes	$\frac{\text{width}}{\text{height}+\varepsilon}$	width, height	
Convex Hull Area* / Perimeter*	Convex shape enclosing team	$A = \frac{1}{2}\left\|\sum_{i=1}^{n}(x_i y_{i+1} - x_{i+1} y_i)\right\|$ $P = \sum_{i=1}^{n}\sqrt{(x_{i+1}-x_i)^2 + (y_{i+1}-y_i)^2}$	x_i, y_i: convex hull points	Pérez-Lantero [24]
Enclosing Rect Area	Bounding rectangle area	$A_{\text{rect}} = (\max x_i - \min x_i) \cdot (\max y_i - \min y_i)$	x_i, y_i: player positions	Frencken et al. [11]
Enclosing Circle Radius	Radius of smallest enclosing circle	$r = \max_i \|p_i - c\|$	p_i: player positions, c: circle center	Welzl et al. [28]
		Team Orientation (PCA)		
Orientation Angle (rad/deg*)	Direction of team shape	$\arctan 2(v_y, v_x)$, $\theta \cdot \frac{180}{\pi}$	v_x, v_y: PCA vector	Cardenas et al. [5]
Eccentricity	Elongation via PCA	$\sqrt{\frac{\lambda_1}{\lambda_2+\varepsilon}}$	λ_1, λ_2: eigenvalues	Cardenas et al. [5]
		Team Compactness Features		
Mean Pairwise Distance*	Avg. player-to-player distance	$\frac{1}{N^2}\sum_{i,j}\|p_i - p_j\|$	p_i, p_j: player vectors	Wenninger et al. [29]
Min / Max / Median* / Std* Pairwise Dist	Distribution of pairwise distances	$\min, \max, \text{median}, \text{std}(\|p_i - p_j\|)$	p_i, p_j: player vectors	
Mean / Std / Min / Max* Dist to Centroid	Spread around centroid	$\frac{1}{N}\sum\|p_i - c\|$, $\text{std}(\|p_i - c\|)$, $\min, \max(\|p_i - c\|)$	c: centroid, p_i: players	Frencken et al. [11]
		Ball-related Features		
Mean* / Min / Max* / Median* Dist to Ball	Player proximity to ball	$\frac{1}{N}\sum\|p_i - b\|$, $\min, \max, \text{median}(\|p_i - b\|)$	b: ball position, p_i: players	
Players within $r = \{5^*, 10, 15^*, 20\}$ meters	Players close to ball	$\sum \mathbb{1}_{\|p_i - b\| < r}$	r: radius, p_i, b	
Ball X / Y	Ball location	(x_{ball}, y_{ball})	Ball coordinates	
		Goal-related Features		
Mean / Min / Max* Dist to Opponent Goal	Player distance to opponent goal	$\frac{1}{N}\sum\|p_i - g_{opp}\|$, etc.	g_{opp}: goal coords	
Mean* / Min / Max Dist to Own Goal	Player distance to own goal	$\frac{1}{N}\sum\|p_i - g_{own}\|$, etc.	g_{own}: goal coords	
Proportion in Attacking Half	Players in opponent half	$\frac{1}{N}\sum \mathbb{1}_{x_i > 0}$	x_i: X coord.	

References

1. Akhanli, S., Hennig, C.: Clustering of football players based on performance data and aggregated clustering validity indexes. J. Quant. Anal. Sports **19**, 1–10 (2023)
2. Anzer, G., Bauer, P.: A goal scoring probability model for shots based on synchronized positional and event data in football (Soccer). Front. Sports Active Living **3**, 1–15 (2021)

3. Bandara, I., Shelyag, S., Rajasegarar, S., Dwyer, D., Kim, E.J., Angelova, M.: Predicting goal probabilities with improved xG models using event sequences in association football. PLoS ONE **19**(10), 1–22 (2024)
4. Bassek, M., Rein, R., Weber, H., Memmert, D.: An integrated dataset of spatiotemporal and event data in elite soccer. Sci. Data **12**(1), 195 (2025)
5. Cardenas, D.G., Zuniga, M.D.: Bullet-proof robust real-time ball tracking. In: 2016 International Conference on Digital Image Computing: Techniques and Applications (DICTA), pp. 1–8 (2016)
6. Christ, M., Braun, N., Neuffer, J., Kempa-Liehr, A.W.: Time Series FeatuRe Extraction on basis of Scalable Hypothesis tests (tsfresh – a Python package). Neural Comput. **307**, 72–77 (2018)
7. Decroos, T., Van Haaren, J., Davis, J.: Automatic discovery of tactics in spatio-temporal soccer match data. In: Proceedings of the 24th ACM SIGKDD International Conference on Knowledge Discovery and Data Mining. KDD '18, pp. 223–232. Association for Computing Machinery, New York, NY, USA (2018)
8. Dempster, A., Schmidt, D.F., Webb, G.I.: QUANT: a minimalist interval method for time series classification. Data Min. Knowl. Disc. **38**(4), 2377–2402 (2024)
9. Fernández, J., Bornn, L.: Wide open spaces: a statistical technique for measuring space creation in professional soccer. In: MIT Sloan Sports Analytics Conference (2018)
10. Feuerhake, U.: Recognition of repetitive movement patterns—the case of football analysis. ISPRS Int. J. Geo Inf. **5**(11), 208 (2016)
11. Frencken, W., Lemmink, K., Delleman, N., Visscher, C.: Oscillations of centroid position and surface area of soccer teams in small-sided games. Eur. J. Sport Sci. **11**(4), 215–223 (2011)
12. Goes, F.R., Brink, M.S., Elferink-Gemser, M.T., Kempe, M., Lemmink, K.A.: The tactics of successful attacks in professional association football: large-scale spatiotemporal analysis of dynamic subgroups using position tracking data. J. Sports Sci. **39**(5), 523–532 (2021)
13. Haaren, J.V., Dzyuba, V., Hannosset, S., Davis, J.: Automatically discovering offensive patterns in soccer match data. In: Fromont, E., De Bie, T., van Leeuwen, M. (eds.) IDA 2015. LNCS, vol. 9385, pp. 286–297. Springer, Cham (2015). https://doi.org/10.1007/978-3-319-24465-5_25
14. Herold, M., Goes, F., Nopp, S., Bauer, P., Thompson, C., Meyer, T.: Machine learning in men's professional football: current applications and future directions for improving attacking play. Int. J. Sports Sci. Coach. 1–20 (2019)
15. Knauf, K., Memmert, D., Brefeld, U.: Spatio-temporal convolution kernels. Mach. Learn. **102**, 247–273 (2016)
16. Lloyd, S.: Least squares quantization in PCM. IEEE Trans. Inf. Theory **28**(2), 129–137 (1982)
17. Lubba, C.H., Sethi, S.S., Knaute, P., Schultz, S.R., Fulcher, B.D., Jones, N.S.: catch22: CAnonical Time-series CHaracteristics. Data Min. Knowl. Disc. **33**(6), 1821–1852 (2019)
18. MacQueen, J.: Some methods for classification and analysis of multivariate observations. In: Proceedings of the Fifth Berkeley Symposium on Mathematical Statistics and Probability, Volume 1: Statistics, vol. 5, pp. 281–298. University of California press (1967)
19. Memmert, D., Raabe, D.: Data Analytics in Football: Positional Data Collection, Modelling and Analysis, 1st edn. Routledge (2018)
20. Memmert, D., Rein, R.: Match analysis, big data and tactics: current trends in elite soccer. Deutsche Zeitschrift für Sportmedizin **69**(3), 65–72 (2018)

21. Plakias, S., Kokkotis, C., Giakas, G., Tsaopoulos, D., Moustakidis, S.: Can artificial intelligence revolutionize soccer tactical analysis? TRENDS Sport Sci. **31**, 151–160 (2024)
22. Poli, R., Besson, R., Ravenel, L.: Attendances in Football Stadia (2003–2018) (2019). cIES Football Observatory Monthly Report, Issue 47
23. Pratas, J.M., Volossovitch, A., Carita, A.I.: Goal scoring in elite male football: a systematic review. J. Hu. Sport Exercise **13**(1), 218–230 (2018)
24. Pérez-Lantero, P.: Area and perimeter of the convex hull of stochastic points. Comput. J. **59**(8), 1144–1154 (2016)
25. Rein, R., Memmert, D.: Big data and tactical analysis in elite soccer: future challenges and opportunities for sports science. Springerplus **5**(1), 1410 (2016)
26. Rico-González, M., Pino-Ortega, J., Méndez, A., Clemente, F.M., Baca, A.: Machine learning application in soccer: a systematic review. Biol. Sport **40**(1), 249–263 (2023)
27. Torres-Ronda, L., Beanland, E., Whitehead, S., Sweeting, A., Clubb, J.: Tracking systems in team sports: a narrative review of applications of the data and sport specific analysis. Sports Med. - Open **8** (2022)
28. Welzl, E.: Smallest enclosing disks (balls and ellipsoids). In: New Results and New Trends in Computer Science, pp. 359–370. Springer, New York (1991)
29. Wenninger, S., Link, D., Lames, M.: Data mining in elite beach volleyball-detecting tactical patterns using market basket analysis. Int. J. Comput. Sci. Sport **18**(2), 1–19 (2019)

Trajectory-Based Retrieval of Similar Soccer Plays Using Time-Warping and Anchor-Based Representations

Shehap Elhadary[1(✉)], Amrou Abdelmawla[1], Mahmoud Nasr[1], Mohamed Hafez[2], and Tamer Basha[1]

[1] Faculty of Engineering, Cairo University, Giza, Egypt
{shehap.elhadary03,amrou.abdelmawla03,mahmoud.nasr03}@eng-st.cu.edu.eg, tamerbasha@eng.cu.edu.eg
[2] Ontario Tech University, Oshawa, ON, Canada
mohamed.hafez1@ontariotechu.net

Abstract. Retrieving similar plays is fundamental to soccer analytics, but the lack of labeled data makes evaluation challenging. We study soccer play retrieval using ball trajectory data from the FIFA World Cup 2022 dataset. We examine Dynamic Time Warping (DTW) and Subsequence DTW, identifying limitations in computational scalability and degenerate alignment patterns. We propose an anchor-based representation that extracts sparse, tactically significant events and applies Subsequence DTW at the anchor level, reducing sequence length by 40%. We evaluate using data augmentation to generate perturbed versions of each play. The anchor-based method achieves 98% recall compared to 42% for full-trajectory DTW, demonstrating substantially improved robustness to sampling variability while maintaining 82.7% zonal precision in spatial context preservation.

Keywords: Soccer Analytics · Soccer Play Representation · Spatiotemporal Retrieval · Dynamic Time Warping · Subsequence Matching

1 Introduction

Soccer analysis increasingly relies on data-based tools that support tactical understanding, performance evaluation, and opponent scouting [4]. Advances in data collection have made spatiotemporal soccer data widely available, enabling detailed analysis of match dynamics. One important task is retrieving soccer plays similar to a given target play [9]. Similarity-based retrieval allows analysts to explore match archives, identify recurring movement patterns, compare tactical behaviors across teams, and support match preparation with historical examples.

Defining what makes soccer plays "similar" remains challenging. Tactical similarity is subjective and context-dependent, often relying on expert interpretation rather than formal definitions. Publicly available datasets do not provide

Z. Liu and V. Misra (Eds.): ISACE 2026, LNCS 16610, pp. 117–132, 2026.
https://doi.org/10.1007/978-3-032-27272-0_9

annotations of tactically similar plays. This lack of labeled data limits supervised approaches and complicates evaluation, motivating unsupervised or weakly supervised similarity measures operating directly on spatiotemporal representations [11].

We address play retrieval using trajectory-based similarity methods. We examine DTW [1] and Subsequence DTW [6] for comparing ball trajectories and identify limitations including computational cost and many-to-one point mappings that yield misleading similarity scores. We propose an anchor-based representation that aligns tactically significant points [3], such as direction changes and zone transitions, reducing computation while focusing on structural elements that define a play.

1.1 Challenges

Soccer play retrieval presents several technical challenges. Plays vary in duration, requiring similarity measures that operate on sequences of unequal length. The exact temporal alignment between tactically similar plays is rare, as similar patterns may unfold at different speeds or shifted timings. Similarity measures must therefore tolerate temporal variability rather than rely on strict time-indexed alignment.

The absence of annotated ground truth for tactical similarity further complicates method selection and evaluation, since conventional accuracy-based metrics cannot be applied [5]. This requires alternative validation strategies.

1.2 Overview of the Approach

We analyze trajectory-based retrieval using FIFA World Cup 2022 ball movement data [7], evaluating both standard and Subsequence Dynamic Time Warping (DTW). We propose an anchor-based representation that distills dense trajectories into sparse, tactically significant moments. Applying DTW at this anchor level reduces sequence length while improving robustness to temporal misalignment and sampling variability. Unlike deep learning methods like Play2Vec [10] that require resource-intensive full tracking data, our approach offers a lightweight, interpretable alternative using only ball trajectories.

1.3 Contributions

The main contributions of this work are: (1) a comparative analysis of DTW-based similarity methods for soccer play retrieval using ball trajectory data; (2) an anchor-based representation that improves robustness to temporal misalignment and sampling variability while reducing computational cost; and (3) a data augmentation–based evaluation framework for validating similarity methods without labeled data.

2 Related Work

2.1 Trajectory Similarity

Similarity measurement between temporal trajectories has been studied extensively in time-series and motion analysis [11]. Dynamic Time Warping (DTW) is among the most widely used techniques for measuring similarity between sequences of unequal length by non-linearly aligning their temporal axes [8]. DTW has been applied in speech recognition, gesture analysis, and movement trajectory comparison, where temporal misalignment is common.

Extensions of DTW have been proposed to address partial matching and localized similarities. Subsequence DTW [6] enables alignment of a shorter sequence within a longer one, suitable for scenarios where patterns of interest occur as subsegments. These methods have been applied in activity recognition, motion retrieval, and anomaly detection.

2.2 Soccer Analytics and Play Representation

In soccer analytics, play representation and retrieval have been approached using both trajectory-based and event-based methods [4]. Trajectory-based approaches rely on spatiotemporal tracking data for players and the ball, enabling detailed modeling of team structure and movement dynamics [9]. Recent work has explored unsupervised deep learning techniques to learn latent representations of plays from tracking data. Play2Vec [10] proposes an embedding-based framework that captures play similarity by learning distributed representations from large collections of player and ball trajectories.

Deep learning approaches can model complex spatial and temporal interactions, but typically require extensive tracking data for all players and substantial computational resources for training and inference. The learned representations are often difficult to interpret and may not generalize well across datasets with different formats or granularity levels.

Event-based modeling offers an alternative that relies on discrete match events and ball movement, which are more widely available and less expensive to obtain [2].

3 Dataset and Preprocessing

3.1 Dataset

This study uses data from the FIFA World Cup 2022 [7], which provides both event-based and tracking-derived information. Event data include passes, shots, and other key actions, while tracking data provide continuous spatial positions of the ball and players.

3.2 Play Definition

A play is defined as a continuous possession sequence by a single team. It begins when a team gains control of the ball and ends upon a change of possession, stoppage, or terminal event such as a shot. We extract ball trajectories at each event of a play, represented as three-dimensional coordinates (x, y, z). The pitch coordinate system is centered at $(0, 0)$, corresponding to the field center.

3.3 Coordinate Normalization

All ball trajectories are expressed in the centered pitch coordinate system.

Teams may attack in either direction, so we apply attacking-direction normalization to align all plays to progress from left to right. For plays attacking toward the left goal, trajectory coordinates are mirrored by multiplying each x and y coordinate by -1:

$$(x, y, z) \to (-x, -y, z) \tag{1}$$

This preserves the internal geometry and dynamics while removing directional asymmetry. Tactically similar plays executed in opposite directions are mapped to a common reference frame, allowing similarity measures to compare spatial and temporal patterns independent of attack direction.

4 Trajectory Similarity Using Dynamic Time Warping

4.1 Ball Trajectory Representation

Each soccer play is represented as a time-ordered sequence of ball positions

$$\mathbf{X} = \{(x_t, y_t, z_t)\}_{t=1}^{T}, \tag{2}$$

where (x_t, y_t, z_t) are the ball coordinates at the t-th event of the play. The distance between two trajectory points (x_i, y_i, z_i) and (x_j, y_j, z_j) is computed using Euclidean distance:

$$d\big((x_i, y_i, z_i), (x_j, y_j, z_j)\big) = \sqrt{(x_i - x_j)^2 + (y_i - y_j)^2 + (z_i - z_j)^2}. \tag{3}$$

4.2 Dynamic Time Warping

Dynamic Time Warping (DTW) [8] measures similarity between two trajectories by computing an optimal alignment under temporal warping. Given two sequences

$$\mathbf{X} = \{x_1, \ldots, x_T\} \quad \text{and} \quad \mathbf{Y} = \{y_1, \ldots, y_S\}, \tag{4}$$

DTW constructs a cost matrix where each entry represents the distance between trajectory points. A warping path is computed to minimize the accumulated cost while preserving temporal order.

4.3 Longer Play Segmentation for Comparison

Standard DTW can align sequences of different lengths, but treats the shorter play as though it must span the entire longer play. Regions of the longer play that do not correspond to the shorter play contribute large distances to the cumulative cost. Even when a segment closely matches, unmatched regions inflate the total alignment cost.

Longer plays are divided into non-overlapping segments equal in length to the query play. For a query of length n, longer plays are subdivided as follows:

- The play is divided into non-overlapping segments of length n
- If a remainder of length $r < n$ exists:
  - If $r \geq n/2$, an additional segment is created by combining the remainder with the final $n - r$ points from the previous segment
  - If $r < n/2$, the remainder is discarded

DTW is computed between the query and each segment separately, with the minimum distance taken as the similarity score.

4.4 Pairwise Similarity Matrix Construction

The dataset contains plays of varying lengths. For each unique play length n, a separate pairwise similarity matrix is constructed. When comparing two plays for target length n:

- If a play has exactly n events, it is used directly
- If a play has more than n events, it is segmented as above, and the minimum DTW distance across all segments is used
- Plays with fewer than n events cannot be compared at this target length

This generates multiple similarity matrices, one for each distinct play length.

Figure 1 shows play retrieval using segmented DTW, where the query play (red) is matched with its top-ranked candidate (blue).

4.5 Limitations

This baseline approach has several limitations:

Computational Complexity: The method requires constructing multiple similarity matrices—one for each distinct play length. For each matrix, DTW must be computed between all pairs of plays, with longer plays requiring segmentation and multiple computations per comparison.

Arbitrary Segment Boundaries: The segmentation strategy divides longer plays at fixed intervals, which may split tactically coherent movement patterns across segment boundaries. The optimal alignment between a query and a longer play may span two segments, but this approach cannot detect such cross-boundary alignments.

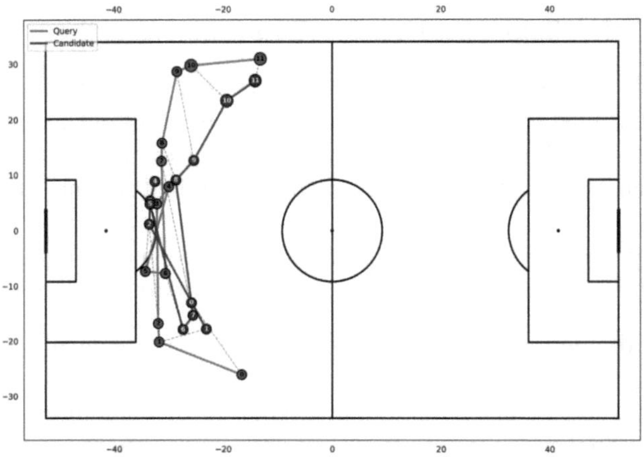

Fig. 1. Segmented DTW retrieval example showing the query play (red) and rank-1 retrieved play (blue). (Color figure online)

Incomplete Coverage: For each target length n, plays shorter than n are excluded. Short plays are systematically excluded from comparisons at larger target lengths, potentially missing similar patterns.

These limitations motivate subsequence DTW [6], which addresses these issues by searching all possible sub-trajectories in a single pass without requiring explicit segmentation or multiple similarity matrices.

5 Subsequence DTW for Play Retrieval

5.1 Motivation

Subsequence Dynamic Time Warping [6] eliminates explicit segmentation by searching for the best-matching sub-trajectory of one play within another. Plays can be compared pairwise regardless of length in a unified similarity space, addressing computational overhead, arbitrary boundary constraints, and incomplete coverage of the segmentation approach.

5.2 Subsequence DTW Definition

Given two ball trajectories

$$\mathbf{X} = \{x_1, \ldots, x_T\} \quad \text{and} \quad \mathbf{Y} = \{y_1, \ldots, y_S\}, \tag{5}$$

Subsequence DTW computes the minimum DTW alignment cost between the shorter trajectory and any contiguous sub-sequence of the longer trajectory. Unlike standard DTW, the warping path need not start and end at sequence boundaries.

This identifies locally similar movement patterns even when surrounding phases differ. Since the method uses absolute pitch coordinates, spatial context is preserved: plays in similar pitch locations yield lower distance scores. Subsequence DTW handles partial pattern matching without explicit segmentation or length normalization.

Figure 2 shows subsequence DTW retrieval for the same query from Fig. 1. The method retrieves a different top-ranked candidate, showing how exploring all possible sub-trajectory alignments without segmentation constraints leads to different retrieval outcomes.

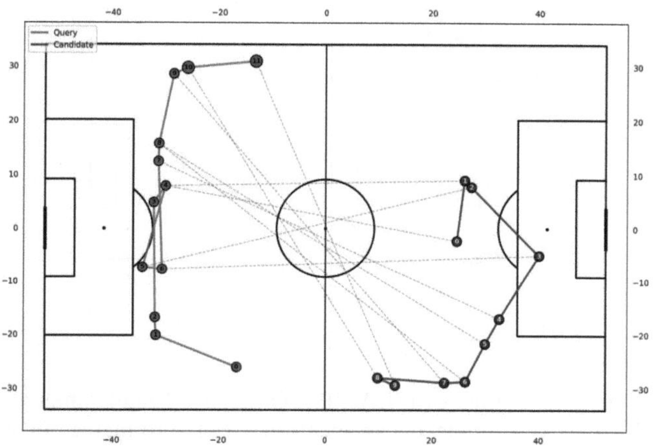

Fig. 2. Subsequence DTW retrieval example showing the query play (red) and rank-1 retrieved play (blue). Using the same query as Fig. 1, this method retrieves a different top-ranked candidate. (Color figure online)

5.3 Limitations

While Subsequence DTW preserves spatial context, it suffers from critical alignment limitations regarding point mapping and tactical weighting.

Many-to-One Mappings. DTW allows multiple candidate points to align to a single query point. Consequently, dense clusters near a single query location can yield artificially low costs despite minimal structural similarity. Figure 3 illustrates a candidate (blue) ranked 4th despite little tactical resemblance, solely because its points cluster near a query segment.

Equal Weighting. DTW treats all points identically, ignoring tactical significance. Critical events like direction changes, through-balls, or switches of play are weighted the same as routine movements. Thus, similarity scores reflect aggregate spatial proximity rather than tactical intent.

Loss of Structural Information. The allowance for arbitrary compression and expansion means a play can achieve low distance via localized clusters while lacking the query's overall movement pattern.

These issues motivate our anchor-based representation, which extracts sparse points at critical moments (e.g., direction changes) to enforce meaningful correspondence and eliminate redundant mappings.

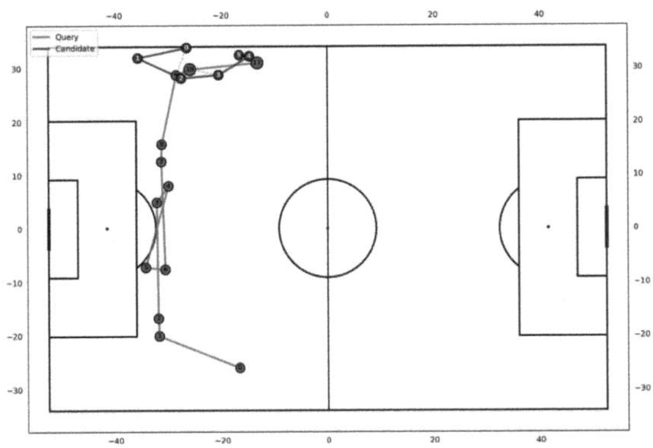

Fig. 3. Limitation of Subsequence DTW: The candidate (blue) ranks 4th due to clustered points aligning to a single query location (red), producing an artificially low distance despite minimal structural similarity. (Color figure online)

6 Anchor-Based Play Representation

6.1 Motivation

Standard DTW weights all trajectory points equally, allowing minor movements to dominate similarity scores over tactically significant events. While Subsequence DTW mitigates segmentation issues, it suffers from degenerate many-to-one mappings that artificially lower distances. Soccer plays are defined by key actions: passes advancing play, structural breaks via direction changes, and tactical transitions. We propose an anchor-based representation extracting only tactically meaningful points from ball trajectories.

6.2 Anchor Point Definition and Extraction

The extraction algorithm reduces trajectories to a sparse set of key points, preserving geometric shape while eliminating redundancy.

Input and Pre-processing: For each match, the event stream includes ball coordinates (x, y, z), event type (e.g., FIRSTKICKOFF, OTB), and possession type (e.g., PA = pass, CR = cross, IT = initial touch), grouped by possession sequence.

Initial Touch Filtering: Initial Touch (IT) events are filtered if the distance to the subsequent pass or cross is $\leq d_{\text{min}}$ (1 m). This removes redundant registrations where a player receives and passes from effectively the same location. IT events exceeding d_{min} from the next pass are retained, indicating a carry or dribble.

Anchor Selection Criteria: Processing events sequentially, a position p is added to the anchor set A if it is a kickoff, or if it meets specific geometric criteria based on the most recent anchor $a_{|A|}$. For pass/cross events, p is added if $d(a_{|A|}, p) > d_{min}$ or if the direction change $\theta > \theta_{min}$. For other events (dribbles), p is added only if both conditions ($d > d_{min}$ and $\theta > \theta_{min}$) are met.

Where A is the anchor set, $a_{|A|}$ the most recent anchor, $d(\cdot, \cdot)$ Euclidean distance, and θ the direction change.

Pass and cross events represent explicit tactical decisions, significant when involving displacement. Other events (dribbles, carries) become anchors only when exhibiting significant directional change.

Direction Change Computation: Given anchors a_{i-1}, a_i and candidate p, the direction change is:

$$\boldsymbol{v_1} = a_i - a_{i-1}, \quad \boldsymbol{v_2} = p - a_i \tag{6}$$

$$\theta = \arccos\left(\frac{\boldsymbol{v_1} \cdot \boldsymbol{v_2}}{\|\boldsymbol{v_1}\|\|\boldsymbol{v_2}\|}\right) \tag{7}$$

Cosine values are clipped to $[-1, 1]$ to handle numerical errors. Zero-length vectors return $\theta = 0°$.

Parameter Selection: We selected an angle threshold $\theta_{\text{min}} = 45°$ to capture meaningful directional changes and filter minor variations, and a minimum distance $d_{\text{min}} = 1$ m to prevent near-duplicates. Additionally, we enforced a match ratio threshold $r_{\text{min}} = 0.5$ to filter degenerate alignments. Applied to 64 FIFA World Cup 2022 matches, these parameters reduced 131,315 points to 78,619 anchors (40% reduction), preserving all passes, crosses, and significant turns.

Figure 4 illustrates the extraction process.

6.3 Anchor-Based Similarity Computation

Similarity is computed by applying Subsequence DTW to the extracted anchor sequences. For plays P_1 and P_2 with anchors $A_1 = \{a_1^{(1)}, \ldots, a_m^{(1)}\}$ and $A_2 = \{a_1^{(2)}, \ldots, a_n^{(2)}\}$:

$$\text{Similarity}(P_1, P_2) = \text{SubsequenceDTW}(A_1, A_2) \tag{8}$$

Since DTW complexity scales quadratically, a 40% length reduction yields $\approx$64% fewer computations ($0.6^2 \approx 0.36$).

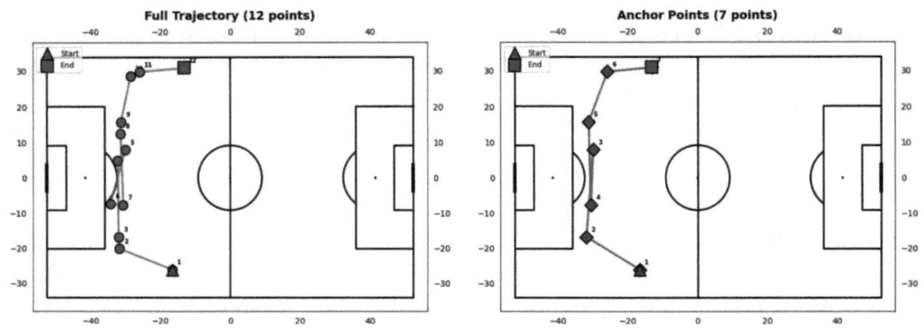

Fig. 4. Trajectory representations. Left: full trajectory. Right: anchor-based representation. The anchor set preserves geometric structure with 41.6% fewer points.

6.4 Filtering Degenerate Matches

Anchor extraction mitigates but does not eliminate many-to-one mappings Sect. 5.3. In subsequence DTW, the query aligns to a reference region. We define **matched span** as the count of unique reference points mapped:

$$\text{matched\_span} = \left|\{j : (i, j) \in \mathcal{P}\}\right| \tag{9}$$

where $\mathcal{P}$ is the set of alignment pairs. This exposes degeneracies by counting distinct reference anchors.

To filter degeneracies, we enforce a minimum match ratio:

$$\text{match\_ratio} = \frac{\text{matched\_span}}{\text{query\_length}} \geq r_{\text{min}} \tag{10}$$

where $r_{\text{min}} = 0.5$. This requires unique reference anchors to number at least half the query length. For example, if a 7-anchor query maps to only 2 unique reference anchors ($2/7 = 0.29$), the match is rejected. Such alignments achieve low distances via redundant mapping rather than genuine similarity.

6.5 Qualitative Example: Anchor-Based Retrieval

Figure 5 shows anchor-based retrieval for the query in Figs. 1 and 2. The approach retrieves a different top candidate, demonstrating how prioritizing tactical points alters similarity assessment.

6.6 Computational Efficiency

Anchor extraction offers specific computational advantages:

- **Versus segmentation-based DTW:** Eliminates multiple similarity matrices and repeated segmentation, producing a single matrix for all plays.

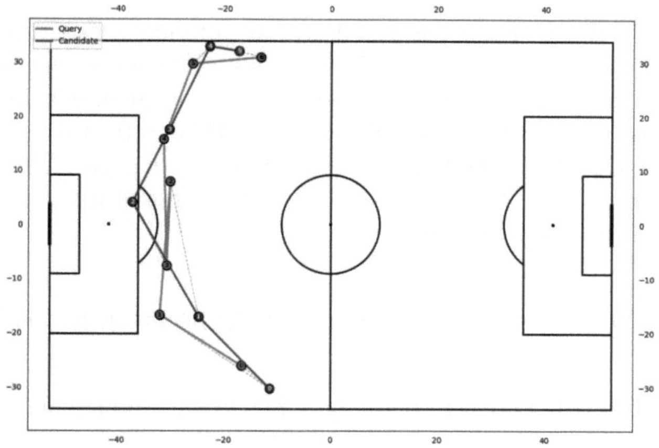

Fig. 5. Anchor-based retrieval: query play (red) and rank-1 retrieved play (blue) using Subsequence DTW on anchor sequences. (Color figure online)

- **Versus full-trajectory subsequence DTW:** Reduces sequence length by 40%, yielding ≈64% fewer distance computations.
- **Match ratio filtering:** Eliminates degenerate alignments, ensuring retrieved plays share genuine structural similarity.

Beyond efficiency, this representation focuses similarity on the events defining tactical structure.

7 Evaluation

7.1 Evaluation Methodology

Without ground-truth labels for tactically similar plays, conventional accuracy metrics cannot be applied. Therefore, we propose a two-part validation framework:

Part 1: Sampling Invariance tests robustness by measuring whether the method retrieves a play's original version after 20% data loss.

Part 2: Zonal Precision measures whether retrieved plays preserve spatial context by originating from the same pitch region as the query.

7.2 Validation Experiment: Sampling Invariance

Experimental Setup. We use 16,994 anchor trajectories from 64 FIFA World Cup 2022 matches. We randomly selected 100 test queries from plays with at least 20 raw events (mean ≈ 30.3).

Validation Pipeline. For each test play, we applied a deterministic stride-5 filter to remove approximately 20% of events while preserving first and last events. Anchors were extracted from these degraded sequences using the criteria in Sect. 6.2. We then performed Subsequence DTW retrieval against the full database of 16,994 trajectories (normalized by query length), filtering matches with a span ratio < 0.5. A trial was considered successful if the original parent play appeared in the top-10 results.

Results. Table 1 summarizes performance of the proposed method.

Table 1. Parent retrieval after 20% event subsampling.

Metric	Value
Test plays	100
Database size	16,994
Mean events (raw → augmented)	30.3 → 25.6
Recall@10	**98.0%**
Rank-1 Accuracy	93.0%
Mean Rank (successful)	1.18
Worst Rank (successful)	9

Baseline Comparison. To contextualize these results, we evaluate a baseline using *full-trajectory standard DTW* without anchor extraction or subsequence alignment. The same 20% subsampling protocol and retrieval evaluation were applied. Table 2 compares both methods.

Table 2. Comparison under 20% subsampling: baseline vs. proposed method.

Method	Recall@10	Rank-1	Mean Rank	Worst Rank
Full-Trajectory DTW (Baseline)	42.0%	36.0%	1.43	10
Anchor Subsequence DTW (Ours)	**98.0%**	**93.0%**	**1.18**	9

The baseline retrieves the parent in only 42 of 100 trials, failing in 58% of cases under identical subsampling conditions. Although its mean rank among successful cases is relatively strong (1.43), the high failure rate indicates brittleness to sampling perturbation. In contrast, the proposed anchor-based subsequence DTW achieves 98% Recall@10 with only 2 failures, reducing the failure rate by a factor of 29×.

Retrieval Performance. The method achieved 98% Recall@10, retrieving the parent in 98 of 100 trials despite 20% data loss. Parents ranked first in 93% of cases (mean rank 1.18). Among 98 successful retrievals, 94.9% placed the parent at rank 1.

Failure Analysis. Only 2 trials failed. The failures represent extremes: a short play (23 events, 10 anchors) and a long play (56 events, 22 anchors), showing retrieval difficulty depends on geometric distinctiveness, not anchor count.

Figure 6 shows the long failure case: an unstructured possession with recursive loops (points 5–12, 28–35) and backward movement. When augmentation removes critical linking events (e.g., point 19), the play decomposes into generic clusters indistinguishable from other sequences.

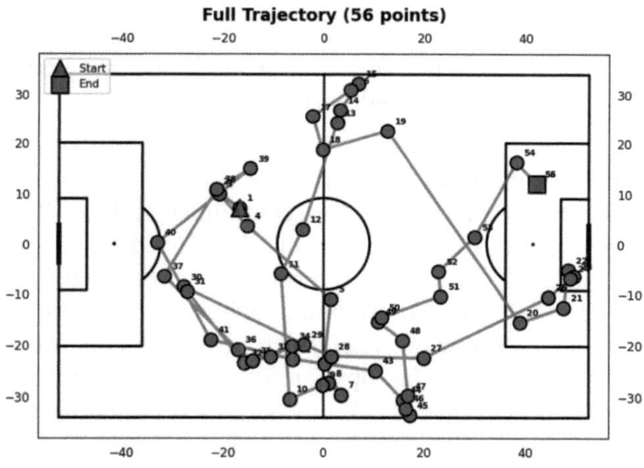

Fig. 6. Failure case (56 events). Removal of critical linking events (e.g., point 19) degrades structure into generic clusters.

Discussion. The 98% Recall@10 and 93% Rank-1 accuracy show the method captures meaningful structure. The comparison with full-trajectory DTW demonstrates that robustness does not arise from DTW alone, but from the combination of anchor abstraction and subsequence alignment. While standard DTW is effective when alignment is preserved, it fails in the majority of cases under sampling perturbation. The matched-span filter (≥ 0.5) eliminated degenerate many-to-one alignments. With only 2 failures, the method is robust to 20% data loss, establishing a lower bound for retrieval quality without ground-truth labels.

7.3 Tactical Context Preservation: Zonal Precision

The sampling-invariance experiment (Sect. 7.2) shows that the retrieval pipeline is stable under data perturbation. However, stability alone does not guarantee that retrieved plays carry equivalent tactical meaning. A method could return geometrically similar trajectories from entirely different pitch regions, limiting practical utility for tactical analysis. We therefore measure whether retrieved plays preserve the spatial context of the query.

Zone Definition. We partition the pitch longitudinally into three equal thirds, following standard soccer analysis conventions. After normalizing all plays so that attacking direction is uniformly left-to-right (pitch $x \in [-52.5,\ 52.5]$, $y \in [-34,\ 34]$), a retrieved play is assigned to the zone in which the **majority** ($> 50\%$) of the anchors within its **matched subsequence** are located:

- **Defensive Third:** $x < -17.5$
- **Middle Third:** $-17.5 \leq x \leq 17.5$
- **Attacking Third:** $x > 17.5$

Using a majority-vote criterion rather than a single starting point captures the predominant spatial region traversed by the play.

Experimental Setup. From the full corpus of 16,994 anchor trajectories (64 matches), we retain the 9,004 plays containing at least 3 anchor points. The resulting zone distribution is imbalanced: 2,594 defensive plays (28.8%), 4,613 middle plays (51.2%), and 1,797 attacking plays (20.0%). We draw 100 query plays via stratified random sampling, balanced across the three zones (34 defensive, 33 middle, 33 attacking), using a fixed seed for reproducibility.

For each query, we retrieve the top-10 most similar plays from the remaining database using the subsequence DTW pipeline, with normalized distance and a matched-span ratio threshold of 0.5. We define the per-query *Zonal Precision@10* as the fraction of the 10 retrieved plays whose majority zone matches that of the query:

$$\text{Zonal Precision@}K = \frac{1}{K} \sum_{i=1}^{K} \mathbb{1}\big[\,\text{zone}(r_i) = \text{zone}(q)\,\big] \tag{11}$$

where r_i denotes the i-th retrieved play and q the query.

A random baseline for this metric is the prior probability that a randomly selected play falls into the same zone as the query:

$$B_z = \frac{|\mathcal{D}_z|}{|\mathcal{D}|} \tag{12}$$

where $\mathcal{D}_z$ is the set of database plays in zone z. This yields baselines of 28.8% (Defensive), 51.2% (Middle), and 20.0% (Attacking). The weighted global baseline under our balanced sampling scheme is $\frac{1}{100}(34 \times 0.288 + 33 \times 0.512 + 33 \times 0.200) = 33.3\%$.

Results. Table 3 reports Mean Zonal Precision@10 for each zone and globally.

Table 3. Zonal Precision@10 results by pitch zone (majority-vote classification, ≥ 3 anchors, $N_{\text{queries}} = 100$). The random baseline B_z reflects the zone's proportion in the database; Lift = P@10/B_z.

Zone	Queries	Mean P@10	Std	Baseline B_z	Lift
Defensive Third	34	0.868	0.187	0.288	3.01×
Middle Third	33	0.879	0.179	0.512	1.72×
Attacking Third	33	0.733	0.284	0.200	3.67×
Global	**100**	**0.827**	**0.231**	**0.333**	**2.48**×

Interpretation Global and Zone-Level Analysis. The global Mean Zonal Precision@10 of **82.7%** (2.48× the 33.3% baseline) confirms that retrieved plays are spatially co-located despite the database's skew toward the Middle Third. The **Attacking Third** shows the strongest retrieval signal (Lift = 3.67×), with 73.3% of retrieved plays coming from the correct zone despite a low 20.0% baseline. The **Defensive Third** follows with Lift = 3.01× (86.8% precision vs. 28.8% baseline), indicating the system actively selects zone-consistent plays rather than reflecting class prevalence.

The **Middle Third** achieves comparable absolute precision at **87.9%**, though its lower Lift (1.72×) reflects its high prior probability (51.2%). The higher standard deviation in the Attacking Third ($\sigma = 0.284$) compared to others ($\sigma \approx 0.18$) reflects the transitional nature of attacking sequences, which often straddle zone boundaries.

Implications. Results show spatial coherence is strongest in the minority zones (Attacking/Defensive), offering 3.0–3.7× improvement over random chance. Combined with the 98% Recall@10 from the stability experiment Sect. 7.2, the pipeline satisfies both structural fidelity and spatial coherence requirements for practical tactical retrieval.

8 Conclusion

In this work, we presented an anchor-based representation for soccer play retrieval that encodes plays as sparse, tactically meaningful events, reducing sequence length by 40% while preserving geometric structure.

The method is robust to missing data, achieving 98% Recall@10 under 20% loss (vs. 42% for DTW) and 82.7% Zonal Precision with up to 3.67× improvement over random in the attacking third. These results show that geometric anchors capture the tactical essence of a play, enabling efficient retrieval. Future work will extend this to multi-agent and off-ball analysis.

References

1. Berndt, D.J., Clifford, J.: Using dynamic time warping to find patterns in time series. In: Proceedings of the 3rd International Conference on Knowledge Discovery and Data Mining, pp. 359–370. AAAI Press (1994)

2. Decroos, T., Bransen, L., Van Haaren, J., Davis, J.: Actions speak louder than goals: valuing player actions in soccer data. In: Proceedings of the 25th ACM SIGKDD International Conference on Knowledge Discovery and Data Mining, pp. 1851–1861 (2019). https://doi.org/10.1145/3292500.3330758
3. Douglas, D.H., Peucker, T.K.: Algorithms for the reduction of the number of points required to represent a digitized line or its caricature. Cartographica: Int. J. Geogr. Inf. Geovisual. **10**(2), 112–122 (1973). https://doi.org/10.3138/FM57-6770-U75U-7727
4. Gudmundsson, J., Horton, M.: Spatio-temporal analysis of team sports. ACM Comput. Surv. (CSUR) **50**(2), 1–34 (2017). https://doi.org/10.1145/3054132
5. Li, H.: Soccer video event detection and retrieval: a survey. Multimedia Tools Appl. **80**, 1–24 (2021). https://doi.org/10.1007/s11042-020-09689-5
6. Müller, M.: Dynamic time warping. In: Information Retrieval for Music and Motion, pp. 69–84. Springer, Cham (2007). https://doi.org/10.1007/978-3-540-74048-3_4
7. PFF FC: 2022 World Cup dataset (2025). https://www.blog.fc.pff.com/blog/pff-fc-release-2022-world-cup-data
8. Sakoe, H., Chiba, S.: Dynamic programming algorithm optimization for spoken word recognition. IEEE Trans. Acoust. Speech Sig. Process. **26**(1), 43–49 (1978). https://doi.org/10.1109/TASSP.1978.1163055
9. Sha, L., et al.: Chalkboarding: a new spatiotemporal query paradigm for sports play retrieval. In: Proceedings of the 21st International Conference on Intelligent User Interfaces, pp. 336–347 (2016). https://doi.org/10.1145/2856767.2856791
10. Wang, Z., Long, C., Cong, G., Ju, C.: Effective and efficient sports play retrieval with deep representation learning. In: Proceedings of the 25th ACM SIGKDD International Conference on Knowledge Discovery and Data Mining, pp. 499–509. Association for Computing Machinery (2019). https://doi.org/10.1145/3292500.3330927
11. Zheng, Y.: Trajectory data mining: an overview. ACM Trans. Intell. Syst. Technol. (TIST) **6**(3), 1–41 (2015). https://doi.org/10.1145/2743025

The Past Informs the Future: Temporal Sliding Window Graph Attention Networks for Real-Time Football Match Outcome Prediction

Miraç Merthan Durdağ(✉), Mustafa Orçun Uçgun, Ege Demir, and Yusuf H. Şahin

Istanbul Technical University, Istanbul, Turkey
{durdag21,ucgun22,demireg20,sahinyu}@itu.edu.tr

Abstract. Real-time football match outcome prediction is challenged by the sport's inherent dynamic nature. While recent graph-based approaches have shown promise, they primarily rely on cumulative passing networks that aggregate data from kickoff, potentially obscuring critical short-term tactical shifts. We propose a Temporal Sliding Window Graph Attention Network (TSW-GAT) that addresses this limitation through a novel dual-graph architecture. Unlike prior models that rely solely on cumulative representations, our framework simultaneously processes global team structures and localized momentum signals through a compact integration of cumulative and interval-specific graphs. Furthermore, we introduce a substitution-aware construction method to ensure network consistency during tactical changes. Trained and validated on 2,806 English matches, TSW-GAT achieves 81.85% accuracy at full-time and 77.94% at halftime. Notably, our model outperforms cumulative-only baselines by up to 20.58% points at the 45-minute mark, demonstrating superior performance when in-match evidence is limited. Cross-league evaluation on 2,800 matches (700 per league) from Bundesliga, La Liga, Ligue 1, and Serie A further confirms strong generalization, with an average accuracy of 84.24% at 90 min. These results highlight the efficacy of temporal decomposition in capturing evolving match contexts. The source code for this work is publicly available at: https://github.com/merthann/The-Past-Informs-the-Future.

Keywords: Football Analytics · Real-Time Match Outcome Prediction · Graph Neural Network · Temporal Sliding Window · Passing Network

1 Introduction

Predicting the outcome of football matches has long been a challenging problem in sports analytics, drawing interest from researchers, betting industries, coaches, and fans alike. Traditional approaches have predominantly relied on

Z. Liu and V. Misra (Eds.): ISACE 2026, LNCS 16610, pp. 133–149, 2026.
https://doi.org/10.1007/978-3-032-27272-0_10

pre-match statistics such as historical win rates, team rankings, and player performance metrics [8,14]. However, these methods fail to capture the dynamic nature of football, where momentum shifts, tactical changes, and in-game events continuously influence match outcomes.

Recent advances in graph neural networks (GNNs) [22] have opened new possibilities for modeling complex relational data in sports. The passing network naturally encodes the tactical structure and coordination patterns of a team. While prior work has demonstrated the utility of passing networks for team performance analysis and outcome prediction [10,11], most existing approaches treat these networks as static snapshots aggregated over an entire match or half.

We argue that static representations often overlook crucial temporal dynamics. Football matches unfold through shifting phases such as early probing, periods of dominance, momentum swings, and late tactical adjustments. Passing behavior in the final minutes of a close match can differ markedly from that in the opening phase. Capturing these variations requires more than a single cumulative graph.

Recent work by Lee et al. [15] demonstrated the effectiveness of Graph Attention Networks (GATs) for real-time match outcome prediction using cumulative passing networks. Their method processes graphs at different time points during a match and outperforms traditional feature-based approaches. However, by relying solely on cumulative graphs that aggregate all passes from kickoff, the model may obscure recent tactical shifts within a single dense representation.

In this work, we extend the graph-based framework by introducing a **Temporal Sliding Window Graph Neural Network (TSW-GAT)** with a dual-graph architecture. Building on the cumulative representation of Lee et al., our model additionally incorporates interval-specific graphs that capture localized passing patterns within discrete time windows. At each prediction time t, the model processes two complementary graph types **(i) Cumulative Graph:** Encodes all passes from kickoff to time t, modeling long-term tactical structure. **(ii) Interval Graphs:** A sequence of k graphs representing passes within N-minute windows preceding t, capturing recent momentum and tactical adjustments.

This temporal decomposition allows the model to learn both macro-level dynamics and short-term momentum signals. For example, at the 90th minute with $k = 2$ and $N = 5$, the model observes the full-match structure alongside focused views of the 80–85 and 85–90 min intervals.

A key challenge stems from player substitutions, which alter the passing network structure, especially in the second half. Existing methods often ignore substitutions or assume a fixed starting eleven, resulting in graphs that do not reflect actual on-field dynamics. We address this with **substitution-aware interval graphs** that dynamically track substitutions and red cards, ensuring each interval includes only the players active in that time window.

We evaluate our approach on 2,806 English Premier League and Championship matches from the 2020/21–2021/22-2022/23 seasons, using the same dataset as Lee et al. [15] to ensure a fair comparison. Unlike prior work that reports results at a single time point, we assess performance at multiple prediction timestamps $t \in \{45, 60, 75, 90\}$, showing how accuracy evolves as additional match information becomes available.

The main contributions of this paper are:

1. TSW-GAT architecture that combines cumulative and interval-based passing graphs for real-time match outcome prediction.
2. A substitution-aware graph construction method that dynamically updates node sets based on player changes and dismissals during the match.
3. Comprehensive experiments demonstrating that temporal graph decomposition outperforms single-graph baselines across different prediction timestamps.
4. An analysis of how different temporal window configurations (varying k and N parameters) affect prediction performance at different stages of a match.

2 Related Work

Early studies on football match outcome prediction primarily focused on statistical modeling and betting market applications, relying on Poisson-type models [7,8,14] and Bayesian dynamic frameworks [20]. Due to limited data availability, these approaches were largely based on aggregated match-level statistics and were mostly restricted to English competitions, establishing important methodological foundations despite their simplified assumptions.

With the increasing availability of digital match data, subsequent work shifted toward feature-based machine learning and deep learning approaches for pre-match prediction [1,2,9,19,23]. These studies relied on engineered features derived from historical performance, rankings, and match statistics, employing artificial neural networks, ensemble models, and hybrid frameworks. While these methods achieved improved predictive accuracy, they primarily operated at the aggregated team level and focused on pre-match settings, limiting their ability to capture in-play interaction patterns and temporal dynamics.

Parallel to predictive modeling, graph theory has been applied to analyze team organization, playing style, and player roles through passing networks. López Peña and Touchette [16] introduced weighted and directed graph representations of teams, while Grund [10] and Cintia et al. [5] demonstrated strong associations between network topology and team performance. McHale and Relton [17] further combined network analysis with pass difficulty modeling to identify influential players. Although these studies provide valuable descriptive and interpretive insights, they mainly rely on static or aggregated representations and focus on tactical evaluation rather than direct outcome prediction.

Building on these foundations, several works incorporated passing network metrics into predictive models. Cintia et al. [5] demonstrated the predictive value of topological indicators, while Ievoli et al. [11,12] integrated handcrafted network features into supervised and Bayesian hierarchical models. Chacoma [4] analyzed temporal passing networks to identify performance phases using logistic regression. Despite their effectiveness, these approaches depend on manually designed summary measures and relatively low-dimensional representations, limiting their capacity to capture complex and evolving interaction dynamics.

A major advancement in learning directly from passing networks using deep graph models was proposed by Lee et al. [15], who introduced a Graph Attention Network framework based on cumulative passing graphs for real-time outcome prediction. By combining graph embeddings with in-game features, their approach achieved substantial improvements over traditional baselines and established a strong benchmark for in-play prediction. However, its reliance on cumulative representations may obscure short-term tactical adjustments and localized momentum shifts.

In parallel, recent research has explored explainable machine learning in football analytics, particularly in the context of expected goals modeling [18]. Cefis and Carpita [3] examined the interpretability of statistical and algorithmic classifiers for shot outcome prediction, emphasizing the influence of spatial and geometric features. While these studies enhance model transparency, they primarily focus on isolated events rather than team-level interaction dynamics.

Overall, existing literature can be grouped into three main directions: (i) statistical and feature-based outcome modeling, (ii) network-oriented analysis of passing structures, and (iii) graph neural network approaches for in-play prediction. However, a unified framework that explicitly integrates temporal decomposition of passing networks with deep graph representation learning remains underexplored. Motivated by this gap, we propose a Temporal Sliding Window Graph Attention Network that jointly models cumulative team structure and short-term interaction dynamics while preserving substitution-aware graph consistency.

3 Methodology

3.1 Data Collection

We collect detailed match event data from WhoScored[1], a comprehensive football statistics platform powered by Opta data, using the `soccerdata` Python library. Our primary dataset comprises matches from two English leagues: the **Premier League** (1,140 matches) and the **Championship** (1,671 matches), spanning the 2020–21, 2021–22, and 2022–23 seasons, totalling 2,806 matches.

From each match, we extract player- and event-level information. For each player, we collect static attributes including position (e.g., GK, DC, MC, FW), height, and weight, together with match-specific metadata such as starting eleven status and pass accuracy. We also extract player ratings (on a scale of 0–10) at each prediction timestamp $t \in \{45, 60, 75, 90\}$, which accumulate throughout the match. These ratings are used as node features in cumulative graphs but are excluded from interval graphs to prevent data leakage, as discussed in Sect. 3.3. In addition, we compute each player's average pitch position (avg_x, avg_y) from event coordinates within each temporal window.

[1] https://www.whoscored.com.

We further collect the full timestamped and geo-located sequence of on-ball actions, including passes, shots, tackles, interceptions, aerial duels, fouls, cards, corners, take-ons, ball touches, recoveries, clearances, blocked passes, dispossessions, offsides provoked, and substitutions. Each event record contains the acting player, associated team, event type, pitch coordinates (x, y), timestamp, and an outcome indicator. Pass events additionally include qualifier tags such as *Cross*, *KeyPass*, *BigChance*, *FinalThirdPasses*, and *IntentionalAssist*. Based on these qualifiers and outcome indicators, we derive six team-level in-game features, including *PassSuccessRate*.

To evaluate cross-league generalization, we additionally collect match data from four major European leagues: **Bundesliga**, **La Liga**, **Ligue 1**, and **Serie A**. For each league, we collect the 700 most recent matches available, spanning back from the 2024–25 season through the 2023–24 and 2022–23 seasons, yielding a total of 2,800 matches. This dataset is used exclusively for cross-league evaluation and is never included in training or validation. The same event extraction pipeline is applied to ensure consistent feature construction. Ground-truth labels are derived from full-time scores and categorized as *home win*, *away win*, or *draw*.

3.2 Temporal Data Preprocessing

To enable in-play prediction, each match is processed at four prediction timestamps, $t \in \{45, 60, 75, 90\}$. For a given t, only events occurring at or before minute t are retained, while future events are discarded. Player ratings are obtained by filtering the minute-by-minute rating records to minute $\leq t$ and selecting the latest available value as the cumulative rating. For each starting player, the mean (x, y) position is computed from events up to time t, representing average spatial positioning. Passes observed up to t define the graph edges, with pass frequencies serving as edge weights.

After temporal filtering, the following data objects are generated for each match and timestamp: player metadata, filtered event logs, pass networks, match-level features, player average positions, and node-level feature matrices. These processed representations form the input for subsequent graph construction and model training stages.

3.3 Graph Construction

We represent each team's on-pitch activity as a pass network graph, where nodes correspond to starting eleven players and directed edges represent passes between them. Our temporal sliding window approach constructs $(1+k)$ graphs per team per match: one *cumulative* graph covering the entire observed period $[0, t]$, and k *interval* graphs capturing recent dynamics in non-overlapping time windows.

The **cumulative graph** G_{cmltv} aggregates all activity from minute 0 to the prediction minute t. Each node (player) carries a 7-dimensional feature vector:

$$\mathbf{x}_i^{\text{cmltv}} = [\text{position, height, weight, rating, pass accuracy, average x, average y}] \quad (1)$$

where *position* is a label-encoded integer (15 categories from GK to Sub), *height* and *weight* are static physical attributes, *rating* is the cumulative WhoScored player rating at minute t, *pass_ accuracy* is the ratio of successful passes to total passes attempted, and (avg_x, avg_y) are the player's average pitch coordinates derived from all events up to t. Edges are directed and weighted by the normalized pass count between each pair of players.

The **interval graph** k most recent time intervals preceding the prediction minute, we construct separate interval graphs $G_{\text{int}}^{(j)}$ for $j = 1, \ldots, k$. With a fixed interval width of N minutes, the j-th interval covers $[t-(k-j+1)N,\ t-(k-j)N)$. Each interval graph uses a 6-dimensional node feature vector:

$$\mathbf{x}_i^{\text{int}} = [\text{position, height, weight, pass\_accuracy, avg\_x, avg\_y}] \qquad (2)$$

Crucially, *rating* is excluded from interval graphs as it is a post-match metric that would introduce data leakage. The *pass_ accuracy* and (avg_x, avg_y) are recomputed from events within the interval only, capturing localized tactical dynamics. Edge structure follows the same pass-based construction, restricted to passes within the interval.

In-Game Features: In addition to graph-structured data, we extract 22 team-level in-game features per window (cumulative and each interval). These comprise **16 event-count features**: ball touches, substitutions, aerials, ball recoveries, blocked passes, cards, clearances, corners awarded, dispossessions, fouls, interceptions, missed shots, saved shots, tackles, take-ons, and offsides provoked; and **6 event-based features**: pass success rate, final-third passes (passes with $x > 66.7$), crosses, key passes, big chances, and shot assists—extracted from event qualifier tags. All 22 features are computed from events within the respective time window only, preventing data leakage from future events.

3.4 Model Architecture

We propose a **Temporal Sliding Window Graph Attention Network** (TSW-GAT) that jointly models cumulative match context and recent tactical dynamics. Figure 1 illustrates the overall architecture.

Graph Attention Encoder: Each graph (cumulative or interval) is processed by a Graph Attention Network (GAT) encoder consisting of three GATConv layers:

$$\mathbf{h}_i^{(l)} = \text{Dropout}\Big(\text{ELU}\Big(\text{GATConv}^{(l)}(\mathbf{h}_i^{(l-1)}, \mathcal{N}(i))\Big)\Big), \quad l = 1, 2, 3 \qquad (3)$$

followed by global mean pooling to produce a fixed-size graph-level embedding $\mathbf{g} \in \mathbb{R}^d$, where $d = 128$ is the hidden dimension. We employ two separate GAT encoders:

- $\text{GAT}_{\text{cmltv}}$: Processes cumulative graphs (input dimension 7).
- GAT_{int}: Processes all interval graphs with *shared weights* (input dimension 6), enabling the model to learn a consistent temporal feature extractor across intervals.

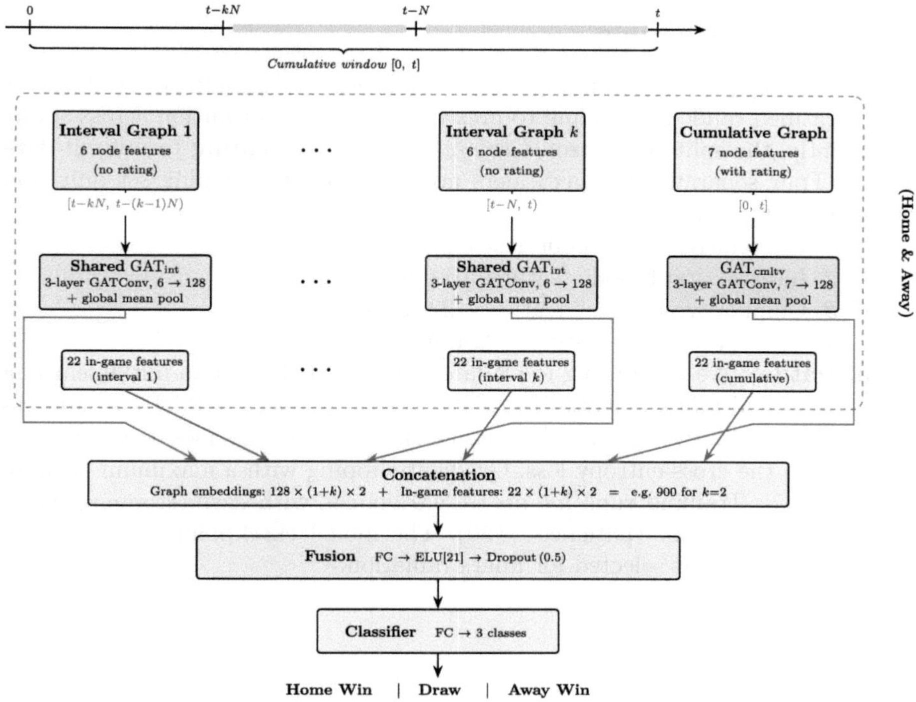

Fig. 1. Architecture of the Temporal Sliding Window GAT (TSW-GAT). For each team, k interval graphs (6 node features, no rating) and one cumulative graph (7 node features, including rating) are encoded by separate GAT modules—$\mathrm{GAT}_{\mathrm{int}}$ shares weights across all intervals while $\mathrm{GAT}_{\mathrm{cmltv}}$ processes the cumulative graph. Graph-level embeddings (via global mean pooling) and 22 in-game features per window are concatenated across both teams and passed through a fusion layer for three-class match outcome prediction.

Temporal Fusion and Classification: The graph embeddings from both teams across all $(1+k)$ temporal windows are concatenated with the corresponding in-game feature vectors:

$$\mathbf{z} = [\mathbf{g}_{\mathrm{home}}^{\mathrm{cmltv}} \| \mathbf{g}_{\mathrm{away}}^{\mathrm{cmltv}} \| \mathbf{g}_{\mathrm{home}}^{\mathrm{int}_1} \| \mathbf{g}_{\mathrm{away}}^{\mathrm{int}_1} \| \cdots \| \mathbf{f}_{\mathrm{home}}^{\mathrm{cmltv}} \| \mathbf{f}_{\mathrm{away}}^{\mathrm{cmltv}} \| \cdots] \tag{4}$$

For $k = 2$ and $d = 128$, the graph component contributes $128 \times (1+k) \times 2 = 768$ dimensions and the feature component contributes $22 \times (1+k) \times 2 = 132$ dimensions, yielding a 900-dimensional fusion vector. This vector is passed through a fully connected fusion layer:

$$\hat{\mathbf{y}} = \mathrm{FC}_{\mathrm{cls}}\Big(\mathrm{Dropout}\big(\mathrm{ELU}(\mathrm{FC}_{\mathrm{fuse}}(\mathbf{z}))\big)\Big) \tag{5}$$

where $\mathrm{FC}_{\mathrm{fuse}} : \mathbb{R}^{900} \rightarrow \mathbb{R}^{128}$ and $\mathrm{FC}_{\mathrm{cls}} : \mathbb{R}^{128} \rightarrow \mathbb{R}^{3}$ outputs raw logits for the three outcome classes. Both linear layers use Xavier initialization.

3.5 Training Procedure

The dataset is split into training (60%), validation (20%), and test (20%) sets using stratified random sampling to preserve the class distribution across splits. Importantly, the split is performed *before* any **feature scaling** to prevent data leakage. Four separate MinMaxScalers are fitted on the training set only and then applied to all sets:

1. Cumulative graph node features (7-dim)
2. Interval graph node features (6-dim)
3. Cumulative in-game features (22-dim)
4. Interval in-game features (22-dim)

Optimization: We train using the Adam optimizer [13] with an initial learning rate of 10^{-3} and an exponential learning rate scheduler ($\gamma = 0.99$). To address class imbalance (draws are underrepresented), we employ inverse-frequency class weighting in the cross-entropy loss. Gradient clipping with a maximum norm of 1.0 is applied. Training runs for up to 300 epochs with early stopping based on validation accuracy (patience = 50). The model checkpoint with the best validation accuracy is selected for final evaluation.

4 Results

We evaluate TSW-GAT on 562 test matches (20% of the 2,806 English matches). All models are trained with early stopping (patience=50) and class-weighted cross-entropy to mitigate class imbalance.

We perform a grid search over temporal window parameters: $k \in \{1, 2, 3, 4\}$ (number of interval graphs) and $N \in \{1, 3, 5, 10, 15\}$ (interval width in minutes). Table 1 reports test accuracy for 45- and 90-minute predictions.

Table 1. Test accuracy (%) for 45- and 90-minute predictions across temporal window configurations. Bold indicates best per timestamp.

$k \backslash N$	45-Min					90-Min				
	1	3	5	10	15	1	3	5	10	15
1	76.33	**77.94**	75.80	77.58	75.62	78.65	77.22	80.25	79.00	80.25
2	76.69	76.16	75.98	75.62	76.69	78.47	78.83	80.78	79.72	**81.85**
3	75.80	76.33	76.33	75.62	75.80	77.58	79.18	79.36	80.60	78.83
4	74.73	77.22	75.80	75.62	—	77.94	77.94	79.72	79.54	79.18

Early predictions favor smaller temporal windows, whereas later predictions benefit from a deeper temporal context. The optimal configuration at halftime is $k = 1, N = 3$, while full-time prediction favors $k = 2, N = 15$.

Table 2 summarizes per-class performance at each prediction timestamp using the corresponding optimal (k, N).

Table 2. Per-class performance across prediction timestamps with optimal (k, N) configurations.

Min	k	N	Class	Prec.	Rec.	F1	Supp.	Macro F1	Accuracy
45	1	3	Home Win	0.86	0.83	0.85	239	0.76	**77.94%**
			Away Win	0.84	0.82	0.83	185		
			Draw	0.58	0.63	0.60	138		
60	1	3	Home Win	0.90	0.81	0.85	239	0.77	**78.47%**
			Away Win	0.86	0.80	0.83	185		
			Draw	0.57	0.72	0.64	138		
75	2	10	Home Win	0.89	0.84	0.86	239	0.79	**80.96%**
			Away Win	0.86	0.85	0.86	185		
			Draw	0.64	0.70	0.66	138		
90	2	15	Home Win	0.92	0.83	0.87	239	0.81	**81.85%**
			Away Win	0.84	0.85	0.85	185		
			Draw	0.65	0.75	0.69	138		

We compare TSW-GAT against the cumulative GAT baseline of Lee et al. [15]. Table 3 reports accuracy across prediction timestamps. The proposed temporal sliding window architecture provides the largest benefit at early timestamps, where cumulative representations remain limited. As more match information becomes available, the performance gap narrows.

Table 3. Test accuracy (%) comparison between Lee et al. [15] and our TSW-GAT model across prediction timestamps.

Model	45 min	60 min	75 min	90 min
Lee et al. [15]	57.36	63.56	75.22	**83.09**
TSW-GAT (Ours)	**77.94**	**78.47**	**80.96**	81.85
Difference	+20.58	+14.91	+5.74	−1.24

Table 4 presents the confusion matrix for the 45-minute model ($k = 1, N = 3$), where halftime is selected because it exhibits the largest performance gap with the baseline, and the parameter setting is chosen due to its superior predictive accuracy.

We further evaluate a substitution-aware variant that updates interval graphs based on substitutions and red cards. Table 5 compares this variant with the base model.

The substitution-aware model shows targeted improvements at mid-game timestamps, suggesting that incorporating dynamic team composition may be beneficial under specific match conditions.

Table 4. Confusion matrix for 45-minute predictions ($k = 1$, $N = 3$). Rows represent actual outcomes, columns represent predicted outcomes.

	Pred. Home Win	Pred. Away Win	Pred. Draw	Total
Home Win	**199**	7	33	239
Away Win	3	**152**	30	185
Draw	29	22	**87**	138
Predicted	231	181	150	562

Table 5. Comparison of base model vs. substitution-aware variant based on accuracy scores.

Pred. Min	Base Model	Substitution-Aware	Difference
45	77.94%	77.22%	-0.72%
60	78.47%	**79.89%**	**+1.42%**
75	80.96%	79.89%	-1.07%
90	81.85%	81.14%	-0.71%

Finally, we evaluate cross-league generalization on Bundesliga, La Liga, Ligue 1, and Serie A matches (Table 6). The model generalizes well at later timestamps but exhibits a degradation in performance at halftime, indicating league-specific early-game interaction patterns.

5 Discussions

5.1 Key Findings and Implications

The consistent accuracy gains over the cumulative-only baseline confirm that interval graphs provide complementary information a single aggregated representation cannot capture. The optimal configuration is timestamp-dependent: early predictions favour narrow intervals (k=1, N=3) while late predictions benefit from broader windows (k=2, N=15), suggesting that **discriminative value** shifts from immediate tactical snapshots to longer-term momentum trajectories as the match progresses.

Draws remain the most challenging class across all configurations (F1: 0.60 at 45 min to 0.69 at 90 min), as they arise from the *absence* of decisive patterns rather than distinctive positive signals, causing graph-level features to overlap substantially with both win classes. Nonetheless, steady improvement with additional match data indicates that **late-game convergence** of passing intensity between evenly matched teams provides useful stalemate indicators that the interval graphs can exploit.

The **substitution-aware** graph construction variant yields a targeted improvement at 60 min (+1.42%), aligning with typical first-substitution timing in professional football (55–65 min). At other timestamps its benefit is negligible

Table 6. Cross-League Generalization Results at 45 and 90 min

League	Class	45 min			90 min		
		Acc.	Overall Acc.	F1	Acc.	Overall Acc.	F1
Bundesliga	Home Win	63.9%	58.6%	57.9%	92.2%	85.0%	82.7%
	Away Win	52.4%			93.8%		
	Draw	57.5%			62.4%		
La Liga	Home Win	54.7%	54.9%	54.9%	91.5%	84.7%	83.0%
	Away Win	48.3%			90.5%		
	Draw	62.3%			67.7%		
Ligue 1	Home Win	60.2%	56.1%	55.4%	91.4%	84.1%	81.2%
	Away Win	50.2%			89.8%		
	Draw	56.9%			61.9%		
Serie A	Home Win	51.6%	55.0%	55.4%	91.9%	83.1%	81.5%
	Away Win	52.1%			92.0%		
	Draw	62.7%			61.8%		
Average			**56.2%**	**55.9%**		**84.2%**	**82.1%**

or slightly negative, since substitutions are rare before halftime and the cumulative graph already absorbs most passing structure by 75–90 minutes. A promising direction is a hybrid strategy that activates substitution tracking selectively around common substitution windows.

Regarding **cross-league generalization**, the model trained exclusively on English football achieves 84.24% average accuracy across four European leagues at 90 min, *exceeding* the 81.85% in-domain result—suggesting that end-of-match passing network structure and outcome share sufficiently universal patterns across leagues. In contrast, 45-minute cross-league accuracy drops to 56.15%, a 22% point gap from in-domain performance, indicating that early-match passing dynamics are more sensitive to league-specific playing styles such as pressing intensity and positional play differences. While the model generalizes well for late-game predictions with minimal performance loss, early-game deployment would benefit from league-specific training data or domain adaptation techniques.

5.2 Model Interpretability and Feature Attribution

To better understand the learned decision patterns of the proposed model, we employ gradient-based attribution methods inspired by Grad-CAM [21] and Input×Gradient. Specifically, we compute the gradient of the predicted class score with respect to the edge attention coefficients, node embeddings, and fusion-layer input features, allowing us to identify which passing interactions and in-game variables contribute most strongly to the final prediction. This approach enables the visualization of both temporally localized and cumulative importance patterns without modifying the training procedure.

For match-level analysis, we apply the Input×Gradient method to the fusion layer to quantify the contribution of individual in-game features. For each test match predicted as a win (Home Win or Away Win), we compute per-feature signed attributions and aggregate them across all 403 winning-team matches using a hybrid grouping strategy: for Home Win predictions, the home team's features are treated as those of the winning team, whereas for Away Win predictions, the away team's features are used. This unified representation enables a consistent comparison between winning and losing teams.

The resulting importance maps and feature attribution profiles provide qualitative insight into how the model differentiates between persistent structural build-up patterns and short-term direct attacking sequences, as well as which contextual variables are most influential in determining match outcomes.

Figure 2 presents the **feature importance heatmap** for the Winning Team, showing the magnitude of Input×Gradient attribution (unsigned) for each of the 22 in-game features across the three temporal windows: Cumulative, Interval 1 (60–75′), and Interval 2 (75–90′).

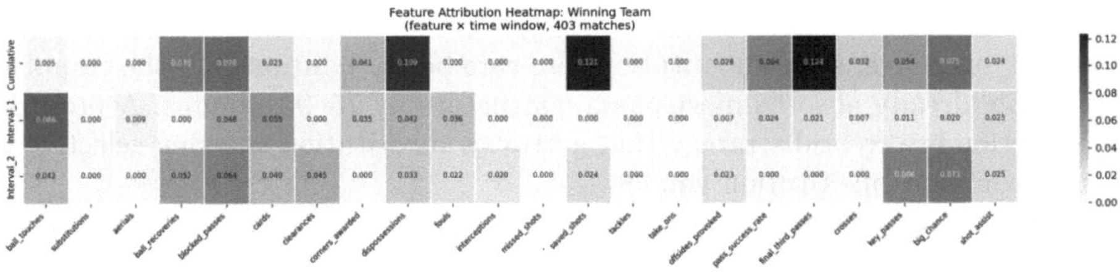

Fig. 2. Feature attribution heatmap (Input×Gradient) for the Winning Team across temporal windows (k=2, N=15, 90-minute model). Darker shading indicates higher attribution magnitude. The cumulative window highlights *pass_success_rate* and *saved_shots* as the most influential features, while the interval windows emphasize *ball_touches* and *key_passes*.

In the cumulative window, *pass_success_rate* (0.124) and *saved_shots* (0.121) emerge as the most important features, followed by *dispossessions* (0.109). This suggests that the model associates winning teams with sustained passing efficiency and goalkeeping interventions accumulated over the full match. In Interval 1 (60–75′), *ball_touches* (0.086) dominates, reflecting the importance of possession control during this transitional phase. In Interval 2 (75–90′), the model shifts attention to *key_passes* (0.066) and *blocked_passes* (0.064), capturing the late-game dynamics where decisive attacking passes and defensive interventions become critical.

Directional Feature Attribution: While the heatmap shows which features the model attends to, it does not reveal the *direction* of influence. Figure 3 presents signed attributions for both the Winning and Losing teams, where positive values (green) indicate features that *support* the predicted outcome and negative values (red) indicate features that *oppose* it.

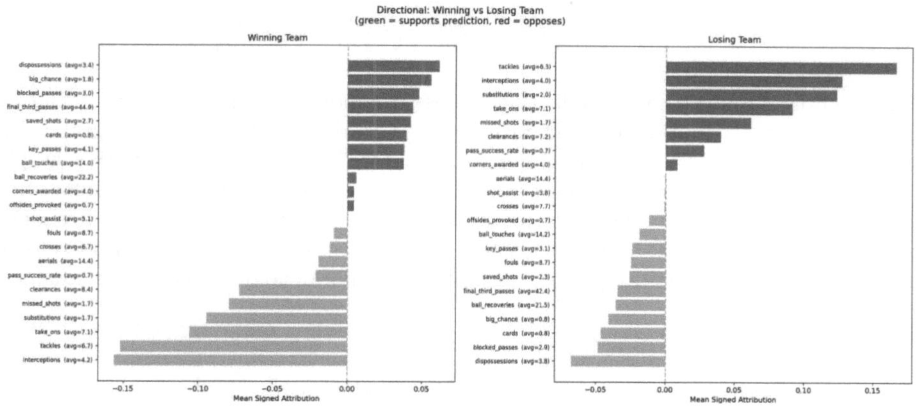

Fig. 3. Directional feature attribution comparison between Winning and Losing teams. Green bars indicate features that support the predicted outcome; red bars oppose it. Average feature values are shown in parentheses. Notably, *dispossessions* positively supports winning while *interceptions* and *tackles* are associated with the losing side.

Several notable patterns emerge from the directional analysis. For the Winning Team, *dispossessions*, *big_ chance*, *blocked_ passes*, and *final_ third_ passes* carry the strongest positive attributions, while *interceptions* and *tackles* exhibit negative attributions. This initially counterintuitive pattern—where being dispossessed supports winning while interceptions oppose it—resolves when viewed at the team level rather than as isolated events. Individually, each interception is a positive defensive action; however, a team that accumulates many interceptions is one that spends prolonged periods without the ball, continuously reacting to the opponent's attacks. Conversely, dispossessions require **prior possession**: a team that is frequently dispossessed is one that **dominates the ball**, attacks regularly, and consequently loses it more often in absolute terms. The model thus learns a coherent macro-level signal—possession-dominant, attacking teams win; defensively reactive teams lose—rather than evaluating each event in isolation.

For the Losing Team, the pattern is symmetrically reversed: *tackles* and *interceptions* carry the strongest positive attributions (supporting the loss prediction), while *dispossessions* is strongly negative. This mirror symmetry confirms that the learned representations are internally consistent and not driven by spurious correlations.

To further investigate how the model's decision-making process evolves throughout the match, Fig. 4 presents edge-importance visualizations derived from a gradient-based attribution method inspired by Grad-CAM for three graph representations: the 60–75 min interval graph (left), the 75–90 min interval graph (middle), and the cumulative graph (right).

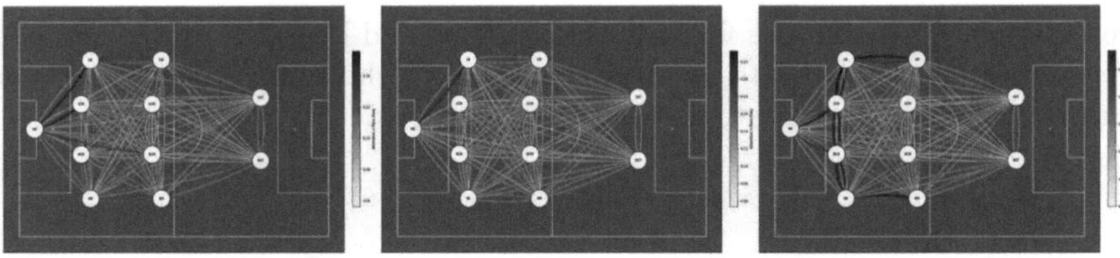

Fig. 4. Edge-importance visualization across temporal graphs obtained using a gradient-based attribution method inspired by Grad-CAM. Left: interval graph for minutes 60–75. Middle: interval graph for minutes 75–90. Right: cumulative graph (0–90 min). Edge thickness and color intensity indicate the relative importance for outcome prediction. The cumulative graph highlights short build-up passes (e.g., defender-to-defender and full-back-to-winger), while late-game interval graphs reveal increased attention to longer vertical passes, suggesting temporal adaptation in the model's decision-making.

The cumulative graph reveals that the model primarily focuses on short-range passing interactions, particularly exchanges between central defenders and lateral build-up patterns from full-backs to wingers. These short passes are both structurally central and highly frequent across the match. Their prominence suggests that sustained build-up structure forms the backbone of the model's long-term reasoning when predicting match outcomes.

In contrast, the interval graphs corresponding to the final 30 min display a more diversified attention pattern. While short passes remain relevant, increased importance is assigned to longer vertical connections, especially passes originating from goalkeepers or central defenders toward advanced players. This shift indicates that the model becomes increasingly sensitive to direct progression patterns in late-game scenarios.

Importantly, this behavior aligns with tactical intuition. Short build-up passes dominate the overall match and thus strongly influence the cumulative representation. However, long balls and direct transitions typically increase in frequency during late stages of the match, particularly when teams chase a result. Because our architecture integrates both cumulative and interval-specific graphs, the model can dynamically adjust its focus, relying on stable structural signals early and incorporating emergent tactical behaviors in later phases.

This analysis demonstrates that the Temporal Sliding Window GAT does not rely solely on static passing structure, but instead adapts its attention to evolving match dynamics.

5.3 Limitations and Future Work

Several limitations of our approach suggest directions for future research. First, our model relies on event-level data from WhoScored, which provides rich tactical information but lacks the granularity of tracking data (e.g., player coordinates at sub-second resolution). Incorporating tracking data could enable more precise interval graphs that capture off-ball movement and spatial formations.

Second, the base model represents each team using the starting eleven, which may limit its ability to fully capture the long-term impact of substitutions in later match phases. While our substitution-aware variant explicitly updates node sets in interval graphs and demonstrates an improvement in performance at the 60-min. mark, it models substitutions primarily at a structural level. Future work could extend this approach by incorporating dynamic player embeddings, substitution-aware message passing, or transition modeling mechanisms that explicitly represent how newly introduced players integrate into existing team interaction patterns.

Third, we treat each match independently and do not incorporate team-level historical context (e.g., recent form, head-to-head records, or league standings). Integrating such contextual priors with our temporal graph framework could improve predictions, particularly for early-game timestamps where in-match evidence is limited.

Finally, our cross-league analysis highlights the need for domain adaptation methods that can bridge stylistic differences between leagues. Transfer learning approaches that fine-tune the interval graph encoder on small amounts of target-league data could potentially recover the performance gap observed at early timestamps while retaining the strong generalization at 90 min.

6 Conclusion

We presented a Temporal Sliding Window Graph Attention Network (TSW-GAT) for real-time football match outcome prediction that jointly processes cumulative and interval-based passing networks. Our approach extends existing graph-based methods by explicitly modeling temporal dynamics through a dual-graph architecture, where a shared interval encoder captures recent tactical variations alongside a cumulative encoder that maintains global match context.

Experiments on 2,806 English Premier League and Championship matches demonstrate that the proposed temporal decomposition achieves up to 81.85% accuracy at 90 min and 77.94% at 45 min, with consistent improvements in draw prediction as more match data becomes available. A comprehensive grid search over temporal window parameters (k and N) reveals that optimal configurations are timestamp-dependent: early predictions benefit from narrow, focused intervals, while late predictions favor broader temporal context.

Our substitution-aware model variant demonstrates a targeted improvement of 1.42% points at the 60-minute mark, confirming the importance of accurately representing on-field player composition during periods of tactical change. Cross-league evaluation on 2,806 matches across Bundesliga, La Liga, Ligue 1, and Serie A reveals strong generalization at 90 min (84.24% average accuracy) but significant domain shift at 45 min (56.15%), suggesting that late-game passing patterns encode more universal outcome signals while early-game dynamics are league-specific.

These findings establish temporal decomposition of passing networks as a promising direction for in-play sports prediction and motivate further research into domain adaptation techniques, tracking data integration, and hybrid substitution-aware architectures.

Disclosure of Interests. The authors declare that they have no competing interests.

References

1. Baboota, R., Kaur, H.: Predictive analysis and modelling football results using machine learning approach for English premier league. Int. J. Forecast. **35**(2), 741–755 (2019). https://doi.org/10.1016/j.ijforecast.2018.01.003
2. Bunker, R.P., Thabtah, F.: A machine learning framework for sport result prediction. Appli. Comput. Inform. **15**(1), 27–33 (2019). https://doi.org/10.1016/j.aci.2017.09.005
3. Cefis, M., Carpita, M.: Accuracy and explainability of statistical and machine learning xg models in football. Statistics **59**(2), 426–445 (2025). https://doi.org/10.1080/02331888.2024.2445305
4. Chacoma, A.: Identification and optimization of high-performance passing networks in football, arXiv preprint arXiv:2502.01444 (2025)
5. Cintia, P., Rinzivillo, S., Pappalardo, L.: A network-based approach to evaluate the performance of football teams (2015)
6. Clevert, D.A., Unterthiner, T., Hochreiter, S.: Fast and accurate deep network learning by exponential linear units (elus) (2016). https://arxiv.org/abs/1511.07289
7. Crowder, M., Dixon, M., Ledford, A., Robinson, M.: Dynamic modelling and prediction of English football league matches for betting. J. Royal Statist. Soc. Ser. D **51**(2), 157–168 (2002)
8. Dixon, M.J., Coles, S.G.: Modelling association football scores and inefficiencies in the football betting market. J. R. Stat. Soc. Ser. C **46**(2), 265–280 (1997). https://doi.org/10.1111/1467-9876.00065
9. Elmiligi, H., Saad, S.: Predicting the outcome of soccer matches using machine learning and statistical analysis. In: Proceedings of the 12th Annual Computing and Communication Workshop and Conference (CCWC), pp. 1–8. (2022). https://doi.org/10.1109/CCWC54503.2022.9720896
10. Grund, T.U.: Network structure and team performance: the case of English premier league soccer teams. Soc. Netw. **34**(4), 682–690 (2012). https://doi.org/10.1016/j.socnet.2012.08.004
11. Ievoli, R., Gardini, A., Palazzo, L.: The role of passing network indicators in modeling football outcomes: an application using bayesian hierarchical models. AStA Adv. Statist. Analy. **107**, 153–175 (2023). https://doi.org/10.1007/s10182-021-00411-x
12. Ievoli, R., Palazzo, L., Ragozini, G.: On the use of passing network indicators to predict football outcomes. Knowl.-Based Syst. **222**, 106997 (2021). https://doi.org/10.1016/j.knosys.2021.106997
13. Kingma, D.P., Ba, J.: Adam: A method for stochastic optimization, arXiv preprint, arXiv:1412.6980 (2014)
14. Koopman, S.J., Lit, R.: A dynamic bivariate poisson model for analysing and forecasting match results in the English premier league. J. R. Stat. Soc. Ser. A **178**(1), 167–186 (2015)

15. Lee, J., Park, E., del Pobil, A.P.: We know who wins: graph-oriented approaches of passing networks for predictive football match outcomes. J. Big Data **12**, 147 (2025). https://doi.org/10.1186/s40537-025-01203-9
16. López Peña, J., Touchette, H.: A network theory analysis of football strategies, arXiv preprint arXiv:1206.6904 (2012)
17. McHale, I.G., Relton, S.D.: Identifying key players in soccer teams using network analysis and pass difficulty. Eur. J. Oper. Res. **268**(1), 339–347 (2018). https://doi.org/10.1016/j.ejor.2018.01.018
18. Mead, J., O'Hare, A., McMenemy, P.: Expected goals in football: improving model performance and demonstrating value. PLoS ONE **18**(4), e0282295 (2023). https://doi.org/10.1371/journal.pone.0282295
19. Rahman, M.A.: A deep learning framework for football match prediction. SN Appli. Sci. **2**, 165 (2020). https://doi.org/10.1007/s42452-019-1821-5
20. Rue, H., Salvesen, Ø.: Prediction and retrospective analysis of soccer matches in a league. J. Royal Statist. Soc. Ser. D **49**(3), 399–418 (2000)
21. Selvaraju, R.R., Cogswell, M., Das, A., Vedantam, R., Parikh, D., Batra, D.: Grad-cam: visual explanations from deep networks via gradient-based localization. In: 2017 IEEE International Conference on Computer Vision (ICCV), pp. 618–626. (2017). https://doi.org/10.1109/ICCV.2017.74
22. Veličković, P., Cucurull, G., Casanova, A., Romero, A., Liò, P., Bengio, Y.: Graph attention networks (2018). https://arxiv.org/abs/1710.10903
23. Wheatcroft, E.: Forecasting football matches by predicting match statistics, arXiv preprint, arXiv:2001.09097 (2020)

A.I. Applications in the NCAA Ecosystem

Don Lee(✉), Michael Cottingham, and Yuxin Mu

Sport and Fitness Administration, Department of Health and Human Performance, University of Houston, Houston, USA

Dlee23@uh.edu, mcotting@central.uh.edu, ymu6@Cougarnet.uh.edu

Abstract. Artificial intelligence (AI) is rapidly transforming the operational, competitive, and managerial dimensions of collegiate athletics. Despite widespread adoption of AI-driven analytics in professional sport, empirical evidence describing how NCAA stakeholders understand and evaluate AI applications remains limited. This study examines perceptions of AI within the NCAA ecosystem, focusing on its perceived benefits, regulatory needs, and potential to exacerbate institutional inequalities. Using a nationwide sample of 562 NCAA-affiliated respondents, participants reported their familiarity with AI, perceived utility across athletic operations, and concerns regarding data use, ethics, and competitive fairness. Descriptive analyses revealed strong support for AI's value in game preparation, operations and logistics, marketing, player development, scouting, and injury prevention, indicating a multidimensional view of AI as a performance and organizational asset. However, 79.5% of respondents endorsed the need for formal regulation, particularly around data governance and recruiting practices, and 43.1% expressed concern that AI may widen competitive gaps between resource-rich and resource-limited institutions. Stakeholders also emphasized preserving the human element in coaching and decision-making. These findings provide one of the first NCAA-focused empirical snapshots of AI perceptions, offering actionable implications for athletic departments, conference governance, and sport-technology developers seeking responsible and equitable AI integration.

Keywords: Artificial Intelligence · Collegiate Athletics · NCAA · Sport Analytics

1 Introduction

1.1 The Rise of AI in Collegiate Athletics

The national collegiate athletic association (NCAA) landscape is evolving at an unprecedented pace, driven by advancements in technology and data-driven decision-making [16, 36]. From recruiting and training to in-game strategy and fan engagement, the integration of emerging technologies is reshaping how collegiate athletic programs operate [21, 50]. This shift is particularly evident in sports management and marketing, where artificial intelligence (AI) is increasingly being adopted to enhance efficiency, optimize performance, and gain a competitive edge [41].

Z. Liu and V. Misra (Eds.): ISACE 2026, LNCS 16610, pp. 150–169, 2026.
https://doi.org/10.1007/978-3-032-27272-0_11

Technology has long played a role in NCAA athletics, but recent advancements in AI, machine learning, and big data analytics have accelerated this transformation [7]. Wearable technology, real-time performance tracking, and biomechanical analysis have become standard tools for teams seeking a deeper understanding of their athletes' capabilities [9, 31]. AI-powered platforms are now being utilized to process vast amounts of performance and tactical data, providing actionable insights that help teams refine their strategies, improve player development, and mitigate injury risks [2, 62].

Beyond performance analytics, AI is also influencing game-day decision-making, fan engagement, and sports marketing strategies [44]. NCAA programs are leveraging AI to optimize ticket sales, social media interactions, and personalized fan experiences, ensuring that athletic departments remain financially sustainable in an increasingly competitive environment [16, 53]. Automated video analysis tools powered by AI can break down plays in real time, helping coaches and analysts refine tactical approaches more efficiently than ever before [24, 54]. Likewise, the integration of emerging technologies into athletic operations is expected to bring numerous benefits; however, there remains a significant lack of empirically supported research on this topic within NCAA contexts [41, 50].

1.2 Strategic Importance of AI in NCAA Operations

One of the most well-known applications of AI in NCAA sports is in talent scouting and player recruitment [41]. Traditionally, scouting relied heavily on manual evaluation, subjective assessments, and limited statistical models [32]. AI, however, has transformed this process by introducing predictive analytics, which can assess an athlete's potential based on historical data, biomechanics, and performance metrics [2, 6]. AI-driven scouting tools can analyze game footage, track player tendencies, and compare athletes across different leagues, providing a data-backed foundation for recruitment decisions [5, 24, 56].

For NCAA programs competing at the highest levels—such as those in the Big 12 Conference—AI-driven performance analytics is becoming an indispensable asset [16]. AI can manage vast amounts of in-game data, identifying patterns and trends that might go unnoticed by human analysts [20]. These insights allow teams to optimize player rotations, adjust tactics on the fly, and develop game strategies tailored to an opponent's weaknesses [43]. Additionally, AI-enhanced injury prediction models are helping teams reduce player downtime, ensuring that key athletes remain healthy throughout the season [9, 62].

Athletic operations that successfully integrate AI into their recruitment, training, and in-game strategy will gain a competitive edge, allowing them to optimize player development and enhance overall team performance [50]. Ultimately, the future of NCAA sports management is becoming increasingly data-driven, with AI playing a vital role in this evolution [16, 41]. While traditional coaching instincts and experience remain invaluable [35], incorporating AI-powered insights into decision-making will be essential for programs striving to compete at the highest levels [44]. As AI technology continues to advance, NCAA institutions that proactively adopt these innovations will position themselves at the forefront of modern sports management, ushering in a new era of intelligent, strategic athletics [41, 50].

1.3 Conceptual Gap

While AI adoption in professional sport has received growing scholarly attention, far less is known about how such innovations take shape within the unique governance, resource, and compliance constraints of the NCAA ecosystem. Unlike professional leagues—where centralized governance, commercial incentives, and technological investment structures are relatively cohesive—NCAA institutions operate within a multilayered system involving athletic departments, conferences, the NCAA national office, and booster- or donor-influenced environments. This study therefore addresses a conceptual gap by examining how AI innovations are interpreted, adopted, and operationalized within a collegiate model that differs substantially from professional sport innovation pathways.

1.4 Research Justification and Theoretical Foundation

The purpose of this research is to investigate how AI-driven analytics influence athlete training, strategic decision-making processes, and overall team performance within NCAA athletics, while also assessing the potential for broader institutional adoption across collegiate sports programs. Additionally, this study identifies and evaluates the most prominent applications of AI within NCAA environments. The next section introduces the two primary research directions, and the subsequent section provides the theoretical justification that grounds these areas of inquiry within established models of technology adoption, sports analytics, and performance optimization.

The Gap in AI-Driven Analytics in NCAA Sports. Despite AI's rapid growth in professional sports, NCAA programs—particularly those competing in Power Five conferences—have yet to fully embrace AI-driven analytics [36, 41]. While some collegiate programs have begun experimenting with AI-based performance tracking and scouting tools—such as Florida's AI-powered wearable monitoring initiative and Arkansas's partnership with WMT Digital—there remains a lack of comprehensive adoption across NCAA athletics [27, 54]. Traditional scouting methods and basic statistical analysis continue to dominate talent evaluation and game preparation at many institutions [32]. The hesitancy to adopt AI in college sports may stem from budget constraints, data privacy concerns, limited staffing, or resistance from coaching staff accustomed to conventional approaches [7, 43]. However, as AI continues to demonstrate its effectiveness in professional leagues, NCAA programs—especially those in highly competitive conferences like the Big 12—will need to accelerate their adoption of AI-powered performance optimization to remain competitive in an increasingly data-driven sports landscape [16, 50].

To move beyond a descriptive account of adoption patterns, this study synthesizes insights across performance analytics, recruiting practices, and strategic decision-making to identify a deeper, structural gap: how NCAA stakeholders interpret, operationalize, and evaluate AI within the constraints of collegiate governance, uneven resource structures, and compliance requirements. While industry reports signal growing interest, peer-reviewed sport analytics literature has not yet established how AI aligns with NCAA-specific organizational realities—such as decentralized decision-making, academic–athletic integration, athlete welfare considerations, and departmental resource variability. This gap sets the stage for an empirical examination that clarifies not just whether AI is being adopted, but how NCAA programs conceptualize its value, barriers, and performance implications, thereby advancing sport innovation scholarship in a collegiate context.

Theoretical Support. The integration of AI into NCAA athletics can also be grounded in established sport analytics and performance-optimization frameworks. Data-driven decision-making models [1, 14] posit that athletic success increasingly depends on the systematic use of objective, high-frequency data to guide both strategic and operational purposes. Similarly, sports performance optimization models emphasize the multifaceted nature of athlete performance—encompassing physiological load, biomechanics, psychological readiness, and tactical behaviors—and highlight the value of integrating multiple data streams for holistic performance enhancement [3, 26, 48]. AI extends these frameworks by enabling coaches and analysts to process larger, more complex datasets than traditional analytics tools can accommodate, uncovering hidden patterns, nonlinear relationships, and predictive indicators related to performance, fatigue, tactical tendencies, and injury risk [6, 31].

To more clearly situate the study's empirical focus, each theoretical lens directly informs one of the study's core research areas. Explicitly mapping these theories to each research dimension strengthens the conceptual foundation and clarifies how the study builds on and extends existing sport innovation literature [20, 41, 50].

- Data-driven decision-making theory supports the research questions concerning strategic decision-making processes, helping explain how AI-derived insights inform adjustments in training loads, tactical preparations, and in-game strategy [13, 46, 59].
- Performance optimization models underpin the examination of athlete training and developmental outcomes, providing a framework for understanding how AI-enabled monitoring affects biomechanics, fatigue management, and individualized training prescriptions [21, 29].
- Human–AI collaboration theory directly informs questions related to coaching adoption and institutional integration, explaining how AI systems complement human expertise and how decision-makers negotiate trust, autonomy, and interpretability when using AI-enhanced analytics [12, 39, 49].

Moreover, evidence-based coaching models argue that coaching decisions should rely on replicable, data-informed processes; AI strengthens this approach by offering real-time, evidence-based insights that reduce uncertainty and supplement experiential knowledge [10, 63]. Conceptualizing AI adoption within these theoretical models positions AI not as an isolated technological trend, but as a continuation of a long-standing evolution in sports analytics toward more sophisticated, data-driven performance optimization. This perspective provides a theoretical foundation for examining how NCAA programs leverage AI to enhance training efficiency, improve decision-making, and strengthen competitive outcomes.

More recent scholarship also highlights the role of human–AI collaboration in high-performance sport environments. Human–AI collaboration theory suggests that optimal decision-making occurs when computational intelligence and human expertise are integrated synergistically, rather than treated as substitutes [8, 33]. In NCAA contexts, AI contributes precision, speed, and scalability in data analysis, while coaches contribute contextual judgment, interpretive insight, and situational nuance. This collaborative perspective further reinforces the theoretical rationale for investigating AI use in collegiate sport settings, as it captures the dynamic interplay between technological capabilities and human decision-makers within athletic departments [15, 49].

Although industry reports provide valuable contextual examples, the theoretical foundation of this study is anchored in peer-reviewed literature across sport analytics, performance science, organizational innovation, and human–technology interaction. Recent scholarship in sport science and analytics highlights the growing role of machine learning in performance prediction, tactical modeling, and injury forecasting [e.g., 51, 18, 34]. Likewise, organizational behavior and sport management research highlight the importance of technological readiness, organizational learning, and innovation culture in shaping the adoption of advanced analytics in sport organizations [e.g., 23, 19]. Integrating these perspectives enhances the study's theoretical grounding and ensures greater alignment with the expectations of today's scholarly community.

2 Methods

Having established the practical significance of AI integration in NCAA environments, outlined the key research gaps in collegiate athletics, and grounded the study in relevant theoretical frameworks, it is essential to describe the empirical approach used to examine these issues. The following Methods section presents the research design, sampling and recruitment procedures, survey measures, and analytical techniques employed to investigate NCAA stakeholders' perceptions of AI-driven analytics. This methodological overview provides the foundation for evaluating how individuals involved in collegiate athletics understand the benefits, concerns, and regulatory implications of AI within their respective roles.

2.1 Participants and Recruitment

Participants were recruited through Prolific, an online crowdsourcing platform commonly used for high-quality human-subjects research [40]. Eligibility criteria required respondents to (a) be at least 18 years old, (b) reside in the United States, and (c) report current or prior involvement with NCAA athletics (e.g., athletes, coaches, analysts, administrators). A total of 562 respondents met eligibility requirements and completed the full survey (with sample details reported in the Results section). All individuals received compensation in accordance with Prolific's recommended pay rates and ethical compensation guidelines [45]. Prior to initiating data collection, the study was reviewed and approved by the authors' Institutional Review Board (IRB). All participants provided informed consent electronically before participating in the study.

2.2 Procedure

Data collection was conducted via an online Qualtrics survey distributed through the Prolific research participant management system. Qualtrics is widely used in behavioral and social science research [47], and its integration with Prolific enabled access to a high-quality, pre-screened participant pool characterized by strong data reliability and diversity [40]. The costs associated with participant recruitment were covered by internal grant funding secured by the research team. After clicking the study link, respondents were routed to a secure Qualtrics environment where they reviewed and electronically signed the IRB-approved consent form. Prolific independently managed recruitment, secure data transfer, and participant compensation, and no personal identifiers were shared with the research team [45]. Participants then completed demographic items, NCAA involvement items, and AI-related measures. The survey required approximately 5–8 min to complete.

2.3 Instrumentation and Measures

A series of measures were administered to assess respondents' background characteristics, levels of engagement within NCAA athletics, and perceptions related to the use of artificial intelligence in collegiate sport contexts. Detailed descriptions of each measure are provided in the subsections below.

Demographics. Participants reported their gender, age, race/ethnicity, educational attainment, NCAA division affiliation, and career length in collegiate athletics.

NCAA Involvement. Respondents selected their primary role(s) within collegiate athletics. Options included current or former athlete, coach, sports analyst/statistician, athletic director, sports medicine professional, and an "other" category that captured administrative, media, and event-operations positions. Multiple selections were permitted to reflect the multifaceted nature of NCAA responsibilities.

Familiarity with Artificial Intelligence. AI familiarity was measured using a single 5-point Likert item ($1 =$ *not at all familiar*, $5 =$ *expert*), assessing respondents' self-reported knowledge of artificial intelligence and its uses within NCAA operations.

Perceived Benefits of AI in NCAA Operations. Participants identified the areas in which they believed AI could provide value. This multi-response item included categories such as:

- Game preparation
- Game-day operations and logistics
- Marketing and revenue generation
- Player development
- Scouting and recruitment
- Injury prevention and rehabilitation
- Fan engagement and experience

Beliefs about AI Regulation. Participants indicated whether they believed AI should be regulated within collegiate athletics. Those who endorsed regulation selected one or more areas needing oversight, including:

- Data collection and usage
- AI in game strategy and decision-making
- AI in recruitment processes
- AI in marketing and revenue generation
- Other (open-ended)

Perceived Inequalities Resulting from AI. Concerns that AI may exacerbate inequalities across collegiate institutions were assessed with a 5-point agreement scale (1 = *strongly disagree*, 5 = *strongly agree*). This item captured beliefs that resource-rich institutions may disproportionately benefit from AI implementation. A multiple-response item assesses areas of concern associated with AI implementation in NCAA environments. Options included:

- Loss of human touch/intuition
- Ethical implications
- Privacy concerns for athletes
- Job displacement
- Unfair advantages for wealthier institutions
- Other concerns (open-ended)

2.4 Data Analysis

Descriptive statistics were analyzed using IBM SPSS Statistics (Version 29), a widely used software package in social science research [25]. Prior to analysis, data were screened for completeness and response quality. Means, standard deviations, and ranges were calculated for continuous variables, while frequencies and percentages were computed for categorical and multi-response items. No inferential analyses were conducted, as the study aimed to provide an exploratory, descriptive overview of stakeholder perceptions of AI within NCAA athletics.

3 Results

3.1 Demographics: Gender/Age/Race/Education/Career Length/Division

The sample consisted of 55.5% male and 40.9% female respondents, with a mean age of 35.9 years (range: 18 to 80). The racial/ethnic composition included 61.4% Caucasian, 15.1% African American, 8.7% Latino, 8.5% Asian, and 2.7% Native American. A highly educated sample, 82% held more than a bachelor's degree. Institutional representation spanned NCAA Division I (39.5%), Division II (25.6%), Division III (23.5%), and NAIA (4.4%). The average career length was 3.37 years, with individual career spans ranging from 1 to 21 years. The largest group came from NCAA Division I, comprising 39.5% of the sample (n = 222). Division II respondents made up 25.6% (n = 144), while Division III accounted for 23.5% (n = 132). NAIA respondents represented a smaller portion at 4.4% (n = 25). Other affiliations (e.g., non-NCAA institutions or unspecified roles) made up 5.2% (n = 29). Detailed demographic characteristics of the sample are presented in Table 1.

Table 1. Participant demographics (N = 562)

Variable	Category	n	%
Gender	Male	312	55.5
	Female	230	40.9
	Other / Not specified	20	3.6
Age	Mean = 35.9 years (Range: 18–80)	–	–
Race / Ethnicity	Caucasian	345	61.4
	African American	85	15.1
	Latino	49	8.7
	Asian	48	8.5
	Native American	15	2.7
	Other / Multi-racial	20	3.6
Education	Bachelor's degree or less	101	18.0
	More than bachelor's degree	461	82.0
NCAA Division Affiliation	Division I	222	39.5
	Division II	144	25.6
	Division III	132	23.5
	NAIA	25	4.4
	Other / Non-NCAA	29	5.2
Career Length in Collegiate Athletics	Mean = 3.37 years (Range: 1–21)	–	–

3.2 NCAA Involvement

Among the 562 eligible respondents, the majority identified as current or former athletes (54.4%). Additional roles included sports analysts/statisticians (10.5%), coaches (8.0%), sports medicine professionals (3.9%), and athletic directors (2.1%). The remaining 21% were classified under "other" roles, encompassing positions such as administrative compliance staff, broadcasters, creative content managers, equipment managers, event coordinators, recruiters, stadium staff, and volunteer managers. Detailed information is presented in Table 2.

Table 2. Respondent NCAA involvement (N = 562)

Role Category	n	%
Current or Former Athlete	306	54.4
Sports Analyst/Statistician	59	10.5
Coach	45	8.0
Sports Medicine Professional	22	3.9
Athletic Director	12	2.1

(continued)

Table 2. (*continued*)

Role Category	n	%
Other Roles*	118	21.0

3.3 Respondent's Familiarity with AI

On a 5-point scale (1 = *not at all familiar*, 5 = *expert*), the mean score of 3.4 suggests that respondents, on average, had more than a moderate level of familiarity with artificial intelligence and its application to NCAA operations. Notably, 99% of respondents indicated at least some level of familiarity with the topic.

3.4 Respondent's Perception on AI Benefits

Analyzing the frequency of each AI benefit category reveals the following insights:

- "Game preparation" was the most frequently cited benefit, mentioned 302 times, representing 53.7% of the total respondents.
- "Game day operations and logistics" followed closely with 270 mentions (48.0%), indicating strong perceived utility in operational efficiency and event execution.
- "Marketing and revenue generation" was cited 259 times (46.1%), highlighting AI's perceived potential in supporting financial sustainability and strategic outreach.
- "Player development" appeared in 250 responses (44.5%), reflecting AI's role in athlete performance improvement.
- "Scouting and recruitment" was identified 236 times (42.0%), showing consistent recognition of AI in talent identification and recruitment analytics.
- "Injury prevention and rehabilitation" was mentioned 206 times (36.7%), emphasizing AI's growing role in athlete health and safety.
- "Fan engagement and experience" received 203 mentions (36.1%), indicating moderate interest in AI's applications for enhancing audience interaction.

These findings suggest that AI is perceived to provide multi-dimensional value in NCAA operations, with the strongest emphasis placed on enhancing game preparation, logistics, and revenue strategies. Detailed information is presented in Table 3.

Table 3. Respondent' perceptions of AI benefits in NCAA operations (N = 562)

AI Benefit Category	n	%
Game preparation	302	53.7
Game-day operations and logistics	270	48.0
Marketing and revenue generation	259	46.1
Player development	250	44.5
Scouting and recruitment	236	42.0

(*continued*)

Table 3. (*continued*)

AI Benefit Category	n	%
Injury prevention and rehabilitation	206	36.7
Fan engagement and experience	203	36.1

3.5 Respondent's Belief on AI Regulation

Regarding the need for AI regulations, the majority of respondents (79.5%) expressed the view that some form of regulation is necessary. The most commonly cited area requiring AI regulation was "*data collection and usage*" (48.9%), followed by "*AI in game strategy and decision-making*" (25.6%) and "*AI in recruitment processes*" (19.4%). Only a small portion identified the need for regulation in "*AI in marketing and revenue strategies*" (4.4%) or selected "*Other*" (1.6%). Detailed information is presented in Table 4.

Table 4. Respondent' beliefs about AI regulation in NCAA athletics (N = 562)

Regulation Category	n	%
Any regulation needed (overall)	447	79.5
Data collection and usage	275	48.9
AI in game strategy and decision-making	144	25.6
AI in recruitment processes	109	19.4
AI in marketing and revenue strategies	25	4.4
Other	9	1.6

3.6 Can AI Cause Inequalities across Collegiate Institutions?

When asked whether the use of AI could create inequalities across collegiate institutions, 43.1% of respondents either agreed (34.7%) or strongly agreed (8.4%), indicating a notable level of concern about potential disparities. However, the largest proportion of respondents (37.5%) remained neutral on the issue, suggesting uncertainty or a need for more information. A smaller segment disagreed (15.1%) or strongly disagreed (4.3%) with the notion.

These findings reflect a cautious yet attentive stance among stakeholders—many acknowledge the risk that resource-rich institutions could disproportionately benefit from AI technologies, potentially widening existing gaps in competitiveness, access, or support services within collegiate athletics.

3.7 Areas for Concerns Due to AI Usage?

Respondents identified a range of concerns associated with AI use in NCAA operations. The most frequently cited issue was the loss of human touch and intuition in decision-making, reported in 80 instances (14.2%), either alone or in combination with other concerns. This was followed by concerns about unfair advantages for wealthier institutions, which appeared in 78 instances (13.9%), suggesting worries over potential resource-driven disparities in AI implementation.

Other commonly reported concerns included:

- Ethical implications (at least 111 instances, 19.8%)
- Privacy concerns for athletes (at least 88 instances, 15.7%)
- Job displacement (at least 69 instances, 12.3%)

These findings indicate that while AI is seen as beneficial, stakeholders are deeply mindful of its ethical, social, and economic implications—especially as they relate to equity, privacy, and the human elements of sports decision-making. Detailed information is presented in Table 5. Then, the figure presents a synthesized overview of the study's conceptual findings (Fig. 1).

Table 5. Areas of concern regarding AI usage in NCAA athletics (N = 562)

Concern Category	n	%
Ethical implications	111	19.8
Privacy concerns for athletes	88	15.7
Loss of human touch/intuition	80	14.2
Unfair advantages for wealthy programs	78	13.9
Job displacement	69	12.3
Other	–	–

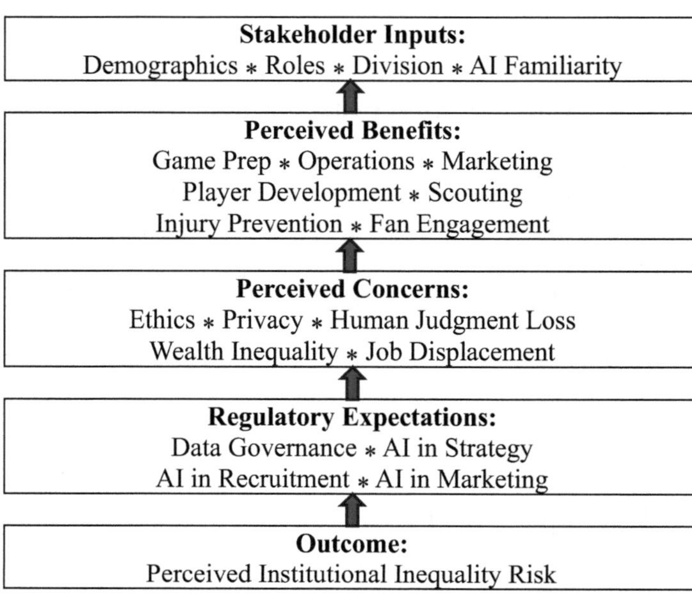

Fig. 1. NCAA AI framework

4 Discussion and Implications

This study provides an NCAA-focused snapshots of how stakeholders understand, value, and question the role of artificial intelligence in collegiate sport operations. While prior work has largely highlighted AI's transformative potential in professional leagues and elite sport analytics [2, 41, 50], empirical evidence from NCAA-affiliated populations has been sparse. By surveying 562 NCAA-related stakeholders across divisions, roles, and career stages, this study offers a baseline map of AI familiarity, perceived benefits, regulatory expectations, and areas of concern within the collegiate ecosystem.

4.1 AI as a Multi-dimensional Value Generator

Overall, respondents perceived AI as a multi-dimensional asset rather than a niche or single-purpose tool. The most frequently endorsed benefit areas—game preparation, game-day operations and logistics, marketing and revenue generation, player development, and scouting and recruitment—mirror how AI has been deployed in professional contexts for performance analytics, tactical decision-making, and fan engagement [16, 20]. That game preparation and operations ranked highest suggests that NCAA stakeholders view AI primarily as a way to enhance competitive readiness and operational efficiency, rather than as a purely experimental or "nice-to-have" innovation.

The strong endorsement of AI for marketing and revenue strategies aligns with growing pressure on athletic departments to sustain or grow revenue in an increasingly competitive and resource-intensive environment [53]. Similarly, substantial support for AI in injury prevention and rehabilitation and player development is consistent with the broader movement toward data-driven athlete monitoring and biomechanical analysis [9, 30, 62]. Collectively, these findings indicate that NCAA stakeholders are conceptually aligned with global sports innovation trends: they see AI as a tool that can simultaneously support performance, health, and financial sustainability.

4.2 Enthusiasm Tempered by Calls for Governance

At the same time, the study reveals that enthusiasm for AI is not uncritical. Nearly four out of five respondents (79.5%) indicated that some form of AI regulation is necessary in collegiate sport. The strongest perceived need for regulation centered on data collection and usage, followed by AI in game strategy and decision-making and AI in recruitment processes. This pattern echoes broader concerns in sport and technology research around data privacy, algorithmic opacity, and competitive fairness [7, 44].

Stakeholders' focus on data practices is particularly salient in NCAA settings, where student-athletes occupy a hybrid status as both students and high-performance performers. Wearables, optical tracking systems, and AI-enhanced video analysis can yield powerful performance insights, but they also generate sensitive biometric and behavioral data. The results suggest that NCAA-affiliated actors are keenly aware that who controls these data, how they are used, and under what safeguards will be central to the legitimacy and acceptance of AI integration.

4.3 Perceived Inequalities and the Risk of a New "Technology Divide"

One of the most consequential findings is that 43.1% of respondents agreed or strongly agreed that AI could exacerbate inequalities across collegiate institutions, with only a minority actively disagreeing and a large neutral segment. This pattern signals a cautious but real concern that AI may act as a force multiplier for already resource-rich institutions—those with larger budgets, deeper analytics infrastructures, and better access to vendor partnerships—thereby widening existing gaps in competitive balance, athlete services, and exposure.

These perceptions dovetail with resource-based views of competitive advantage and prior work on innovation diffusion, which suggest that early adopters with greater financial and human capital are best positioned to benefit from complex technologies [41, 50]. In the NCAA context, this may mean that Power Five or similar resource-rich programs are able to institutionalize AI across recruiting, performance, and fan engagement more quickly and comprehensively than their less resourced peers. The concerns about unfair advantages for wealthier institutions and job displacement further underscore that AI is not perceived as a neutral tool, but as a potential generator of structural shifts in how success and opportunity are distributed.

4.4 Protecting the "Human Element" in Collegiate Sport

Another prominent theme in the data is concern over the loss of human touch and intuition in decision-making. Even as respondents acknowledged AI's benefits, the most frequently mentioned concern involved the erosion of interpersonal judgment, relational coaching, and holistic decision-making that considers context beyond what is captured in data.

This is particularly important in the NCAA ecosystem, where coach–athlete relationships, educational missions, and developmental priorities extend beyond winning and losing. The findings suggest that stakeholders do not want AI to replace the human side of coaching and leadership, but rather function as a decision-support system that augments, rather than overrides, human expertise. For innovators and athletic leaders, this implies that framing and implementation matter: AI tools that are positioned as collaborative aids are likely to face less resistance than those that appear to automate or displace core human roles.

4.5 Managerial and Policy Implications for the NCAA Ecosystem

The descriptive nature of this study does not test causal relationships, but it offers several actionable implications for NCAA leaders, conference offices, and technology providers:

1. Develop AI Readiness and Literacy Initiatives

   With a mean familiarity score of 3.4 on a 5-point scale, stakeholders report more than moderate familiarity with AI, yet not at an expert level. Athletic departments and conferences could:

- Offer professional development workshops on AI basics, ethical use, and case examples.

- Create cross-functional AI task forces involving coaches, analysts, compliance officers, and sport medicine staff to guide responsible adoption.

2. Prioritize Governance Frameworks Around Data and Strategy Use

   Given strong support for regulation—especially around data collection and strategic use—NCAA governance bodies and conferences should:

- Establish clear guidelines for data ownership, consent, and retention for athlete performance and biometric data.
- Consider guardrails on in-game AI decision support (e.g., limits on real-time algorithmic coaching aids) to preserve competitive integrity.
- Provide model policies or best-practice frameworks that athletic departments can adapt.

3. Mitigate Emerging Inequalities Through Shared Resources

   If AI risks widening gaps between resource-rich and resource-limited programs, conference offices and the NCAA could:

- Support shared analytics platforms or consortium-based vendor agreements to reduce cost barriers for smaller programs.
- Encourage knowledge-sharing initiatives, such as conference-wide data analytics workshops or open technical playbooks.
- Consider grant or subsidy mechanisms for programs with limited resources to experiment with AI tools in a structured, ethical way.

4. Design AI Tools That Preserve Human Relationships and Values

   Technology providers and athletic leaders should intentionally design and implement AI systems that:

- Emphasize coach control and interpretability, rather than "black-box" outputs.
- Support dialogue between data and lived experience, encouraging coaches and staff to question, contextualize, and validate AI recommendations.
- Align with the educational and developmental mission of collegiate sport by considering impacts on athlete autonomy, identity, and well-being.

5. Leverage Case Examples Strategically, Not Just Tactically

   Emerging use cases—such as automated game recaps, AI-powered performance monitoring, social media threat detection, and AI-driven recruiting—illustrate the breadth of AI's footprint in college sport. However, this study suggests that adoption should be guided by overarching strategy and governance, not just tool availability. Athletic departments should:

- Evaluate AI initiatives through a multi-criteria lens (competitive impact, ethics, equity, data protection, and alignment with institutional values).
- Treat early AI implementations as learning laboratories, with built-in evaluation and feedback loops rather than one-off tech purchases.

4.6 Addressing NCAA Policy Feasibility and Institutional Pathways

While this study highlights stakeholder demand for clearer AI governance, the feasibility of implementing such policies requires acknowledging the NCAA's decentralized regulatory structure and the varying capacities of institutions across divisions [22, 61]. Unlike fully centralized professional leagues, the NCAA operates through layered authority—national office legislation, conference-level policies, and institution-specific compliance practices [11, 37]—which affects how quickly and uniformly new technology regulations can take hold. For AI-related policies to be actionable, several realistic pathways merit consideration.

First, the NCAA is more likely to implement principle-based guidelines rather than highly prescriptive rules, given the diversity of sports, resource levels, and technological maturity across member institutions [28, 57]. Feasible starting points include establishing baseline standards for data governance, consent procedures, athlete privacy, and algorithmic transparency [43, 52], which can then be operationalized by conferences and institutions according to their own infrastructures.

Second, the NCAA frequently adopts policy changes only after pilot testing and cross-institutional consultation [61]. An attainable model for AI governance would involve conference-level pilot programs that evaluate the competitive, ethical, and operational consequences of AI tools. This approach aligns with how past technology policies (e.g., wearable GPS devices, optical tracking systems) were gradually normalized [9, 38].

Third, because resource inequity emerged as a major stakeholder concern in this study, policy feasibility may hinge on mechanisms that reduce adoption burdens for lower-resourced programs. The NCAA could realistically support this through shared vendor contracts, pooled analytics services, model consent templates, and optional compliance toolkits—low-cost interventions that do not require full-scale rule changes but still promote equity [42, 50].

Fourth, conferences are likely to play a pivotal intermediary role [11]. Conferences already govern sideline technologies, video exchange standards, and officiating protocols [17, 55]; AI governance could logically extend from these existing domains. Conference-level rules may therefore become the earliest and most practical sites of regulation, especially around real-time AI decision support, recruiting analytics, and competitive fairness safeguards [7].

Finally, any feasible policy trajectory must respect the NCAA's educational mission [61]. Policies that frame AI as a tool for enhancing student-athlete welfare—such as injury prevention analytics, academic support algorithms, or mental health risk detection—are significantly more likely to gain early adoption than policies focused solely on competitive optimization [4, 32, 58]. Aligning AI governance with institutional values increases both political viability and stakeholder acceptance [41].

4.7 Theoretical Contributions

From a scholarly standpoint, this study contributes to the sport innovation and sport management literature in three main ways. First, it empirically grounds discussions of AI in the NCAA context by providing systematic evidence of how a large and diverse group of stakeholders understand AI's benefits and risks. Second, it highlights the tension between innovation and equity, showing that stakeholders simultaneously view AI as a critical tool for performance optimization and as a potential driver of inequality and ethical concern. Third, it underscores the importance of governance and human-centered design in sport innovation, reinforcing that technological advancement, without appropriate structures, may conflict with collegiate sport's educational and developmental missions.

4.8 Limitations and Directions for Future Research

This study is not without limitations. It relies on self-reported perceptions collected via an online survey panel, which may introduce selection and response biases. The cross-sectional design also precludes any causal inferences about how AI familiarity shapes beliefs about benefits, regulation, or inequality. Additionally, while the sample was diverse across divisions and roles, the study did not formally test between-group differences (e.g., by division, role, or resource level).

Because most variables in this study were assessed using single-item measures, it was not possible to evaluate psychometric properties typically examined with multi-item scales, such as internal consistency reliability. Also, future research should build on this descriptive baseline by incorporating inferential analyses and longitudinal designs, examining how AI familiarity varies across NCAA divisions, how different stakeholder roles prioritize AI benefits, and whether familiarity predicts heightened concern about inequality and ethical risks. Such work could deepen our understanding of how AI diffuses within the NCAA ecosystem, who benefits most, and under what conditions AI supports—not undermines—the values that collegiate sport aspires to uphold.

4.9 Opportunity for Future Research

The findings of this study reveal several promising avenues for future scholarly inquiry into the role of artificial intelligence within NCAA athletics. As AI adoption accelerates across collegiate sports, deeper empirical analyses will be essential for understanding how familiarity, stakeholder roles, and institutional characteristics shape attitudes toward AI technology. Based on the present dataset and emergent trends, at least three specific research opportunities warrant further investigation:

Comparative Analysis of AI Familiarity across NCAA Divisions. Future research should examine whether AI familiarity varies meaningfully across NCAA competitive divisions. A theoretically grounded expectation is that Division I stakeholders may report higher AI familiarity than their counterparts in Divisions II, III, or NAIA, due to greater resource availability, budget capacity, and access to advanced technological tools. Inferential tests—such as ANOVA—could determine whether significant between-division differences exist, shedding light on how competitive level influences technological literacy and readiness for AI adoption. This line of inquiry may also reveal structural disparities that influence how AI diffuses across collegiate sport ecosystems.

Role-Based Differences in Perceived AI Benefits. Another promising direction involves investigating whether stakeholder role predicts the types of AI benefits valued most within NCAA settings. Because coaches, athletes, athletic trainers, analysts, and administrators engage with sport operations in different ways, their strategic interests and technological priorities are likely to differ. For example, coaches may place higher value on AI for scouting, recruitment, and player development, whereas sports analysts may prioritize game preparation, predictive modeling, and performance analytics. Role-based multivariate analyses could reveal meaningful patterns of preferential AI applications. Understanding such variations could help athletic departments tailor AI tools to stakeholder needs and optimize adoption across functional areas.

Predictive Link Between AI Familiarity and Perceived Inequality. The current findings indicate substantial concern that AI may widen competitive disparities between resource-rich and resource-limited institutions. Future research should empirically test whether AI familiarity predicts heightened perceptions of inequality. That is, do individuals with greater AI experience or expertise express stronger worries that AI could amplify existing gaps in financial resources, competitive performance, or operational capacities across NCAA institutions? A simple regression or path model could help determine whether familiarity drives concerns—or whether unfamiliarity and uncertainty amplify fear of negative outcomes. Exploring this relationship would contribute to theory on technological inequality, innovation diffusion, and resource-based competitive advantage in collegiate athletics.

References

1. Alamar, B.C.: Sports Analytics: A Guide for Coaches, Managers, and Other Decision Makers. Columbia University Press (2013)
2. Barron, D., Ball, G., Robins, T.: Artificial intelligence applications in sport performance analysis: a review. J. Sports Sci. **38**(14), 1583–1590 (2020). https://doi.org/10.1080/02640414.2020.1744818
3. Bishop, D.: An applied research model for the sport sciences. Sports Med. **38**(3), 253–263 (2008)
4. Breslin, G., Shannon, S., Fitzpatrick, B., Hanna, D.: Artificial intelligence and digital mental health tools for athletes: opportunities and limitations. Int. J. Sport Exerc. Psychol. **20**(4), 1012–1028 (2022)
5. Brown, M.: What are actual ways an athletic department could be using AI? Extra Points (2023). https://www.extrapointsmb.com/p/actual-ways-athletic-department-using-ai
6. Bunker, R., Thabtah, F.: A machine learning framework for sport result prediction. Appl. Comput. Informatics. **15**(1), 27–33 (2019)
7. Carter, E., Morgan, K.: Machine learning and data analytics in modern sport organizations: enhancing performance and decision-making. Sport Manage. Rev. **25**(3), 356–370 (2022)
8. Castelo, N., Bos, M.W., Lehmann, D.R.: Task-dependent algorithm aversion. J. Mark. Res. **56**(5), 809–825 (2019)
9. Sports, C.: The impact of wearable technology on athlete monitoring. Catapult Sports White Pap. (2022). https://www.catapultsports.com
10. Collins, D., Collins, R., Carson, H.J.: Appreciating the complexity of talent development. Sports Med. **46**(7), 935–948 (2016)

11. Cooper, C.G., Weight, D.F.: A model for institutional governance in sport organizations. J. Issues Intercollegiate Athletics. **4**, 1–24 (2011)
12. Daugherty, P.R., Wilson, H.J.: Human + Machine: Reimagining Work in the Age of AI. Harvard Business Review Press (2018)
13. Davenport, T.H.: The AI Advantage: how to Put the Artificial Intelligence Revolution to Work. MIT Press (2018)
14. Davenport, T.H.: Big data at work. Harvard Business Review Press (2014)
15. Davenport, T.H., Mittal, N.: All-in on AI: how Smart Companies Win Big with Artificial Intelligence. Harvard Business Review Press (2022)
16. Deloitte: 2023 Deloitte Sports Industry Outlook. Deloitte Insights (2023) https://www2.deloitte.com
17. DeSchriver, T.D., Jensen, T.D.: The role of conferences in shaping NCAA competitive and commercial policy. J. Intercollegiate Sport. **11**(1), 1–22 (2018)
18. Drust, B., Green, M.: Science and football: evaluating the influence of science on performance. J. Sports Sci. **31**(13), 1377–1382 (2013). https://doi.org/10.1080/02640414.2013.820471
19. Filo, K., Lock, D., Karg, A.: Sport and social media research: a review. Sport Manage. Rev. **18**(2), 166–181 (2015). https://doi.org/10.1016/j.smr.2014.11.001
20. Funk, D.C., Pizzo, A.D., Baker, B.: Sport consumer behavior and technology adoption: emerging trends in AI-driven sport engagement. J. Glob. Sport Manag. **6**(3), 245–263 (2021)
21. Halson, S.L.: Monitoring training load to understand fatigue in athletes. Sports Med. **44**(S2), 139–147 (2014). https://doi.org/10.1007/s40279-014-0253-z
22. Hextrum, K.: Special Admission: how College Sports Recruitment Favors White Suburban Athletes. Rutgers University Press (2021)
23. Hoeber, L., Hoeber, O.: Advancements in technology and innovation in sport organizations: a review and future directions. Int. J. Sport Manag. Mark. **11**(3–4), 198–220 (2012). https://doi.org/10.1504/IJSMM.2012.048746
24. Hudl: AI-Enhanced Video Breakdown for Team Performance. Hudl Innovation Report (2022). https://www.hudl.com
25. Corp, I.B.M.: IBM SPSS Statistics for Windows (Version 29.0). [Computer software]. IBM Corp (2022)
26. Impellizzeri, F.M., Agosti, F., Marcora, S.M.: Training load and its role in injury prevention. J. Sports Sci. **37**(3), 1–11 (2019). https://doi.org/10.1080/02640414.2018.1528739
27. Jenkins, S.: University of Florida to strengthen its sports program through AI-powered athletics. University of Florida College of Engineering. (2024). https://www.eng.ufl.edu
28. Katz, M., Schaefer, A.: The shifting landscape of NCAA regulation: implications for institutional compliance. Sport Manage. Rev. **25**(4), 567–580 (2022)
29. Künzell, S., Krüger, A.: Performance analysis and optimization in elite sports: current state and future directions. Int. J. Sports Sci. Coaching. **14**(1), 1–10 (2019)
30. Li, X., Chen, S., Hou, J.: Wearable sensors and biomechanical analytics in athletic performance evaluation: a systematic review. Sensors. **21**(12), 4037 (2021). https://doi.org/10.3390/s21124037
31. Li, X., Zhao, K., Xu, Y.: Deep learning in sports analytics: a survey. IEEE Trans. Knowl. Data Eng. (2021)
32. Liu, T., Liu, H., Gómez, M.A.: Data-driven sports scouting: a systematic review. Int. J. Perform. Anal. Sport. **20**(6), 770–793 (2020)
33. Longo, L.: Human-AI teaming and cognitive support. AI Soc. **37**, 1207–1220 (2022)
34. Lupo, C., Minganti, C., King, N., Cortis, C., Capranica, L.: Machine learning approaches in performance analysis and talent identification in sport: a systematic review. Int. J. Sports Sci. Coaching. **16**(4), 1156–1168 (2021). https://doi.org/10.1177/17479541211024145
35. Nash, C., Martindale, R., Collins, D., Martindale, A.: The development of coaching expertise. Int. Sport Coaching J. **6**(1), 43–52 (2019)

36. NCAA: NCAA launches initiative to study and understand online abuse in college sports. NCAA Press Release. (2023). https://www.ncaa.org
37. NCAA: 2024–2025 NCAA Division I Manual. National Collegiate Athletic Association (2024)
38. NCAA Sport Science Institute: Best practices and guidelines for wearable technologies in collegiate athletics. National Collegiate Athletic Association (2019)
39. Parasuraman, R., Manzey, D.H.: Complacency and bias in human use of automation: an attentional integration. Hum. Factors. **52**(3), 381–410 (2010). https://doi.org/10.1177/0018720810376055
40. Peer, E., Rothschild, D., Gordon, A., Evernden, Z., Damer, E.: Data quality of platforms and panels for online behavioral research. Behav. Res. Methods. **53**(5), 1951–1968 (2021). https://doi.org/10.3758/s13428-021-01694-3
41. Pitts, B.G., Zhang, J.: Sport management in the age of artificial intelligence: opportunities and challenges. Sport Manage. Rev. **25**(4), 543–559 (2022)
42. Popp, N., McEvoy, C., Morse, A.: Resource sharing and collaborative strategies among collegiate sport organizations. J. Appl. Sport Manage. **10**(1), 45–60 (2018)
43. Pradhan, A., Erwin, A., Lee, J., Perry, M.: Ethical considerations for artificial intelligence in sports science and athlete monitoring. Sports Technol. **16**(1), 45–59 (2023)
44. Pradhan, A., Saha, S., O'Reilly, N.: Artificial intelligence and fan engagement: implications for sport marketing. Int. J. Sports Mark. Spons. **24**(2), 377–395 (2023)
45. Prolific: Prolific participant recruitment and data quality guidelines (2024).https://www.prolific.co
46. Provost, F., Fawcett, T.: Data Science for Business: What you Need to Know about Data Mining and Data-Analytic Thinking. O'Reilly Media (2013)
47. Qualtrics.: Qualtrics XM Platform. Qualtrics International Inc. (2024). https://www.qualtrics.com
48. Raab, M., Lobinger, B., Hoffmann, S.O., Pizzera, A., Laborde, S.: Performance Science: Understanding the Human Factors behind Peak Performance. Oxford University Press (2015)
49. Rai, A.: Explainable AI: from black box to glass box. J. Acad. Mark. Sci. **48**(1), 137–141 (2020)
50. Ratten, V.: Sport innovation management: developing AI-driven strategies in sport organizations. J. Bus. Res. **121**, 569–576 (2020)
51. Ruddy, J.D., Opar, D.A., Timmins, R.G., Maniar, N.: Big data and machine learning applications in elite sport: a systematic review. Sports Med. **52**(1), 1–18 (2022). https://doi.org/10.1007/s40279-021-01568-7
52. Sanderson, J., Weathers, M.R.: Governing the athlete body: wearable technologies, data collection, and athlete privacy in elite sport. Commun. Sport. **8**(1), 26–52 (2020)
53. Smith, J.T.: AI applications in sport marketing and fan analytics. Sport Mark. Q. **31**(1), 43–55 (2022)
54. Sports Business Journal: WMT's The Six uses AI to automate game recaps for college sports. Sports Business Journal (2023). https://www.sportsbusinessjournal.com
55. Southeastern Conference (SEC): SEC Football Operations Manual. Southeastern Conference (2023)
56. Stats Perform: AI-powered player evaluation and recruitment analytics (2023).https://www.statsperform.com
57. Staurowsky, E.J., Sack, A.L.: Reconsidering the student-athlete: navigating academic and commercial obligations in college sport. J. Sport Manag. **19**(4), 380–398 (2005)
58. Torres-Ronda, L., Schelling, X.: Data-driven performance and health monitoring in team sports: challenges and opportunities. Strength Conditioning J. **43**(1), 33–48 (2021)

59. Wang, Y., Kung, L.A., Byrd, T.A.: Big data analytics: understanding its capabilities and potential benefits for healthcare organizations. Technol. Forecast. Soc. Chang. **126**, 3–13 (2018). https://doi.org/10.1016/j.techfore.2015.12.019
60. Weight, D.F., Harry, M., Huml, M.R.: Navigating organizational change in intercollegiate athletics. J. Issues Intercollegiate Athletics. **13**, 1–25 (2020)
61. Weight, D.F., Huml, M.R.: Education through athletics: how does the delivery of the NCAA mission influence student-athlete Well-being? J. Intercollegiate Sport. **9**(3), 352–378 (2016). https://doi.org/10.1123/jis.2016-0028
62. Weiss, E., Ray, M.: Artificial intelligence for injury prediction and performance optimization in collegiate athletics. J. Athl. Train. **58**(5), 421–430 (2023)
63. Williams, A.M., Hodges, N.J.: Skill Acquisition in Sport: Research, Theory and Practice. Routledge (2020)

Decoding Defensive Coverage Responsibilities in American Football Using Factorized Attention-Based Transformer Models

Kevin Song[1(✉)], Evan Diewald[1], Ornob Siddiquee[1], Chris Boomhower[1], Keegan Abdoo[2(✉)], Mike Band[2], and Amy Lee[2]

[1] Amazon Web Services, Seattle, WA, USA
kcsong@amazon.com
[2] National Football League, New York, NY, USA

Abstract. Defensive coverage schemes in the National Football League (NFL) represent complex tactical patterns requiring coordinated assignments among defenders who must react dynamically to the offense's passing concept. This paper presents a factorized attention-based transformer model applied to NFL multi-agent play tracking data to predict individual coverage assignments, receiver-defender matchups, and the targeted defender on every pass play. Unlike previous approaches that focus on post-hoc coverage classification at the team level, our model enables predictive modeling of individual player assignments and matchup dynamics throughout the play. The factorized attention mechanism separates temporal and agent dimensions, allowing independent modeling of player movement patterns and inter-player relationships. Trained on randomly truncated trajectories, the model generates frame-by-frame predictions that capture how defensive responsibilities evolve from pre-snap through pass arrival. Our models achieve approximately 89%+ accuracy for all tasks, with true accuracy potentially higher given annotation ambiguity in the ground truth labels. These outputs also enable novel derivative metrics, including disguise rate and double coverage rate, which enable enhanced storytelling in TV broadcasts as well as provide actionable insights for team strategy development and player evaluation.

Keywords: Football · Transformer · Multi-agent Trajectory · Factorized Attention

1 Introduction

Defensive coverage schemes in the National Football League (NFL) represent some of the most complex tactical patterns in modern team sports, involving coordinated assignments among as many as eight defensive players who must react dynamically to offensive formations and play development while maintaining specific coverage responsibilities [8,12,14]. The ability to automatically

Z. Liu and V. Misra (Eds.): ISACE 2026, LNCS 16610, pp. 170–187, 2026.
https://doi.org/10.1007/978-3-032-27272-0_12

predict individual coverage assignments, identify target defenders, and forecast receiver-defender matchups has profound implications for tactical analysis, player evaluation, and strategic decision-making. However, modeling defensive strategies is challenging, and previously, it was found that defensive backs are the most challenging position to model trajectories, noting their complex trajectory patterns involving long-distance travel and frequent direction changes based on ball perception and receiver movement [6,10].

Despite significant advances in sports analytics, current approaches to defensive coverage analysis face fundamental limitations. Previously, a CNN-LSTM model was introduced to predict coverage classification system at the play level, reaching 88.9% accuracy across eight coverage types. However, this system focuses primarily on post-hoc coverage classification rather than predictive modeling of individual player assignments and matchup dynamics. Recent advances in multi-agent trajectory modeling have demonstrated the potential for sophisticated defensive analysis. The scene transformer architecture introduced unified approaches for multi-agent trajectory prediction using factorized attention mechanisms while AutoBots achieved state-of-the-art performance on multi-agent prediction tasks through interleaved temporal and social attention mechanisms [9,11]. These architectures demonstrate strength in handling variable numbers of agents and complex interaction patterns, making them well-suited for NFL applications where player formations and tactical schemes vary dynamically. In addition, in other sports such as basketball, factorized attention architecture was applied to basketball plays to identify offensive plays [13].

Here, in this paper, we apply factorized attention transformer models on NFL multi-agent play tracking data to predict individual coverage assignments, receiver-defender matchups, and target defenders, and demonstrate the effectiveness and applicability of these models. We also demonstrate how these models together can provide additional derivative metrics, such as disguise rate and double coverage, that elucidate the effectiveness of defensive backs in American football.

2 Related Work

2.1 Football Coverage Scheme Classification

This effort builds on earlier collaborative work between the NFL Next Gen Stats (NGS) team and the Amazon ML Solutions Lab to classify NFL defensive schemes at the team coverage level (e.g. Cover 1, Cover 3) [12]. Their ensemble CNN-attention model achieved 88.9% accuracy across eight coverage types using frame-level tracking data, with temporal dynamics via self-attention being critical for capturing complex player interactions as plays unfold.

2.2 Architectures for Modeling Spatio-Temporal Sequences

Spatio-temporal predictive models are widely used across robotics [10], traffic flow [7], video analytics [4], and sports [5] to model causal relationships between multiple agents over time. The HoopTransformer architecture [13] demonstrated effective factorized attention for NBA play classification by applying attention along the agent axis at each timestep, then along the time axis for each agent independently. This factorized approach efficiently aggregates spatio-temporal relationships in multi-agent scenarios, making it well-suited for NFL applications.

3 Methodology

3.1 Model Architecture

Our model architecture implements a factorized attention mechanism that is well suited for multi-agent trajectory data. Unlike traditional transformer attention mechanisms that apply full spatio-temporal attention, this architecture separates attention across temporal and agent dimensions for improved understanding of multi-agent relationships in both dimensions [13].

In addition to the attention-based encoding of player trajectories, our models also incorporate categorical metadata like player positions and a binary indicator of team (offense or defense) via learnable embeddings. These static features are fused with the outputs of the transformer to produce latent vectors corresponding to each player, which are then fed into a final classification head for the appropriate task. For coverage assignment specifically, additional situational features are added, such as down, distance, yard line, time left in the game, and importantly, the overall team coverage scheme. During training, the ground truth team coverage scheme label is provided directly as an input feature. At inference time, a separate model [12] predicts the team coverage scheme, and this prediction is used as the input feature in place of the ground truth label. These features are then broadcast into the latent player representations described above.

While each task shares this common model backbone, there are subtle nuances specific to each objective. The main differences are in the nature of the output classification which are highlighted in Fig. 1B. At a high level, all prediction heads apply a temporal pooling layer to get an average representation of each player at the play level. These player features are then extracted and fed to a feed-forward neural network (FFN) for final predictions.

For the coverage assignment task, only defensive player features are extracted and each feature set is fed to the coverage assignment FFN with an output shape of [num_defenders, 20], where there are 20 different types of coverage assignments, including "no assignments" for pass rushers. For target defenders, only defensive player features are extracted, and the output of shape [num_defenders + targeted_receiver] contains probabilities for each defender being the primary target on a given play. For receiver-defender matchups, the features from eligible receivers and defenders are extracted, and we create a pairwise feature concatenation of all possible receiver-defender matchups. Then, the concatenated pairwise features are fed to a FFN and the output shape is [num_defenders, num_receivers + 1], corresponding to the probability that each defender is matched up to each receiver, including a class for "no matchup".

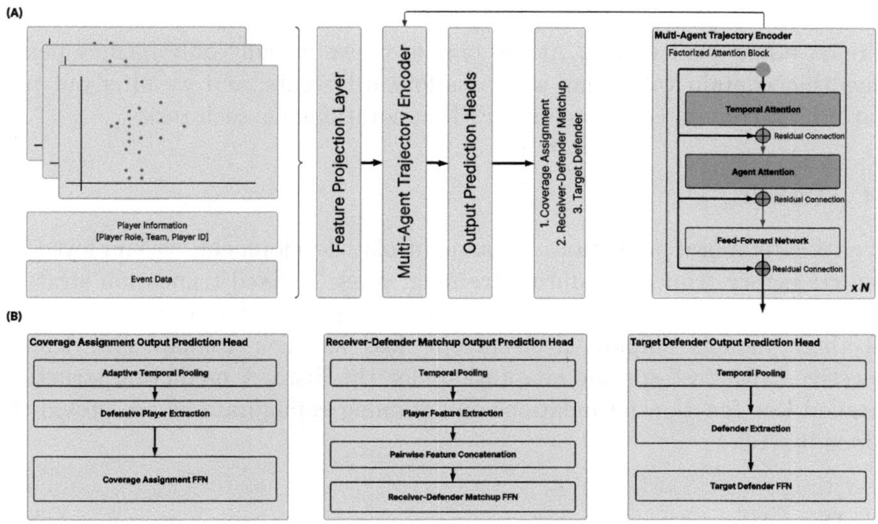

Fig. 1. Model architecture of the three coverage responsibility models. (A) General architecture that's shared amongst the 3 models (B) Different output heads for each model.

3.2 Data Overview

For all tasks, the NFL NGS data from seasons 2020 through 2024 were used, where seasons 2020–2023 were used for training and season 2024 data was used for testing. Broadly speaking, there are 5 data sources: tracking, play events, participation, Pro Football Focus (PFF) ground truth labels, and play data. The tracking data contains player and ball x,y coordinates within the field at 10 Hz sample rate. Events data contains game event markers such as snap, pass forward, and pass arrival, which are used to identify key events in a play. Participation data contains player roster information. PFF labels contain coverage responsibility ground truth annotation that includes individual coverage assignment, defender-receiver matchups, and target defender. The play data contains metadata such as play direction and field position.

3.3 Data Processing

The NGS dataset is processed into structured sequences suitable for transformer-based machine learning models by integrating data sources above and applying filtering to train the transformer model. First, we frames at 10 Hz to pass forward frame, where frame 0 indicates the snap frame. After we extract the play sequence, we apply directional normalization, where all plays are normalized to run left-to-right regardless of the original play direction. In addition to tracking x and y coordinates, the NGS data also traces player orientation and movement direction. So, after normalizing overall play direction, we apply the same angular transformation on player orientation and movement direction vectors to ensure

$0°$ represents rightward play movement. Then, we apply a series of filtering logic to remove low quality data. At the play level, we initially only include passing plays that contain valid snap and pass forward events, and we filter out plays that do not contain corresponding PFF annotations for each task.

3.4 Training

To enable temporal predictions throughout play development, we employed random trajectory truncation during training, using 11 fixed truncation strategies combined with random truncation as discussed in more detail in Appendix A.1. All three models employ cross-entropy loss as their fundamental training objective, with task-specific adaptations for the distinct prediction structures. Detailed loss function formulations and training configurations are provided in Appendix A.2.

4 Results

Four seasons from 2020 to 2023 were used for training, and season 2024 was used as the final test set. The ground truth labels for target defender, receiver-defender matchups, and coverage assignment were annotated at the play-level by human labelers, meaning each play received a single set of labels typically reflecting the state at the end of the play. This labeling approach, while practical for large-scale annotation, does not fully capture the dynamic nature of defensive coverage as it evolves throughout a play. For example, defenders may switch assignments, hand off receivers, or rotate into different zones as the play develops. However, because our model was trained on randomly truncated trajectories as described in Sect. 3.4 and Appendix A.1, the model learned to generalize and predict purely on trajectory and spatial patterns. The model is capable of generating predictions at a frame-by-frame level, producing coverage assignment, matchup, and target defender outputs at any point during the play's development. This temporal prediction capability allows us to evaluate model performance across different time points throughout the play, comparing predictions made with varying amounts of trajectory context—from pre-snap alignments through post-snap development to pass arrival. We leverage this capability in the following subsections by systematically evaluating each model across 11 distinct trajectory truncation strategies.

4.1 Receiver-Defender Matchups

To evaluate temporal robustness and real-time deployment feasibility, we implemented an evaluation framework that assesses model performance across 11 distinct trajectory truncation strategies. Each strategy defines a temporal window by combining a start boundary with an end boundary. Start boundaries include 30, 20, or 10 frames before the snap, as well as the snap itself. End boundaries include the snap, pass forward, or pass arrival events. For example, one strategy

Table 1. Receiver-defender matchup accuracy across different time frames.

Time frame	Accuracy	F1
–30 to pass arrival	0.894	0.894
–20 to pass arrival	0.894	0.894
–10 to pass arrival	0.894	0.894
Snap to pass arrival	0.893	0.893
–20 to pass forward	0.873	0.872
–10 to pass forward	0.873	0.872
Snap to pass forward	0.872	0.871
–30 to pass forward	0.872	0.871
–20 to snap	0.752	0.746
–30 to snap	0.751	0.746
–10 to snap	0.750	0.745

uses frames from 30 frames pre-snap through pass arrival, while another uses only the snap frame through pass forward. This systematic approach allows us to assess how prediction accuracy varies with the amount of available trajectory context. Accuracy is computed per-defender, where a prediction is counted as correct if the receiver assigned to a given defender matches the ground truth label for that defender.

As shown in Table 1, the model achieves up to 89.4% accuracy in predicting the correct receiver-defender matchups when using trajectory data through pass arrival. Importantly, this accuracy likely underestimates the model's true performance because the ground truth labels were assigned at the play level, reflecting a single snapshot of matchup assignments typically captured at the end of the play. On plays where matchups shift mid-play due to coverage rotations, route exchanges, or zone handoffs, the model may produce predictions that are correct for a given moment in the play but differ from the end-of-play label. In general, accuracy improves as more temporal context is provided: pre-snap trajectory data alone yields approximately 75% accuracy, while including post-snap trajectories raises performance to 87%+ across all configurations. This gap reflects the natural evolution of matchup assignments after the snap, and further reinforces that the model is effectively learning to track how coverage responsibilities develop in real time.

4.2 Coverage Assignments

The coverage assignment model employs the same 11 trajectory truncation strategies described in Appendix A.1 to evaluate temporal robustness. The key differentiator in performance is whether the model has access to post-snap data. As shown in Table 2, all truncation strategies that include post-snap trajectories, ending at either pass forward or pass arrival, achieve approximately 92% accuracy on coverage defenders. In contrast, strategies limited to pre-snap data yield approximately 88% accuracy, a roughly 4-percentage-point gap. It is notable that the model can detect substantial signal from pre-snap alignments alone, and the performance gap between pre- and post-snap predictions may reflect deliberate deception by the defense, a topic we explore further in the Discussion section.

Table 2. Individual coverage assignment accuracy across different time frames.

Time frame	Accuracy	F1
–30 to pass arrival	0.918	0.879
–20 to pass arrival	0.918	0.879
–10 to pass arrival	0.918	0.878
–10 to pass forward	0.919	0.879
–20 to pass forward	0.918	0.878
–30 to pass forward	0.918	0.878
Snap to pass forward	0.917	0.877
Snap to pass arrival	0.917	0.877
–30 to snap	0.883	0.827
–20 to snap	0.883	0.827
–10 to snap	0.882	0.825

4.3 Target Defender

Unlike receiver-defender matchups and coverage assignments where there was no previous classification mechanism, the NFL NGS team was previously using a rule-based approach to determine target defenders. This metric leveraged the nearest defender to the targeted receiver at pass arrival. This metric provides a benchmark for comparison.

Another key difference is the application of rule-based logic that considers the situation surrounding the play, applied to augment predictions when probabilities are below 50%. This post-processing step increases the accuracy of predictions by assigning a "no target defender" label when the defense is in a preventative alignment or when receptions occur behind the line of scrimmage. In other low-confidence cases, it defaults to the receiver-defender matchup model's assignment for targeted receiver classification. Target defender accuracy is calculated via the ratio between the number of plays with a correctly classified target defender over the total number of plays in the holdout season (Table 3).

Overall, the model with post-processing rules achieves an 88.2% accuracy in predicting the true target defender at the play-level. This deployed target defender classification process achieves about 12% points of lift over the previous nearest defender approach.

Table 3. Target defender classification accuracy against rule-based method and with and without post-processing rules.

Implementation	Accuracy
Rules-Based Nearest Defender	0.764
Transformer	0.862
Transformer + Post-Processing Rules	0.882

5 Discussion

5.1 Receiver-Defender Matchups

The receiver-defender matchup model demonstrates robust performance across different temporal contexts, achieving up to 89.4% accuracy when using trajectory data from pre-snap through pass arrival. Previously, receiver-defender matchups were approximated by simply determining who lined up against who at the snap [3]. This ignored key dynamics of what happened after the snap, especially when the defense played zone coverage. In comparison to this previous distance-based algorithm, which was unable to capture the nuanced dynamics of coverage matchups throughout play development, the new model represents a significant improvement. Unlike simple proximity-based heuristics, the factorized attention-based transformer models utilize player trajectories and spatial information to best predict the corresponding matchups, which allows tracking of how matchup assignments evolve as players' routes develop.

In addition, a key strength of the transformer-based approach is its temporal robustness. The model maintains approximately 75% accuracy using only pre-snap data (from -30, -20, or -10 frames to snap), which provides valuable insights into defensive pre-snap alignment and initial coverage intentions. Performance improves substantially to 87–89% when post-snap trajectory data is included, reflecting the model's ability to confirm matchup assignments as the play unfolds.

Figure 2 illustrates how matchup predictions evolve throughout the play. At pre-snap (Fig. 2A) and at full play (Fig. 2C), the model incorrectly predicts 2 out of 5 matchup assignments. However, at mid-play (Fig. 2B), the model achieves perfect accuracy, correctly identifying all 5 matchups. This temporal variation is particularly evident in the TE-CB matchup shown at the bottom of Figs. 2A and 2B. Initially, the cornerback appears to be covering the tight end, but as the play develops, the tight end cuts inside while the cornerback transitions to zone coverage. The ground truth annotations were likely labeled based on mid-play context, which explains why the model's full-play predictions appear reasonable despite conflicting with the ground truth label.

This discrepancy highlights a key advantage of the model: it adapts its predictions dynamically based on available context, whereas human annotators were constrained to provide a single label per play. The model's capacity for generating temporal predictions throughout play development reveals valuable tactical insights, such as identifying when defenders execute coverage handoffs mid-

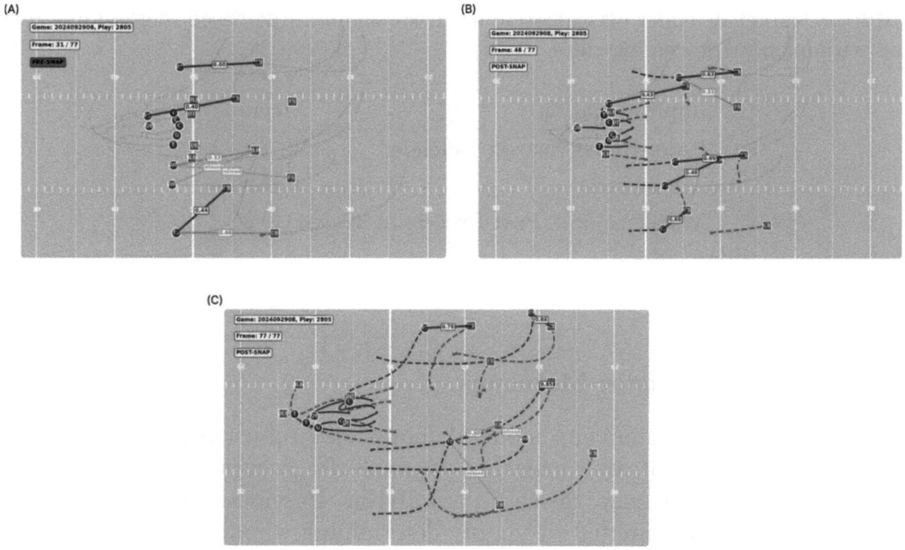

Fig. 2. Receiver-defender matchup results over time. Receiver-defender matchup predictions at (A) pre-snap, (B) mid-play, and (C) pass arrival.

play. Training the model on randomly truncated plays enabled it to learn robust spatio-temporal pattern recognition across varying trajectory lengths, from brief pre-snap sequences to complete play development, and this allows the model to flexibly make predictions with any amount of play context.

These matchup predictions serve as a critical foundation for downstream metrics and analyses, including double coverage identification and tight coverage evaluation. By reliably attributing which defenders are responsible for covering specific receivers, we enable more sophisticated defensive performance evaluation and tactical insights.

5.2 Coverage Assignment

For the coverage assignment task, the model generates predictions for all 11 defenders on every play. On approximately 70% of 2024 plays, all coverage defenders were correctly classified at pass arrival. An additional 20% had between 1 and 3 incorrect predictions—"judgment calls" representing annotation ambiguity, quick passes where coverage cannot fully develop, or genuinely borderline situations.

Figure 3 shows an example where all defenders' assignments were correctly classified at pass arrival. This particular play is illustrative of the model's flexibility because in conventional Cover 2, the two high safeties would take the deep left and right halves, outside cornerbacks cover the flats, and slot corners cover hook/curl routes in the middle of the field. The pre-snap predictions (Fig. 3A) show that the model has internalized this concept. However, as the play unfolds,

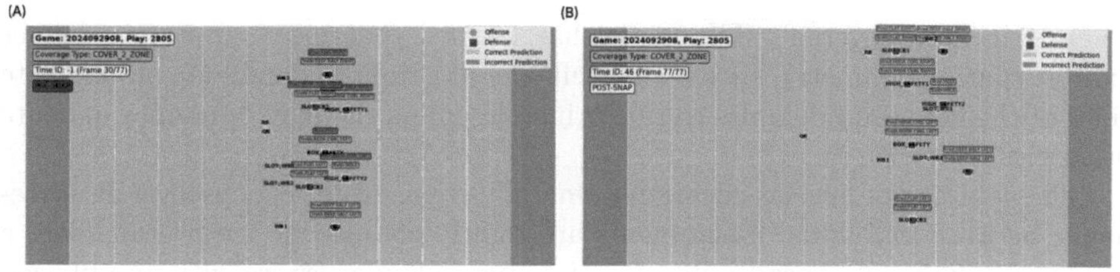

Fig. 3. Coverage assignment prediction over time. From left to right, the frames show snapshots of predictions (A) 3 s before the snap and at (B) pass arrival.

the defensive backs rotate such that the outside cornerbacks drop back to occupy the deep left and right halves, the high safeties step forward into the middle of the field, and the slot corners shift to the flats. By the time of pass arrival (Fig. 3B), the model has detected this disguise and updated its predictions accordingly. This example also presents an added benefit of classifying individual coverage responsibilities, as it captures the "Invert Cover 2" team coverage scheme. These adjustments and more specific coverage concepts are unlocked, moving into more detailed classifications of team coverage schemes beyond the general families.

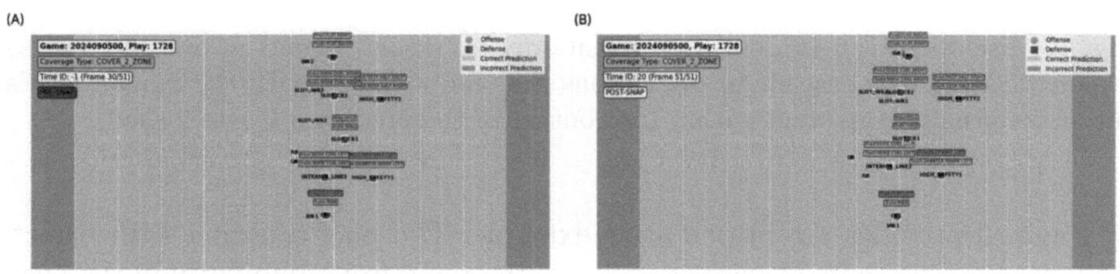

Fig. 4. Misclassified individual assignments due to potential mislabeled samples (HIGH_SAFETY1) and/or genuine ambiguity in man vs. zone assignments (CB1). (A) Coverage assignment predictions at pre-snap and (B) coverage assignments at full play both show misclassified predictions. This example shows the model's bias toward symmetry and respecting the overall coverage scheme.

The play shown in Fig. 4 contains 2 incorrect classifications. At just 2.1 s from snap to pass arrival, the compressed timeline adds inherent difficulty, yet the model still correctly identifies the overall Cover 2 shell. One of the misclassifications involves the deep safety on the left side: the model predicts a left deep half zone assignment, while the human label indicates quarters inside left. This discrepancy is likely attributable to human labeling error, as the quarters inside left label violates the charting guidelines since no teammate is assigned the outside quarters area on that side of the field. In reality, the available label set may be insufficient to describe what this safety is doing; upon review of the all-22 film, the safety appears to be "poaching" any route from the three-receiver side that crosses the field, while the cornerback to his side locks onto the isolated receiver in man coverage. The model has learned that most coverage schemes exhibit spatial symmetry, such as flat left and flat right assignments on opposite sides of the field, and defaults to this principle unless the play dynamics indicate otherwise.

The next tier of misclassifications generally stems from scheme-level disagreement: because individual assignments are tightly coupled to the overall shell, a single misalignment cascades into multiple per-defender errors with an outsized effect on accuracy. These scheme disagreements often occupy a gray area where the model's predictions are plausible, if not preferable, to the human-generated labels. The most extreme cases (3% of plays, with 6+ errors) arise from disagreements on specialized schemes such as Prevent, where the model assigns Prevent labels to all coverage defenders, concentrating misclassifications on a single play.

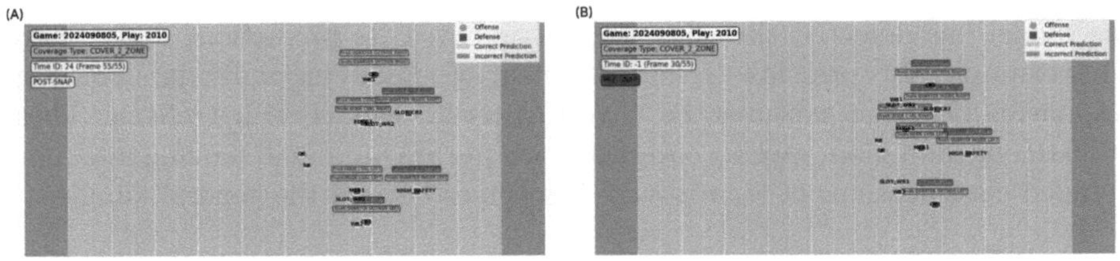

Fig. 5. Misclassified individual assignments due to disagreement on overall coverage scheme, leading to a cascade of predictions that do not align with the human labels, but are internally consistent within the context of the predicted Cover 2 shell.

Figure 5 provides a representative example. The play contains 4 "incorrect" individual assignments at pass arrival, all stemming from ambiguity in the overall coverage scheme. The human labelers classified the play as Cover 4, while the model identified it as Cover 2. This uncertainty is compounded by a quick-game passing concept in which the quarterback releases the ball within 2 s of the snap, leaving little time for the coverage to fully develop. The human labelers may have inferred deep quarters coverage based on the outside corners' initial alignment depth. In contrast, the model observes that the two deep safeties gain significantly more depth than the corners, who remain relatively stationary, suggesting flat responsibilities consistent with a Cover 2 scheme. Critically, the model's individual assignments are internally consistent with its identified scheme, demonstrating that it considers the relationships between defenders within the broader coverage context rather than classifying each defender in isolation.

Overall, the model consistently produces plausible predictions. In cases of disagreement with the ground truth labels, our inspection suggests that the discrepancy reflects either a genuine gray area in the labeling or an error in the human-generated annotations. This interpretation is supported both by anecdotal review of "incorrect" classifications and by the model's Top-2 accuracy of 97% across 20 possible assignment classes. In other words, the reported 89%+ accuracy may still understate the model's true performance, as many of the "errors" represent defensible alternative interpretations rather than genuine prediction failures.

5.3 Target Defender

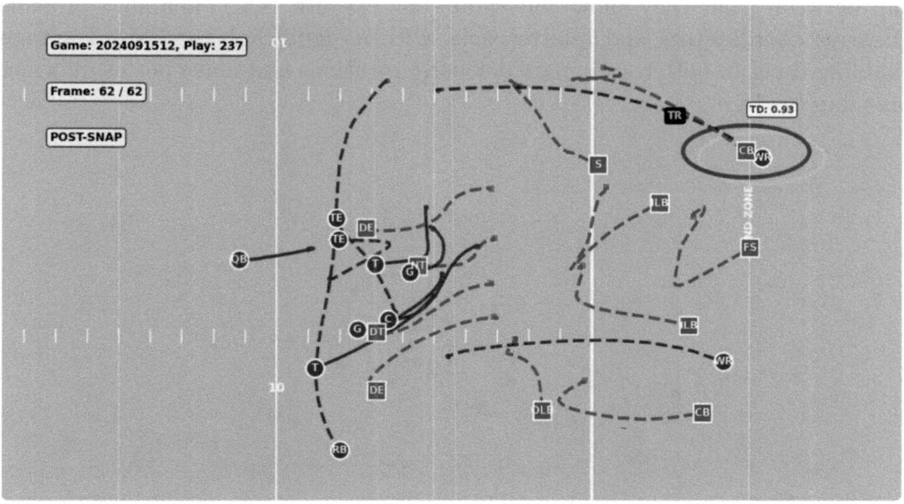

Fig. 6. Play level target defender prediction illustrated at pass forward.

The factorized attention-based transformer model demonstrates significant improvement over the previous rules-based approach for identifying the target defender, achieving 88.2% accuracy compared to 76.4% for the nearest defender heuristic. This 12-percentage-point lift represents a substantial advancement in the ability to identify which defender the quarterback is targeting across various coverage schemes, and it is driven by a key property of the factorized attention mechanism.

Most notably, the transformer architecture incorporates temporal context that the rules-based approach cannot. While the nearest defender heuristic only considers defender proximity at a single point in time, the model analyzes the full sequence of player movements leading up to the pass. As illustrated in Fig. 6, the model correctly predicts the targeted defender by integrating both trajectory dynamics and final positioning. More broadly, the model learns to detect subtle cues in defender movement patterns and receiver route concepts that signal which defender is the true target of the play.

The strong performance of the target defender model has important implications for defensive player evaluation. Accurately attributing coverage responsibility to the correct defender, rather than approximating credit based on physical proximity, is essential for fair and meaningful assessment of individual performance in coverage. This capability lays the groundwork for more reliable player grading and schematic evaluation across the league.

5.4 Disguise Rate

Predicting pre-snap coverage assignments in the NFL offers valuable insights into one of football's most critical strategic elements: defensive deception [1, 2]. By accurately identifying coverage schemes before the snap, analysts can quantify how effectively defenses disguise their true intentions, revealing the gap between what they show and what they execute. This capability provides offensive coordinators and quarterbacks with a significant tactical advantage, enabling them to better anticipate defensive rotations and make better informed pre-snap reads.

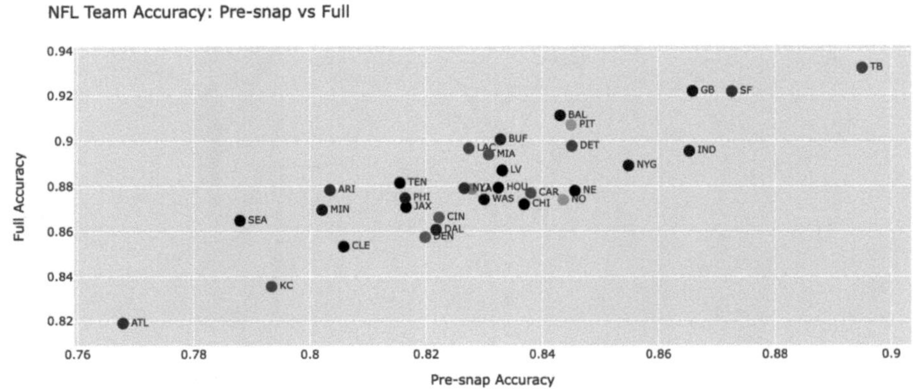

Fig. 7. Disguise rate was approximated by calculating pre-snap coverage assignment accuracy and full accuracy.

Because the coverage assignment model was trained to see a range of truncated plays, including combinations of pre- and post-snap trajectories, it can make robust predictions before the ball is snapped. The model could make an "accurate" prediction at pre-snap based on the defensive players' spatial arrangements, but the players may move into a completely different formation as soon as the ball is snapped. Accuracy at pre-snap predictions can provide a proxy for deception, as defenses attempt to disguise the coverage as the quarterback makes his initial reads. The teams that have the lowest pre-snap accuracy can be thought of as those demonstrating the most deceptive pre-snap. One notable example is the Kansas City Chiefs as shown in Fig. 7; Defensive Coordinator Steve Spagnuolo is famous for his bold stunts and exotic blitz packages. At the other end of the spectrum, Tampa Bay and San Francisco appear to show more predictable schemes. While the Tampa Bay Buccaneers Head Coach Todd Bowles is also known for his more unpredictable blitz packages, the high accuracy rate here might indicate that his coverage rotations are easily identified by the model based on his secondary's timing of their movement before the snap.

This concept of "disguise rate" and the difference between pre- and post-snap labels can unlock other advanced capabilities, like instances of inverted coverages.

5.5 Double Coverage Rate

Another example of a derivative metric that can be calculated with the three models presented here is double coverage rate. An instance of a double coverage is defined as a play where at least 2 defenders playing man coverage have a primary matchup against the same receiver. We can therefore derive these cases by combining the outputs from the Receiver-Defender Matchups and Coverage Assignment models, where we define a double coverage as greater than or equal to 2 defenders with man coverage assignments matched to a single receiver.

True double coverage is a relatively rare phenomenon reserved for specific scenarios and for dominant receivers. For example, when analyzing the human-labeled ground truth, there were only 1,179 instances of double coverage across 21,567 eligible pass plays during the 2024 season (5.5%). The objective of this analysis is to calibrate the sensitivity of the upstream models to ensure that the global population of model-defined instances of double coverage approximately matches the ground truth. We then aggregate the results at the team defense and receiver level to find Double Coverage Rates across the league.

Using the coverage assignment and defender-receiver matchup models, the number of double coverages was calculated per receiver. The results are shown in Fig. 8. The top-20 most double-covered receivers according to the model show general alignment with the human labels and generally pass the "eye test" in

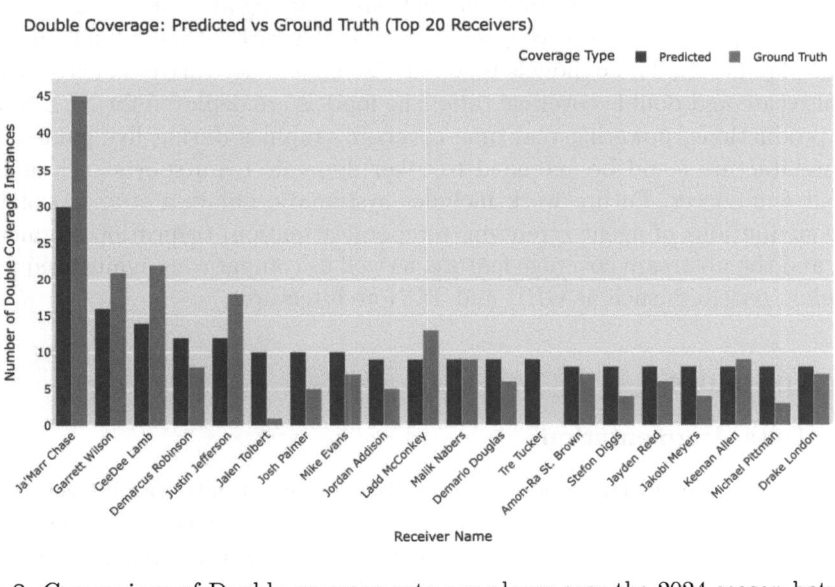

Fig. 8. Comparison of Double coverage rate per player over the 2024 season between the prediction and ground truth.

terms of the names at the top of the list. It comes as no surprise that Ja'Marr Chase, Garrett Wilson, CeeDee Lamb, and Justin Jefferson are in the top 5.

Outside of the top 5 double covered receivers, there were a few notable surprises like Jalen Tolbert and Tre Tucker. For Tre Tucker specifically, we found 9 instances of double coverage whereas the human labels identified 0. It is plausible that there is a "reputation bias" in the human labels compared to the model, where labelers are more likely to identify double coverage on well-known, dominant players like Chase, Lamb, and Jefferson. This bias may truly be more in line with what NFL defensive coordinators are game-planning for, but on the other hand, the model may be more objective in capturing the on-field realities or "leading indicators" about underrated receivers. It's also important to caveat this analysis with the reality that this is a rare phenomenon, and disagreements on a handful of "judgment call" plays can look drastic with the small sample size. For example, even Mike Evans saw only 10 double coverages over the whole season.

6 Conclusion

In this paper, we demonstrated the application and effectiveness of factorized attention-based transformers for classifying individual coverage responsibilities across three tasks: target defender identification, receiver-defender matchup prediction, and coverage assignment classification. While the models achieve approximately 89%+ accuracy, true accuracy may be higher given human labeling ambiguity, with the model's predictions consistently defensible and often preferable to human annotations in gray-area situations. A key contribution is the model's ability to generate frame-by-frame predictions, enabling analysts to observe how defensive responsibilities evolve throughout the play rather than relying on static end-of-play labels. These models together also enable derivative metrics such as disguise rate and double coverage rate. The models are deployed for NFL broadcast productions, powering real-time coverage graphics during live games, and the architecture could be extended to other dynamic team sports such as basketball and soccer. Future work includes systematic ablation studies isolating the contributions of agent attention, temporal attention, truncation augmentation, and the upstream coverage feature, as well as comparisons against sequence modeling baselines such as GRU and TCN architectures.

A Appendix

A.1 Data Augmentation

To extend the transformer model's capabilities to predict better at different times on any given play, a data augmentation with random truncation scheme was applied to help the model learn more effectively. For any given play, there are 11 fixed truncation strategies where the play can be truncated to any of the following combinations where the first item in the tuple represents the start frame, and the second item in the tuple represents the end frame. The following combinations were used: (–30, snap), (–30, pass forward), (–30, pass arrival), (–20, snap), (–20, pass forward), (–20, pass arrival), (–10, snap), (–10, pass forward), (–10, pass arrival), (0, pass forward), and (0, pass arrival), where 0 represents the snap frame and negative frame numbers denote frames prior to snap. In addition to the 11 fixed truncation strategies, a truly random truncation strategy was also added, which will truncate the start and end frames anywhere from -30 to pass arrival. With the two fixed and random truncation strategies in place during training, each play is truncated with either fixed truncation or random truncation at a 60% and 40% split, respectively.

A.2 Training Objectives and Loss Functions

All three models employ cross-entropy loss as their fundamental training objective due to their shared nature as classification tasks. Each model processes multi-agent trajectory data through factorized transformer encoders that separate temporal and spatial attention mechanisms, ultimately producing logits that are compared against ground truth labels using cross-entropy loss.

While the three models share the same fundamental loss function, the three models differ in how cross-entropy is applied due to their distinct prediction structures and task requirements. The target defender model performs single-label classification across all defenders on a play, computing cross-entropy over a categorical distribution where exactly one defender is selected as the primary target. The receiver-defender matchup model, in contrast, computes cross-entropy independently for each defender, treating each as a separate multi-class classification problem over receivers plus a "no matchup" class. The coverage assignment model extends this further by performing independent multi-class classification for each of the 11 defensive players, predicting 20 coverage responsibilities (e.g. hook curl left, deep right, etc.) with cross-entropy computed per defender and averaged across the defensive unit.

Receiver-Defender Matchups. For each defender, the model predicts which eligible receiver they are matched to in a prediction format of (batch_size, num_defenders, num_receivers + 1), where the additional dimension represents a "no matchup" class for defenders not assigned to cover any receiver. For defenders with no coverage assignments, indicated by zero-sum rows in the transposed target matrix, the "no matchup" class label is set to 1.0, while defenders with valid assignments retain their original one-hot encoded receiver assignments. Then, the loss for matchup is computed as:

$$\mathcal{L}_{\text{matchup}} = -\frac{1}{D}\sum_{d=1}^{D}\sum_{r=0}^{R} z^*_{d,r} \log\left(\frac{\exp(Z_{d,r})}{\sum_{r'=0}^{R}\exp(Z_{d,r'})}\right) \tag{1}$$

where $Z_{d,r}$ is the logit score for defender d covering receiver r, R is the number of eligible receivers, and $z^*_{d,r}$ is the ground truth receiver assignment for defender d.

Coverage Assignment. For individual coverage assignments, the training objective is to assign a single assignment for each of the 11 defenders on a given play. The prediction output shape is (batch_size, num_defenders, 20), where there are 19 total coverage assignment classes with 1 no assignment class. The goal of training is to minimize cross entropy loss for the 20 possible coverage assignments, defined as:

$$\mathcal{L}_{\text{coverage}} = -\frac{1}{D}\sum_{d=1}^{D}\sum_{c=1}^{C} \mathbb{1}[c = c^*] \log \left(\frac{\exp(z_{d,c})}{\sum_{c'=1}^{C} \exp(z_{d,c'})} \right) \tag{2}$$

where $z_{d,c}$ is the logit score for each defender having coverage assignment c, C is the number of coverage classes, and c^* is the ground truth coverage class for defender d.

Target Defender. For passing plays, the quarterback attempts to beat a defender to make a successful completion to an eligible receiver and advance offensive field position. The target defender model determines which of the 11 defenders present in each passing play is the primary defender that quarterback is looking to beat. For each play, only one defender is the true target defender.

The model outputs logits for each player with the following shape: (batch_size, num_defenders + targeted receiver). These are then masked to only consider defensive players as valid candidates by setting the offensive player's (targeted receiver) logit to a large negative value (-1e9) before the softmax operation. The training process minimizes the following cross-entropy loss function where N is the number of players, z_j is the logit for player j, and z_d refers to the logit of the ground truth primary defender:

$$\mathcal{L}_{\text{target}} = -\log \left(\frac{\exp(z_d)}{\sum_{j=1}^{N} \exp(z_j)} \right) \tag{3}$$

Table 4. Training Optimization and Hyperparameter settings

Training Task	Target Defender	Receiver-Defender Matchups	Coverage Assignments
Batch Size	16	16	16
Num Epochs	100	200	150
Learning Rate and Scheduler	OneCycleLR (max_lr = $2e^{-4}$, $total\_steps$ = $train\_len * 100$, $pct\_start = 0.1$, $div\_factor = 10.0$, $final\_div\_factor$= 100.0)	OneCycleLR (max_lr = $2e^{-4}$, $total\_steps$= $train\_len * 200$, $pct\_start = 0.1$, $div\_factor = 10.0$, $final\_div\_factor$ = 100.0)	Cosine Annealing Warm Restarts $init\_lr = 2e^{-5}$ $T_0 = 15$ $T_mult = 1$ $eta\_min = 2e^{-7}$
Optimizer	AdamW weight decay=1e-4, betas=(0.9, 0.999)	AdamW weight decay=1e-4, betas=(0.9, 0.999)	AdamW weight decay=1e-4, betas=(0.9, 0.999)
Num Heads	4	4	8
Num Layers	3	3	6
Dropout	0.1	0.2	0.1

A.3 Training Hyperparameters

Hyperparameters used for training the final models are shown in Table 4.

References

1. Exposing coverage tells in the presnap. https://kaggle.com/code/smitbajaj/exposing-coverage-tells-in-the-presnap
2. NFL big data bowl 2025. https://kaggle.com/nfl-big-data-bowl-2025
3. NFL next gen stats. https://nextgenstats.nfl.com/stats
4. Wang, Y., et al.: PredRNN: A recurrent neural network for spatiotemporal predictive learning. IEEE J. Mag. IEEE xplore. https://ieeexplore.ieee.org/document/9749915
5. Capellera, G., Ferraz, L., Rubio, A., Agudo, A., Moreno-Noguer, F.: Footbots: a transformer-based architecture for motion prediction in soccer. In: 2024 IEEE International Conference on Image Processing (ICIP), pp. 2313–2319. https://doi.org/10.1109/ICIP51287.2024.10647396, https://ieeexplore.ieee.org/document/10647396, ISSN: 2381-8549
6. Cheong, L.L., Zeng, X., Tyagi, A.: Prediction of defensive player trajectories in NFL games with defender CNN-LSTM model. https://www.amazon.science/publications/prediction-of-defensive-player-trajectories-in-nfl-games-with-defender-cnn-lstm-model
7. Deng, L., Wu, C., Lian, D., Zhou, M.: Transposed variational auto-encoder with intrinsic feature learning for traffic forecasting. https://doi.org/10.48550/arXiv.2211.00641
8. Dutta, R., Yurko, R., Ventura, S.: Unsupervised methods for identifying pass coverage among defensive backs with NFL player tracking data. https://doi.org/10.48550/arXiv.1906.11373
9. Girgis, R., et al.: Latent variable sequential set transformers for joint multi-agent motion prediction. https://doi.org/10.48550/arXiv.2104.00563
10. Lee, N., Kitani, K.M.: Predicting wide receiver trajectories in American football. In: 2016 IEEE Winter Conference on Applications of Computer Vision (WACV), pp. 1–9. https://doi.org/10.1109/WACV.2016.7477732, https://ieeexplore.ieee.org/abstract/document/7477732
11. Ngiam, J., et al.: Scene transformer: a unified architecture for predicting multiple agent trajectories. https://doi.org/10.48550/arXiv.2106.08417
12. Song, H., et al.: Explainable defense coverage classification in NFL games using deep neural networks. https://www.amazon.science/publications/explainable-defense-coverage-classification-in-nfl-games-using-deep-neural-networks
13. Wang, X., Tang, Z., Shao, J., Robertson, S., Gómez, M.Á., Zhang, S.: HoopTransformer: advancing NBA offensive play recognition with self-supervised learning from player trajectories, vol. 54(10), pp. 2663–2673. https://doi.org/10.1007/s40279-024-02030-3
14. Yurko, R., Nguyen, Q., Pelechrinis, K.: NFL ghosts: a framework for evaluating defender positioning with conditional density estimation. https://doi.org/10.48550/arXiv.2406.17220

A Bootstrap Method for Persistent Homology Analysis of NBA Lineups

Jim Wiseman(✉)

Agnes Scott College, Decatur, GA 30030, USA
jwiseman@agnesscott.edu

Abstract. We demonstrate a novel way to analyze lineup usage among sports teams, and to use bootstrap methods to validate the results. We use a weighted simplicial complex to capture information about which groups of players are in lineups together, rather than using network methods, which are restricted to pairs of players. As an example, we analyze the 2024-2025 NBA season. The results reflect different approaches to roster construction and usage. Applications include predicting improvement in team winning percentage from year to year, measuring the importance of individual players and groups of players to lineup flexibility, and the effect of a team's lineup choices on those of its opponent, as well as applications to other sports.

Keywords: Lineup analysis · Persistent homology · Bootstrap

1 Introduction

Typically, sports lineup analysis uses network methods (focusing on *pairs* of players) and fails to capture information about complete lineups and subgroups of players. (For example, basketball players A and B may be in lineups together, but only if C is also playing; or A, B, and D may never play together – some of them may be poor defenders who need a strong center behind them, or poor shooters who cannot play together because of spacing concerns.) We capture this information in a simplicial complex, a higher-dimensional analog of a network. Each element (simplex) corresponds to an individual lineup and is weighted by the number of possessions played. The topology of the simplicial complex reflects the team's lineup usage patterns.

We analyze this topology using persistent homology. Roughly, it counts the number of "holes" in each dimension of the data, and measures how long they last as we include more and more of the individual lineups. A fundamental challenge in the use of persistent homology is assessing statistical significance, i.e., separating signal from noise. We demonstrate a bootstrap method in this context, interpreting individual possessions as samples.

As a demonstration, we analyze lineup data for the 2024-25 NBA season, and obtain four-dimensional simplicial complexes. Comparing them reveals different

Z. Liu and V. Misra (Eds.): ISACE 2026, LNCS 16610, pp. 188–197, 2026.
https://doi.org/10.1007/978-3-032-27272-0_13

approaches to lineup management. As a simple, concrete example, we measure the maximum "length" of holes (as a percentage of each team's total possessions), and apply the bootstrap to get 95%-confidence intervals. In Fig. 1, we see that SAS and WAS have large values, reflecting more complicated lineup patterns. DET and NYK have values which we are confident are lower than San Antonio's and Washington's and larger than 0, but not necessarily different from each other. MIL has a nonzero length, but it is not statistically significant, since the confidence interval contains 0.

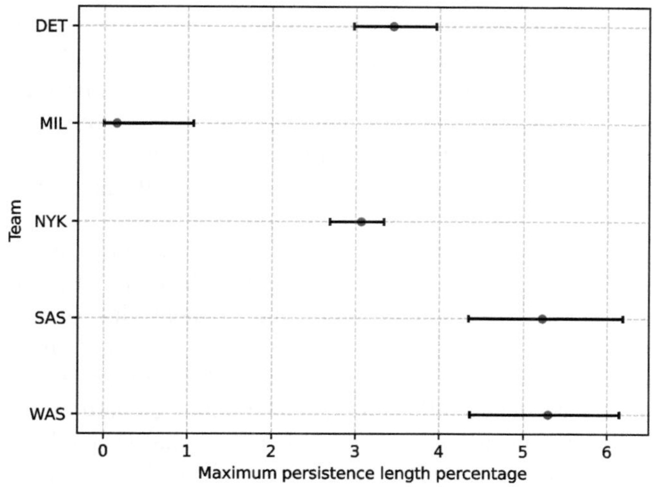

Fig. 1. Confidence intervals for maximum persistence length, selected teams.

These results reflect differences in lineup usage among the teams. For example, as shown in [24], they can detect heavy usage of starters, for the whole season or in the playoffs; the growth of young players; and improvements in team winning percentage correlated with lineup flexibility. Other potential applications include comparing teams' approaches to roster-building and substitution patterns, measuring the importance of individual players and groups of players to lineup flexibility, and the effect of a team's lineup choices on those of its opponent, as well as applications to other sports.

The paper is organized as follows. We present the background material and describe the analytical methods in Sect. 2, and discuss the results and interpretations, using the 2024-25 NBA season as an example, in Sect. 3. In Sect. 4 we discuss future work and applications of the methods. We give technical details of the methods in the appendix, Sect. 5.

2 Background and Methods

We review the application of persistent homology to team lineups from [24], then explain the bootstrap method for statistical analysis of the results.

2.1 Collaboration Simplicial Complexes and Persistent Homology

The intuition behind simplicial complexes and persistent homology is relatively clear, but the details can be somewhat technical. Here we give only the minimal level of detail necessary for our results. For more details, see, for example, [8], and for a more informal, intuitive explanation of homology, see [13].

For ease of exposition, we will use basketball terminology in our discussion, but everything applies essentially unchanged to other team sports.

Typically, mathematical analysis of team lineups uses network or graph methods. The nodes are players on a given team, and there is an edge between two players if they appeared on the court together. This approach has been very fruitful; see, as just a few examples, [1–3,5,6,11,12,15,16,18,23]. However, by focusing only on *pairs* of players, this method loses information on complete lineups, as well as trios and quartets. For example, it can reflect that players A and B played together, as well as the pair B and C and the pair A and C, but it can not show whether or not the trio A, B, and C all played together at the same time.

A simplicial complex is a generalization of networks that captures the information about which groups of players have shared the court. To make the geometry easier to visualize, let us assume for the moment that a complete lineup consists of only three players, rather than five. If players A, B, and C have been in a lineup together, then they form a simplex ABC, which we can visualize as a solid triangle with vertices A, B, and C. If B, C, and D were in another lineup, then BCD would be another simplex, and it would share the edge BC with the simplex ABC. By putting together in this way all of the simplices corresponding to lineups that a given team played, we get the team's *simplicial complex.* (This is an example of a collaboration simplicial complex; see [17,21]. Similar complexes have been used to analyze interactions in academic collaborations, scientific ideas, neural networks, actors, wireless networks, and social contagion, among others [7,14,19,20,22].)

"Holes" in the simplicial complex represent groups of players who never all played together. For example, if A and B played together, B and C played together, and A and C played together, then the triangle with edges AB, BC, CA would be in the simplicial complex. If A, B, and C all played together, then the triangle would be solid (the simplex ABC would be part of the simplicial complex.) However, if A, B, and C *did not* play together simultaneously, then the simplex would be missing and the triangle would be hollow – there would be a hole in the simplicial complex.

Similarly, imagine that lineups have four players. Then a lineup that played together would correspond geometrically to a solid tetrahedron. The faces of the tetrahedron would be solid triangles, corresponding to the three-person subgroups (trios) who of course also played together. However, if there were four players who never played together, but any three of whom played together in some lineup, then the simplicial complex would have a hollow tetrahedron, corresponding to a higher-dimensional hole.

By counting all of the holes in a team's simplicial complex, we get a measure of the complexity of the set of lineups that they use. (For example, if every possible combination of players played together at some point, then there would be no holes.) Since a basketball lineups has five players, the corresponding simplex is four-dimensional. We can no longer visualize the resulting simplicial complex, but the algebra of higher-dimensional simplicial complexes is essentially identical to that of two- and three-dimensional ones.

Homology theory is a tool from algebraic topology. For our application, we do not need to know the details, but we do need to know two important features. First, the homology of a simplicial complex essentially counts the numbers of "holes" in each dimension algebraically (although the precise meaning of what it is measuring can be quite subtle). Second, homology has algebraic properties that make it relatively easy to calculate compared to other topological invariants, and there exist efficient computational algorithms.

The last piece that we need to add to a team's simplicial complex is information about how often a given lineup (simplex) played together. The lineups that played together frequently are more important to our analysis, and that should be reflected in the simplicial complex. We do that by assigning a weight to each lineup/simplex; the weight is simply the number of possessions that the lineup played together. The result is a weighted simplicial complex.

Given the weights, we can imagine constructing the simplicial complex piece by piece. Start with the lineup/simplex with the highest weight, then add the second highest, and so on. As we lower the possessions threshold, more and more simplices are added. As this happens, holes of different dimensions may appear and disappear in the simplicial complex. For a given threshold, this is measured by the homology. If we keep track of the homology over all of the threshold levels, we get *persistent homology.* We record the evolution of the homology in a barcode, which shows when each hole is created and when it disappears.

In [24], we analyzed the persistent homology for all NBA teams over thirty seasons. This is a lot of information to keep track of. As a very simple example, we might measure the maximum persistence of any homology element for each team in a given season. Roughly, greater persistence corresponds to more complicated lineup patterns.

For example, in Fig. 2 we show the results for the 2024-25 Milwaukee Bucks and San Antonio Spurs. For the Bucks, we see a hole in dimension 2 for possession thresholds between 108 and 112. This is the only hole, so the maximum persistence length is 4. (The total number of possessions was 2625, so the maximum persistence length proportion is $\frac{4}{2625} = 0.0015$, or 0.15%.) For the Spurs, we see that holes appear simultaneously in dimensions 1 and 2 at threshold value 131 and then do not disappear, so the maximum persistence length is 131. (The Spurs had 2507 possessions, giving a maximum persistence length proportion of $\frac{131}{2507} = 0.052$, or 5.2%.)

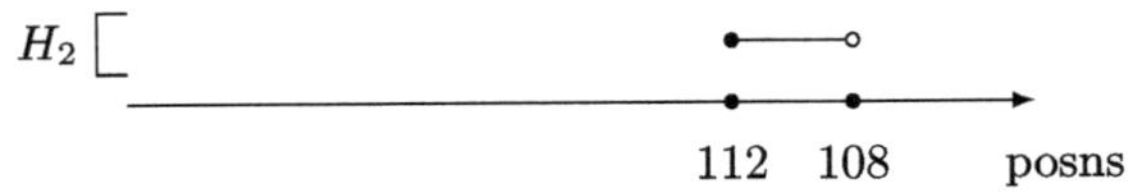

(a) Barcode for 2024-25 Milwaukee Bucks

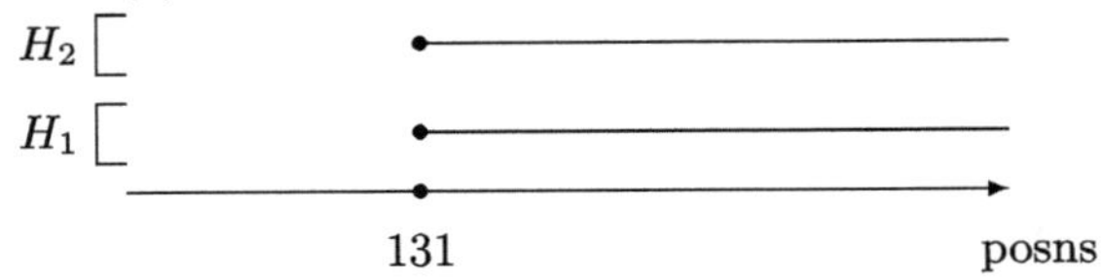

(b) Barcode for 2024-25 San Antonio Spurs

Fig. 2. Homology barcodes.

2.2 Statistical Analysis

Persistent homology is a relatively new data analysis tool that has been applied in many different areas, with a great deal of success. (See [8] for an introduction and references.) One of the central challenges is assessing the statistical significance of the results. We may find "holes" (nontrivial homology) in our data, but do they really reflect something fundamental in the population structure, or are they simply noise in the data? Statistical analysis is challenging, because in general, it is not at all clear what the underlying distributions should look like, or what hypotheses are appropriate. Bootstrapping, which generates new "samples" from the given sample, can be a useful approach (see [4,10], for example), but it is often difficult to see how it might be applied. Here, we propose a bootstrap method that fits naturally with the construction of our weighted collaboration simplicial complexes.

The method is as follows. For a given team in a given season, we start with the collection of all of their lineups. (We use a minimum threshold of 100 possessions, to avoid lineups that did not play any significant role in the season.) We construct the weighted collaboration simplicial complex and compute the maximum persistence length, measured as percentage of all of the team's possessions.

We then create a new sample (an imaginary set of lineups, including possessions played, for the season) by bootstrapping. We randomly sample, with replacement, from the original set of lineups, with probabilities given by the proportion of possessions played by each lineup. This new sample gives a new weighted simplicial complex, for which we compute the maximum persistence length.

We repeat this procedure many times (100 times per team, in this example). The middle 95% of the bootstrap maximum persistence lengths give a 95% confidence interval for the team's true persistence.

3 Results and Applications

3.1 Results

We apply the methods to lineup data for the 2024-25 NBA season, using the gudhi package to compute persistent homology. The results are shown in Fig. 3. Several features stand out.

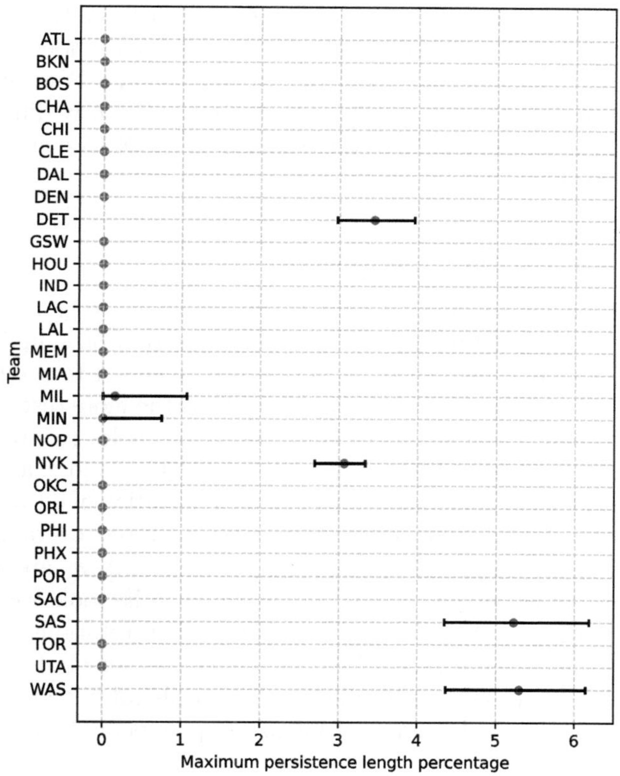

Fig. 3. Confidence intervals for maximum persistence length, all teams.

First, most of the teams have zero persistence length, and their confidence intervals consist only of the point 0. That means that their weighted simplicial complexes have no homology (holes) at any possession threshold level. That does not, of course, mean that their lineup patterns are trivial in a practical sense, or identical to each other; they simply do not have any nontrivial structure that is detectable by this method, and that would not change even if they changed their lineup usage slightly. (As discussed in [24], teams tend to have more nontrivial homology during times of transition in playing styles, either for the team itself or for the league as a whole.)

Second, although Milwaukee has nonzero persistence, it is not statistically significant, since the confidence interval contains zero. In practical terms, this means that if the team had put in different lineups for a few possessions, there might have been no holes in their lineup pattern.

Third, although Minnesota has zero persistence, the confidence interval contains nonzero lengths. Thus their lineup pattern could be perturbed into one that does demonstrate complexity in the form of nontrivial persistent homology.

Fourth, we are confident that San Antonio and Washington do have nonzero lengths, but we are not confident that the difference between them is significant. Similarly, we are confident that Detroit and New York have nonzero lengths and that those lengths are less than those of San Antonio and Washington, but we are not confident that Detroit and New York are significantly different.

We discuss the interpretation of these results in the NBA context in the next section.

3.2 Interpretation and Applications

Recall that in a lineup network, missing edges correspond to pairs of players who are never in a lineup together. In contrast, in a collaboration simplicial complex, missing simplices (as measured by homology), correspond to groups of players who are never all in a lineup at the same time. Thus the more restrictions a team puts on which players can share the court, the more holes (greater persistence length) we might expect to see. See [24] for more details and examples.

For example, Coach Tom Thibodeau had the reputation of playing his starters longer than other teams, and having more rigid rotations overall, which could result in holes in the simplicial complex. As shown in [24], we are able to detect this, in the form of increased persistence length when he took over teams.

Similarly, in the playoffs teams tend to shorten their rotations, and this shows up as increased persistence length [24]. We see similar effects for young teams, with players that might not yet be able to fill multiple roles, and teams with less three-point shooting, which might not be able to play poor shooters together for spacing reasons.

As another example, we saw in [24] that teams with nontrivial persistence tended to improve their record the following season. This could be explained by nontrivial homology resulting from a rigidity in possible lineups due to limited roles for players; as the players gain more experience and expand their roles, the team gets better and more lineups are possible.

4 Conclusion and Future Work

We have demonstrated a method for detecting statistically significant features of team lineup usage patterns. By analyzing the structure of the set of complete lineups, rather than just pairs of players, and applying an adapted bootstrap technique, we are able to compare team's lineup patterns and discern effects of rotation constraints.

These results are just a demonstration, however, and the method has the potential to be applied much more broadly. A few examples: We can identify the most important players, or groups of players, in lineup construction – not just the most individually productive, but the "glue guys" who allow other groups to play together. We can make comparisons from team-to-team (to compare different approaches to roster-building, player usage, and substitution patterns), season-to-season (to measure growth and decline of players), within a single team during a single season (to analyze the effects of injuries, load management, or player development), or within a single game (by looking at all ten players on the court, and measuring the effects of a team's lineup on its opponent's).

Finally, the method applies to other team sports besides basketball, many of which have very different patterns of lineup usage.

5 Appendix

5.1 Persistent Homology

We refer to [8] for standard definitions of simplicial complexes, homology, and persistent homology. Here we give the details of their application in our setting; see [24] for more discussion.

For a given team, denote by $\{a_k\}$ the set of players. Let $L_i = \{a_{i,1}, \ldots, a_{i,5}\}$ be a lineup. We consider only lineups that played some minimum number $n_{\min}$ of possessions. (For the examples in this paper, we take $n_{\min} = 100$.) Let n_i be the number of possessions played by lineup L_i, and set $N = \sum_{i=1}^{l} n_i$, the total number of possessions played by such lineups.

We construct the weighted abstract simplicial complex Δ by making the nodes players and each of the lineups L_i a simplex with weight n_i. For each possession threshold t, define the sub-complex Δ_t by including only the lineups with weight at or above the threshold, $n_i \geq t$.

For each t, we compute the homology (with coefficients in $\mathbb{Z}/11\mathbb{Z}$ for the examples in this paper). This gives the persistent homology of the weighted simplicial complex, which can be expressed as a barcode. We define the maximum persistence length of Δ to be the maximum length of a bar in the barcode in dimension 1 or greater. Finally, the maximum persistence length percentage is that maximum length as a percentage of the total number of possessions N.

5.2 Bootstrap

The bootstrap is a powerful general technique [9]; here we give details on our method of applying it in the setting of persistent homology of weighted collaboration simplicial complexes.

As in the previous section, for a given team, let $\{L_i\}_{i=1}^{l}$ be the set of lineups that played at least some minimum number $n_{\min}$ of possessions. Let n_i be the number of possessions played by lineup L_i, and set $N = \sum_{i=1}^{l} n_i$, the total number of possessions played by such lineups. The team's lineup data set is the collection of pairs $\mathcal{L} = \{(L_i, n_i)\}_{i=1}^{l}$.

To construct a bootstrap lineup data set $\mathcal{L}_j$, we first assign to each lineup L_i its probability $p_i = \frac{n_i}{N}$. Define a random variable X by setting $P(X = i) = p_i$, $1 \leq i \leq l$. Then let $X_1^j, \ldots, X_l^j$ be independent random variables distributed identically to X.

We define the bootstrap lineup data set $\mathcal{L}_j$ to be $\mathcal{L}_j = \{(L_{X_i^j}, n_i)\}_{i=1}^l$. To create a set of such bootstrap samples, we let j range from 1 to m, where m is the desired number of samples. (For the examples in this paper, we use $m = 100$.)

Acknowledgments. I am grateful to Thomas Wiseman for his helpful comments and ideas for this paper.

Disclosure of Interests. The author has no competing interests to declare that are relevant to the content of this article.

References

1. Ahmadalinezhad, M., Makrehchi, M.: Basketball lineup performance prediction using edge-centric multi-view network analysis. Soc. Netw. Anal. Min. **10**, 1–11 (2020)
2. Bai, Z., Bai, X.: Towards understanding the analysis, models, and future directions of sports social networks. Complexity **2022**, 5743825 (2022)
3. Brave, S.A., Butters, R.A., Roberts, K.A.: Uncovering the sources of team synergy: player complementarities in the production of wins. J. Sports Anal. **5**(4), 247–279 (2019)
4. Chazal, F., Fasy, B., Lecci, F., Rinaldo, A., Singh, A., Wasserman, L.: On the bootstrap for persistence diagrams and landscapes. Modelirovanie i Analiz Informacionnyh Sistem **20** (2013). https://doi.org/10.18255/1818-1015-2013-6-111-120
5. Clemente, F.M., Martins, F.M.L.: Who are the prominent players in the UEFA champions league? An approach based on network analysis. Walailak J. Sci. Technol. (WJST) **14**(8), 627–636 (2017)
6. Clemente, F.M., Martins, F.M.L., Mendes, R.S.: Social Network Analysis Applied to Team Sports Analysis. Springer, Cham (2016). https://doi.org/10.1007/978-3-319-25855-3
7. Ebli, S., Defferrard, M., Spreemann, G.: Simplicial neural networks. arXiv preprint arXiv:2010.03633 (2020)
8. Edelsbrunner, H., Harer, J.L.: Computational Topology: An Introduction. American Mathematical Society (2010). https://doi.org/10.1090/mbk/069
9. Efron, B.: Bootstrap methods: another look at the jackknife. Ann. Stat. **7**(1), 1–26 (1979). http://www.jstor.org/stable/2958830
10. Fasy, B., Lecci, F., Rinaldo, A., Wasserman, L., Balakrishnan, S., Singh, A.: Confidence sets for persistence diagrams. Ann. Stat. **42**, 2301–2339 (2014)
11. Fewell, J.H., Armbruster, D., Ingraham, J., Petersen, A., Waters, J.S.: Basketball teams as strategic networks. PLoS ONE **7**(11), e47445 (2012)
12. Hambrick, M.E.: Social Network Analysis in Sport Research. Cambridge Scholars Publishing (2019)
13. Houston-Edwards, K.: How mathematicians use homology to make sense of topology (2021). https://www.quantamagazine.org/how-mathematicians-use-homology-to-make-sense-of-topology-20210511/. Accessed 31 Aug 2023

14. Iacopini, I., Petri, G., Barrat, A., Latora, V.: Simplicial models of social contagion. Nat. Commun. **10**(1), 2485 (2019)
15. Korte, F., Lames, M.: Characterizing different team sports using network analysis. Curr. Issues Sport Sci. (CISS) **3**, 005 (2018)
16. Korte, F., Link, D., Groll, J., Lames, M.: Play-by-play network analysis in football. Front. Psychol. **10**, 1738 (2019)
17. Moore, T.J., Drost, R.J., Basu, P., Ramanathan, R., Swami, A.: Analyzing collaboration networks using simplicial complexes: a case study. In: 2012 Proceedings IEEE INFOCOM Workshops, pp. 238–243. IEEE (2012)
18. Mora-Cantallops, M., Sicilia, M.Á.: Team efficiency and network structure: the case of professional league of legends. Soc. Networks **58**, 105–115 (2019)
19. Pal, S., Moore, T.J., Ramanathan, R., Swami, A.: Comparative topological signatures of growing collaboration networks. In: Gonçalves, B., Menezes, R., Sinatra, R., Zlatic, V. (eds.) CompleNet 2017. SPC, pp. 201–209. Springer, Cham (2017). https://doi.org/10.1007/978-3-319-54241-6_18
20. Patania, A., Petri, G., Vaccarino, F.: The shape of collaborations. EPJ Data Sci. **6**, 1–16 (2017)
21. Ramanathan, R., et al.: Beyond graphs: capturing groups in networks. In: 2011 IEEE Conference on Computer Communications Workshops (INFOCOM WKSHPS), pp. 870–875. IEEE (2011)
22. Salnikov, V., Cassese, D., Lambiotte, R., Jones, N.S.: Co-occurrence simplicial complexes in mathematics: identifying the holes of knowledge. Appl. Network Sci. **3**, 1–23 (2018)
23. Wäsche, H., Dickson, G., Woll, A., Brandes, U.: Social network analysis in sport research: an emerging paradigm. Eur. J. Sport Soc. **14**(2), 138–165 (2017)
24. Wiseman, J.: Persistent homology of NBA lineups usage. J. Sports Anal. **11**, 22150218251324876 (2025). https://doi.org/10.1177/22150218251324877

TANS-Agent: Structured, Multi-agent Tactical Reasoning for Tennis Match Analysis and Strategy Recommendation

Emma Y. Cai[1(✉)], Yuexi Song[2,4], Chuanfei Li[3], and Zhenkai Liang[2]

[1] Johns Creek High School, Johns Creek, USA
emmaycai@gmail.com
[2] National University of Singapore, Singapore, Singapore
yuexi06@u.nus.edu, liangzk@nus.edu.sg
[3] Raffles Institution, Singapore, Singapore
[4] Georgia Institute of Technology, Atlanta, USA

Abstract. Tennis match analysis and tactical recommendation remain challenging due to the lack of structured, machine-readable representations that capture high-level spatial and strategic dynamics. Most existing AI-based approaches rely on unstructured textual descriptions or coarse-grained statistics, which limits their ability to support fine-grained tactical reasoning and actionable decision support. In this paper, we propose TANS-Agent, a multi-agent AI framework that leverages the Tennis Algebraic Notation System (TANS) to enable structured and interpretable tennis analysis. By using TANS as a unified high-level representation, TANS-Agent grounds Large Language Model (LLM) agents in explicit spatial and tactical semantics and supports statistical analysis, spatial pattern discovery, and tactical reasoning within a staged multi-agent pipeline. Due to the limited availability of fully structured match data, we study six professional matches between Qinwen Zheng and Aryna Sabalenka, which are manually charted into TANS. We systematically compare three types of input data—web-based match descriptions, TennisAbstract-based data, and TANS-based representations—and show that increased levels of tactical structure and spatial precision lead to more interpretable, consistent, and tactically grounded strategy recommendations.

Keywords: Multi-Agent Sport Analytics · Tennis Tactical Recommendations

1 Introduction

Tennis match analysis and tactical reasoning are inherently challenging due to the sequential and spatial nature of in-play decision making. During a match, players adapt shot selection, movement, and rally construction in response to

Y. Song—Exchange student at Georgia Institute of Technology.

Z. Liu and V. Misra (Eds.): ISACE 2026, LNCS 16610, pp. 198–214, 2026.
https://doi.org/10.1007/978-3-032-27272-0_14

their opponents' actions. While modern tennis analytics provides match-level statistics, such as serve percentages, rally length distributions, and winner-to-error ratios, these aggregate measures primarily support descriptive evaluation. By summarizing outcomes at a coarse level, they obscure shot-to-shot dependencies and spatial configurations within rallies, limiting their ability to explain how tactical advantages arise during play. As a result, existing analytical approaches struggle to connect match-level statistics with the fine-grained tactical reasoning that governs in-play decision making.

Recent advances in Large Language Models (LLMs) and agent-based AI systems have made it possible to automate sports analysis over heterogeneous data sources, including web articles, match commentary, and structured databases. In tennis, however, AI-driven analysis remains at a relatively early stage, with most existing work focusing on descriptive statistics and limited tactical scopes rather than high-level strategic analysis. Most existing studies rely on basic statistical analysis of match data, using aggregate performance metrics to summarize outcomes and identify broad tendencies, such as serve effectiveness or point correlations. While these approaches are useful for descriptive analysis and performance characterization, they provide limited insight into the tactical structure of rallies or specific shot decision processes that determine success against a specific opponent.

A primary reason for this limitation lies not in the lack of modeling techniques, but in the coarse granularity and structure of the data available for analysis. Web-based sources are largely narrative in nature, consisting of match commentary and high-level summaries accompanied by basic statistics, with little explicit encoding of spatial context or tactical intent. Widely used structured resources such as TennisAbstract [1] provide extensive historical match statistics and result summaries and are well suited for aggregate analysis; however, they are not designed to capture the detailed spatial and tactical dynamics of in-play decision making. Although community-driven extensions introduce high-level annotations for selected matches, coverage remains limited, and many variables required for fine-grained reasoning are not consistently available. Consequently, existing data representations provide insufficient grounding for LLMs and AI agents to move beyond high-level summarization toward deeper tactical analysis and systematic understanding of match play.

To address this representation gap, we previously proposed the Tennis Algebraic Notation System (TANS) [8], a chess-inspired language for encoding tennis rallies with explicit spatial, temporal, and tactical semantics. TANS represents a rally as an ordered sequence of shots, where each shot encodes player identity, stroke type, ball landing location, player positioning, and point outcome at rally resolution. This compact, machine-readable representation preserves the spatial structure and sequential dependencies of in-play decision making while remaining amenable to systematic computational analysis. Importantly, although TANS was originally introduced as a standalone notation framework for high-level analysis, its design naturally aligns with the requirements of modern AI systems. By making tactical relations, spatial context, and high-level structure explicit, TANS provides a compact and interpretable representation that effectively grounds large language models and agent-based reasoning. This structured abstraction enables reliable tactical analysis beyond what unstructured text or raw visual inputs can support.

Beyond professional match analysis, an important motivation for this work is the limited access to high-quality tactical guidance for non-professional players, especially in early-stage training. Many recreational players or young learners lack consistent coaching that provides detailed, high-level feedback, leading to fragmented or heuristic-based tactical understanding. Owing to its simplicity and compositional design, TANS allows AI models to generate precise yet interpretable recommendations, making tactically grounded guidance accessible to non-expert users.

Building on TANS, we propose TANS-Agent, a multi-agent AI framework for tennis match analysis and strategy recommendation. Rather than introducing a new notation system, this work investigates how a structured tactical representation can be integrated with multi-agent reasoning to support deeper and more interpretable tennis analytics. By grounding agent reasoning in explicit spatial and tactical semantics, TANS-Agent moves beyond descriptive analysis toward systematic tactical interpretation. Based on this data, we design a pipeline-based multi-agent framework (Fig. 1) that performs event parser, statistical analysis, spatial pattern mining, weakness identification, and tactical recommendation within a unified workflow. Beyond post-match analysis, TANS-Agent further supports interactive operation by ingesting sequences of opponent shots and generating response strategies expressed directly in TANS, enabling high-level, step-by-step tactical decision support.

This study is guided by following research questions:

- First, can a structured tactical representation combined with multi-agent reasoning produce strategy recommendations that are more detailed, interpretable, and actionable than those derived from unstructured text or aggregate statistics?
- Second, inspired by AI-assisted training in strategy-intensive domains such as chess and Go, can a similar move-by-move decision-support paradigm be applied to tennis? Specifically, given an incoming opponent shot, can an AI agent generate a tactically sound and context-aware response at a professional level?

To explore these questions, we analyze six complete professional matches between Qinwen Zheng and Aryna Sabalenka, selected based on the availability of full-match video. All matches are manually charted into TANS, enabling accurate reconstruction of high-level spatial and tactical dynamics. We systematically compare three types of input data—web-based match descriptions, TennisAbstract-based data, and TANS-based representations—and show that increased levels of tactical structure and spatial precision lead to more interpretable, consistent, and tactically grounded strategy recommendations.

Our contributions are summarized as follows:

- We propose **TANS-Agent**, a multi-agent AI framework that integrates structured TANS representations with agent-based reasoning for tennis analysis and strategy recommendation. To the best of our knowledge, this is the first work to employ a multi-agent AI architecture for high-level tennis strategy recommendation.
- We systematically compare three analysis paradigms—web-based descriptions, TennisAbstract-based data, and TANS-based representations—to isolate the impact of tactical structure and spatial grounding.
- We show that TANS-grounded analysis yields more precise, interpretable, and tactically coherent insights, especially in head-to-head matchups.
- We demonstrate that TANS-Agent supports interactive, high-level decision support by generating context-aware response strategies expressed directly in TANS.

2 Related Work

With the rapid advancement of large language models and artificial intelligence, AI-driven applications in sports have expanded significantly [6], particularly in domains requiring strategic reasoning and decision-making. While AI systems such as AlphaGo [7] have achieved remarkable success in structured games like chess, tennis presents a far greater challenge due to its complex stroke mechanics, continuous uncertainty in ball trajectories, and highly dynamic player movements. Elite tennis performance requires not only speed, agility, power, but also strong cognitive and psychological skills, including anticipation, rapid decision-making, and mental resilience under pressure. As computational intelligence continues to evolve as a powerful tool for performance optimization, applying AI to tennis highlights both the promise and the challenges of modeling strategy in complex, real-world sports environments.

In an early work on AI-assisted tennis analysis, Makino et al. [3] employed logistic regression together with a custom charting language to identify features associated with hitting winners. Vives et al. [9] trained a deep learning model to determine optimal serve angles in men's doubles tennis. Although effective, these approaches address only specific aspects of play rather than overall match strategy. Moving toward a more comprehensive framework, Match Point AI [4] leveraged match-level statistics from TennisAbstract and employed Monte Carlo Tree Search to simulate tennis matches. However, despite its scale, the Tennis-Abstract dataset lacks fine-grained information such as precise ball and player positioning, limiting realism of the simulations. Moreover, as a statistical-based framework, Match Point AI is unable to provide strategic or tactical advice to players. In general, these approaches struggle to deliver personalized strategic insights, particularly when only a small number of matches are available between a specific player and opponent.

Similarly, Li et al. [2] utilized TennisAbstract data to develop an agentic AI framework capable of generating player-specific coaching advice. While this represents a meaningful step toward personalized tennis analytics, the approach remains constrained by the coarse granularity of the underlying data. As a result, the generated recommendations strive to be high-level, but they lack the detailed technical and tactical precision necessary for effective player improvement.

3 Multi-agent Pipeline Architecture for Tactical Analysis

3.1 Multi-agent Pipeline Architecture

TANS-Agent adopts a modular, staged analysis pipeline that transforms heterogeneous tennis match data into structured tactical insights. Figure 1 provides an overview of the system architecture, illustrating how different data sources are processed through a sequence of specialized agents to generate interpretable tactical reports.

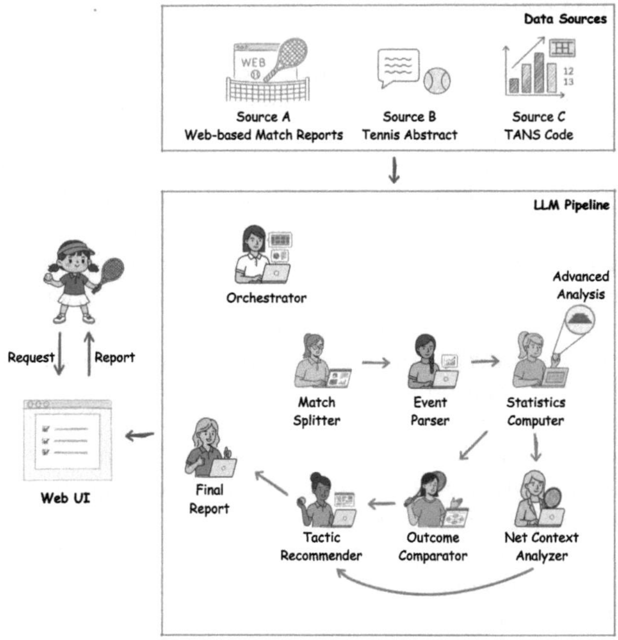

Fig. 1. Overview of the knowledge-grounded, multi-agent reasoning architecture of TANS-Agent.

As shown in Fig. 1, the pipeline accepts three categories of input data with increasing levels of structure: web-based match reports (Source A), TennisAbstract data (Source B), and fully structured TANS rally representations

(Source C). These sources differ substantially in granularity and tactical precision. The pipeline normalizes these heterogeneous inputs into a shared internal representation, enabling consistent downstream analysis regardless of the original data format.

An orchestrator component manages the overall execution of the pipeline. It coordinates the invocation order of analysis modules, enforces data dependencies between stages, and ensures that all agents operate on a consistent match representation. This centralized control enables reproducible execution and systematic comparison across different input configurations. The pipeline begins with the Match Splitter, which constructs a hierarchical backbone of the match by segmenting raw inputs into sets, games, and individual points. This hierarchical structure supports multi-granularity analysis and provides a stable foundation for high-level reasoning. Next, the Event Parser maps input data into a canonical event representation. For textual sources, this stage extracts shot descriptions, outcomes, and contextual cues using natural language processing techniques. For TANS inputs, algebraic codes are directly translated into structured fields, including player identity, stroke type, spatial coordinates, player positioning, and point outcomes. As a result, downstream modules operate on a unified representation that abstracts away differences in input format. Based on the parsed events, the Statistics Computer aggregates both usable and match-level statistics. These include stroke frequency distributions, winner and error counts, serve performance indicators, and rally length. The resulting statistical summaries provide the quantitative foundation for subsequent tactical analysis. Following statistical aggregation, the Net Context Analyzer evaluates net-play patterns to validate hypothesized opponent tendencies, such as a preference for down-the-line passing shots against net approaches, under predefined pattern share and sample size thresholds. With TANS coordinate data, the analysis incorporates spatial features including approach depth, landing distributions, and opponent positioning. The resulting tactical insights and prioritized game plan are passed to downstream modules for cross-match comparison and report generation. To move beyond descriptive statistics, the pipeline invokes a set of Advanced Analysis Modules in parallel, each targeting a distinct class of tactical signals. These modules include pressure-sensitive performance analysis under critical score states, spatial pattern mining based on ball landing and player positioning data, identification of technical and tactical weaknesses from error patterns, and analysis of net-play and transition behaviors. Together, these modules enrich the statistical baseline with contextual, spatial, and failure-mode evidence. The Outcome Comparator then consolidates evidence across multiple matches between the same players. By contrasting successful and unsuccessful tactical choices across head-to-head encounters, this module identifies stable, opponent-specific patterns that generalize beyond single-match variability.

Finally, the Tactic Recommender synthesizes outputs from all preceding stages to generate coherent tactical reports. The resulting recommendations are grounded in statistical evidence, spatial patterns, and contextual analysis, ensuring that high-level tactical conclusions remain traceable to the underlying match data.

By organizing analysis as a staged, agent-based pipeline, TANS-Agent enables inspection of intermediate representations and constrains higher-level reasoning to validated evidence. This design improves the controllability, interpretability, and robustness of tactical reasoning, particularly when large language models are used for semantic analysis and synthesis.

3.2 LLM-Based High-Level Recommendation

Beyond post-match analysis, the proposed pipeline is also designed to support a high-level recommendation capability as a direct extension of its analytical output, rather than as an independent subsystem. The Tactic Recommender can operate in a high-level mode. At each rally, an incoming opponent shot is encoded in TANS and treated as a structured query over previously analyzed matches. The system retrieves relevant tactical patterns conditioned on score context, spatial configuration, and opponent-specific tendencies, and generates candidate response strategies consistent with observed statistical regularities and identified weaknesses. Recommended responses are expressed directly in TANS format, specifying stroke type, target zone, and positional adjustment. This ensures unambiguous tactical interpretation and compatibility with TANS-based training environments. All recommendations are grounded in the same statistical profiles and weakness analyses produced during post-match processing, without relying on hand-crafted heuristics or isolated prompt engineering. This high-level capability is presented as a functional outcome of the pipeline design rather than a fully validated decision-support system. While expert-in-the-loop evaluation is required to assess practical coaching value, the capability demonstrates how structured tactical knowledge can be operationalized into context-aware, actionable guidance during training.

3.3 Implementation

The TANS-Agent pipeline is implemented in Python using a modular, agent-based execution framework. LangChain is used to manage agent invocation, prompt construction, and inter-agent data flow. Each analytical stage is realized as an independent module with well-defined inputs and outputs, enabling controlled execution and flexible composition across experimental settings. An orchestrator component coordinates the execution order of agents and enforces data dependencies between stages, ensuring consistency of intermediate representations throughout the pipeline. Only a subset of stages relies on LLM. Early stages, including match segmentation, structured event parsing, and statistical aggregation, are implemented as deterministic or near-deterministic modules. These stages generate stable intermediate representations that constrain downstream reasoning. LLM-based agents are applied primarily in higher-level stages that require semantic interpretation and explanation, such as contextual analysis, cross-match comparison, and tactical synthesis. This design balances analytical rigor with expressive reasoning capability. Structured data derived from TANS is processed using symbolic and relational representations, while textual inputs are normalized before entering the shared internal format. All intermediate results are logged and inspectable, supporting transparent and traceable tactical reasoning.

TANS Abstraction and Translation. TANS data can be obtained through both manual human charting and computer vision techniques. Ball landing positions, player coordinates, and stroke information captured in videos can be directly converted into the TANS representation. TANS can also be directly translated into natural language. For example, the spatial relationships between consecutive ball landing positions are explicitly modeled. This allows shot directions to be described using commonly used terms such as cross-court and down-the-line, giving users a more intuitive understanding of matches. We build tools to carry out the translation to bridge the three type of data sources and enhance the information captured in TANS representation.

Directly feeding raw video into a large language model (LLM) is computationally expensive and overly complex, while using only natural language descriptions is often too coarse for an LLM to extract precise tactical information. Therefore, TANS serves as an intermediate, structured representation that bridges low-level visual data and high-level language-based analysis.

4 Experiments

This section evaluates how different data representations affect the quality of tactical reasoning in TANS-Agent. The experiments are designed to address three research questions. RQ1 examines whether structured spatial representations improve tactical analysis compared to text-based inputs. RQ2 investigates how different data sources interact and which combinations yield the most effective reasoning performance.

We evaluate TANS-Agent on six professional WTA matches between Qinwen Zheng and Aryna Sabalenka played from 2023 to 2025, covering both hard-court and clay-court surfaces [10–14]. Using the same player pair across all experiments controls for player-specific playing styles and isolates the effect of data representation. Due to the limited public availability of fully structured high-level data, all matches are manually charted into TANS based on complete broadcast videos, enabling accurate reconstruction of shot sequences, spatial configurations, and rally outcomes. We consider three representative input data sources with increasing levels of structure. Source A consists of web-based match reports and expert commentary. Source B contains TennisAbstract-derived narratives and aggregate statistics [1]. Source C provides structured TANS representations with explicit spatial and tactical information. Together, these sources form a spectrum from unstructured text to fine-grained, machine-readable tactical descriptions.

Based on these sources, we construct seven ablation configurations: A-only, B-only, C-only, A+B, A+C, B+C, and ABC (Table 1). This design enables evaluation of both the standalone performance of each data source and their marginal contributions when combined, while keeping the analysis pipeline fixed across all configurations.

Table 1. Ablation Experiment Configurations: Data Source Combinations

Config	Source A	Source B	Source C	Description
A-only	✓	×	×	Web reports (traditional news analysis)
B-only	×	✓	×	Text narratives (manual match records)
C-only	×	×	✓	TANS coordinates (pure data-driven capability)
A+B	✓	✓	×	Traditional data sources (no coordinate data)
A+C	✓	×	✓	Web reports + coordinate data
B+C	×	✓	✓	Text narratives + coordinate data
ABC	✓	✓	✓	All data sources

DeepSeek-chat is used as the primary pipeline model. Claude Sonnet 4.5, GPT-5.2, and Gemini-3 are used for cross-model validation. All judge-based evaluations use the same fixed judge model to ensure consistency.

4.1 Evaluation Setting

The experiments evaluate the tactical reasoning quality produced by the system. Rather than assessing the correctness of individual tactical decisions, we focus on how tactical conclusions are derived, structured, and supported by evidence. Tactical reasoning quality is assessed through the generated tactical analysis reports, which reflect evidence selection, use of spatial and contextual information, and synthesis of tactical insights. Report quality therefore serves as an observable proxy for reasoning quality. We adopt a two-part evaluation protocol that combines automatic metrics with LLM-based judgment. Both components evaluate reports along four shared dimensions: Content Quality, Analysis Depth, Data Quality, and Reliability, enabling complementary assessment of reasoning quality from different perspectives. Automatic metrics quantify reproducible and observable report properties, including structural completeness, evidence density, spatial specificity, and internal consistency. These metrics enable controlled comparison across experimental configurations. The definitions and weights of the automatic indicators are summarized in Table 2. The LLM-based judge is used exclusively for evaluation and does not participate in report generation. It evaluates only the generated reports, without access to external match knowledge or ground-truth outcomes. All judgments are conducted under a fixed prompt and scoring rubric and are applied uniformly across all experimental configurations, ensuring consistency and comparability of evaluation results.

Table 2. Unified evaluation metrics combining automatic metrics (60%) and LLM-as-Judge metrics (40%).

Dimension	Automatic (60%)		LLM-as-Judge (40%)	
	Weight	Indicators	Weight	Indicator
Content Quality	20%	Report Completeness (8%), Content Richness (5%), Evidence Density (7%)	12%	Professional Quality
Analysis Depth	18%	Statistical Precision (6%), Contextual Coherence (4%), Strategic Insight (4%), Spatial Analysis Depth (4%)	13%	Analytical Depth
Data Quality	15%	Coordinate Coverage (6%), Position Precision (5%), Error Detail Coverage (4%)	10%	Practical Utility
Reliability	7%	Cross-Source Consistency (4%), Claim Verifiability (3%)	5%	Report Readability

The LLM-based judge Table 2 is used exclusively for evaluation and does not participate in report generation. It evaluates only the generated reports, without access to external match knowledge or ground-truth outcomes. All judgments are conducted under a fixed prompt and scoring rubric and are applied uniformly across all experimental configurations, ensuring consistency and comparability of evaluation results.

4.2 Impact of Data Representation on Tactical Reasoning

Figure 2 summarizes the ablation results across seven data source configurations using the DeepSeek-chat model, reporting total tactical reasoning scores with error bars indicating standard deviation over six matches. Across all configurations, a consistent pattern emerges: settings that include Source C achieve substantially higher scores than those without it. Notably, using Source C alone yields a large improvement over the A-only configuration, indicating that structured coordinate data provides essential spatial information that cannot be recovered from unstructured reports.

Among all configurations, the B+C combination achieves the highest overall score, suggesting a complementary effect between textual narratives and structured coordinates. While Source C provides precise spatial grounding for tactical reasoning, Source B contributes contextual framing that improves report completeness. In contrast, incorporating Source A yields marginal gains only when Source C is absent, and introduces a slight negative effect when added to C-containing configurations. The full ABC configuration scores lowest among all C-containing settings, suggesting that adding unstructured web content introduces noise rather than providing diminishing positive returns. Performance variance across matches remains low, as reflected by the small error bars across config-

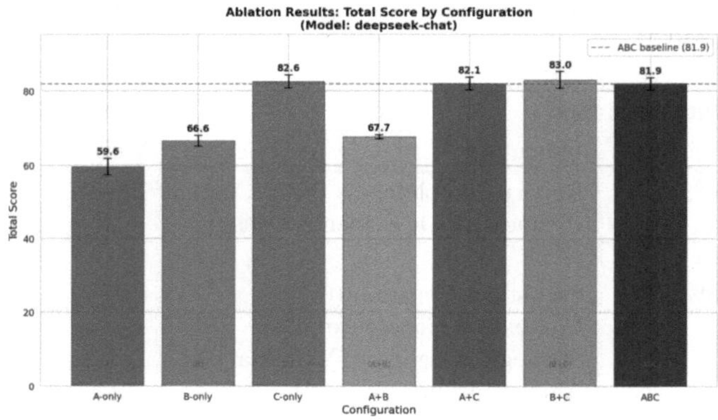

Fig. 2. Ablation results showing total scores across seven data source configurations using the DeepSeek-chat model. Error bars denote standard deviation. Configurations including Source C (TANS coordinates) consistently outperform those without it.

urations, suggesting that the observed trends are stable rather than driven by individual matches.

Overall, these results indicate that structured spatial data forms the core of effective tactical reasoning, while textual narratives provide secondary but complementary support. These findings directly address RQ1 and RQ2, demonstrating that input data representation plays a central role in tactical reasoning quality, with structured coordinate data as the dominant contributing factor.

4.3 Performance Breakdown Across Evaluation Dimensions

Figure 3 presents a breakdown of performance across the four evaluation dimensions for all data source configurations. A clear separation emerges in the Data Quality dimension. Configurations that include Source C consistently achieve high Data Quality scores, while configurations without Source C collapse toward the center of the radar. This sharp contrast indicates that spatial and error-related information is almost entirely provided by structured coordinate data, aligning with the intended design of this dimension. Other dimensions exhibit more gradual and complementary patterns. Content Quality remains relatively stable across configurations and reaches its highest values under C-only and A+C, suggesting that textual narratives improve report completeness and readability when combined with structured spatial grounding. However, gains in Content Quality alone do not compensate for the absence of explicit spatial information. Analysis Depth is highest under C-only, and adding more sources slightly reduces this score, indicating that diverse inputs support more complex tactical reasoning. Reliability varies less dramatically across configurations, with text-based settings achieving moderate consistency despite lacking spatial precision.

Overall, the dimension-level analysis explains the trends observed in overall performance. Structured coordinate data dominates Data Quality and underpins

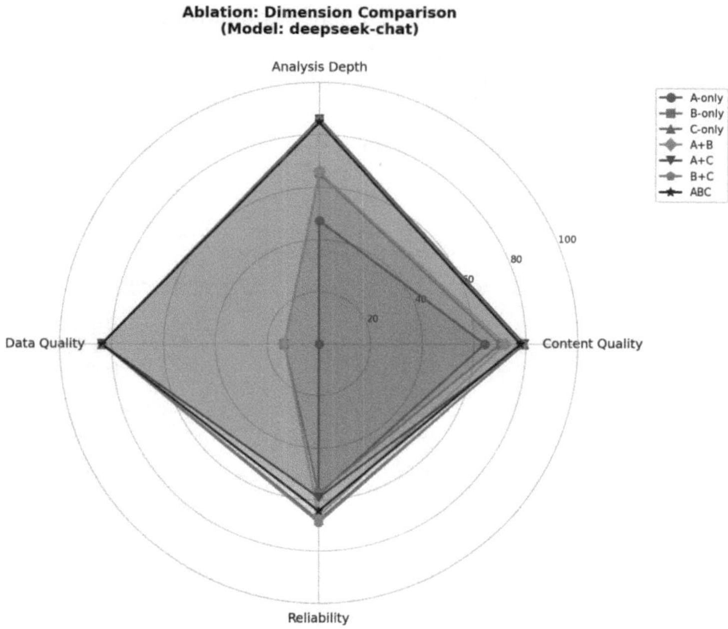

Fig. 3. Radar chart comparing four evaluation dimensions across seven data source configurations. Configurations including Source C (TANS coordinates) achieve substantially higher Data Quality scores, while textual inputs primarily affect Content Quality and Reliability.

effective tactical reasoning, while textual inputs provide complementary benefits in content-related and interpretative dimensions.

4.4 Contribution of Individual Data Sources

To further isolate the contribution of each data source, we analyze performance from two complementary perspectives: standalone usage and marginal contribution when combined with other sources. Figure 4 shows that Source C achieves the strongest standalone performance and provides the largest positive marginal gain across configurations. This result confirms that structured coordinate data contributes essential spatial and error-related information that cannot be recovered from textual inputs alone.

Source B exhibits moderate standalone performance; however, its marginal contribution becomes negligible once Source C is present (+0.4 when added to C-only and −0.1 when added to A+C). This pattern suggests that textual narratives primarily contribute to contextual framing rather than providing core tactical grounding. By contrast, Source A demonstrates the weakest standalone performance and consistently yields negative marginal gains when Source C is already included (−0.5 when added to C-only and −1.1 under the full configuration). This indicates that unstructured web content may introduce noise when richer representations are available. A likely explanation is the heterogeneous and occasionally inconsistent nature of tactical advice across web sources, which can dilute or obscure coherent tactical signals.

Overall, this analysis reinforces the central role of structured spatial data in tactical reasoning, while highlighting the secondary and complementary contributions of textual sources.

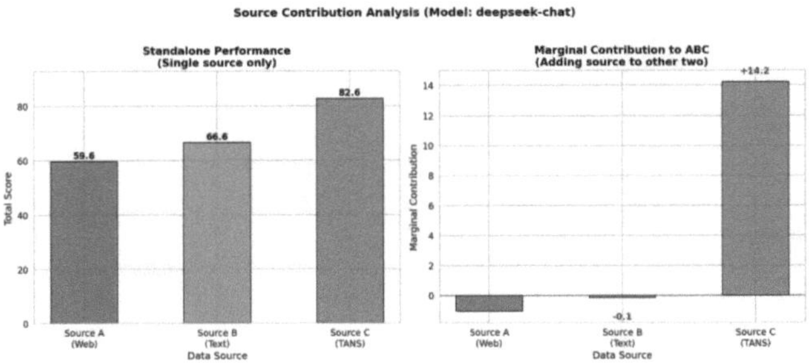

Fig. 4. Source contribution analysis under the DeepSeek-chat model. Left: standalone performance. Right: marginal contributions, highlighting the dominant role of Source C (TANS coordinates).

4.5 Consistency Across Language Models

To examine whether the observed effects generalize across different large language models, we repeat the data source ablation experiments using multiple LLMs.

Figure 5 compares total performance across seven data source configurations for four representative models. While absolute scores vary across models, the relative ranking of configurations remains highly consistent. In all cases, configurations including Source C substantially outperform those without it, confirming that the benefit of structured coordinate data is not model-specific.

The relative improvement from A-only to C-only is consistently large across models, indicating that gains in tactical reasoning quality are driven primarily by data representation rather than by model choice. Stronger models exhibit higher baseline performance under weak data conditions, but structured spatial data consistently narrows these gaps.

Overall, these results demonstrate that the effectiveness of TANS-based representations is robust across different language models, directly addressing RQ3.

4.6 Case Study: Passing Shot Direction Under Net Pressure

Prior professional analysis has noted that Aryna Sabalenka exhibits a strong preference for down-the-line (DTL) passing shots when facing opponents who

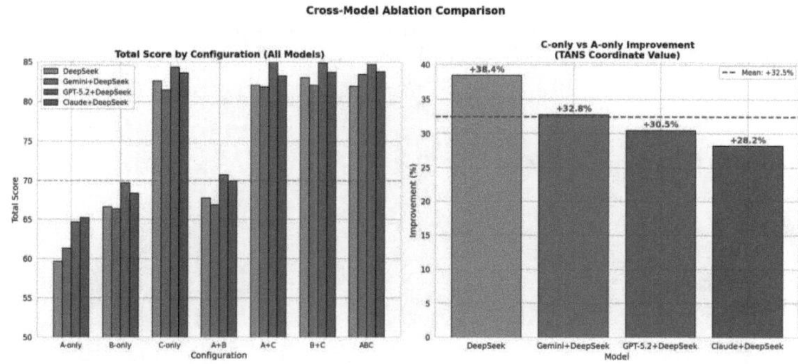

Fig. 5. Cross-model ablation comparison across four language models. Relative improvement from A-only to C-only is consistently large across models, indicating robust gains from structured coordinate data.

approach the net [5]. We use this observation as a case study to examine whether TANS-Agent can recover and explain such opponent-specific tactical tendencies from structured data.

Using TANS-based representations, the system identifies net-approach situations through explicit volley actions and player positioning, and extracts the subsequent passing shot directions. Analysis of six head-to-head matches shows that when Zheng Qinwen approaches the net, Sabalenka predominantly selects DTL passing shots (77.8%), compared to 11.1% crosscourt and 11.1% middle(in Fig. 6). This preference is consistently reflected in both the statistical summaries and the tactical reports generated by TANS-Agent, closely aligning with prior professional observations.

For comparison, we also examine the inverse situation. When Sabalenka approaches the net, Zheng Qinwen also favors DTL passing shots (57.9%), followed by crosscourt (36.8%) and middle options (5.3%). While both players prefer DTL responses under net pressure, Sabalenka's preference is notably stronger (77.8% vs 57.9%), reflecting a more pronounced tactical commitment to the down-the-line passing lane.

Importantly, these patterns emerge without manual rule encoding or prior knowledge of the specific tactical bias. Instead, they are derived from structured spatial representations and contextual filtering within the pipeline. This case study demonstrates that TANS-Agent not only reproduces known professional insights, but also provides transparent, data-grounded explanations of opponent-specific tactical behavior.

4.7 Discussion and Future Work

Beyond offline tactical analysis, our results indicate that TANS-Agent naturally supports interactive, high-level decision support. By ingesting opponent shot sequences and current match context, the system can generate context-aware response strategies at match-level resolution, expressed directly in TANS. This

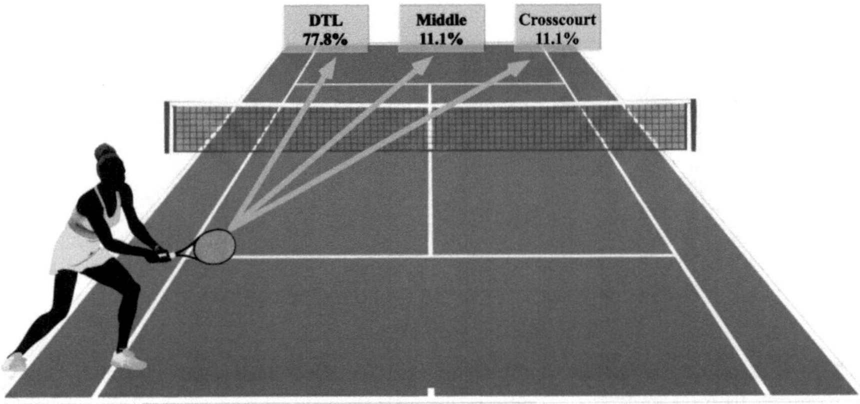

Fig. 6. Passing shot direction distribution for Sabalenka when Zheng Qinwen approaches the net, aggregated across six head-to-head matches, showing a dominant preference for down-the-line responses.

capability extends the utility of structured tactical reasoning from retrospective analysis toward interactive, decision-oriented use. Such a direction aligns with established practices in other strategic domains, including Go and chess, where AI systems are widely used not only for optimization but also for training human decision-making through iterative, strategy-aligned practice. In these settings, players internalize AI-recommended patterns by repeatedly responding to structured prompts, thereby refining their tactical intuition. In contrast, comparable high-level, AI-driven decision support remains largely unexplored in tennis, where analytical tools are typically limited to post-match summaries or coarse statistical feedback. By enabling per-shot tactical recommendations grounded in opponent-specific behavior and spatial context, TANS-Agent highlights a new opportunity for fine-grained, opponent-aware training support in tennis.

An important direction for future work is the integration of high-level tactical recommendations into interactive training environments. The structured nature of TANS representations makes them well-suited for deployment in immersive AR and VR systems, enabling simulation of opponent shot patterns and requiring athletes to respond according to AI-derived strategies. Such environments support repeated rehearsal of tactical responses under controlled conditions, which may help players develop anticipatory decision-making and opponent-specific tactical familiarity over time. Evaluating the effectiveness of these interactive training paradigms will require expert-in-the-loop studies involving coaches and athletes, and remains beyond the scope of the present work. Future work will incorporate such expert evaluation to assess the practical coaching value of the recommendations, including their interpretability and usability in real training settings. We also plan to conduct controlled user studies with athletes to better understand how AI-driven tactical guidance influences decision-making and skill development. In parallel, future work will focus on improving

Table 3. Automated Evaluation Metrics: Definitions, Formulas, and Parameter Explanations

Metric	Description	Formula	Parameters
Content Quality (20%): Measures report completeness and richness			
Report Completeness	Covers all required analytical sections	$\frac{N_{\text{det}}}{N_{\text{req}}} \times 100$	N_{det}, N_{req} [a]
Content Richness	Lexical diversity and descriptive depth	$0.4 \cdot \text{TTR} + 0.3 \cdot \bar{L} + 0.3 \cdot D_a$	TTR, $\bar{L}$, D_a [b]
Evidence Density	Density of quantitative evidence	$\min(100, \frac{N_e}{N_s} \times 50)$	N_e, N_s [c]
Analysis Depth (18%): Evaluates tactical analysis depth			
Statistical Precision	Precision level of numerical statistics	Ordinal: 0–100 [d]	–
Contextual Coherence	Logical flow and semantic consistency	$0.5 \cdot C + 0.3 \cdot R + 0.2 \cdot T$	C, R, T [e]
Strategic Insight	Depth of causal reasoning and recommendations	$\sum_i w_i \cdot \frac{N_i}{N_p}$	N_i, N_p, w_i [f]
Spatial Analysis	Depth of positioning and trajectory analysis	Ordinal: 0–100 [g]	–
Data Quality (15%): Coordinate coverage and precision (Source C exclusive)			
Coordinate Coverage	Coverage rate of coordinate types in shot events	$\frac{0.5N_l + 0.25N_h + 0.25N_o}{N} \times 100$	N, N_l, N_h, N_o [h]
Position Precision	Diversity and logical validity of position data	$0.6 \cdot \frac{\|Z\|}{50} \times 100 + 0.4 \cdot S$	$\|Z\|$, S [i]
Error Detail Coverage	Errors with specific type annotation	$\frac{N_t}{N_e} \times 100$	N_t, N_e [j]
Reliability (7%): Cross-source agreement and claim traceability			
Validation Strength	Agreement of facts across sources	$B(n) + \beta(1 - r_c)$	$B(n)$, β, r_c [k]
Claim Verifiability	Claims backed by traceable evidence	$\frac{N_v}{N_c} \times 100$	N_v, N_c [l]

[a] N_{det}: detected sections; N_{req}: required sections (=5).
[b] TTR: unique/total words; $\bar{L}$: avg sentence length; D_a: adjective ratio.
[c] N_e: evidence count (numbers, %, coordinates); N_s: sentence count.
[d] Scoring: 100: decimal%; 80: integer%; 60: vague; 40: qualitative; 0: none.
[e] C: discourse connector freq; R: coreference accuracy; T: topic similarity.
[f] N_i: count of pattern i; N_p: paragraph count; w_i: pattern weight.
[g] Scoring: 100: heatmap; 75: zones; 50: mentions; 25: vague; 0: none.
[h] N: total events; N_l: landing coord; N_h: hitter pos; N_o: opponent pos.
[i] $|Z|$: unique zones (out of 50, 5×10 grid); S: logic consistency score.
[j] N_t: typed errors (wide/long/net); N_e: total errors.
[k] $B(n)$: base (60/70/80 for 1/2/3 sources); β: cap; r_c: contradiction rate.
[l] N_v: verified claims; N_c: total claims.

generality and scalability by extending the analysis to a larger and more diverse set of matches and players. In addition, we will explore automated extraction of TANS representations from raw match data to reduce reliance on manual annotation and enable scalable deployment. Nevertheless, our results demonstrate that TANS-Agent provides a concrete foundation for extending structured tactical reasoning from offline analysis to interactive, opponent-aware training scenarios (Table 3).

References

1. Tennisabstract.com. https://www.tennisabstract.com/ Accessed Apr 2025
2. Li, Z., Liu, Z., Jiang, K.: Scalable tactical tennis insights: hybridizing automated reports and LLM-powered analytics. In: International Sports Analytics Conference and Exhibition (ISACE 2025). Lecture Notes in Computer Science, vol. 15925, pp. 126–141. Springer, Cham (2025). https://doi.org/10.1007/978-3-032-06167-6_10
3. Makino, M., Odaka, T., Kuroiwa, J., Suwa, I., Shirai, H.: Feature selection to win the point of ATP tennis players using rally information. Int. J. Comput. Sci. Sport **19**(1), 1–16 (2020). https://doi.org/10.2478/ijcss-2020-0003
4. Nübel, C., Dockhorn, A., Mostaghim, S.: Match point AI: a novel AI framework for evaluating data-driven tennis strategies. arXiv preprint arXiv:2408.05960 (2024)
5. Report: Sportinsights. https://depintel.pythonanywhere.com/report Accessed Apr 2025
6. Sampaio, T., Oliveira, J.P., Marinho, D.A., Neiva, H.P., Morais, J.E.: Applications of machine learning to optimize tennis performance: a systematic review. Appl. Sci. **14**(13), 5517 (2024). https://doi.org/10.3390/app14135517
7. Silver, D., et al.: Mastering the game of go with deep neural networks and tree search. Nature **529**(7587), 484–489 (2016). https://doi.org/10.1038/nature16961
8. Song, Y., Li, C., Cao, H., Wu, L., Zheng, H., Liang, Z.: TANS: a chess-inspired notation system for strategy analysis of tennis games. In: International Sports Analytics Conference and Exhibition, pp. 253–267. Springer, Cham (2025). https://doi.org/10.1007/978-3-032-06167-6_19
9. Vives, F., Lázaro, J., Guzmán, J.F., Martínez-Gallego, R., Crespo, M.: Optimizing sporting actions effectiveness: a machine learning approach to uncover key variables in the men's professional doubles tennis serve. Appl. Sci. **13**(24), 13213 (2023). https://doi.org/10.3390/app132413213
10. WTA: 2023 us open women's singles quarterfinal: Qinwen Zheng vs. Aryna Sabalenka (2023). https://www.youtube.com/watch?v=7IqnqJXJ2OE, full match video
11. WTA: 2024 Australian open women's singles final: Qinwen Zheng vs. Aryna Sabalenka (2024). https://www.youtube.com/watch?v=8EShbWpBm_0, full match video
12. WTA: 2024 us open women's singles quarterfinal: Qinwen Zheng vs. Aryna Sabalenka (2024). https://www.youtube.com/watch?v=Q4UB3yY_C2k, full match video
13. WTA: 2024 Wuhan open women's singles final: Qinwen Zheng vs. Aryna Sabalenka (2024). https://www.youtube.com/watch?v=xJCy7Vveofk, full match video
14. WTA: 2025 Roland-garros women's singles quarterfinal: Qinwen Zheng vs. Aryna Sabalenka (2025). https://www.youtube.com/watch?v=96YeQSrIS_E, full match video

Geometrically Aware Ice Hockey Puck Tracking via Stable Planar Representations

Liam Salass(✉), John Zelek, and David Clausi

University of Waterloo, Waterloo, ON N2L 3G1, Canada
{liam.salass,jzelek,dclausi}@uwaterloo.ca

Abstract. Accurate puck tracking from broadcast ice hockey video remains challenging due to the puck's small size, frequent occlusions, motion blur, and rapid camera motion. Recent advances in puck detection have improved per-frame localization, but robust tracking is often undermined by geometric instability arising from image-space motion modelling. We argue that representation stability, rather than tracker complexity, is the primary bottleneck in broadcast puck tracking. We propose a three-stage pipeline that combines reliable puck detections with a temporally stable planar representation of the rink surface. Using monocular 3D reconstruction, we estimate a single, consistent rink plane across an entire broadcast sequence and map image-space puck detections into this stable planar coordinate system. Unlike traditional rink registration approaches, the proposed representation prioritizes temporal and geometric consistency over absolute metric scale or orientation, enabling smooth and coherent puck-motion modelling without relying on per-frame homographies or camera calibration. Geometry-aware motion estimation is then performed directly in the planar space using simple sequence models. Experimental results demonstrate that enforcing temporal geometric consistency enables robust puck tracking with simple models, particularly under severe occlusion, and provides a strong alternative to complex image-space tracking pipelines.

Keywords: Ice hockey analytics · Puck tracking · Monocular 3D reconstruction · Planar motion modeling · Homography stability

1 Introduction

Computer vision has become a central tool in ice hockey analytics, enabling applications such as player tracking, pose estimation, jersey recognition, and gameplay analysis [2,3,21,23,30,33,35–37]. These tasks require accurate estimates of puck location, which serve as primary indicators of possession, play development, and event dynamics. Despite its importance, reliable puck tracking from broadcast video remains a challenging and largely unresolved problem.

Z. Liu and V. Misra (Eds.): ISACE 2026, LNCS 16610, pp. 215–232, 2026.
https://doi.org/10.1007/978-3-032-27272-0_15

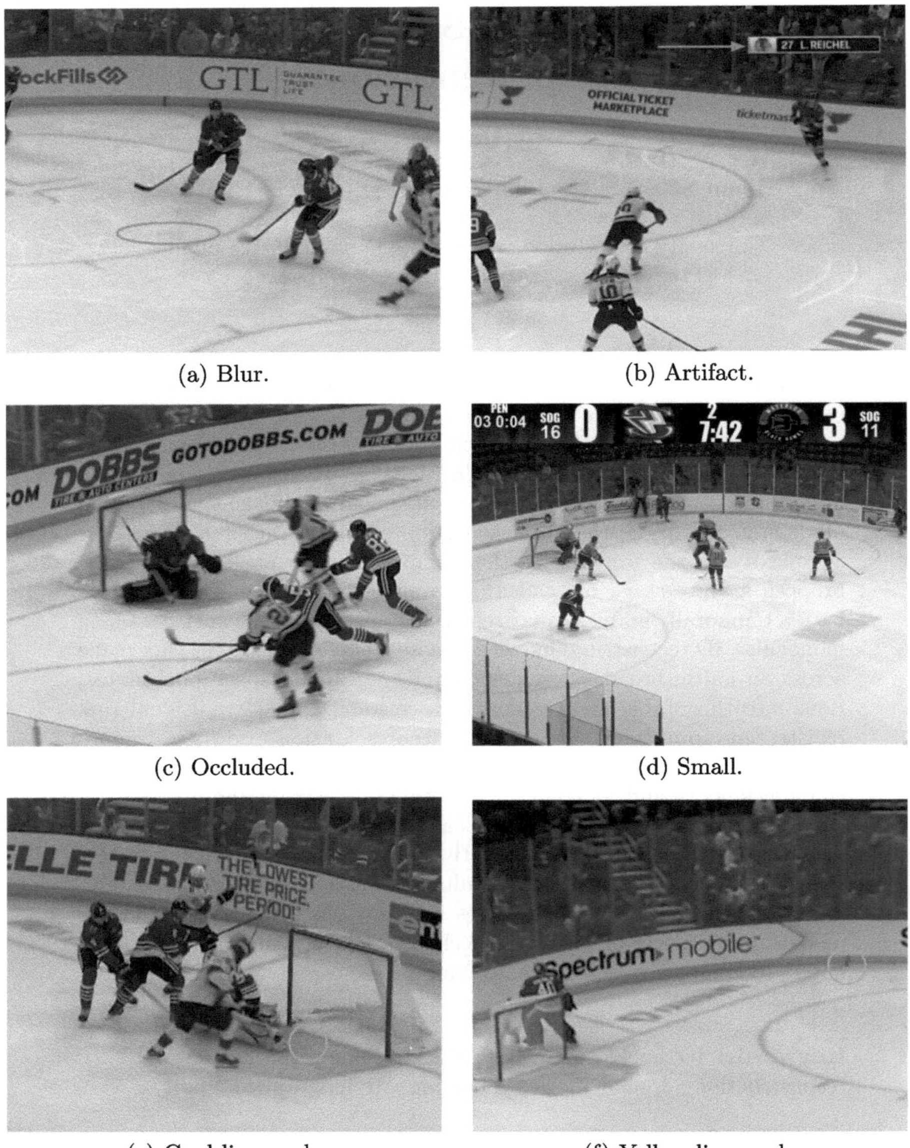

(a) Blur. (b) Artifact. (c) Occluded. (d) Small. (e) Goal-line puck. (f) Yellow-line puck.

Fig. 1. Test set examples of challenges faced in automated puck detection from ice hockey broadcast video: (a) motion blur causing deformation; (b) artifacts introduced by broadcast overlays; (c) occlusions from player bodies obstructing camera views; (d) small puck size, occupying approximately 0.005% of the frame pixels; (e) goal-line puck where the contour is harder to visualize due to reduced contrast; (f) puck on the yellow line of rink borders being difficult to distinguish due to similar colors. (Color figure online)

Unlike balls in many other sports, the hockey puck occupies a small fraction of the image area, undergoes severe motion blur, and is frequently occluded by players, sticks, and boards. These challenges are further exacerbated by broadcast camera motion, zooming, overlays, and viewpoint changes. As illustrated in Fig. 1, such conditions significantly degrade tracking performance when puck motion is modelled directly in image coordinates. While ball tracking has been extensively studied in sports such as soccer, volleyball, table tennis, and basketball [1,4,6,7,9,14], comparatively little work has addressed puck tracking in ice hockey [18,22,29,36,42].

Prior approaches focus on improving detection robustness through temporal aggregation or contextual cues [18,22,36,42]. Recent single-frame detectors such as PLUCC [28] demonstrate strong per-frame localization, but accurate detection alone is insufficient for reliable long-term tracking and occlusion handling. When motion is modelled in image space, even small geometric inconsistencies—arising from camera motion or per-frame homography estimation—introduce artificial motion that accumulates over time, corrupting velocity and acceleration estimates.

In this work, we argue that the primary bottleneck in broadcast puck tracking is not detection accuracy or tracker design, but the lack of a temporally stable geometric representation. Common rink registration pipelines independently estimate homography for each frame, introducing jitter that affects the puck's rink-space trajectory. To address this limitation, we propose a representation-level solution that constructs a single, temporally stable planar representation of the rink surface across an entire sequence using 3D reconstruction, without the need for domain (sport) specific training.

Building on reliable puck detections, we map image-space puck locations to a stable planar coordinate system and perform geometry-aware motion estimation directly on the plane. Rather than enforcing an absolute metric scale or orientation, the proposed representation prioritizes geometric and temporal consistency, enabling smooth trajectory modelling without reliance on precise camera calibration. We show that once puck motion is expressed in a stable planar space, even simple temporal models achieve robust tracking, highlighting the importance of representation stability over tracker complexity.

Our contributions are summarized as follows:

- We introduce a temporally stable rink-plane representation derived from 3D reconstruction that eliminates frame-to-frame homography jitter common in broadcast hockey video.
- We demonstrate that image-space tracking fails under geometric instability, while stable planar representations enable accurate puck motion estimation.
- We evaluate puck detection and tracking performance in both image space and metrically calibrated rink space.

2 Related Works

2.1 Puck Localization

Existing puck detection approaches can be broadly grouped into three categories: single-frame detection, short temporal aggregation, and context-driven localization. Early methods struggle with high false-positive rates due to the puck's visual similarity to ice markings, sticks, and skates. Yang et al. [42] demonstrated that detectors such as YOLOv3 [26] and Mask-RCNN [15] perform poorly on puck detection, thus introducing an architecture that incorporates limited temporal context by processing short frame sequences to regress a single puck location. Pidaparthy et al. [22] regress the location of play using player positions and motion, enabling camera control rather than precise puck localization. Sarkhoosh et al. [16,29] fine-tuned object detectors to regress puck locations for automated video cropping, citing improved detection accuracy with larger YOLOv8 models [34]. These approaches demonstrate that incorporating temporal and contextual information is beneficial, but they remain constrained by unstable image-space representations and do not address downstream tracking robustness.

2.2 Visual Object Tracking for Small, Fast Objects

Visual object tracking has progressed through several architectural paradigms aimed at improving robustness to appearance variation, background clutter, and temporal uncertainty. Early deep trackers were dominated by Siamese architectures such as SiamFC [8], which learn a similarity function between an initial target template and a local search region. While computationally efficient, these methods rely on a fixed appearance representation and degrade rapidly under occlusion, motion blur, and distractors.

Subsequent approaches introduced discriminative online model prediction to mitigate these limitations. DiMP [5] and SuperDiMP [10] adapt target-specific classifiers during tracking, improving resilience to background clutter but remaining vulnerable to corrupted updates when the target appearance is unreliable. PrDiMP [11] extends this framework by modeling uncertainty over target states, yet still depends on stable image-space observations.

More recent Transformer-based trackers replace online optimization with global model prediction. ToMP [19] and TaMOs [20] leverage attention mechanisms to improve adaptation and re-detection. Despite these advances, all such trackers fundamentally assume that the target's appearance remains informative in image space—a premise that breaks down for tiny, fast-moving objects and a rapidly panning camera.

Several works have explored incorporating structured priors for tracking small objects. Physics-guided fusion methods [14,32] integrate kinematic constraints to stabilize motion estimates, while TrackNetV4 [24] introduces motion-attention mechanisms tailored to sports broadcasts. Implementing these methods for puck-tracking would require substantial architectural changes to accommodate the differing physics modelling in ice hockey.

Puck-specific tracking methods further highlight these limitations. Vats et al. [36] propose *PuckNet*, which predicts spatio-temporal heatmaps from short video clips, mitigating brief occlusions but relying on contextual heuristics that limit long-term stability. Li et al. [18] introduce a two-state framework that alternates between appearance-based matching and motion estimation, yet acknowledge frequent identity switches caused by visual ambiguity. These works underscore that appearance-driven tracking alone is insufficient for reliable puck tracking in broadcast video.

2.3 Rink Homography Estimation

Ice-rink registration in broadcast hockey video is commonly formulated as a per-frame homography estimation problem. Fani et al. [12] regress four control points on a canonical rink template from each frame using a ResNet-based model, recovering homographies via DLT. Because each frame is processed independently, temporal consistency is enforced only *post hoc* through smoothing of control-point trajectories, resulting in residual frame-to-frame jitter. Shang et al. [31] segment rink markings and iteratively refine homographies between broadcast frames and an overhead rink template, enabling generalization across rink geometries. Similarly, the HockeyRink dataset [17] introduces dense landmark annotations and keypoint-based homography estimation using YOLOv8, achieving high per-frame accuracy.

Across these approaches, homography estimation ultimately relies on single-frame visual evidence, with temporal stability either ignored or approximated via smoothing. These approaches introduce small but persistent coordinate inconsistencies that can significantly degrade downstream motion estimation. In contrast, our approach enforces temporal consistency by fitting a single planar surface to a 3D reconstruction across the entire sequence, yielding a stable mapping for puck-motion analysis.

3 Methodology

We propose a three-stage pipeline for puck analysis in broadcast ice hockey video. As a first step, we leverage PLUCC [28], a previously introduced context-aware detector, to localize the puck in individual frames. We then introduce a temporally stable rink-plane estimation method that maps image-space predictions into a canonical planar coordinate system. Finally, we perform geometry-aware puck motion estimation directly in this normalized space to model puck trajectories over time.

The primary methodological contribution of this work lies in the temporally stable rink-plane representation and its use as a geometric coordinate system for downstream motion modelling; puck detection and trajectory models are treated as modular components.

3.1 Puck Localization Using Contextual Cues

Puck localization is performed using PLUCC [28], a previously proposed single-frame heatmap-based detector that incorporates player-derived contextual information to localize the puck under occlusion and motion blur. PLUCC is adopted as a detection module in our pipeline and is not modified in this work.

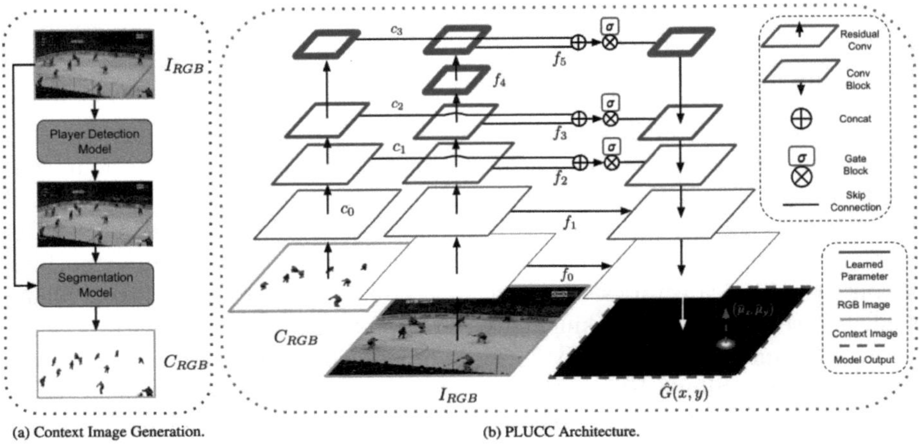

Fig. 2. Left image (a) shows context image generation pipeline, a combination of detection and segmentation models frozen in training. I_{RGB} is the full-resolution RGB frame, and C_{RGB} is the half-resolution context image. Latent features are denoted as f_n and c_n for the feature pyramid encoder and context encoder, respectively. The right image (b) is the trained PLUCC model architecture, where $\hat{G}(x, y)$ is the predicted Gaussian heatmap.

As illustrated in Fig. 2, PLUCC consists of three components: (1) a feature pyramid encoder operating on the full-resolution RGB image, (2) a context encoder operating on a player-only context image, and (3) a gated decoder that fuses multi-scale visual and contextual features to produce a puck likelihood heatmap. The context image is constructed by detecting and segmenting all players in the frame using pretrained models, and contains only RGB player pixels at half resolution. Full architectural details, ablations, and training procedures are provided in the original PLUCC paper [28] and are omitted here for brevity.

3.2 Temporally Stable Rink Plane Estimation

The primary contribution of this work is the construction of a *temporally stable* rink-plane representation from broadcast hockey video. Rather than estimating homography independently for each frame, we leverage 3D reconstruction to recover a single, consistent rink plane across the entire sequence, thereby avoiding the frame-to-frame jitter inherent to single-frame 2D methods, which corrupts velocity and acceleration estimates in downstream tracking. This process consists of two stages: (1) 3D reconstruction with dynamic point filtering, and (2) planar surface localization, as illustrated in Fig. 3.

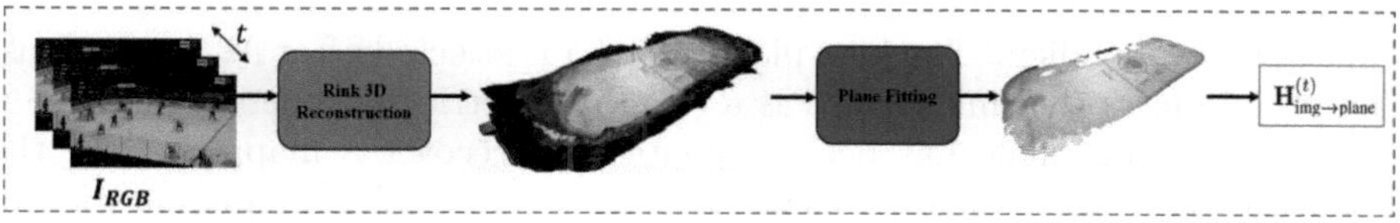

Fig. 3. Temporally stable rink-plane reconstruction pipeline illustrating the two main stages: (1) 3D reconstruction with dynamic point filtering, and (2) plane fitting.

3D Reconstruction and Dynamic Point Filtering. Each broadcast frame is processed using the Pi3 monocular depth estimation model [38], which produces: (1) a dense local point cloud $\mathbf{P}_{\text{local}} \in \mathbb{R}^{H\times W\times 3}$ in the camera coordinate frame, (2) its corresponding world-coordinate point cloud $\mathbf{P}_{\text{world}}$, and (3) the camera pose matrix $\mathbf{T} \in \mathbb{R}^{4\times 4}$.

Local points are mapped into the global frame by

$$\mathbf{P}_{\text{world}} = \mathbf{R}\mathbf{P}_{\text{local}}^{T} + \mathbf{t}, \tag{1}$$

where $\mathbf{R}$ and $\mathbf{t}$ are extracted from $\mathbf{T}$. Because Pi3 predicts consistent camera pose trajectories, the resulting 3D world points vary smoothly across frames, giving us a more stable geometric foundation than using 2D image evidence alone.

Raw reconstructions include both the ice surface and dynamic objects (players, officials), which must be removed to isolate the rink plane. These dynamic points act as strong outliers, degrading downstream plane estimation. To address this, we use **PLUCC**'s context image binary mask $\mathbf{C}_{\mathbf{RGB}}$ of player pixels. The mask is resized to match the point cloud resolution:

$$\mathbf{M}_{\text{local}} = \text{Resize}(\mathbf{C}_{\mathbf{RGB}}, (H_{\text{local}}, W_{\text{local}}), \text{Nearest}). \tag{2}$$

Player-associated 3D points are then removed from the reconstruction:

$$\mathbf{P}_{\text{cleaned}}[i,j] = \begin{cases} \text{NaN}, & \mathbf{M}_{\text{local}}[i,j] = 1, \\ \mathbf{P}_{\text{local}}[i,j], & \text{otherwise.} \end{cases} \tag{3}$$

By filtering out these dynamic points, the resulting point cloud contains predominantly static rink geometry, yielding a substantially cleaner set of candidate points for the subsequent RANSAC-based plane fitting step. The filtered reconstruction is shown in Fig. 4a.

Planar Surface Localization. To recover the worldplane geometry, we fit a plane to the cleaned point cloud using RANSAC [13]. Each iteration samples three non-collinear points ($\mathbf{p}_n$), estimates a candidate normal $\mathbf{n}_k$ and plane offset d_k,

$$\mathbf{n}_k = \frac{(\mathbf{p}_2 - \mathbf{p}_1) \times (\mathbf{p}_3 - \mathbf{p}_1)}{\|(\mathbf{p}_2 - \mathbf{p}_1) \times (\mathbf{p}_3 - \mathbf{p}_1)\|}, \qquad d_k = -\mathbf{n}_k \cdot \mathbf{p}_1, \tag{4}$$

and evaluates its inliers. The best plane $(\mathbf{n}^*, d^*)$ is selected after N_{iter} iterations. This step isolates the rink surface as a clean, geometrically coherent plane.

Once the rink plane has been estimated, we recover a mapping from the broadcast image to the plane by constructing a canonical 2D representation of the fitted surface. Let $\mathcal{P}_{\text{inlier}}$ denote the set of 3D points whose distance to the plane is less than $\epsilon = 0.001$. These points form a dense sampling of the physical ice surface.

Flattening the Plane. We first construct an orthonormal basis $(\mathbf{u}, \mathbf{v})$ spanning the plane. All inlier points are projected onto this basis,

$$\mathbf{p}_{\text{plane}} = \begin{bmatrix} (\mathbf{p} - \mathbf{p}_0) \cdot \mathbf{u} \\ (\mathbf{p} - \mathbf{p}_0) \cdot \mathbf{v} \end{bmatrix}, \tag{5}$$

producing a 2D point cloud lying on the rink surface. The width of the plane image is chosen as the longest spatial extent of this flattened point set, while the height corresponds to the largest extent along the orthogonal direction. This yields a normalized 2D "plane image" whose coordinate system is aligned with the physical rink surface, shown in Fig. 4b.

(a) 3D ice hockey rink reconstruction after filtering dynamic player points.

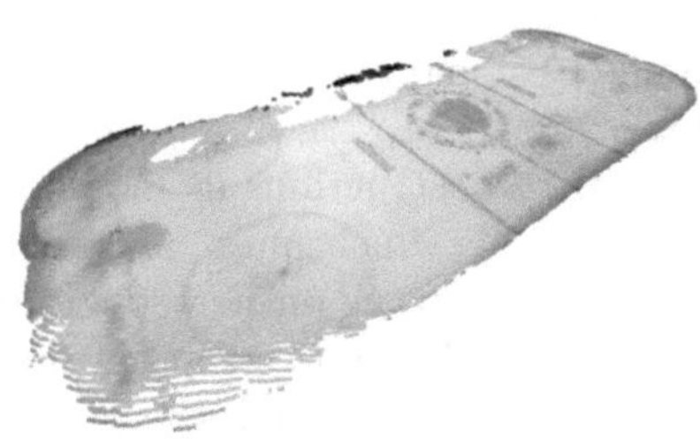

(b) Planar surface localization showing points within $\epsilon = 0.001$ of the fitted plane.

Fig. 4. Rink plane estimation from monocular 3D reconstruction. (a) Filtered 3D reconstruction containing predominantly static rink geometry after removing dynamic players. (b) Resulting planar surface obtained via RANSAC-based plane fitting.

Constructing Image-to-Plane Correspondences. For each inlier pixel (x_i, y_i) in the broadcast frame, Pi3 provides the associated 3D point $\mathbf{p}_i$. Since $\mathbf{p}_i$ is also mapped to a plane coordinate $\mathbf{p}_{\text{plane},i}$, we obtain direct correspondences

$$(x_i, y_i) \longleftrightarrow (u_i, v_i)$$

between image-space pixels and plane-image coordinates. Importantly, this step does not require camera intrinsics or knowledge of the camera matrix K; all correspondences are derived solely from the plane geometry and the Pi3-predicted 3D structure.

Estimating the Homography. Given these 2D–2D correspondences, the initial image-to-plane homography $\mathbf{H}_{\text{img}\to\text{plane}}$ is estimated using the Direct Linear Transform (DLT) with RANSAC to reject outliers:

$$\lambda \begin{bmatrix} u_i \\ v_i \\ 1 \end{bmatrix} = \mathbf{H}_{\text{img}\to\text{plane}} \begin{bmatrix} x_i \\ y_i \\ 1 \end{bmatrix}. \tag{6}$$

The resulting planar representation prioritizes temporal and geometric consistency rather than absolute metric scale or orientation. Scale and rotation are intentionally unconstrained, as downstream motion estimation relies on relative displacement and smoothness rather than physical distance measurements.

4 Experimentation

4.1 Datasets

Experiments are conducted on the VIP-PuckDataset, which contains 4,813 broadcast hockey sequences (~150,000 frames) annotated with puck bounding boxes. Sequences are grouped by challenge type, including standard, blurry, yellow-line, and goal-line scenarios (Fig. 1). Typical clips contain 16–40 visible-puck frames before occlusion, and across all splits the puck is visible in only ~68% of frames, reflecting the inherent difficulty of broadcast puck tracking.

4.2 Baselines and Metrics

All experiments use 1280×720 broadcast footage and are conducted on two NVIDIA A6000 GPUs. We evaluate three classes of methods: detection models, image-space visual trackers, and planar trajectory models.

Detection Baselines. We compare PLUCC against Faster R-CNN [27], YOLOv5 [25], the HockeyAI YOLOv8 model [16], and a heatmap-based FCN-ResNet152 [40]. The FCN-ResNet152 serves as an architectural ablation of PLUCC, isolating the effect of contextual encoding and gated fusion. The HockeyAI model was not trained on our dataset and is included as a publicly available, off-the-shelf detection baseline.

Tracking Baselines. We evaluate several state-of-the-art visual trackers with domain-specific fine-tuning: SiamFC [8], ARTrack [39], DiMP-50 [5], SuperDiMP-50 [10], ToMP-50 [19], PrDiMP-50 [11], and TaMOs-Swin Base [20]. Trackers are re-initialized after 10 consecutive missed frames, in accordance with standard evaluation practice.

Artificial Occlusion. To evaluate tracker robustness under occlusion, we follow the synthetic occlusion protocol of [41]. For each frame, the ground-truth puck bounding box region is masked by replacing pixel values with the mean RGB computed from a surrounding ring of radius $r = 5$ pixels. This removes direct visual evidence of the puck while preserving local background statistics, simulating realistic occlusion scenarios without introducing unnatural artifacts. The three frames of each sequence remain unoccluded to allow tracker initialization.

Trajectory-Based Baselines. To assess whether explicit appearance modeling is necessary once stable geometry is available, we include lightweight LSTM-based models that operate purely on 2D planar puck trajectories. These models receive only projected puck coordinates (x_t, y_t) and model temporal dynamics without visual input. We evaluate Forward, Bidirectional, and Dual-Path LSTMs, all trained with masked trajectories and MSE loss to handle missing detections. Unlike the tracker comparisons, we do not evaluate resets because of the non-causal temporal processing in Bidirectional and Dual-Path LSTMs.

Importantly, these models are not evaluated under the artificial occlusion setting. Since LSTM inputs consist solely of projected coordinates and do not depend on visual appearance, masking the puck in image space does not affect their inputs. Instead, robustness to occlusion is inherently captured through trajectory masking, where ground-truth (x_t, y_t) observations are removed during training and evaluation to simulate missing detections.

Evaluation Metrics. Detection performance is measured using mean Average Precision (mAP^{τ}) at pixel thresholds $\tau \in \{5, 10, 25\}$ and average pixel localization error. For rink-space evaluation, detections are projected using a metrically calibrated homography [31] and evaluated using rink-space AP and average localization error in meters. Tracking performance is evaluated using AUC, mAP^{20}, and the average number of tracker re-initializations per sequence.

4.3 Detection Results

Detection results (Table 1) show that PLUCC provides the strongest per-frame puck localization among all evaluated detectors in both image space and rink-space evaluation. Qualitative examples in Fig. 5 illustrate robust detections under blur, occlusion, and low-contrast scenarios. These results confirm that detection accuracy is not the limiting factor for downstream tracking performance. The reported PLUCC FPS includes both context image generation and detection, with overall throughput dominated by the cost of context construction.

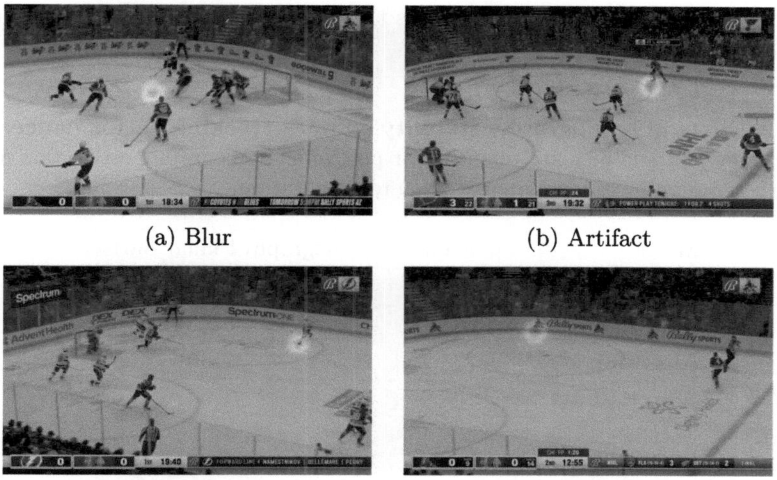

(a) Blur (b) Artifact

(c) Occluded (d) Yellow-line

Fig. 5. Qualitative PLUCC detections under challenging conditions. (a) Motion blur, (b) broadcast artifacts, (c) full occlusion, and (d) yellow-line puck. (Color figure online)

Table 1. Combined performance comparison of puck detection models in image coordinate space and homographic rink-space coordinates. Image-space metrics include mean Average Precision (mAP^{τ}) for all $\tau \in \{5, 10, 25\}$, Average Precision at each threshold (AP^{τ}), and average pixel localization error ($\mathcal{D}_{pixel}$). Rink-space metrics report Average Precision within puck radius (AP^{r}), four times the radius ($AP^{r\times4}$), and the average rink-space localization error ($RSLE_{avg}$) in meters. Inference speed is reported separately as frames per second (FPS).

Method	Image Coordinate Space					Homographic Rink Space			Speed
	mAP^{τ}	AP^{5}	AP^{10}	AP^{25}	$\mathcal{D}_{pixel}$	AP^{r}	$AP^{r\times4}$	$RSLE_{avg}$ (m)	FPS
YOLOv5-Large [25]	56.3	51.5	57.5	57.9	55.2	0.17	43.11	3.14	–
Faster-RCNN [27]	71.3	69.6	70.9	72.0	71.4	18.58	20.06	3.76	32.3
HockeyAI (YOLOv8) [16]	41.5	41.3	41.4	41.5	81.3	18.87	40.9	1.58	60.1
FCN-ResNet152 [40]	79.6	74.8	79.9	81.3	52.11	41.85	62.74	3.89	45.8
PLUCC ($\sigma = 15$)	81.6	76.2	82.0	83.7	48.8	20.69	67.68	1.10	6.0
PLUCC ($\sigma = 5$)	**83.5**	**82.2**	**83.6**	**84.2**	**47.0**	**43.59**	**81.23**	**1.05**	6.0

4.4 Effect of Homography Stability

To isolate the role of geometric stability, we compare two Kalman filterbased tracking pipelines that differ only in how planar coordinates are constructed. The first uses per-frame homographies estimated independently for each frame, while the second uses a single temporally stable planar representation derived from 3D reconstruction. As shown in Table 2, the stable planar representation significantly improves all tracking metrics, reducing localization error and tracker restarts. This experiment demonstrates that homography stability is critical for reliable motion estimation.

Table 2. Effect of homography stability on puck tracking performance. Tracking accuracy and stability are reported for per-frame homography estimation and the proposed temporally stable planar surface representation.

Metric	Per-Frame Homography	Planar Surface
$\mathcal{D}_{pixel}$ (px)	183.20	**42.96**
mAP^{20}(%) (%)	33.88	**51.34**
AUC (%)	5.17	**7.39**
Avg. Restarts/Seq	2.10	**1.54**
Total Restarts	762	**560**

4.5 Tracking and Motion Estimation Results

Table 3 presents a comparison of image-space visual trackers under both standard and artificial occlusion settings. Under standard evaluation, PrDiMP achieves the highest AUC (31.25%), while TaMOs attains the best localization precision (mAP^{20}) and the fewest tracker restarts. However, under artificial occlusion, all visual trackers exhibit a substantial drop in performance, with increased restart frequency and degraded localization accuracy, highlighting their reliance on visual appearance.

Table 3. Tracking performance of image-space visual trackers. *Standard test:* unmodified GT. *Artificial occlusion:* GT puck region masked using ring-based mean RGB ($r = 5$ px).

Method	Standard			Artificial Occlusion		
	AUC (%)	mAP^{20} (%)	Restarts	AUC(%)	mAP^{20} (%)	Restarts
Siamese-FC	22.09	34.46	1.33	-	-	-
ToMP-50	25.38	46.11	1.12	6.59	11.64	2.07
ARTrack	20.0	52.2	1.35	**9.19**	24.3	**1.02**
DiMP-50	27.05	40.61	1.29	5.12	8.20	2.21
Super DiMP-50	29.85	44.75	1.20	6.74	11.14	2.11
PrDiMP-50	**31.25**	47.75	1.12	6.68	11.17	2.09
TaMOs-Swin Base	14.66	**55.65**	**0.64**	6.43	**26.96**	1.13

Table 4. Tracking performance of trajectory-based planar models. Models operate solely on projected puck coordinates and are evaluated under standard conditions without image-space occlusion.

Method	AUC (%)	mAP^{20} (%)
Forward LSTM	24.4	**48.8**
Bidirectional LSTM	**30.9**	46.0
Dual-Path LSTM	22.2	46.2

Table 4 reports the performance of trajectory-based models operating in planar coordinates. The Bidirectional LSTM achieves an AUC of 30.9%, closely matching the strongest image-space tracker despite using no visual information and requiring no re-initialization.

Importantly, the artificial occlusion setting provides a closer comparison between the two paradigms. While visual trackers are evaluated by masking the puck in image space, trajectory models are evaluated by masking ground-truth (x_t, y_t) observations, removing direct access to the puck location. In both cases, the models must infer motion in the absence of explicit puck information, making the comparison more consistent across input modalities.

Although image-space trackers achieve competitive AUC scores under standard evaluation, these metrics are largely driven by performance on frames where the puck is visible and ground-truth annotations are available. As shown in

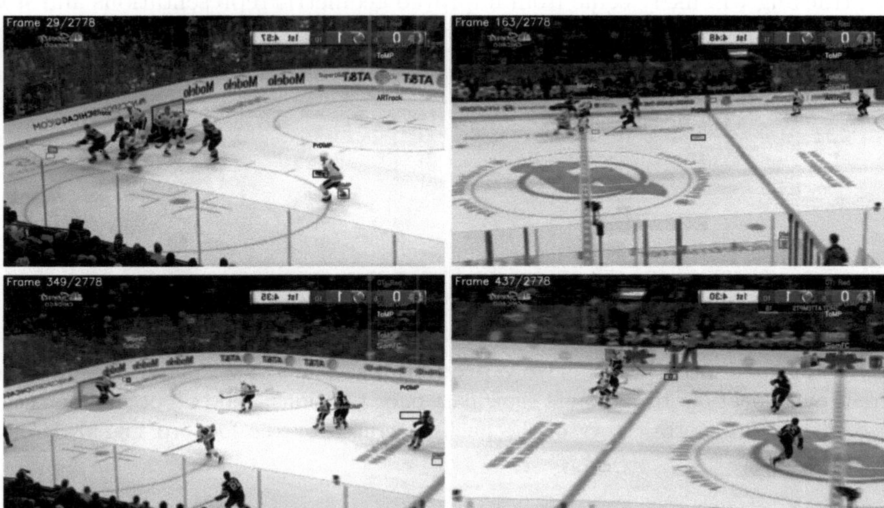

Fig. 6. Tracking failure examples showing predictions from multiple trackers overlaid with colored bounding boxes: **Red** = Ground Truth, **Magenta** = DiMP, **Orange** = SuperDiMP, **Cyan** = ToMP, **Blue** = PrDiMP, Green = TaMOs, Yellow = SiamFC, **Purple** = ARTrack. (Color figure online)

Fig. 6, these aggregate metrics obscure a consistent qualitative failure mode. Under occlusion, where visual evidence of the puck is absent, image-space trackers frequently drift toward visually similar distractors such as sticks, skates, or ice markings. These failures result in abrupt trajectory jumps, unstable motion, and eventual target loss, often requiring explicit re-initialization to recover. Consequently, strong quantitative performance does not necessarily translate to physically plausible or temporally coherent puck trajectories.

In contrast, the planar trajectory models produce smoother and more coherent motion estimates, as shown in Fig. 7. Operating in a temporally stable rink-plane coordinate system, these models extrapolate puck motion through occlusions using only past trajectory information, yielding continuous paths that better reflect expected puck dynamics. While these results are visually more consistent, we note that the LSTM-based models are evaluated offline and rely on the stability of the underlying planar representation. Minor geometric inconsistencies, such as slight warping in the estimated plane, can still introduce small discontinuities in isolated frames, although these effects are substantially less severe than the failures observed in image-space tracking.

Robust puck tracking in broadcast hockey video is constrained less by tracker design and more by the stability of the geometric representation. While visual trackers achieve strong quantitative performance on visible frames, their qualitative behaviour degrades significantly under occlusion. By contrast, simple trajectory models operating in a stable planar space recover comparable aggregate accuracy while producing motion estimates that are smoother, more interpretable, and more physically plausible. This suggests that future progress in puck tracking will likely come from improved geometric representations and stability rather than from increased tracker complexity.

Fig. 7. Forward LSTM trajectory predictions. The yellow marker denotes the current puck location, **blue** points show past puck positions, and red points represent the predicted future trajectory of the puck generated by the forward LSTM. (Color figure online)

Table 5. Runtime breakdown (ms). Hardware: NVIDIA RTX 6000 Ada; 16-frame clip.

Component	ms
Context image generation	144.84
PLUCC	21.83
Pi3 preprocess	6.37
Pi3 DNN forward (amortized)	213.84
Plane RANSAC (once)	396.06
Plane RANSAC (per frame, amortized)	24.75
Homography projection (each direction)	< 0.02
LSTM (causal, T=10)	0.28
Sum (illustrative)	**411.91**

Runtime Analysis. We provide a per-component runtime breakdown of the proposed pipeline in Table 5. All measurements are reported in milliseconds on an NVIDIA RTX 6000 Ada GPU over a 16-frame clip. Costs that are incurred once per clip (e.g., plane RANSAC) are excluded from the illustrative total, while amortized components are reported on a per-frame basis. The runtime is dominated by context generation and geometric processing, while detection and trajectory modeling contribute comparatively little overhead.

5 Conclusion

Modern visual object trackers have demonstrated strong performance on generic benchmarks; however, our results show that their underlying assumptions fundamentally break down for the task of tracking ice hockey pucks. Scale variation, motion blur, frequent occlusions, rapid camera panning, and broadcast artifacts cause appearance-based trackers operating in image space to drift irreversibly, locking onto visually similar distractors such as sticks, skates, or ice markings.

We show that puck tracking begins not with more sophisticated tracking heads, but with stronger spatial grounding. First, context-aware single-frame detection substantially improves puck localization by leveraging player positioning and orientation as implicit cues, enabling robust predictions even under occlusion. Second, projecting detections into a temporally stable planar coordinate system is critical for preserving motion continuity. Our 3D reconstructionbased rink-plane estimation enforces geometric consistency across frames, eliminating frame-to-frame jitter introduced by traditional per-frame homography estimation, which destabilizes downstream tracking and motion models.

Once puck trajectories are expressed in a stable planar space, simple temporal models become highly effective. Lightweight LSTM-based models operating solely on 2D rink-plane coordinates—without any visual appearance information—achieve performance comparable to many state-of-the-art visual trackers, while avoiding common failure modes such as drift, re-initialization, and appearance confusion. Although these models are evaluated offline, their trajectories are qualitatively smoother and more physically plausible under occlusion, reinforcing the importance of representation stability over tracker complexity.

Importantly, the proposed planar surface localization requires no task-specific training and relies only on geometric reconstruction and filtering, making it readily adaptable to other sports domains with planar playing surfaces. We view this as a promising direction for future work, including the extension of the approach to sports such as soccer, basketball, and tennis. More broadly, this work highlights the need for future rink and field registration pipelines to explicitly address temporal stability, as downstream tasks—including tracking, motion estimation, and tactical analysis—are highly sensitive to geometric inconsistency. Our results underscore a key principle: in sports analytics, the choice of representation is often more consequential than the choice of tracker.

Acknowledgments. This work was supported by a grant with the Natural Sciences and Engineering Research Council (NSERC) partnered with Stathletes, Inc. Stathletes also provided the puck annotation data used in this research.

References

1. Ariki, Y., Takiguchi, T., Yano, K.: Digital camera work for soccer video production with event recognition and accurate ball tracking by switching search method. In: 2008 IEEE International Conference on Multimedia and Expo, pp. 889–892 (2008). https://doi.org/10.1109/ICME.2008.4607578
2. Balaji, B., Bright, J., Chen, Y., Rambhatla, S., Zelek, J., Clausi, D.: Seeing beyond the crop: using language priors for out-of-bounding box keypoint prediction. Adv. Neural. Inf. Process. Syst. **37**, 102897–102918 (2024)
3. Balaji, B., et al.: Domain-guided masked autoencoders for unique player identification
4. Beetz, M., et al.: Aspogamo: automated sports games analysis models. Int. J. Comput. Sci. Sport **8** (2009). https://api.semanticscholar.org/CorpusID:15332987
5. Bhat, G., Danelljan, M., Van Gool, L., Timofte, R.: Learning discriminative model prediction for tracking, pp. 6181–6190 (2019). https://doi.org/10.1109/ICCV.2019.00628
6. Chakraborty, B., Meher, S.: 2D trajectory-based position estimation and tracking of a ball in a basketball video (2011)
7. Chen, H.T., Chen, H.S., Lee, S.Y.: Physics-based ball tracking in volleyball videos with its applications to set type recognition and action detection. In: 2007 IEEE International Conference on Acoustics, Speech and Signal Processing - ICASSP '07, vol. 1, pp. I-1097–I-1100 (2007). https://doi.org/10.1109/ICASSP.2007.366103
8. Chen, X., He, K.: Exploring simple Siamese representation learning (2020). https://arxiv.org/abs/2011.10566
9. Choi, K., Seo, Y.: Probabilistic tracking of the soccer ball. In: Comaniciu, D., Mester, R., Kanatani, K., Suter, D. (eds.) SMVP 2004. LNCS, vol. 3247, pp. 50–60. Springer, Heidelberg (2004). https://doi.org/10.1007/978-3-540-30212-4_5
10. Choi, S., Lee, J., Lee, Y., Hauptmann, A.: Robust long-term object tracking via improved discriminative model prediction (2020). https://arxiv.org/abs/2008.04722

11. Danelljan, M., Gool, L.V., Timofte, R.: Probabilistic regression for visual tracking (2020). https://arxiv.org/abs/2003.12565
12. Fani, M., Walters, P.B., Clausi, D.A., Zelek, J., Wong, A.: Localization of ice-rink for broadcast hockey videos (2021). https://arxiv.org/abs/2104.10847
13. Fischler, M.A., Bolles, R.C.: Random sample consensus: a paradigm for model fitting with applications to image analysis and automated cartography. Commun. ACM **24**(6), 381–395 (1981)
14. Gossard, T., Ziegler, A., Zell, A.: TT3D: table tennis 3D reconstruction. In: Proceedings of the IEEE/CVF Conference on Computer Vision and Pattern Recognition (CVPR) Workshops (2025)
15. He, K., Gkioxari, G., Dollár, P., Girshick, R.: Mask R-CNN (2018). https://arxiv.org/abs/1703.06870
16. Houshmand Sarkhoosh, M., Gautam, S., Midoglu, C., Shafiee Sabet, S., Kupka, T., Halvorsen, P.: Hockeyai: a multi-class ice hockey dataset for object detection. In: Proceedings of the 16th ACM Multimedia Systems Conference. MMSys '25, pp. 228–234. Association for Computing Machinery, New York, NY, USA (2025). https://doi.org/10.1145/3712676.3718335
17. Houshmand Sarkhoosh, M., Gautam, S., Midoglu, C., Shafiee Sabet, S., Kupka, T., Halvorsen, P.: Hockeyrink: a dataset for precise ice hockey rink keypoint mapping and analytics. In: Proceedings of the 16th ACM Multimedia Systems Conference. MMSys '25, pp. 249–255. Association for Computing Machinery, New York, NY, USA (2025). https://doi.org/10.1145/3712676.3718338
18. Li, M., Hu, H., Yan, H.: Ice hockey puck tracking through broadcast video. Neurocomputing **551**, 126484 (2023)
19. Mayer, C., et al.: Transforming model prediction for tracking. In: 2022 IEEE/CVF Conference on Computer Vision and Pattern Recognition (CVPR), pp. 8721–8730 (2022). https://doi.org/10.1109/CVPR52688.2022.00853
20. Mayer, C., Danelljan, M., Yang, M.H., Ferrari, V., Van Gool, L., Kuznetsova, A.: Beyond sot: tracking multiple generic objects at once. In: Proceedings of the IEEE/CVF Winter Conference on Applications of Computer Vision (WACV), pp. 6826–6836 (2024)
21. Nsiempba, K., Nazemi, A., Clausi, D., Zelek, J.: Leveraging player tracking for event detection in ice hockey. J. Comput. Vision Imaging Syst. **10**(1), 69–74 (2024)
22. Pidaparthy, H., Elder, J.H.: Keep your eye on the puck: Automatic hockey videography. In: Winter Conference on Applications in Computer Vision (WACV) (2019)
23. Prakash, H., Shang, J.C., Nsiempba, K.M., Chen, Y., Clausi, D.A., Zelek, J.S.: Multi player tracking in ice hockey with homographic projections. arXiv preprint arXiv:2405.13397 (2024)
24. Raj, A., Wang, L., Gedeon, T.: Tracknetv4: enhancing fast sports object tracking with motion attention maps (2024). https://arxiv.org/abs/2409.14543
25. Redmon, J.: You only look once: unified, real-time object detection. In: Proceedings of the IEEE Conference on Computer Vision and Pattern Recognition (2016)
26. Redmon, J., Farhadi, A.: YOLOv3: an incremental improvement (2018). https://arxiv.org/abs/1804.02767
27. Ren, S., He, K., Girshick, R., Sun, J.: Faster R-CNN: towards real-time object detection with region proposal networks (2016). https://doi.org/10.48550/arXiv.1506.01497, http://arxiv.org/abs/1506.01497, arXiv:1506.01497 [cs]
28. Salass, L., Bright, J., Nazemi, A., Chen, Y., Zelek, J., Clausi, D.: Ice hockey puck localization using contextual cues. In: 2025 IEEE/CVF Conference on Computer Vision and Pattern Recognition Workshops (CVPRW), pp. 6050–6059 (2025). https://doi.org/10.1109/CVPRW67362.2025.00603

29. Sarkhoosh, M.H., et al.: AI-based cropping of ice hockey videos for different social media representations. IEEE Access **12**, 118227–118249 (2024)
30. Shahi, M., Clausi, D., Wong, A.: Goalienet: a multi-stage network for joint goalie, equipment, and net pose estimation in ice hockey. arXiv preprint arXiv:2306.15853 (2023)
31. Shang, J.C., Chen, Y., Shafiee, M.J., Clausi, D.A.: Rink-agnostic hockey rink registration. In: Proceedings of the 6th International Workshop on Multimedia Content Analysis in Sports. MMSports '23, pp. 73–81. Association for Computing Machinery, New York, NY, USA (2023). https://doi.org/10.1145/3606038.3616161
32. Singh, P.R., Gottumukkala, R., Maida, A.S., Barhorst, A.B., Gopu, V.: Physics-guided fusion for robust 3D tracking of fast moving small objects (2025). https://arxiv.org/abs/2510.20126
33. Tian, S.: Group event recognition in ice hockey. Ph.D. thesis. University of British Columbia (2018)
34. Varghese, R., Sambath, M.: YOLOv8: a novel object detection algorithm with enhanced performance and robustness. In: 2024 International Conference on Advances in Data Engineering and Intelligent Computing Systems (ADICS), pp. 1–6 (2024). https://doi.org/10.1109/ADICS58448.2024.10533619
35. Vats, K., Fani, M., Clausi, D.A., Zelek, J.: Multi-task learning for jersey number recognition in ice hockey. In: Proceedings of the 4th International Workshop on Multimedia Content Analysis in Sports, pp. 11–15 (2021)
36. Vats, K., Fani, M., Clausi, D.A., Zelek, J.: Puck localization and multi-task event recognition in broadcast hockey videos. In: Proceedings of the IEEE/CVF Conference on Computer Vision and Pattern Recognition, pp. 4567–4575 (2021)
37. Vats, K., Walters, P., Fani, M., Clausi, D.A., Zelek, J.S.: Player tracking and identification in ice hockey. Expert Syst. Appl. **213**, 119250 (2023)
38. Wang, Y., et al.: π^3: Permutation-equivariant visual geometry learning (2025). https://arxiv.org/abs/2507.13347
39. Wei, X., Bai, Y., Zheng, Y., Shi, D., Gong, Y.: Autoregressive visual tracking. In: Proceedings of the IEEE/CVF Conference on Computer Vision and Pattern Recognition (CVPR), pp. 9697–9706 (2023)
40. Wu, Y., Zand, M., Etemad, A., Greenspan, M.: Vote from the Center: 6 DoF Pose Estimation in RGB-D Images by Radial Keypoint Voting (2022). https://doi.org/10.48550/arXiv.2104.02527, http://arxiv.org/abs/2104.02527
41. Xu, H., Baniya, A.A., Wells, S., Bouadjenek, M.R., Dazely, R., Aryal, S.: Totnet: occlusion-aware temporal tracking for robust ball detection in sports videos (2025). https://arxiv.org/abs/2508.09650
42. Yang, X.: Where is the puck? Tiny and fast-moving object detection in videos (2021)

Quantifying Off-Ball Attacking Influence Using Additive Pitch Control Attribution

Bassel Hammad[1(✉)], Mahmoud Nasr[1], Omar Refaat[1], Mohamed Hafez[2], and Tamer Basha[1]

[1] Cairo University, Faculty of Engineering, Giza, Egypt
{bassel.shahat03,mahmoud.nasr03,omar.refaat03}@eng-st.cu.edu.eg, tamer.basha@eng1.cu.edu.eg

[2] Ontario Tech University, Oshawa, Canada
mohamed.hafez1@ontariotechu.net

Abstract. Quantifying individual attacking influence in soccer remains challenging, particularly for off-ball movement that does not directly result in observable events. While event-based metrics such as Expected Possession Value (EPV) capture changes in possession value, they systematically undervalue spatial contributions that create or constrain space. Pitch control models provide a continuous representation of team-level spatial dominance, but they do not offer a principled mechanism for attributing this dominance to individual players.

This paper proposes an additive attribution framework that decomposes short-term variations in pitch control into individual attacking player contributions. By evaluating counterfactual pitch control surfaces in which only a single attacker's movement is applied, the method isolates the marginal spatial impact of each player over fixed temporal intervals. Player influence scores are aggregated across attacking possessions to produce match-level metrics that reflect off-ball space creation.

To assess the validity of the proposed measure in the absence of ground-truth labels, we evaluate its relationship with EPV-based player metrics. Empirical results demonstrate a positive and interpretable association between additive pitch control influence and possession value creation, while also highlighting complementary insights provided by spatial attribution. These findings suggest that additive pitch control attribution offers a meaningful framework for quantifying attacking off-ball influence in soccer.

Keywords: player influence · pitch control · off-ball movement · spatial attribution · soccer

1 Introduction

Quantifying individual player performance remains a core challenge in modern sports analytics. While established metrics effectively evaluate on-ball actions, such as passes and shots, a significant portion of attacking contribution occurs

Z. Liu and V. Misra (Eds.): ISACE 2026, LNCS 16610, pp. 233–243, 2026.
https://doi.org/10.1007/978-3-032-27272-0_16

off the ball. Tactical movements shape passing lanes, vacate space for teammates, and disrupt defensive structures, yet their impact is often indirect and difficult to quantify via traditional event data [2]. Consequently, players who consistently generate spatial advantages through intelligent positioning may be systematically undervalued by frameworks that rely primarily on observable ball events.

Current event-based models, including Expected Possession Value (EPV) [3] and related possession value frameworks, have become the standard for quantifying attacking effectiveness by estimating the value added by discrete actions. While these approaches provide high-resolution insights into on-ball decision-making, they are inherently limited to moments of direct ball interaction. Off-ball contributions are captured only residually through subsequent events, complicating the attribution of value to players whose primary influence lies in movement and space creation rather than direct ball involvement.

Pitch control models offer a continuous spatial representation of team dominance by estimating the probability of ball control across every location on the pitch [4]. By incorporating probabilistic movement models, these frameworks capture the collective effect of player positioning and velocity [1]. However, standard formulations typically operate at the team level, lacking a principled mechanism to attribute spatial control changes to individual players. While pitch control reveals *where* space is created or constrained, it does not inherently explain *who* is responsible for these changes.

This paper addresses this attribution gap by proposing an additive pitch control framework to quantify individual off-ball attacking influence. The methodology decomposes short-term variations in spatial control into marginal contributions by evaluating counterfactual scenarios—a technique increasingly utilized to isolate player-specific spatial impact [5]. By aggregating these time-local influence estimates, we derive player-level metrics that reflect sustained space creation. To validate these measures in the absence of ground-truth labels, we analyze their relationship with EPV-based metrics, demonstrating that additive pitch control aligns with possession value creation while offering a distinct, movement-based perspective on performance.

2 Methods

Dataset and Preprocessing. Our analysis is based on professional soccer tracking and event data provided by Pro Football Focus (PFF). The dataset comprises four full matches (IDs: 3822, 10514, 10515, and 10517), for which both tracking and event annotations are available. Player and ball positions are recorded at an original sampling rate of approximately 30 Hz in a metric coordinate system centered at the pitch midpoint.

To ensure compatibility with existing pitch control implementations, the PFF data are converted into the Metrica Sports data format using a custom adapter. During this conversion, raw metric coordinates are transformed into normalized pitch coordinates in the $[0, 1] \times [0, 1]$ range with a fixed pitch dimension of 105 m by 68 m. Only regulation time (the first two periods of each match) is considered in the analysis.

Given the high temporal resolution of the raw tracking data, a smart sampling strategy is employed to reduce computational cost while preserving tactically relevant moments. Tracking frames are sampled at a base rate of approximately 7.5 Hz by retaining every fourth frame from the original data stream, with additional frames included at event timestamps such as passes and shots. This strategy avoids interpolation artifacts while ensuring that all critical on-ball actions are captured with temporal precision.

Attacking possessions are defined using PFF's native possession sequence annotations. Each possession segment corresponds to a continuous period of team control as identified by PFF's proprietary event labeling system and includes all associated events such as passes, carries, dribbles, and shots. No additional filtering is applied to remove set pieces; consequently, corners, free kicks, throw-ins, kick-offs, and goal kicks are all included.

To ensure spatial consistency across possessions and matches, all sequences are normalized to a single attacking direction prior to analysis. Possessions are transformed such that the team in possession always attacks from left to right, with coordinate flipping applied on a period-specific basis. Influence metrics are computed separately for both teams in each match, considering each team only during its attacking phases.

Pitch Control Model. Pitch control is used to represent spatial dominance during attacking possessions as a continuous probability surface over the pitch. At each time instant, the model estimates, for every spatial location, the likelihood that the team in possession would be first to gain control of the ball if it were played to that location. This representation captures the collective effect of player positioning and movement, providing a spatial abstraction of team structure beyond discrete on-ball events.

Pitch control is computed using a standard Spearman-style model originally introduced by Spearman [4], in which each player's ability to reach a given location is determined by a time-to-intercept function based on their current position, velocity, reaction time, and maximum running speed. For each spatial location, the arrival times of attacking and defending players are compared, and control probabilities are derived based on the relative likelihood that either team would reach the location first. Defensive players therefore contribute implicitly through spatial competition, but no defensive influence scores are computed in this work.

The pitch is discretized into a fixed grid of 50 cells along the longitudinal axis and 32 cells along the lateral axis, preserving the pitch aspect ratio. Pitch control probabilities are evaluated independently at each grid cell, resulting in a spatial control surface that is recomputed at each sampled tracking frame. In this work, pitch control is computed only for the team in possession and restricted to the attacking half of the pitch, reflecting the focus on attacking influence and space creation during possession phases.

Importantly, the pitch control model itself is not modified or reparameterized. Instead, it is used as a foundational spatial representation upon which the proposed attribution framework operates. The subsequent analysis focuses on explaining short-term changes in pitch control over time, rather than redefining the underlying spatial control model.

Additive Influence Attribution. The objective of the proposed attribution framework is to quantify the marginal off-ball attacking influence of individual players by isolating their contribution to short-term changes in pitch control. Rather than attributing influence retrospectively based on observed outcomes, the method adopts a counterfactual perspective in which player movement is treated as an intervention on the spatial control surface.

For each attacking possession, pitch control is evaluated at consecutive time instants separated by a fixed interval of one second. This produces a baseline pitch control surface at time t and an observed surface at time $t+1$, reflecting the combined effect of all player movements during that interval. While the observed difference between these surfaces captures the net spatial evolution of control, it does not reveal the individual contribution of each player.

To attribute influence at the player level, we construct counterfactual pitch control scenarios in which only a single attacker's movement from time t to $t+1$ is applied, while the positions of all other players—both teammates and opponents—are held fixed at their locations at time t. Pitch control is then recomputed under this counterfactual configuration. The resulting surface represents the spatial dominance that would have emerged if only that player had moved, thereby isolating the marginal spatial impact of their movement.

A player's additive influence for a given time interval is defined as the difference between the counterfactual pitch control surface and the baseline surface at time t. This difference yields a spatial map indicating regions where the player's movement increases or decreases attacking control. To obtain a scalar influence value, the spatial difference map is integrated over the attacking half of the pitch. Grid cells outside the attacking half are excluded from the integration, ensuring that influence is attributed only to tactically relevant attacking space. Both positive and negative contributions are retained, allowing the measure to capture space creation as well as space loss.

This procedure is repeated independently for each attacker and for each time interval within an attacking possession. Because each player's influence is computed relative to the same baseline state and without modifying the movements of other players, the resulting contributions are additive by construction. The framework therefore avoids double counting while preserving a direct causal interpretation: the influence score reflects the spatial control gained or lost as a direct consequence of a player's off-ball movement during the interval.

Temporal and Player-Level Aggregation. The additive attribution procedure produces a scalar influence value for each attacking player at every one-second interval within an attacking possession. To obtain player-level metrics, these time-local influence values are aggregated across time and possessions.

For a given attacking possession, a player's influence values are summed across all one-second intervals during which the player is on the pitch and the team is in possession. This yields a possession-level influence score that reflects the cumulative spatial impact of the player's off-ball movement during that sequence. Both positive and negative influence values are retained, allowing the aggregation to capture space creation as well as space loss.

Possession-level influence scores are then aggregated across all attacking possessions for a given team within a match, producing match-level player influence metrics. Aggregation is performed independently for each team, considering only the periods in which the team is in possession, thereby ensuring that influence is attributed exclusively to attacking phases.

No normalization by minutes played or possession duration is applied in this work. Consequently, the reported influence scores reflect total spatial impact over the course of a match rather than rate-based measures, which aligns with the subsequent validation against aggregate possession value metrics.

EPV Computation and Validation. To assess the validity of the proposed additive influence metric in the absence of ground-truth influence labels, we evaluate its relationship with Expected Possession Value (EPV). EPV provides an event-based estimate of the expected future value of a possession and is widely used to quantify attacking effectiveness in soccer [2,3].

EPV is computed using a grid-based spatial model that assigns a value to each pitch location based on the expected probability of scoring from that position. For each successful pass, we extract the EPV value associated with the ball reception location, referred to as *reception EPV*. This measure reflects the value of the spatial context in which a player receives the ball and serves as the primary validation metric, as it is conceptually aligned with off-ball spatial influence.

For completeness, we also compute two additional EPV-based player metrics: *added EPV*, defined as the difference between reception EPV and the EPV at the pass origin, and *EPV per touch*, which aggregates EPV values across all ball receptions and touches. These variants capture complementary aspects of on-ball contribution and are included for comparative analysis. Player-level EPV metrics are obtained by aggregating the respective EPV values across all relevant events during a match.

Validation is performed by comparing match-level additive influence scores with player-level EPV aggregates. The relationship between the proposed influence metric and each EPV variant is quantified at the player level using both Pearson and Spearman correlation coefficients, allowing assessment of both linear association and rank consistency.

3 Results

3.1 Relationship Between Additive Influence and Reception EPV

We first examine the relationship between additive off-ball influence and reception Expected Possession Value (EPV), which reflects the value of the spatial context in which a player receives the ball. This comparison serves as a primary evaluation of whether the proposed influence metric aligns with possession value arising from advantageous positioning and space creation.

Across the analyzed matches, teams, and periods, additive influence exhibits a consistently positive association with reception EPV at the player level. In each match, players with higher cumulative additive influence tend to receive the ball in spatial locations associated with higher EPV values. This pattern is observed for both teams and across both periods, although the strength of the association varies depending on match context.

Correlation analysis using both Pearson and Spearman coefficients indicates moderate to strong positive relationships in many cases, with statistical significance frequently observed. These results demonstrate that the proposed influence metric aligns with reception-based possession value despite being computed independently of ball events. The consistency of this association across multiple matches suggests that additive influence captures spatial contributions that are

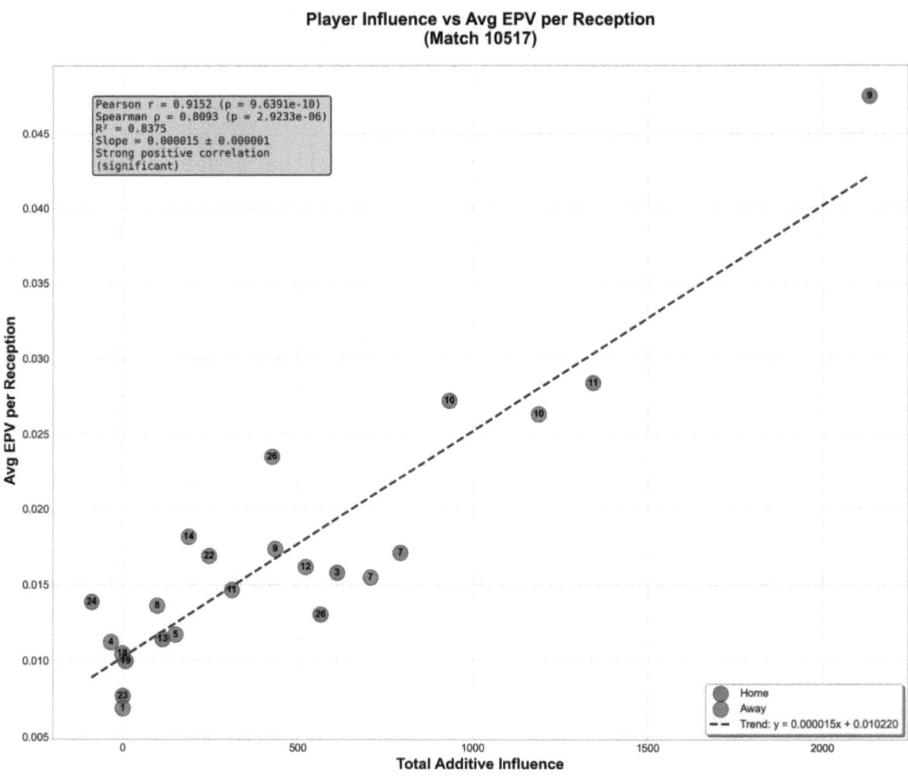

Fig. 1. Relationship between total additive influence and reception EPV at the player level for a representative match. Each point corresponds to a player, with separate panels shown for each team and period.

relevant to the quality of attacking contexts at the moment of ball reception (Fig. 1).

3.2 Comparison with Other EPV Variants

In addition to reception EPV, we examine the relationship between additive influence and two alternative EPV-based metrics: added EPV per pass and EPV per touch. These variants capture different aspects of attacking contribution and provide a comparative baseline for assessing the specificity of the proposed influence measure.

Across matches, teams, and periods, the relationship between additive influence and added EPV is weak and inconsistent. Correlation coefficients vary in magnitude and sign, and statistical significance is rarely observed, indicating that additive influence does not systematically align with action-based measures of value added through passing.

In contrast, both reception EPV and EPV per touch exhibit consistently positive and often statistically significant associations with additive influence. The strength of these correlations is comparable across the two metrics, suggesting that additive influence aligns with possession value measures that reflect the spatial context in which players receive and operate on the ball. These findings indicate that the proposed metric captures off-ball spatial contributions that shape the quality of attacking contexts, rather than the execution quality of individual actions (Fig. 2).

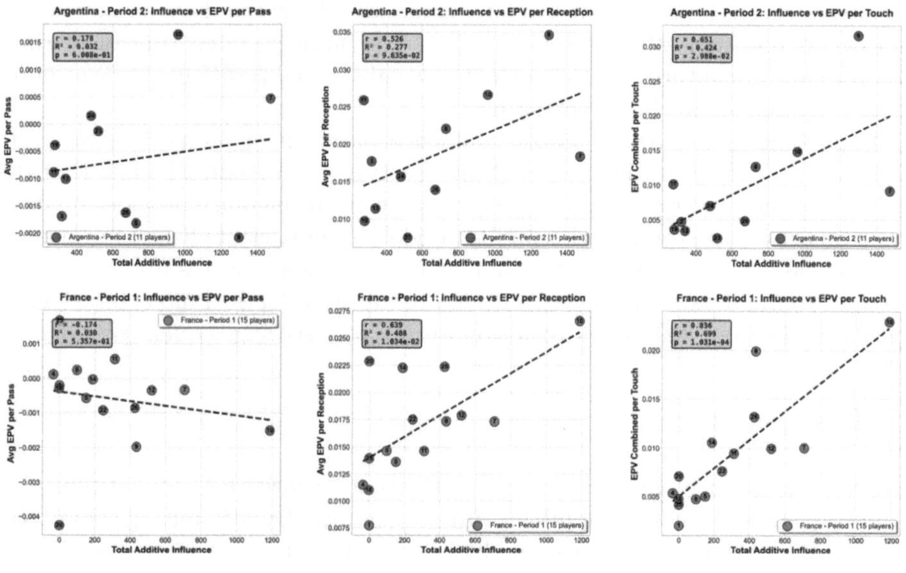

Fig. 2. Comparison of player-level additive influence with different EPV variants, including added EPV per pass and EPV per touch, across teams and periods.

3.3 Comparison with Distance Covered

To examine whether additive influence is related to overall physical workload, we analyze its relationship with total distance covered by each player during the match. Distance covered is computed as the cumulative displacement of each player across all tracking frames and serves as a general measure of physical activity.

Across matches, teams, and periods, no meaningful association is observed between additive influence and distance covered. Correlation coefficients are consistently close to zero and are not statistically significant, indicating that players with higher additive influence do not necessarily cover greater distances.

These results suggest that additive influence is not driven by raw running volume. Instead, the metric captures spatial contributions arising from positioning and movement quality rather than physical workload alone.

3.4 Case Study: Goal Sequence Attribution

To provide qualitative insight into the interpretability of the proposed metric, we examine an attacking sequence resulting in Argentina's second goal. Figure 3 illustrates the spatial configuration during the sequence together with the aggregated additive influence scores for all attackers involved in the possession.

The figure highlights the top five players ranked by total additive influence over the sequence. Ángel Di María, the eventual goal scorer, exhibits the highest additive influence. This aligns with the tactical context of the play: Di María initiates an aggressive run on the left flank, stretching the defensive structure and occupying high-value attacking space. The additive pitch control attribution framework captures this movement as a substantial positive contribution to spatial dominance in the attacking half.

Importantly, the metric assigns influence based on cumulative short-term pitch control changes rather than the final scoring event itself. The fact that the highest-ranked player corresponds to the scorer in this instance provides qualitative support for the framework's ability to identify impactful off-ball movement.

This case study demonstrates that additive influence scores are not merely abstract spatial quantities but correspond to intuitive tactical interpretations of space creation and defensive disruption during goal-scoring sequences.

4 Discussion

This work introduced an additive, counterfactual framework for quantifying off-ball attacking influence using pitch control dynamics. By attributing short-term changes in spatial control to individual player movement, the proposed metric captures aspects of attacking contribution that are not directly observable through ball events alone. The results demonstrate that this approach provides meaningful and complementary insight into attacking behavior.

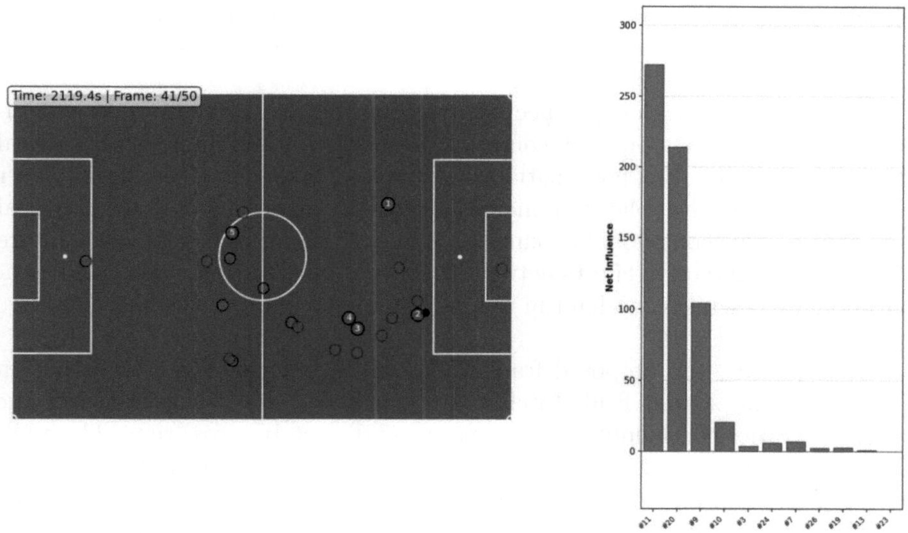

Fig. 3. Additive pitch control influence during Argentina's second goal sequence. The left panel shows the spatial configuration at a representative frame, while the right panel displays cumulative additive influence for all attacking players. The top five contributors are highlighted, with Di María ranked first.

A central finding of the study is the consistent positive association between additive influence and EPV variants that reflect spatial context, namely reception EPV and EPV per touch. This alignment indicates that players who generate higher additive influence through off-ball movement tend to receive the ball in more valuable locations and operate within more advantageous attacking contexts. Importantly, this relationship emerges despite additive influence being computed independently of ball interactions, reinforcing the idea that spatial control dynamics encode information that is directly relevant to possession value.

In contrast, the weak and inconsistent relationship between additive influence and added EPV highlights an important distinction between spatial contribution and action-based value creation. Added EPV primarily reflects the quality of on-ball decisions and execution, such as pass selection and accuracy, whereas additive influence captures how off-ball movement reshapes the spatial landscape in which those actions occur. The absence of strong correlation between these measures suggests that the proposed metric does not replicate existing event-based evaluations, but instead captures a complementary dimension of attacking contribution.

The lack of association between additive influence and total distance covered further supports the construct validity of the proposed approach. Distance covered is a coarse measure of physical workload that does not account for spatial relevance or tactical context. The observed independence between influence and running volume indicates that additive influence is driven by where and how players move, rather than by raw physical output. This distinction is particularly important in soccer, where intelligent positioning and timing often outweigh sheer running volume.

From a methodological perspective, framing influence attribution as a counterfactual intervention on pitch control provides a clear and interpretable causal structure. By evaluating how spatial control would change if only a single player moved while all other players remained fixed, the framework isolates marginal contributions without double counting. While this approach does not capture higher-order interaction effects between players, it offers a transparent and computationally tractable mechanism for individual attribution within a collective system.

Conceptually, the proposed framework can be interpreted as operating on a time-evolving spatial field. Pitch control defines a scalar function over the pitch that varies continuously across space and discretely across time. The additive attribution procedure evaluates localized temporal changes in this field and decomposes them into marginal contributions associated with individual agents. In this sense, the method resembles a discretized field-evolution process, analogous to how partial differential equations describe the evolution of physical quantities over space and time. However, the framework does not assume a specific governing differential equation; instead, it operates directly on empirically estimated spatial control surfaces derived from tracking data.

While the empirical results are consistent across all four analyzed matches, teams, and periods, the evaluation is conducted on a limited set of professional matches. The observed consistency suggests that the proposed metric captures stable spatial patterns of off-ball influence; however, broader evaluation across additional competitions, tactical contexts, and playing styles would be required to assess robustness at scale.

The framework also relies on a specific pitch control formulation. Although player velocities are estimated directly from tracking data, influence estimates remain dependent on model-level parameters such as reaction times and control rate functions. Alternative pitch control parameterizations or spatial dominance models may lead to variations in absolute influence values. Investigating the sensitivity of additive attribution to these modeling choices represents an important direction for future work.

Overall, the findings indicate that additive pitch control attribution provides a principled and interpretable measure of off-ball attacking influence. By bridging continuous spatial models with player-level evaluation, the proposed approach offers a promising direction for analyzing tactical contributions that are not captured by traditional event-based metrics.

5 Conclusion

This paper proposed an additive, counterfactual framework for quantifying off-ball attacking influence using pitch control dynamics. By attributing short-term changes in spatial control to individual player movement, the method captures tactical contributions that are not directly observable through ball events. Empirical results across multiple matches demonstrate consistent alignment between additive influence and possession value measures that reflect spatial context, while remaining distinct from action-based and physical workload metrics. These findings highlight the potential of pitch control attribution as a complementary tool for player evaluation and tactical analysis. Future work will focus on large-scale validation, defensive influence modeling, and sensitivity analysis with respect to spatial dominance formulations.

References

1. Brefeld, U., Lasek, J., Mair, S.: Probabilistic movement models and spatial control in soccer. Mach. Learn. **108**(8), 1267–1284 (2019)
2. Fernández, J., Bornn, L.: Wide open spaces: A statistical technique for measuring space creation in professional soccer. MIT Sloan Sports Analytics Conference (2018)
3. Fernández, J., Bornn, L.: Evaluating the efficiency of the high press in soccer. MIT Sloan Sports Analytics Conference (2019)
4. Spearman, W.: Beyond expected goals. MIT Sloan Sports Analytics Conference (2018)
5. Terlow, M., Kempe, M.: Evaluating player positioning in soccer: A counterfactual pitch control approach. Journal of Sports Sciences (2022)

Synthetic Data Generation for NCAA Basketball Performance Analytics

Ryan Mastropaolo[1], Srishti Sharma[2], Jui Shah[3], Andrea Hudy[3], N. Sertac Artan[4], Alexander Young[5], Tolga Kaya[1](✉), Christopher Taber[5], and Mehul S. Raval[2]

[1] School of Computer Science and Engineering, Sacred Heart University, Fairfield, CT, USA
{mastropaolor2,kayat}@sacredheart.edu

[2] School of Engineering and Applied Science, Ahmedabad University, Gujarat, India
mehul.raval@ahduni.edu.in

[3] Department of Kinesiology, University of Connecticut, Storrs, CT, USA

[4] College of Engineering and Computing Sciences, New York Institute of Technology, New York, NY, USA

[5] Department of Exercise and Sports Science, Sacred Heart University, Fairfield, CT, USA

Abstract. Access to athlete monitoring data in NCAA Division 1 basketball is limited by privacy and proprietary restrictions, despite the growing use of wearable analytics for training, recovery, and performance decision-making. This study introduces a privacy-preserving synthetic data generation framework explicitly designed for collegiate basketball performance analytics. The real dataset consists of wearable-derived workload measurements collected from collegiate women's basketball athletes across practices, training sessions, and games. Key metrics include Total Athlete g-Load, limb-specific load, impact, push-off, intensity, and asymmetry measurements. The proposed pipeline preprocesses and anonymizes raw data, imputes missing values using Multiple Imputation by Chained Equations (MICE), and generates synthetic data via Gaussian resampling based on athlete-specific statistical profiles. Real and synthetic datasets are then used for model development, including a downstream multivariate regression model with regularization and feature-importance analysis. We evaluated the following train–test protocols for assessing synthetic data fidelity: Train Real–Test Real (TRTR, gold-standard baseline), train synthetic–test real (TSTR), train real–test synthetic (TRTS), and train synthetic–test synthetic (TSTS). Predictive results for TSTR (train R^2 0.99 / test R^2 0.76) closely follow those for TRTR (train R^2 0.91 / test R^2 0.91), showcasing good generalization ability. The TSTS train and test R^2 values are 0.91, indicating good internal consistency of the dataset. Results demonstrate strong statistical fidelity and preservation of meaningful workload relationships, with correlations among load, impact, and push-off metrics consistent with biomechanical expectations. Overall, the framework provides a valuable approach for enabling reproducible research and predictive model development in NCAA basketball while addressing data scarcity and athlete privacy concerns.

Keywords: Basketball analytics · Data Augmentation · Data Imputation · Predictive Modeling · Synthetic Data Generation

Z. Liu and V. Misra (Eds.): ISACE 2026, LNCS 16610, pp. 244–257, 2026.
https://doi.org/10.1007/978-3-032-27272-0_17

1 Introduction

In recent years, data analytics has become increasingly crucial for competitive team sports, including basketball, as a tool for improving performance and making informed decisions across training, recovery, and game strategies [1]. Advances in wearable metric-recording technologies have enabled the measurement of athletes' intensity, workload, and other key metrics with greater precision than previously possible. While data-driven innovations have been recognized, limited access to high-quality datasets due to privacy and proprietary concerns has been a barrier for practitioners and researchers [2]. This work proposes a synthetic data generation framework that mitigates data scarcity and privacy constraints in sports data analytics while preserving key statistical and domain properties of real competition data, enabling widespread use of anonymized data generated from field-collected sensor data.

Existing synthetic sports datasets are typically validated only for statistical similarity, which does not guarantee that they retain the predictive relationships required by machine learning models. It remains unclear whether models trained on synthetic athlete monitoring data can reliably generalize to real athlete observations. As a result, the field lacks a shareable and validated dataset that supports reproducible modeling while maintaining privacy.

To address this gap, a privacy-preserving data framework for NCAA Division 1 basketball athlete monitoring was developed in this work. Raw wearable workload data was first anonymized and preprocessed to ensure consistency and remove identifying information. Missing observations were reconstructed using Multiple Imputation by Chained Equations (MICE) by filling time-based gaps while maintaining realistic relationships among workload variables and reducing the risk of re-identification. Next, a synthetic dataset was generated via Gaussian resampling based on athlete- and metric-specific statistical profiles, preserving the realistic ranges and structural characteristics of the original data. The effectiveness of this framework was evaluated using both statistical and predictive validation. Pearson correlation analysis and feature-importance stability were used to assess the preservation of relationships.

For prediction, a multivariate regression model was tested across four protocols: Train Real–Test Real (TRTR), Train Synthetic–Test Real (TSTR), train Real–Test Synthetic (TRTS), and Train Synthetic–Test Synthetic (TSTS). TRTR is a gold baseline indicating the best achievable performance. Every other protocol score could be interpreted with respect to the TRTR. In TSTR, the downstream model is trained on synthetic data and tested on handheld real data. It shows how well synthetic-data-trained models generalize to real data. Comparing TRTR, it indicates whether synthetic data can substitute real data for training. A small gap between TRTR and TSTR indicates that synthetic data preserves the statistical fidelity of the real data. TRTS checks how learning by an ML model is transferred to synthetic data. It can be seen as a diagnostic tool to assess how well synthetic data look real to the trained model. TSTS helps evaluate internal consistency and check the structure of the synthetic data. In summary, they determine whether models trained on synthetic data can generalize to real-world observations of athletes.

The remainder of the paper is as follows: Section 2 discusses related work and the literature review; Section 3 describes the dataset, and Section 4 explains the pipeline methodology for generating synthetic data. The experiment evaluation, results, and discussion were summarized in Section 5, and a conclusion was presented in Section 6.

2 Background and Related Work

High-performance athlete monitoring relies on high-frequency measurements recorded from wearable sensors such as accelerometers, inertial measurement units (IMUs), and GPS tracking systems. These systems record workload, impact, and intensity metrics that are directly tied to training design, performance evaluation, and injury prevention. However, datasets that include these metrics are often inaccessible to the public because they contain sensitive performance and health information and may expose private details about individual athletes. As a result, synthetic data has emerged as a practical alternative for enabling research and model development while mitigating risks to athletes' privacy and confidentiality. Synthetic data was proposed as a sports science strategy for navigating privacy and confidentiality constraints, demonstrates sport-oriented generation workflows through the synthpop framework, and emphasizes that "good" synthetic data must preserve relationships and analytical validity rather than marginal distributions or visual similarity [3]. Moreover, by examining the realities of high-performance deployment, including governance, use cases, and risk management, it was revealed that practical adoption depends on balancing realism and utility against privacy and risks, such as bias amplification and misuse of the dataset [4].

Athlete monitoring data are typically tabular, including continuous workload and intensity measures alongside discrete labels, categorical context, and frequently imbalanced classes. These characteristics make it challenging to generate high-fidelity synthetic data, particularly when preserving cross-feature relationships that reflect physiological behavior. Recent sports analytics research demonstrates that synthetic datasets can support performance modeling and training-load prediction while protecting privacy. Hybrid training strategies that combine real and synthetic samples can outperform models trained on either source alone [1]. Although synthetic data can be applied across sports, its use in basketball data analytics remains limited. Basketball-specific monitoring introduces additional structure, including athlete positions, asymmetrical movement patterns, and session-dependent workloads. As a result, conditional generation approaches capable of modeling player-specific distributions are particularly relevant to this area of focus.

Synthetic data generation methods for tabular datasets can be broadly classified into statistical modeling approaches and deep generative learning methods. Early approaches relied on statistical synthesis, including parametric sampling and imputation based generation, which approximate joint distributions by estimating correlations between variables [3]. While these strategies are computationally efficient, they often struggle to capture complex nonlinear dependencies found in athlete monitoring data. As a result, deep generative models have been developed to address these limitations.

There are several approaches to generative modeling for tabular data in athlete monitoring. Generative Adversarial Networks (GANs), for example, learn the data distribution through competition between a generator and a discriminator, enabling them to model complex feature relationships [5]. The Conditional Tabular GAN (CTGAN) is a widely utilized architecture designed explicitly for mixed-type tabular datasets [6]. CTGAN uses conditional sampling and mode-specific normalization to address class imbalance and heterogeneous feature distributions; a desired application is sports monitoring data, where rare events and categorical variables are common. Beyond adversarial approaches, generative modeling can also be achieved through probabilistic latent-variable frameworks that explicitly learn compressed representations of the data. Variational Autoencoders (VAEs) provide an alternative framework that learns a latent representation of the dataset and generates new samples by decoding from this latent space [7]. VAE-based tabular generators help capture smooth feature relationships and can be combined with conditional inputs to model player- or session-specific patterns. Conditional generation is therefore vital for athlete monitoring, as individual players exhibit persistent workload profiles and movement characteristics.

Recent benchmarking research shows that no single generator consistently outperforms the others across all datasets, with performance strongly dependent on dataset structure [8]. These findings underscore the need to evaluate multiple generation strategies rather than relying on a single model class. Complementary work on privacyaware synthetic data generation expands the evaluation framework by incorporating formal privacy guarantees and explicitly examining the trade-off between privacy and utility [2]. It stresses the need for realistic, domain-representative benchmarks and empirical validation under meaningful privacy budgets that protect individuals in the dataset [2]. Together, these studies emphasize that meaningful deployment requires both a realistic, domain-representative data structure and quantifiable privacy protection.

Evaluating synthetic data is, therefore, challenging because visual similarity does not imply analytical validation. Hence, modern validation frameworks separate fidelity, utility, and privacy risk [8]. Statistical fidelity measures, such as feature-wise distribution similarity metrics, Kolmogorov-Smirnov (KS) tests, and correlation-structure preservation analyses, assess whether synthetic data resemble real-data marginals and inter-feature dependencies, thereby verifying that relationships between workload variables are preserved. In addition, utility evaluation assesses whether synthetic data supports downstream modeling.

In addition to predictive accuracy, feature stability analysis is proper. When feature importance rankings and learned relationships remain consistent between real and synthetic training regimes, the generated data preserves meaningful structure rather than superficial resemblance. These validation strategies align with the intended use cases in athlete analytics, where datasets are shared to develop and test predictive models. Accordingly, the following section describes the athlete monitoring dataset used in this study.

3 Dataset

The real-world dataset includes metrics for collegiate women's basketball players. All data were collected across all session types labeled "session," including practices, shoot-arounds, pre-game warm-ups, competitive games, quarters, and individual training sessions. This data was collected to translate high-frequency wearable metrics into actionable workload and performance insights that coaches and staff can use to gauge recovery, tailor training to specific athletes, prevent injuries, and make informed decisions for in-game success.

The real data were collected during a competitive basketball season, during which Plantiga was used as the wearable recording device [10]. A cleaned, anonymized subset of the complete team data was provided to the researchers to prevent linking data to players.

The *total player load* was quantified by summing the workloads across all sessions. It is calculated as the sum of the peak resultant accelerations on each toe-off and foot strike [10]. In addition, a *left total athlete load* and a *right total athlete load* were collected to measure the load each player exerted on each leg. These features help quantify the mechanical load accumulated during an activity.

Athlete intensity was also collected during the entire season. This feature is quantified by the athlete's acceleration load experienced per minute of activity [10]. It is used to provide context across training sessions of varying lengths and types by normalizing the total load. For example, a 10-minute warm-up may have the same total load as a 2minute hard training session. However, the intensity of the hard training session would be significantly higher.

Impact is defined as the peak acceleration at foot contact with the ground. It is calculated each time the foot touches the ground [10]. In this study, the *total and average impacts* were measured across the entire session to provide both a total and a session-level summary of the per-contact impact peaks. The *push-off* data were quantified as the peak acceleration at foot-off. They calculated each time the foot left the ground [10]. Similarly, both total and average push-off data were utilized.

In addition to performance data, asymmetry data were collected for each of the metrics listed above, including *player load*, *intensity*, *impact*, and *push-off*. Asymmetry was used to monitor the athlete's use of each leg to find any imbalances or biases in which leg was predominantly used per athlete. The basic asymmetry calculation that can be used for all metrics is the percent difference between accelerations exerted on the left and right feet, defined by:

$$(R - L) / max\,(R,\ L) \tag{1}$$

The *R* or *L* signifier after the asymmetry percent indicates the side that experiences greater acceleration [10]. In this study, three asymmetry thresholds were used to monitor athletes, consistent with [11]. Table 1 summarizes the athlete symmetry ranges.

During the various sessions, athletes' move time and idle time were also measured. Move time is the total duration within a recorded session that is classified as active movement. In contrast, idle time is the total duration within a recorded session during which the athlete is not actively moving [10]. The 14 features include in the study

Table 1. Athlete asymmetry range.

Label	Range
Ideal asymmetry	0–10%
Acceptable, but worth monitoring	10–20%
High asymmetry, potential injury, or compensation risk	20% +

are: *Total Athlete g-Load*, *Total Athlete g-Load* Asymmetry, Left *Total Athlete g-Load*, *Right Total Athlete g-Load*, *Athlete* Intensity, *Athlete Intensity* Asymmetry, *Total Impact*, *Average Impact*, *Average Impact Asymmetry*, *Total Push-off*, *Average Push-off*, *Average Push-off Asymmetry*, *Move time*, and *Idle Time*.

4 Methodology

An end-to-end synthetic data pipeline was proposed in this work (Fig. 1), in which raw wearable workload data undergoes preprocessing to ensure privacy and consistency, thereby making it ready for modeling. Missing data was imputed via the MICE imputer. A privacy-preserving synthetic dataset was then generated through Gaussian resampling based on athlete- and metric-specific statistical profiles. Validation of the synthetic data was performed using three different approaches: (1) Pearson correlation analysis to assess relationship preservation, (2) evaluating predictive models through four train-test regimes (TRTR, TSTR, TRTS, TSTS), and (3) feature importance results to inform prediction mechanisms. Across all experiments, Total *Athlete g-Load* is designated as the target variable because it exhibits strong relationships with other metrics. Fig. 1 exhibits the overall methodology.

4.1 Data Collection

First, real-time training and game data were collected across all session types (practices, shoot-arounds, pre-game warm-ups, competitive games, quarters, and individual training sessions) for each of the players (mean age: 20.0 years; average height: 185.06 cm) using Plantiga (Plantiga Technologies, Vancouver, BC, CA) wearable devices [10]. The 14 primary features collected as shown in Section 3.

4.2 Data Preprocessing

Prior to analysis, the raw dataset (6,882 rows × 10 columns) underwent preprocessing steps to ensure data quality, privacy, and analytical readiness. To protect the identity of each athlete, all personally identifiable information was removed from the dataset. The players' names were replaced with generic pseudonyms (Player 1 through Player n) using an alphabetical mapping. In addition, the original data were recorded in long format, with each row representing a single metric observation for a given player-session combination across 14 workload variables and 493 unique activity sessions. The data

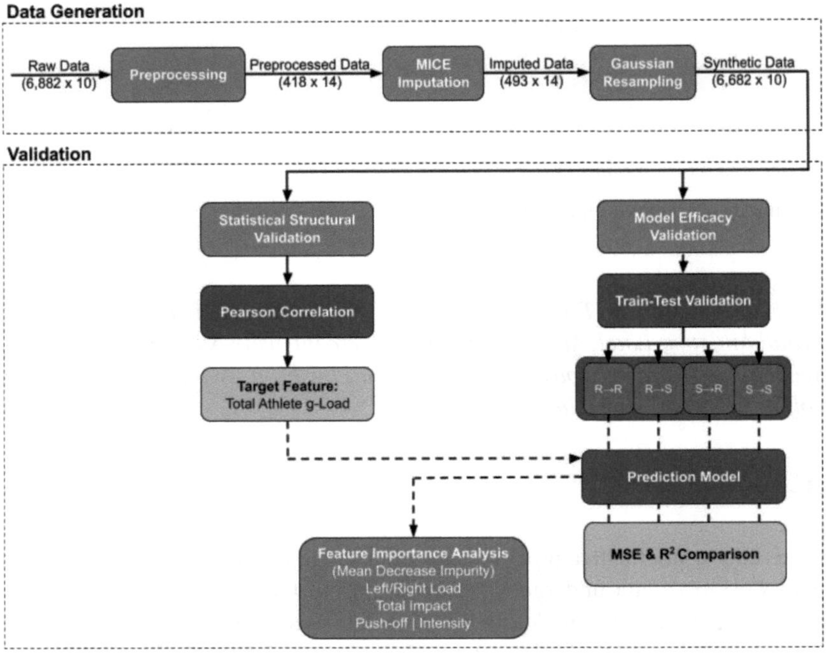

Fig. 1. Proposed methodology of the privacy-preserving synthetic data generation and validation framework for NCAA basketball athlete monitoring.

were then reshaped to a wide format for downstream modelling, and columns with zero variance or with excessive null values (>50%) were removed. In addition, any duplicate records were dropped.

4.3 Data Imputation

In the synthetically generated dataset, missing values were retained to preserve the structure of the original dataset. Short gaps (1-3 days) were observed in the data, occurring sporadically due to routine data-collection issues. However, extended periods of missing sequences (> 4 consecutive days) corresponded to post-injury periods for some athletes. Such a pattern could serve as a quasi-identifier, enabling an individual with prior knowledge of the original dataset to exploit temporal gaps to link records and infer athlete identities. Therefore, targeted imputation was performed using the MICE algorithm to mitigate the risk of re-identification. First, the raw timestamps were converted to UTC and reduced to the date level. The dataset was then transformed from long to wide format, with each row representing a unique athlete-date pair as the key and 14 biomechanical metric columns corresponding to it. Temporal gaps (interval of 4 or more missing days) were then identified. Missing values were estimated using the MICE imputer (Random Forest base estimator with 200 trees, maximum depth = 10, fixed random state; maximum 15 iterations; convergence tolerance = 1×10^{-3}), increasing the dataset from 418 $\times$ 14 to 493 $\times$ 14. This imputation was applied to continuous numeric performance metrics. In contrast, the identifier (player_id), temporal (date), and categorical variables (activity type, movement type) were excluded and retained in their original form.

4.4 Synthetic Data Generation

To preserve each athlete's privacy while maintaining the utility of the data for public release, a statistical resampling approach was developed to generate synthetic workload data from the original dataset. This approach was selected due to the relatively small sample size of athlete monitoring data and the need for transparent, interpretable generation methods suitable for sports science research settings. This generation process preserves the data's structural integrity while introducing controlled variation to prevent others from identifying the athletes in the dataset. The original dataset comprised 6,882 observations from 7 athletes and 14 biomechanical metrics collected over an NCAA Division I basketball season. Each observation contained time-related information, unique player identifiers that were deidentified to the primary author, activity metadata, metric classifications, and corresponding values with units. The synthetic data generation methodology operates as follows:

Statistical Profile Extraction: For each unique player-feature combination, descriptive statistics, including mean (μ), standard deviation (σ), minimum, and maximum values from the original dataset, were computed. This approach captures individual athlete patterns and feature-specific distributions.

Normalization and Outlier Handling: For each row in the original dataset, a new value was generated from a normal distribution $N(\mu, 0.8\sigma)$. The reduced standard deviation factor of 0.8 was chosen to balance realistic variability with distributional fidelity to the original data. Generated values were clipped to the range $[0.5 \times \text{min}, 1.5 \times \text{max}]$ to prevent physiologically implausible outliers while allowing natural variation beyond observed bounds.

Structure Preservation: All non-value columns remained unchanged from the original dataset, including timestamps, activity identifiers, metric names, and units. This ensures that time-based patterns, session structures, and measurement contexts are preserved exactly as they are.

Reproducibility: A fixed random seed (42) was used to ensure reproducibility of the synthetic dataset for validation.

After the generation process, player names were anonymized by mapping original identifiers to generic labels (Player 1 through Player 7) in alphabetical order, ensuring consistent anonymization across all records. The resulting synthetic dataset maintained the same dimensionality (6,882 rows $\times$ 10 columns) as the original, with only the *Value* column generated from synthetic data. This approach ensures that downstream analyses operate on structurally equivalent data while protecting athlete identities.

5 Experimentation Evaluation

To validate the internal consistency and utility of the synthetic dataset, a series of analyses were conducted on it, including correlation analysis, supervised machine learning regression with four protocols, and feature-importance evaluation.

Pearson's correlation coefficients were computed across all 14 numeric workload variables. Correlation values were interpreted using Hopkins' scale (0.0–0.1, 0.1–0.3, 0.3–0.5, 0.5–0.7, 0.7–0.9, and 0.9–1.0), with descriptors of trivial, small, moderate, large, very large, and nearly perfect, respectively [12]. Fig. 2 shows the correlation map, which revealed strong positive correlations among *Total Load*, limb-specific loads (*Left and Right Total Athlete g-Load*), *Total Impact*, and *Total Push-off* metrics. This is consistent with established biomechanical principles and IMU-derived workload theory [11]. In contrast, asymmetry metrics showed weak correlations with absolute load variables, consistent with the expected independence between bilateral imbalance measures and overall workload magnitude. These patterns confirm that the synthetic data preserves physiologically meaningful inter-variable relationships.

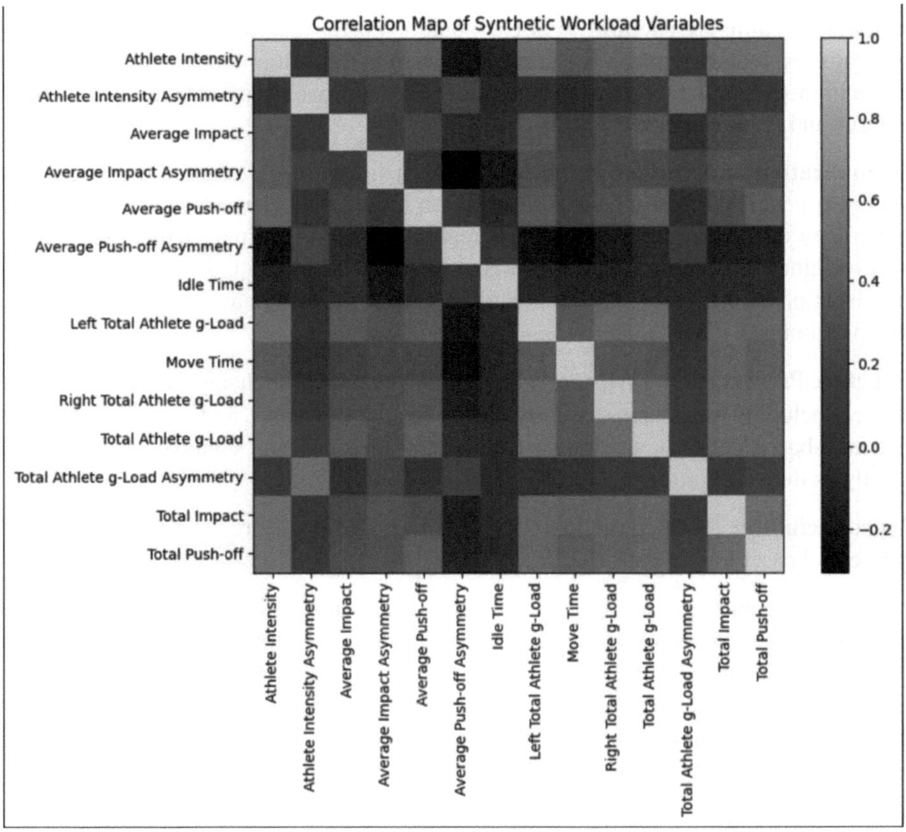

Fig. 2. Correlation map of synthetic workload variables.

From the correlation analysis, *Total Athlete g-Load* was selected as the prediction target because Pearson correlation analysis across all 14 numeric workload variables revealed strong positive associations between *Total Athlete g-Load* and *Total Load*, limb-specific loads (*Left and Right Total Athlete g-Load*), *Total Impact*, and *Total Push-off* metrics. The comparative outcomes are consistent with domain expectations that *Total Athlete g-Load* is driven primarily by cumulative workload and impact-derived metrics, with limb-specific load variables contributing directly to the composite target. Next, a multivariate regression model with regularization was implemented under an 80/20 shuffled train–test split to predict Total Athlete g-load from the remaining 13 biomechanical features.

Four train–test performance protocol scores are shown in Table 2. They validate whether the synthetic dataset preserved the functional predictive structure of the real data rather than merely marginal similarity. This approach evaluates cross-domain generalization to determine if predictive structure learned in one domain (real or synthetic) reliably transfers to the other without significant degradation [13]. Performance was reported using R^2 and Mean Squared Error (MSE), consistent with the validation framework used in prior modeling work, in which utility is judged by predictive error and variance explained on held-out evaluation splits [14].

Table 2. Train – test protocol scores for synthetic data fidelity.

Protocol	R^2 [Train, Test]	MSE[Train, Test]
TRTR	0.9198, 0.9193	1.32e8, 1.38e8
TSTR	0.9994, 0.7696	1.42e8., 6.1e8
TRTS	0.9198, 0.4403	1.32e8, 9.62e8
TSTS	0.9994, 0.9993	1.42e8, 1.91e8

In this context, the near-identical TRTR and TSTR results provide indirect evidence that the generator preserved relative contributions and interactions among the high-signal predictors, rather than only matching marginal distributions. These results indicate a generalization penalty under TSTR, supporting the conclusion that the synthetic generation process preserves predictive structure relevant to workload modeling. In essence, training on synthetic samples does not improve real-test performance, which is the most decisive criterion for synthetic utility when real data access is constrained. The performance under TRTS shows limited decision-making capability, but comparing TRTR vs TSTR indicates that synthetic data is helpful for training models that generalize to the real world. TSTS results indicate that the model generalizes well within the synthetic distribution and that the task is almost perfectly predictable.

Following predictive validation, we assessed model interpretability using feature importance scores derived from the TRTR protocol. The importance score was derived directly from the estimated multiple linear regression coefficients, enabling identification of variables that most contribute to variance reduction in predicting Total Athlete g-Load. As shown in Fig. 3, cumulative workload indicators such as Total Push-Off,

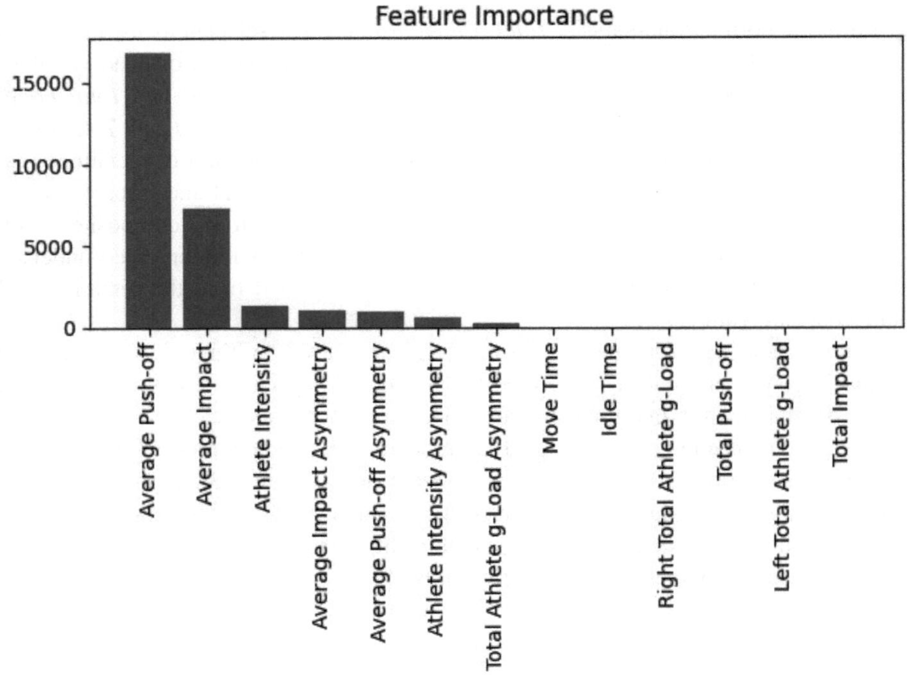

Fig. 3. Feature importance scores with respect to *Total Athlete g-Load* using multivariate regression.

Average Impact, and Athlete Intensity, and asymmetry measures such as Average Impact Asymmetry, Average Push-Off Asymmetry, Athlete Intensity Asymmetry, and Total Athlete g-Load Asymmetry consistently ranked highest. The ranking aligns with sports science principles, as Total Athlete g-Load is a composite workload metric derived from bilateral limb contributions and accumulated impact forces captured by IMU sensors.

Overall, the transfer results demonstrate that the synthetic dataset supports downstream workload prediction without observable loss in real-test performance. This framework shows that synthetic datasets can reproduce statistical workload relationships for a single collegiate team under monitoring; however, our study has several limitations. First, the dataset consists of a relatively small number of athletes from a single collegiate team and season. As a result, the observed workload distributions may reflect team-specific training structures, players' roles, and the competitive context. While synthetic data reproduces statistical relationships within this sample, it may not capture the full variability across teams with different training structures or levels of competition. Second, the synthetic data generation process uses Gaussian resampling combined with MICE imputation and does not explicitly model nonlinear interactions or temporal workload dynamics. As a result, rare measurements of high-intensity events, sequential fatigue effects, and session-to-session progression patterns may be underrepresented. Thus, the generated dataset should be interpreted as preserving general statistical structure rather than physiological behavior. Finally, validation was performed using a single target variable (*Total Athlete g-Load*) and a specific set of wearable-derived biomechanical metrics. As a result, the conclusions primarily apply to workload modeling tasks using similar monitoring variables. Thus, application to other sports, different sensor systems, injury prediction problems, or long-term performance forecasting requires additional evaluation before the framework can be assumed to generalize beyond this context.

6 Conclusion

In this work, the challenge of restricted access to athlete monitoring datasets in NCAA Division 1 women's basketball was addressed. Although wearable technologies provide detailed measurements of athlete workload and performance, privacy and proprietary constraints prevent data sharing, limiting reproducible research and model development. To address this limitation, a privacy-preserving synthetic data generation framework was proposed that reconstructs complete workload profiles using MICE imputation and generates synthetic observations via Gaussian resampling, while preserving the original dataset structure.

Validation results demonstrated that the generated dataset preserved meaningful statistical relationships and predictive structure. Correlation analysis showed physiologically plausible associations between workload variables and feature-importance rankings aligned with biomechanical expectations for *Total Athlete g-Load* predictors. Machine learning evaluation further confirmed preservation of predictive behavior. Across two training-testing regimes, the TSTR performance remained lower than the TRTR baseline but comparable to it. This indicates moderate but acceptable generalization degradation relative to the TRTR baseline and confirms that models trained on synthetic data perform effectively on real athlete observations.

By enabling a shareable dataset that retains analytical usefulness, this framework directly addresses the data scarcity challenge in NCAA basketball analytics. It supports model development when real-athlete monitoring data cannot be shared. In practice, synthetic data can serve as a substitute training source, allowing analysis to develop predictive workload models while maintaining athlete confidentiality. This also improves reproducibility by allowing researchers to distribute datasets with publications and to compare modeling approaches across institutions without requiring direct access to team data.

Future research should investigate more advanced generative approaches capable of modeling complex relationships and time-dependent behavior in athlete monitoring data. Deep generative and time-series methods may better represent nonlinear interactions and sequential workload patterns than the current Gaussian resampling approach. Specifically, future work will investigate tabular generative models such as Conditional Tabular GANs (CTGAN) and Variational Autoencoder (VAE)-based methods to benchmark performance across different generator classes. In addition, expanding the dataset to include multiple seasons and additional teams will improve generalizability and allow the framework to capture broader variability in athlete workload patterns. Further evaluation across multiple teams and predictive tasks, such as injury risk estimation, return-to-play monitoring, and workload classification, would help establish the framework's broader usefulness and reliability. Future work will also incorporate additional statistical fidelity metrics, including Kolmogorov-Smirnov tests, Wasserstein distances, and mutual information preservation, to further quantify distributional similarity between real and synthetic datasets. Finally, a formal privacy risk evaluation, such as membership inference testing or differential privacy guarantees, was not conducted in this study and remains an important direction for ensuring the safe deployment of synthetic athlete monitoring datasets.

Disclosure of Interests The authors have no competing interests to declare that are relevant to the content of this article.

References

1. Cordeiro, M.C., Cathain, C.O., Daly, L., Kelly, D.T., Rodrigues, T.B.: A synthetic datadriven machine learning approach for athlete performance attenuation prediction. Front. Sports Active Living **7**, 1607600 (2025)
2. Schlegel, V., Bharath, A.A., Zhao, Z., Yee, K.: Generating synthetic data with formal privacy guarantees: State of the art and the road ahead. arXiv preprint arXiv:2503.20846 (2025)
3. Naughton, M., Weaving, D., Scott, T., Compton, H.: Synthetic data as a strategy to resolve data privacy and confidentiality concerns in the sport sciences: Practical examples and an R Shiny application. Int. J. Sports Physiol. Perform. **18**(10), 1306–1314 (2023)
4. Warmenhoven, J., et al.: Synthetic data for sharing and exploration in highperformance sport: Considerations for application. Sports Med. (2025)
5. Goodfellow, I., et al.: Generative adversarial nets. In: Advances in Neural Information Processing Systems (NeurIPS), pp. 2672–2680 (2014)
6. Xu, L., Skoularidou, M., Cuesta-Infante, A., Veeramachaneni, K.: Modeling tabular data using conditional GAN. arXiv preprint arXiv:1907.00503 (2019)
7. Kingma, D.P., Welling, M.: Auto-encoding variational Bayes. arXiv preprint arXiv:1312.6114 (2013)
8. Hansen, L., Seedat, N., van der Schaar, M., Petrovic, A.: Reimagining synthetic tabular data generation through data-centric AI: A comprehensive benchmark. arXiv preprint arXiv:2310.16981 (2023)
9. Esteban, C., Hyland, S.L., Rätsch, G.: Real-valued (medical) time series generation with recurrent conditional GANs. arXiv preprint arXiv:1706.02633 (2017)
10. Plantiga Technologies Inc.: Plantiga. https://plantiga.com/, Accessed 5 Feb 2026
11. Impellizzeri, F.M., Rampinini, E., Maffiuletti, N., Marcora, S.M.: A vertical jump force test for assessing bilateral strength asymmetry in athletes. Med. Sci. Sports Exerc. **39**(11), 2044–2050 (2007)
12. Hopkins, W.G., Marshall, S.W., Batterham, A.M., Hanin, J.: Progressive statistics for studies in sports medicine and exercise science. Med. Sci. Sports Exerc. **41**(1), 3–13 (2009)
13. Ganesan, D.G.: Synthetic time-series data generation using Generative Adversarial Networks. Master's thesis (Complex Adaptive Systems), Department of Physics, Chalmers University of Technology, Gothenburg, Sweden (2021). https://odr.chalmers.se/bitstreams/19befa5e-d571-4666-bc4ec9f5f865c665/download
14. Sharma, S.U., Divakaran, S., Kaya, T., Raval, M.: A hybrid approach for interpretable game performance prediction in basketball. In: Proceedings of the International Joint Conference on Neural Networks (IJCNN), pp. 1–8. IEEE, Padua (2022)
15. Senbel, S., et al.: Impact of sleep and training on game performance and injury in Division-1 women's basketball amidst the pandemic. IEEE Access **10**, 15516–15527 (2022)

16. Sharma, S., Barot, V., Divakaran, S., Kaya, T., Taber, C.B., Raval, M.S.: A data-driven imputation scheme for cohort studies: A collegiate basketball case study. In: Dong, J.-S., Sun, J., Xie, X., Jiang, K. (eds.) Sports Analytics (ISACE 2025). LNCS, vol. 15925, pp. 235–252. Springer, Cham (2026)

The Impact of Strength of Schedule Balance on Tournament Efficacy

João P.L. Marchetti(✉), João P.F. Batista, and Pedro O.S. Vaz-de Melo

Computer Science Department, Universidade Federal de Minas Gerais (UFMG), Belo Horizonte, Brazil
jplm.marchetti@gmail.com

Abstract. Professional sports leagues rely on the double round-robin format to promote competitive fairness, yet the temporal ordering of opponents—whether a team faces a sequence of elite rivals early or begins with a more favorable schedule—remains a persistent source of debate. Theoretical accounts suggest that such sequencing may generate psychological feedback loops: front-loaded difficulty could induce a discouragement effect, whereas early success may foster momentum, potentially affecting final standings. This paper introduces the *Strength of Schedule Balance* (**SSB**) metric to quantify the temporal distribution of opponent difficulty and applies a stratified non-parametric framework to a validated dataset of 306 seasons from 20 professional football leagues ($N = 5{,}944$ schedules). Our results indicate that the double round-robin format is generally robust to schedule imbalance at the aggregate level, with most competitions showing no large or systematic distortions in final ranking outcomes attributable solely to fixture sequencing. However, league-level analysis reveals localized anomalies, particularly for unbalanced-weak schedules, where easier starts are more consistently associated with advantageous outcomes than harder starts are with disadvantageous ones. These findings suggest that schedule balance is not a universal determinant of tournament efficacy, but neither is it a purely logistical artifact; its impact appears to depend on the competitive environment of each league.

Keywords: Tournament Scheduling · Competitive Balance · Sports Analytics · Strength of Schedule · Causal Inference

1 Introduction

Professional sports leagues face a fundamental design challenge: ensuring that the tournament format yields a final ranking that accurately reflects the true skill levels of the participants. While several works [17,20,27,36] emphasized the importance of outcome uncertainty for sustaining fan interest, the structural integrity of the schedule itself plays a distinct, yet equally critical, role in competitive fairness. As noted by Szymanski [32], the specific rules and organization of a contest shape the incentives for effort. As the sequence of opponents defines

Z. Liu and V. Misra (Eds.): ISACE 2026, LNCS 16610, pp. 258–276, 2026.
https://doi.org/10.1007/978-3-032-27272-0_18

the competitive path a team must navigate, it can influence whether the final standings accurately reflect teams' true latent abilities.

Traditionally, tournament scheduling has been treated primarily as an operations research problem focused on minimizing travel costs and logistical constraints [10,13]. However, there is an ongoing discussion regarding whether scheduling significantly impacts the accuracy of team rankings. Empirical evidence suggests that the sequence of matches matters. Krumer and Lechner [18], for instance, found that the ordering of opponents in round-robin tournaments can create significant "first-mover"' advantages in knockout UEFA championships. In contrast, Goossens and Spieksma [14] found that "carry-over effects" [28] —where a team's performance is influenced by the strength of its previous opponent—were non-existent in the Belgian football league.

Despite these insights, the consequences of *structural* schedule imbalance remain understudied. Contest theory suggests that "front-loaded" or "back-loaded" sequences can distort incentives, triggering either a "discouragement effect" [32]—where early losses reduce rational effort—or a "momentum effect" [8], where early success catalyzes performance. Consequently, it remains unclear whether such imbalances introduce systematic bias into final standings, thereby compromising the tournament's efficacy in recovering the true ordering of team abilities.

This paper addresses this gap by introducing the *Strength of Schedule Balance* (**SSB**) to quantify the temporal distribution of opponent difficulty. Analyzing 20 major professional football leagues over 19 seasons [33], we compute the metric using two proxies for team strength—final league standing and team market value—and classify schedules as (i) **balanced**, (ii) **unbalanced-strong**, or (iii) **unbalanced-weak**. We then statistically assess whether these structural imbalances are associated with distortions in tournament efficacy, that is, with the league's ability to recover latent team rankings.

Contrary to theoretical concerns regarding schedule fairness, our findings indicate that the standard double round-robin format is generally robust. While the aggregate evidence suggests that, in most competitions, intrinsic team quality outweighs scheduling nuances, the league-level analysis reveals localized anomalies. In particular, easier starts are more consistently associated with advantageous outcomes than harder starts are with disadvantageous ones, suggesting that the impact of schedule imbalance is conditional rather than universal. These findings challenge the view of fixture ordering as a purely logistical artifact and instead position schedule balance as a context-dependent factor in competitive fairness.

The remainder of this paper proceeds as follows. We first review relevant literature on tournament scheduling and efficacy determinants. We then present our **SSB** metric and describe the dataset. Subsequently, we report our empirical findings on both research questions before concluding with implications for league design.

2 Related Work

Tournament Scheduling and Fairness. Tournament scheduling has traditionally focused on operational constraints such as travel distance and fixture breaks, aiming to reduce costs for clubs and organizers [13]. However, current research recognizes that the schedule structure itself affects fairness and competitive balance by systematically favouring some teams through the timing of opponents [10,35]. Bartsch, Drexl, and Kröger [3] introduced the partitioning of teams into strength groups to avoid long runs of matches against similar-quality opponents, a notion formalized by Briskorn and Knust [6] to mitigate carry-over effects, that is, situations where a team's performance influences subsequent matches [28]. While designing "fair" schedules requires solving complex combinatorial optimization problems [7], empirical evidence on how these operational imbalances translate to on-field outcomes remains scarce.

Tournament Efficacy and Competitive Incentives. Tournament efficacy refers to the ability of a format to recover the true latent ordering of team abilities. It is typically assessed by comparing the final ranking to an underlying "true" ranking of team strengths, using metrics such as Kendall's τ, Spearman's footrule distance, or the fraction of tournaments where the best team wins on Monte Carlo simulations [2,19].

Several factors may impact tournament efficacy. The most extensively studied factor in the literature is tournament format [2,9,19,21,29–31]—with the double round-robin generally considered one of the most reliable formats—and seeding [11,15,16,25], as noted by [10]. However, other factors have been shown to influence game outcomes which, if not regulated, can lead to diminished efficacy in the overall tournament, such as home advantage [22,23] and referee bias [4].

While standard efficacy models treat match outcomes as stochastic processes, theoretical and empirical work suggests that schedule structure creates path dependence. Szymanski [32] argues that a sequence of elite opponents can trigger a "discouragement effect," where early losses induce a rational reduction in effort. Conversely, favorable schedules may generate a "momentum effect"; Cohen-Zada, Krumer, and Shtudiner [8] demonstrate that past success causally increases the probability of future victory through psychological mechanisms, independent of strategic incentives. Consequently, if structural imbalances systematically induce either discouragement or momentum, the tournament's efficacy in recovering the true ordering of team abilities is compromised.

Research Gap. Despite the extensive literature on constructing balanced schedules from an operations research perspective [5–7,24,28,34], a significant disconnect remains between algorithmic scheduling and its actual impact on tournament efficacy. Existing empirical studies on schedule-induced bias often yield mixed conclusions and are typically limited to single competitions or specific knockout contexts [1,12,14,18]. Consequently, there is a lack of a unified, quantitative framework to assess how the temporal distribution of opponent strength affects the accuracy of league standings. Specifically, the literature has yet to determine whether theoretical phenomena like the "discouragement effect" [32] or its counterpart, the "momentum effect" [8], are merely localized anomalies or systematic features of professional league structures.

3 Data

3.1 Data Acquisition and Source

The empirical analysis utilizes a longitudinal dataset of professional football competitions, restricted to the **2004–2024** period to ensure the synchronization of performance metrics with financial valuation data. Data were programmatically extracted via web scraping from *Transfermarkt* [33], a comprehensive repository for association football statistics. To facilitate a multi-granular analysis, the extraction pipeline targeted three distinct data structures:

1. **Final League Standings**: These records capture the aggregate seasonal performance for each team. Specifically, the dataset includes the final position, team name, total matches played, and the specific distribution of outcomes (won, drawn, and lost). Furthermore, we extracted the total points accumulated by each team, which are used to assess the efficacy of the league's final ranking.
2. **Match-Level Records**: To reconstruct the chronological sequence of the season, we extracted granular fixture data. This includes temporal metadata—date and time—alongside the specific round (matchday) number. For each fixture, we identified the home and away teams, along with the official match result.
3. **Market Valuations**: We extracted the total market value of each participating squad, denominated in Euros (€). These values serve as a high-fidelity proxy for latent team strength, allowing the model to distinguish between schedule-induced performance variance and intrinsic quality disparities.

3.2 Data Preprocessing and Validation Protocols

To ensure the structural integrity of the analysis, a multi-stage preprocessing pipeline was implemented. Data were subjected to rigorous validation based on the following **business rules** to filter out anomalous or incomplete seasons:

- **Tournament Structure**: Inclusion was strictly limited to double round-robin formats. Competitions utilizing multi-stage playoffs or irregular structures that deviate from the standard home-and-away parity were excluded to maintain the consistency of our proposed Strength of Schedule Balance metric.
- **Operational Stability and Reporting Fidelity**: Seasons were retained only if at least 95% of match records contained non-null attendance values. While attendance is not a primary variable of interest, this threshold serves as

a proxy for operational continuity and data reliability. The absence of attendance records often correlates with external disruptions—such as the COVID-19 pandemic, geopolitical instability, or administrative failures—which result in "behind-closed-doors" matches or irregular competitive conditions. By applying this filter, we ensure the dataset represents standardized seasons where environmental and institutional factors remained consistent.
- **Financial Data Completeness**: A season was retained only if market valuation data were available for all participating clubs. This ensures that every scheduling data point is paired with a corresponding financial proxy for team ability.

3.3 Dataset Composition

The final validated dataset comprises 306 seasons across 20 distinct leagues, representing 11 countries and 3 continents (Europe, Asia, and South America). Table 1 provides a detailed summary of the coverage and valid seasons per competition. The dataset exhibits a mean of 15.30 valid seasons per league, with the French *Ligue 1* providing one of the highest longitudinal depth (19 seasons). Conversely, the Turkish *Süper Lig* represents the most constrained subset due to stricter validation outcomes.

The preprocessing pipeline culminated into two high-fidelity datasets, *Validated Standings* and *Validated Games*, which restrict the analytical scope exclusively to the seasons and championships verified as structurally sound. To ensure longitudinal consistency, we implemented an Entity Resolution protocol: raw strings for teams and leagues underwent sanitization—involving case normalization and the removal of diacritics—followed by a canonical mapping of team names to unique identifiers.

This procedure accounts for historical club rebrands and nomenclature variations, ensuring that the deterministic unique identifiers[1] remain invariant across the 306 valid seasons. Furthermore, temporal variables were subjected to rigorous parsing and conversion into unified *datetime* objects, supplemented by manual curation via targeted online research to resolve persistent null values. These consolidated dataframes provide the empirical foundation for the statistical assessment of tournament efficacy and schedule-driven discouragement effects explored in the subsequent sections.

4 Methodology

The analytical framework of this study isolates the impact of temporal schedule sequencing on tournament outcomes. We transform raw data into a structured

[1] To guarantee data integrity and record traceability, we employed the SHA-256 (Secure Hash Algorithm 256-bit) to generate fixed-size, collision-resistant cryptographic hashes for each entry. This ensures that identifiers remain invariant across datasets regardless of string variations in raw sources.

Table 1. Descriptive statistics of the validated longitudinal dataset by league. The *Avg. Teams* column reflects the mean number of participants per season, accounting for historical expansions or contractions in league size. *Coverage (%)* represents the data density, defined as the ratio of successfully validated seasons to the total chronological span from the *Start* year through 2024.

League Name	Seasons	Avg. Teams	Country	Start	Coverage (%)
Ligue 1	19	19.79	France	2004	90.48
Premier League	19	20.00	England	2004	90.48
Championship	19	24.00	England	2004	90.48
Serie A	19	20.00	Italy	2004	90.48
Serie B	19	21.42	Italy	2004	90.48
Liga Portugal	19	16.95	Portugal	2004	90.48
Bundesliga	18	18.00	Germany	2004	85.71
2. Bundesliga	18	18.00	Germany	2004	85.71
La Liga	18	20.00	Spain	2005	90.00
La Liga 2	16	22.00	Spain	2007	88.89
Liga Portugal 2	16	18.25	Portugal	2007	88.89
Série A (Brazil)	15	20.00	Brazil	2007	83.33
Challenger Pro League	14	15.43	Belgium	2006	73.68
Ligue 2	13	20.00	France	2004	61.90
J1 League	13	18.31	Japan	2009	81.25
J2 League	13	21.69	Japan	2011	92.86
Série B (Brazil)	13	20.00	Brazil	2010	86.67
Jupiler Pro League	13	16.31	Belgium	2008	76.47
Saudi Pro League	7	15.43	Saudi Arabia	2014	63.64
Süper Lig	5	19.00	Turkey	2014	45.45

inferential pipeline comprising three stages: (i) computation of the Strength of Schedule Balance, (ii) heuristic-based classification of schedule types, and (iii) non-parametric statistical evaluation of ranking disparities conditioned on schedule type.

4.1 Measuring Strength of Schedule Balance (SSB)

To quantify how opponent difficulty is distributed across a team's schedule, we introduce the *Strength of Schedule Balance* (**SSB**) metric. Let $R = \{r_1, \ldots, r_n\}$ represent the set of teams ordered by a latent strength or skill rank, denoted as s_i, such that r_1 is the strongest team and r_n is the weakest. In our evaluation, this skill rank s_i is empirically measured using two proxies: the team's final league standing (the oracle rank) and the team's market value.

For a specific team r_i, the schedule S_i is the ordered sequence of opponents faced in the first half of the season. We define the Strength of Schedule Balance, $\rho(S_i)$, as the Spearman's rank correlation coefficient between the actual schedule S_i of team r_i and a theoretical perfectly unbalanced schedule R_{-i}. In this generalized model, R_{-i} is the ordered list of all opponents excluding r_i sorted by their strength s_i. For example, in a tournament composed of four teams, $R_{-2} = \{r_1, r_3, r_4\}$ denotes the perfectly unbalanced schedule of the second-best team r_2. In this formulation, $\rho(S_i) \in [-1, 1]$ serves as a proxy for the "loading" of the schedule:

- $\rho(S_i) \approx 1$: Indicates a **front-loaded** or **unbalanced-strong** schedule, in which the team faces elite opponents early in the competition, with difficulty decreasing over time.
- $\rho(S_i) \approx -1$: Indicates a **back-loaded** or **unbalanced-weak** schedule, in which the team initially faces weaker opponents, with difficulty escalating toward the season's conclusion.
- $\rho(S_i) \approx 0$: Indicates a **balanced** schedule, characterized by a uniform distribution of opponent difficulty across rounds.

4.2 Threshold Selection and Group Classification

To facilitate comparative analysis, we categorize the continuous $\rho(S_i)$ values into three discrete cohorts: **Balanced** (G_0), **Unbalanced-Weak** (G_-), and **Unbalanced-Strong** (G_+). We consider two criteria for assigning schedules to these categories. First, by the magnitude of $\rho(S_i)$:

Definition 1 (Magnitude Criterion). *Given a threshold* $\tau \in [0, 1]$, *a schedule* S_i *is categorized according to the value of* $\rho(S_i)$ *as follows:*

- G_0 ***(balanced)****:* $-\tau \leq \rho(S_i) \leq \tau$, *corresponding to a balanced schedule.*
- G_- ***(unbalanced-weak)****:* $\rho(S_i) < -\tau$, *corresponding to a back-loaded schedule.*
- G_+ ***(unbalanced-strong)****:* $\rho(S_i) > \tau$, *corresponding to a front-loaded schedule.*

Second, based on the statistical significance of $\rho(S_i)$, assessed via Spearman's rank correlation coefficient between S_i and R_{-i}:

Definition 2 (Statistical Significance Criterion). *Given a significance level* $\alpha \in (0, 1)$ *and the corresponding p-value obtained from Spearman's rank correlation test between* S_i *and* R_{-i}, *a schedule* S_i *is categorized as follows:*

- G_0 ***(balanced)****:* $p \geq \alpha$, *indicating no statistically significant schedule loading.*
- G_- ***(unbalanced-weak)****:* $p < \alpha$ *and* $\rho(S_i) < 0$, *indicating a statistically significant back-loaded schedule.*

– *G_+ (**unbalanced-strong**): $p < \alpha$ and $\rho(S_i) > 0$, indicating a statistically significant front-loaded schedule.*

The magnitude-based and statistical-significance criteria capture complementary aspects of schedule imbalance. The magnitude criterion offers a direct and interpretable measure of the extent to which a schedule is front- or back-loaded, enabling controlled comparisons across different threshold values. In contrast, the statistical-significance criterion accounts for uncertainty arising from schedule length and opponent variability, distinguishing meaningful temporal patterns from fluctuations that may occur by chance. Together, these criteria allow us to distinguish structurally unbalanced schedules from those that are only weakly or spuriously correlated with opponent strength, thereby supporting a more robust comparative analysis.

As expected, the resulting group distributions depend on the choice of parameters τ and α. To ensure the robustness of the **SSB** metric, we evaluated its behavior using two distinct proxies for team skill: final league standings and squad market valuations. Table 2 reports the proportion of schedules assigned to each group across these classification frameworks, computed over the validated dataset.

Table 2. Group distributions across different classification thresholds for ranking and market value classifications.

	Final Standing			Market Value		
Classification Criterion	G_- (%)	G_0 (%)	G_+ (%)	G_- (%)	G_0 (%)	G_+ (%)
$\alpha = 0.10$ (Significance)	4.1	91.8	4.1	4.5	91.9	3.7
$\alpha = 0.05$ (Significance)	1.9	96.1	2.0	2.3	96.1	1.6
$\tau = 0.2$ (Magnitude)	19.5	61.3	19.2	19.2	61.7	19.1
$\tau = 0.3$ (Magnitude)	**9.6**	**80.9**	**9.5**	**9.5**	**81.5**	**9.0**
$\tau = 0.4$ (Magnitude)	3.8	92.3	3.9	4.2	92.4	3.4

The empirical distribution reveals a high degree of convergence between the two proxies. While p-value thresholds ($\alpha = 0.05$) offer high statistical confidence, they result in extremely sparse groups ($< 2.5\%$) that lack the variance necessary to detect systemic bias. Conversely, $\tau = 0.2$ captures nearly 40% of the population as unbalanced, potentially diluting the effect of extreme scheduling.

Consequently, we adopted the **Magnitude Criterion** with $\tau = 0.3$ as the optimal threshold for both classification types. This heuristic ensures that approximately **10%** of the total sample is captured in each unbalanced extreme (G_- and G_+), providing a robust and balanced subset for testing the discouragement and momentum effect hypotheses. The alignment between ranking-based and valuation-based distributions suggests that the structural loading of a schedule is a persistent feature, independent of how team quality is operationalized.

4.3 Empirical Illustrations of Schedule Imbalance

To illustrate the structural variance captured by the **SSB** metric, we examine the Premier League in the season 2024/2025 using both final league rankings and squad market valuations.

Consider Chelsea, who finished 4th in the final standings. When utilizing the final ranking as the strength proxy (s_i), their schedule $\mathbf{S}_4$ is represented as the sequence of opponent ranks: $\mathbf{S}_4 = \{3, 16, 12, 9, 14, 8, 7, 1, 5, 15, 2, 18, 6, 20, 17, 10, 13, 11, 19\}$. This yields a Strength of Schedule Balance of $\rho(\mathbf{S}_4) = 0.3474$. When applying the market value proxy—where Chelsea is ranked 2nd in squad valuation—the schedule sequence becomes $\mathbf{S}_2 = \{1, 13, 10, 11, 15, 9, 12, 4, 8, 5, 3, 20, 7, 18, 6, 14, 16, 17, 19\}$, resulting in a higher correlation of $\rho(\mathbf{S}_2) = 0.4351$. In both frameworks, Chelsea is categorized into the **unbalanced-strong** group (G_+), indicating a consistently identified front-loaded schedule.

In contrast, Leicester City (ranked 18th in standings and 20th in market value) provides an illustration of a back-loaded or **unbalanced-weak** schedule. Under the final ranking proxy, their schedule $\mathbf{S}_{18} = \{17, 11, 6, 12, 13, 2, 9, 20, 7, 19, 15, 4, 10, 14, 8, 5, 16, 1, 3\}$ yields $\rho(\mathbf{S}_{18}) = -0.3053$. Using the market value proxy, the sequence $\mathbf{S}_{20} = \{6, 17, 7, 10, 16, 3, 11, 18, 12, 19, 5, 2, 14, 15, 9, 8, 13, 4, 1\}$ results in $\rho(\mathbf{S}_{20}) = -0.2386$.

4.4 Inferential Framework: Efficacy and Effect Size

The terminal stage of our methodology assesses whether the group assignment (G_-, G_0, G_+) significantly distorts the final league standings. Formally, let $R = \{r_1, r_2, \ldots, r_n\}$ denote the ordered list of teams according to their final positions in the league standings, where r_1 is the champion, r_2 the runner-up, and so on. Let $G(r_i) \in \{G_-, G_0, G_+\}$ denote the group assignment of team r_i. We formulate our hypothesis as follows:

$$
\begin{aligned}
H_0: &\ \text{The final league ranking is independent of the group assignment,}\\
&\ \Pr(r_i \mid G(r_i) = G_-) = \Pr(r_i \mid G(r_i) = G_0) = \Pr(r_i \mid G(r_i) = G_+)\,,\ \forall i.\\
H_1: &\ \text{The group assignment distorts the final standings,}\\
&\ \exists i \text{ such that } \Pr(r_i \mid G(r_i) = g) \neq \Pr(r_i \mid G(r_i) = g')\,,\ \text{for some } g \neq g'.
\end{aligned}
$$

Mann-Whitney U Test for Distributional Shift. We begin testing these hypotheses using the non-parametric MannWhitney U test to compare the distributions of final ranks between pairs of groups (e.g., G_+ vs. G_0). Because the test is rank-based and makes no assumptions about the normality of the data, it is well suited to ordinal outcomes such as league standings. The test assesses the null hypothesis that team rank is independent of group assignment. A statistically significant result ($p < 0.05$) indicates that certain ranks are disproportionately represented in one group relative to another, suggesting that schedule imbalance induces a systematic advantage or disadvantage that the round-robin format does not fully neutralize.

Effect Size: Cliff's Delta (δ). Because our large sample size ($N = 5,944$) may yield significant p-values even for negligible differences, we employ **Cliff's Delta** (δ) to quantify the actual magnitude of the effect. This non-parametric effect size metric, bounded by $[-1, 1]$, measures how often values in one distribution are larger than values in another, providing a robust evaluation of distributional overlap.

Formally, we compare the rank of the teams in a unbalanced group $\mathcal{U} \in \{G_+, G_-\}$ with the rank of the teams in the balanced group $\mathcal{B} \equiv G_0$. For a given rank $u \in \mathcal{U}$ and rank $b \in \mathcal{B}$, we define the dominance function $d(u, b)$ as:

$$d(u,b) = \begin{cases} +1 & \text{if } u > b \quad \text{(Unbalanced performed worse)} \\ -1 & \text{if } u < b \quad \text{(Unbalanced performed better)} \\ 0 & \text{if } u = b \end{cases} \tag{1}$$

We apply this framework in two distinct contexts to isolate the impact of strength of schedule imbalance:

1. Season-Level Effect Size (δ. To analyze individual seasons, we compute the standard Cliff's Delta as a measure of effect size. Let $\mathcal{U}$ and $\mathcal{B}$ denote the sets of final ranks for teams with unbalanced and balanced schedules in a given season, with cardinalities $n_{\mathcal{U}}$ and $n_{\mathcal{B}}$, respectively. The seasonal effect size is defined as the average dominance across all pairwise comparisons between ranks in $\mathcal{U}$ and $\mathcal{B}$:

$$\delta = \frac{1}{n_{\mathcal{U}} n_{\mathcal{B}}} \sum_{u \in \mathcal{U}} \sum_{b \in \mathcal{B}} d(u,b) \tag{2}$$

A positive δ indicates that teams with unbalanced schedules tend to finish in worse positions (i.e., higher rank values) than those with balanced schedules. For instance, if every rank in $\mathcal{B}$ is strictly lower than every rank in $\mathcal{U}$, then $\delta = 1$, reflecting complete dominance of balanced over unbalanced teams.

2. League-Wide Stratified Effect Size ($\delta_{\mathcal{L}}$) To aggregate results across an entire league history while controlling for inter-season and inter-league variance, we implement a **League-Wide Stratified Cliff's Delta**. This ensures that a team is only compared against its contemporaries within the same season, preventing confounding factors—such as varying league sizes or historical shifts in competitive balance—from skewing the results. For a league $\mathcal{L}$ comprising m seasons $L_1, L_2, \ldots, L_m$, we compute the aggregated effect size as

$$\delta_{\mathcal{L}} = \frac{\sum_{L \in \mathcal{L}} \sum_{u \in \mathcal{U}_L} \sum_{b \in \mathcal{B}_L} d(u,b)}{\sum_{L \in \mathcal{L}} (|\mathcal{U}_L| \times |\mathcal{B}_L|)}, \tag{3}$$

where $\mathcal{B}_L$ and $\mathcal{U}_L$ denote the sets of balanced and unbalanced teams in season L, with cardinalities $|\mathcal{B}_L|$ and $|\mathcal{U}_L|$, respectively. This formulation corresponds to a weighted average of the seasonal Cliff's Delta values, where each season is weighted by the total number of pairwise comparisons between balanced and unbalanced teams.

This stratified approach allows for a clean isolation of the schedule's structural impact across our longitudinal dataset, summarizing whether specific competitions consistently penalize unbalanced schedules over decades of play without confounding the data across different years.

Finally, to interpret the magnitude of the resulting coefficients, we adopt the thresholds established by Romano et al. [26]. Specifically, an effect size is considered **negligible** if $|\delta| < 0.147$, **small** if $|\delta| < 0.33$, **medium** if $|\delta| < 0.474$, and **large** otherwise.

5 Results

5.1 Prevalence of Schedule Imbalance

Table 3 summarizes the schedule classifications across the 20 competitions by highlighting the most extreme deviations alongside the global average. Both metrics reveal high structural consistency, with the English Championship consistently demonstrating the highest stability ($G_0 > 85\%$). Additionally, Brasileiro Série A exhibits the highest financial balance ($G_0 = 89.00\%$). Conversely, the Saudi Pro League is the most volatile under the ranking proxy ($G_0 = 68.52\%$), while Liga Portugal 2 shows a significant divergence, dropping to a 68.49% balance rate under the market value classification. Despite these localized outliers, the global average for balanced schedules (G_0) securely anchors at approximately 80% across both proxies, confirming the double round-robin format's overall structural resilience.

5.2 Aggregate Impact on Ranking Efficacy

In this section, we examine whether the observable imbalance identified in the previous section translates into distortions in final league standings. To this end, we first analyze the aggregate distribution of final positions across the dataset.

To quantify the magnitude of these distributional shifts, we analyze the effect sizes for individual seasons. Figure 1 presents the distribution of Cliff's Delta (δ) values for the G_- vs. G_0 and G_+ vs. G_0 comparisons. The results indicate a conditional rather than universal effect. Under the traditional final ranking classification, the median effect size for both groups is centered strictly at zero ($\delta \approx 0.00$), but the inter-quartile ranges (IQRs) reveal a distinct directional asymmetry. The G_- cohort (Easy Start) consistently extends into the negative "medium" effect zone ($-0.474 < \delta < -0.33$), suggesting that while an easy start does not guarantee success, it significantly widens the potential for overperformance. Conversely, the G_+ cohort (Hard Start) exhibits a mirrored skew toward the positive "medium" zone, indicating a higher susceptibility to underperformance.

Table 3. Prevalence of schedule types across the 20 analyzed football leagues. For each league, the table reports the percentage of schedules classified as unbalanced-weak (G_-), balanced (G_0), and unbalanced-strong (G_+) when **SSB** is computed using two alternative team-strength proxies: final standing and market value. The column N denotes the number of valid schedules available for that league, and the last row reports the global average across all leagues.

		Final Standing			Market Value		
League Name	N	% G_-	% G_0	% G_+	% G_-	% G_0	% G_+
Saudi Pro League	108	16.67	68.52	14.81	12.96	74.07	12.96
Challenger Pro League	216	12.96	72.69	14.35	11.11	80.56	8.33
Bundesliga 2	324	13.27	75.93	10.80	9.57	77.47	12.96
Jupiler Pro League	212	13.21	76.42	10.38	11.32	79.72	8.96
J1 League	238	12.61	77.31	10.08	12.18	76.89	10.92
Bundesliga	324	9.57	79.01	11.42	7.10	83.95	8.95
Brasileiro Série B	260	10.38	79.62	10.00	9.23	80.00	10.77
Liga Portugal 2	292	8.90	79.79	11.30	15.41	68.49	16.10
Ligue 2	260	10.00	80.77	9.23	11.15	78.85	10.00
Premier League	380	10.00	80.79	9.21	10.00	81.58	8.42
Liga Portugal	322	9.32	81.37	9.32	8.70	81.68	9.63
Serie A	380	10.79	81.58	7.63	8.42	82.89	8.68
La Liga 2	352	7.95	82.10	9.94	10.80	78.98	10.23
J2 League	282	8.16	82.27	9.57	7.45	82.98	9.57
Serie B	407	8.35	82.56	9.09	9.83	81.82	8.35
Ligue 1	376	8.78	82.71	8.51	8.78	84.84	6.38
La Liga	360	6.94	83.61	9.44	9.44	83.06	7.50
Brasileiro Série A	300	7.33	84.33	8.33	6.00	89.00	5.00
Süper Lig	95	10.53	85.26	4.21	8.42	87.37	4.21
Championship	456	7.46	85.96	6.58	7.46	86.62	5.92
Global Average (20 Leagues)	**5944**	**10.16**	**80.13**	**9.71**	**9.77**	**81.04**	**9.19**

Crucially, this directional asymmetry persists when transitioning to the exogenous market value proxy. While substituting the final standing with pre-season financial data shifts the median of the G_- cohort slightly below zero, the overall spread and structural behavior remain consistent across both methodologies. This comparison show a consolidation of this variance into the directional patterns described above, supporting the hypothesis that schedule imbalances act as a latent risk factor rather than a deterministic outcome.

5.3 League-Specific Significance

To ensure that the aggregate patterns are not masking localized anomalies, we analyze the impact of schedule imbalance on a per-league basis using the Strat-

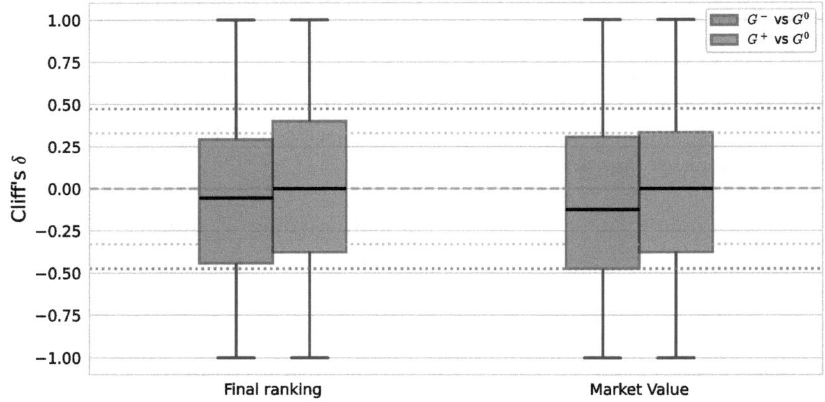

Fig. 1. Cliff's δ distributions for ranking efficiency comparing evaluation metrics. Comparisons are shown for G_- vs. G_0 (red) and G_+ vs. G_0 (blue) using both Final Ranking and Market Value to compute the Strength of Schedule Balance. Dotted lines denote effect size thresholds: small ($|\delta| = 0.33$, yellow) and medium ($|\delta| = 0.474$, red). The grey dashed line at $\delta = 0$ represents the null effect.

ified Cliff's Delta ($\delta_{\mathcal{L}}$) and Mann–Whitney significance tests. We perform this analysis using the **SSB** metric under both market value and final standing proxies, which yield broadly similar qualitative patterns. However, we present the plots using the market value proxy in order to reduce concerns regarding endogeneity. Figure 2 maps each league according to its effect size (y-axis) and statistical significance (x-axis, $-\log_{10}(p\text{-value})$), while Table 4 compares the significant results between proxy choices as a robustness check.

Overall, both proxies suggest that the double round-robin format is broadly robust: most leagues remain to the left of the $p = 0.05$ threshold, and the major European leagues do not exhibit statistically significant deviations under either schedule extreme.

Table 4. Comparison of league-level results that are statistically significant in the Mann–Whitney tests (p-value < 0.05) under the two **SSB** proxy choices. Results are reported separately for the G_- vs. G_0 and G_+ vs. G_0 comparisons.

Proxy	Sig. Better ($\delta_{\mathcal{L}} < 0$)	Sig. Worse ($\delta_{\mathcal{L}} > 0$)
G_- vs. G_0		
Final Standing	Saudi Pro; Jupiler Pro	—
Market Value	Saudi Pro; Jupiler Pro; Liga Portugal 2; Ligue 2; Camp. Bras. Série B	—
G_+ vs. G_0		
Final Standing	J1 League; Liga Portugal 2	Jupiler Pro
Market Value	J2 League; Camp. Bras. Série B	—

Notes: "Sig. Better" denotes significantly better final ranks for the unbalanced group (negative $\delta_{\mathcal{L}}$); "Sig. Worse" denotes significantly worse ranks (positive $\delta_{\mathcal{L}}$). "—" indicates no leagues in that category for the given proxy.

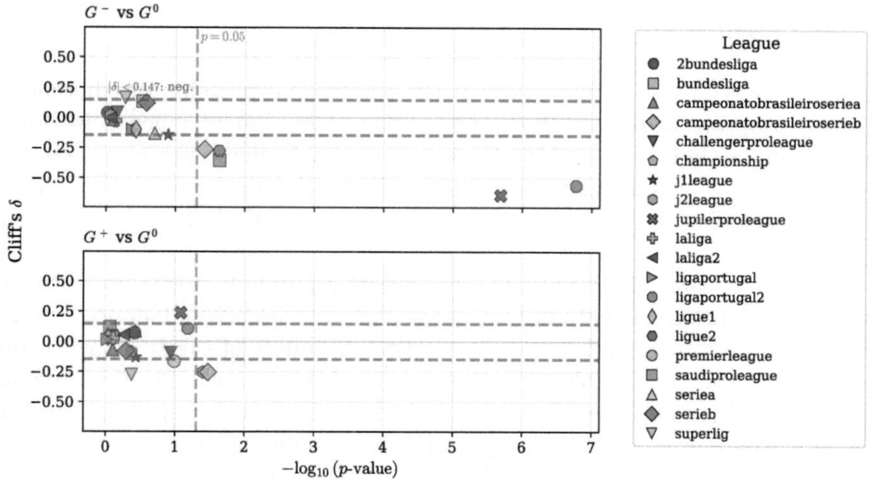

Fig. 2. Significance tests per league for the G_- and G_+ groups based on market value classification. Points to the right of the red dashed line ($p < 0.05$) represent statistically significant deviations from the balanced baseline. The region between the blue dashed lines ($|\delta| \leq 0.147$) denotes a negligible effect size. (Color figure online)

The clearest league-specific effects emerge for unbalanced-weak schedules (G_- vs. G_0). In this comparison, the Jupiler Pro League ($\delta_{\mathcal{L}} = -0.643, p < 10^{-5}$) and Liga Portugal 2 ($\delta_{\mathcal{L}} = -0.562$, $p < 10^{-6}$) stand out as the strongest anomalies, with additional significant negative effects in the Saudi Pro League ($\delta_{\mathcal{L}} = -0.356$, $p = 0.023$), Ligue 2 ($\delta_{\mathcal{L}} = -0.278$, $p = 0.024$), and Campeonato Brasileiro Série B ($\delta_{\mathcal{L}} = -0.265$, $p = 0.038$). As shown in Table 4, the Jupiler Pro League and Saudi Pro League remain significant under both proxy choices. Because negative Cliff's Delta indicates that teams in the unbalanced group tend to finish in better positions than those in the balanced baseline, these results are consistent with a momentum-type advantage associated with easier starts.

In contrast, the evidence for unbalanced-strong schedules (G_+ vs. G_0) is more limited and does not support a generalized discouragement pattern under the market value proxy. No league presents a statistically significant positive $\delta_{\mathcal{L}}$, and the only significant deviations are observed in J2 League ($\delta_{\mathcal{L}} = -0.254$, $p = 0.040$) and Campeonato Brasileiro Série B ($\delta_{\mathcal{L}} = -0.254$, $p = 0.034$), both indicating that teams with front-loaded difficult schedules finished better than their balanced counterparts. Unlike the G_- comparison, these league-level results do not align closely with the findings obtained under the final standing proxy, which suggests that the evidence for hard-start effects is less stable across alternative definitions of team strength.

Taken together, these findings indicate that league-level anomalies are concentrated in a small subset of competitions and are not symmetric across schedule extremes. Thus, the evidence is more consistent with league-specific associations than with a universal schedule mechanism affecting tournament efficacy.

6 Discussion

The main contribution of this study is the empirical evaluation of whether the temporal ordering of opponent strength affects tournament efficacy in double round-robin football leagues. At the aggregate level, the evidence points to a predominantly robust format: most competitions do not exhibit large or systematic distortions in final rank distributions attributable solely to schedule sequencing.

At the same time, the results do not support a purely neutral view of fixture ordering. The distributional analysis suggests that schedule imbalance acts less as a deterministic force and more as a conditional source of variation, with some seasons exhibiting noticeable deviations even when the median effect remains close to zero. In this sense, the timing of strong and weak opponents appears capable of shaping competitive trajectories in specific settings, even if it does not consistently alter outcomes across the ecosystem as a whole.

The clearest league-level deviations emerge for unbalanced-weak schedules (G_{-}), where several competitions display significant negative effect sizes relative to the balanced baseline. Because negative Cliff's Delta indicates that teams in the unbalanced group tend to finish in better final positions, these patterns are consistent with an advantage associated with easier starts. The recurrence of this signal across multiple leagues, and its partial stability across alternative strength proxies, suggests that back-loaded schedules may in some environments create a meaningful pathway to overperformance.

By contrast, the evidence for unbalanced-strong schedules (G_{+}) is considerably weaker. Although isolated league-level deviations appear under both strength definitions, they are fewer in number, less stable across proxies, and do not reveal a coherent pattern of systematic underperformance. As a result, the present findings provide limited support for a generalized discouragement effect linked to front-loaded schedules.

This asymmetry between G_{-} and G_{+} is substantively important. If schedule imbalance operated through a uniform mechanism, one would expect easier starts and harder starts to generate roughly symmetric effects in opposite directions. Instead, the empirical picture is more uneven: easier starts appear more consistently associated with advantageous outcomes than harder starts are with disadvantageous ones. This suggests that any schedule effect is likely mediated by contextual factors such as league stratification, competitive volatility, or the interaction between early results and the broader dynamics of a season.

The comparison between market value and final standing proxies also helps clarify the interpretation of the **SSB** metric. On the one hand, the persistence of the broad qualitative pattern under both definitions indicates that the metric is not merely capturing an artifact of a single operationalization of team strength. Although some league-specific anomalies differ across proxy choices, the overall empirical pattern remains consistent.

From a tournament-design perspective, the results suggest that schedule sequencing is usually not the dominant driver of ranking efficacy, particularly in competitions where differences in team quality are strong enough to be revealed over a full double round-robin season. However, the existence of recurrent anomalies in a subset of leagues indicates that fixture ordering should not be treated as a purely logistical detail. Even under a formally symmetric format, the schedule may still influence the path by which teams accumulate points and, in some environments, affect the degree to which final standings reflect underlying team strength and thus tournament efficacy.

7 Conclusion

This paper introduced the Strength of Schedule Balance (**SSB**) metric and applied a stratified non-parametric framework to evaluate whether the temporal ordering of opponent strength affects tournament efficacy in professional football leagues. Using a validated longitudinal dataset of 306 seasons across 20 competitions, we examined whether balanced, unbalanced-weak, and unbalanced-strong schedules are associated with systematic differences in final league standings.

Our findings indicate that the double round-robin format is generally robust to schedule imbalance. At the aggregate level, most competitions do not exhibit large or systematic distortions in final ranking outcomes attributable solely to fixture sequencing. However, league-level analysis reveals localized anomalies, particularly for unbalanced-weak schedules, where easier starts are more consistently associated with advantageous outcomes than harder starts are with disadvantageous ones. Overall, the evidence provides limited support for a generalized discouragement effect under front-loaded difficult schedules, while suggesting that back-loaded schedules may, in some competitive environments, be associated with overperformance.

8 Limitations and Future Work

This study has important limitations. First, although the **SSB** metric is defined as a continuous measure of schedule imbalance, our empirical analysis relies on stratifying it into discrete groups. This design facilitates interpretation and non-parametric comparison, but it may obscure more gradual relationships between schedule imbalance and tournament efficacy.

A natural extension would be to analyze the impact of **SSB** as a continuous variable. In principle, this could be done through a regression-based framework that estimates the coefficient associated with schedule imbalance and its statistical significance. However, such an approach raises methodological challenges, including the choice of an appropriate model specification, the treatment of potential non-linearity, the dependence structure among covariates, and the need to control for confounding factors that may also influence final standings, such as market value, injuries, and home-away scheduling effects.

Future work should address these issues and explore whether schedule imbalance affects outcomes beyond final rankings. In particular, it would be valuable to investigate its relationship with other indicators of competitive dynamics, such as stadium attendance or other measures of team performance and engagement.

A Appendix: Sensitivity Analysis of Threshold Parameters

Table 5. Leagues in statistically significant zones across thresholds τ and α, by proxy

		Final Standing Proxy		*Market Value Proxy*	
Scenario	Thresh.	Sig. worse	Sig. better	Sig. worse	Sig. better
G_- *vs.* G_0	$\tau = 0.2$	—	Süper Lig; C. Br. B; Saudi Pro; Jupiler Pro; Champ.	—	Ligue 2; Liga Portugal 2; Jupiler Pro
	$\tau = 0.3$	—	Saudi Pro; Jupiler Pro	—	C. Br. B; Ligue 2; Saudi Pro.; Jupiler Pro.; Lig. Port. 2
	$\tau = 0.4$	—	Saudi Pro; Jupiler Pro	—	Serie A; Saudi Pro.; Jupiler Pro.; Liga Portugal 2
	$\alpha = 0.1$	—	Jupiler Pro; Ligue 2	—	Serie A; Jupiler Pro; Lig. Port. 2
G_+ *vs.* G_0	$\tau = 0.2$	Jupiler Pro; La Liga	J1 League; J2 League	Jupiler Pro	J2 League
	$\tau = 0.3$	Jupiler Pro	J1 League; J2 League	—	J2 League; C. Br. B
	$\tau = 0.4$	—	C. Brasileiro A; J1 League	—	—
	$\alpha = 0.1$	—	C. Brasileiro A; J1 League	Jupiler Pro; Lig. Port. 2	—

Notes: "—" indicates no leagues in that category.

To assess whether the league-specific effects identified in the main analysis depend on the choice of classification threshold, we performed a sensitivity analysis across alternative magnitude criteria, $\tau \in \{0.2, 0.3, 0.4\}$, as well as a statistical-significance criterion ($\alpha = 0.1$) based on the Spearman correlation test used in the definition of the **SSB** metric $\rho(\mathbf{S})$. The results, summarized in Table 5, indicate that the broad qualitative conclusions of the paper are robust to parameter variation, although the stability of league-level anomalies differs markedly across schedule extremes and proxy choices.

Stability in G_- vs. G_0. The most persistent pattern appears in the comparison between unbalanced-weak and balanced schedules. Under the final-standing proxy, the Saudi Pro League and Jupiler Pro League remain in the statistically significant "better" zone across all magnitude thresholds, while under the market-value proxy the Jupiler Pro League and Liga Portugal 2 recur consistently, with the Saudi Pro League also appearing at $\tau = 0.3$ and $\tau = 0.4$. This repeated concentration of significant negative effects supports the interpretation that the main league-specific anomalies are more stable for easier starts than for harder starts.

Instability in G_+ vs. G_0. By contrast, the results for unbalanced-strong schedules are considerably less stable. Under the final-standing proxy, the significant leagues vary across thresholds, with Jupiler Pro League and La Liga appearing in the "worse" zone at $\tau = 0.2$, while J1 League and J2 League appear repeatedly in the "better" zone and Campeonato Brasileiro Série A emerges only at stricter definitions. Under the market-value proxy, the pattern is even weaker: J2 League is the only league recurring in the "better" zone for $\tau = 0.2$ and $\tau = 0.3$, while no significant leagues remain at $\tau = 0.4$. Overall, these results do not indicate a robust or universal discouragement effect.

Role of the significance-based criterion. The significance-based grouping ($\alpha = 0.1$) yields conclusions that are directionally consistent with the threshold analysis, but it also highlights the sensitivity of specific leagues to the grouping rule. In the G_- comparison, Jupiler Pro League remains significant under both proxies, while Ligue 2, Serie A, and Liga Portugal 2 appear depending on the choice of team-strength proxy. In the G_+ comparison, the significant leagues differ substantially across proxies, reinforcing the view that hard-start effects are less stable and more dependent on the operational definition of imbalance.

Justification for $\tau = 0.3$. These findings support the use of the Magnitude Criterion with $\tau = 0.3$ in the main analysis. Relative to $\tau = 0.2$, this threshold reduces the inclusion of weaker or noisier cases while preserving the recurring league-specific anomalies. Relative to $\tau = 0.4$, it avoids an overly restrictive definition that removes a substantial portion of the detectable signal. Thus, $\tau = 0.3$ provides a reasonable balance between sample size and effect isolation in the identification of schedule-related distortions.

References

1. Amez, S., Baert, S., Neyt, B., Vandemaele, M.: No evidence for second leg home advantage in recent seasons of European soccer cups. Appl. Econ. Lett. **27**(2), 156–160 (2020)
2. Appleton, D.R.: May the best man win? The Statistician **44**, 529 (1995)
3. Bartsch, T., Drexl, A., Kröger, S.: Scheduling the professional soccer leagues of Austria and Germany. Comput. Oper. Res. **33**(7), 1907–1937 (2006). https://doi.org/10.1016/j.cor.2004.09.037
4. Boyko, R.H., Boyko, A.R., Boyko, M.G.: Referee bias contributes to home advantage in English premiership football. J. Sports Sci. **25**(11), 1185–1194 (2007)
5. Briskorn, D., Drexl, A.: IP models for round robin tournaments. Comput. Oper. Res. **36**(3), 837–852 (2009)
6. Briskorn, D., Knust, S.: Constructing fair sports league schedules with regard to strength groups. Discret. Appl. Math. **158**(2), 123–135 (2010)
7. Briskorn, D.: Combinatorial properties of strength groups in round robin tournaments. Eur. J. Oper. Res. **192**(3), 744–754 (2009)
8. Cohen-Zada, D., Krumer, A., Shtudiner, Z.: Psychological momentum and gender. Journal of Economic Behavior & Organization **135**, 66–81 (2017)
9. Csató, L.: A simulation comparison of tournament designs for the world men's handball championships. Int. Trans. Oper. Res. **28**(5), 2377–2401 (2021)
10. Devriesere, K., Csató, L., Goossens, D.: Tournament design: A review from an operational research perspective (7 2025). https://doi.org/10.1016/j.ejor.2024.10.044
11. Engist, O., Merkus, E., Schafmeister, F.: The effect of seeding on tournament outcomes: Evidence from a regression-discontinuity design. J. Sports Econ. **22**(1), 115–136 (2021). https://doi.org/10.1177/1527002520955212
12. Flores, R., Forrest, D., de Pablo, C., Tena, J.: What is a good result in the first leg of a two-legged football match? Eur. J. Oper. Res. **247**(2), 641–647 (2015)
13. Goossens, D.R., Spieksma, F.C.R.: Soccer schedules in Europe: an overview. J. Schedul. **15**, 641–651 (10 2012). https://doi.org/10.1007/s10951-011-0238-9, http://link.springer.com/10.1007/s10951-011-0238-9
14. Goossens, D.R., Spieksma, F.C.: The carryover effect does not influence football results. J. Sports Econ. **13**(3), 288–305 (2012)

15. Groh, C., Moldovanu, B., Sela, A., Sunde, U.: Optimal seedings in elimination tournaments. Econ. Theor. **49**(1), 59–80 (2012)
16. Horen, J., Riezman, R.: Comparing draws for single elimination tournaments. Oper. Res. **33**(2), 249–262 (1985)
17. Knowles, G., Sherony, K., Haupert, M.: The demand for major league baseball: a test of the uncertainty of outcome hypothesis. Am. Econ. **36**(2), 72–80 (1992)
18. Krumer, A., Lechner, M.: First in first win: Evidence on schedule effects in round-robin tournaments in mega-events. Eur. Econ. Rev. **100**(11), 412–427 (2017). https://doi.org/10.1016/j.euroecorev.2017.09.006
19. Lasek, J., Gagolewski, M.: The efficacy of league formats in ranking teams. Stat. Modell.**18**, 411–435 (12 2018). https://doi.org/10.1177/1471082X18798426
20. Lee, Y.H., Fort, R.: Attendance and the uncertainty-of-outcome hypothesis in baseball. Rev. Ind. Organ. **33**(4), 281–295 (2008)
21. McGarry, T., Schutz, R.: Efficacy of traditional sport tournament structures. J. Oper. Res. Society **48**(1), 65–74 (1997)
22. Moskowitz, T., Wertheim, L.J.: Scorecasting: The hidden influences behind how sports are played and games are won. Crown Archetype , (2011)
23. Neave, N., Wolfson, S.: Testosterone, territoriality, and the 'home advantage'. Physiol. Behav. **78**(2), 269–275 (2003)
24. Nemhauser, G.L., Trick, M.A.: Scheduling a major college basketball conference. INFORMS Inst. Oper. Res. Manage. Sci. **46**, 1–8 (1998). https://doi.org/10.1287/opre.46.1.1. Operations Research
25. Prince, M., Cole Smith, J., Geunes, J.: Designing fair 8-and 16-team knockout tournaments. IMA J. Manag. Math. **24**(3), 321–336 (2013)
26. Romano, J., Kromrey, J.D., Coraggio, J., Skowronek, J.: Appropriate statistics for ordinal level data: Should we really be using t-test and cohen'sd for evaluating group differences on the NSSE and other surveys. In: annual meeting of the Florida Association of Institutional Research, vol. 177 (2006)
27. Rottenberg, S.: The baseball players' labor market. J. Polit. Econ. **64**(3), 242–258 (1956)
28. Russell, K.G.: Balancing carry-over effects in round robin tournaments. Biometrika **67**(1), 127–131 (1980). https://doi.org/10.1093/biomet/67.1.127
29. Ryvkin, D.: The selection efficiency of tournaments. Eur. J. Oper. Res. **206**(3), 667–675 (2010)
30. Scarf, P., Yusof, M.M., Bilbao, M.: A numerical study of designs for sporting contests. Europ. J. Oper. Res. **198**, 190–198 (10 2009). https://doi.org/10.1016/j.ejor.2008.07.029
31. Sziklai, B.R., Biró, P., Csató, L.: The efficacy of tournament designs. Comput. Oper. Res. **144** (8 2022). https://doi.org/10.1016/j.cor.2022.105821
32. Szymanski, S.: The economic design of sporting contests. J. Econom. Lit. **41**(4), 1137–1187 (2003)
33. Transfermarkt: Football transfers, market values, rumours and statistics. https://www.transfermarkt.com
34. Urban, T.L., Russell, R.A.: Scheduling sports competitions on multiple venues. Eur. J. Oper. Res. **148**(2), 302–311 (2003)
35. Utt, J., Fort, R.: Pitfalls to measuring competitive balance with gini coefficients. J. Sports Econ. **3**(4), 367–373 (2002)
36. Vassoler, E.B., de Melo, P.O.S.V.: An interpretable and probabilistic competitive balance metric for sports leagues. J. Quant. Anal. Sports **22**(1), 17–34 (2026).https://doi.org/10.1515/jqas-2025-0056

Risk Parity vs. Kelly Criterion: An Empirical Evaluation of Bankroll Allocation Strategies in Football Value Betting

René Manassé Galekwa[1,2], Jean Marie Tshimula[2,3], Etienne Gael Tajeuna[4], Selain K. Kasereka[1,2], and Kyandoghere Kyamakya[1(✉)]

[1] Institute of Smart Systems Technologies, University of Klagenfurt, 9020 Klagenfurt am Wörthersee, Austria
kyandoghere.kyamakya@aau.at

[2] Mathematics, Statistics and Computer Science Department, University of Kinshasa, Kinshasa, Democratic Republic of the Congo

[3] Applied Artificial Intelligence Institute, Université TÉLUQ, Montreal, Canada

[4] Department of Computer Science and Engineering, Université du Québec en Outaouais, Gatineau, QC J8X 3X7, Canada

Abstract. This paper looks at how to best manage money in sports betting, focusing on the top five European football leagues from 2015 to 2025. The Kelly Criterion is the best way to grow money over time, but it can be risky and unstable, especially when dealing with related events. Many models ignore this issue. To solve this, we suggest a new method that uses a logistic regression model to find value and a Risk Parity strategy to balance risk in each bet. We tested this on over 17,403 matches and compared it to Flat Staking and Fractional Kelly strategies. The results showed that while Full Kelly had the highest peak, it was not stable and led to big losses (>80%). The Optimal Fractional Kelly (15%) gave the best returns (+10.5% ROI) with smaller losses (<52%). The Risk Parity method did not do well overall because of similar "favorite" bets, but it did better in low-risk markets like the Italian Serie A (+83% ROI). Overall, fixed fractional Kelly is a strong choice, while Risk Parity works well in certain low-risk leagues. This study offers a clear, data-based way to separate profit-making from risk management in sports betting.

Keywords: Risk Parity · Kelly Criterion · Sports Betting · Bankroll Management

1 Introduction

Optimizing investment portfolios in sports betting markets presents a unique challenge. It lies at the intersection of financial mathematics, machine learning,

Z. Liu and V. Misra (Eds.): ISACE 2026, LNCS 16610, pp. 277–291, 2026.
https://doi.org/10.1007/978-3-032-27272-0_19

and game theory. Unlike traditional financial markets, sports betting markets are characterized by discrete event occurrences. They also feature binary outcomes (in the simplified home/draw/away context) and expiring assets [20,29]. For algorithmic bettors, the problem is twofold. First, one must identify the "value." This refers to situations in which market odds imply a probability lower than the outcome's true probability [8]. Second, the optimal capital (bankroll) allocation to these opportunities must be determined [21].

The Kelly Criterion [13] is a canonical benchmark for capital allocation: under idealized assumptions, maximizing expected log utility yields the maximum asymptotic wealth growth rate. However, full-Kelly betting is notoriously volatile. This often leads to unacceptable drawdowns. These can threaten the investor's psychological or financial stability [1]. Furthermore, typical Kelly applications in sports betting assume independence between simultaneous bets. This flaw becomes critical when betting on multiple matches within the same league. Here, latent factors such as weather, fatigue, or league-wide trends introduce correlations [3,27].

In financial portfolio management, Risk Parity strategies [18,25] have emerged as a robust alternative to mean–variance optimization [7]. Risk Parity equalizes the risk contribution of each asset. This offers resilience to estimation errors in the expected returns. It also provides smoother equity curves [5,14]. More robust formulations have recently been proposed to handle parameter uncertainties [4,6]. Despite its success in asset management, the application of Risk Parity to sports betting portfolios remains underexplored.

This paper bridges this gap. We evaluate the efficacy of Risk Parity allocation versus traditional Kelly strategies in European football. We employed a logistic regression model trained on the rolling performance metrics to generate alpha (see Sect. 4.1 and Fig. 1). We then rigorously tested various allocation strategies via Walk-Forward Validation on 10 years of data.

2 Related Work

The literature on sports betting can be categorized into predictive modeling and staking strategies. A recent comprehensive review by [11] highlighted the shift from simple statistical models to complex machine learning architectures in this domain.

2.1 Predictive Modeling in Sports

The early approaches relied on simple statistical modeling. These included the Poisson distribution of goals. Recently, machine learning techniques have dominated. Studies by [12,19] demonstrate the superiority of gradient boosting and neural networks over bookmaker odds in specific niches. Advanced state-space models have also been explored to capture team dynamics [24]. Research by [26] highlighted the importance of feature engineering. This is particularly true for advanced metrics such as Expected Goals (xG) and rolling form. This directly informs our choice of features. Moreover, the risk-adjusted returns of such strategies have been investigated by [10]. This emphasizes the need for a robust evaluation.

2.2 Staking and Bankroll Management

The optimality of the Kelly Criterion is well documented [1]. However, its practical limitations have also been noted. [3] proposed tail-risk control strategies to mitigate Kelly's risks. Although effective, such approaches, such as conditional value-at-risk (CVaR) optimization face challenges. They typically require estimating the full tail distribution of the returns. This requires extensive historical data and is sensitive to outliers. In contrast, Risk Parity focuses on equalizing risk contributions based on volatility. This is a second-moment metric. It is robustly estimable, even in lower-sample regimes. In the broader financial context, [2,22] have shown how machine learning and advanced risk measures like Expected Shortfall can refine portfolio weights. [23] emphasized the importance of diversification in out-of-sample performance. [16] extended portfolio optimization to multi-period frameworks using model predictive control. However, most sports betting literature defaults to flat staking or ad hoc fractional Kelly. They ignore the covariance structure of the simultaneous bets. [18] identified this structure as crucial for risk parity.

3 Preliminaries

Kelly Criterion. The Kelly Criterion is derived from information theory. It maximizes the expected logarithmic utility of the wealth. For a single bet with probability p and gross odds $b = \Omega - 1$, the optimal fraction of bankroll to wager is:

$$f^* = \text{argmax}_f \mathbb{E}[\ln(1 + f \cdot X)] = \frac{p \cdot b - (1-p)}{b} \tag{1}$$

This is theoretically optimal for growth [13]. However, full-Kelly betting is extremely risky in practice. This is due to the parameter uncertainty (estimation error in p). To mitigate this, we employ a fractional adjustment $f_{adj} = \lambda_K f^*$, where $\lambda_K = 0.15$ is a fixed risk-reduction multiplier used in our experiments (not optimized out-of-sample).

Risk Parity. In contrast to the Kelly criterion, Risk Parity aims to construct a diversified portfolio. The Kelly criterion focuses solely on maximizing returns. Risk Parity ensures that each asset contributes equally to the total portfolio risk [2,18]. Let Σ be the covariance matrix of the bet returns. The portfolio volatility is $\sigma_p(\mathbf{w}) = \sqrt{\mathbf{w}^T \Sigma \mathbf{w}}$. The Marginal Risk Contribution (MRC) of bet i is defined as:

$$MRC_i = w_i \frac{\partial \sigma_p}{\partial w_i} = w_i \frac{(\Sigma \mathbf{w})_i}{\sqrt{\mathbf{w}^T \Sigma \mathbf{w}}} \tag{2}$$

The optimization problem seeks to find the weight vector $\mathbf{w}$. This vector minimizes the variance of the risk contributions.

$$\min_{\mathbf{w}} \sum_i \sum_j (MRC_i - MRC_j)^2 \tag{3}$$

This approach was popularized in asset management [25]. This ensures that no single match dominates the risk profile of the betting portfolio. It provides theoretical resilience against correlation breakdowns [5].

4 Methodology

4.1 Problem Statement

We define the sports betting challenge as a stochastic control problem. The agent seeks to optimize the long-term growth of a capital reservoir (bankroll) C_t over a finite horizon T. This involves two distinct but coupled sub-problems:

1. **Alpha generation (value identification)**: The estimation of the true probability $p_i = P(Y_i = 1|\mathbf{x}_i)$ of an event i given a feature vector $\mathbf{x}_i$. A betting opportunity exists if a condition is satisfied. The estimated probability must exceed the implied probability of market odds Ω_i. That is, $p_i > 1/\Omega_i$.
2. **Risk management (capital allocation)**: The determination of the optimal weight vector $\mathbf{w}_t = [w_1, ..., w_N]^T$ for a portfolio of N simultaneous bets. The objective was to maximize the expected geometric growth rate. It must also adhere to risk constraints (e.g., maximum drawdowns). This concept is rooted in modern portfolio theory [15].

4.2 Predictive Framework: Logistic Regression

To model the binary outcome of a match (Home Win vs. Not Home Win), we employed logistic regression. Unlike "black box" models, this generalized linear model provides interpretable coefficients. It also provides well-calibrated probabilities [12,26]. The probability of a Home Win ($Y = 1$) is modeled as a sigmoid function of a linear combination of features:

$$P(Y = 1|\mathbf{x}) = \sigma(\mathbf{w}^T\mathbf{x} + b) = \frac{1}{1 + e^{-(\beta_0 + \sum_{j=1}^{m} \beta_j x_j)}} \tag{4}$$

where β are the learnable parameters. These parameters were estimated by maximizing the likelihood of the observed data. This is equivalent to minimizing the log loss (cross-entropy) function:

$$J(\beta) = -\frac{1}{N} \sum_{i=1}^{N} [y_i \log(\hat{y}_i) + (1 - y_i)\log(1 - \hat{y}_i)] + \lambda||\beta||_2^2 \tag{5}$$

Here, the term $\lambda||\beta||_2^2$ represents L_2 regularization (Ridge). This term is critical in the noisy domain of sports data. It penalizes the large coefficients. This prevents the model from overfitting to the idiosyncratic noise in historical matches [17].

4.3 Feature Engineering

The feature vector $\mathbf{x}$ combines the long-term strength (static capability) with short-term form (dynamic momentum).

Elo Rating. The Elo rating R_A captures the long-term strength of team A. It is updated Bayesian-style after each match:

$$R'_A = R_A + K \cdot (S_A - E_A) \tag{6}$$

where S_A is the actual score and E_A is the expected score. This metric provides a robust baseline for team strength [28].

Rolling Performance Metrics. We compute 5-match rolling averages ($W = 5$) to capture the immediate team form. Elo effectively smooths this process. We used Goals Scored (GF), Goals Conceded (GA), and Shots on Target (SOT).

$$\text{Form}_{SOT}^{(T)} = \frac{1}{W} \sum_{k=1}^{W} m_{T-k,\text{Target}} \tag{7}$$

We selected a window of $W = 5$ as the optimal trade-off between responsiveness and stability of the model. Shorter windows were excessively noisy. Longer windows lag behind the tactical shifts. Furthermore, we deliberately excluded qualitative variables such as injuries and managerial changes. Although potentially informative, these factors lack consistent structure across leagues and seasons. We therefore restricted the inputs to reproducible quantitative match statistics, thereby reducing subjective bias in feature construction. Short-term changes in team condition are captured indirectly through recent performance indicators such as goals scored, goals conceded, and shots on target.

The overall data flow and model architecture are illustrated in Fig. 1.

4.4 Value Identification

We formalize the "edge" (Expected Value, $\mathcal{E}$) for a bet on the home team with decimal odds Ω:

$$\mathcal{E} = p \cdot \Omega - 1 \tag{8}$$

A trade is executed if the following two conditions are met. First, $\mathcal{E} > \tau$ (Minimum Edge). Second, $\Omega \leq \Omega_{max}$ (Volatility Control). This filtering step acts as a preliminary risk control mechanism [1].

4.5 Bankroll Allocation Strategies

As established in Sect. 3, Risk Parity aims to construct a portfolio where each asset contributes equally to the total portfolio risk [2,18]. The Marginal Risk

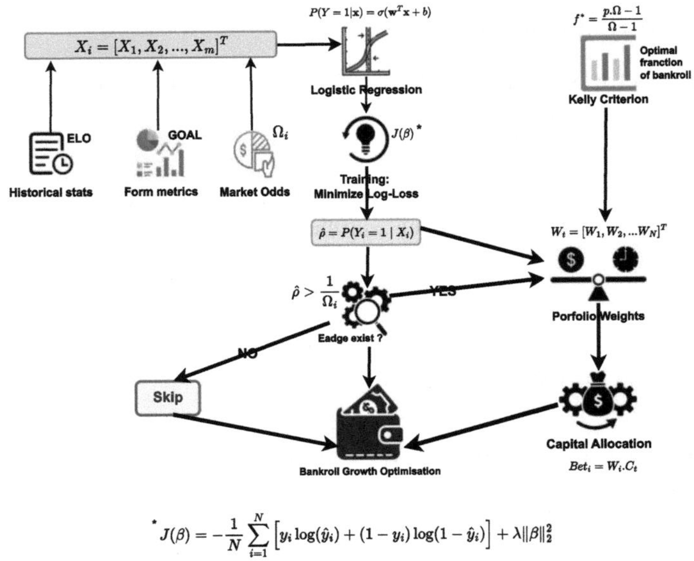

Fig. 1. System Architecture: The pipeline integrates (1) Rolling Feature Extraction ($W = 5$), (2) Logistic Regression for probability estimation $P(Y|\mathbf{x})$, and (3) Risk Parity Allocation for portfolio construction.

Contribution (MRC) of each bet and the optimization problem that minimizes the variance of these contributions are given by Eqs. 2 and 3, respectively.

In the context of sports betting, this approach ensures that no single match or league dominates the portfolio's risk profile. However, the practical implementation of Risk Parity for matching portfolios hinges critically on one fundamental challenge: estimating the covariance matrix Σ of the bet returns. Unlike financial assets, matches are discrete, non-repeating events with no continuous price histories. We address this challenge through the structural covariance construction described in the next section.

4.6 Covariance Matrix Construction

A critical challenge exists in applying Risk Parity to sports betting. This is the estimation of the covariance matrix Σ. Matches are discrete, non-repeating events with no continuous price history. We address this by constructing a *Structural Correlation Matrix* based on latent factors. The volatility of a single bet i follows the variance of the Bernoulli trial. It is scaled by the odds Ω_i:

$$\sigma_i = \Omega_i \sqrt{p_i(1-p_i)} \tag{9}$$

The correlation ρ_{ij} between the two bets is modeled structurally. This captures the hierarchical dependencies as follows:

$$\rho_{ij} = \rho_{base} + \mathbb{I}(L_i = L_j) \cdot \rho_{league} + \mathbb{I}(T_i = T_j) \cdot \rho_{time} \tag{10}$$

where $\mathbb{I}(\cdot)$ is the indicator function. We set $\rho_{base} = 0.15$ to capture the global market sentiment (e.g., favorite-longshot bias). We set $\rho_{league} = 0.1$ for the intra-league and $\rho_{time} = 0.05$ for simultaneous matches. The covariance terms are then $\Sigma_{ij} = \rho_{ij}\sigma_i\sigma_j$. This formulation actively penalizes the concentration in single leagues or time slots. Crucially, this structural approach addresses the "noisy covariance" critique. This critique is often leveled at Risk Parity. We imposed a logical correlation structure. We do not rely on unstable sample covariance matrices derived from limited historical data. This ensures that the diversification mechanism is robust and theoretically sound. This is true, even in low-sample regimes.

5 Experiments and Results

5.1 Experimental Setup

An experimental evaluation was conducted on a dataset of 17,403 matches. These data were obtained from Football-Data.co.uk[1]. We applied a standardized data-cleaning pipeline to remove incomplete records, align league labels, and enforce chronological consistency before walk-forward evaluation [9]. The data cover the top five European leagues (EPL, La Liga, Bundesliga, Serie A, Ligue 1) from 2015/2016 to 2024/2025. Following recent protocols for profitability evaluation [21], we employed a Walk-Forward Validation protocol. The model was trained on the accumulated seasons $1..t$. It is then tested in the subsequent season $t+1$. This ensures that no future information guides betting decisions. The simulation initializes with a bankroll of $C_0 = 1000$ units.
Parameter Integrity: To rigorously avoid look-ahead bias, we established the filtering parameters *a priori*. These are Minimum Edge $\tau = 0.05$ and Maximum Odds $\Omega_{max} = 2.00$. They were selected based on the well-documented favorite–longshot bias [8]. This bias indicates that high-odds bets systematically underperform in the long run. We also adhered to strict safety margins. These parameters were fixed for the entire duration of Walk-Forward Validation. The test data were not tuned.

5.2 Model Reliability Verification

To address the dependency of Kelly based strategies on accurate probability estimates, we evaluated the calibration of our model. The Brier Score for the 15,856 out-of-sample predictions was 0.2131. This was better than the reference value of 0.25 for an uninformative classifier.

Figure 2 shows the reliability diagram, indicating that the predicted probabilities $\hat{p}$ align closely with observed win frequencies. This diagnostic supports the interpretation that the catastrophic drawdowns observed under Full Kelly (discussed below) are driven primarily by the staking rule's variance amplification and by correlated outcomes, rather than by gross miscalibration of the underlying probability signal.

[1] https://www.football-data.co.uk/.

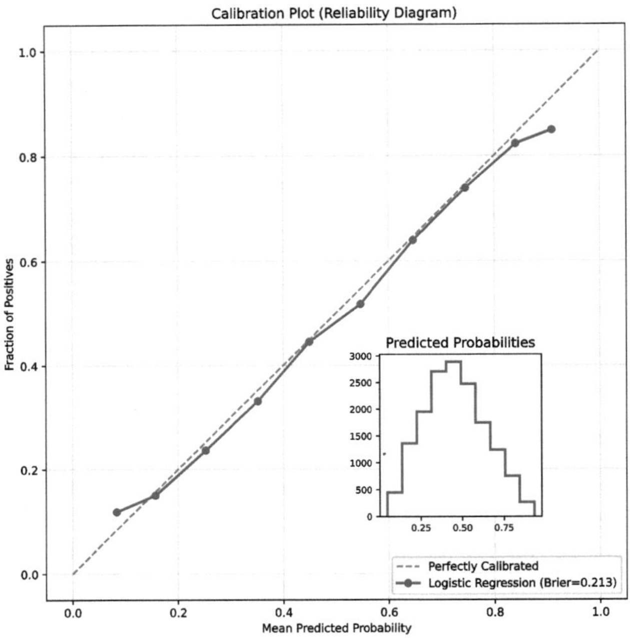

Fig. 2. Reliability Diagram (Calibration Curve) for the Logistic Regression Model. The blue line tracks a perfect calibration diagonal. The Brier Score of 0.2131 confirms that the predicted probabilities reliably estimate the true win frequency, validating the input signal for Kelly sizing. (Color figure online)

An examination of the fitted coefficients suggests that the 5-match rolling average of shots on target (SOT) is the most informative short-term predictor of match outcomes. Home SOT contributes positively to the probability of a home win ($\beta = 0.0940$), whereas Away SOT contributes negatively ($\beta = -0.1146$). By contrast, recent goals scored exhibit weaker effects ($\beta = -0.0430$ for Home GF and $\beta = 0.0062$ for Away GF), consistent with goals being a noisier realization of underlying attacking pressure. Combined with longer-term team strength captured by Elo ratings (Home Elo $\beta = 0.6316$, Away Elo $\beta = -0.5126$), these features yield a Brier Score of 0.2131, supporting the use of the resulting probabilities as inputs to staking rules.

5.3 Global Performance

Table 1 summarizes the comprehensive performances of all the strategies. It covers the entire 10-year period across all the leagues. Full Kelly reached the highest interim peak bankroll during simulation (approximately +457%) but proved unsustainable, ultimately suffering a catastrophic 99.8% maximum drawdown and ending in near-total ruin. By contrast, the global underperformance of Risk Parity (−38.7% ROI) appears to stem from the high positive correlation inherent in our restricted universe of home-favorite bets ($\Omega \leq 2.00$), a limitation analyzed in detail in 6.3. These findings align with the well-known gambler's ruin risk associated with aggressive sizing in non-stationary betting environments. The Optimal Fractional Kelly (15%) achieves the best balance. It yielded a +10.5% ROI with a manageable 51.4% maximum drawdown.

Table 1. Global Strategy Comparison (All Seasons)

Strategy	ROI	Max DD	Sharpe	Final Bankroll
Flat Staking	+4.6%	45.1%	0.26	$1,045
Full Kelly	−99.1%	99.8%	−0.28	$9
Quarter Kelly	−10.9%	73.7%	−0.05	$891
Frac. Kelly (15%)[a]	**+10.5%**	51.4%	**0.37**	**$1,105**
Risk Parity	−38.7%	71.3%	−0.12	$612

[a]Frac. Kelly: Optimized Fractional Kelly ($\lambda = 0.15$).

5.4 League-Specific Analysis

The most significant finding of this paper is the divergence of strategy performance across different leagues. The predictive model struggled in Germany (Bundesliga) and France (Ligue 1). It yielded negative returns, regardless of staking. However, it performed exceptionally well in Spain (La Liga) and in England (Premier League). Table 2 presents the performances across all five major leagues. It provides a complete picture of the strategy's robustness (or lack thereof) in terms of different market efficiencies.

Table 2. Performance by League (All Strategies)

League	Flat	Risk Parity	Frac. Kelly[a]	Sharpe (RP)
EPL (England)	+19.6%	+31.2%	+62.7%	1.07
La Liga (Spain)	+62.7%	**+151.7%**	+61.9%	**2.42**
Serie A (Italy)	+17.4%	**+82.9%**	+22.4%	1.71
Bundesliga (Germany)	−26.3%	−57.9%	−31.6%	−2.25
Ligue 1 (France)	−38.2%	-70.6%	−49.0%	−3.48

[a]Frac. Kelly (15%): Fractional Kelly with fixed multiplier $\lambda_K = 0.15$.

In La Liga, Risk Parity delivered a large +151.7% ROI. This matched the aggressive full-Kelly returns. However, it had materially lower volatility (Max DD 25.2% vs. 65.6%). In Serie A, Risk Parity was the best-performing strategy in our experiments (+82.9% ROI). It outperformed Flat Staking (+17.4%) by a factor of four. This suggests that the covariance structure of Italian matches allows for highly efficient risk diversification. Conversely, in the Bundesliga and Ligue 1, the core predictive signal (α) was negative. This implies that no staking method can salvage the portfolio. This validates the "Garbage In, Garbage Out" principle.

To assess whether cross-league profitability differences were primarily driven by the predictive signal, we compared out-of-sample Brier Scores across leagues. The results indicate an association between calibration quality and profitability: Serie A achieved the best predictive accuracy (Brier Score = 0.2025), followed by the Premier League (0.2106) and La Liga (0.2141), whereas the Bundesliga (0.2218) and Ligue 1 (0.2187) exhibited weaker calibration and poorer investment outcomes. This pattern suggests that portfolio construction can redistribute risk across bets, but it cannot compensate for a weak alpha signal (Fig. 3).

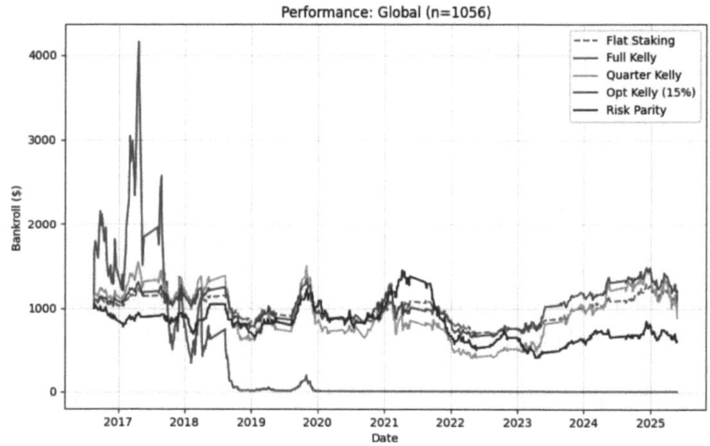

Fig. 3. Global Bankroll Evolution (2015–2025). The figure compares the equity curves of Flat Staking, Full Kelly, Quarter Kelly, Fractional Kelly (15%), and Risk Parity over the full sample. The Full Kelly curve illustrates rapid early growth followed by collapse; the more conservative strategies exhibit improved survivability. Note Risk Parity's lower volatility and superior survival characteristics compared to the aggressive Kelly methods.

5.5 Recent Performance (2023-2025)

To assess the model's current relevance, we evaluated performance on the last two seasons. During this period, Risk Parity demonstrated superior robustness. It achieved a +24.8% ROI in the Premier League (vs. +3.4% for Flat). It also achieved +28.0% in La Liga.

We performed a paired t-test on the daily returns of Risk Parity versus Flat Staking. This was done to assess whether the observed return difference was distinguishable from sampling variability. For La Liga (2023–2025), the paired

t-test produced $p = 0.19$, and for the full 10-year period the test produced $p = 0.117$; thus, we do not reject the null hypothesis of equal mean daily returns at the 5% level. This outcome highlights the inherent high variance in sports betting. Claiming a "strategic edge" purely based on short-term ROI is perilous. Risk Parity demonstrates superior risk-adjusted metrics (lower drawdown and higher Sharpe). However, its pure stochastic dominance over the baseline is not guaranteed at standard confidence levels.

6 Discussion

6.1 The Risk-Return Trade-Off in Staking

Our results empirically validate the theoretical trade-off between growth and survival. The full Kelly criterion maximizes the expected logarithmic wealth. However, it assumes precise probability estimates. In sports betting, estimated probabilities $P(Y \mid x)$ are subject to unavoidable estimation error. Consequently, Full Kelly tends to overbet and can lead to ruin. Fractional Kelly (15%) effectively mitigated this parameter uncertainty. It acts as a regularization term for the stake size.

Beyond the mathematical expectation, the practical implications of a 99.8% drawdown are prohibitive. For a professional bettor, the utility function of wealth is rarely logarithmic. The psychological pressure of losing 90% of the capital typically leads to strategy abandonment. It can also cause emotional decision-making ("tilting") long before the theoretical ruin is reached. Therefore, the Full Kelly might be optimal for a robot with infinite psychological capital and perfect calibration. However, it is practically unimplementable in real-world scenarios. Fractional Kelly and Risk Parity provide practical risk control and improve long-run implementability. These are required for long-term adherence to strategies.

6.2 The "Holy Grail" in Low-Variance Markets

Risk Parity's performance in La Liga and Serie A is particularly noteworthy. In these markets, the Risk Parity algorithms successfully identified that portfolio volatility could be minimized. This was achieved by diversifying the weights across matches. This finding aligns with the evolution of ML-driven forecasting [19]. Figure 4 illustrates this phenomenon for Serie A. Flat betting yields a slow, steady upward trend. In contrast, Risk Parity accelerates exponentially during winning streaks. It also dampens the drawdowns during losing streaks.

6.3 Diversification vs. Quality: A Control Experiment

As anticipated in Sect. 5.3, the global underperformance of Risk Parity (-38.7% ROI) can be directly attributed to the nature of our filtered bet universe. A critique of our methodology is the restriction to home favorites ($\Omega_{max} \leq 2.00$). This potentially limits the diversification benefits of Risk Parity. To address this issue, we conducted a control experiment. We removed the odds cap. This

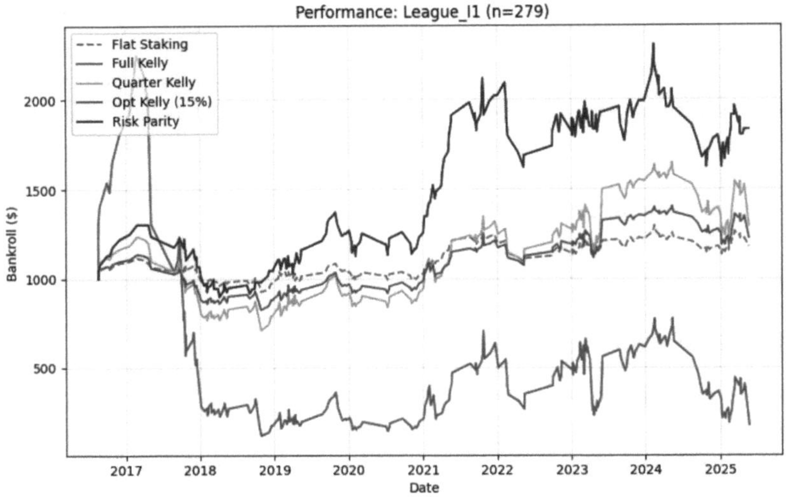

Fig. 4. Serie A Bankroll Evolution. Risk Parity (blue curve) demonstrates a convex payout profile and outperforms Flat Staking over the observed sample. This illustrates the strategy's ability to compound returns effectively in efficient, low-variance markets. (Color figure online)

allowed bets on the full spectrum of home teams (including underdogs with odds of up to 10.0). The results were unequivocally negative for all samples. The unconstrained Risk Parity portfolio suffered a -92.6% loss over the 10-year period (Flat Staking: -99.1%). This confirms that Risk Parity requires heterogeneous assets to minimize variance. However, it cannot alchemize positive returns from a universe of assets with negative expected value. The "Favorite-Longshot Bias" [20] dominates the benefits of structural diversification. Thus, pre-filtering for quality (positive α) is a prerequisite for effective risk allocation. Risk Parity's global underperformance can be interpreted as a correlation-concentration effect: by restricting the universe to home favorites ($\Omega \leq 2.00$), the strategy operates over assets with highly positive latent correlations, limiting diversification benefits in adverse joint-outcome episodes (e.g., league-wide upsets). This suggests that globally effective Risk Parity would require a broader, more correlation-heterogeneous bet universe (e.g., mixing markets such as home win, draw, and totals), while preserving positive expected value.

6.4 Practical Implementation Constraints

Finally, we must acknowledge the gap between simulations and execution. Our model assumes unlimited liquidity at the closing prices. In practice, implementing a Risk Parity strategy requires placing bets proportional to precise weights. This may be hindered by bookmaker limits, especially for profitable betting accounts. Furthermore, our odds data include the bookmaker's margin (typically 2–5%). However, we did not account for additional transaction costs, such as exchange commissions or price slippage during execution. Risk Parity's diversified nature reduces the need for massive single bets, unlike the Full Kelly. However, the rebalancing required for a large portfolio could incur higher operational friction. Advanced multiperiod optimization frameworks [16] aim to overcome this challenge.

6.5 Heuristic Variables and Look-Ahead Bias Limitations

Our framework has an important limitation: several key parameters are fixed ex ante rather than dynamically estimated. In particular, the fractional Kelly multiplier ($\lambda_K = 0.15$) and the structural correlation coefficients ($\rho_{base} = 0.15$, $\rho_{league} = 0.10$, $\rho_{time} = 0.05$) were specified as heuristic settings rather than obtained through formal out-of-sample optimization. The empirical results suggest that stake reduction is necessary in sports betting environments, but labeling $\lambda_K = 0.15$ as 'optimal' would be overstated and may implicitly introduce look-ahead bias. Likewise, the structural covariance specification provides a pragmatic alternative to unstable sample covariance estimation, yet its components remain only partially validated. Future work should estimate these parameters adaptively and test their stability across leagues, seasons, and market regimes.

7 Conclusion

This paper provides a comprehensive evaluation of bankroll allocation strategies in European football. Our results indicate that a conservative fractional Kelly strategy of 10–15% constitutes the most robust baseline across diverse market conditions. Nevertheless, the Risk Parity approach outperformed traditional staking methods in selected stable and relatively efficient leagues, notably La Liga and Serie A, where it generated superior realized risk-adjusted returns. These findings emphasize the limitations of a one-size-fits-all staking rule and support the adoption of league-specific allocation strategies to mitigate persistent exposure to high-variance markets. Future research will extend the asset universe by incorporating over/under markets, thereby improving the covariance structure necessary for the effective deployment of Global Risk Parity. Overall, the main empirical implication is that bankroll management in sports betting should be approached as a context-dependent portfolio construction problem rather than a universal staking rule.

References

1. Baker, R.D., McHale, I.G.: Robust sports betting strategies using the kelly criterion. Eur. J. Oper. Res. **258**(1), 269–281 (2017)
2. Cajas, D.: Risk parity optimization. In: Advanced Portfolio Optimization: A Cutting-edge Quantitative Approach, pp. 277–306. Springer (2025)
3. Consiglio, A., Zenios, S.A.: Tail risk control strategies in betting markets. Eur. J. Oper. Res. **253**(2), 525–539 (2016)

4. Costa, G., Kwon, R.: A robust framework for risk parity portfolios. J. Asset Manag. **21**(5), 447–466 (2020)
5. Costa, G., Kwon, R.H.: Risk parity portfolio optimization under a Markov regime-switching framework. Quant. Finan. **19**(3), 453–471 (2019)
6. Costa, G., Kwon, R.H.: Generalized risk parity portfolio optimization: An ADMM approach. J. Global Optim. **78**(1), 207–238 (2020)
7. DeMiguel, V., Garlappi, L., Uppal, R.: Optimal versus naive diversification: How inefficient is the 1/n portfolio strategy? Rev. Finan. Stud. **22**(5), 1915–1953 (2009)
8. Feddersen, A.: Market efficiency and the favorite–longshot bias: evidence from handball betting markets. In: The economics of sports betting, pp. 105–117. Edward Elgar Publishing (2017)
9. Gábor, A.: (2025), oRCID: https://orcid.org/0009-0001-9252-5976
10. Galekwa, R.M., Tshimula, J.M., Tajeuna, E.G., Kyamakya, K.: Towards sports betting as a financial asset: An investigative analysis of risk, investment potential, and future perspectives. Authorea Preprints (2025)
11. Galekwa, R.M., Tshimula, J.M., Tajeuna, E.G., Kyandoghere, K.: A systematic review of machine learning in sports betting: Techniques, challenges, and future directions. arXiv preprint arXiv:2410.21484 (2024)
12. Hubáček, O., Šourek, G., Železný, F.: Exploiting sports-betting market using machine learning. Int. J. Forecast. **35**(2), 783–796 (2019)
13. Kim, S.K.: Kelly criterion extension: advanced gambling strategy. Mathematics **12**(11), 1725 (2024)
14. Klasen, S.: In search of the holy grail: how to achieve pro-poor growth? Toward pro poor policies-aid, institutions, and globalization, pp. 63–94 (2004)
15. Kolm, P.N., Tütüncü, R., Fabozzi, F.J.: 60 years of portfolio optimization: Practical challenges and current trends. Eur. J. Oper. Res. **234**(2), 356–371 (2014)
16. Li, X., Uysal, A.S., Mulvey, J.M.: Multi-period portfolio optimization using model predictive control with mean-variance and risk parity frameworks. Eur. J. Oper. Res. **299**(3), 1158–1176 (2022)
17. Liu, F., Cai, M., Wang, L., Lu, Y.: An ensemble model based on adaptive noise reducer and over-fitting prevention LSTM for multivariate time series forecasting. IEEE Access **7**, 26102–26115 (2019)
18. Maillard, S., Roncalli, T., Teïletche, J.: The properties of equally weighted risk contribution portfolios. J. Portfolio Manage. **36**(4), 60–70 (2010)
19. Mandadapu, P.: The evolution of football betting-a machine learning approach to match outcome forecasting and bookmaker odds estimation. arXiv preprint arXiv:2403.16282 (2024)
20. Newall, P.W., Walasek, L.: Structural characteristics of fixed-odds sports betting products. J. Behav. Addict. **10**(2), 201–209 (2021)
21. Pál, J.G., Bíró, C.: Evaluating profitability in sports betting using probabilistic models and betting strategies. In: Annales Mathematicae et Informaticae, vol. 61, pp. 202–214 (2025)
22. Pinelis, M., Ruppert, D.: Machine learning portfolio allocation. J. Finan. Data Sci. **8**, 35–54 (2022)
23. Lopez de Prado, M.: Building diversified portfolios that outperform out-of-sample. J. Portfolio Manage. (2016)
24. Ridall, P.G., Titman, A.C., Pettitt, A.N.: Bayesian state-space models for the modelling and prediction of the results of English premier league football. J. R. Stat. Soc.: Ser. C: Appl. Stat. **74**(3), 717–742 (2025)
25. Roncalli, T.: Introduction to risk parity and budgeting. Chapman and Hall/CRC Financial Mathematics Series (2013)

26. Walsh, C., Joshi, A.: Machine learning for sports betting: should model selection be based on accuracy or calibration? Mach. Learn. Appl. **16**, 100539 (2024)
27. Wheatcroft, E.: Forecasting football matches by predicting match statistics. J. Sports Anal. **7**(2), 77–97 (2021)
28. Wunderlich, F., et al.: Assessing machine learning and data imputation approaches to handle the issue of data sparsity in sports forecasting. Mach. Learn. **114**(2), 48 (2025)
29. Zonaro—francesco, F.: Data-driven sports forecasting: Analyzing the profitability of machine learning in the football betting industry (2024)

Expected Possession Value of Control and Duel Actions for Soccer Player Skills Estimation

Andrei Shelopugin(✉)

Moscow, Russia
shelopuginandrey@gmail.com

Abstract. Estimating football player skills is a key task in sports analytics. This paper introduces several extensions to the widely used Expected Possession Value (EPV) model to address the selection problem challenge. First, we assign greater weight to events occurring immediately before a shot (decay effect). Second, our model more accurately accounts for possession risk by incorporating both the decay effect and effective playing time. Third, we assess individual player abilities in winning aerial and ground duels. Using the extended EPV model, we develop a Pass-Carry Reward (PCR) metric that characterizes a player's skill in improving team possession. Furthermore, we predict values of this metric for various football players in the upcoming season, particularly considering the strengths of their teams and opponents by utilizing a modified Glicko-2 rating system.

Keywords: soccer analytics · evaluation metrics · rating systems · Glicko · performance prediction · EPV

1 Introduction

Estimating players' skills is a key challenge for football managers, scouts, and analysts. While video analysis can offer insights [1], conducting it for all players in the market is impractical. Analysts must therefore use filtering mechanisms to narrow down the selection pool. This can involve basic profile data such as age, position, and nationality. Alternatively, leveraging statistics or metrics correlated with actual player performance offers a more effective approach. By using these metrics, analysts can make more informed decisions in player selection.

Currently, accurately assessing the skill levels of players based on historical data has become a complex task. Soccer, being a complicated game, presents various challenges in this regard. One of the challenges is the fact that out of the 22 players on the field, only one possesses the ball at any given time. In recent years, sports analytics, including soccer analytics, has made significant advancements in understanding how to effectively estimate players' abilities, particularly in terms of ball possession skills. In the past, player analysis predominantly relied on basic statistics such as goals scored, successful passes, and fouls committed.

A. Shelopugin—Independent Researcher.

Z. Liu and V. Misra (Eds.): ISACE 2026, LNCS 16610, pp. 292–314, 2026.
https://doi.org/10.1007/978-3-032-27272-0_20

However, there has been a shift towards utilizing advanced metrics, which provide a more comprehensive and nuanced evaluation of player performance.

The challenge with such advanced metrics lies in their reliance on historical data, limiting their use in predicting future performance. While they may work well in "closed" leagues like the NBA, where teams share similar strengths, soccer's diverse leagues present a more complex scenario. This complicates player selection, as managers must understand how players will adapt to new clubs or leagues. Analysts need to assess the resistance levels of different leagues and the stylistic characteristics of new clubs for optimal player hiring decisions.

In this paper, we propose the extension of the Expected Possession Value (EPV) model. Using this model, we calculate a reward accumulated by each player during the season, which characterizes a footballer's ability to play with the ball, and we predict the values of this reward for the next season.

2 Related Work

In the realm of sports analytics, various metrics have been introduced to assess player performance and decision-making. One of the earliest and most influential contributions was made by [10], who developed the Player Efficiency Rating (PER) to evaluate NBA players using basic statistics. His work introduced the concept of possession value and formulated a system that rewards or penalizes players based on successful or unsuccessful actions, thus quantifying their overall impact on the game. [3] [4] extended this to the Expected Possession Value (EPV) model for basketball tracking data, which accounts for individual player skills.

In soccer, [14] proposed using the expected goals (xG) model to evaluate possessions in risk-reward terms. They assigned an xG value to shots taken during a possession and a negative xG value to shots taken by the opponent in the subsequent possession. [22] introduced the term Off-Ball Scoring Opportunities (OBSO), which represents the posterior probability of scoring with the next on-ball event at a particular location based on tracking data. As a result, his method allows to estimate a player's skill to create shot opportunities, even when no shots occur.

[12] proposed the concept of pitch control to estimate the quality of possession using Voronoi diagrams with tracking data. [23] later developed a more complex version of pitch control based on a physical model that predicts whether a pass will be accurate. [15] developed a pass model to analyze decision-making in risk-reward contexts.

[21] introduced the Expected Threat (xT) metric, based on a Markov chain approach, while [7] applied the EPV model to soccer data.

[8] employed deep reinforcement learning (RL) techniques [24] to introduce a metric called Expected Discounted Goal (EDG). Similarly, [13] approached the estimation of EPV as a reinforcement learning task, developing the Goal Impact Metric (GIM) as part of their RL-based solution.

[5] predicted various player metrics for the next 1,000 min at a new or current club, incorporating the Elo ratings [6] of both clubs and leagues to adjust for team and league strength.

Garry Gelade introduced an approach using the Bradley-Terry model [2] to calculate player ratings for duels[1]. This method incorporates opponent strength, facilitating future duel scenario modeling and providing cross-league comparability through a standardized rating system. However, it has limitations, as it assumes equal chances of winning duels, which may not always reflect real-world contexts. While valuable, the Bradley-Terry model is not considered state-of-the-art. Therefore, a modified version of the Glicko-2 system [9] has been employed, as described in [19], to enhance player rating in duels.

3 Proposed Approach for EPV

3.1 Background

This section introduces our customized version of the Expected Possession Value (EPV) model. The model is built using event data, which includes actions such as passes, shots, dribbles, and more. Each event is described by relevant details, including coordinates, time, and other contextual information. This paper employs the following notation to formalize the problem:

- i - index of event,
- c_i - control action,
- d_i - duel action,
- t_i - effective playing time of event i in seconds,
- s_i - index of possession of event i,
- xG_i - xG of event i, if the event is a shot,
- $PV(e_i)$ - possession value of event i,
- $EPV(e_i)$ - expected possession value of event i (prediction of EPV model).

By *control actions*, we refer to actions such as a pass, shot, dribble, carry (ball control), free kick, goal kick, penalty, corner kick, or throw-in. The rationale behind this definition is that it is clear which player possesses the ball during these actions.

We distinguish between symmetrical and asymmetrical duels. Aerial and ground duels are considered symmetrical duels, whereas a dribble is an asymmetrical duel that is already included in the control action category.

We define *possession* as a series of control actions by the same team, uninterrupted by the opponent. In theory, a team may touch the ball during the opponent's possession, such as through an interception, but if this does not lead to their own control action, the opponent's possession continues. For instance, a goalkeeper's save that leads to a corner or offensive rebound does not interrupt the opponent's possession. Therefore, one possession may include multiple shots.

Effective Playing Time refers to the total amount of time that the ball is in play during a match. Most football metrics are normalized based on *dirty* playing time, which includes pauses. The duration of pauses during VAR reviews,

[1] https://www.statsperform.com/resource/a-new-metric-for-evaluating-1v1-ability, Accessed: 2024-10-10.

substitutions, and set-piece situations should be excluded. Thus, we recalculate our metrics based on effective playing time, considering only the actual time of active gameplay. Furthermore, when we refer to playing time, minutes, seconds, etc., we mean effective playing time.

3.2 Possession Value of Control Actions

We define the target variable of our model as the *possession value* and refer to the model's prediction as the *expected possession value (EPV)*. Traditionally, there are two approaches to defining the EPV model's target. The first assigns a value of 1 to each event within a possession if it results in a goal, and 0 otherwise. However, we avoid this approach due to the limited number of goals per game, which could lead to class imbalance and overfitting.

The alternative approach involves assigning each event within a possession the cumulative sum of xG from *future* shots during that possession.

$$PV(c_i) = (1 - \prod_{j=1}^{\infty}(1 - xG_j[t_j \geq t_i][s_i = s_j])) \tag{1}$$

We would like to highlight a few key points. First, this equation applies only to control actions, as these are the only instances where we can definitively determine which player has possession. Second, we consider only the xG of shots that occur after a specific event, since the reward is determined by future events rather than past ones. Third, we account for the possibility of a subsequent goal if the initial shot does not result in a goal, which is why the term $(1 - xG_j)$ is included in Eq. (1). A detailed description of our xG model can be found in Chap. 4.

3.3 Adding Decay Effect

Equation 1 has a significant drawback: it assigns the same possession value (PV) to all events preceding the corresponding shots, implying equal importance for each action. This assumption is invalid. Therefore, we introduce a decay effect, where actions leading to shots carry more weight. We modify the equation as follows:

$$PV(c_i) = (1 - \prod_{j=1}^{\infty}(1 - \gamma^{(t_j - t_i)} xG_j[t_j \geq t_i][s_i = s_j])) \tag{2}$$

The discount factor, introduced by [17], is widely applied in fields like economics and reinforcement learning. It emphasizes the importance of receiving rewards sooner rather than later. However, in our context, the interpretation of the discount factor differs. We do not encourage earlier shots; instead, we suggest that if an action does not lead to a shot soon, it may not significantly advance the attacking phase. We use a discount factor of 0.95. This value is a hyperparameter that can be adjusted based on analyst's preferences. Analysts favoring a vertical attacking style might use a lower γ, such as 0.9, while those preferring a *tiki-taka* style might choose a higher value, like 0.99.

Another point to highlight is that the Eq. (2) operates correctly due to our consideration of effective playing time. For example, if a player draws a penalty, they receive a substantial reward since the penalty kick occurs immediately after. This ensures that rewards accurately reflect the timing and impact of events in the game.

The concept of employing a discount factor in soccer is not entirely new. For instance, in [8], the discounted expected number of goals that a team will score (or concede) was used as a target value for a reinforcement learning algorithm. However, this target value lacks precision without considering the xG and effective time concepts.

3.4 Accounting for Possession Risk

Some EPV models incorporate *possession risk* [14]. An accurate forward pass not only increases the team's scoring chances but also reduces the threat near their own goal. These models consider the difference between the team's PV and the opponent's PV in the subsequent possession, rather than just the team's possession value.

The penalty for possession risk in this approach has a significant drawback. For instance, consider a player who completes a pass, but the team loses possession 10 s later, leading to the opponent earning a penalty kick 20 s after that. In this case, the player's pass would be assigned a target value of -0.75 (the xG value of the penalty kick), which is counterintuitive given the elapsed time. To address this, we incorporate the decay effect from (2). Using the decay factor, the value is calculated as $-0.95^{30} \times 0.75 = -0.16$, showing that the player's action was less influential with respect to the opponent's penalty kick.

Another issue with the original approach to assessing possession risk is that it considers only one possession change. However, a team might lose possession, quickly regain it, and score on the third possession. By incorporating the decay effect, we can account for a larger number of possessions.

Thus, we derive Eq. (3) for the PV, which is used as the target value in our EPV model for control actions:

$$\begin{aligned} PV(c_i) = &\sum_{s_j \in \text{team}} \left(1 - \prod_{j=1}^{\infty}(1 - \gamma^{(t_j - t_i)} xG_j[t_j \geq t_i])\right) \\ &- \sum_{s_j \in \text{opponent}} \left(1 - \prod_{i=1}^{\infty}(1 - \gamma^{(t_j - t_i)} xG_j[t_j \geq t_i])\right) \end{aligned} \tag{3}$$

3.5 Possession Value of Symmetrical Duels

We also calculate EPV for symmetrical duels. To address the challenge of assigning possession to duel events, we assign the possession value of the first control action following the duel to that duel. If there is a series of symmetrical duels, all are recursively assigned the same possession value.

$$PV(d_i) = \begin{cases} PV(e_{i+1}) & \text{if } s_i = s_{i+1} \\ -PV(e_{i+1}) & \text{if } s_i \neq s_{i+1} \end{cases} \tag{4}$$

3.6 Reward Metrics

Before building the EPV model, we define our research goal. Our objective is to implement a metric that measures a player's or team's ability to "improve" possession. We highlight five possible outcomes of a player's actions:

1. **The action leads to a control action by the same team.** If a control action or symmetrical duel maintains possession, the player receives a *reward* equal to the difference between the EPV values of consecutive events.
2. **The action leads to a control action by the opposing team.** If a control action or duel results in a turnover, the next event $(i+1)$ is performed by the opposing team. Thus, the player is penalized twice: once for the turnover and again for creating a goal-scoring opportunity for the opponent.
3. **A goal is scored.** If possession ends with a goal, the player receives a reward of $(1 - EPV(c_i) - EPV(c_{i+1}))$, where c_{i+1} denotes the pass from the center circle following the goal.
4. **The action is the last in the half.** In this case, we assign a reward value of zero to neither reward nor penalize the player.
5. **The action leads to a symmetrical duel.** This is the most challenging scenario. For example, a pass leading to an aerial duel initially incurs a negative reward for creating a 50/50 situation. However, we account for possible mismatches between the players involved. We address this using an enhanced approach to estimate symmetrical duel skills [19]. By incorporating the probability of winning the duel as a feature in the EPV model, we can more accurately evaluate the reward. If the teammate has a high probability of winning the duel, the passing player receives a greater reward. However, when calculating the reward for players involved in symmetrical duels, we do not consider the probability of winning the duel. Instead, we compare the actual outcome with the "average" outcome to avoid penalizing a player with superior skills by inflating the EPV.

Different feature sets describe control actions and symmetrical duels. Therefore, we build three types of models: one for control actions, one for symmetrical duels for the "average" player, and one for symmetrical duels with player duel skill estimation. These are denoted as EPV, EPV_{duel}^{avg}, and EPV_{duel}^{ind}, respectively. Thus, we design the following reward equations to evaluate players' control actions and symmetrical duels.

If i is a control action:

$$\Delta EPV(c_i) = \begin{cases} EPV(c_{i+1}) - EPV(c_i), & \text{if scenario 1} \\ -EPV(c_{i+1}) - EPV(c_i), & \text{if scenario 2} \\ 1 - EPV(c_i) - EPV(c_{i+1}), & \text{if scenario 3} \\ 0, & \text{if scenario 4} \\ EPV_{duel}^{ind}(d_{i+1}) - EPV(c_i), & \text{if scenario 5} \end{cases} \quad (5)$$

If i is a symmetrical duel:

$$\Delta EPV(d_i) = \begin{cases} EPV(c_{i+1}) - EPV_{duel}^{avg}(d_i), & \text{if scenario 1} \\ -EPV(c_{i+1}) - EPV_{duel}^{avg}(d_i), & \text{if scenario 2} \\ 0, & \text{if scenario 4} \\ EPV_{duel}^{ind}(d_{i+1}) - EPV_{duel}^{avg}(d_i), & \text{if scenario 5} \end{cases} \quad (6)$$

Regarding our target function, it's crucial to understand that pass accuracy does not directly affect rewards. For instance, an inaccurate cross that leads to a defender's handball, resulting in a penalty kick, is still rewarded for creating the penalty. This underscores the importance of the concept of *possession* in our approach. Additionally, our analysis excludes certain events, such as interceptions. Therefore, when calculating rewards, we omit these actions. For example, a sequence like "pass-interception-shot" is interpreted as "pass-shot" in our analysis.

4 Empirical Implementation of EPV

4.1 Expected Goals

Soccer's low-scoring nature, averaging 2.6 goals per game, poses challenges in assessing player performance. The emergence of xG as a measure of scoring opportunities addresses this challenge, representing the probability of a shot resulting in a goal based solely on the game situation, not individual player skills. Our goal is to develop a model that evaluates scoring opportunities for an average player.

We create two distinct models: one for set-piece shots and another for open-play shots. Factors such as shot coordinates, distance, angle from the goal, and set-piece type (penalty, free-kick, corner) were considered. For open-play shots, attributes like body part used and preceding actions (e.g., aerial duel, pass) were included, along with spatial details. A separate model was built for set-pieces, as xG should be independent of previous events.

Certain features, like the current game score, championship, and player's team, were omitted due to their correlation with player skill. Another challenge is that the dataset revealed a non-uniform distribution of shots, with top players having more scoring opportunities. To tackle this, we implement a custom loss function, using a log-loss function as the basic loss function for each shot. We divide the loss function value for each shot by its appearance count in the training set, reducing the focus on overrepresented players.

$$customlogloss_i = \frac{1}{|player_i \in D|}[y_i \log(p_i) + (1 - y_i)\log(1 - p_i)] \tag{7}$$

We train the LightGBM [11] and CatBoost [16] frameworks, with LightGBM showing superior accuracy. We implement equation (7) as an *objective* in this framework, a parameter responsible for the loss function, which determines how the model is trained.

4.2 Symmetrical Duels

Here, we present an improved version of approach [19], focusing specifically on *symmetrical duels.*

Analysts often use win percentage as a measure of player duel skill; however, this metric overlooks opponent strength. Players may achieve high win rates against weaker opponents, which skews the evaluation. Additionally, coaches frequently match players of similar strength, particularly during set-pieces, resulting in win rates converging to fifty percent as strong players face strong opponents, while weak players encounter weaker ones.

We introduce a definition of a duel winner. In both cases (aerial and ground duels), we will adhere to the following logic:

1. If a player suffers a foul, he is considered the winner.
2. A player who makes the first touch on the ball is considered the winner.
3. If no one touches the ball, we consider the player whose team gains possession after the duel as the winner.

We consider that duels aren't fully symmetrical. Outcomes depend not only on players' skills but also on external factors, such as the location of the duel or the type of pass leading to it. The original Glicko-2 version updates rating in this way:

$$\mu' = \mu + \phi'^2 g(\phi_j)(s_j - E(\mu, \mu_j, \phi_j)) \tag{8}$$

We modify it for a defender:

$$\mu' = \mu + \phi'^2 g(\phi_j)(s_j - E(\mu + a, \mu_j, \phi_j)) \tag{9}$$

where E is the probability of winning a duel, s_j is the outcome (1 if the player won the duel, 0 otherwise), μ is the rating being updated, and ϕ and g control the learning speed. The advantage a is determined using a model that predicts duel outcomes based on contextual features such as duel and pass coordinates, pass type (e.g., corner, free kick), and the number of opponents, while excluding player skill-related features to create an "average" model that describes duel difficulty.

Two factors contribute to a data leak. First, the defending team generally has an advantage in aerial duels. Second, central defenders typically excel in aerial duels compared to players in other positions; however, they often play more frequently in defensive roles, resulting in underestimated ratings. To mitigate this, player positions are categorized into six groups: central defenders, full-backs, midfielders, central forwards, wingers, and goalkeepers. The model is trained by filtering aerial duels in which the players involved belong to the same position category, applying the same logic as described in Eq. (7). However, the majority of duels occur between players from different position groups, and filtering to same-position duels may result in an unrepresentative training subset. We plan to address this limitation in future work.

Therefore, we train a LightGBM model to calculate the probability of winning a duel. Based on this probability, we calculate the average advantage (a from (9)) for a Glicko-2-based model. This allows us to determine individual aerial and ground duel ratings for each player, considering the duel context. The ratings are presented in Tables 4 and 5.

4.3 Expected Possession Value

We built the EPV model in a similar way to the xG model, utilizing spatial characteristics of the action and the preceding one. Six separate models were trained:

1. For control actions in open-player situations.
2. For set pieces, as they should depend only on the current action.

3-4. Aerial and ground average EPV models, EPV_{duel}^{avg}. These models describe the context of the duel while ignoring the player's skill in aerial duels. We use the predictions of the LightGBM model from Sect. 4.2 as a feature to describe the context of the duel. These models help calculate the reward (6), which allows to estimate players' abilities to "improve" possession in situations where the player participates in a duel.

5–6. In contrast to the previous point, here we want to describe the aerial or ground duel situation considering player skills. It helps calculate pass reward more accurately, as seen in scenario 5 of Eqs. (5), (6). We used the following features: the probability to win the duel (taking into account player ratings), the player's rating, the opponent's rating, as well as the spatial features of the duel and the pass leading to the duel.

Analogously to Eq. (7), we implemented a custom mean squared error:

$$customMSE_i = \frac{1}{|player_i \in D|}(y_i - \hat{y}_i)^2 \qquad (10)$$

5 Metrics Prediction for the Upcoming Season

5.1 Season Pass Carry Reward

We introduce the metric *Pass Carry Reward* (PCR) as a measure of how a player enhances possession through passes or carries over the season. For the term *carry*, we encompass all events where a player controls the ball, including dribbles, carries, or simply maintaining possession without significant movement.

By summing all $\Delta EPV(e_i)$ values throughout the season, we derive a season reward, designated as PCR, focusing solely on pass and carry events. To assess a player's season performance accurately, it's crucial to normalize this reward based on the player's effective playing time, specifically their effective time per 60 min of play.

$$PCR(player) = \frac{60 \times \sum \Delta EPV(e_i | player, e_i = pass \vee e_i = carry)}{\sum \text{minutes}} \tag{11}$$

The idea behind this paper is straightforward: to predict players' PCR for the upcoming season. However, there are certain limitations and restrictions that we need to address and discuss.

5.2 Data

First and foremost, it is important to define the group of players for whom we will train our model. Our decision is to focus only on players who have accumulated at least 100 min in both the current season and the next season. This criterion is implemented to ensure the stability of PCR predictions, as values of PCR for players with limited playing time tend to be less reliable. The potential drawbacks of dropping data based on this criterion will be discussed in the Subsects. 5.3, 5.3.

The calculated features, approximately 600 in total, can be categorized into several groups.

Player-specific features. These include attributes such as age, height, position, and other characteristics that describe the individual player.

Performance Features. This group encompasses metrics like PCR, xG, goals, played minutes, and other raw statistics from the previous seasons. Additionally, average values of these metrics over the past three or five seasons are also considered.

Contribution to Team Success. These statistics capture the player's impact on the team's overall performance. For instance, features like the player's share of the team's total xG when they were on the field are included. These features are crucial as they provide insights into a player's effectiveness, especially when playing for a weaker team where their absolute metrics may be lower.

League Style Features. This category includes metrics that describe the prevalent playing style in the league. For example, the average PCR of the league in the previous season is considered. These features help address challenges such as the influence of league-specific playing styles on PCR. For a player in a league that prioritizes attacking play, it may be easier to achieve higher PCR values.

Team and League Strength Features. These features account for factors such as team and league strength, particularly in the context of player transfers. They provide information regarding a player's transfer, such as moving from a strong team to a weaker one, and help contextualize the player's performance accordingly. A detailed discussion regarding this last group of features will be presented in the Subsect. 5.3.

5.3 Estimation Challenges

Ratings of Clubs and Leagues To address the issue of player transfers and the potential impact on PCR prediction, it is important to consider the information associated with changes in clubs or leagues. One approach could involve introducing a categorical feature that indicates the transfer from one league to another, such as "player transfers from Denmark Superliga to France Ligue 1". However, this approach may encounter challenges related to the curse of dimensionality, as there may not be a significant number of transfers between specific leagues. Additionally, it is worth noting that the strengths of leagues can vary over time.

To overcome these challenges, we propose utilizing a modified Glicko-2 rating system [20]. This model calculates ratings for teams based on match outcomes, allowing for the estimation of team strength. The strength of a league is defined as the average rating of a specified number of teams, with the exact number being adjustable to account for variations across leagues.

With this modified rating system, we can calculate various features, such as the rating of the player's old team, the rating of the player's new team, and the difference in ratings between the player's old league and the new league. These features provide valuable information related to the player's transition and enable us to account for changes in team and league strength. Additionally, we calculate the average rating of team opponents, as two players can demonstrate similar metrics; however, the level of opponents can differ.

It is important to note that we utilized the actual club/league ratings at the start of the season. This approach allows the model to incorporate up-to-date information about the strength of the clubs/leagues, considering that their levels may change over time. Moreover, we must adhere to the natural constraint that we cannot use the future ratings of the clubs/leagues.

Probability to Stay in the Data. As mentioned earlier, our training set includes only instances where players have played at least 100 min in the next season. This limitation poses a challenge as it is not possible to know in advance how many minutes a player will play in the next season. To address this issue, we build an auxiliary model.

We predict whether a football player will play at least 100 min in the next season. A player may have less than 100 min for various reasons: retirement from professional football, injury, underperformance resulting in exclusion from matches by the coach, or transfer to a team or league not presented in the dataset, indicating the transfer to a less competitive league.

We train the model using the same features as those employed in the previous model, excluding the features related to the ratings of a new team or league. In addition, we incorporated data on players' contract durations at the beginning of the season, leveraging information sourced from the FIFA video game series[2].

---

[2] https://kaggle.com/datasets/stefanoleone992/ea-sports-fc-24-complete-player-dataset, Accessed: 2024-10-10.

Presence-Only Data Problem. Another challenge in training our model is the non-random nature of real-world transfers. Football club managers make informed decisions when acquiring players, leading to two key scenarios. When a player moves from a weaker club to a stronger one, it suggests the new club sees potential or talent in the player. When a player moves from a strong club to a weaker one, it suggests a decline in performance. These scenarios introduce bias in our predictions. We use features like the "rating of the new team" to inform the model about transfers, but the outcomes remain uncertain. Consequently, predictions can be overly optimistic in the first scenario and overly pessimistic in the second, reflecting the uncertainties and biases inherent in real-world transfers.

This problem is known as *presence-only data* or *learning from positive and unlabeled data* [25]. First, account for the data leak from leaving data, assigning a probability pl. Second, consider the data leak from subsequent transfers, which is highly correlated with league rating differences. Assign this as $\Delta ratings$, with 1500 as the average club rating.

$$\Delta ratings = \frac{(rating(league_{new}) - rating(league_{old}))}{1500} \tag{12}$$

$$PCR_{adj} = PCR * 0.8^{(\Delta ratings + pl)} \tag{13}$$

5.4 Results

As a baseline, we calculate the root mean squared error (RMSE) and mean absolute error (MAE) between the PCR from the previous season and the next season (refer to Table 1). This imitates a selection process based on historical data without applying machine learning. We separate the data into several groups based on the following binary rules: whether the player is in the same team/league as in the previous season or not, and whether the player played more than 100 or 1000 min in the previous season. Remember that we are trying to solve a selection problem; therefore, we assume that a player may change clubs or even leagues.

Table 1. Baseline Metrics Without Applying Machine Learning

Data Sample	$RMSE_{100}$	MAE_{100}	$RMSE_{1000}$	MAE_{1000}
all data	0.053	0.036	0.042	0.029
same team, same league	0.050	0.034	0.039	0.027
same team, new league	0.051	0.035	0.042	0.031
new team, same league	0.055	0.038	0.044	0.031
new team, new league	0.061	0.043	0.051	0.036

By comparing the RMSE and MAE of our model's predictions (without adjustments), we can estimate the contribution of our approach (see Table 2).

Table 2. Achieved Metrics Based On Our Approach

Data Sample	$RMSE_{100}$	MAE_{100}	$RMSE_{1000}$	MAE_{1000}
all data	0.033	0.023	0.031	0.021
same team, same league	0.032	0.022	0.029	0.02
same team, new league	0.031	0.021	0.027	0.019
new team, same league	0.034	0.024	0.032	0.023
new team, new league	0.037	0.026	0.036	0.025

The proposed evaluation approach has certain limitations. Our end product is a player ranking based on predicted PCR, and there is no guarantee that the calculated shortlist is accurate. Additionally, there is no mathematical way to prove that EPV-based metrics truly correlate with player skills. We see two ways to evaluate our shortlists. The first is to ask experts, which may be done in future work. The second way is to assume that the transfer market is enough effective at least at the top level and compare top players from our shortlists with actual transfers to top clubs.

Table 6 presents the top season performances based on the PCR metric among players who played at least 1,000 min during the season. The PCR predictions for Manchester City, Barcelona, Milan, and Brighton can be found in Tables 7, 8, 9, 10. Brighton was chosen because this club has a reputation for having a strong data analysis department and making transfers based on data. The actual date is June 2, 2024.

As a retrospective validation, the arxiv version of this paper [18] was published on June 2, 2024, based on data available as of mid-May 2024. Since then, several players from our top-50 ranking (Table 7) have transferred to top European clubs: Sávio (Girona → Manchester City), M. Olise (Crystal Palace → Bayern Munich), K. Kvaratskhelia (Napoli → PSG), F. Conceição (Porto → Juventus), Pedro Neto (Wolverhampton → Chelsea), David Neres (Benfica → Napoli), and Y. Minteh (Feyenoord → Brighton). Additionally, Nico Williams and Lamine Yamal demonstrated excellent performance at UEFA Euro 2024, where Spain won the tournament.

There is also a case study Sect. A in the appendix that demonstrates the advantage of using individual duel skills in the EPV model.

6 Conclusion

We improve the EPV model by accurately accounting for effective playing time, decay effect, and possession risk. The incorporation of player duel skills allows us to calculate rewards more accurately. Therefore, we partially solve the problem of reward distribution between the passing player and the target player in cases of passes leading to duels. However, the problem still exists in cases of accurate passes, and we do not have a solution based on event data.

This model can potentially demonstrate higher performance with tracking data due to the consideration of more features. The inclusion of injury data is promising not only for enhancing the predictive capacity of the model that calculates the probability of a player remaining in the dataset but also for improving the prediction of PCR for the next season. Additionally, we need to consider the context of new and old teams more accurately. For instance, we can replace PCR with a conditional expectation that takes into account the player's position in the next club. For example, our model lacks accuracy when a center forward starts to play as a winger in a new club. Finally, the presence-only data problem should be tackled with a more elegant approach, which is a subject for further research.

Acknowledgments. The author is thankful to Nikita Kozodoi, Viktoria Lokteva, Nikita Vasyukhin, Iskander Safiulin, Daniil Babaev, and Alexander Sirotkin for their invaluable consultations on machine learning and soccer analytics.

A A Case Study: Gianluigi Donnarumma Passes to Duels in Seasons 19/20, 20/21

In this paper, we focus on addressing the selection problem by proposing a mechanism to narrow the selection pool. Our approach, however, is versatile and can be applied not only to selection tasks but also to team performance and opposition analysis. Below, we provide an example of such an analysis.

Gianluigi Donnarumma was an exceptional shot-stopper during his time at AC Milan but struggled with passing under pressure. Coach Stefano Pioli suggested that when Donnarumma was pressured, he should make a long forward pass (typically leading to a duel); otherwise, he should pass short to a defender or defensive midfielder.

We define a long forward pass as one exceeding 40 m in distance and with a y-projection increment of more than 10 m. Donnarumma's most common targets were Zlatan Ibrahimovic (35 aerial duels, 8 ground duels) and Rafael Leao (28 aerial duels, 11 ground duels).

The traditional EPV model does not account for players' duel skills, whereas our approach offers a more detailed analysis. In Table 3, we compare passes to Leao and Ibrahimovic. Both faced similar challenges in winning duels, but despite slightly stronger opponents, Zlatan had a higher success rate: his average win probability in aerial duels was 61%, compared to Leao's 35.8%. Consequently, Ibrahimovic's EPV values are higher than Leao's. Note that Glicko ratings adjust over time; thus, the column r reflects Ibrahimovic's and Leao's average ratings against opponents following Donnarumma's passes.

Table 3. Gianluigi Donnarumma Passes to Rafael Leao or Zlatan Ibrahimovic Duels[5]

$player$	$duel$	$duels$	$saved$	p_{avg}	p_{ind}	r	r_{opp}	epv_{duel}^{avg}	epv_{duel}^{ind}
Leão	aerial	35	28.6	40.5	35.8	1519	1545	0.00075	0.00069
Zlatan	aerial	28	53.6	39.2	61.1	1746	1573	0.00077	0.00135
Leão	ground	8	12.5	45.0	28.2	1408	1534	0.00073	0.00062
Zlatan	ground	11	54.5	44.8	44.9	1539	1533	−0.00012	−0.0001

Table 4. Aerial Duel Ratings

#	player	position	rating	#duels	wins%
1	V. van Dijk	central_def	1762	2167	71.9
2	L. Sobiech	central_def	1761	1239	72.2
3	B. Matić	midfielder	1757	1076	71.1
4	M. Djurić	central_forward	1744	2763	67.7
5	L. Došek	central_forward	1743	253	66.0
6	S. Coates	central_def	1742	1729	69.3
7	Rafael Donato	central_def	1742	868	71.5
8	P. Budkivskyi	central_forward	1738	1238	56.2
9	A. Papazoglou	wing	1734	1137	61.3
10	M. Jakubko	central_forward	1726	239	63.6
11	S. Memišević	central_def	1725	762	67.2
12	N. Bendtner	central_forward	1725	742	52.4
13	S. Ganvoula	central_forward	1722	1364	58.7
14	J. Tarkowski	central_def	1721	2097	66.3
15	R. Uldriķis	central_forward	1721	1615	56.6
16	C. Bolger	central_def	1715	670	74.0
17	F. Benković	central_def	1715	690	77.2
18	A. Flint	central_def	1713	2676	68.8
19	R. Rodelin	wing	1713	1461	65.6
20	K. Moore	central_forward	1713	2478	58.2
21	C. Keeley	central_def	1712	687	72.6
22	J. Greaves	lateral	1712	774	71.2
23	J. Cooper	central_def	1712	2915	69.6
24	R. Leeuwin	central_def	1711	754	67.8
25	L. Lindsay	central_def	1711	1732	68.7
26	E. Sipović	central_def	1711	266	76.3
27	M. Papadopulos	central_forward	1710	1807	55.2
28	J. Owens	central_forward	1709	1590	59.7
29	C. Casadei	wing	1708	106	70.8
30	V. Posmac	central_def	1707	870	77.2
31	J. Arango	wing	1706	165	64.2
32	F. Mayembo	central_def	1705	446	69.7
33	R. Sykes	central_def	1705	195	73.3
34	V. Koskimaa	central_def	1704	596	74.8
35	Y. Khacheridi	central_def	1704	532	76.3
36	N. Ziabaris	central_def	1704	262	72.9
37	I. Soumaré	wing	1703	684	61.3
38	C. Stewart	central_def	1702	458	63.3
39	J. Chabot	central_def	1702	808	63.2
40	C. Bocşan	central_def	1700	235	71.1
41	J. Blayac	central_forward	1700	720	59.9
42	Héliton	central_def	1700	360	70.8
43	Nilton	midfielder	1699	356	64.0
44	M. Janko	central_forward	1699	647	59.7
45	M. Baša	central_def	1699	242	76.9
46	D. Lemajić	central_forward	1699	1420	54.7
47	Kim Min-Jae	central_def	1699	485	67.2
48	A. Taylor	central_def	1699	1353	71.2
49	M. Beevers	central_def	1698	787	67.0
50	A. Zabolotny	central_forward	1698	1572	57.8

Table 5. Ground Duel Ratings

#	player	position	rating	#duels	wins%
1	B. Ostojić	central_def	1695	279	73.1
2	Felipe	central_def	1672	643	67.8
3	Vasco Fernandes	central_def	1671	408	66.4
4	V. van Dijk	central_def	1669	742	71.6
5	R. García	central_def	1666	427	68.1
6	L. Valenti	central_def	1666	135	74.1
7	V. Mudrac	central_def	1665	274	69.3
8	M. Vítor	central_def	1663	691	68.7
9	Raúl Navas	central_def	1663	350	70.9
10	N. Elvedi	central_def	1660	735	66.9
11	L. McCullough	central_def	1658	317	75.7
12	G. Valsvik	central_def	1656	702	64.2
13	P. Jagielka	central_def	1656	388	69.8
14	J. Matip	central_def	1655	543	69.2
15	A. Maxsø	central_def	1655	552	65.4
16	A. Flint	central_def	1655	917	68.5
17	J. Kucka	midfielder	1654	877	55.6
18	Marcão	central_def	1654	427	65.6
19	A. Bengtsson	lateral	1654	118	72.0
20	Rodrigão	central_def	1654	293	68.9
21	Aleksandar Luković	central_def	1653	120	76.7
22	T. Petrášek	central_def	1653	254	72.0
23	C. McJannet	central_def	1653	445	67.2
24	N. Belaković	wing	1652	351	61.5
25	Gabriel Magalhaes	central_def	1651	566	67.3
26	M. Hasebe	midfielder	1651	572	63.5
27	M. Peersman	lateral	1651	817	62.5
28	G. Mancini	central_def	1650	759	63.9
29	O. Bačo	central_def	1648	478	61.3
30	H. Moukoudi	central_def	1647	408	61.3
31	L. Querfeld	central_def	1647	330	67.9
32	C. Halkett	central_def	1646	374	68.2
33	W. Pacho	central_def	1646	269	66.2
34	S. Bell	central_def	1646	543	61.7
35	Luiz Otávio	central_def	1645	344	68.0
36	B. Utvik	central_def	1644	398	64.3
37	S. Papagiannopoulos	central_def	1644	716	70.4
38	L. Nielsen	central_def	1644	708	65.5
39	R. Grodzicki	central_def	1644	171	70.2
40	A. Sørensen	central_def	1644	589	65.9
41	C. Goldson	central_def	1644	820	72.8
42	F. Aguilar	central_def	1644	117	72.6
43	O. Kúdela	central_def	1644	465	66.2
44	J. Boller	central_def	1643	280	68.2
45	M. Lovato	central_def	1643	267	69.7
46	L. Morgillo	central_def	1643	130	73.1
47	Tiago Ilori	central_def	1643	200	67.5
48	M. Connolly	central_def	1642	380	69.7
49	T. Vion	lateral	1642	419	59.4
50	A. Seck	central_def	1642	444	68.7

Table 6. Top Season Performances Based on PCR

#	player	team	competition	season	PCR	time
1	H. Ziyech	Ajax	Netherlands. First	19/20	0.355	1237
2	J. Iličić	Atalanta	Italy. First	20/21	0.315	1143
3	A. Zoubir	Qarabag	Azerbaijan. First	20/21	0.314	1465
4	H. Ziyech	Ajax	Netherlands. First	17/18	0.308	2257
5	O. Dembélé	Barcelona	Spain. First	21/22	0.305	1008
6	J. Hauge	Bodo Glimt	Norway. First	20	0.305	1149
7	J. Grealish	Aston Villa	England. First	20/21	0.301	1481
8	J. Doku	Manchester City	England. First	23/24	0.299	1207
9	Malcom	Zenit	Russia. First	20/21	0.297	1184
10	A. Zoubir	Qarabag	Azerbaijan. First	23/24	0.287	1134
11	A. Schjelderup	Nordsjaelland	Denmark. First	23/24	0.283	1207
12	L. Messi	Barcelona	Spain. First	18/19	0.277	2058
13	T. Ali	Malmo FF	Sweden. First	23	0.277	1258
14	K. Mbappé	PSG	France. First	19/20	0.276	1146
15	J. Ito	Genk	Belgium. First	21/22	0.273	2286
16	Neymar	PSG	France. First	17/18	0.272	1353
17	L. Abada	Celtic	Scotland. First	22/23	0.271	1078
18	Y. Soteldo	Santos	Brazil. First	23	0.27	1105
19	Musa Al Tamari	APOEL	Cyprus. First	18/19	0.27	1387
20	J. Clarke	Sunderland	England. Second	23/24	0.268	2503
21	R. Mahrez	Manchester City	England. First	19/20	0.268	1506
22	G. Kanga	Crvena Zvezda	Serbia. First	16/17	0.268	1261
23	M. Marin	Crvena Zvezda	Serbia. First	18/19	0.262	1145
24	Dodo	Hamrun Spartans	Malta. First	20/21	0.258	1033
25	P. Zinckernagel	Bodo Glimt	Norway. First	20	0.254	1818
26	Daniel Podence	Olympiacos	Greece. First	23/24	0.252	1199
27	C. McCloskey	Glenavon	N. Ireland. First	20/21	0.251	1107
28	K. Mbappé	Monaco	France. First	16/17	0.25	1088
29	J. Cooper	Linfield	N. Ireland. First	19/20	0.249	1463
30	A. Limbombe	Almere City	Netherlands. Second	22/23	0.248	1360
31	I. Kallon	Cambuur	Netherlands. Second	20/21	0.248	1530
32	Antony	Ajax	Netherlands. First	21/22	0.244	1323
33	N. Lang	Club Brugge	Belgium. First	22/23	0.242	1646
34	A. Abreu	UT Petange	Luxembourg. First	22/23	0.241	1437
35	D. Payet	Marseille	France. First	17/18	0.241	1660
36	Ângelo Gabriel	Santos	Brazil. First	22	0.24	1085
37	H. Ziyech	Ajax	Netherlands. First	18/19	0.24	1794
38	J. Croux	Roda JC	Netherlands. Second	19/20	0.236	1856
39	L. Messi	Barcelona	Spain. First	15/16	0.236	2025
40	Á. Di María	PSG	France. First	20/21	0.235	1372
41	Marquinhos	Ferencvaros	Hungary. First	23/24	0.234	1391
42	K. De Bruyne	Manchester City	England. First	19/20	0.234	2133
43	F. Conceicão	Porto	Portugal. First	23/24	0.233	1133
44	V. Birmančević	Cukaricki	Serbia. First	20/21	0.233	1217
45	A. Gómez	Atalanta	Italy. First	19/20	0.233	2095
46	Neymar	PSG	France. First	20/21	0.233	1051
47	M. Melikson	Hapoel Beer-Sheva	Israel. First	16/17	0.232	1341
48	Cesc Fàbregas	Chelsea	England. First	16/17	0.231	1006
49	M. Tomasov	Astana	Kazakhstan. First	23	0.231	1347
50	N. Lang	Club Brugge	Belgium. First	21/22	0.231	2052

Table 7. Player Ranking Based on PCR Predictions in the Case of Their Transfer to Manchester City

#	player	team	age	PCR	PCR_{pred}	PCR_{adj}	p_{stay}
1	J. Doku	Manchester City	21.2	0.299	0.197	0.196	0.961
2	O. Dembélé	PSG	26.3	0.215	0.173	0.166	0.868
3	Sávio	Girona	19.4	0.174	0.165	0.162	0.96
4	Nico Williams	Athletic Bilbao	21.1	0.199	0.157	0.154	0.956
5	Bryan Zaragoza	Bayern Munchen	21.9	0.162	0.154	0.151	0.961
6	K. Kvaratskhelia	Napoli	22.5	0.195	0.153	0.15	0.954
7	F. Conceicão	Porto	20.7	0.233	0.156	0.149	0.905
8	M. Olise	Crystal Palace	21.7	0.182	0.152	0.148	0.862
9	O. Sahraoui	Heerenveen	22.2	0.151	0.155	0.146	0.882
10	Vinícius Júnior	Real Madrid	23.1	0.136	0.148	0.144	0.938
11	K. Coman	Bayern Munchen	27.2	0.095	0.149	0.144	0.861
12	R. Sterling	Chelsea	28.7	0.152	0.149	0.144	0.828
13	O. Niang	Riga	21.4	0.296	0.161	0.144	0.734
14	C. Ejuke	Antwerp	25.6	0.158	0.152	0.143	0.848
15	N. Lang	PSV	24.2	0.196	0.156	0.143	0.74
16	Rafael Leão	Milan	24.2	0.178	0.145	0.142	0.913
17	J. Dompé	Hamburger SV	28.0	0.158	0.155	0.141	0.768
18	F. Chiesa	Juventus	25.8	0.195	0.144	0.141	0.932
19	M. Edwards	Sporting CP	24.7	0.277	0.149	0.141	0.866
20	T. Corbeanu	Granada	21.2	0.152	0.148	0.14	0.869
21	B. Gruda	Mainz 05	19.2	0.163	0.144	0.138	0.823
22	S. Ltaief	Winterthur	23.3	0.114	0.148	0.137	0.786
23	I. Akhomach	Villarreal	19.3	0.094	0.14	0.137	0.936
24	J. Enciso	Brighton	19.6	0.215	0.147	0.137	0.677
25	Pedro Neto	Wolverhampton	23.4	0.131	0.14	0.136	0.855
26	T. Kubo	Real Sociedad	22.2	0.162	0.139	0.135	0.933
27	T. Ali	Malmo FF	24.8	0.277	0.145	0.135	0.828
28	J. Bynoe-Gittens	Borussia D	19.0	0.208	0.139	0.135	0.898
29	J. Sancho	Borussia D	23.4	0.224	0.14	0.135	0.858
30	A. Mitriţă	Univ. Craiova	28.4	0.195	0.143	0.135	0.906
31	A. Nusa	Club Brugge	18.3	0.143	0.142	0.134	0.872
32	J. Bakayoko	PSV	20.3	0.194	0.141	0.134	0.928
33	E. Zhegrova	Lille	24.4	0.097	0.139	0.134	0.907
34	Y. Minteh	Feyenoord	19.1	0.217	0.145	0.134	0.79
35	Lamine Yamal	Barcelona	16.1	0.136	0.138	0.134	0.922
36	Haissem Hassan	Sporting Gijon	21.5	0.125	0.144	0.133	0.873
37	K. Mitoma	Brighton	26.2	0.215	0.137	0.133	0.856
38	A. Sbaï	Grenoble	22.8	0.185	0.145	0.132	0.818
39	Serginho	Viborg	22.5	0.182	0.144	0.132	0.719
40	R. Sottil	Fiorentina	24.2	0.097	0.137	0.132	0.84
41	A. Schjelderup	Nordsjaelland	19.2	0.283	0.137	0.131	0.936
42	N. Madueke	Chelsea	21.4	0.177	0.136	0.131	0.823
43	M. Fofana	Lyon	18.3	0.169	0.136	0.131	0.93
44	Milson	Maccabi Tel Aviv	23.9	0.178	0.14	0.13	0.856
45	Ângelo Gabriel	Strasbourg	18.6	0.125	0.134	0.13	0.918
46	Dudu	Palmeiras	31.3	0.172	0.147	0.13	0.57
47	A. Garnacho	Manchester Unt	19.1	0.088	0.132	0.129	0.922
48	David Neres	Benfica Portugal	26.5	0.25	0.142	0.129	0.708
49	Gabriel Martinelli	Arsenal	22.2	0.132	0.133	0.129	0.874
50	Luis Guilherme	Palmeiras	17.2	0.127	0.144	0.129	0.62

Table 8. Player Ranking Based on PCR Predictions in the Case of Their Transfer to Barcelona

#	player	team	Age	PCR	PCR_{pred}	PCR_{adj}	p_{stay}
1	J. Doku	Manchester City	21.2	0.299	0.182	0.182	0.961
2	O. Dembélé	PSG	26.3	0.215	0.179	0.173	0.868
3	Sâvio	Girona	19.4	0.174	0.163	0.162	0.96
4	Nico Williams	Athletic Bilbao	21.1	0.199	0.155	0.153	0.956
5	Bryan Zaragoza	Bayern Munchen	21.9	0.162	0.153	0.152	0.961
6	K. Kvaratskhelia	Napoli	22.5	0.195	0.151	0.15	0.954
7	Vinícius Júnior	Real Madrid	23.1	0.136	0.148	0.146	0.938
8	E. Zhegrova	Lille	24.4	0.097	0.147	0.143	0.907
9	M. Olise	Crystal Palace	21.7	0.182	0.146	0.143	0.862
10	Lamine Yamal	Barcelona	16.1	0.136	0.144	0.141	0.922
11	N. Lang	PSV	24.2	0.196	0.152	0.14	0.74
12	T. Kubo	Real Sociedad	22.2	0.162	0.142	0.14	0.933
13	I. Akhomach	Villarreal	19.3	0.094	0.142	0.14	0.936
14	Rafael Leão	Milan	24.2	0.178	0.142	0.14	0.913
15	C. Ejuke	Antwerp	25.6	0.158	0.146	0.14	0.848
16	R. Sterling	Chelsea	28.7	0.152	0.143	0.139	0.828
17	F. Conceicão	Porto	20.7	0.233	0.144	0.139	0.905
18	O. Niang	Riga	21.4	0.296	0.153	0.138	0.734
19	O. Sahraoui	Heerenveen	22.2	0.151	0.145	0.138	0.882
20	F. Chiesa	Juventus	25.8	0.195	0.139	0.137	0.932
21	K. Coman	Bayern Munchen	27.2	0.095	0.14	0.137	0.861
22	T. Corbeanu	Granada	21.2	0.152	0.143	0.137	0.869
23	J. Dompé	Hamburger SV	28.0	0.158	0.147	0.136	0.768
24	Pedro Neto	Wolverhampton	23.4	0.131	0.138	0.135	0.855
25	J. Sancho	Borussia D	23.4	0.224	0.138	0.135	0.858
26	T. Ali	Malmo FF	24.8	0.277	0.142	0.134	0.828
27	M. Edwards	Sporting CP	24.7	0.277	0.14	0.133	0.866
28	Haissem Hassan	Sporting Gijon	21.5	0.125	0.141	0.133	0.873
29	Ângelo Gabriel	Strasbourg	18.6	0.125	0.135	0.132	0.918
30	J. Bynoe-Gittens	Borussia D	19.0	0.208	0.134	0.132	0.898
31	R. Sottil	Fiorentina	24.2	0.097	0.135	0.13	0.84
32	K. Mitoma	Brighton	26.2	0.215	0.133	0.13	0.856
33	A. Nusa	Club Brugge	18.3	0.143	0.135	0.129	0.872
34	M. Politano	Napoli	30.1	0.188	0.134	0.129	0.796
35	B. Gruda	Mainz 05	19.2	0.163	0.133	0.128	0.823
36	J. Bakayoko	PSV	20.3	0.194	0.133	0.128	0.928
37	Ez Abde	Real Betis	21.7	0.126	0.13	0.128	0.948
38	N. Madueke	Chelsea	21.4	0.177	0.132	0.128	0.823
39	A. Garnacho	Manchester Unt	19.1	0.088	0.129	0.128	0.922
40	M. Fofana	Lyon	18.3	0.169	0.131	0.127	0.93
41	A. Mitriță	Univ. Craiova	28.4	0.195	0.133	0.127	0.906
42	A. Schjelderup	Nordsjaelland	19.2	0.283	0.13	0.127	0.936
43	Milson	Maccabi Tel Aviv	23.9	0.178	0.134	0.126	0.856
44	S. Ltaief	Winterthur	23.3	0.114	0.134	0.126	0.786
45	M. Simon	Nantes	28.1	0.125	0.132	0.126	0.801
46	J. Boga	Nice	26.6	0.079	0.129	0.125	0.894
47	Dudu	Palmeiras	31.3	0.172	0.14	0.125	0.57
48	J. Clarke	Sunderland	22.7	0.268	0.131	0.125	0.939
49	Serginho	Viborg	22.5	0.182	0.135	0.124	0.719
50	M. Daramy	Reims	21.6	0.077	0.127	0.124	0.926

Table 9. Player Ranking Based on PCR Predictions in the Case of Their Transfer to Milan

#	Player	Team	Age	PCR	PCR_{pred}	PCR_{adj}	p_{stay}
1	J. Doku	Manchester City	21.2	0.299	0.173	0.173	0.961
2	O. Dembélé	PSG	26.3	0.215	0.168	0.162	0.868
3	Sávio	Girona	19.4	0.174	0.159	0.157	0.96
4	Nico Williams	Athletic Bilbao	21.1	0.199	0.151	0.15	0.956
5	K. Kvaratskhelia	Napoli	22.5	0.195	0.148	0.147	0.954
6	Bryan Zaragoza	Bayern Munchen	21.9	0.162	0.147	0.145	0.961
7	Vinícius Júnior	Real Madrid	23.1	0.136	0.145	0.142	0.938
8	Rafael Leão	Milan	24.2	0.178	0.145	0.142	0.913
9	R. Sterling	Chelsea	28.7	0.152	0.142	0.137	0.828
10	M. Olise	Crystal Palace	21.7	0.182	0.141	0.137	0.862
11	N. Lang	PSV	24.2	0.196	0.149	0.137	0.74
12	O. Sahraoui	Heerenveen	22.2	0.151	0.144	0.137	0.882
13	C. Ejuke	Antwerp	25.6	0.158	0.144	0.137	0.848
14	T. Ali	Malmo FF	24.8	0.277	0.143	0.134	0.828
15	K. Coman	Bayern Munchen	27.2	0.095	0.137	0.133	0.861
16	J. Dompé	Hamburger SV	28.0	0.158	0.145	0.133	0.768
17	T. Kubo	Real Sociedad	22.2	0.162	0.135	0.133	0.933
18	T. Corbeanu	Granada	21.2	0.152	0.139	0.132	0.869
19	F. Conceicão	Porto	20.7	0.233	0.137	0.132	0.905
20	Pedro Neto	Wolverhampton	23.4	0.131	0.135	0.132	0.855
21	E. Zhegrova	Lille	24.4	0.097	0.135	0.131	0.907
22	F. Chiesa	Juventus	25.8	0.195	0.133	0.131	0.932
23	K. Mitoma	Brighton	26.2	0.215	0.134	0.131	0.856
24	I. Akhomach	Villarreal	19.3	0.094	0.133	0.131	0.936
25	J. Sancho	Borussia D	23.4	0.224	0.134	0.13	0.858
26	Haissem Hassan	Sporting Gijon	21.5	0.125	0.139	0.13	0.873
27	O. Niang	Riga	21.4	0.296	0.144	0.129	0.734
28	J. Bynoe-Gittens	Borussia D	19.0	0.208	0.132	0.129	0.898
29	R. Sottil	Fiorentina	24.2	0.097	0.134	0.129	0.84
30	M. Edwards	Sporting CP	24.7	0.277	0.134	0.128	0.866
31	Lamine Yamal	Barcelona	16.1	0.136	0.129	0.127	0.922
32	Ângelo Gabriel	Strasbourg	18.6	0.125	0.129	0.126	0.918
33	M. Politano	Napoli	30.1	0.188	0.132	0.126	0.796
34	Milson	Maccabi Tel Aviv	23.9	0.178	0.134	0.126	0.856
35	Ez Abde	Real Betis	21.7	0.126	0.127	0.125	0.948
36	B. Gruda	Mainz 05	19.2	0.163	0.128	0.124	0.823
37	A. Garnacho	Manchester Unt	19.1	0.088	0.125	0.124	0.922
38	A. Nusa	Club Brugge	18.3	0.143	0.129	0.124	0.872
39	N. Madueke	Chelsea	21.4	0.177	0.127	0.123	0.823
40	J. Bakayoko	PSV	20.3	0.194	0.128	0.123	0.928
41	David Neres	Benfica Portugal	26.5	0.25	0.133	0.122	0.708
42	J. Clarke	Sunderland	22.7	0.268	0.128	0.122	0.939
43	A. Mitriță	Univ. Craiova	28.4	0.195	0.128	0.122	0.906
44	Daniel Podence	Olympiacos Piraeus	27.8	0.252	0.131	0.121	0.8
45	A. Schjelderup	Nordsjaelland	19.2	0.283	0.125	0.121	0.936
46	Dudu	Palmeiras	31.3	0.172	0.136	0.121	0.57
47	M. Fofana	Lyon	18.3	0.169	0.125	0.121	0.93
48	Serginho	Viborg	22.5	0.182	0.129	0.119	0.719
49	A. Sbaï	Grenoble	22.8	0.185	0.128	0.118	0.818
50	J. Boga	Nice	26.6	0.079	0.122	0.118	0.894

Table 10. Player Ranking Based on PCR Predictions in the Case of Their Transfer to Brighton

#	Player	Team	Age	PCR	PCR_{pred}	PCR_{adj}	p_{stay}
1	J. Doku	Manchester City	21.2	0.299	0.161	0.159	0.961
2	O. Dembélé	PSG	26.3	0.215	0.15	0.143	0.868
3	Sávio	Girona	19.4	0.174	0.141	0.139	0.96
4	R. Sterling	Chelsea	28.7	0.152	0.134	0.129	0.828
5	K. Kvaratskhelia	Napoli	22.5	0.195	0.13	0.127	0.954
6	Nico Williams	Athletic Bilbao	21.1	0.199	0.129	0.127	0.956
7	M. Olise	Crystal Palace	21.7	0.182	0.13	0.126	0.862
8	J. Dompé	Hamburger SV	28.0	0.158	0.138	0.126	0.768
9	C. Ejuke	Antwerp	25.6	0.158	0.133	0.125	0.848
10	O. Sahraoui	Heerenveen	22.2	0.151	0.131	0.124	0.882
11	Bryan Zaragoza	Bayern Munchen	21.9	0.162	0.126	0.124	0.961
12	Haissem Hassan	Sporting Gijon	21.5	0.125	0.132	0.123	0.873
13	T. Corbeanu	Granada	21.2	0.152	0.127	0.12	0.869
14	Vinícius Júnior	Real Madrid	23.1	0.136	0.123	0.12	0.938
15	T. Ali	Malmo FF	24.8	0.277	0.127	0.119	0.828
16	N. Lang	PSV	24.2	0.196	0.128	0.117	0.74
17	K. Mitoma	Brighton	26.2	0.215	0.12	0.117	0.856
18	O. Niang	Riga	21.4	0.296	0.13	0.116	0.734
19	R. Sottil	Fiorentina	24.2	0.097	0.121	0.116	0.84
20	Pedro Neto	Wolverhampton	23.4	0.131	0.12	0.116	0.855
21	I. Akhomach	Villarreal	19.3	0.094	0.119	0.116	0.936
22	Rafael Leão	Milan	24.2	0.178	0.118	0.115	0.913
23	F. Conceicão	Porto	20.7	0.233	0.12	0.114	0.905
24	K. Coman	Bayern Munchen	27.2	0.095	0.118	0.114	0.861
25	Ângelo Gabriel	Strasbourg	18.6	0.125	0.117	0.114	0.918
26	E. Zhegrova	Lille	24.4	0.097	0.117	0.113	0.907
27	A. Mitriță	Univ. Craiova	28.4	0.195	0.12	0.113	0.906
28	J. Clarke	Sunderland	22.7	0.268	0.119	0.112	0.939
29	S. Ltaief	Winterthur	23.3	0.114	0.121	0.112	0.786
30	A. Nusa	Club Brugge	18.3	0.143	0.118	0.112	0.872
31	N. Madueke	Chelsea	21.4	0.177	0.116	0.112	0.823
32	Milson	Maccabi Tel Aviv	23.9	0.178	0.12	0.112	0.856
33	M. Edwards	Sporting CP	24.7	0.277	0.118	0.111	0.866
34	F. Chiesa	Juventus	25.8	0.195	0.114	0.111	0.932
35	J. Boga	Nice	26.6	0.079	0.115	0.111	0.894
36	A. Garnacho	Manchester Unt	19.1	0.088	0.112	0.111	0.922
37	T. Kubo	Real Sociedad	22.2	0.162	0.113	0.11	0.933
38	J. Bynoe-Gittens	Borussia D	19.0	0.208	0.112	0.109	0.898
39	A. Schjelderup	Nordsjaelland	19.2	0.283	0.113	0.109	0.936
40	Serginho	Viborg	22.5	0.182	0.119	0.109	0.719
41	M. Fofana	Lyon	18.3	0.169	0.113	0.108	0.93
42	B. Gruda	Mainz 05	19.2	0.163	0.113	0.108	0.823
43	Y. Soteldo	Santos	25.8	0.27	0.125	0.108	0.485
44	Dudu	Palmeiras	31.3	0.172	0.122	0.108	0.57
45	J. Sancho	Borussia D	23.4	0.224	0.111	0.107	0.858
46	Danilo Al Saed	Sandefjord	24.1	0.11	0.118	0.107	0.741
47	C. Hudson-Odoi	Nottingham Forest	22.8	0.114	0.11	0.107	0.884
48	J. Enciso	Brighton	19.6	0.215	0.114	0.106	0.677
49	A. Sbaï	Grenoble	22.8	0.185	0.116	0.106	0.818
50	David Neres	Benfica Portugal	26.5	0.25	0.117	0.106	0.708

References

1. Bergkamp, T.L., Frencken, W.G., Niessen, A.S.M., Meijer, R.R., den Hartigh, R.J.: How soccer scouts identify talented players. Eur. J. Sport Sci. **22**(7), 994–1004 (2022)
2. Bradley, R.A., Terry, M.E.: Rank analysis of incomplete block designs: I. the method of paired comparisons. Biometrika **39**(3/4), 324–345 (1952)
3. Cervone, D., D'amour, A., Bornn, L., Goldsberry, K.: Pointwise: predicting points and valuing decisions in real time with nba optical tracking data. In: Proceedings of the 8th MIT Sloan Sports Analytics Conference, Boston, MA, USA, vol. 28 (2014)
4. Cervone, D., D'Amour, A., Bornn, L., Goldsberry, K.: A multiresolution stochastic process model for predicting basketball possession outcomes. J. Am. Stat. Assoc. **111**(514), 585–599 (2016)
5. Dinsdale, D., Gallagher, J.: Transfer portal: Accurately forecasting the impact of a player transfer in soccer. arXiv preprint arXiv:2201.11533 (2022)
6. Elo, A.E.: The proposed USCF rating system, its development, theory, and applications. Chess Life **22**(8), 242–247 (1967)
7. Fernández, J., Bornn, L., Cervone, D.: Decomposing the immeasurable sport: A deep learning expected possession value framework for soccer. In: 13th MIT Sloan Sports Analytics Conference (2019)
8. Garnier, P., Gregoir, T.: Evaluating soccer player: From live camera to deep reinforcement learning. arXiv preprint arXiv:2101.05388 (2021)
9. Glickman, M.E.: Example of the glicko-2 system. Boston University 28 (2012)
10. Hollinger, J.: Pro basketball forecast (2005). No Title
11. Ke, G., et al.: Lightgbm: A highly efficient gradient boosting decision tree. In: Advances in Neural Information Processing Systems, p. 30 (2017)
12. Kim, S.: Voronoi analysis of a soccer game. Nonlinear Anal.: Modell. Contr. **9**(3), 233–240 (2004)
13. Liu, G., Luo, Y., Schulte, O., Kharrat, T.: Deep soccer analytics: learning an action-value function for evaluating soccer players. Data Min. Knowl. Disc. **34**(5), 1531–1559 (2020). https://doi.org/10.1007/s10618-020-00705-9
14. Pollard, R., Reep, C.: Measuring the effectiveness of playing strategies at soccer. J. Royal Stat. Society Series D: Stat. **46**(4), 541–550 (1997)
15. Power, P., Ruiz, H., Wei, X., Lucey, P.: Not all passes are created equal: Objectively measuring the risk and reward of passes in soccer from tracking data. In: Proceedings of the 23rd ACM SIGKDD international conference on knowledge discovery and data mining, pp. 1605–1613 (2017)
16. Prokhorenkova, L., Gusev, G., Vorobev, A., Dorogush, A.V., Gulin, A.: Catboost: unbiased boosting with categorical features. In: Advances in neural information processing systems, p. 31. (2018)
17. Samuelson, P.A.: A note on the pure theory of consumer's behaviour. Economica **5**(17), 61–71 (1938)
18. Shelopugin, A.: Expected possession value of control and duel actions for soccer player's skills estimation. arXiv preprint arXiv:2406.00814 (2024)
19. Shelopugin, A., Sirotkin, A.: Evaluating of football player 1v1 abilities based on the glicko-2 with modifications. In: 2023 IEEE 28th Pacific Rim International Symposium on Dependable Computing (PRDC), pp. 287–291. IEEE (2023)
20. Shelopugin, A., Sirotkin, A.: Ratings of European and south American football leagues based on glicko-2 with modifications. arXiv preprint arXiv:2310.11459 (2023)

21. Singh, K.: Introducing expected threat. https://karun.in/blog/expected-threat.html (2018). Accessed 30 June 2024
22. Spearman, W.: Beyond expected goals. In: Proceedings of the 12th MIT Sloan Sports Analytics Conference, pp. 1–17. (2018)
23. Spearman, W., Basye, A., Dick, G., Hotovy, R., Pop, P.: Physics-based modeling of pass probabilities in soccer. In: Proceeding of the 11th MIT Sloan Sports Analytics Conference (2017)
24. Sutton, R.S.: Reinforcement learning: An introduction, A Bradford Book (2018)
25. Ward, G., Hastie, T., Barry, S., Elith, J., Leathwick, J.R.: Presence-only data and the EM algorithm. Biometrics **65**(2), 554–563 (2009)

From Skeletons to Pixels: Few-Shot Precise Event Spotting via Representation and Prediction Distillation

Zhong Han Ervin Yeoh(✉) and Kan Jiang(✉)

School of Computing, National University of Singapore, Singapore, Singapore
ervinyeohzh@u.nus.edu, jiangkan@comp.nus.edu.sg

Abstract. Precise Event Spotting (PES) is essential in fast-paced sports such as tennis, where fine-grained events occur within very short temporal windows. Accurate frame-level localization is challenging due to motion blur, subtle action differences, and limited annotated data. We study two complementary distillation strategies for few-shot PES: 1) **Adaptive Weight Distillation (AWD)**, a prediction-level method that adaptively weights teacher supervision on unlabeled data, and 2) **Annealed Multimodal Distillation for Few-Shot Event Detection (AMD-FED)**, a representation-level framework that transfers robust skeleton knowledge into visual modalities through annealed pseudo-labeling. Both methods leverage multimodal distillation to improve generalization under limited supervision. Experiments on F^3Set-Tennis(sub) under two few-shot settings, 50-clip and 100-clip, show that our methods consistently outperform single-modality baselines and previous PES approaches. In particular, AMD-FED achieves the best overall performance, reaching 80.24% and 83.84% Edit score in the 50-clip and 100-clip settings, respectively, exceeding the strongest single-modality baseline by 9.17 and 7.19% points.

Keywords: Precise Event Spotting · Few-Shot Learning · Multimodal Knowledge Distillation · Semi-Supervised Learning · Action Recognition

1 Introduction

Precise Event Spotting (PES) aims to localize key events in continuous video streams and is fundamental to modern sports analytics. In fast-paced sports such as tennis, where hits, serves, and bounces occur within very short temporal windows, accurate event localization is essential for downstream applications including highlight generation [23], player and tactic analysis [5,30], workload estimation [2], and referee support [34]. Therefore, PES serves as a core component of scalable sports understanding systems.

Large-scale datasets [31,41,50] have been introduced to advance research in precise event spotting (PES), but typically require dense temporal annotations

Z. Liu and V. Misra (Eds.): ISACE 2026, LNCS 16610, pp. 315–332, 2026.
https://doi.org/10.1007/978-3-032-27272-0_21

(see Fig. 1), incurring substantial human effort and time costs. Moreover, fully supervised training paradigms often suffer from limited generalization to unseen scenarios, long training durations, and a tendency to overfit when annotations are scarce. **In this work, we focus on a few-shot setting, where the model must detect events and classify actions given only k video clips in total, simulating realistic low-data conditions.** Existing approaches [21,31] also predominantly rely on a single modality, further exacerbating overfitting in few-shot settings. From a modeling perspective, fine-grained action detection methods can be broadly categorized into end-to-end visual models [3,12,29,47] and skeleton-based approaches [33]. Visual models operate directly on raw RGB frames, often incorporating optical flow to improve robustness, but their heavy dependence on pixel-level patterns causes them to latch onto static visual cues rather than learning generalizable motion representations, particularly in low-data regimes. Skeleton-based methods, on the contrary, leverage structured pose representations to model human motion and exhibit stronger generalization, yet they discard rich visual context and rely on accurate pose estimation. In fast-paced sports scenarios, even state-of-the-art pose detectors [44,48] frequently fail due to motion blur, occlusions, and rapid movements, often in frames critical for event recognition. As a result, both paradigms struggle to generalize to fine-grained sports actions under limited supervision.

While knowledge distillation has been widely explored to improve few-shot learning, prior work predominantly focuses on multi-class classification tasks on datasets such as CIFAR [25], or on coarse-grained action recognition videos [4,15] , where either representation-level [9,16] or prediction-layer distillation [22,24] is applied. In contrast, the challenges of Precise Event Spotting—short temporal windows, multi-label per-frame annotations, and subtle motion cues—have rarely been addressed within a distillation framework.

In this work, we embed both representation-level and prediction-layer distillation strategies into the PES setting, enabling robust few-shot learning by transferring knowledge from skeleton-based motion priors to visual modalities. Unlike prior distillation work that mainly targets multi-class classification or coarse-grained action recognition, our approach explicitly addresses the challenges of Precise Event Spotting, including short temporal windows, multi-label per-frame annotations, and subtle motion cues. We also introduce improvements specific to each distillation paradigm to enhance performance in this domain.

To this end, we propose two complementary frameworks:

- **Annealed Multimodal Distillation for Few-Shot Event Detection (AMD-FED)**, a representation-level distillation framework that improves teacher robustness through an **Annealed Pseudo-Labeling Strategy**, gradually incorporating unlabeled samples during semi-supervised pretraining.
- **Adaptive Weight Distillation (AWD)**, a prediction-level distillation framework that adapts teacher supervision to the multi-label PES setting using confidence-aware weighting and tennis-specific post-processing.

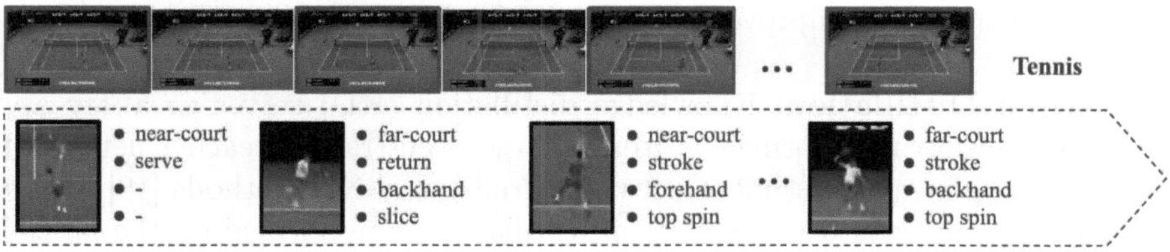

Fig. 1. Example of fine-grained event annotation in fast-paced sports, with event timestamps highlighted in red, adopted from [31] (Color figure online).

We evaluate both methods on F^3Set-Tennis(sub) under two few-shot settings, 50-clip and 100-clip. Both AWD and AMD-FED consistently outperform single-modality baselines and prior PES methods, while AMD-FED achieves the best overall results with **80.24%** and **83.84%** Edit score, exceeding the strongest single-modality baseline by 9.17 and 7.19% points, respectively. These results demonstrate the effectiveness of distillation for few-shot PES, and in particular the advantage of representation-level transfer for fine-grained event spotting.

2 Related Work

Few-Shot Temporal Action Detection. Few-shot learning (FSL) aims to enable models to generalize to novel classes using only a limited number of labeled examples, addressing the scalability challenges of fully supervised learning [11,39]. A predominant paradigm for FSL is supervised meta-learning, where models are trained across episodic tasks to rapidly adapt to unseen classes [13,18]. Existing meta-learning approaches can be broadly categorized into three groups: metric-based methods, which learn embedding spaces that facilitate similarity-based classification [45,46]; memory-based methods, which store and retrieve task-specific knowledge to support generalization [35,40]; and gradient-based methods, which learn optimization strategies that enable fast adaptation of a base learner to new tasks [13,14,28].

Extending FSL to temporal action detection (TAD) introduces additional challenges due to the need for precise temporal localization. Early work integrated sliding-window proposals with metric learning frameworks to perform few-shot TAD in untrimmed videos [46]. More recently, Transformer-based architectures have been adopted to better align support and query features in untrimmed video settings [36]. Unlike traditional k-shot formulations, where each support example contains a single action instance and background [36], several works—including ours—evaluate few-shot temporal event detection using sparsely annotated clips that may contain multiple events and timestamps [20]. Despite these advances, existing FSL-based action detection methods often struggle in fine-grained sports scenarios, where events are brief, visually subtle, and subject to high intra-class variation. In this work, we address few-shot fine-grained sports event detection by emphasizing precise temporal localization and leveraging multimodal distillation to improve robustness and adaptation under limited labeled data.

Knowledge Distillation. Knowledge distillation (KD) serves as a key approach for transferring information from a large, well-trained teacher network to a smaller or less capable student network. Traditional KD methods [19] operate under a fully supervised setting, when distillation is performed on the labelled training data of the teacher model, rather than on new, unlabelled data. Extensions, such as variational [1] framework, aim to further align the student's outputs and intermediate representations [6] with those of the teacher.

In cases where labelled data is scarce and unlabelled samples dominate, the reliability of teacher-generated pseudo-labels becomes uncertain. Studies [43] have shown that over-reliance on noisy pseudo-labels can degrade student performance. To mitigate this, recent works [8,22] propose confidence-based filtering or reweighting of pseudo-labels using uncertainty estimates (e.g., entropy or margin scores), or explicitly modelling the teacher's noise to adjust the student's learning objective. These approaches highlight the importance of robust distillation techniques for scenarios involving unlabelled or weakly labelled data. In this work, we evaluate the performance of pseudo-label-based approaches in comparison to representation-level distillation.

3 Our Approach

We study the problem of few-shot precise event detection and propose two distillation-based frameworks that adapt knowledge transfer techniques—commonly used in action recognition—to the precise event spotting (PES) setting.

Specifically, we consider two standard distillation paradigms: *(i) representation-level distillation* and *(ii) prediction-layer distillation.* While both paradigms have been extensively explored for video-level action recognition, their application to fine-grained, timestamp-level event detection remains underexplored.

Based on these paradigms, we introduce:

- **AMD-FED**, which performs *representation-level multimodal distillation*, transferring domain-adapted motion features from skeletons to visual modalities; and
- **AWD**, which performs *prediction-layer distillation* by directly supervising student predictions using weighted teacher outputs.

An overview of the AMD-FED framework is illustrated in Fig. 2. Unless otherwise stated, AMD-FED serves as our primary model, while AWD is used as a complementary distillation strategy for comparison.

3.1 Problem Statement

We study the few-shot Precise Event Spotting (PES) task under limited supervision, following the standard formulation adopted in prior work [32]. Given

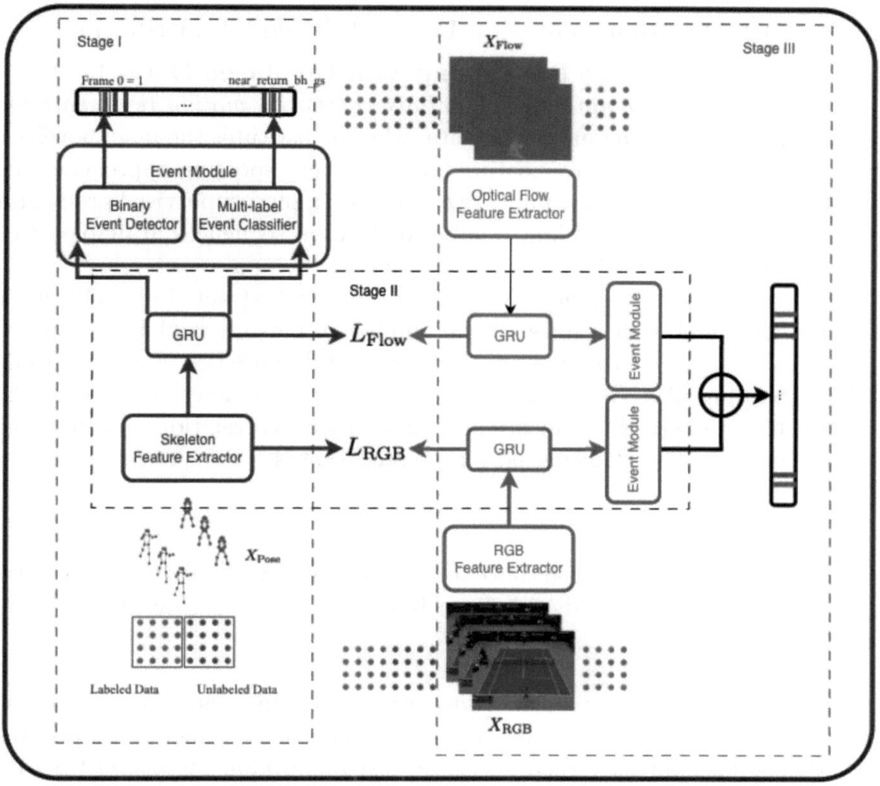

Fig. 2. The framework of our proposed method, AMD-FED has three training stages: 1. learning domain-specific skeleton features from both labeled and unlabeled data, 2. distilling the skeleton feature (freezed) into student(s) RGB & optical flow encoders through self-supervised training using both labeled and unlabeled data, 3. few-shot learning for adapting to the temporal event detection task in target sports using only the labeled data.

an input video clip $\mathbf{X} \in \mathbb{R}^{T \times H \times W \times 3}$ consisting of T RGB frames with spatial resolution $H \times W$, the objective is to localize a sequence of M events in time, represented as $\{(E_1, t_1), \ldots, (E_M, t_M)\}$. Here, E_i denotes the event category drawn from C possible classes, and t_i corresponds to the temporal timestamp of the i-th event.

We consider a target dataset $\mathcal{D}$ comprising $|\mathcal{D}|$ video clips, partitioned into a labeled subset $\mathcal{D}_{\text{label}} \subset \mathcal{D}$ and an unlabeled subset $\mathcal{D}_{\text{unlabel}} \subset \mathcal{D}$, such that $\mathcal{D} = \mathcal{D}_{\text{label}} \cup \mathcal{D}_{\text{unlabel}}$.

We specifically focus on the few-shot PES setting, where only a small number of labeled video clips $k = |\mathcal{D}_{\text{label}}|$ are available for training. We refer to this regime as the *k-clip setting.*

3.2 AMD-FED: Representation-Level Multimodal Distillation

Domain-Specific Feature Pretraining with Unlabeled Data. In Stage I, we focus on learning *domain-adapted and discriminative motion representations* by explicitly incorporating unlabeled data, which constitutes the main novelty of our framework. In contrast to existing few-shot event spotting approaches that rely solely on limited labeled samples, we introduce a semi-supervised pretraining strategy that leverages abundant unlabeled skeleton sequences available in the target domain.

Given an input pose sequence $X_{\text{pose}} \in \mathbb{R}^{T \times P \times V \times 2}$ (extracted by [44]), where T denotes the number of frames, P the number of persons, and V the number of joints with (x, y) coordinates, we employ a skeleton-based teacher encoder $\varepsilon_{\text{pose}}^{\text{teacher}}$ consisting of a GCN backbone followed by a bidirectional GRU. This design enables the model to capture both spatial joint correlations and temporal motion dynamics. The resulting pose representation is

$$F_{\text{pose}} = \varepsilon_{\text{pose}}^{\text{teacher}}(X_{\text{pose}}). \tag{1}$$

The pose features are fed into a temporal event detector with coarse-grained and fine-grained prediction branches to produce dense event predictions at each timestamp.

Semi-supervised Training with Pseudo-Labeling. Training is conducted in two phases to ensure stability. During the first 30 epochs, the model is optimized using labeled data only. We then select the *best-performing checkpoint* from this warm-up phase and use it to initialize the subsequent semi-supervised training. Afterward, labeled and unlabeled samples are mixed with a 1:1 sampling ratio. Pseudo-labels for unlabeled samples are generated online using the model's own predictions and are used as supervisory signals.

This progressive introduction of unlabeled data, together with an epoch-dependent weighting schedule, alleviates the impact of noisy pseudo-labels while effectively expanding the training set. As a result, the model learns more robust domain-specific motion representations, which are crucial for few-shot event spotting.

Labeled Coarse-Grained Loss. The coarse-grained branch predicts whether any event occurs at each timestamp. For labeled samples, let $\hat{p}_{b,t,c}$ denote the predicted probability for coarse class $c \in \{0, 1\}$ at batch index b and timestamp t, and $y_{b,t,c}$ be the corresponding one-hot ground-truth label. The coarse-grained loss for labeled data is computed using standard cross-entropy:

$$L_{\text{coarse}}^{\text{lab}} = -\frac{1}{B \times T} \sum_{b=1}^{B} \sum_{t=1}^{T} \log \hat{p}_{b,t,c}. \tag{2}$$

Labeled Fine-Grained Loss. The fine-grained branch predicts multiple event categories at each timestamp. Let $\hat{Y}_{b,t,c}$ denote the predicted logit for fine-grained event class $c \in \{1, \ldots, C\}$, and let $Y_{b,t,c} \in \{0, 1\}$ be the corresponding ground-truth label. The fine-grained loss for labeled data is computed using binary cross-entropy:

$$L_{\text{fine}}^{\text{lab}} = \frac{1}{B \times T \times C} \sum_{b=1}^{B} \sum_{t=1}^{T} \sum_{c=1}^{C} \Big[- Y_{b,t,c} \log \sigma(\hat{Y}_{b,t,c}) \\ - (1 - Y_{b,t,c}) \log \big(1 - \sigma(\hat{Y}_{b,t,c})\big) \Big], \tag{3}$$

where $\sigma(\cdot)$ denotes the sigmoid function.

Unlabeled Loss with Pseudo-Labeling. For unlabeled samples, pseudo-labels are generated using the model's current predictions. Let $\tilde{y}_{b,t}$ and $\tilde{Y}_{b,t,c}$ denote the pseudo-labels for the coarse-grained and fine-grained predictions, respectively. The unlabeled loss is defined analogously as

$$L_{\text{unlab}} = L_{\text{coarse}}^{\text{unlab}} + L_{\text{fine}}^{\text{unlab}}. \tag{4}$$

Total Training Objective. The overall loss for Stage I is defined as

$$L_{\text{total}} = L_{\text{lab}} + \lambda(e)\, L_{\text{unlab}}, \tag{5}$$

where

$$L_{\text{lab}} = L_{\text{coarse}}^{\text{lab}} + L_{\text{fine}}^{\text{lab}}. \tag{6}$$

The weighting coefficient $\lambda(e)$ is scheduled based on the training epoch e:

$$\lambda(e) = \begin{cases} 0, & e < 30, \\ \text{anneal}(0 \to 0.4), & 30 \le e < 90, \\ 0.4, & e \ge 90. \end{cases} \tag{7}$$

Multimodal Distillation. In Stage II, we transfer the domain-adapted motion knowledge learned from skeletons to visual modalities, namely RGB and optical flow. The pretrained skeleton encoder from Stage I serves as a teacher, while RGB and optical-flow encoders act as student networks.

For each modality $m \in \{\text{RGB}, \text{Flow}\}$, the student encoder projects the input X_m into the same embedding space as the teacher:

$$F_m = \varepsilon_{\text{student}}^{m}(X_m). \tag{8}$$

Knowledge distillation is achieved by minimizing the ℓ_2 distance between student features and the teacher's pose embeddings:

$$L_m = \|F_{\text{pose}} - F_m\|_2. \tag{9}$$

This stage follows standard multimodal distillation practices; further details can be found in related work such as [16,32]. In the final stage, we train the temporal event detector on the target domain using the few-shot labeled dataset D_{label}. The pretrained RGB and optical-flow student encoders obtained in Stage II are retained, and the loss is computed in the same manner as in Stage I to obtain the final model.

MD-FED. MD-FED is a reduced version of AMD-FED that removes unlabeled data from Stage I pretraining. It follows the same multimodal distillation pipeline but relies solely on labeled skeleton sequences when learning domain-specific pose representations. This variant isolates the effect of unlabeled data and annealed pseudo-labeling on downstream few-shot event detection.

3.3 AWD: Adaptive Weight Distillation

In contrast to AMD-FED, which distills knowledge at the representation level, AWD adopts a *prediction-layer distillation* strategy. Instead of aligning intermediate embeddings, the student network directly learns from the teacher's output predictions. To account for the teacher's reliability on unlabeled samples, AWD introduces a weighting term W that scales the distillation loss adaptively based on the agreement between teacher and student:

$$W = \frac{1}{1 + p\,(d-1)}, \quad d = \frac{\text{loss(teacher, student)}}{\text{loss(student, label)}}, \tag{10}$$

where p is a binary indicator representing whether the teacher's prediction is correct ($p = 0$) or incorrect ($p = 1$). When the teacher is correct, $W = 1$ and the student fully follows the teacher. When the teacher's prediction is incorrect ($p = 1$), the weight W is reduced according to the ratio

$$\frac{1}{d}. \tag{11}$$

If the student performs better than the teacher (i.e., has a smaller loss with respect to the ground-truth labels), the ratio becomes small, which decreases W and thus limits the influence of the unreliable teacher. For stability, W is clipped to the range $[0, 1]$.

In the original paper [22], the weight parameters are estimated using a validation set via a nearest-neighbors regression approach. The validation samples provide a mapping between the teacher's and student's confidence scores and their corresponding reliability measures (p, d). Each validation example contributes a pair of confidence values—one from the teacher and one from the student—as regression inputs, and a target pair consisting of the teacher's correctness p (1 or 0) and the observed distortion ratio d. During inference on unlabeled data, the same mapping is used to predict p and d, enabling the model to assign adaptive weights based on the confidence and relative performance of the teacher. This approach mitigates error propagation from uncertain teacher predictions and enhances the robustness of the distillation process.

Extension to Multi-label Classification Setting. The original paper designs the weighting mechanism for a multi-class classification task, where each sample belongs to exactly one class. In our setup, the action recognition problem is formulated as a multi-label classification task, where multiple labels can co-occur within a frame of a single clip. Therefore, we adapt the confidence estimation, validation mapping, and weight computation process accordingly.

Averaged Confidence and Weight Estimation. For each clip, we may have several frames each containing a multi-labelled action such as `near_return_bh_gs`. We will have individual p and d values for each frame containing action, as well as the confidences for teacher and student models. We then average them clip-level, across the frames. The validation set is then constructed using input pairs

$$(\bar{C}_s, \bar{C}_t) \tag{12}$$

where $\bar{C}_s$ and $\bar{C}_t$ denote the averaged student and teacher confidences, respectively. The corresponding targets are the averaged $(\bar{p}, \bar{d})$. During inference, we compute the weight W for a clip using the averaged confidence pair $(\bar{C}_s, \bar{C}_t)$ as query to the k-Nearest Neighbours (kNN) model, which returns the averaged $(\bar{p}, \bar{d})$ from the validation mapping. The final weight is the computed as

$$W = \frac{1}{1 + \bar{p}(\bar{d} - 1)}, \quad \bar{p}, \bar{d} = kNN(\bar{C}_s, \bar{C}_t) \tag{13}$$

Confidence Computation for Multi-label Predictions. In the original multi-class setup, confidence is typically defined as the margin between the largest and second-largest softmax probabilities:

$$C = \max(y) - 2^{nd} \max(y) \tag{14}$$

For our multi-label setting, we define confidence within mutually exclusive label groups to reflect structured dependencies among action categories, as implemented in Listing 1.1. The specific mapping of indices to classes is detailed in Table 1. Specifically, labels [0,1] form a binary pair where one is active and the other inactive, representing mutually exclusive states such as "near" and "far." Similarly, labels [2,3,4] represent a three-way exclusivity, where only one class within the group can be active at any time. The next set of groups, [5,6] and [7,8,...,12] are conditional on earlier decisions. Finally, label [13] is treated as an independent binary indicator that does not depend on other groups. Within each group g, the confidence is computed as the difference between the largest and second largest predicted probabilities, interclass this time, while for label [13], confidence is defined as the absolute difference between the two possible states,

$$C_{13} = |y_{13} - (1 - y_{13})|. \tag{15}$$

The overall clip-level confidence is then obtained by averaging across all label groups,

$$\bar{C} = \frac{1}{G} \sum_{g=1}^{G} C_g \tag{16}$$

where G is the number of label groups.

```python
def fine_label_postprocess(pred):
    """
    Fine label post-processing logic for tennis pseudo labels.
    Ensures mutual exclusivity within label groups and rule-based
    hierarchy.
    """

    # [0,1]: near / far
    activate_one(pred, [0, 1])

    # [2,3,4]: serve / return / stroke
    activate_one(pred, [2, 3, 4])

    # if not serve
    if pred[2] != 1:
        # [5,6]: forehand / backhand
        activate_one(pred, [5, 6])
        # [7-12]: gs / slice / volley / smash / drop / lob
        activate_one(pred, [7, 8, 9, 10, 11, 12])

    # [13]: approach
    pred[13] = 1 if pred[13] >= 0.5 else 0

    return pred
```

Listing 1.1. Fine Label Post-processing Logic

Table 1. Label Indices and Classes

Index	Class
0	near
1	far
2	serve
3	return
4	stroke
5	fh
6	bh
7	gs
8	slice
9	volley
10	smash
11	drop
12	lob
13	approach

Table 2. Statistics of the F^3Set-Tennis(sub) dataset. Each sub-class contains multiple elements with corresponding event counts and proportions.

Sub-Class	Element	Count	Proportion (%)
SC1	Near	21,467	50.1
	Far	21,362	49.9
SC2	Forehand	27,802	64.9
	Backhand	15,027	35.1
SC3	Serve	11,584	27.0
	Return	8,216	19.2
	Stroke	23,029	53.8
SC4	Ground stroke	38,287	89.4
	Slice	3,358	7.8
	Volley	497	1.2
	Lob	334	0.8
	Drop	236	0.5
	Smash	117	0.3
SC5	Approach	964	2.3
	Non-approach	41,865	97.7

4 Experimental Results

This section presents datasets, evaluation metrics, ablation study, and baselines comparison.

4.1 Dataset

F^3Set-Tennis [31] consists of 11,584 clips from 114 professional tennis matches, with each clip containing 1 to 34 shots. Each shot is annotated with the exact frame of racket-ball contact and its corresponding event type. We focus on a subset, which we will denote as F^3Set-Tennis(sub) in this paper, comprising 5 pose-related sub-classes, resulting in 67 event types, having statistics in Table 2.

In this course of research, we focus on the evaluation of models under the 100-clip few shot setting for the dataset.

4.2 Evaluation Metrics

Following [31], we assess our approach using two metrics that capture both temporal accuracy and classification performance: Edit score and mean F1 with temporal tolerance.

(1) Edit Score [26] measures the structural alignment between predicted and ground-truth event sequences using Levenshtein distance. It penalizes missing, redundant, and misordered predictions, making it suitable for tasks that require accurate event ordering and completeness.

(2) Mean F1 Score with Temporal Tolerance evaluates both classification and localization accuracy. A prediction is considered correct if it matches the event class and falls within a temporal window of δ frames around the ground-truth timestamp. We report the average F1 across all event categories, denoted as $F1_{\mathrm{evt}}$. Unless otherwise specified, we adopt a strict tolerance of $\delta = 1$ frame.

4.3 Ablation on Unlabeled Data Integration in Stage I

Stage I of AMD-FED adopts a semi-supervised training paradigm to pretrain the skeleton-based teacher encoder using both labeled and unlabeled data. While the overall objective in Eq. (5) defines how unlabeled samples contribute through pseudo-labeling and an annealed loss weight, the manner in which unlabeled data is introduced during training can significantly affect the stability and quality of the learned representations. In this subsection, we conduct an ablation study to systematically examine different strategies for incorporating unlabeled samples in Stage I.

Experimental Protocol. We evaluate three unlabeled-data integration strategies inspired by pseudo-labeling-based semi-supervised learning [27]:

1. **Joint training**, where labeled and unlabeled samples are used together from the first training epoch;
2. **Delayed integration**, in which the teacher encoder is trained solely on labeled data for the first n epochs before unlabeled samples are introduced; and
3. **Best-model continuation**, where training with both labeled and unlabeled data resumes from the best checkpoint obtained during the labeled-only phase ($e \leq n$).

For unlabeled samples, supervision is provided via pseudo-labels generated online from the model's current predictions. Since pseudo-labels are particularly noisy during early training when the model is not yet sufficiently adapted to the target domain, directly incorporating unlabeled data can degrade learning. To mitigate this issue, the contribution of the unlabeled loss is modulated by the epoch-dependent weighting coefficient $\lambda(e)$, which gradually increases from zero to its target value as training progresses. This annealing strategy reduces the influence of unreliable pseudo-labels in early epochs and stabilizes optimization.

Results and Analysis. The experimental results in Table 3 show that **best-model continuation** consistently outperforms both joint training and delayed integration strategies. By initializing semi-supervised learning from the strongest labeled-only checkpoint, this strategy effectively reduces the impact of noisy pseudo-labels while still benefiting from abundant unlabeled data.

Table 3. Ablation study on different strategies for incorporating unlabeled data in Stage I of AMD-FED. "From epoch 1" indicates that unlabeled samples are used from the beginning of training, while "After 30" denotes delayed integration following 30 epochs of labeled-only training. The notation $0 \to \alpha$ (e_s–e_e) specifies the annealing schedule of the unlabeled loss weight $\lambda(e)$, which linearly increases from 0 to α between epochs e_s and e_e. Best-model continuation yields the highest edit score and is adopted in the final AMD-FED model.

Setting	Edit (%)
Stage I (labeled only)	75.79
(a) Joint training	
From epoch 1, $0 \to 1$ (20–60)	70.14
From epoch 1, $0 \to 1$ (20–80)	75.12
(b) Delayed integration	
After 30, $0 \to 3$ (30–60)	74.26
After 30, $0 \to 1$ (30–60)	76.43
After 30, $0 \to 1$ (30–90)	77.55
After 30, $0 \to 0.7$ (30–90)	78.26
After 30, $0 \to 0.4$ (30–90)	78.66
(c) Best-model continuation	
After 30, $0 \to 0.4$ (30–90)	**79.43**

In contrast, **joint training** consistently performs worse than the labeled-only baseline. This degradation can be attributed to the training batch construction strategy: during dataset sampling, each mini-batch has a 50% probability of being drawn from labeled or unlabeled data. Because the unlabeled loss weight $\lambda(e)$ is set to zero before epoch 20, the model effectively receives supervision from only half of the labeled data during early training. As a result, joint training under-utilizes labeled samples in the critical early optimization phase, leading to inferior representations compared to delayed integration and best-model continuation.

Moreover, adopting best-model continuation in Stage I of AMD-FED leads to a clear performance improvement over labeled-only training. Across multiple 100-clip sets, the edit score increases from 76.12 ± 0.30 to 79.51 ± 0.18. Note that Table 3 reports an exploratory result on a single 100-clip set, while the reported averages summarize performance across several such sets. Based on these observations, AMD-FED adopts the best-model continuation strategy for incorporating unlabeled data in Stage I.

4.4 Baseline Comparisons

Table 4 reports the Edit score and event-level F1 under the 50-clip and 100-clip settings.

Table 4. Edit score (%) and event $F1_{\mathrm{evt}}$ (mean ± standard deviation) on the F^3Set-Tennis(sub) dataset under 50-clip and 100-clip few-shot settings.

	50-clip		100-clip	
	Edit	$F1_{evt}$	Edit	$F1_{evt}$
(a) RGB modality				
RegNet-Y-200MF(TSM) [29,38]	47.90 ± 2.12	9.06 ± 0.26	55.35 ± 1.19	12.31 ± 1.34
RegNet-Y-800MF(TSM) [29,38]	47.11 ± 9.42	8.83 ± 2.22	59.31 ± 1.84	14.93 ± 1.81
ResNet-50(TSM) [17,29]	49.29 ± 1.84	8.37 ± 0.33	52.69 ± 4.46	11.67 ± 1.56
(a) 2D skeleton modality				
STGCN [51]	69.39 ± 2.58	19.24 ± 1.49	76.29 ± 0.46	24.16 ± 0.80
MSG3D [33]	71.07 ± 3.13	21.97 ± 1.76	76.65 ± 1.00	23.17 ± 3.06
AAGCN [42]	68.93 ± 0.89	21.63 ± 1.75	76.19 ± 2.12	24.22 ± 2.86
CTRGCN [7]	69.56 ± 2.59	20.26 ± 0.46	76.58 ± 1.35	23.59 ± 1.18
STGCN++ [10]	68.17 ± 0.83	19.48 ± 1.38	76.12 ± 0.30	24.30 ± 1.24
(c) SOTA PES Methods				
F^3ED (contextualized) [31]	47.94 ± 3.28	9.17 ± 0.22	58.94 ± 1.06	12.16 ± 1.28
T-DEED$_{200MF}$ [49]	38.67 ± 9.05	6.45 ± 1.04	49.72 ± 1.55	10.17 ± 0.87
T-DEED$_{800MF}$ [49]	51.00 ± 2.27	10.32 ± 1.67	54.48 ± 0.99	11.22 ± 0.70
(b) Our approach				
AWD (Pred-Distillation)	72.58 ± 5.12	18.47 ± 2.89	77.03 ± 0.81	20.52 ± 0.67
MD-FED (Repr-Distillation)	77.91 ± 1.67	25.13 ± 2.10	81.89 ± 1.14	29.76 ± 1.21
AMD-FED (Repr-Distillation)	$\mathbf{80.24 \pm 1.35}$	$\mathbf{25.93 \pm 1.59}$	$\mathbf{83.84 \pm 0.96}$	$\mathbf{30.37 \pm 2.09}$

First, **skeleton-based baselines consistently outperform RGB methods**. Under the 100-clip setting, all skeleton models achieve Edit scores above 76%, while the best RGB model reaches only 59.31%. A similar gap is observed in $F1_{evt}$, where skeleton models achieve $23\% - 24\%$, compared to $11\% - 15\%$ for RGB baselines. This highlights the robustness of pose representations under limited supervision.

Second, **RGB baselines remain comparatively unstable**. Although RegNet-Y backbones outperform ResNet-50 overall, their variance is noticeably larger, particularly in the 50-clip setting. Prior PES methods **F^3ED and T-DEED** also fail to close this modality gap, suggesting that improved temporal modeling alone is insufficient without robust representations. This suggests that appearance-driven models struggle to learn robust event semantics from limited supervision, even when equipped with temporal shift modules. The gap between RGB and skeleton baselines therefore justifies using the skeleton branch as the teacher modality in our framework.

Against these baselines, **our distillation-based methods provide substantial gains**. AWD improves the 100-clip Edit score to 77.03±0.81%, surpassing the best RGB baseline by 17.72 points and slightly exceeding the strongest skeleton-only baseline. This shows that even prediction-level distillation can effectively transfer useful supervisory signals from the skeleton teacher to the student model.

More importantly, **representation-level distillation is markedly more effective**. MD-FED raises the Edit score further to 81.89 ± 1.14%, while AMD-FED achieves the best overall result of 83.84 ± 0.96% with an event F1 of 30.37 ± 2.09%. Compared with AWD, AMD-FED improves Edit by 6.81 points under the 100-clip setting, demonstrating the effectiveness of intermediate feature alignment. The additional gain of AMD-FED over MD-FED further demonstrates the value of incorporating unlabeled data through semi-supervised annealed pseudo-labeling.

Finally, **model capacity plays a critical role in few-shot settings**. Lower-capacity models such as ResNet-50 and RegNet-Y exhibit better generalization due to stronger inductive biases. In contrast, high-capacity architectures like SlowFast [12] and VTN [37] tend to overfit, quickly driving training and validation losses to near zero. This suggests over-parameterization in low-data regimes, where models memorize dataset-specific patterns rather than learning transferable representations.

Overall, these results indicate that robust representation learning—rather than temporal modeling alone—is the key to effective few-shot event detection, and AMD-FED achieves the strongest generalization.

5 Conclusion and Future Work

We introduced two distillation frameworks for few-shot precise event spotting: **AWD**, which transfers supervision at the prediction level, and **AMD-FED**, which performs representation-level distillation with semi-supervised annealed pseudo-labeling. By exploiting the robustness of skeleton-based teachers, both methods substantially improve over RGB-only baselines in the low-data regime.

On F^3Set-Tennis(sub), our results show that distillation is highly effective for bridging the gap between appearance-based models and structurally robust skeleton models. AWD already surpasses the strongest RGB baseline, while **AMD-FED** achieves the best overall performance, reaching **83.84% Edit** and **30.37% event F1** in the 100-clip setting. These gains indicate that representation-level transfer is more effective than prediction-level supervision for fine-grained event spotting under limited supervision.

For future work, we aim to evaluate the proposed framework on additional sports datasets and investigate stronger semi-supervised and teacher-adaptation strategies for handling noisy pseudo-labels and broader domain shifts.

References

1. Ahn, S., Xu, S.: Variational information distillation for knowledge transfer. In: Proceedings of the IEEE/CVF Conference on Computer Vision and Pattern Recognition (CVPR), pp. 9163–9171 (2019)

2. Antonini, V., Mileo, A., Roantree, M.: Engineering features from raw sensor data to analyse player movements during competition. Sensors **24**(4), 1308 (2024)
3. Carreira, J., Zisserman, A.: Quo vadis, action recognition? A new model and the kinetics dataset. In: Proceedings of the IEEE Conference on Computer Vision and Pattern Recognition (CVPR), pp. 6299–6308 (2017). https://doi.org/10.1109/CVPR.2017.671, https://openaccess.thecvf.com/content_cvpr_2017/html/Carreira_Quo_Vadis_Action_CVPR_2017_paper.html
4. Chen, D., Kasarla, T., Bang, Y., Shukor, M., Chung, W., Yu, J., et al.: ACTION100M: a large-scale video action dataset (2026). https://arxiv.org/abs/2601.10592
5. Chen, G.: Retracted article: an interpretable composite CNN and GRU for fine-grained martial arts motion modeling using big data analytics and machine learning. Soft Comput. (Berlin, Germany) **28**(3), 2223–2243 (2024). https://doi.org/10.1007/s00500-023-09565-z, retracted
6. Chen, H., Wang, Y.: Learning student networks via feature embedding. IEEE Trans. Neural Netw. Learn. Syst., 25–35 (2020)
7. Chen, Y., Zhang, Z., Yuan, C., Li, B., Deng, Y., Hu, W.: Channel-wise topology refinement graph convolution for skeleton-based action recognition. In: Proceedings of the IEEE/CVF International Conference on Computer Vision (ICCV), pp. 13359–13368 (2021)
8. Dehghani, M., Mehrasa, A.: Fidelity-weighted learning. arXiv preprint arXiv:1711.02799 (2017)
9. Du, P., Zhao, S., Sheng, Z., Li, C., Chen, H.: Semi-supervised learning via weight-aware distillation under class distribution mismatch (2023). https://arxiv.org/abs/2308.11874
10. Duan, H., Wang, J., Chen, K., Lin, D.: PYSKL: towards good practices for skeleton action recognition. In: Proceedings of the 30th ACM International Conference on Multimedia, pp. 7351–7354. ACM (2022)
11. Fei-Fei, L., Fergus, R., Perona, P.: One-shot learning of object categories. IEEE Trans. Pattern Anal. Mach. Intell. **28**(4), 594–611 (2006)
12. Feichtenhofer, C., Fan, H., Malik, J., He, K.: Slowfast networks for video recognition. In: Proceedings of the IEEE/CVF International Conference on Computer Vision (ICCV), pp. 6202–6211 (2019)
13. Finn, C., Abbeel, P., Levine, S.: Model-agnostic meta-learning for fast adaptation of deep networks. In: Proceedings of the 34th International Conference on Machine Learning (ICML) (2017)
14. Grant, E., Finn, C., Levine, S., Darrell, T., Griffiths, T.L.: Recasting gradient-based meta-learning as hierarchical bayes. In: International Conference on Learning Representations (ICLR) (2018)
15. Grauman, K., Westbury, A., Byrne, E., Chavis, Z.: Ego4D: around the world in 3,000 hours of egocentric video. In: Proceedings of the IEEE/CVF Conference on Computer Vision and Pattern Recognition (CVPR) (2022)
16. Hatano, M., Hachiuma, R., Fujii, R., Saito, H.: Multimodal cross-domain few-shot learning for egocentric action recognition. In: Proceedings of the European Conference on Computer Vision (ECCV) (2024)
17. He, K., Zhang, X., Ren, S., Sun, J.: Deep residual learning for image recognition. In: Proceedings of the IEEE Conference on Computer Vision and Pattern Recognition (CVPR), pp. 770–778 (2016)
18. Hinton, G.E., Plaut, D.C.: Using fast weights to deblur old memories. In: Proceedings of the Ninth Annual Conference of the Cognitive Science Society (CogSci) (1987)

19. Hinton, G.E., Vinyals, O., Dean, J.: Distilling the knowledge in a neural network. CoRR abs/1503.02531 (2015). https://arxiv.org/abs/1503.02531
20. Hong, J., Fisher, M., Gharbi, M., Fatahalian, K.: Video pose distillation for few-shot, fine-grained sports action recognition. In: Proceedings of the IEEE/CVF International Conference on Computer Vision (ICCV) (2021)
21. Hong, J., Zhang, H., Gharbi, M., Fisher, M., Fatahalian, K.: Spotting temporally precise, fine-grained events in video. In: European Conference on Computer Vision (ECCV), pp. 33–51. Springer (2022). https://doi.org/10.1007/978-3-031-19833-5_3
22. Iliopoulos, F., Karypis, V.: Weighted distillation with unlabeled examples. In: Advances in Neural Information Processing Systems (NeurIPS) (2022)
23. Javed, A., Bajwa, K., Malik, H., Irtaza, A.: An efficient framework for automatic highlights generation from sports videos. IEEE Signal Process. Lett. **23**(7), 954–958 (2016)
24. Kontonis, V., Iliopoulos, F., Trinh, K., Baykal, C., Menghani, G., Vee, E.: Slam: student-label mixing for distillation with unlabeled examples (2023). https://arxiv.org/abs/2302.03806
25. Krizhevsky, A.: Learning Multiple Layers of Features from Tiny Images. University of Toronto, Tech. rep. (2009)
26. Lea, C., Flynn, M.D., Vidal, R., Reiter, A., Hager, G.D.: Temporal convolutional networks for action segmentation and detection. In: Proceedings of the IEEE Conference on Computer Vision and Pattern Recognition (CVPR), pp. 156–165 (2017)
27. Lee, D.H.: Pseudo-label: the simple and efficient semi-supervised learning method for deep neural networks. In: Workshop on Challenges in Representation Learning, ICML (2013)
28. Lee, Y., Choi, S.: Gradient-based meta-learning with learned layerwise metric and subspace. In: Proceedings of the 35th International Conference on Machine Learning (ICML) (2018)
29. Lin, J., Gan, C., Han, S.: TSM: temporal shift module for efficient video understanding. In: Proceedings of the IEEE/CVF International Conference on Computer Vision (ICCV), pp. 7083–7093 (2019)
30. Liu, Z., Jiang, K., Hou, Z., Lin, Y., Dong, J.S.: Insight analysis for tennis strategy and tactics. In: 2023 IEEE International Conference on Data Mining (ICDM), pp. 1169–1174. IEEE (2023). https://doi.org/10.1109/ICDM58522.2023.00143
31. Liu, Z., Jiang, K., Ma, M., Hou, Z., Lin, Y., Dong, J.S.: F^3set: Towards analyzing fast, frequent, and fine-grained events from videos. In: International Conference on Learning Representations (ICLR) (2025)
32. Liu, Z., Jiang, K., Ma, M., Hou, Z., Lin, Y., Dong, J.S.: Few-shot precise event spotting via unified multi-entity graph and distillation. In: Proceedings of the 40th AAAI Conference on Artificial Intelligence (AAAI) (2026). https://github.com/LZYAndy/UMEG-Net
33. Liu, Z., Zhang, H., Chen, Z., Wang, Z., Ouyang, W.: Disentangling and unifying graph convolutions for skeleton-based action recognition. In: Proceedings of the IEEE/CVF Conference on Computer Vision and Pattern Recognition (CVPR), pp. 140–149 (2020). https://doi.org/10.1109/CVPR42600.2020.00022
34. Ma, E., Kabala, Z.J.: Refereeing the sport of squash with a machine learning system. Mach. Learn. Knowl. Extract. **6**(1), 506–553 (2024)
35. Mishra, N., Rohaninejad, M., Chen, X., Abbeel, P.: Snail: a simple neural attentive meta-learner. In: International Conference on Learning Representations (ICLR) (2018)

36. Nag, S., Zhu, X., Xiang, T.: Few-shot temporal action localization with query adaptive transformer. arXiv preprint arXiv:2110.10552 (2021)
37. Neimark, D., Bar, O., Zohar, M., Asselmann, D.: Video transformer network. In: Proceedings of the IEEE/CVF Conference on Computer Vision and Pattern Recognition (CVPR), pp. 3163–3172 (2021)
38. Radosavovic, I., Kosaraju, R.P., Girshick, R., He, K., Dollár, P.: Designing network design spaces. In: Proceedings of the IEEE/CVF Conference on Computer Vision and Pattern Recognition (CVPR), pp. 10428–10436 (2020)
39. Salakhutdinov, R., Tenenbaum, J.B., Torralba, A.: Learning with hierarchical-deep models. IEEE Trans. Pattern Anal. Mach. Intell. **35**(8), 1958–1971 (2013)
40. Santoro, A., Bartunov, S., Botvinick, M., Wierstra, D., Lillicrap, T.P.: Meta-learning with memory-augmented neural networks. In: Proceedings of the 33rd International Conference on Machine Learning (ICML) (2016)
41. Shao, D., Zhao, Y., Dai, B., Lin, D.: FineGym: a hierarchical video dataset for fine-grained action understanding. In: Proceedings of the IEEE/CVF Conference on Computer Vision and Pattern Recognition (CVPR), pp. 2616–2625 (2020)
42. Shi, L., Zhang, Y., Cheng, J., Lu, H.: Skeleton-based action recognition with multi-stream adaptive graph convolutional networks. IEEE Trans. Image Process. **29**, 9532–9545 (2020)
43. Stanton, S., Iscen, P.: Does knowledge distillation really work? In: Advances in Neural Information Processing Systems (NeurIPS), pp. 6906–6919 (2021)
44. Sun, K., Xiao, B., Liu, D., Wang, J.: Deep high-resolution representation learning for human pose estimation. In: Proceedings of the IEEE/CVF Conference on Computer Vision and Pattern Recognition (CVPR) (2019)
45. Sung, F., Yang, Y., Zhang, L., Xiang, T., Torr, P.H.S., Hospedales, T.M.: Learning to compare: Relation network for few-shot learning. In: Proceedings of the IEEE Conference on Computer Vision and Pattern Recognition (CVPR) (2018)
46. Vinyals, O., Blundell, C., Lillicrap, T., Kavukcuoglu, K., Wierstra, D.: Matching networks for one-shot learning. In: Advances in Neural Information Processing Systems (NeurIPS) (2016)
47. Wang, L., et al.: Temporal segment networks for action recognition in videos. IEEE Trans. Pattern Anal. Mach. Intell. **41**(11), 2740–2755 (2018)
48. Wu, Y., Kirillov, A., Massa, F., Lo, W.Y., Girshick, R.: Detectron2 (2019). https://github.com/facebookresearch/detectron2
49. Xarles, A., Escalera, S., Moeslund, T.B., Clapés, A.: T-Deed: temporal-discriminability enhancer encoder-decoder for precise event spotting in sports videos. In: Proceedings of the IEEE/CVF Conference on Computer Vision and Pattern Recognition (CVPR), pp. 3410–3419 (2024)
50. Xu, J., Rao, Y., Yu, X., Chen, G., Zhou, J., Lu, J.: FineDiving: a fine-grained dataset for procedure-aware action quality assessment. In: Proceedings of the IEEE/CVF Conference on Computer Vision and Pattern Recognition (CVPR), pp. 2949–2958 (2022)
51. Yan, S., Xiong, Y., Lin, D.: Spatial temporal graph convolutional networks for skeleton-based action recognition. In: Proceedings of the AAAI Conference on Artificial Intelligence (AAAI) (2018)

Integrating Team Pursuit Video Analysis in Track Cycling

Robbe Decorte(✉), Maarten Slembrouck, and Steven Verstockt

Ghent University - imec, Technologiepark-Zwijnaarde 126, 9052 Ghent, Belgium
robbe.decorte@ugent.be

Abstract. In elite track cycling, performance gains increasingly depend on event-level analysis of training and competition data. However, current practices rely heavily on manual tasks, limiting scalability and real-time feedback. This paper presents an integrated system for team pursuit analysis that unifies multimodal sensor data (timing loops, athlete-worn sensors) and automatic video annotations from pan-tilt-zoom footage within a centralized Wireless Cycling Network (WCN). Sensor and timing data are leveraged to generate rule-based annotations for key events, such as lead switches, which serve as ground truth labels for training vision models. A RF-DETR model is fine-tuned on a diverse track cycling dataset to detect track cyclists and is integrated into a semantic tracking pipeline specific to the team pursuit formation. Instead of continuous identity tracking, the method exploits domain-specific priors on rider order and train geometry to detect lead transitions. Evaluations across training and competition footage demonstrate reliable cyclist detection (F1-score up to 0.96 at IoU 0.50) and lead switch detection (95%). By combining both sensor and video based data, the system can self-annotate new data and provide a unified analysis interface for both training and races while simultaneously lowering the manual input for coaches.

Keywords: Track Cyling · Computer Vision · Team Pursuit

1 Introduction

In elite track cycling, marginal gains are increasingly achieved through data-driven insights [16,22,30]. Yet, manual annotation of on-track events remains a time-consuming process post race and often ignored during practice. With the current state of the technology, track cycling has moved towards performance related monitoring sensors on the athlete and bike such as for measuring power, speed and cadence. This remains challenging due to non real time collection (proxy through head unit) and decentralization, which requires coaches to collect it after each exercise from all athletes before they can even start reviewing the captured data manually. This area remains largely unexplored, yet addressing these limitations could greatly alleviate the data-collection burden and extend analytical capabilities.

Z. Liu and V. Misra (Eds.): ISACE 2026, LNCS 16610, pp. 333–350, 2026.
https://doi.org/10.1007/978-3-032-27272-0_22

The system presented in this work introduces a synchronized Wireless Cycling Network (WCN) to collect multimodal data from timing loops, rider sensors and annotated footage from (PTZ-)cameras. A dashboard is provided for real time statistics of the riders (heart rate, speed, etc.), integrations with external energetic reserve capacity models [25,39] and allows exercise tagging all without interfering with the bike's head unit. Furthermore, sensor and timing data are used to automatically generate labels for on-track events. For example, a sudden increase in speed coupled with a timing-loop crossing can mark the beginning of a sprint phase, while changes in rider proximity can indicate a lead exchange in a team pursuit. These automatically derived labels (together with exercise tags) can serve as ground truth annotations for subsequent training of machine learning models to identify events directly from accompanying video footage. This approach bridges the gap between traditional rule-based analytics and modern methods, supporting self-annotating datasets in track cycling. By integrating sensing, timing, and vision systems into a single automated workflow, this research contributes towards the shift to a smart velodrome. This setup also aims to connect training environments to competition settings. Models can be developed and validated in the controlled conditions of the velodrome, where synchronized sensor data are available, and later applied to race footage where such sensors are impractical or forbidden under race regulations.

While the proposed system is applicable across various track-cycling disciplines, this work primarily focuses on the team pursuit event. In this type of race two teams of four riders start on opposite sides of the track and compete over 4 km. The winning team is the one that manages to catch its opponents or records the fastest time. Teammates take turns at the front of the formation (train) to optimize power delivery and aerodynamic efficiency. The final time is taken when the third rider of the team crosses the finish line (i.e., three out of four riders must complete the distance) [21]. During the qualifying rounds, teams ride alone against the clock, whereas from round one onwards, two teams compete head-to-head as described above.

2 Related Work

2.1 Sensor and Video-Based Monitoring in Track Cycling

Early research on athlete monitoring targeted wearable and wireless sensing techniques and further evolved towards Wireless Sensor Networks (WSNs). Several studies have investigated the use of these networks to capture physiological and biomechanical data in real time [7,29,50]. For the tracking aspect, indoor positioning systems have been previously explored to track rider movement and group dynamics. Minne et al. [31] evaluated ultra-wideband positioning for indoor track cycling, demonstrating sub-meter localization accuracy for real-time performance analysis. In training this could be used (analogously to integrated timing loops, but continuous) to track rider positions in the train but suffers from the same limitations where this is impractical or banned in competition and lacks the relationship to track or train geometry (travel direction, corner progress, etc.) unless it's calibrated for each track.

Compared to wearable sensing, video-based analysis in track cycling remains underexplored. Most cycling specific research focuses on outdoor cycling, where helmet-mounted cameras [20,28] or roadside optical tracking systems [27,43] are used to estimate speed, drafting position, or crash detection. Some of the multi-object tracking pipelines that you'd typically find in this type of research (not limited to cycling) are further explored in Sect. 3, but the datasets are too different from a velodrome environment to be useful in this study (as we also require a spectators point-of-view).

From a broader viewpoint, it's clear that video-based approaches have distinct advantages though. Not relying on direct sensor instrumentation of athletes, which in turn could affect the athletes' performance or limit its applicability, is a strong factor. Its use has also been discussed at length for various sports domains [19,34]. And more specifically, for instance in a study from Einfalt and Lienhart [9] where event detection in swimming and athletics is achieved by decoupling human motion (in the form of pose sequences) from the video and applying a domain specific tracker instead of a separate end-to-end system for both.

2.2 Team Pursuit Dynamics and Analysis

The team pursuit event in track cycling presents unique challenges due to its dynamic nature and the need for precise coordination among team members. Recent efforts have focused on applying machine learning techniques to analyze team pursuit strategies. For instance, USA Cycling's Project 4:05 utilized data-driven strategies to optimize race performance, leading to a gold medal at the Paris 2024 Olympics [41]. Beyond this case study, several works have investigated pacing and formation strategies in the individual and team pursuit using physics-based simulations and optimization models [1,13,18,46,49]. These approaches primarily focus on the physical and aerodynamic aspects of performance, such as optimal rider order and energy expenditure. These are valuable pre-race but do not directly provide feedback on performed rides.

Stadnyk et al. [42] showed that, at that time, most track cycling related research is performed in the physical component (70.4%) compared to tactical and the technical aspects (22.5%). There is no stated reason why but a likely reason is the high cost and effort associated with creating annotated video datasets or convoluted sensor setups required for technical and tactical analyses. Manual labelling of spatio-temporal events and technical actions is labour-intensive and scales poorly: large activity benchmarks (e.g., AVA [15], ActivityNet [11], SoccerNet [14], MultiSports [24]) required thousands of annotator hours and often rely on sparse or semi-automated strategies to remain tractable. Prior work therefore emphasizes that the annotation burden is a major methodological bottleneck for tactical research in sport [4,12,37,48]. This motivates efforts toward automated labeling, model-assisted annotations and sensor-driven ground truth generation which will be further discussed in Sect. 3 [6,12,17,23].

When the lack of annotated videos can be overcome, it becomes possible to quantify or assess different stages of the race. For instance the changeover, an important aspect of team pursuit, where the lead cyclist rotates to the back of the group. But what makes a good changeover? There are many components involved: changeover time, or the height on the track (riding line), the loss of pedal power, the energy expenditure, or the transition back into the group. These are all interconnected and required for a well executed changeover but the literature does not provide a clear answer towards structured optimization. Correlations between these parameters and race time were studied by Sigrist et al. [38] but still warrant more specific and focused research interventions.

3 Methods

In this section we will start from a pure sensor-based system used during training and describe how some of its collected data can be reused to further extend visual analysis of race and training video footage. For races, one of the coaches would typically place a camera on a tripod in the stands and record hand steered footage (with zoom) from a fixed location. This has, in part, been emulated through an automatically steered pan-tilt-zoom (PTZ) camera in the training facility. Therefore, the dataset used for training and analysis consists primarily of footage originating from these two setups. The training related data for this study was collected at the Centrum Eddy Merckx in Ghent and the Sport Vlaanderen Heusden-Zolder Velodroom Limburg in collaboration with Cycling Vlaanderen. At both sites, a permanent setup of this system has been installed.

3.1 Wireless Cycling Network

Through WCN, coaches can access an aggregated view on all available sensor data with real time feedback on power delivery, energetic reserves, etc., and review previous recordings with exercise summaries of tagged segments.

The first step to provide such system is to unify various data sources. Modern fitness sensors communicate wirelessly via standardised protocols from the sensor to the receiving devices. Most off-the-shelf sports sensors support data

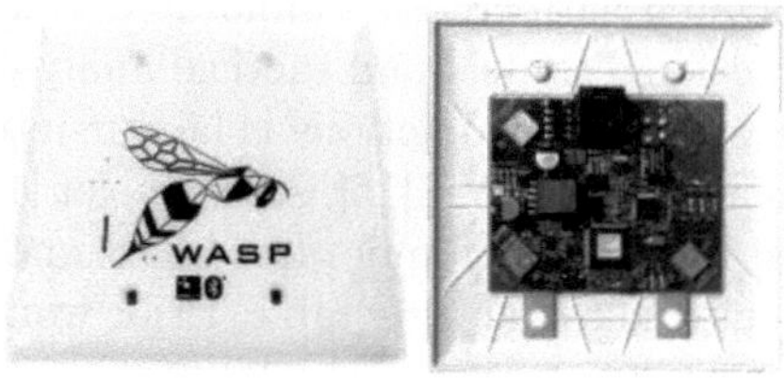

(a)

(b)

Fig. 1. NPE bridging devices for ANT+ to Ethernet using WASP-PoE (a) or WiFi using WASP-N (b).

transmission via either ANT+ or Bluetooth Low Energy (BLE). In the context of a centralized collection system inside a velodrome, the ANT+ protocol is best suited for our goal as it does not require pairing and broadcasts data to bridging devices (i.e. collection points) listening on the ANT+ network. Furthermore, ANT+ is not encrypted by default, as it is designed for observability and allows a many-to-one relationship to collect data from multiple riders simultaneously.

To capture signals sent from the sensors we rely on North Pole Engineering's (NPE) WASP devices (Fig. 1). These devices bridge messages from ANT+ to a WiFi or Ethernet network. The more devices that are positioned along the course, the better coverage we will have for the track. In Centrum Eddy Merckx in Ghent we have full coverage on the track with overlapping zones using four fixed WASP-PoE mounted to support pillars on the inside of the track. Alternatively, the wireless WASP-N devices can be mounted on a tripod or strapped to the outside railing (which we do for our mobile setup). In the collection network, a dotnet application works as a local aggregator that deduplicates (since WASP coverage may overlap) and parses messages using an SDK provided by NPE. This application also powers the live dashboard and other WCN capabilities (camera controls, exercise reporting, etc.) and implements the protocol used by MYLAPS P3 and X2 decoders to collect passes on timing loops installed under the track in real time. Figure 2 shows a schematic overview of the WCN setup.

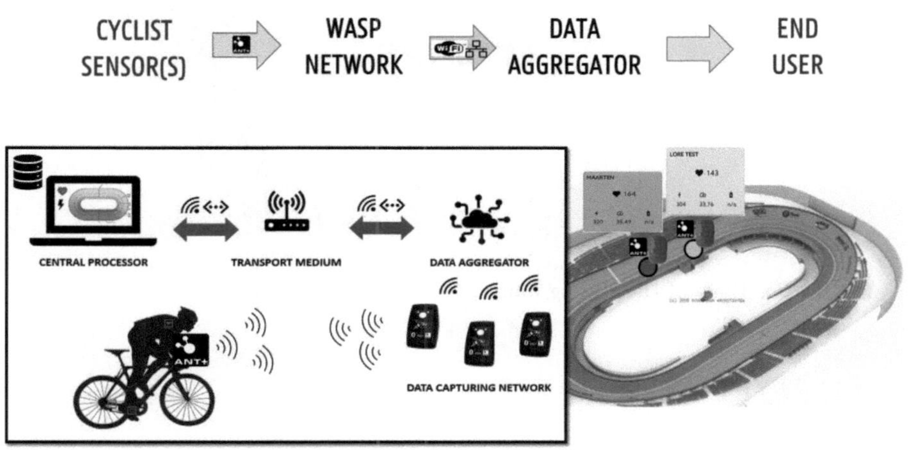

Fig. 2. Schematic overview of the WCN setup on the cycling track. [5]

Capturing Automated PTZ Steered Video Footage. To support automated video capture during track cycling sessions, we permanently installed a PTZ camera in the velodrome. This camera can be steered using position and timing information derived from the timing loop infrastructure embedded in WCN. Each rider is identified by a transponder, and loop crossing events at known track locations are used to estimate the rider's progression on track. These estimates are translated into camera pan, tilt, and zoom commands, enabling continuous framing of a rider without manual operation. Practical challenges and implementation details will not be addressed in this publication but have been previously presented by Slembrouck et al. [40].

Sensor Annotations for Lead Switch Events. The training tracks in this study are equipped with 7 timing loops (Fig. 3). These are used for various track cycling activities but for the team pursuit we're focusing mostly on corner entry (L2/5) and the straights (L7/4). Planned lead changes always occur in the corners, where the track's banking allows for a smoother, more energy-efficient transition and minimizes speed loss compared to transitions on the straights. Therefore, if an order change is observed on the straight, the timestamp of the previous corner entry is used to initialize a switch event. For annotations on video recordings, the frame where the first rider enters the corner is used (typically indicated by a painted line segment).

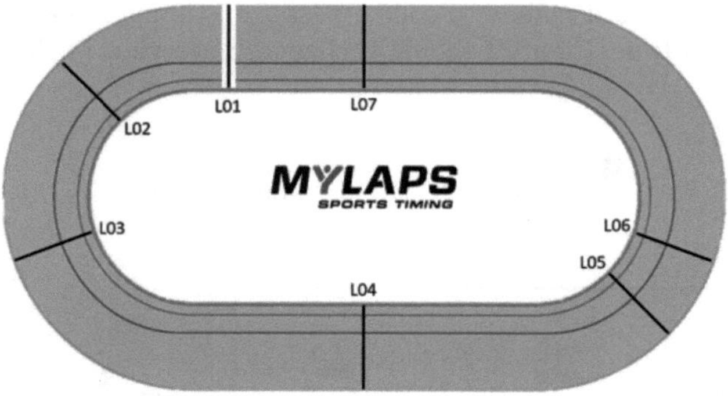

Fig. 3. Positions of the timing loops at Eddy Merckx Flemish Cycling Centre.

3.2 Cyclist Detector

As with many domains in deep learning, transformer architectures have shown improvements over well established convolutional based techniques for image detection tasks [8]. DETR-style detectors simplify the detection pipeline via an end-to-end trainable framework that directly predicts sets of bounding boxes and class labels without the need for region proposal networks or post-processing heuristics like anchor generation and non-maximum suppression [2,36].

This, together with the lack of a stable enough track cyclist detection model, led us to fine-tune the RF-DETR model [33] on our track cycling dataset. Detection stability is a critical requirement, as the detector directly powers the downstream semantic tracking component. Longer periods of false negatives would propagate further down, possibly resulting in missed events, or wrong position estimates (w.r.t. the pursuit train). These issues are exacerbated in track cycling by frequent occlusions, particularly in the banked corners when footage is captured from the stands and riders move in tight train formations. In such scenarios, cyclists partially or fully occlude one another for multiple frames, requiring a detector that can maintain consistent detections even with severe overlap. By not using on a generic cyclist detector from an urban or competitive (road) setting, we can further incorporate concepts that are mostly relevant in track cycling, such as distinguishing riders from the derny (motorized pacemaker) or focusing on cyclists on track and not in warm up zones by adding more of such negative samples to the dataset.

Dataset. In total, the dataset contains 4428 annotations. Most annotations were created from footage obtained through Cycling Vlaanderen's training facilities (25%) or competition recordings (59%), and supplemented with open track cycling datasets after manual verification (16%) [3,35,45]. To reduce temporal redundancy, frames were not labeled exhaustively. Videos were uniformly downsampled with a small random offset to obtain a diverse and representative subset of each recording. Figure 4 shows four sample predictions and highlights some of the variation of the velodromes. Furthermore, annotations were not restricted to team pursuit and thus include various bike positions, number of riders, etc. from different track cycling disciplines. This also leads to a more general detector.

Fig. 4. Four sample predictions from the validation set with prediction confidence. Displays the variety of velodrome color and reflection and also varying levels of occlusion caused by other riders, roof pillars or other materials.

Evaluation. The rider detection model was trained for 24 epochs using an approximate 80/20 train-test split. Splits on video level to avoid data leakage, i.e. all annotations from a single video are always assigned to the same split. Table 1 summarizes performance for medium, large, and all objects using AP and F1-score at IoU thresholds of 0.50, 0.75, and the average of the [0.50;0.95] interval in 5% increments. The model performs well with AP/F1 of 0.90/0.84 for medium objects and 0.96/0.96 for large objects at IoU 0.50. Performance decreased at higher IoU thresholds, particularly for medium riders, reflecting the increased challenge of overlapping riders. This typically occurs when riders are smaller because of the distance between the camera and the corners (unless zoomed in).

Table 1. Rider detection model results for medium, large, and all predictions. Following COCO [26] standards for object sizing. Note that because of the zooming, there were no small and limited medium objects.

	AP			F1-score			N
IoU @	0.50	0.75	[0.50;0.95]	0.50	0.75	[0.50;0.95]	
Medium	0.90	0.65	0.63	0.84	0.70	0.66	107
Large	0.96	0.82	0.70	0.96	0.85	0.75	770
All	0.95	0.80	0.70	0.96	0.83	0.74	877

3.3 Team Pursuit Formation

Most race statistics require some variation of tracking (not necessarily continuous) or sparse re-identifcation to relate rider identities in on-track events. Current tracking SOTA algorithms and models like SAM [32], including extensions that aim to increase robust tracking by introducing motion [51] and distractor-aware memory [47], still struggle to accurately track detections in multi-rider events when they significantly overlap and occlude each other. Coupled with nearly identical visual representations, a semantically driven tracking based on events is more appropriate to analyze these types of races. Specifically for team pursuits, this corresponds to: the rider order did not change unless a (detectable) lead switch occurs. We can link rider identity to this as well because lead switches are always circular (i.e. the first rider always goes to the back and the second in line continues). Identity tracking then simplifies to sorting riders along the traveling direction but shifted by the number of detected switches, starting from the initial ordering decided by the coach.

To detect these events we've designed a computer vision pipeline to estimate the train's formation and travel direction using the detected bounding boxes from Sect. 3.2. Identifying the main clusters of riders (i.e. trains) is done through a customized clustering procedure based on DBScan [10]. In previous work, Theiner et al. [44] showed the use of DBScan for team assignment in football. Similarly, we will utilize it to assign cyclists to the correct train. However, in our case the inter-rider spacing, the apparent scale of the riders, zoom, and the camera motion vary continuously throughout the recording requiring several adaptive mechanisms. Perhaps the most important assumption used to preprocess inputs, is that train formation is not arbitrarily shaped but rectangular along the travel direction.

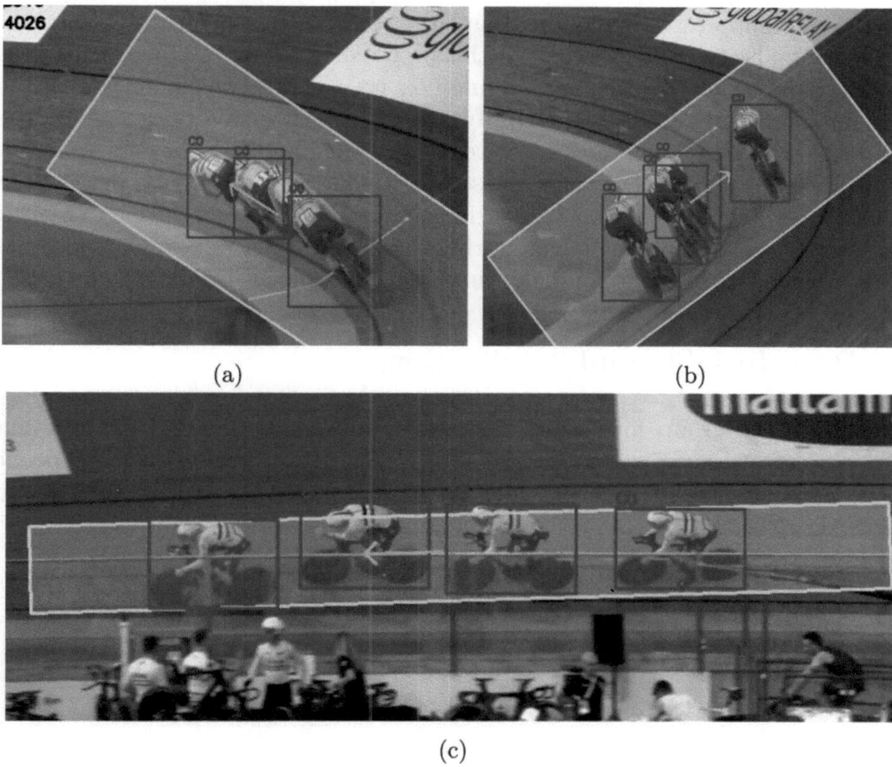

Fig. 5. Train region of acceptance (ROA) and alignment direction visualized in different race scenarios. (a) During a corner without position switches. (b) Corner in combination with a lead switch. (c) Corner entry on the opposite side of the track without rider overlap. Note the ROA shape elongates when riders are not overlapping w.r.t. the camera and grows when this is the case.

First, the clustering distance parameter ϵ is dynamically scaled according to the apparent size of the riders in the image. The mean bounding-box height, normalized by the image size, is used as a proxy for camera zoom or distance between riders and the camera. A running baseline of this normalized height is maintained, and the clustering radius is inversely adjusted to compensate for variations in perceived scale. This allows the algorithm to maintain approximately constant physical spacing thresholds even as the zoom level changes. Second, we exploit temporal and directional priors derived from the train's previously estimated motion which is initialized on the first frame on a straight with the horizontal direction given as input (left or right). Using the centroid position and direction of travel from the preceding frame, the relative positions of current detections are projected onto two orthogonal axes: one aligned with the direction of motion and one lateral to it. A directional filter is then applied to retain only those detections lying within a narrow acceptance region that is elongated along the direction of travel but constrained laterally. This ensures that the clustering operates primarily within the expected train region of acceptance (ROA) and suppresses detections that are geometrically inconsistent with the formation. The shape and extent of this acceptance region are further adapted based on inter-rider overlap. Bounding-box intersection-over-union (IoU) values are computed pairwise to quantify overlap, which increases during corners when the travel direction moves towards codirectionality with the camera's view direction. A mean overlap value is used to widen the lateral part of the ROA dynamically and the length across shrinks naturally (due to occlusion), creating a less elongated acceptance region during turns (Fig. 5). A full sample video has been provided at https://cloud.ilabt.imec.be/index.php/s/9GGH4tNsqnGc9s9.

4 Race Insights and Applications

Extracting the group formation is an essential step for further analysis but requires extra derivatives or act as input for subsequent steps in the pipeline to be useful for coaches. We've outlined some relevant metrics in Table 2 and clarified further below with some discussion on positive and negative cases.

Table 2. Race insights derived from the semantic tracking and ride formation.

Race metric	Description
Lead time	Time spent at the front of the train. Grouped per rider.
Lead distance	Distance (# laps) spent at the front of the train. Calculated using the direction indicator given that transitions occur in a corner.
Transition time	Time between leaving and rejoining the train cluster during a leader transition.
Rejoin distance	Distance between the back and front wheel of the two back riders after a transition is completed.
Rejoin time	Time it takes to reach a distance threshold towards the back of the train. Differs from transition time by using the wheel-to-wheel distance instead of cluster size.

For coaches, transition time typically starts from the "intent" of the transition. Because this is visually indistinguishable without detecting passes on the transition line (if painted on at all), we start this measurement the moment that the front rider leaves the train cluster (Fig. 6). This causes a delay at the start because the sweeping rider needs to be far enough from the other riders. This should not cause significant errors between tagged events in the system but should be handled with care when compared to other data sources. For instance hand timed, or how timing loops are used to generate timestamps in Sect. 3.1.

Fig. 6. Lead switch event where the front rider leaves the train cluster.

4.1 Detecting Lead Switch Events

While lead switches can be inferred directly from the clustering, additional post-processing is required to eliminate temporary missed detections and to handle death pulls. For reference, a death pull is an all out turn at the front after which the leading rider does not rejoin after switch. This is allowed because only 3/4 rider are required to finish. Both types of transitions are illustrated for an exercise in Fig. 7. Because no training is involved in this part of the pipeline, it allows for fast customization on how the algorithm works and since it's built around explainable parameters there are no black box transformations required.

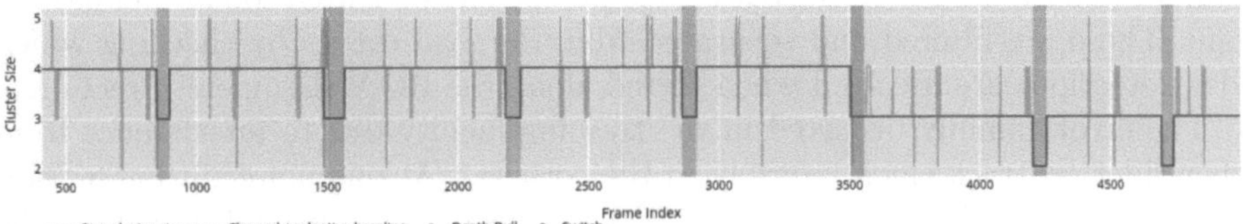

Fig. 7. Train cluster size progression in an exercise shown by the red line. Lead transitions indicated with green bars and death pull, after which they continue with 1 less rider, with a red bar. Cleans detection jitter and adapts to the number of remaining riders. (Color figure online)

As part of the regularization scheme of the clustering/direction assignment we disallow opposite rotation during the corners and in some situations counter steer when a rotation is expected. This allows the algorithm to consider a subset of the previous cluster earlier in the corner. In some cases, like Fig. 5b, a rotation is expected because of overlapping detections but because the lead switch is initiated early, the ROA and direction will point towards the rider that sweeps outward, not snap him out of the cluster, and eventually fall backwards 90° when the rider rejoins if no counter steering is performed. The incorrect ROA motion following the situation in Fig. 5b and the result after a steering correction is shown in Fig. 8.

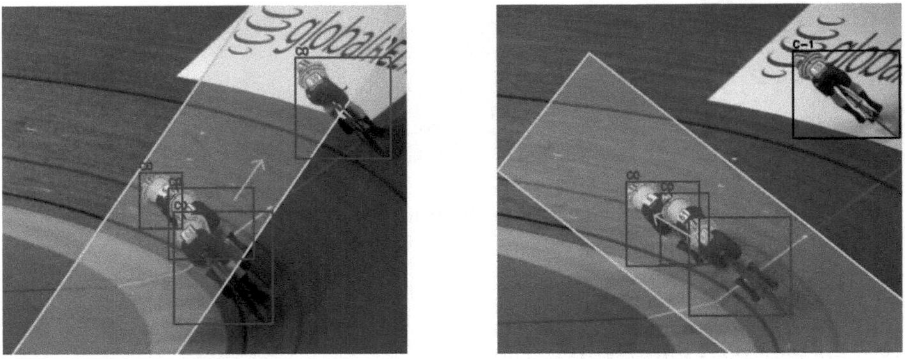

(a) (b)

Fig. 8. Example showing the frame before and after a counter steer was triggered. Note the unwanted ROA rotation due to an early switch initiation.

Evaluation. In total we've evaluated 78 lead transitions which were mostly collected through WCN (46/78) while the other 32 are manually annotated from racing footage. The system was able to detect 95% of these lead switch events, did not detect false positives within the evaluated set, and flagged another 4% of unannotated events where the back rider (temporarily) drifted too far behind the train. These are filtered and separated from the lead events by checking which rider detections are involved when sorted along the ROA alignment direction.

The errors mainly occurred in the training facility due to interference from other rider on track (most notably in the corners). At one point during a transition, we observed that the leading rider sweeps out but instead of leaving the cluster, it grows towards the top of the corner because another rider not involved in the exercise (e.g. in a warm up waiting until the team pursuit ends) is riding too close to the train. Another is due to a rider's mistake that the transition occurs very late when the corner banking is already decreasing. What may happen then is that the leader can't sweep up anymore and the transition happens alongside and not far enough (laterally) from the train. Note that for transitions in competition, no errors were made so to minimize errors in training it may be beneficial to limit the number of riders on track during team pursuit related exercises.

4.2 Unified Performance Analysis for Training and Competition

For competitions, coaches would typically collect FIT files from the riders' head unit. On its own, the sensor data inside these activity files are not well suited to evaluate multi-rider competitions. The lack of event annotations causes decoupling during the analysis because, in case of a team pursuit, four files are individually interpreted and would require large manual efforts to overcome without automated tooling. Discrepancies between the analysis of training and competition rides also makes it harder to compare how riders performed between settings.

One of WCN's strengths is that the same analysis views are supported for both data sources even though the underlying data is sourced differently. In training we can utilize the automated collection platform from Sect. 3.1, which provides the sensor data, event annotations from a ground truth source and video automatically. Then for competitions, after inputting the video and FIT files, the system will predict the annotations. An example of such unified analysis is shown in Fig. 9

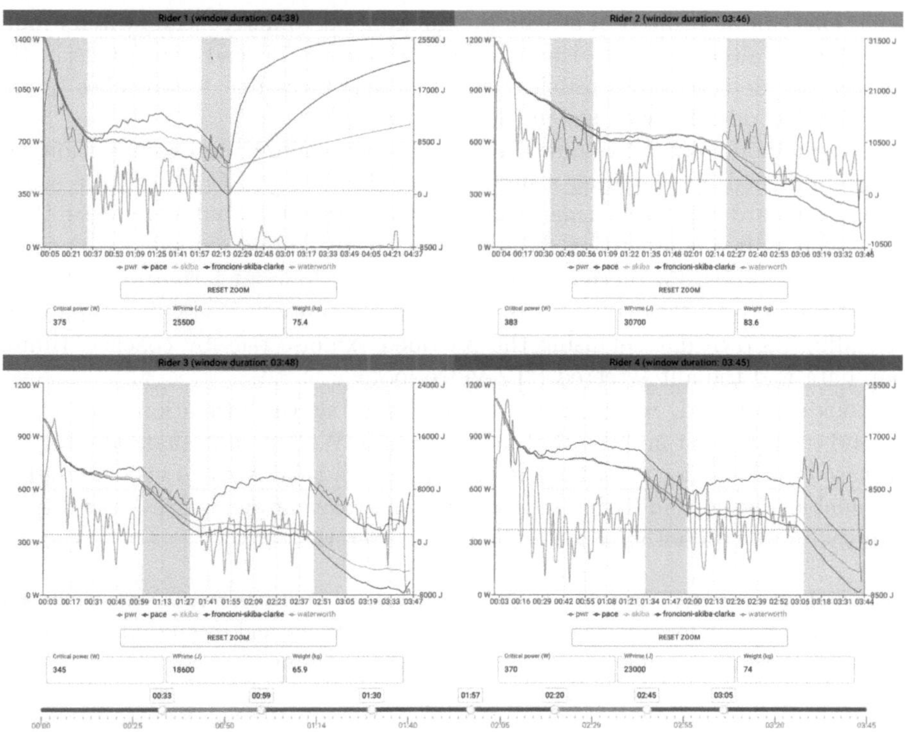

Fig. 9. Sample analysis view focused on team pursuit. Shows the power output and critical power level per rider vs energetic reserve capacity of multiple models. The highlights in red indicate lead position time with the full leader timeline given on the bottom. (Color figure online)

This links both situations together from the analysis point-of-view but also creates a feedback loop where using the system in training improves the diversity and grows the number of annotations in the dataset (and implicitly the detection capabilities). Transitions from exercises annotated as team pursuit by coaches are sourced automatically, linked to PTZ footage or manual recordings and extended by on-rider sensors and timing loops. This not only generates more usable data for researchers and coaches but also does it without imposing on the federation's training schedules as such autonomous recording setups don't require technical staff on-site (allowing sessions to be recorded at any time without coordination constraints).

5 Conclusion and Future Work

In this paper, we presented a computer vision pipeline to integrate event annotations extracted from team pursuit videos into a sensor-based analysis platform. At its base we finetuned an RF-DETR model to detect track cyclists ($N = 4428$) with an F1-score of 0.96/0.75 at IoU 0.50/[0.50-0.95]. We've shown how these detections can be utilized in a team pursuit context to detect lead switch events and offer an alternative to visual trackers. From the 78 lead transitions in the dataset, we detected 95% missing only four instances due to mistakes in the transition or rider interference in the training facility.

The methodology shows how the link between training and competition can be strengthened by providing a unified analysis platform. Coaches have access to a dashboard with real time sensor data in training, but can reuse these components after competition data has been ingested and extended with automatic annotations. Furthermore, because the team pursuit formation detection is partly based on data collected during training through WCN, it's capable of extending its own dataset using the provided exercise tags by coaches, timing loop data and the auto-steered PTZ video footage.

Looking forward, we're interested in extending the formation capabilities beyond team pursuit and use that information in WCN to automatically tag the exercise type for video recordings in the training facility. Next to visible insights, this enables the system to link sensor data (and relevant derivatives) and display it in the most optimal view for each specific exercise.

Acknowledgements. We'd like to express our gratitude to Jan Vancompernolle and Cycling Vlaanderen for granting us access to the velodrome and technical facilities and for their cooperation in implementing the monitoring system.

Data Availability Statement. The code, examples and models for the rider detection and team pursuit formation will be made available in this repository: https://cloud.ilabt.imec.be/index.php/s/9GGH4tNsqnGc9s9. Access to the full video dataset can be requested through Cycling Vlaanderen.

Disclosure of Interests. The authors have no competing interests to declare that are relevant to the content of this article.

References

1. Boillet, A., Noble, M., Sachet, I., Messonnier, L.A., Cohen, C.: Individualized optimal strategy in team pursuit for track cycling. Sci. Rep. **14**(1), 25308 (2024). https://doi.org/10.1038/s41598-024-75963-4
2. Carion, N., et al.: End-to-end object detection with transformers. CoRR abs/2005.12872 (2020). https://arxiv.org/abs/2005.12872
3. Cycling, T.: Track cycling KP dataset (2025). https://universe.roboflow.com/track-cycling/track-cycling-kp. Accessed 14 Dec 2025
4. Davis, J., et al.: Methodology and evaluation in sports analytics: challenges, approaches, and lessons learned. Mach. Learn. **113**(9), 6977–7010 (2024). https://doi.org/10.1007/s10994-024-06585-0
5. Bock, D.: Jelle: Data-driven performance and safety analysis in cycling races, Ghent University (2023). Ph.D. thesis
6. Deng, D., et al.: Eventanchor: reducing human interactions in event annotation of racket sports videos. In: Proceedings of the 2021 CHI Conference on Human Factors in Computing Systems. CHI '21, Association for Computing Machinery, New York, NY, USA (2021). https://doi.org/10.1145/3411764.3445431
7. Dias, A.C., Postolache, O.: Cyclist performance assessment based on WSN and cloud technologies. In: 2018 International Conference and Exposition on Electrical And Power Engineering (EPE), pp. 1041–1046 (2018). https://doi.org/10.1109/ICEPE.2018.8559950
8. Dosovitskiy, A., et al.: An image is worth 16x16 words: transformers for image recognition at scale. In: International Conference on Learning Representations (2021). https://openreview.net/forum?id=YicbFdNTTy
9. Einfalt, M., Lienhart, R.: Decoupling video and human motion: towards practical event detection in athlete recordings. CoRR abs/2004.09776 (2020). https://arxiv.org/abs/2004.09776
10. Ester, M., Kriegel, H.P., Sander, J., Xu, X.: A density-based algorithm for discovering clusters in large spatial databases with noise. In: Proceedings of the Second International Conference on Knowledge Discovery and Data Mining, pp. 226–231. KDD'96, AAAI Press (1996)
11. Fabian Caba Heilbron, V., Escorcia, B.G., Niebles, J.C.: Activitynet: A large-scale video benchmark for human activity understanding. In: Proceedings of the IEEE Conference on Computer Vision and Pattern Recognition, pp. 961–970 (2015)
12. Fassmeyer, D., Anzer, G., Bauer, P., Brefeld, U.: Toward automatically labeling situations in soccer. Front Sports Act Living **3**, 725431 (2021)
13. Fitzgerald, S., Kelso, R., Grimshaw, P., Warr, A.: Measurement of the air velocity and turbulence in a simulated track cycling team pursuit race. J. Wind Eng. Ind. Aerodyn. **190**, 322–330 (2019). https://doi.org/10.1016/j.jweia.2019.05.014. https://www.sciencedirect.com/science/article/pii/S0167610519301527
14. Giancola, S., Amine, M., Dghaily, T., Ghanem, B.: SoccerNet: A scalable dataset for action spotting in soccer videos. In: 2018 IEEE/CVF Conference on Computer Vision and Pattern Recognition Workshops (CVPRW), pp. 1792–179210. IEEE Computer Society, Los Alamitos, CA, USA (2018). https://doi.org/10.1109/CVPRW.2018.00223. https://doi.ieeecomputersociety.org/10.1109/CVPRW.2018.00223
15. Gu, C., et al.: Ava: a video dataset of spatio-temporally localized atomic visual actions. In: 2018 IEEE/CVF Conference on Computer Vision and Pattern Recognition, pp. 6047–6056 (2018). https://doi.org/10.1109/CVPR.2018.00633

16. Hall, D., James, D., Marsden, N.: Marginal gains: Olympic lessons in high performance for organisations. HR Bulletin Res. Pract. **7**(2), 9–13 (2012)
17. Heilbron, F.C., Lee, J.-Y., Jin, H., Ghanem, B.: What do I annotate next? An empirical study of active learning for action localization. In: Ferrari, V., Hebert, M., Sminchisescu, C., Weiss, Y. (eds.) ECCV 2018. LNCS, vol. 11215, pp. 212–229. Springer, Cham (2018). https://doi.org/10.1007/978-3-030-01252-6_13
18. Heimans, L., Dijkshoorn, W.R., Hoozemans, M.J., de Koning, J.J.: Optimizing the team for required power during track-cycling team pursuit. Int. J. Sports Physiol. Perform. **12**(10), 1385–1391 (2017). https://doi.org/10.1123/ijspp.2016-0451. https://journals.humankinetics.com/view/journals/ijspp/12/10/article-p1385.xml
19. Host, K., Ivašić-Kos, M.: An overview of human action recognition in sports based on computer vision. Heliyon **8**(6) (2022). https://doi.org/10.1016/j.heliyon.2022.e09633
20. Ibrahim, M.R., Haworth, J., Christie, N., Cheng, T.: Cyclingnet: detecting cycling near misses from video streams in complex urban scenes with deep learning (2021). https://arxiv.org/abs/2102.00565
21. Internationale, U.C.: Union Cycliste Internationale: Track overview. https://www.uci.org/discipline/track/5bBV0EMQvb3ZiTcXbKFLJz?tab=discover. Accessed 27 Oct 2025
22. Jeukendrup, A.E., Martin, J.: Improving cycling performance. Sports Med. **31**(7), 559–569 (2001). https://doi.org/10.2165/00007256-200131070-00009
23. Li, J., Fan, Y., Lyu, X., Yang, L., Zhao, Y.: Dynamic multisensor fusion framework with adaptive spatiotemporal optimization for IoT-based motion recognition. IEEE Internet Things J. **12**(13), 23182–23194 (2025). https://doi.org/10.1109/JIOT.2025.3551082
24. Li, Y., et al.: Multisports: a multi-person video dataset of spatio-temporally localized sports actions. In: Proceedings of the IEEE/CVF International Conference on Computer Vision (ICCV), pp. 13536–13545 (2021)
25. Lievens, M., et al.: Characterizing the exponential profile of W' recovery following partial depletion. Med. Sci. Sports Exerc. **56**(9), 1770–1781 (2024). https://doi.org/10.1249/mss.0000000000003468
26. Lin, T., et al.: Microsoft COCO: common objects in context. CoRR abs/1405.0312 (2014). http://arxiv.org/abs/1405.0312
27. Liu, C., Huynh, D.Q., Sun, Y., Reynolds, M., Atkinson, S.: A vision-based pipeline for vehicle counting, speed estimation, and classification. IEEE Trans. Intell. Transp. Syst. **22**(12), 7547–7560 (2021). https://doi.org/10.1109/TITS.2020.3004066
28. Ma, S., Zhang, W., Noland, R.B., Andrews, C.J.: Eye tracking measures of bicyclists' behavior and perception: a systematic review. Transport. Res. F Traffic Psychol. Behav. **107**, 52–68 (2024). https://doi.org/10.1016/j.trf.2024.08.026. https://www.sciencedirect.com/science/article/pii/S136984782400233X
29. Marin-Perianu, R., et al.: A performance analysis of a wireless body-area network monitoring system for professional cycling. Personal Ubiquitous Comput. **17**(1), 197–209 (2013). https://doi.org/10.1007/s00779-011-0486-x
30. Migliaccio, G.M., Padulo, J., Russo, L.: The impact of wearable technologies on marginal gains in sports performance: an integrative overview on advances in sports, exercise, and health. Appl. Sci. **14**(15) (2024). https://doi.org/10.3390/app14156649. https://www.mdpi.com/2076-3417/14/15/6649

31. Minne, K., et al.: Experimental evaluation of UWB indoor positioning for indoor track cycling. Sensors **19**(9) (2019). https://doi.org/10.3390/s19092041. https://www.mdpi.com/1424-8220/19/9/2041
32. Ravi, N., et al.: Sam 2: segment anything in images and videos. arXiv preprint arXiv:2408.00714 (2024). https://arxiv.org/abs/2408.00714
33. Robinson, I., Robicheaux, P., Popov, M., Ramanan, D., Peri, N.: RF-DETR: neural architecture search for real-time detection transformers (2025). https://arxiv.org/abs/2511.09554
34. Rossi, L.F., Sanna, A., Manuri, F., Donna Bianco, M.: How AI-based computer vision algorithms are impacting the sports industry: a survey. Discov. Artif. Intell. **5**(1), 374 (2025). https://doi.org/10.1007/s44163-025-00586-1
35. School: Cycle riders dataset (2023). https://universe.roboflow.com/school-jhocg/cycle-riders. Accessed 14 Dec 2025
36. Shehzadi, T., et al.: Object detection with transformers: a review. Sensors **25**(19) (2025). https://doi.org/10.3390/s25196025. https://www.mdpi.com/1424-8220/25/19/6025
37. Shih, H.C.: A survey of content-aware video analysis for sports. IEEE Trans. Circuits Syst. Video Technol. **28**(5), 1212–1231 (2018). https://doi.org/10.1109/TCSVT.2017.2655624
38. Sigrist, S., Maier, T., Faiss, R.: Qualitative video analysis of track cycling team pursuit in world-class athletes. Int. J. Sports Physiol. Perform. **12**(2017). https://doi.org/10.1123/ijspp.2016-0596
39. Skiba, P.F., Chidnok, W., Vanhatalo, A., Jones, A.M.: Modeling the expenditure and reconstitution of work capacity above critical power. Med. Sci. Sports Exerc. **44**(8) (2012). https://journals.lww.com/acsm-msse/fulltext/2012/08000/modeling_the_expenditure_and_reconstitution_of.15.aspx
40. Slembrouck, M., Decorte, R., De Bock, J. Verstockt, S.: Automated PTZ framing of track cyclists using timing loops. In: Science and Cycling 2023, Abstracts, p. 3 (2023)
41. Smith, A.: USA cycling awarded the 2025 informs Edelman award for data-driven Olympic gold strategy (2025). https://usacycling.org/article/usa-cycling-awarded-the-2025-informs-edelman-award-for-data-driven-olympic-gold-strategy. Accessed 27 Oct 2025
42. Stadnyk, A.M.J., Impellizzeri, F.M., Stanley, J., Menaspà, P., Slattery, K.M.: Testing, training, and optimising performance of track cyclists: a systematic mapping review. Sports Med. **52**(2), 391–401 (2022)
43. Stipancic, J., Zangenehpour, S., Miranda-Moreno, L., Saunier, N., Granié, M.A.: Investigating the gender differences on bicycle-vehicle conflicts at urban intersections using an ordered logit methodology. Accid. Anal. Prev. **97**, 19–27 (2016). https://doi.org/10.1016/j.aap.2016.07.033. https://www.sciencedirect.com/science/article/pii/S0001457516302627
44. Theiner, J., et al.: Extraction of positional player data from broadcast soccer videos. In: 2022 IEEE/CVF Winter Conference on Applications of Computer Vision (WACV), pp. 1463–1473 (2022). https://doi.org/10.1109/WACV51458.2022.00153
45. Track: 1-wcn-bbox-comp dataset (2025). https://universe.roboflow.com/track-1z9nc/1-wcn-bbox-comp-thqoe. Accesed 14 Dec 2025
46. Underwood, L., Jermy, M.: Determining optimal pacing strategy for the track cycling individual pursuit event with a fixed energy mathematical model. Sports Eng. **17**(4), 183–196 (2014). https://doi.org/10.1007/s12283-014-0153-3

47. Videnovic, J., Lukezic, A., Kristan, M.: A distractor-aware memory for visual object tracking with SAM2. In: Proceedings of the Computer Vision and Pattern Recognition Conference (2025)
48. Vondrick, C., Ramanan, D., Patterson, D.: Efficiently scaling up video annotation with crowdsourced marketplaces. In: Daniilidis, K., Maragos, P., Paragios, N. (eds.) ECCV 2010. LNCS, vol. 6314, pp. 610–623. Springer, Heidelberg (2010). https://doi.org/10.1007/978-3-642-15561-1_44
49. Wagner, M., Day, J., Jordan, C.D., Kroeger, T., Neumann, F.: Evolving pacing strategies for team pursuit track cycling. CoRR abs/1104.0775 (2011). http://arxiv.org/abs/1104.0775
50. Xu, J.Y., et al.: Integrated inertial sensors and mobile computing for real-time cycling performance guidance via pedaling profile classification. IEEE J. Biomed. Health Inform. **19**(2), 440–445 (2015). https://doi.org/10.1109/JBHI.2014.2322871
51. Yang, C.Y., Huang, H.W., Chai, W., Jiang, Z., Hwang, J.N.: Samurai: adapting segment anything model for zero-shot visual tracking with motion-aware memory (2024). https://arxiv.org/abs/2411.11922

Shot and Technical Error Detection in Tennis Using Graph Convolutional Networks

Pierre Hellich[1(✉)], Jiang Kan[2], Jin Song Dong[2], and Mathieu Salzmann[1]

[1] Computer Vision Laboratory, Swiss Federal Technology Institute of Lausanne (EPFL), Lausanne, Switzerland
{pierre.hellich,mathieu.salzmann}@epfl.ch

[2] Computer Science Department, National University of Singapore, Singapore, Singapore
{jiangkan,dcsdjs}@nus.edu.sg

Abstract. Recent developments in Large Language Models bring a personal AI coach closer to reality. However, to apply this to sport activities, multimodal LLMs still struggle to provide precise technical advice from videos. This study demonstrates that Graph Convolutional Networks (GCN) can help bridge the gap between human and AI coaching by extracting meaningful features from human skeletons. Using limited data consisting only of the player's pose without ball or racket tracking, GCNs show strong capabilities to detect events frame-wise and correctly classify them, through learning new topologies and spatio-temporal relationships between physically distant joints. The proposed framework uses a two-stage approach: first, a Channel-wise Topology Refinement-GCN (CTR-GCN) is trained on professional athletes to learn canonical tennis motions and strikes; second, the backbone is frozen and transfer learning is applied to identify technical errors and their root-cause joints. To support this, we introduce a dataset of in-the-wild videos from amateur tennis players with semi-automated error annotations.

Keywords: Graph Convolutional Network · AI Coaching · Tennis Dataset

1 Introduction

Improving technical skills in tennis typically relies on expert feedback. While online tutorials provide general guidance, they lack the precision and personalization required for iterative practice and correction. Identifying subtle technical errors in movements such as serves or forehands requires expert knowledge to evaluate a player's execution and provide targeted advice. However, personalized coaching is often costly and limited by coach availability. AI therefore offers a promising opportunity to make personalized feedback more accessible to amateur players.

Automatically diagnosing technical errors from video is a challenging task. It requires both accurate pose estimation and a detailed understanding of the

Z. Liu and V. Misra (Eds.): ISACE 2026, LNCS 16610, pp. 351–376, 2026.
https://doi.org/10.1007/978-3-032-27272-0_23

spatio-temporal dynamics of body motion during a stroke. The problem is further complicated by the large variability in amateur executions compared to the more consistent movements of professional players. General-purpose models such as multimodal LLMs often struggle with this fine-grained motion analysis [5,9, 10]. Skeleton-based graph models provide a promising alternative by explicitly modeling relationships between body joints over time.

This work proposes a framework for detecting tennis strokes and identifying technical errors from skeleton sequences. The approach uses a Channel-wise Topology Refinement Graph Convolutional Network (CTR-GCN) [1] to model spatio-temporal joint dynamics. The model is first pre-trained on professional match data from the F^3Set dataset [7] to perform Precise Event Spotting (PES) of serves, forehands, and backhands. The learned representation is then transferred to a smaller dataset of amateur players, where additional classification heads are trained to detect technical errors. This two-stage training strategy allows the model to learn correct motion patterns from professional players and identify deviations corresponding to common technical mistakes in amateur executions.

In summary, the contributions of this study are as follows:

- **An amateur tennis player dataset:** We introduce a dataset featuring video, technical error labels, and 3D-skeleton data with frame-level annotations of shot type (forehand, backhand, or serve) and technique (e.g., slice, groundstroke, volley). This addresses the scarcity of data on imperfect movements in existing tennis datasets.
- **A two-stage transfer learning framework:** We propose a model that leverages professional motion as a baseline to learn correct dynamics, followed by transfer learning to accurately categorize common technical errors in amateur players. The framework is generic and can be adapted to other sports or technical activities without requiring architectural modifications.

2 Related Work

2.1 AI-Based Sports Coaching

Recent advances in large language models (LLMs) have enabled the development of AI coaching systems that combine video or sensor data with the reasoning capabilities of LLMs. These approaches aim to provide personalized feedback to athletes by analyzing motion data and generating natural language explanations.

Ma et al. [9] introduced T3Set, a multimodal dataset aligning sensor, video, and textual data for sports analysis. Their framework uses inertial measurement unit (IMU) data to identify problematic joints and generates feedback through an LLM. To improve domain-specific reasoning, Ma et al. [10] later incorporated a retrieval-augmented generation (RAG) architecture supported by a knowledge base of common beginner errors. More recently, Li et al. [5] proposed ZARA, a multi-agent reasoning framework for human action recognition that combines structured knowledge bases with LLM prompting to produce interpretable predictions. While these approaches provide high-level feedback, they often struggle with the fine-grained motion analysis required to detect subtle technical errors.

2.2 Skeleton-Based Human Action Recognition

To capture detailed body dynamics, recent research has increasingly relied on skeleton-based representations. These methods reduce visual complexity while preserving the underlying biomechanical structure of human motion.

Yan et al. [13] introduced the Spatio-Temporal Graph Convolutional Network (ST-GCN), which models skeleton sequences as graphs where joints correspond to nodes and bones define edges. Building on this idea, later work explored more flexible graph topologies to better capture correlations between distant joints. Chen et al. [1] proposed the Channel-wise Topology Refinement GCN (CTR-GCN), where the skeleton topology becomes a learnable parameter that can adapt to different motion patterns. Other variants, such as HD-GCN [4], STA-GCN [12], InfoGCN [2], and ProtoGCN [6], further improve representation learning through hierarchical structures, attention mechanisms, or information bottleneck techniques.

2.3 Skeleton-Based Methods in Sports Analysis

Skeleton-based models have also been applied to sports analytics, where accurate temporal modeling is crucial due to the structured phases of athletic movements. In tennis, Liu et al. [8] proposed UMEG-Net, which integrates player, court, and ball graphs to achieve frame-level event detection. Other models, such as ST-GCN-CAD [14] and FFGCAN [11], improve multi-scale temporal modeling and robustness to noisy skeleton data.

Despite these advances, many existing approaches either rely on additional information such as ball trajectories or focus primarily on action recognition rather than detailed error diagnosis. This work explores the use of graph convolutional networks to jointly perform Precise Event Spotting (PES), action recognition, and technical error detection using only player skeleton data.

3 Method

3.1 Problem Statement

We categorize tennis actions into three primary shot types: the *Forehand*, the *Backhand*, and the *Serve*. Frames that do not contain ball-racket contact are labeled as *No-shot*. Furthermore, the shot techniques considered in this work include: *Groundstroke (GS)*, *Slice*, *Volley*, *Drop shot*, *Smash*, and *Lob*. This typology follows the definition introduced in F^3Set [7].

Certain joints experience significant mechanical loading during a tennis stroke and are therefore considered potential points of technical failure: *Shoulder*, *Elbow*, *Wrist*, *Chest*, *Hip*, *Knee*, and *Foot*.

In collaboration with a certified professional tennis coach, technical errors were categorized into four groups: *Ready Position*, *Unit Turn*, *General Balance*, and *Strike*. Each category is described in the LLM system prompt provided in the Appendix A.4.

3.2 Proposed Framework

To achieve a high model performance, this study proposes a two-stage method illustrated in Fig. 1. The first stage consists of pre-training and fine-tuning in order to learn a robust skeleton feature extractor. In the second stage, the framework reuses the CTR-GCN backbone and applies transfer learning to identify technical errors and their associated joints.

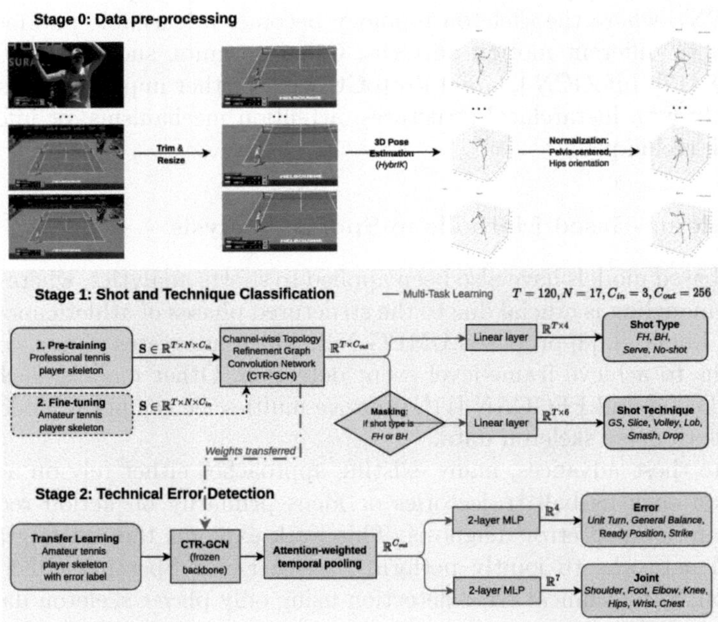

Fig. 1. Overview of the proposed two-stage framework. Stage 1 involves training the CTR-GCN backbone on professional skeleton data for shot type and technique classification. Stage 2 utilizes transfer learning on amateur data to identify technical errors and their root-cause joints.

Stage 1: Shot and Technique Classification. To construct a powerful feature extractor, the model is initially trained to classify shot types and shot techniques. This strengthens the representation for error detection later. This multi-task learning approach has two parallel objectives:

1. Classifying each frame as *No-shot*, *Forehand*, *Backhand*, or *Serve*
2. Identifying the specific technique (see Sect. 3.1) if the shot type is *Forehand* or *Backhand*

The loss function is defined as the sum of the shot detection loss and the shot technique classification loss, the latter weighted by a factor $\lambda = 0.5$. This weighting factor was chosen to prioritize the primary task of shot detection while providing enough gradient signal for technique classification:

$$\mathcal{L}_{\text{total}} = \mathcal{L}_{\text{shot detection}} + \lambda \cdot \mathcal{L}_{\text{shot technique}} \tag{1}$$

In this formulation, $\mathcal{L}_{\text{shot detection}}$ has a $\delta = \pm 1$ frame tolerance and uses the Cross-Entropy (CE) loss.

$$\mathcal{L}_{\text{shot detection}} = -\sum_{c=1}^{M} w_c y_c \log(p_c) \tag{2}$$

where M is the number of technique classes, w_c is the class weight, and y_c is a binary indicator of the ground-truth label. The CE loss $\mathcal{L}_{\text{shot technique}}$ is computed using a masking mechanism, ensuring it is only applied to frames where the true shot type label is either *Forehand* or *Backhand*.

Stage 2: Technical Error Detection. In the second stage, the CTR-GCN backbone is frozen. To retain the maximum amount of information during the temporal pooling of extracted features, a linear attention layer learns to assign greater weight to the most relevant frames. The feature vectors of all frames are then summed proportionally to their weights. The resulting clip-level representation is fed into a Multi-Layer Perceptron (MLP) of two linear layers separated by a ReLU activation and a dropout layer. A separate MLP is used for each task (error and root-cause joint classification).

3.3 Professional Tennis Dataset

Pose Estimation for Videos of Professional Players. The model is first pre-trained on skeletons extracted from videos of professional tennis players. The F^3Set dataset [7] comprises 11,584 tennis rallies containing 42,846 shots across 114 broadcast matches. Each rally contains one or more strokes annotated with attributes such as the specific frame of occurrence, shot type, and technique.

The professional tennis dataset is derived from F^3Set by augmenting it with 3D skeleton data, and is used for pre-training of the CTR-GCN. To ensure the quality of the pose estimation, only the skeleton of the player closest to the camera is extracted. Rallies in which the foreground player does not hit the ball were filtered out, and clips were re-centered around the bounding box of this player with a margin of 300 pixels. A heuristic was applied to limit the clip duration and the number of *No-shot* frames. This heuristic also excludes transitional frames where the broadcast switches between slow-motion replays or close-ups and the actual live rally, as shown in Fig. 3 in Appendix A.1. After manual verification of the results, the enhanced F^3Set dataset consists of 9,487 clips with 20,407 events. Table 1 and Fig. 4 in Appendix A.3 highlight the existing class imbalances. The dataset was randomly split into 65% for training (6,085 clips), 15% for validation (1,515 clips), and 20% for testing (1,887 clips).

Skeleton Data Normalization. The 3D joints estimated by HybrIK follow the Human3.6M [15] convention (see Fig. 2 in Appendix A.1). The skeleton consists of 17 joints in a root-relative coordinate system centered on the pelvis $(0, 0, 0)$ and normalized within a range of $[-0.5, 0.5]$. A significant advantage of 3D coordinates is that they allow camera-view invariance. All skeletons were therefore normalized to face a consistent direction. First, the vector between the right and left hips was averaged across all frames to determine the player's average orientation. The normal vector in the xy-plane was then rotated to align with the x-axis.

Data Sanity Check. The Mean Per Joint Position Error (MPJPE) Fig. 4drepresents the mean Euclidean distance between joints across consecutive frames. Although MPJPE is commonly used to evaluate pose estimation accuracy against ground truth data, it serves here as an indicator of temporal smoothness. Joint displacement naturally increases during strokes, but remains low during preparation phases. The correlation between frames of shot events and peaks in MPJPE, observed in Fig. 4cand Fig. 4din Appendix A.3, confirms the sanity of the data. The model may implicitly leverage these peaks in joint displacement to identify the occurrence of specific shot events.

3.4 Amateur Tennis Dataset

Once the CTR-GCN has been trained to extract skeleton features, the second stage uses its backbone to detect technical errors in amateur players. This study introduces a dataset of amateur tennis players comprising video clips, skeleton data, and technical error annotations.

A total of 1,015 tennis videos were collected from the Reddit subreddit r/10 s, where users frequently request technical advice. Additional metadata were also collected, including post titles, descriptions, and comments with their respective upvote and downvote counts. Non-relevant, humorous, blurry, or poorly framed videos were filtered out. Slow-motion videos were also excluded to ensure that the clips matched the temporal dynamics on which the model was pre-trained. Long videos were split into several shorter clips, each containing a number of shots representative of a real tennis rally (see Fig 5a and 5b).

All frames were manually annotated by shot type (*No-shot*, *Forehand*, *Backhand* and *Serve*) and the technique was specified for frames with a shot. This dataset follows a similar structure to the enhanced F^3Set to facilitate performance comparisons of the CTR-GCN between professional players (recorded with stable broadcast cameras) and amateur "in the wild" videos. The amateur players in the Reddit posts include both males and females of various ages and skill levels, recorded from various camera angles, and performing either repetitive drills or edited rally highlights. The dataset consists of 1,442 clips containing 4,495 shots (see Table 2), partitioned into 70% for training (1,009 clips), 15% for validation (217 clips), and 15% for testing (216 clips).

3.5 Amateur Tennis Dataset with Technical Error Labels

Technical error annotation for each clip was semi-automated using Google Gemini-3 models (Pro and Flash). This choice was motivated by its SoTA performance in visual reasoning and spatial understanding. Racket sport technical analysis is highlighted as one of the potential applications of Gemini-3 by Google.

The system and user prompts (Appendix A.4) guide the LLM through the classification of technical errors. The error classes and associated joints are described in Sect. 3.1. These error categories were defined under the supervision of a certified and experienced tennis coach, who also provided detailed descriptions of typical symptoms for each error type across different shots (e.g., errors in the ready position for a forehand vs a serve).

To improve annotation reliability, the LLM was also provided with the Reddit post title for context. To help the LLM focus on critical frames during shot execution, the API request was supplemented with additional static frames corresponding to key phases of the stroke: preparation (frames -9, -6, and -3 relative to ball-racket contact), contact, and follow-through (frames $+3$ and $+6$). For a clip containing two shot events, the LLM therefore receives 12 sampled frames. Empirically, these additional frames improved the consistency of the LLM. Annotation consistency is vital to ensure that the CTR-GCN model can effectively learn the underlying patterns. The LLM also determines whether the post is requesting technical advice, as some Reddit posts are intended for humor or highlight sharing. This filtering step resulted in the exclusion of 73 clips.

Final labels were determined by majority voting across three independent LLM runs. Clips with ties (391 clips) were excluded to ensure label reliability and training consistency. From the initial 1,442 clips, 978 were retained (67.8%). Although this strategy is restrictive, it prioritizes annotation quality over dataset size. Table 7 in Appendix A.2 shows one annotation example of the same video by the tennis coach and the LLM. The dataset was randomly split into 70% for training (684 clips), 15% for validation (146 clips), and 15% for testing (148 clips).

Table 3 shows the distribution of error types and root-cause joints. The *Shoulder* is identified as the cause of failure in nearly half of the cases (49.80%), followed by the *Foot* (26.48%). In contrast, the *Wrist* and *Chest* appear only once and were excluded from training due to insufficient samples. This is partly due to the restrictive tie-breaking assumption and the fact that the *Chest* and *Shoulder* can act as similar indicators. Furthermore, the wrist angle is particularly difficult to evaluate accurately using just video and static frames which are often blurry. Figure 6 in Appendix A.5 illustrates the correlation between joints and error types.

Table 1. Professional dataset statistics (9,487 clips, 1,401,254 frames, 20,407 events)

Shot type	Forehand	Backhand	Serve	Total
Groundstroke	6,984	5,707	—	12,691 (62.2%)
Slice	473	1,040	—	1,513 (7.4%)
Volley	169	113	—	282 (1.4%)
Lob	42	106	—	148 (0.7%)
Drop	43	70	—	113 (0.6%)
Smash	54	1	—	55 (0.3%)
Serve	—	—	5,605	5,605 (27.5%)
Total	7,765 (38.1%)	7,037 (34.5%)	5,605 (27.5%)	20,407 (100%)

Table 2. Amateur tennis dataset statistics (1,442 clips, 481,188 frames, 4,495 events)

Shot Type	Forehand	Backhand	Serve	Total
Groundstroke	2,392	914	—	3,306 (73.7%)
Slice	25	68	—	93 (2.1%)
Volley	20	16	—	36 (0.8%)
Lob	3	3	—	6 (0.1%)
Drop	9	5	—	14 (0.3%)
Smash	21	2	—	23 (0.5%)
Serve	—	—	1,017	1,017 (22.7%)
Total	2,470 (54.9%)	1,008 (22.5%)	1,017 (22.7%)	4,495 (100%)

Table 3. Amateur tennis dataset with technical error labels (978 clips)

Joint	**Count**	**Percentage**
Shoulder	487	49.80
Foot	259	26.48
Elbow	116	11.86
Knee	70	7.16
Hips	44	4.50
Wrist*	1	0.10
Chest*	1	0.10

Error	**Count**	**Percentage**
Unit turn	457	46.73
Ready position	328	33.54
Strike	118	12.07
General Balance	75	7.67

* Excluded from training due to insufficient samples.

3.6 Implementation Details

Loss Function Weighting. As shown in Table 1, the professional video dataset is highly imbalanced between background frames and frames containing events (20,000 events vs 1.40M total frames) and across shot techniques (12,000 groundstrokes vs 113 drop shots). To compensate, we used square-root inverse frequency weights $w_c = \sqrt{\frac{N}{n_c}}$, where w_c and n_c denote the weight and number of samples for class c, and N is the total number of samples. Square-root inverse frequency weighting produces less extreme weight differences than standard inverse frequency weighting, leading to improved generalization in this study.

Pre-Training on Professional Tennis Dataset. The models were optimized using the AdamW optimizer, with the learning rate controlled by a cosine annealing schedule. Training was performed for 85 epochs. Each epoch processed 150,000 frames randomly sampled with probability proportional to video length. The full training took approximately 40 minutes on an NVIDIA RTX 4090 GPU. The initial learning rate was set to 0.001, with a five-step linear warm-up phase before followed by cosine decay. Weight decay and dropout were set to 0.0001 and 0.3 respectively. The clip length was set to $T = 120$ frames, and the batch size was $B = 16$. The CTR-GCN backbone contains 1.421M trainable parameters.

Transfer Learning on Amateur Tennis Dataset with Technical Error Labels. The second stage aims to classify errors and root-cause joints. To mitigate class imbalance, the CE loss is weighted using inverse frequency weights for both classification tasks. The learning rate and weight decay are both set to 0.001. The MLP has a dropout rate of 0.2. A single optimizer is shared between the two MLP heads, as their training objectives are aligned. This configuration contains 70,292 trainable parameters. During evaluation, the model processes input clips of 120 frames, while some videos may be longer. To handle this mismatch, sliding inference windows are applied across the entire clip. The logits from each window are aggregated until the full clip is covered, and the final classification is obtained from the aggregated logits. Model selection across epochs is based on the macro-F1 score, which assigns equal importance to all classes regardless of their frequency.

4 Experiments and Results

4.1 Evaluation Metrics

To evaluate the temporal precision and classification accuracy of the events occurring in tennis rallies, this study adopts the metrics proposed in the F^3Set paper [7], alongside additional metrics introduced in this work.

Edit Score. The Edit Score reflects the similarity between predicted and ground-truth event sequences using the Levenshtein distance, capturing errors in sequence structure. This is particularly valuable for evaluating models where temporal order and sequence completeness are essential. Event sequences are derived from frame-level predictions by collapsing consecutive frames with identical labels into single events. The Levenshtein distance L quantifies the minimum number of operations (insertions, deletions, or substitutions) needed to transform the predicted sequence into the ground truth. The distance is normalized to account for different sequence lengths and produces a score out of 100:

$$\text{Edit score} = \left(1 - \frac{L}{\max(|s_{gt}|, |s_{pred}|)}\right) \times 100, \tag{3}$$

where $|s_{gt}|$ and $|s_{pred}|$ are the lengths of the ground-truth and predicted sequences.

F1 with Temporal Tolerance. The F1 score evaluates both classification accuracy and temporal localization. A prediction for a frame is considered correct only if its timestamp falls within a strict temporal tolerance of $\delta = \pm 1$ frame relative to the ground truth frame and if its class is correctly predicted. This ensures the model is evaluated on its ability to achieve Precise Event Spotting alongside accurate classification. The macro-F1 scores presented in Tables 4 and 5 are averaged across shot types, excluding *No-shot* frames.

4.2 Stage 1 Analysis: Shot and Technique Classification

Table 4 presents the Edit score, macro-F1, and other global metrics for the first task of frame classification. Table 5 reports the same metrics for the second task of classifying the shot technique. In Appendix A.6, Table 8 details the F1, precision, and recall scores for each class using the baseline model, while Table 9 provides the same information for the fine-tuned model.

Baseline Performance. The baseline model, trained with the hyperparameters specified in Sect. 3.6, achieves strong results on the professional video dataset. As shown in Table 4, the model reaches an Edit Score of 96.10 and an F1 score of 0.94. Across all models, recall is approximately 10% higher than precision. A high recall indicates few false negatives, meaning the model correctly identifies nearly all instances of a class. While the model rarely misses a shot, the slightly lower precision indicates a tendency toward false positives and over-prediction, as illustrated in Table 10 in Appendix A.7. This behavior results from the low loss associated with the *No-shot* class, making the model less deterred from making a guess, whereas missing a shot incurs a higher penalty. This over-prediction is qualitatively visible when a shot is identified across more frames than the temporal tolerance of $\delta \pm 1$ frame allows. It can also create duplicate detections (e.g., detecting the same shot at frames n and $n+2$, while frame $n+1$ is classified as *No-shot*), thereby decreasing the Edit Score.

Serves. Analysis by class reveals that the model recognizes *Serves* with high accuracy (F1: 0.986) and maintains similar performance for *Forehands* and *Backhands* (F1 $\approx$ 0.91 for both). This is expected because serve mechanics are more consistent across players, while forehand and backhand executions vary (e.g., one-handed vs. two-handed, slice vs. smash). Furthermore, serves consistently occur within the first 40 frames of a rally in the professional video dataset.

Table 4. Model performance for frame classification

Model	Professional				Amateur			
	Edit	F1	Prec.	Rec.	Edit	F1	Prec.	Rec.
Baseline	96.10	**0.94**	0.89	0.98	81.38	0.81	0.79	0.85
Left-handers only	*90.70*	*0.92*	*0.88*	*0.96*				
FT on amateur clips	90.80	0.89	0.82	0.97	**91.31***	**0.86***	0.77*	**0.97***
1-layer GRU	95.42	0.93	0.88	0.98	84.18	0.83	0.80	0.87
Shorter seq. (96 f.)	**96.36**	**0.94**	0.89	**0.99**	83.15	0.81	0.79	0.84
Inv. freq. (norm.)	86.49	0.74	0.60	**0.99**	54.57	0.55	0.44	0.89
Without skel. norm.	96.00	0.93	0.89	**0.99**	69.06	0.67	0.68	0.71

Table 5. Model performance for shot technique classification

Model	Professional				Amateur#			
	Edit	F1	Prec.	Rec.	Edit	F1	Prec.	Rec.
Baseline	91.34	0.55	0.68	0.52	68.65	0.37	0.39	0.37
FT on amateur clips	87.54	0.42	0.48	0.39	**85.28***	0.38*	0.43*	0.36*
1-layer GRU	91.19	0.53	0.64	0.49	75.97	0.35	0.37	0.34
Shorter seq. (96 f.)	92.41	0.53	0.64	0.50	75.60	0.37	0.39	0.35
Inv. freq. (norm.)	71.96	**0.58**	0.74	**0.58**	31.82	0.35	0.53	**0.40**
Without skel. norm.	91.94	0.52	0.60	0.49	64.18	0.33	0.40	0.29

* Indicates evaluation on amateur test set only

\# Indicates that annotation is uncertain for the amateur dataset.

Left-handers. Evaluation on a smaller test set of left-handed players (183 clips) shows a decrease in Edit score to 90.70 and F1 to 0.92. This indicates that the model retains a strong understanding of tennis motion, although with increased confusion between *Forehand* and *Backhand.* Specifically, *Forehand* recall drops from 0.97 to 0.92, while *Backhand* precision decreases from 0.84 to 0.77, suggesting occasional misclassification of *Forehand* as *Backhand.*

Technique-Specific Challenges. Regarding technique classification (Table 5), Edit scores remain high but are not fully informative due to strong class imbalance, as over-predicting the majority class (*Groundstrokes*) can yield inflated results. We therefore focus on F1, precision, and recall. While F1 scores are high for *Groundstroke* (0.986), *Slice* (0.839), and *Lob* (0.991), they drop to 0.200 for *Drop*, 0.276 for *Volleys*, and 0.0 for *Smashes.*

The strong performance on *Lobs*, despite their rarity (148 instances, comparable to *Drop* (113), *Smash* (55), and *Volley* (282)), can be explained by their distinctive biomechanical pattern, characterized by pronounced upward arm motion and a low knee position. In contrast, *Drop* shots and *Volleys* are difficult to distinguish from *Slices* without ball tracking. In the test set, 8 drops and 12 volleys were misclassified as slices. *Smashes*, which occur 17 times, are never correctly predicted and are consistently misclassified as serves due to similar skeleton dynamics.

Results on the amateur dataset should be interpreted with caution. Manual annotations for amateur techniques are ambiguous and uncertain, especially in clips where the camera faces the player, making it difficult to see ball trajectory and player intent.

Generalization to Amateur Data. The model generalizes well to the amateur dataset, achieving an Edit score of 81.38. However, several factors explain the performance gap compared to the professional dataset. First, Table 2 shows a strong class imbalance, with more than twice as many forehands as backhands or serves (2,470 vs. 1,008 and 1,017), which is not reflected in the loss weighting of the training. Second, amateur videos are longer and contain more shots (see Fig. 5a5b vs. Figure 4a, 4b in Appendix A.3), increasing the likelihood of misclassification, especially given the higher motion variability of beginners. Third, event frequency is less consistent than in professional rallies, ranging from high-frequency wall practice to slower serve drills. Some clips are also edited, introducing abrupt transitions in skeleton sequences (e.g., from follow-through to preparation). Fourth, amateur players more frequently use one-handed backhands, which can confuse the model. Finally, orientation normalization can fail when players turn their backs to the net between strokes, a situation absent in professional match play.

A notable result is the drop in *Serve* F1-score to 0.822 (vs. 0.986 on professional data). Precision (0.89) exceeds recall (0.76), indicating missed detections, likely due to the absence of consecutive serve sequences during training.

Variations of Baseline

Fine-tuned baseline. The model fine-tuned on amateur videos demonstrates more balanced performance across both datasets. On the amateur dataset, the Edit Score improves by 10 points compared to the baseline model. Precision and recall also improve for all classes. Notably, *Serve* recall reaches 0.99, exceeding the corresponding precision of 0.81, indicating that fine-tuning successfully corrected the model's behavior for this class. While the model experiences a slight loss in precision on the professional dataset, suggesting minor over-prediction, precision remains stable on amateur videos. Furthermore, recall on the amateur dataset increases significantly (+0.12), indicating that nearly all shots are correctly detected and identified.

CTR-GCN combined with GRU. Model combined with a 1-layer GRU models achieves performance comparable to the baseline on the professional dataset and the best overall performance on amateur videos. Despite this improvement, it was not selected as the final backbone due to its increased number of parameters for the relatively small amateur dataset, as well as a preference for maintaining the interpretability of the learned CTR-GCN topology rather than relying on additional black-box temporal layers. Nevertheless, these results confirm that additional temporal modeling can help the model more precisely localize the frames where events occur.

Shorter Sequences. Using shorter skeleton sequences leads to slightly higher Edit and F1 scores. This is likely because such a time window reflects a typical duration of a single tennis stroke. However, since the performance gain remains limited, a longer sequence length of 120 frames is retained. This allows the model to capture multiple consecutive shots and provides additional temporal context, which is beneficial for detecting technical errors in the second stage of the proposed framework.

Weighting Strategy in Loss Function. Normalized inverse frequency loss weights lead to poor results. Precision for the *Forehand* and *Backhand* classes drops to 0.49, reinforcing the over-prediction effect. This is likely because these weights are more extreme than their square-rooted counterparts for rare classes, encouraging the model to avoid false negatives at the expense of increased false positives.

Normalization Impact. Finally, the model trained without skeleton normalization achieves strong results on professional data, which is consistently broadcast from a fixed perspective (the back of the nearest player). However, its Edit Score on amateur clips drops to 69.06, which is 23 points lower than on the professional dataset. This underlines the critical need for skeleton normalization when dealing with amateur footage, where videos are recorded from a wide range of camera angles, distances, and orientations.

CTR-GCN's Topologies. As described in the original CTR-GCN paper [1], the model first learns a shared topology and refines it using channel-specific correlation matrices. Figure 9 in Appendix A.9 reproduces Figs. 4 and 5 from the original work.

Figure 9a presents the shared topology along with the refined channel-wise topologies **R** for a forehand action performed by an amateur player. The diagonal values are higher due to the initialization of the **A** matrix. These visualizations show that the refined topologies differ from the shared one and vary across channels, indicating that the model learns distinct correlation patterns from different motion features.

Figure 9b illustrates the shared topology across three layers among the ten CTR-GCN blocks. The 15 strongest correlations from the **Q** matrices are projected onto a human skeleton. Some correlations focus on local joints, while others capture long-range interactions between distant joints (e.g., right foot and left hand), reflecting the coordinated full-body dynamics of tennis strokes.

4.3 Stage 2 Analysis: Technical Error Detection

Table 6. Classification results for the Joint and Technical Error

Joint	Precision	Recall	F1
Shoulder	0.640	0.727	0.681
Foot	0.407	0.250	0.310
Elbow	0.464	0.722	0.565
Knee	0.300	0.300	0.300
Hips	0.375	0.300	0.333
Average	0.437	0.460	0.438

Error	Precision	Recall	F1
Unit turn	0.659	0.862	0.747
Ready position	0.458	0.208	0.286
Strike	0.314	0.786	0.449
General Balance	0.750	0.188	0.300
Average	0.545	0.511	0.445

Error Classification. The macro-F1 score for error classification is 0.445 (Table 6). The model performs well on the dominant class, *Unit turn* (F1: 0.747). However, its precision (0.659), combined with the very low recall of *Ready position* (0.208), indicates that *Unit turn* predictions often absorb *Ready position* instances. This likely stems from the model's difficulty in capturing preparation-phase features, instead focusing on frames around the strike (see Fig. 8 in Appendix A.8).

The *Strike* class shows high recall (0.786) but low precision (0.314), suggesting it acts as a fallback when confidence in other classes is low. Conversely, *General Balance*, the smallest class, achieves high precision (0.750) but low recall (0.188), indicating conservative predictions. This is likely due to inverse-frequency loss weighting penalizing errors on rare classes.

Joint Classification. Joint classification yields similar results (macro-F1: 0.438; Table 6). The *Shoulder* class achieves strong performance (F1: 0.681) with a good precision–recall balance. In contrast, *Foot*, the second-largest class, performs poorly (F1: 0.310), suggesting difficulty in capturing lower-body features. This may be because the CTR-GCN encoder emphasizes strike moments, dominated by upper-body motion, while the feet remain relatively static (see Fig. 7 in Appendix A.8).

The *Elbow* class reaches an F1 of 0.565, driven by high recall (0.722), further indicating that features near the racket are well captured. Finally, *Knee* and *Hips* show balanced but moderate performance, with similar precision and recall. Overall, results highlight a clear gap between upper- and lower-body joint classification.

5 Conclusion

This study highlights the strong potential of Graph Convolutional Networks for sports analytics tasks such as Precise Event Spotting and action recognition. The

CTR-GCN model achieves solid performance on both professional and amateur datasets with relatively few parameters. It also offers interpretability through the analysis of learned topologies and attention weights, providing insight into motion patterns. Notably, the approach relies solely on skeleton data, without ball, racket, or court tracking, and remains robust to varying camera angles via orientation normalization. These properties make it easily transferable to other sports requiring precise technical analysis.

The second stage yields more mixed results. While shot recognition remains robust on in-the-wild videos, the amateur dataset is relatively small and the labeling process introduces limitations. Due to resource constraints, gold-standard annotations of technical errors could not be fully provided by expert coaches. Instead, labeling was partially automated using predefined error classes and an LLM prompt designed with a certified coach.

LLM outputs are inherently probabilistic, leading to inconsistencies for ambiguous sequences. Moreover, beginner players often exhibit multiple simultaneous errors, complicating label assignment. Multimodal LLMs also remain limited in capturing complex biomechanical patterns such as kinetic chains.

Despite these challenges, the model produces coherent predictions and captures meaningful error patterns. Performance would likely improve with a larger, higher-quality dataset, enabling strategies such as multi-head attention for *Ready position* detection or backbone fine-tuning for lower-body features.

Future work includes training on the Ego-Exo4D dataset [3], which provides skeleton data with expert annotations, and integrating an LLM to convert predictions into precise, actionable feedback. This reasoning layer could approximate real coaching more effectively than approaches relying solely on raw video prompting.

A Appendices

A.1 Pose Estimation

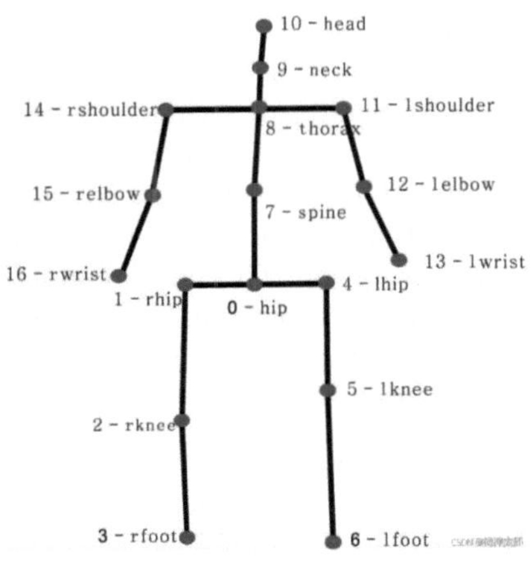

Fig. 2. Human3.6M format of skeleton.

Ex. 1, fr. 1 Ex. 1, fr. 9 Ex. 2, fr. 1 Ex. 1, fr. 3

Fig. 3. Two examples of hallucinations produced by the HybrIK pose estimator caused by poor clip framing. To remove these undesirable frames, a heuristic was implemented to start each clip five frames before the first shot of the closest player. If the first event occurs within the first five frames of the clip, the sequence instead begins exactly one frame earlier. The same rule is applied symmetrically to the end of the clip. This heuristic does not introduce bias into the model, as the starting time of each clip during training is randomly selected and supplemented with padding when necessary.

A.2 Error Semi-Automated Annotation

Table 7. Both LLM and tennis coach identify a lack of unit turn and a late preparation. The video was finally labeled as *Unit turn* with a joint failure at the *Shoulders* level.

Error	Unit turn
Joint	Shoulder
AI Analysis	The most significant technical issue is a consistent delay in preparation. Across all analyzed sequences, the unit turn is initiated far too late; in frame 7, the ball is already mid-flight while the player is still facing forward with no shoulder rotation. This late preparation prevents the player from using the kinetic chain effectively, resulting in a rushed strike where the body lacks a solid anchor at contact, often leading to 'tip-toeing' or jumping during the hit.
Coach Analysis	Late preparation and insufficient unit turn caused by insufficient usage of non-dominant arm to prepare the swing.

A.3 Datasets Statistics

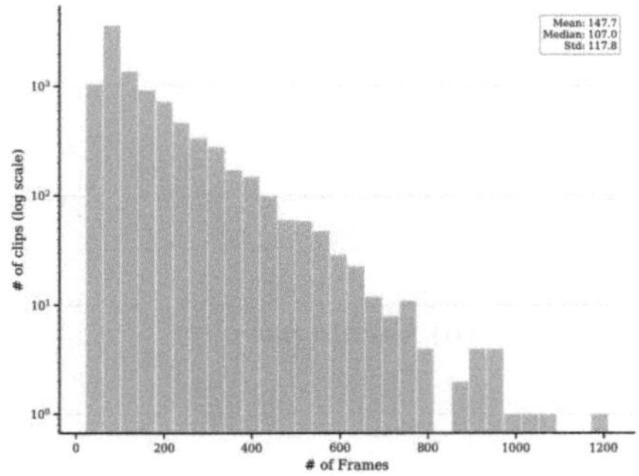

(a) Clip lengths

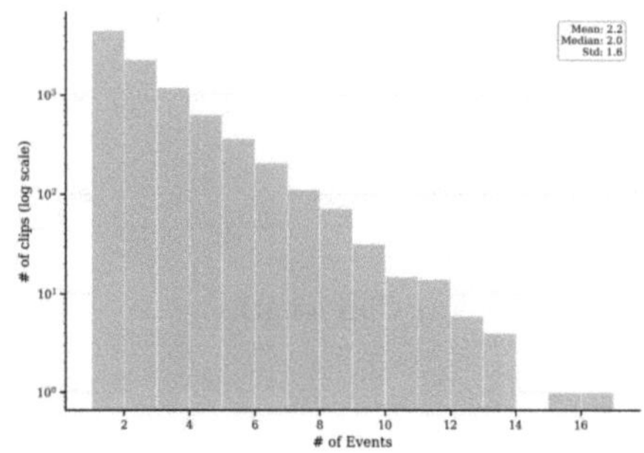

(b) Events per clip

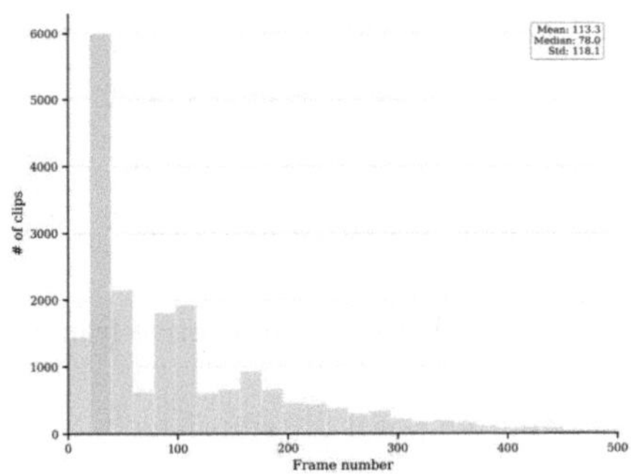

(c) Frames with a shot

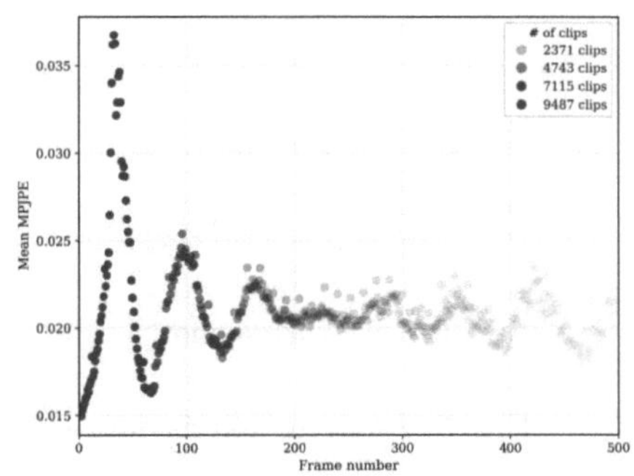

(d) MPJPE between consecutive frames

Fig. 4. Professional tennis dataset and temporal distributions.

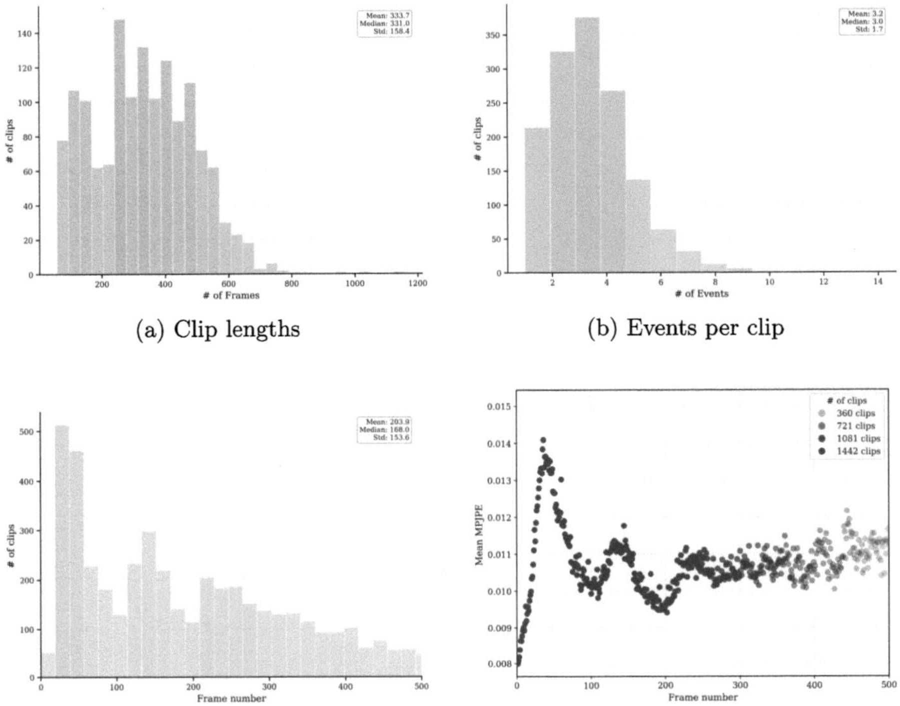

(a) Clip lengths (b) Events per clip

(c) Frames with a shot (d) MPJPE between consecutive frames

Fig. 5. Amateur tennis dataset statistics and temporal distributions.

A.4 System and User Prompts

User Prompt

Analyze the tennis technique shown in this video.

Video Context
Title: `post_title`

Uploaded Frames
I have uploaded `N` individual frames showing key moments:
`frame 1`
...
`frame N`
The frames show: preparation (-9, -6, -3), contact point (0), and follow-through (+3, +6).

Analysis Instructions
Identify only the most significant technical error that is **consistently present across ALL shots** shown in the frames. Do not report errors that appear in only one shot - focus only on systematic errors.

System Prompt

Role
Analyze the technique of a tennis player. Act as a certified Tennis coach. Provide a technical performance audit, identifying main areas of improvement.

Error Definitions

1. Ready position
Success Criteria: Effective use of light contacts for movement and heavy anchor for hitting.
Manifestation of Errors:
- **Forehand:** Non Dominant Arm role hindering unit turn - Chronology: Orientation of racket, shoulder turn, feet motion not respected.
- **Backhand:** Late preparation, Backswing too high, first step forward placing the player too close to the ball.
- **Serve:** Check if the player follows this chronology: Toss and then bent knees and not bending during toss resulting in a loss of platform. Body needs to be balanced, with player standing tall, front foot fixed during the toss. *Errors to identify:* Moving Hips during toss, Bending knees during toss, Moving front foot
- **General:** Right before contact and at contact time one foot (at least) must be well anchored (flat and long). *Errors to identify:* No foot has a strong anchor, player jumping, tip toeing at contact.

2. Unit turn
Success Criteria: A synchronized unit turn where the non-dominant arm is key for the rotation.
Manifestation of Errors:
- **Forehand:** Check if player's non dominant arm hold the racket properly and follow the unit turn move at the beginning of unit turn. *Error to identify:* The non dominant arm does not participate into the unit turn, ie is not holding the racket when the movement is initiated. Check if player's non dominant arm is stable during the player motion. *Error to identify:* During the player motion toward the ball the non dominant arm is shaking upwards/downwards or left and right. Check if a non-dominant arm is dropping or shaking or rotating heavily, or coming back to players belly at contact point. It should be stable and slowly rotate to allow racket follow-through and upper body turn. *Errors to identify:* Non dominant arm is dropping at contact, is shaking at contact, is turning fast at contact, is coming back to the player's belly
- **Backhand:** Check the timing of preparation and level of preparation. *Errors to identify:* Player prepare too late, Player prepare to high, Player does not turn the shoulders enough
- **Serve:** *Errors to identify:* Non-dominant arm up during trophee position, Height of the contact point

3. General Balance
Success Criteria: Stability throughout the rotation.
Manifestation of Errors:
- **Forehand/Backhand:** "Falling backward" or lateral leaning, often caused by the hips failing to provide a stable "anchor" into the ground.
- **Serve:** check position and movement of the elbow which should act as throwing articulation. *Error to identify:* Elbow too high during trophy position, Racket/wrist speed during the strike. Does the racket accelerate continuously until contact

4. Strike
Success Criteria: Full extension through the contact zone with a shot-specific wrist state.
Manifestation of Errors:
- **Groundstrokes:** Excessive wrist flicking, where a steady wrist is required for stability. Racket head to finish above contact.
- **Serve:** Hips or shoulder collapse, contact point height.

A.5 Joint and Errors Occurrences in Amateur Tennis Dataset

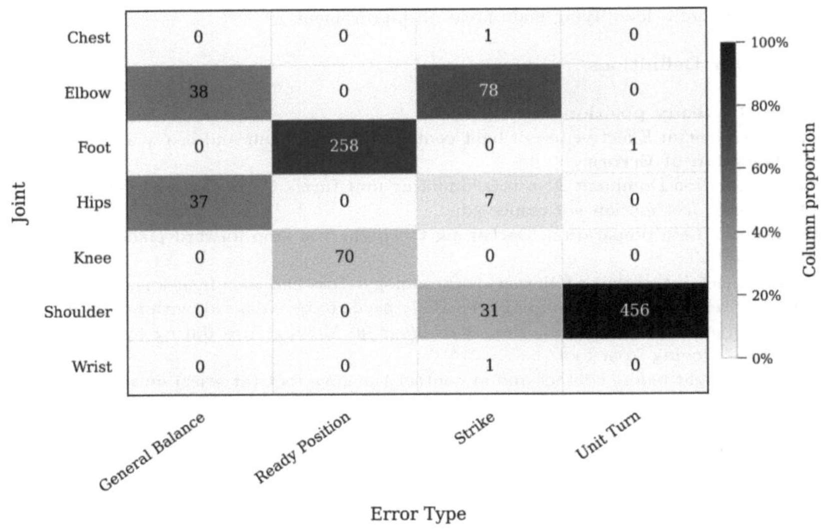

Fig. 6. Correlations for the Amateur tennis dataset with technical error labels.

A.6 Model Performance by Class

Table 8. Details of Baseline model performances

Model	Professional			Amateur*		
	F1	Prec.	Rec.	F1	Prec.	Rec.
Forehand	0.917	0.866	0.974	0.824	0.758	0.901
Backhand	0.906	0.840	0.985	0.793	0.719	0.884
Serve	0.986	0.976	0.996	0.822	0.892	0.762
Groundstroke	0.986	0.992	0.980	0.832	0.997	0.715
Slice	0.839	0.847	0.831	0.281	0.284	0.278
Volley	0.276	0.571	0.182	0.048	0.029	0.143
Lob	0.991	1.000	0.981	1.000	1.000	0.999
Drop	0.200	0.667	0.118	0.037	0.025	0.071
Smash	0.000	0.000	0.000	0.000	0.000	0.000

* Indicates that shot technique annotation is uncertain for the amateur dataset. Fine-tuned model is evaluated on a smaller subset of amateur videos with limited occurrences.

Table 9. Details of Fine-tuned model performances

Model	Professional			Amateur*		
	F1	Prec.	Rec.	F1	Prec.	Rec.
Forehand	0.861	0.777	0.966	0.847	0.753	0.967
Backhand	0.876	0.806	0.958	0.831	0.738	0.951
Serve	0.928	0.871	0.992	0.896	0.818	0.991
Groundstroke	0.979	0.982	0.977	0.972	0.994	0.952
Slice	0.558	0.906	0.403	0.320	0.571	0.222
Volley	0.000	0.000	0.000	0.000	0.000	0.000
Lob	0.993	1.000	0.986	0.994	1.000	0.988
Drop	0.000	0.000	0.000	0.000	0.000	0.000
Smash	0.000	0.000	0.000	0.000	0.000	0.000

Table 10. Comparison between predicted (baseline model) and ground-truth events (289 frames). Novak Djokovic vs. Rafael Nadal (Roland Garros Semi-Final 2013). This rally illustrates the model's tendency to over-predict, evidenced by the false positive at frames 185–186. The frames show that the player's arm movement during recovery mimics a hitting motion, leading to a misclassification when relying only on skeletal data. Notably, all ground-truth events were accurately localized within the $\delta \pm 1$ frame tolerance.

Frame 40

Frame 101

Frame 171

Frame 186

Frame 248

Real Event	Pred. Event	Real Frame	Pred. Frame Range
fh - gs	fh - gs	40	[39–40]
fh - gs	fh - gs	101	[100–102]
bh - slice	bh - slice	171	[169–172]
-	**fh - gs**	-	[185–186]
bh - gs	bh - gs	248	[248–249]

A.7 Shot Detection Example

A.8 Error Detection Examples

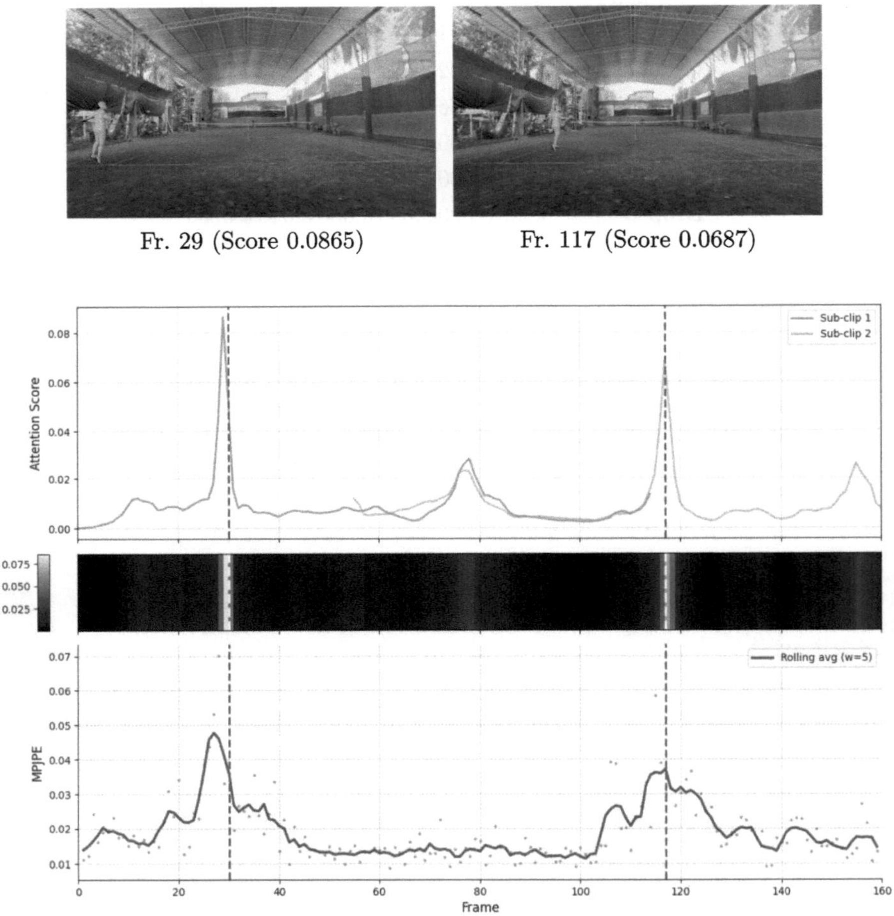

Fig. 7. The ground truth is [*Foot*, *Ready position*], while the prediction is [*Hips*, *Ready position*]. The images show that the player lacks a stable ground anchor during the stroke, a flaw identified by the LLM-generated feedback. The small jump of the player, visible in the frames, also acts as a motion cue for the LLM. However, accurately identifying errors related to the *Foot* is challenging because the skeleton representation provides only joint positions (knees and feet) without detailed information about foot orientation. As a result, the model lacks sufficient information to detect errors such as tip-toeing. A similar limitation affects the detection of errors involving the *Wrist*.

Fr. 34 (Score 0.0483) Fr. 142 (Score 0.0362) Fr. 241 (Score 0.0390)

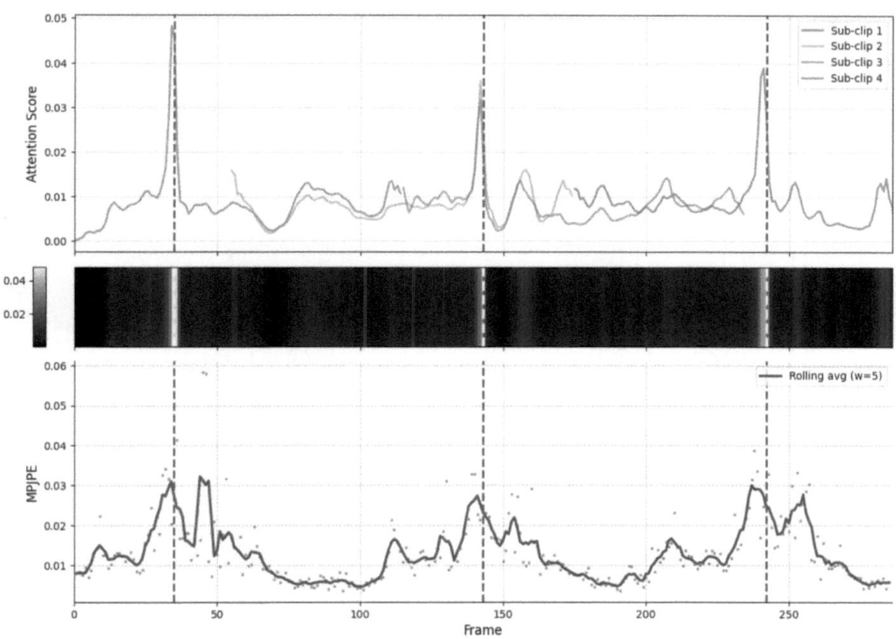

Fig. 8. Attention weights assigned to all frames in a clip. Different colors correspond to distinct sub-clips, each of 120 frames. Red lines indicate the moment the player hits the ball. The three displayed frames are those with the highest attention scores. The bottom plot shows the MPJPE between consecutive frames, revealing a correlation between motion magnitude and attention score. Frames preceding the shot generally receive higher attention than those following it, with the peak attention occurring 1–3 frames before the stroke. The ground truth is [*Shoulder* (Color figure online), *Unit turn*], and the prediction is correct for both. This indicates that the player does not rotate enough through the shot or fails to properly engage the non-dominant arm.

A.9 CTR-GCN Learned Topologies

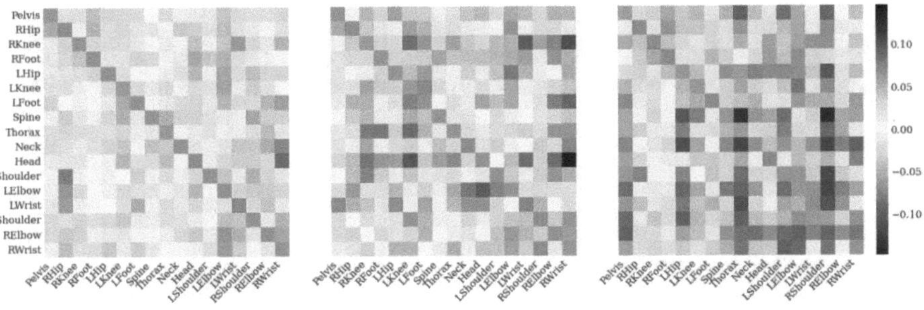

(a) Shared topology and two refined topologies

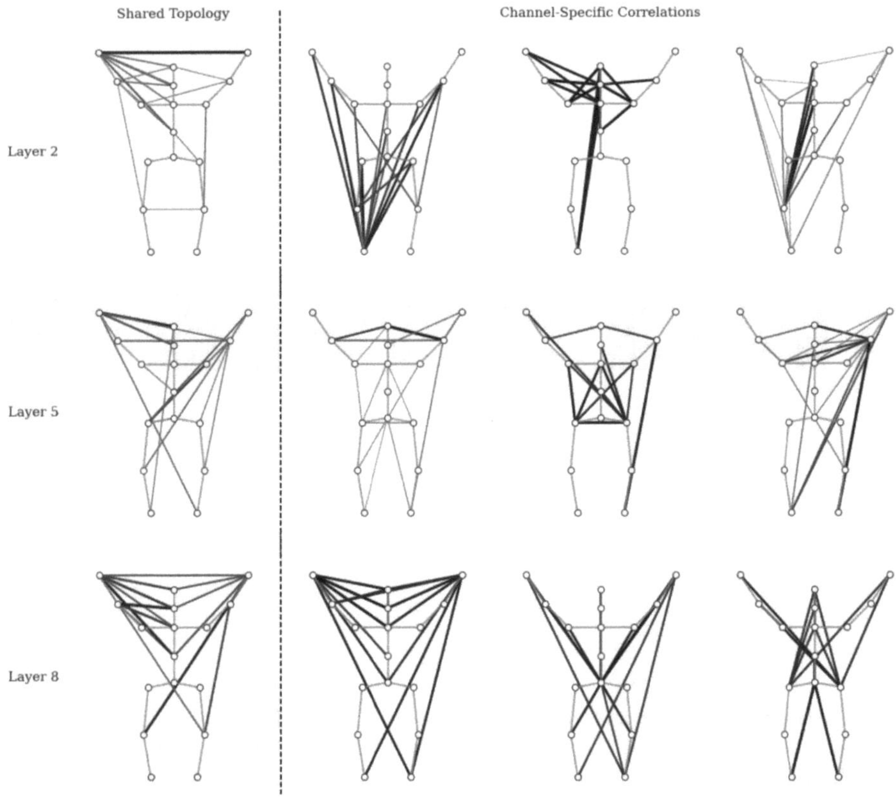

(b) Shared topology and illustrative channel-specific correlations for layers 2, 5, 8

Fig. 9. CTR-GCN's learned Topologies.

A.10 Ethical Considerations

The amateur dataset is constructed from publicly available videos sourced from Reddit, specifically from a subreddit where tennis amateurs and coaches ask for and give advice.

The videos are recorded and voluntarily shared by the authors of the posts. To comply with Reddit's Terms of Service, we provide only video URLs and do not store or distribute local copies unless permitted by Creative Commons or similar licenses. No personally identifiable information is collected or inferred.

Annotations focus exclusively on event-based information. The dataset is intended strictly for academic research, and users are required to ensure ethical compliance in their applications.

References

1. Chen, Y., et al.: Channel-wise topology refinement graph convolution for skeleton-based action recognition. https://doi.org/10.48550/ARXIV.2107.12213, https://arxiv.org/abs/2107.12213. Accessed 19 Jan 2026
2. Chi, H.G., et al.: InfoGCN: representation learning for human skeleton-based action recognition. In: 2022 IEEE/CVF Conference on Computer Vision and Pattern Recognition (CVPR), pp. 20154–20164. IEEE (2022). https://doi.org/10.1109/CVPR52688.2022.01955, https://ieeexplore.ieee.org/document/9879266/. Accessed 19 Jan 2026
3. Grauman, K., et al.: Ego-exo4d: understanding skilled human activity from first- and third-person perspective (2023). https://doi.org/10.48550/ARXIV.2311.18259, https://arxiv.org/abs/2311.18259. Accessed 19 Jan 2026
4. Lee, J., et al.: Hierarchically decomposed graph convolutional networks for skeleton-based action recognition (2022). https://doi.org/10.48550/ARXIV.2208.10741, https://arxiv.org/abs/2208.10741. Accessed 19 Jan 2026
5. Li, Z., et al.: ZARA: zero-shot motion time-series analysis via knowledge and retrieval driven LLM agents (2025). https://doi.org/10.48550/ARXIV.2508.04038, https://arxiv.org/abs/2508.04038. Accessed 19 Jan 2026
6. Liu, H., et al.: Revealing key details to see differences: a novel prototypical perspective for skeleton-based action recognition (2025). https://doi.org/10.48550/ARXIV.2411.18941, https://arxiv.org/abs/2411.18941. Accessed 22 Jan 2026
7. Liu, Z., et al.: F\$^3\$set: towards analyzing fast, frequent, and fine-grained events from videos (2025). https://doi.org/10.48550/ARXIV.2504.08222, https://arxiv.org/abs/2504.08222. Accessed 19 Jan 2026
8. Liu, Z., et al.: Few-shot precise event spotting via unified multi-entity graph and distillation (2025). https://doi.org/10.48550/ARXIV.2511.14186, https://arxiv.org/abs/2511.14186. Accessed 19 Jan 2026
9. Ma, J.: T3set: table tennis training multimodal dataset (2025). https://doi.org/10.5281/ZENODO.15516143, https://zenodo.org/doi/10.5281/zenodo.15516143. Accessed 19 Jan 2026
10. Ma, W., et al.: Table tennis coaching system based on a multimodal large language model with a table tennis knowledge base. In: PLOS ONE 20.2 (Feb. 13, 2025). Ed. by Peter Andreas Federolf, e0317839 (2025). https://doi.org/10.1371/journal.pone.0317839, https:/dx.plos.org/10.1371/journal.pone.0317839. ISSN: 1932-6203. Accessed 19 Jan 2026

11. Powroznik, P., et al.: Feature fusion graph consecutive-attention network for skeleton-based tennis action recognition. Appl. Sci. **15**(10), 532 (2025). https://doi.org/10.3390/app15105320, https://www.mdpi.com/2076-3417/15/10/5320. ISSN: 2076-3417. Accessed 19 Jan 2026
12. Shiraki, K., et al.: Spatial temporal attention graph convolutional networks with mechanics-stream for skeleton-based action recognition. In: Ishikawa, H., Liu, C.L., Pajdla, T., Shi, J. (eds.) Computer Vision – ACCV 2020, vol. 12626, pp. 341–357. Springer International Publishing (2021). https://doi.org/10.1007/978-3-030-69541-5_21, http://link.springer.com/10.1007/978-3-030-69541-5_21, ISBN: 9783030695408 9783030695415. Accessed 19 Jan 2026
13. Yan, S., et al.: Spatial temporal graph convolutional networks for skeleton-based action recognition (2018). https://doi.org/10.48550/ARXIV.1801.07455, https://arxiv.org/abs/1801.07455. Accessed 19 Jan 2026
14. Yu, Y.: Construction of tennis pose estimation and action recognition model based on improved ST-GCN. Molecular Cell. Biomech. **21**(4), 605 (2024). https://doi.org/10.62617/mcb605, https://ojs.sin-chn.com/index.php/mcb/article/view/605. ISSN: 1556-5300, 1556-5297. Accessed 19 Jan 2026
15. Zhu, Y., et al.: H3wb: Human3.6m 3d WholeBody dataset and benchmark (2022). https://doi.org/10.48550/ARXIV.2211.15692, https://arxiv.org/abs/2211.15692. Accessed 27 Jan 2026

Predicting the NBA Finals Most Valuable Player: Using a Dual Approach for Small Datasets

Tung Wai Chen[1](✉) and Michael Johnson[2]

[1] University of British Columbia, Vancouver, BC, Canada
tchen67@student.ubc.ca
[2] Beedie School of Business, Simon Fraser University, Vancouver, BC, Canada
michael_johnson@sfu.ca

Abstract. This paper examines NBA Finals Most Valuable Player (FMVP) prediction using a dual framework that combines backward stepwise logistic regression with a cross-validated machine learning pipeline. The analysis uses Finals statistics from championship-team players across the 2005–06 to 2024–25 seasons ($N = 237$; 20 FMVP winners, 217 non-winners), yielding a small and class-imbalanced prediction setting. In the logistic framework, Points Per Game (PTS) and Defensive Rating (DRtg) emerge as key predictors, and the final parsimonious specification achieves 90% retrodictive accuracy. Across machine learning models, Random Forest performs best, reaching 95% per-year accuracy and correctly identifying 19 of 20 historical winners. SHAP (SHapley Additive exPlanations) analysis complements global importance rankings by clarifying model-specific local contributions, confirming the central role of scoring while highlighting the additional influence of efficiency- and defense-related signals in difficult cases. Overall, the results show that a combined inference-plus-prediction strategy can deliver both interpretability and strong performance in small-sample sports analytics.

Keywords: Sports Analytics · NBA · Machine Learning · Logistic Regression · Random Forest · Small-sample Prediction · Ensemble Methods

1 Introduction

The NBA Finals Most Valuable Player (FMVP) award is voted by a panel of 11 media members and recognizes the most impactful player in the NBA Finals. Since its introduction in 1969, the FMVP has typically been awarded to the highest scorer on the championship team. However, notable exceptions (e.g., Andre Iguodala in 2015) imply multifaceted criteria in the selection process. Although FMVP voting is subjective, the decision is largely grounded in observable player statistics such as points, efficiency, and defense. Understanding the statistical drivers of FMVP selection is relevant to teams, analysts, and betting markets, and offers a rich case study for predictive modeling with limited sample sizes.

Z. Liu and V. Misra (Eds.): ISACE 2026, LNCS 16610, pp. 377–391, 2026.
https://doi.org/10.1007/978-3-032-27272-0_24

This study investigates the relationship between Finals-series statistics and the probability of winning the FMVP award from the 2005–06 through 2024–25 seasons. The selected timeframe focuses on the "Modern NBA Era": a period characterized by the 3-point revolution and analytics-driven evaluation [1]. Kilcoyne [2] documents a significant decline in mid-range jump-shot attempts beginning in the 2005–06 season. Limiting the dataset to this period reduces confounding effects from earlier eras with different gameplay dynamics and improves the comparability of players' statistics across seasons.

A primary contribution of this paper is the development and empirical evaluation of a dual framework that pairs backward stepwise logistic regression with a cross-validated machine learning pipeline, addressing the challenges of predictive modeling with small, imbalanced datasets—a frequent limitation in sports analytics. Parametric models alone suffer from multicollinearity and limited degrees of freedom, while complex machine learning models risk overfitting; our dual approach leverages the complementary strengths of both paradigms.

Applied to FMVP prediction using box-score and efficiency statistics ($N = 237$; 20 winners vs. 217 non-winners), the framework reveals that: (1) Points Per Game (PTS) and Defensive Rating (DRtg) are the dominant statistical drivers of FMVP selection; (2) Random Forest achieves the highest per-year retrodictive accuracy (95%), correctly identifying 19 of 20 historical winners; (3) SHAP analysis provides post-hoc interpretability, confirming the centrality of scoring while revealing that both the Random Forest and Neural Network converge on an "efficiency-defense" archetype that emphasizes two-way dominance over raw offensive volume; and (4) the substantially imbalanced class distribution presents a realistic prediction task that tests model discrimination under real-world conditions.

2 Literature Review

Existing research on basketball award prediction has concentrated primarily on regular-season Most Valuable Player (MVP) awards rather than Finals MVP (FMVP). For example, Tummala [3] used random forest models and highlighted win shares as an important predictor, while Li and Jia [4] applied gradient-boosting methods (CatBoost) and emphasized value-based and efficiency metrics.

A key challenge in FMVP prediction is the small-sample and context-dependent nature of a single playoff series, where defensive assignments and matchup effects influence voting. Basketball analytics research also notes that commonly reported statistics tend to capture offensive ability more reliably than defensive contributions [5]. Cervone et al. [6] proposed expected possession value (EPV) models using optical tracking data to better quantify within-possession impacts, while work on event prediction suggests outcomes influenced by public perception may benefit from incorporating text-derived signals such as media sentiment [7]. More broadly, panel-based awards can exhibit systematic voting bias [8]. This paper addresses a key literature gap by developing and evaluating a dual statistical machine learning framework tailored to FMVP prediction challenges, particularly the constraints imposed by small datasets.

Methodologically, this dual framing is motivated by a common trade-off in small-sample prediction problems: simple parametric models can remain stable and interpretable but may be misspecified, whereas flexible machine learning models can capture nonlinearities but are more prone to overfitting without careful internal validation. Prior work on prediction modeling emphasizes the importance of internal validation and shrinkage when sample size is limited [9].

3 Data Description

3.1 Dataset Construction

NBA Finals series data were collected from Basketball-Reference for the 2005–06 through 2024–25 seasons [10]. To capture the full range of player contributions and maximize the number of negative cases, the dataset includes all rostered players from the championship team in each season who recorded playing time, yielding 237 player-season observations. Among these, 20 observations are FMVP winners and 217 are non-winners, forming a substantially imbalanced binary classification problem (8.4% positive rate).

3.2 Dataset Variables

The variables were categorized into a set of explanatory (independent) variables and an outcome (dependent) variable (Table 1) .

Independent Variables The independent variables include box-score and advanced statistics:

Dependent Variable The dependent variable is a binary indicator,

$$FMVP_i = \begin{cases} 1, & \text{if player } i \text{ won the NBA Finals Most Valuable Player (FMVP)} \\ 0, & \text{otherwise.} \end{cases} \tag{1}$$

Table 2 reports summary statistics for selected variables. Differences between FMVP winners and non-winners are pronounced across scoring volume and offensive involvement: the mean PTS for FMVP winners was 27.79 compared to 7.24 for non-winners, and the mean USG% was 30.30% versus 17.61%. The mean GmSc (Game Score) for winners was 22.27 compared to 5.66 for non-winners, reflecting the comprehensive performance gap between award recipients and the rest of the roster.

Table 1. Independent variables and definitions

Abbrev.	Variable	Definition
Age	Age	Player age as of January 31 of the corresponding season.
MP	Minutes Played Per Game	Average minutes played per game in the Finals series.
PTS	Points Per Game	Average points scored per game in the Finals series.
AST	Assists Per Game	Average assists per game in the Finals series.
TRB	Total Rebounds Per Game	Average total rebounds per game in the Finals series.
STL	Steals Per Game	Average steals per game in the Finals series.
BLK	Blocks Per Game	Average blocks per game in the Finals series.
TS%	True Shooting Percentage	Shooting-efficiency measure accounting for field goals and free throws.
TOV%	Turnover Percentage	Estimated turnovers committed per 100 plays.
USG%	Usage Percentage	Estimated proportion of team plays used by a player while on court.
ORtg	Offensive Rating	Estimated points produced per 100 possessions.
DRtg	Defensive Rating	Estimated points allowed per 100 possessions.
GmSc	Game Score	PTS + 0.4×FG - 0.7×FGA - 0.4×(FTA-FT) + 0.7×ORB + 0.3×DRB + STL + 0.7×AST + 0.7×BLK - 0.4×PF - TOV.

Table 2. Summary statistics for FMVP winners versus non-winners

Variable	FMVP Winners ($N = 20$)		Non-Winners ($N = 217$)	
	Mean	Median	Mean	Median
PTS	27.79	28.70	7.24	5.60
USG%	30.30	30.80	17.61	16.90
GmSc	22.27	23.00	5.66	4.40
MP	40.02	40.05	19.44	17.20
DRtg	104.60	105.00	107.8	108.00

4 Traditional Approach: Backward Stepwise Logistic Regression

4.1 Initial Model and Multicollinearity

The traditional modeling approach begins with a full logistic regression that includes all 13 independent variables. Variance inflation factors (VIFs) reveal substantial multicollinearity, particularly among scoring and efficiency metrics such as PTS, TS%, USG%, and ORtg. Several VIFs exceed commonly used thresholds (e.g., VIF > 10), indicating unstable coefficient estimates and limiting the interpretability of individual effect sizes. This multicollinearity is also evident in the pairwise Pearson correlation matrix reported in Table 3, where strong correlations are observed among key offensive variables—most notably between PTS and GmSc ($r = 0.972$), and TS% and ORtg ($r = 0.908$). These patterns confirm that the elevated VIFs reflect genuine redundancy in the predictor space rather than sampling noise.

Table 3. Correlation matrix of predictors (Pearson correlations)

	Age	MP	PTS	TRB	AST	STL	BLK	TS%	TOV%	USG%	ORtg	DRtg	GmSc
Age	1.000	0.041	-0.039	-0.001	0.050	0.009	-0.002	-0.021	0.229	-0.104	-0.066	-0.102	-0.026
MP	0.041	1.000	0.847	0.800	0.730	0.771	0.523	0.118	0.021	0.223	0.159	-0.095	0.838
PTS	-0.039	0.847	1.000	0.741	0.758	0.697	0.528	0.181	-0.057	0.531	0.206	-0.089	0.972
TRB	-0.001	0.800	0.741	1.000	0.609	0.574	0.661	0.096	0.051	0.276	0.157	-0.208	0.802
AST	0.050	0.730	0.758	0.609	1.000	0.671	0.377	0.047	0.105	0.370	0.115	-0.052	0.798
STL	0.009	0.771	0.697	0.574	0.671	1.000	0.421	0.089	0.058	0.243	0.115	-0.190	0.710
BLK	-0.002	0.523	0.528	0.661	0.377	0.421	1.000	0.124	0.038	0.181	0.149	-0.223	0.607
TS%	-0.021	0.118	0.181	0.096	0.047	0.089	0.124	1.000	-0.027	-0.054	0.908	0.086	0.234
TOV%	0.229	0.021	-0.057	0.051	0.105	0.058	0.038	-0.027	1.000	-0.068	-0.204	-0.147	-0.052
USG%	-0.104	0.223	0.531	0.276	0.370	0.243	0.181	-0.054	-0.068	1.000	-0.050	-0.210	0.461
ORtg	-0.066	0.159	0.206	0.157	0.115	0.115	0.149	0.908	-0.204	-0.050	1.000	0.094	0.277
DRtg	-0.102	-0.095	-0.089	-0.208	-0.052	-0.190	-0.223	0.086	-0.147	-0.210	0.094	1.000	-0.105
GmSc	-0.026	0.838	0.972	0.802	0.798	0.710	0.607	0.234	-0.052	0.461	0.277	-0.105	1.000

In the full model, no predictor attains statistical significance at conventional levels, largely due to multicollinearity and the limited sample size. This motivates a systematic variable reduction procedure aimed at achieving a more parsimonious and stable specification.

4.2 Backward Stepwise Selection

Backward stepwise selection is applied starting from the full model, iteratively removing the predictor with the highest p-value. Over 11 iterations, highly collinear and statistically weak variables are dropped in the following order: GmSc (p = 0.967), Age (p = 0.891), USG% (p = 0.857), STL (p = 0.778), TRB (p = 0.651), AST (p = 0.614), ORtg (p = 0.677), TOV% (p = 0.608), MP (p = 0.500), BLK (p = 0.555), and TS% (p = 0.128).

The procedure converges to a final model retaining only PTS and DRtg as statistically significant predictors at the 5% level. In this specification, multicollinearity is substantially reduced, and both coefficients have intuitive signs: higher scoring and better (lower) defensive rating are associated with a greater probability of winning FMVP (Table 4).

4.3 Final Model Specification

The estimated logistic regression equation for the final model is:

$$\ln\left(\frac{P(FMVP=1)}{1-P(FMVP=1)}\right) = \beta_0 + \beta_1\, PTS + \beta_2\, DRtg + \epsilon. \tag{2}$$

The estimated odds ratio for PTS is $e^{0.424} \approx 1.528$, suggesting that one additional point in Points Per Game increases the odds of winning FMVP by approximately 52.8%, holding DRtg constant. The estimated odds ratio for DRtg is $e^{-0.191} \approx 0.826$, indicating that a one-point increase in DRtg (i.e., allowing

Table 4. Final model coefficient estimates

Predictor	Coefficient	Std. Error	z-value	p-value
PTS	0.424	0.095	4.477	< 0.001
DRtg	-0.191	0.085	-2.250	0.0245
Constant	9.732	7.938	1.226	0.2202

the opponent to score one more point per 100 possessions) reduces the odds of winning FMVP by 17.4%, holding PTS constant.

4.4 Model Performance and Retrodiction

The model exhibited strong discrimination (AUC $= 0.987$ and McFadden $R^2 = 0.728$). In each season, we predicted the FMVP as the player with the highest estimated probability. Under this rule, the model correctly identified the FMVP winner in 18 of 20 seasons (Table 5).

Table 5. Retrospective FMVP predictions by season (2006–2025)

Year	Actual Winner	Predicted Winner	Pred. Prob.	Correct
2006	Dwyane Wade	Dwyane Wade	0.997	TRUE
2007	Tony Parker	Tony Parker	0.730	TRUE
2008	Paul Pierce	Paul Pierce	0.214	TRUE
2009	Kobe Bryant	Kobe Bryant	0.987	TRUE
2010	Kobe Bryant	Kobe Bryant	0.949	TRUE
2011	Dirk Nowitzki	Dirk Nowitzki	0.662	TRUE
2012	LeBron James	LeBron James	0.733	TRUE
2013	LeBron James	LeBron James	0.593	TRUE
2014	Kawhi Leonard	Kawhi Leonard	0.115	TRUE
2015	Andre Iguodala	Stephen Curry	0.776	FALSE
2016	LeBron James	LeBron James	0.953	TRUE
2017	Kevin Durant	Kevin Durant	0.945	TRUE
2018	Kevin Durant	Kevin Durant	0.886	TRUE
2019	Kawhi Leonard	Kawhi Leonard	0.794	TRUE
2020	LeBron James	LeBron James	0.790	TRUE
2021	Giannis Antetokounmpo	Giannis Antetokounmpo	0.968	TRUE
2022	Stephen Curry	Stephen Curry	0.936	TRUE
2023	Nikola Jokić	Nikola Jokić	0.954	TRUE
2024	Jaylen Brown	Jayson Tatum	0.211	FALSE
2025	Shai Gilgeous-Alexander	Shai Gilgeous-Alexander	0.872	TRUE

Misclassifications occur in 2015 (Andre Iguodala vs. Stephen Curry) and 2024 (Jaylen Brown vs. Jayson Tatum). Although the final model achieved strong predictive power, the misclassifications in 2015 and 2024 highlight the limitations of using purely statistical summaries to predict a subjectively voted award.

2015 (Actual Winner: Andre Iguodala; Predicted Winner: Stephen Curry). The model predicted that Stephen Curry had 77.6% chance of being named FMVP while Andre Iguodala won the award in 2015. He was awarded FMVP primarily for his matchup against LeBron James, a contextual factor that Defensive Rating (DRtg) cannot fully capture. The voters valued the narrative of"stopping the best player" over Curry's offensive impact.

2024 (Actual Winner: Jaylen Brown; Predicted Winner: Jayson Tatum). Jayson Tatum had the highest probability of 21.1% winning the FMVP. However, the 2024 FMVP trophy went to Jaylen Brown. This suggests that the model struggles to differentiate in cases where two teammates have very similar stats, and voters may rely on intangibles, efficiency consistency, or "clutch" moments that are not accounted for in players' stats.

5 Machine Learning Pipeline

5.1 Preprocessing and Validation Strategy

To complement the traditional analysis, a machine learning pipeline is constructed using the same FMVP dataset. The data are restricted to the FMVP indicator and the 13 numeric predictors. The FMVP outcome is treated as a binary factor with "0" (non-winner) and "1" (winner). A preprocessing recipe is applied that (i) removes zero-variance predictors and (ii) normalizes all numeric predictors via centering and scaling, ensuring that models sensitive to feature scales are treated fairly.

Model evaluation relies on a 5-repeat, 5-fold stratified cross-validation strategy (25 total resamples). Due to the extreme sparsity of the target class (20 FMVP winners among 237 observations), this design was prioritized over higher k-fold counts or a single held-out test set. The stratified folds maintain a sufficient number of positive instances in each validation slice to ensure metric stability, while the 25 iterations reduce the variance of performance estimates and yield robust 95% confidence intervals.

5.2 Models Considered

Within this standardized framework, four classification models are specified:

- **Logistic regression**: baseline generalized linear model.
- **Random forest**: ensemble of decision trees.
- **XGBoost**: gradient-boosted decision trees.
- **Multilayer perceptron**: feed-forward neural network classifier.

For logistic regression, we fit a standard binomial model without extensive hyperparameter tuning. For the more flexible models, key hyperparameters are tuned, including the number of trees, maximum tree depth, learning rate, minimum node size, subsampling proportions, number of hidden units, regularization penalties, and training epochs.

5.3 Hyperparameter Tuning and Metrics

Hyperparameter tuning is performed using grid-based and Latin hypercube designs over plausible ranges, evaluated via the cross-validation strategy described in Sect. 5.1. A unified metric set provides a multi-faceted view of performance: ROC AUC captures overall ranking ability, balanced accuracy reflects minority-class sensitivity under severe class imbalance, and Brier score together with log loss evaluates probability calibration, helping distinguish well-calibrated models from those that are accurate but overconfident.

5.4 Cross-Validation Results

The results of the cross-validation evaluation are summarized in Table 6. The Neural Network achieves the highest Balanced Accuracy (0.864) and ROC AUC (0.988), while the Random Forest follows closely (Balanced Accuracy: 0.858; ROC AUC: 0.984) and achieves the best calibration with the lowest Brier score (0.031) and Log Loss (0.106). XGBoost's degenerate Balanced Accuracy of 0.500 indicates that the model predicts all observations as the majority class in some folds—a known risk when the positive rate is below 10%.

Although the Neural Network achieved the highest ROC AUC (0.988), its higher Log Loss (0.356) suggests weaker probability calibration, whereas the Random Forest's Log Loss of 0.106 indicates more reliable probability estimates. Probability calibration matters in this context because a model can rank candidates well (high ROC AUC) while still producing unreliable probability estimates. The robust cross-validation performance of both the Random Forest and Neural Network (mean ROC AUC > 0.98) indicates a narrow generalization gap, suggesting that high training accuracy reflects the models' capacity to capture complex, non-linear feature interactions rather than a failure to generalize due to over-parameterization. Random Forest was selected as the primary model because it offered the best balance of predictive performance, cross-validation stability, and post-hoc interpretability (via SHAP).

5.5 Per-Year Retrodictive Comparison

To complement aggregate cross-validation metrics with a season-level view, each model is trained on the full dataset and used to predict the FMVP in each season by selecting the player with the highest predicted probability. Table 7 summarizes per-model per-year accuracy. Random Forest performs best (95%), correctly identifying 19 of 20 historical winners (missing only 2024). Logistic

Table 6. Comparative model performance metrics (mean ± SE with 95% CI). *Best in column.

Model	Bal.Acc. [95% CI] (SE)	ROC AUC [95% CI] (SE)	Accuracy [95% CI] (SE)	Brier [95% CI] (SE)	Log Loss [95% CI] (SE)
Random Forest	0.858 [.805, .911] (.026)	0.984 [.976, .993] (.004)	**0.964*** [.951, .977] (.006)	**0.031*** [.023, .039] (.004)	**0.106*** [.081, .131] (.012)
Neural Net	**0.864*** [.811, .916] (.025)	**0.988*** [.981, .994] (.003)	0.963 [.951, .975] (.006)	0.092 [.088, .096] (.002)	0.356 [.348, .365] (.004)
XGBoost	0.500 [.500, .500] (.000)	0.984 [.976, .993] (.004)	0.931 [.917, .946] (.007)	0.065 [.051, .079] (.007)	0.260 [.197, .323] (.031)
Logistic Reg.	0.753 [.676, .829] (.037)	0.771 [.702, .839] (.033)	0.925 [.910, .940] (.007)	0.075 [.060, .089] (.007)	2.450 [1.96, 2.95] (.238)

Table 7. Per-year FMVP prediction accuracy by model.

Model	Correct	Accuracy	Missed Years
Random Forest	19 / 20	95.0%	2024
Logistic Regression	18 / 20	90.0%	2014, 2024
XGBoost	18 / 20	90.0%	2015, 2024
Neural Network	17 / 20	85.0%	2014, 2015, 2024

regression and XGBoost each achieve 90%, and the neural network achieves 85%.

All four models miss the 2024 FMVP (Jaylen Brown), instead selecting his teammate Jayson Tatum. In 2015 (Andre Iguodala), both Logistic Regression and Random Forest identify the winner correctly, while XGBoost and the Neural Network predict Stephen Curry.

5.6 Variable Importance and Interpretability

To bridge the predictive performance of the machine learning models with the interpretability of the stepwise logistic regression, variable importance measures are examined for the tree-based classifiers. Gain-based importance (XGBoost) and permutation-based importance (Random Forest) are computed across all 13 predictors and visualized side by side in Fig. 1.

Usage Percentage (USG%) estimates the proportion of team possessions a player concludes through field-goal attempts, free-throw attempts, or turnovers. In the context of FMVP voting, elevated USG% reflects offensive centrality, since the award is typically given to the player through whom a team channels its most consequential possessions. The prominence of USG% in both tree-based models, together with the distributional separation shown in Fig. 2, suggests that offensive workload captures information beyond raw scoring totals, particularly in seasons where multiple players post similar point averages but differ in play-ending responsibility.

This pattern also highlights a methodological trade-off between parametric and nonparametric approaches: in the logistic regression framework, substan-

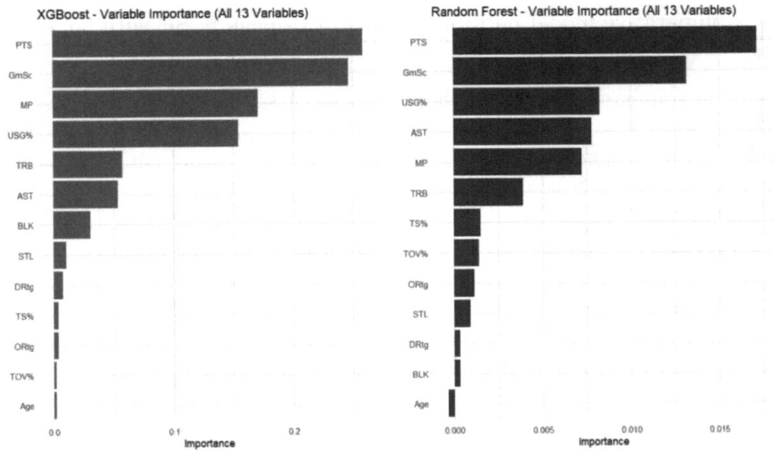

Fig. 1. Variable importance for XGBoost and Random Forest across all 13 predictors.

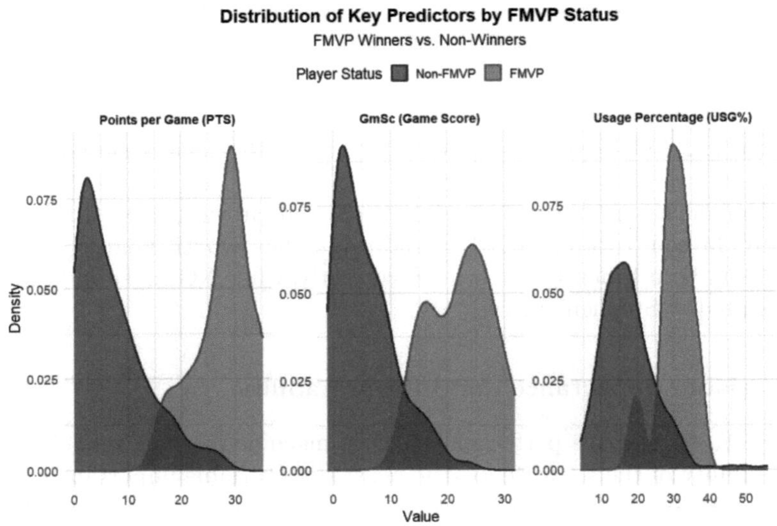

Fig. 2. Density distributions of PTS, GmSc, and USG% by FMVP outcome class.

tial multicollinearity among offensive metrics and the limited number of positive cases attenuate the coefficient estimate for USG%, rendering it statistically insignificant once correlated scoring and efficiency variables are included; by contrast, tree-based models flexibly accommodate nonlinearities and feature interactions, allowing USG% to emerge as a stable secondary predictor. Collectively, these results indicate that FMVP selection is driven primarily by scoring volume, with usage capturing an additional dimension of offensive influence and defensive impact contributing in a supporting role. To further decompose these feature contributions at the individual-prediction level, the following section applies SHAP analysis.

5.7 SHAP Explanations

To provide deeper post-hoc interpretability beyond aggregate importance scores, SHAP (SHapley Additive exPlanations) analysis was conducted for both the Random Forest and Neural Network models. SHAP values decompose each prediction into individual feature contributions, offering a principled, game-theoretic measure of how much each variable pushes the predicted probability toward or away from the FMVP class for each observation. While the variable importance plot in Fig. 1 reveals which features matter most globally, the SHAP beeswarm plots in Figs. 3 and 4 reveal how each feature's value directionally influences individual predictions.

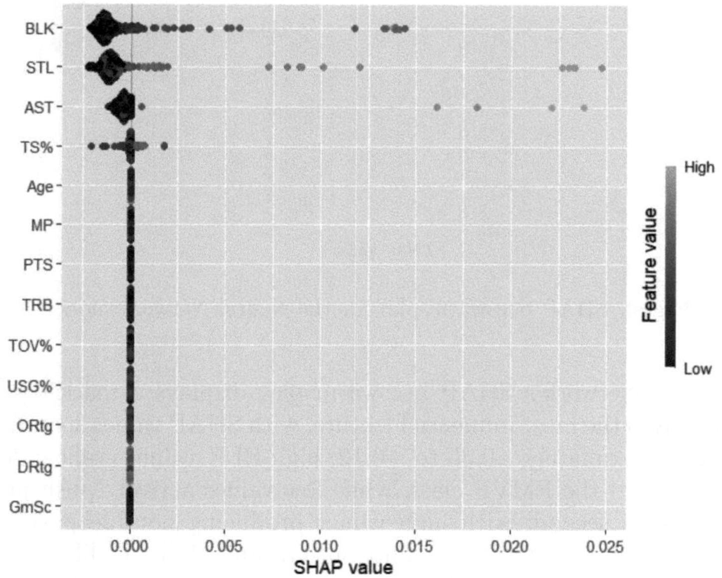

Fig. 3. SHAP beeswarm plot for the Random Forest model.

The Random Forest's SHAP beeswarm plot reveals that defensive stats (BLK, STL) and assists (AST) are the dominant contributors at the individual-prediction level, with shooting efficiency (TS%) playing a supporting role. High feature values (yellow dots) push SHAP values strongly positive for these variables, while the remaining predictors—including PTS, GmSc, DRtg, USG%, and ORtg—cluster almost entirely at zero, contributing negligibly to individual predictions. Notably, SHAP values are concentrated on the positive side, with most observations near zero and only a small number of outliers exhibiting large positive contributions. This one-sided pattern suggests that the Random Forest uses scoring volume as a coarse initial filter but relies on defensive and efficiency thresholds as binary gatekeepers: players who clear these thresholds receive a sharp boost in predicted FMVP probability, while those who do not remain indistinguishable from the majority class.

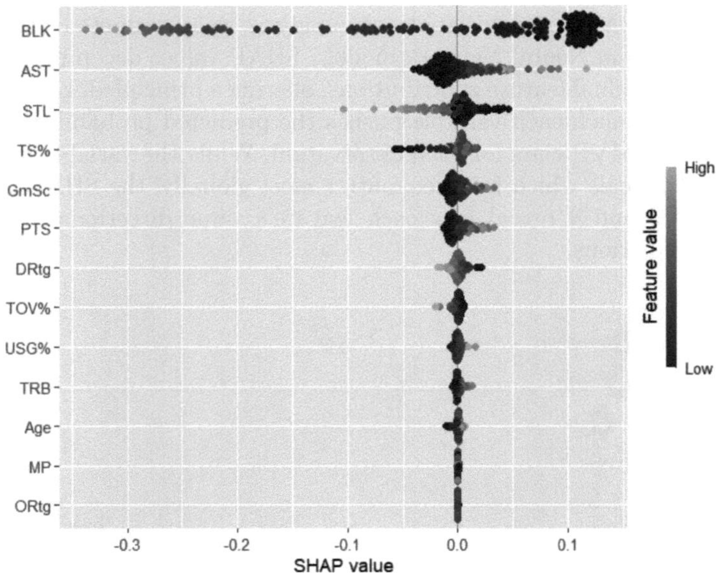

Fig. 4. SHAP beeswarm plot for the Neural Network model.

The Neural Network's SHAP beeswarm plot displays a markedly different structure. BLK is the most influential feature, with SHAP values spanning a wide range from approximately -0.35 to $+0.12$; high BLK values (yellow dots) push predictions toward the FMVP class, while low values actively push predictions away. AST ranks second, with high values producing notable positive SHAP contributions. STL and TS% also contribute meaningfully. Unlike the Random Forest, the Neural Network exhibits substantial negative SHAP values across multiple features, indicating that it actively penalizes players who lack defensive and playmaking credentials rather than simply ignoring them. PTS and GmSc, which dominate in the tree-based variable importance rankings, show modest SHAP contributions clustered near zero, suggesting that the network encodes scoring information indirectly through correlated features rather than relying on raw point totals.

Despite their architectural differences, both models converge on a consistent "efficiency-defense" archetype. Both demote raw scoring volume (PTS, GmSc) to a negligible role in the SHAP decomposition, instead emphasizing high-leverage defense (BLK, STL) and playmaking (AST). The key divergence lies in mechanism: the Random Forest employs a "stepped" gatekeeper logic, where defensive thresholds produce sharp, one-sided boosts for qualifying players, while the

Neural Network captures smoother, bidirectional effects that both reward defensive excellence and penalize its absence. That different architectures arrive at the same feature subspace—through distinct internal mechanisms—strengthens confidence that these patterns reflect genuine structure in FMVP voting rather than model-specific artifacts.

6 Integrated Results and Discussion

6.1 Complementary Insights

The dual approach yields complementary insights. The backward stepwise logistic regression offers a concise, interpretable model that explicitly quantifies how scoring and defensive rating affect the log-odds of winning FMVP. Its strong retrodictive performance demonstrates that much of the historical voting pattern can be captured with just two carefully selected predictors, once multicollinearity is addressed.

The machine learning pipeline, by contrast, emphasizes robustness and model comparison. It shows that more flexible algorithms such as random forests, gradient boosting, and neural networks do not necessarily outperform a well-specified logistic regression when the dataset is small and the predictors are relatively low-dimensional and structured. However, the pipeline is readily extensible to richer feature spaces (e.g., tracking data, play-by-play metrics, text features), where more complex models may have clearer advantages.

6.2 Narrative-Driven Misclassifications

As discussed in Sect. 4.4, the 2015 and 2024 misclassifications persist across both the logistic and machine learning frameworks, confirming that these errors stem from unobserved narrative and contextual factors rather than model-specific weaknesses. Such cases suggest that additional features—such as player-tracking metrics, lineup-level impact measures, or media sentiment indicators—may be required for consistently accurate prediction of subjectively voted awards.

6.3 Methodological Lessons

This study demonstrates that in small samples with highly correlated predictors, careful variable selection remains essential for interpretable parametric models, while a standardized machine learning workflow with cross-validation and multiple evaluation metrics provides a robust benchmark for assessing whether additional model complexity is warranted. For subjectively voted awards, even strong statistical models are limited by unobserved contextual and narrative factors, reinforcing the value of integrating non-box-score data sources.

7 Limitations and Future Work

A key limitation of this study is the small number of positive outcomes: there is only one FMVP winner per season. This constrains the complexity of models that can be reliably estimated and increases the risk of overfitting, a concern that is widely discussed in small-sample prediction settings and internal validation for logistic models [5,9]. The reliance on aggregate series-level statistics also omits possession-level dynamics, matchup details, and high-leverage situational performance. Moreover, the models do not incorporate qualitative information such as media narratives, public sentiment, or historical reputations.

Future work should prioritize richer contextual features (e.g., player-tracking, play-by-play, matchup, and clutch indicators) and text-derived narrative signals, while extending the same cross-validated framework to more complex models without sacrificing robust model selection.

8 Conclusion

This paper integrates backward stepwise logistic regression, a cross-validated machine learning pipeline, and SHAP-based model explanations into a unified study of NBA Finals MVP prediction. Using 237 player-season observations from the 2005–06 through 2024–25 seasons, the logistic regression identifies PTS and DRtg as the key predictors and achieves 90% retrodictive accuracy with a parsimonious, interpretable model. The machine learning pipeline complements this with systematic model comparison, revealing Random Forest as the strongest classifier at 95% per-year retrodictive accuracy (19/20 correct), supported by the best probability calibration among all models tested.

SHAP analysis adds a third layer of insight by decomposing individual predictions. Despite their architectural differences, both the Random Forest and Neural Network converge on an "efficiency-defense" archetype: at the individual-prediction level, defensive contributions (BLK, STL) and playmaking (AST) emerge as critical differentiators, while raw scoring volume—though dominant in global importance rankings—contributes negligibly to individual SHAP decompositions. The key divergence lies in mechanism: the Random Forest employs a one-sided gatekeeper logic that sharply boosts qualifying players, while the Neural Network captures bidirectional effects that both reward defensive excellence and penalize its absence. This cross-model convergence strengthens confidence that the patterns reflect genuine structure in FMVP voting rather than model-specific artifacts.

Together, the three analytical layers demonstrate that structured statistical modeling can capture much of the FMVP voting pattern even in a small-sample, narrative-sensitive setting. At the same time, the persistent misclassifications—particularly the universal failure to predict the 2024 Jaylen Brown case—underscore that subjectively voted awards are shaped by intangibles, matchup narratives, and perceived leadership that no box-score model can fully encode. Closing this gap will require richer data sources, including player-tracking metrics, clutch-time performance indicators, and text-derived narrative signals.

References

1. Schuhmann, J.: NBA's 3-point revolution: how 1 shot is changing the game. NBA.com (2021). https://www.nba.com/news/3-point-era-nba-75. Accessed 01 Apr 2026
2. Kilcoyne, S.: The decline of the mid-range jump shot in basketball: a study of the impact of data analytics on shooting habits in the NBA. Bachelor's thesis, Bryant University (2020). https://digitalcommons.bryant.edu/honors_mathematics/35/. Accessed 01 Apr 2026
3. Tummala, R.: Using machine learning to predict the NBA MVP. Samford University (2023). https://www.samford.edu/sports-analytics/fans/2023/Using-Machine-Learning-to-Predict-the-NBA-MVPAccessed 01 Apr 2026
4. Li, Z., Jia, L.: NBA most valuable player projection model: based on traditional and advanced metrics. In: Proceedings of the 2024 4th International Conference on Computing and Data Science, pp. 178–183 (2024). https://doi.org/10.1145/3723936.3723963
5. Fearnhead, P., Taylor, B.M.: On estimating the ability of NBA players. J. Quant. Anal. Sports **7**(3), 11 (2011). https://doi.org/10.2202/1559-0410.1298
6. Cervone, D., D'Amour, A., Bornn, L., Goldsberry, K.: A multiresolution stochastic process model for predicting basketball possession outcomes. J. Am. Stat. Assoc. **111**(514), 585–599 (2016). https://doi.org/10.1080/01621459.2016.1141685
7. Iyer, R.R., Zheng, R., Li, Y., Sycara, K.: Event outcome prediction using sentiment analysis and crowd wisdom in microblog feeds. arXiv:1912.05066 (2019)
8. Johnson, M.R., McCarthy, I.P.: Cultural similarity and impartiality on voting bias: the case of FIFA's world's best male football player award. PLoS ONE **17**(7), e0270546 (2022). https://doi.org/10.1371/journal.pone.0270546
9. Steyerberg, E.W., Harrell, F.E., Jr., Borsboom, G.J., Eijkemans, M.J., Vergouwe, Y., Habbema, J.D.: Internal validation of predictive models: efficiency of some procedures for logistic regression analysis. J. Clin. Epidemiol. **54**(8), 774–781 (2001). https://doi.org/10.1016/S0895-4356(01)00341-9
10. Basketball-Reference: NBA Finals player statistics database (2006–2025). Sports Reference LLC (2025). https://www.basketball-reference.com/. Accessed 01 Apr 2026

Rethinking the Shooting Foul: Evaluating Two Alternative Penalty Models for Enhanced Game Flow, Competitive Balance, and Fan Experience

Jeff Rickords[1] and Willie K. Harrison[2](✉)

[1] Independent Researcher, Springville, USA
jrickords@gmail.com
[2] Brigham Young University, Provo, UT 84602, USA
willie.harrison@byu.edu

Abstract. The traditional free-throw system in basketball has remained largely unchanged for decades, despite persistent concerns regarding game flow, entertainment value, and strategic distortions created by foul-baiting and intentional fouling. This paper evaluates two alternative models for penalizing shooting fouls on missed field-goal attempts: (1) a 5-on-4 power-play possession, in which the offending player must sit out for one defensive possession, and (2) a one-free-throw plus retained-possession model. Using comparative logic, time-efficiency analysis, and strategic modeling across youth, high school, collegiate, and professional levels, we assess how each option affects pace of play, late-game strategy, fairness, and fan engagement. We also explore secondary rule reforms enabled by these changes, including the potential removal of personal-foul disqualification limits. The potential results from adopting both models are significantly improved game flow and entertainment value, with the power-play model offering the most dramatic transformation.

Keywords: Basketball Analytics · Fouls and Free Throws · Rule Reform · Game Flow · Pace of Play · Entertainment Value

1 Introduction

Basketball's free-throw system has long been a focal point of debate among analysts, coaches, and fans [7]. While free throws serve an important function, penalizing illegal contact and attempting to preserve fairness, they also introduce substantial inefficiencies and additional problems. Free-throw sequences slow the game, reduce continuous action, and disproportionately influence late-game outcomes. At the youth and high-school levels, where free-throw percentages are

J. Rickords—Independent Researcher.

Z. Liu and V. Misra (Eds.): ISACE 2026, LNCS 16610, pp. 392–402, 2026.
https://doi.org/10.1007/978-3-032-27272-0_25

significantly lower, the system often produces long, disjointed stretches of inactivity. At the professional level, free throws contribute to strategic distortions such as foul-baiting, intentional fouling, and "Hack-a-Player" tactics [6,10].

As of mid-February 2026, the NBA's league-wide free-throw percentage during the 2025–26 season is approximately 78% [2], with NCAA Division I at roughly 72% [11,12]. High School play produces free throw percentages around 50–60% [3], and youth recreational leagues are much lower [9]. These statistics are summarized in Table 1. These disparities highlight a structural issue with the free-throw system: the same foul produces vastly different expected outcomes depending on the level of play. In other words, the penalties associated with fouling are less severe for recreational and high-school leagues compared to higher-level play. Thus, the same basic construct for administering these penalties is unlikely to produce fair and balanced deterrents for all levels of play.

Table 1. Free-throw accuracy by competition level.

Level	Average FT%	Sources
Youth	40–50%	[9]
High School	50–60%	[3]
NCAA Men	~72%	[11]
NCAA Women	~71%	[12]
NBA	~78%	[2]

In response to these issues, this paper proposes two alternative models for penalizing shooting fouls on missed field-goal attempts. Both models preserve the current rule for made baskets while being fouled, preserving some continuity with existing scoring logic. For shooting fouls that do not end in a made basket, the goal of the reform on free throw rules is to create a more dynamic, continuous, and strategically rich game environment while maintaining fairness and competitive balance across all levels of basketball competition.

The rest of the paper is organized as follows. Section 2 outlines the background and motivation for rule reform of the penalties associated with the shooting foul. Section 3 outlines two options for rule reform. In Sect. 4 we analyze the potential benefits and drawbacks of both options, and we conclude the paper in Sect. 5.

2 Background and Motivation

To motivate rule reform with respect to basketball fouls that result in free throws, we consider data from NBA.com [8]. Figure 1 presents data from 431 NBA games that took place in December 2025 and January 2026. Histograms of game duration in minutes and free throw attempts (FTA) per game are both given. Note the wide range of both of these variables within those two months of NBA play.

The range of NBA game duration in this dataset stretches between 116 and 179 min, while the number of FTA per game ranges between 15 and 86.

NBA commissioner, Adam Silver, has publicly stated that he thinks NBA games are too long. For example, in [5], he mentions that making quarters 10 min long, rather than 12 min long, could help to shorter NBA games to roughly two hours, which would make a better fan experience. The average of our data signifies that NBA games are roughly 138 min long right now, meaning 15-20 min of game time would need to be cut to reach Commissioner Silver's goal.

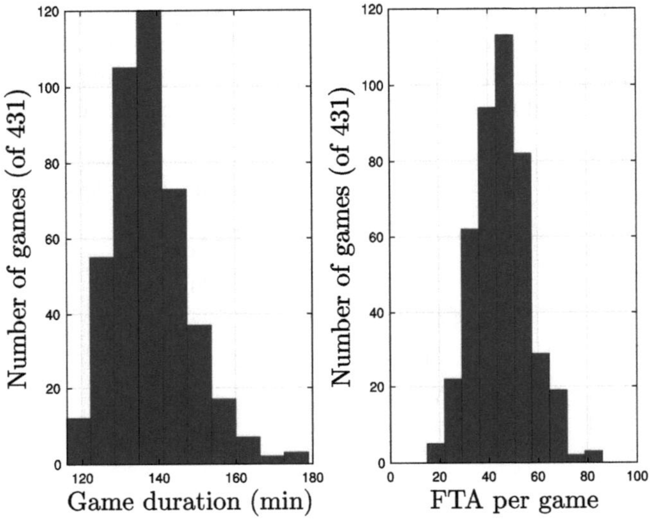

Fig. 1. Histograms of game duration (left) and FTA per game (right) using only two months of NBA regular season game data.

We note in Fig. 2 that the number of FTA is well correlated with the duration of NBA games. A simple linear regression model using the 431 games from two recent months of play yields

$$d = 113.3 + 0.54 \times f, \tag{1}$$

where d is the duration of games, and f is the number of free throws per game. It is clear from the figure that there are other factors that affect game duration besides just the number of FTA, but it is also clear that free throws are a significant contributor to longer game durations. If the linear model is to be blindly considered, then NBA games are roughly 113 min long with no free throws, but each FTA adds roughly half a minute to the length of the game. This simple model suggests that if the number of FTA could be reduced to roughly 14, games would be two hours in duration on average.

Game duration is certainly one factor that could be altered by limiting the number of FTA per game; however, there are other considerations as well. The current free-throw system introduces several issues:

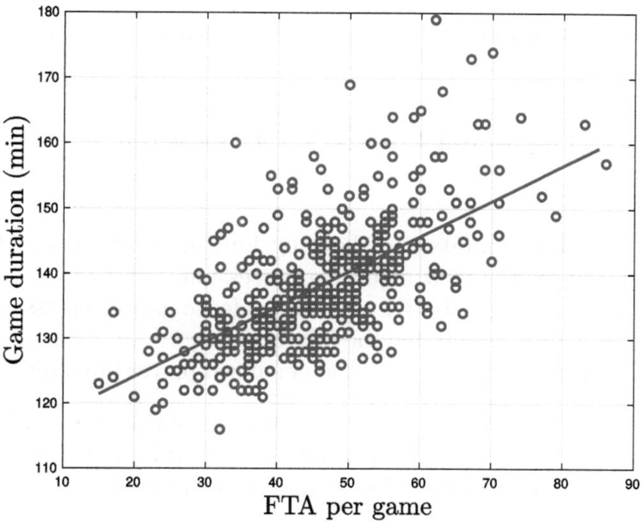

Fig. 2. FTA per game vs. game duration (in minutes). NBA data from the 431 games played in December 2025 and January 2026. The line fit is a linear regression model.

- **Time inefficiency:** Free throws consume 15–20 min of game time for an average NBA game [1].
- **Strategic distortion:** Teams exploit fouling rules to stop the clock or target poor shooters [6,10].
- **Entertainment decline:** Fans frequently rank free throws among the least exciting game sequences [1].
- **Skill imbalance:** Free-throw accuracy varies widely across levels [2,3,9,11, 12].

Many of these issues allow players to foul other players to gain an advantage, all while lengthening games with boring basketball events.

3 Proposed Rule Alternatives

This paper provides alternative solutions to penalizing fouls besides the current free-throw system. Our new ideas promote fairness, and reward good game play rather than fouling. They also achieve a speed-up of the game that equates to roughly the desired speed-up mentioned by Adam Silver in [5]. This paper is not the first attempt at proposing rule reform for free throws in basketball. For instance, in [1], we learn of a proposal to remove multiple free throws for any one foul. The proposed action was to simply make one free throw worth the total number of points associated with the foul. For example, if a person was fouled shooting a three-point shot and missed, then the player would take a single free throw worth three points. While this idea would speed up games, the idea of different free throws being worth a different number of points is a bit odd. Our proposals also manage to speed up play, but present fairer solutions that focus on bringing excitement to the game as well.

3.1 Option 1: The 5-on-4 Power-Play Possession

Under this model:

- The defender who commits the shooting foul must sit or stand beside the basket standard for the next defensive possession.
- The offensive team plays 5-on-4 until the defense gains possession.
- The clock stops only briefly for the inbound.
- Once the defense gains possession, the penalized player immediately re-enters.

This model mirrors power-play systems in hockey and lacrosse. Note that free throws are basically eliminated from basketball with this approach, and the main emphasis is on resuming regular play as quickly as possible.

3.2 Option 2: One Free Throw + Retained Possession

Under this model:

- The fouled player shoots one free throw.
- Regardless of make or miss, the offensive team retains possession, inbounding near half-court.

This model preserves the free-throw skill component while eliminating multi-shot sequences. Regular play is resumed reasonably quickly in this scenario, but foul shots retain their value of a single point, rather than foul shots being worth multiple points as in the proposal in [1].

4 Analysis of the Proposed Rule Alternatives

The proposed systems would dramatically reduce the number of free throws per game, especially under the power play option. In this section, we consider the two options for replacing the penalty for shooting fouls across several different dimensions:

1. Game flow and time efficiency,
2. Strategic implications for offense and defense,
3. Late-game scenarios,
4. Fan experience and entertainment value,
5. Secondary rule reforms enabled,
6. Unintended consequences,
7. Cross-level applicability.

Each of these issues is considered in turn, mostly focusing on the impact to the NBA. The final dimension of the analysis covers items that specifically apply to lower levels of competition.

4.1 Game Flow and Time Efficiency

Free-throw sequences are among the most time-consuming stoppages in basketball, particularly when combined with intentional fouling and late-game timeouts. By reducing the number of free throws and eliminating the need for multiple attempts, the proposed rules promise substantial time savings.

The effect on game flow is somewhat obvious, as Option 1 removes most FTA in NBA games, and the action resumes almost immediately in a 5-on-4 power play. Option 2 still provides a break in the game flow for each shooting foul, but only free throws associated with made baskets would require the other players to line up for the FTA. Thus, most FTA would resemble the current technical foul shot, which tends to happen quite quickly in practice.

In the remainder of this section, we attempt to estimate the reduction in overall game duration imposed by each of the two rule reform options. The single variable linear regression model in (1) ascribes 0.54 min (approximately 32 s) to each FTA in a regular season NBA game. Not all FTA are alike in terms of how long they take to complete. For example, consider a foul committed under the basket vs. a foul committed at the opposite end when a team is in a "bonus" status. Clearly, the first scenario allows players to line up quickly, whereas the second scenario requires players to walk to the opposite end to line up for the free throws. Furthermore, Option 1 (Power-Play) would almost surely remove the large majority of all FTA in a game, while Option 2 (1 FT + Possession) would likely remove slightly less than half of the FTA in a game.

For this analysis, we attempt to put some numbers to several example games from the dataset. We only include five games here because the games chosen cover the breadth of possibilities for the effect on game duration: (1) the game with the fewest FTA from the dataset (Celtics at Pacers on 01/12/26), (2) the shortest game from the dataset (Spurs at Hawks on 12/19/25), (3) an average game in terms of both FTA and game duration (Heat at Kings on 01/20/26), (4) the longest game from the dataset (T-wolves at Nuggets on 12/25/25), and (5) the game with the most FTA from the dataset (Lakers at Jazz on 12/18/25). An average NBA game lasts roughly 138 min and has 45-46 FTA. The Heat/Kings game matches these numbers almost exactly. Table 2 shows the data for each of the five games, along with estimates of the speed-up for each game.

To estimate the length of the five sample games under Options 1 and 2, we must first identify the number of free throws that would be affected by the rule reform options. Free throws that would always remain are those associated with technical fouls and those associated with made baskets (often referred to as 3-pt plays or 4-pt plays). All other FTA would be removed by Option 1, and replaced with 5-on-4 power plays with the clock still running. Option 2 would remove the 2nd (and 3rd, when appropriate) FTA associated with a single foul, and the game would then resume by the shooting team retaining possession. In that option, fewer FTA would be removed. The remaining FTA for each game is indicated in the table for both options.

On the high-end of time reduction, we may assume the 32 s per FTA from the model in (1). This is almost certainly a high estimate for several reasons.

Table 2. Estimate of time savings for five regular season NBA games from the dataset (Dec 2025 - Jan 2026). The column labeled FTA Opt1/Opt2 gives the numbers of FTA that would remain in the game under Option 1 and Option 2, respectively, for FTA rule reform. The column labeled Est Dur Opt1/Opt2 gives the estimated duration of each game under the two options, respectively. All durations are in minutes.

Game	Duration	FTA	FTA Opt1/Opt2	Est Dur Opt1/Opt2
Celtics @ Pacers - 01/12/26	123	15	3/9	116.5–117.8/119.8-120.4
Spurs @ Hawks - 12/19/25	116	32	5/18	101.4-104.3/108.4–110
Heat @ Kings - 01/20/26	138	45	5/25	116.4-120.7/127.2–129.4
T-wolves @ Nuggets - 12/25/25	179	62	9/34	150.4-156.1/163.9–166.9
Lakers @ Jazz - 12/18/25	157	86	13/48	117.6-125.5/136.5-140.6

First, the data in Fig. 2 appear to have larger errors above the best fit line than below. Thus, there are likely to be factors not associated with FTA that are lengthening these games. Furthermore, Option 2 still requires one free throw for all shooting fouls, although only those associated with made baskets require players to line up for the free throw. Finally, estimates from other sources appear to come in lower than 32 s per FTA [1]. We present time reductions of 80% of the model estimate to 100% of the model estimate (i.e., ~26-32 s per FTA) in Table 2. Note that the average game (see the third game in the table) is likely to be right around the two-hour mark under Option 1, but closer to 128 min for Option 2.

4.2 Strategic Implications for Offense and Defense

For both options for rule reform, the expected penalty for a shooting foul grows in value for the offensive team. This removes many of the incentives that currently exist for defensive teams to foul, which should lead to cleaner games in general.

Option 1: Power-Play. A 5-on-4 advantage dramatically alters offensive behavior. The following are just a few possibilities of adjustments that may be made on the offensive side of a power play:

- Specially designed "power-play" sets may be developed by coaches,
- 5-out spacing to stretch the defense,
- Corner overloads to force rotations,
- Slip screens for uncontested dunks,
- High-low actions exploiting the missing defender.

These strategies are likely to result in:

- More open three-point attempts,
- More dunks,
- Higher points per possession (PPP).

Defenses forced to play in 5-on-4 power plays must then:

- Use zone shells to compensate for being down a player,
- Decide whether to prioritize protecting the rim or the three-point line, depending on game situation and strategy,
- Force longer passes to burn the clock.

Defensive stands that result in no points being scored in a power play are likely to be very exciting as well. The new rule would surely invite innovation on both sides of the game.

Option 2: 1 FT + Possession. The second option is less of a change from the current system. The offense gains:

- A chance at 1 point through a traditional FTA,
- A full possession following the FTA worth approximately 1.0–1.2 expected points.

Again, due to the increase in the penalty from the current state of the game, defensive strategies would further attempt to:

- Remain disciplined and continue to defend,
- Avoid fouling shooters,
- Emphasize verticality and walling up,
- Reduce "take fouls."

All of these are likely to improve the beauty of the game and increase the skill required by defensive players.

4.3 Late-Game Scenarios

Current System. In close games, teams often exploit the free throw system for strategic advantage. Trailing teams intentionally foul poor shooters to stop the clock and force low-probability scoring attempts ("Hack-a-Shaq"), while leading teams seek to maximize the ball in the hands of their best free throw shooters. The predictability of these tactics can slow the game, frustrate fans, and reduce the variety of late-game scenarios. Free-throw accuracy becomes disproportionately important towards the end of games for these reasons, which often also incentivizes coaches to substitute players in and out of games, often seconds removed from the last player substitution. The endgame in basketball is clunky at best. For this reason, alternate endings, such as the Elam Ending have been proposed [4]. These additional endgame options could be coupled with the rule reforms we propose in this paper.

Option 1: Power-Play. Intentional fouling becomes significantly less advantageous, as the offense is likely to generate an open shot or easy basket during the 5-on-4 power play. Furthermore, the clock is not effectively stopped, removing fouling as an endgame strategy. Coaches would need to emphasize disciplined defense, leading to more organic, skill-based endgame play. Endgame flow would become continuous, similar to soccer or hockey. Comebacks would rely on defensive stops rather than whistle manipulation.

Option 2: 1 FT + Possession. The incentive to foul poor shooters is diminished from the current state of the game under this option, as a missed free throw does not result in a change of possession. Offenses may prioritize high-percentage shooters or design plays to maximize the value of retained possessions. Endgame scenarios become less predictable, with greater emphasis on execution and less on exploiting the clock. Intentional fouling largely disappears, since it awards opponents a free point attempt and retained possession. Endgame strategy returns to continuous basketball play.

4.4 Fan Experience and Entertainment Value

Fan surveys and engagement studies consistently show that live sports audiences, especially younger fans, value pace, excitement, and highlight plays over repetitive stoppages and static sequences. Free throws, while dramatic in high-pressure moments, are often cited as the least engaging aspect of basketball, with many fans tuning out or multitasking during these sequences. The power-play option:

- Creates immediate, visually striking mismatches (5-on-4), leading to more open dunks, alley-oops, and uncontested three-point attempts,
- Increases the frequency of high-leverage, crowd-pleasing plays, especially in late-game situations,
- Reduces dead time, keeping fans engaged and invested in every possession.

The free throw + possession option:

- Maintains the drama of the free throw while adding strategic intrigue, as the offense can capitalize on a missed shot with a designed set play,
- Encourages creative play-calling and dynamic offensive schemes, appealing to fans who appreciate tactical depth.

4.5 Secondary Rule Reforms Enabled

Because both proposed penalties are more severe than the current free-throw based model, there may no longer be a need to disqualify players who acrue a set number of fouls. This is likely to be true because players who foul excessively naturally harm their team at a greater penalty. Coaches can manage players' court time without requiring a five- or six-foul disqualification limit, and incentives would be aligned for players to learn to play clean basketball. Another benefit is that officiating is simplified and controversy surrounding foul limits is reduced.

Under both options for rule reform, non-shooting fouls remain unchanged. Bonus fouls could simply trigger the new penalty model, which could simplify rules for teams reaching bonus levels of fouls.

4.6 Potential Unintended Consequences

Given the current focus of analytics in determining winning strategies, we have no doubt that rules changes regarding shooting fouls would result in new tactics being deployed by teams. While it is difficult to anticipate all possible actions that a team may take to gain a competitive advantage, we note that the rule changes proposed in this paper generally increase the penalty of the shooting foul. Perhaps the most likely consequence, thus, would be an increase in foul-baiting strategies. Without careful consideration, this could result in some comical situations during games. For example, under Option 2, it may be possible for a team to draw a shooting foul, take a free throw, and then draw another shooting foul, and continue in this way in perpetuity. While we think the rule changes would encourage a more beautiful brand of basketball, we readily admit that the ideas presented in this paper may need to be adapted based on strategies that teams deploy if the new rules ever were established.

4.7 Cross-Level Applicability

All levels of play benefit from the increased flow of the game with fewer stoppages. The emphasis on good defensive tactics and skills that would naturally arise would also benefit all levels of play. Since free-throw accuracy grows as players develop, the lowest levels of play are the most likely to benefit from either of these two rule reform options. Fouling unskilled players would no longer be an advantage for the fouling team, which aligns incentives with the rules of the game. If the rule reform is coupled with a simplification of bonus rules, as mentioned in the previous section, this would eliminate the one-and-one free throw scenarios, which highly favor the fouling team. Fairness of play and less reckless play are both enhanced.

5 Conclusion

This paper presents two options for free-throw reform in basketball. Both proposed models significantly improve basketball's pace, fairness, and entertainment value. The power-play model offers the most dramatic transformation, creating dynamic, high-action possessions that reward aggression and punish fouling with immediate tactical consequences. The one-free-throw-plus-possession model preserves tradition while mitigating inefficiencies. They also open the door to broader rule reforms, including the removal of personal-foul disqualification limits. While implementation will require careful pilot testing and stakeholder engagement, this paper highlights the potential for transformative improvement at every level of play. As basketball continues to evolve, embracing evidence-based rule reform is essential to preserve the sport's integrity and appeal in the modern era.

Disclosure of Interests. The authors have no competing interests to declare that are relevant to the content of this article.

References

1. Arnovitz, K.: Is one trip to the free-throw line enough? ESPN TrueHoop (July 2014). https://www.espn.com/blog/truehoop/post/_/id/70581/hoopidea-is-one-trip-to-the-free-throw-line-enough. Accessed 15 Feb 2026
2. Basketball Reference: NBA league averages - per game. https://www.basketball-reference.com/leagues/NBA_stats_per_game.html
3. Carter, J.: Basketball shooting percentages and statistics. Noah Basketball (July 2012). https://www.noahbasketball.com/blog/basketball-shooting-percentages-and-statistics
4. Elam, N.: An examination of the effectiveness of the Elam ending at TBT2018 and TBT2019. Sports Innovation Journal 1, 120–133 (2020). https://doi.org/10.18060/23969. Accessed15 Feb 2026
5. Herring, C., Williams, M.: NBA commissioner Adam Silver floats idea of shortening games to 10-minute quarters. ESPN (Jan 2025). https://www.espn.com/nba/story/_/id/43617073/nba-commissioner-adam-silver-floats-idea-shortening-games-10-minute-quarters. Accessed 15 Jan 2026
6. Kenter, F.H.J.: An analysis of the basketball endgame: when to foul when trailing and leading. In: Proceedings MIT Sloan Sports Analytics Conference. Boston, MA (Feb 2015). https://www.stat.berkeley.edu/~aldous/157/Papers/kenter.pdf
7. Moskowitz, T., Wertheim, L.J.: Scorecasting: The hidden influences behind how sports are played and games are won. Crown Archetype , (2011)
8. NBA.com: Boxscore NBA data. https://cdn.nba.com/static/json/liveData/boxscore/
9. Petreanu, A.G., Petreanu, M.: Study on statistical parameters in basketball for junior female players in the age categories under 13, under 14, under 15 and under 16 years old. Research and Science Today: Physical Education and Sports Science (5.2026) (2026). https://www.rstjournal.com/adrian-gheorghe-petreanu-manuela-petreanu-study-on-statistical-parameters-in-basketball-for-junior-female-players-in-the-age-categories-under-13-under-14-under-15-and-under-16-years-old/
10. Skinner, B.: Scoring strategies for the underdog: a general, quantitative method for determining optimal sports strategies. J. Quant. Anal. Sports **7**(4), (2011)
11. Sports Reference: 2025–26 men's college basketball school stats. https://www.sports-reference.com/cbb/seasons/men/2026-school-stats.html
12. Sports Reference: 2025–26 women's college basketball school stats. https://www.sports-reference.com/cbb/seasons/women/2026-school-stats.html

SoccerRef-Agents: Multi-agent System for Automated Soccer Refereeing

Zi Meng[1,2], Wanli Song[1], Yi Hu[2], Jiayuan Rao[2(✉)], and Gang Chen[2(✉)]

[1] University of Michigan, Michigan, USA
{mengzi,wanlis}@umich.edu
[2] Shanghai Jiao Tong University, Shanghai, China
{huyi_0811,jy_rao,chengang76}@sjtu.edu.cn

Abstract. Refereeing is vital in sports, where fair, accurate, and explainable decisions are fundamental. While intelligent assistant technologies are being widely adopted in soccer refereeing, current AI-assisted approaches remain preliminary. Existing research mostly focuses on isolated video perception tasks and lacks the ability to understand and reason about foul scenarios. To fill this gap, we propose **SoccerRef-Agents**, a holistic and explainable multi-agent decision-making framework for soccer refereeing. The main contributions are: (i) constructing the multimodal benchmark **SoccerRefBench** with over 1,200 referee theory questions and 600 foul video clips; (ii) building a vector-based knowledge base **RefKnowledgeDB** using the latest *"Laws of the Game"* and a classic case database for precise, knowledge-driven reasoning; (iii) designing a novel multi-agent architecture that collaborates via cross-modal RAG to bridge the semantic gap between visual content and regulatory texts. This work explores the technical capability of integrating MLLMs with refereeing expertise, and evaluations show our system significantly outperforms general-purpose MLLMs in decision accuracy and explanation quality. All databases, benchmarks, and code will be made available.

Keywords: AI Referee · Sports Understanding · Multi-Agent System · Multimodal Reasoning

1 Introduction

Competitive sports captivate global audiences with their inherent dynamism and passion. Among them, soccer, hailed as the most beautiful game, enjoys unparalleled worldwide attention. In modern soccer, with advancements in science and technology, particularly the recent development of AI, technology is being applied across all aspects from training and competition to broadcasting. Within this context, soccer refereeing occupies a special position, as it is tasked with the crucial work of maintaining the orderly conduct of matches. The fairness and integrity of a match are highly dependent on the accuracy of refereeing

Z. Liu and V. Misra (Eds.): ISACE 2026, LNCS 16610, pp. 403–427, 2026.
https://doi.org/10.1007/978-3-032-27272-0_26

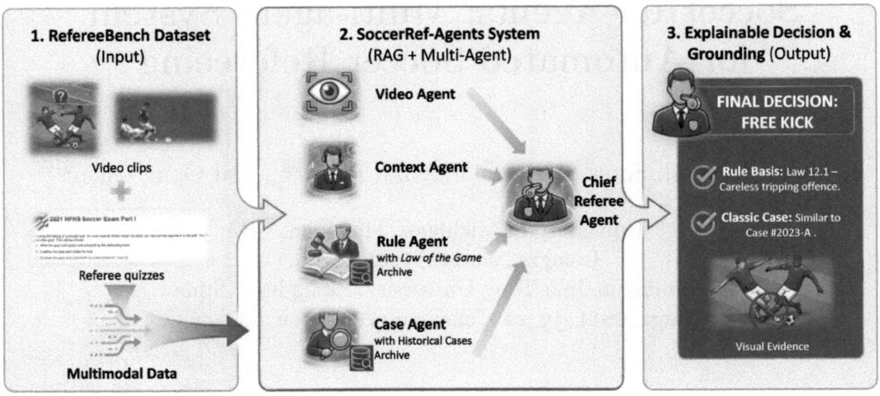

Fig. 1. Overview of **SoccerRef-Agents**. The system mimics a professional officiating team by decomposing the task into perception (Video Agent), background analysis (Context Agent), legal interpretation (Rule Agent), and precedent retrieval (Case Agent), culminating in a final decision by the Chief Referee Agent.

decisions. Currently, the latest advancements in artificial intelligence have been applied to many aspects of soccer understanding, including video comprehension [20,28,37–39,43] However, in the domain of automated refereeing, despite some attempts, three main challenges remain: **(i) The Gap Between Perception and Reasoning:** Most existing systems [14,15] treat foul detection as a simple visual classification task. However, effective officiating requires a cognitive leap from visual data to rule-based logic. For instance, determining disciplinary actions such as distinguishing between "reckless" and "using excessive force" is a knowledge-intensive process that necessitates explicit reference to the *"Laws of the Game(LOTG)"* [33], a capability largely absent in current vision-only models. **(ii) Unreliable and Unexplainable Outputs:** General-purpose multimodal large models often struggle to provide reliable justifications for their decisions. Due to a lack of internalized domain knowledge, these models [3,5,16] may generate seemingly plausible but factually incorrect explanations, known as hallucinations. They typically fail to ground their judgments in specific rules or similar historical cases, limiting their practical utility as transparent decision-support systems. **(iii) Limitations in Sample Size:** Most current researches [12,41] focus on analyzing and processing small-scale samples, lacking a truly large-scale benchmark for the comprehensive evaluation of AI refereeing systems.

To bridge this gap, we propose a comprehensive framework for holistic and explainable soccer refereeing. Recognizing that a valid judgment requires both accurate perception and authoritative knowledge, we first construct **SoccerRef-Bench**, a multimodal benchmark specifically designed to evaluate refereeing logic. Unlike general sports datasets, **SoccerRefBench** integrates theoretical knowledge derived from professional certification exams with practical judgment from controversial broadcast replay clips. Furthermore, to enable knowledge-driven reasoning, we construct **RefKnowledgeDB** by digitizing and vectorizing the latest *Laws of the Game* [33] and a curated database of classic historical cases, serving as the long-term memory of our system.

To tackle the complexity of decision-making, we introduce **SoccerRef-Agents**, a novel multi-agent system that mimics the collaborative workflow of a professional officiating team. As illustrated in Fig. 1, our system decomposes the refereeing task into specialized roles: a *Video Agent* for perception, a *Rule Agent* for legal interpretation, a *Case Agent* for precedent retrieval, and a *Chief Referee Agent* for final adjudication. By leveraging a cross-modal Retrieval-Augmented Generation (RAG) mechanism, our agents can consult the rulebook based on visual analysis, ensuring decisions are not only accurate but also legally cited.

Concretely, we make the following contributions in this paper:

(i) We construct **SoccerRefBench**, a specialized multimodal benchmark for soccer officiating. It comprises 1,218 theoretical exam questions and 600 annotated video clips of fouls, mapped to standard disciplinary outcomes (No Offence, Normal, Yellow, Red).
(ii) We establish a specialized vector knowledge base: the **RefKnowledgeDB**. The database enables precise and fine-grained retrieval of regulations and historical precedents, mitigating model hallucinations.
(iii) We introduce **SoccerRef-Agents**, a multi-agent framework featuring a novel cross-modal reasoning pipeline. By utilizing video descriptions to drive textual knowledge retrieval, our system effectively bridges the semantic gap between visual footage and legal texts.
(iv) Extensive evaluations on **SoccerRefBench** demonstrate the superiority of our agentic system. **SoccerRef-Agents** significantly outperforms general-purpose MLLMs in decision accuracy and achieves state-of-the-art performance in generating legally grounded explanations.

2 Related Works

2.1 Sports Understanding

Sports understanding has emerged as a pivotal testbed for evaluating Multimodal Large Language Models (MLLMs) due to its dynamic nature and complex rules. Early research primarily focused on atomic tasks such as action recognition [20,37,39,43] and automated scoring [29,36,40]. With the advent of large-scale benchmarks [8,13,42], the focus has shifted towards holistic understanding. For instance, Sports-QA [19] and SPORTU [35] evaluate models on QA tasks across multiple sports disciplines, requiring agents to perceive actions and reason about game states. Recent works have also explored dense video captioning [22,25] and commentary generation [28,38] to enhance fan engagement. However, these general benchmarks often treat sports rules as implicit background knowledge rather than explicit logic constraints, limiting their ability to evaluate fine-grained professional judgment.

2.2 Soccer Understanding

As the world's most popular sport, soccer has attracted significant research attention. The field is largely driven by extensive datasets like SoccerNet [9], which facilitates tasks ranging from action spotting to replay grounding. Beyond perception, recent studies have ventured into higher-level cognitive tasks. MatchTime [28] and SoccerNet-Caption [22] focus on generating time-aligned commentary, while other works explore tactical analysis [18,24] and game state reconstruction [30]. Despite these advancements, existing soccer understanding models predominantly focus on descriptive tasks [26,27] or statistical analysis [2,6,17]. They rarely address the normative aspect of the game—specifically, judging player actions against the strict, textual framework of the Laws of the Game [33].

2.3 Soccer Refereeing

The automation of refereeing has advanced significantly in both industrial applications and academic research, albeit with distinct focuses. In professional leagues, hardware-centric systems like Video Assistant Referee (VAR) [31] and Semi-Automated Offside Technology (SAOT) [7] provide precise spatial measurements. However, they lack the semantic reasoning capabilities required to judge subjective fouls or interpret player intent. Conversely, academic research focuses on vision-based foul recognition from broadcast footage. For instance, VARS [14] treats refereeing as a multi-view classification problem, while X-VARS [15] explores utilizing MLLMs to generate descriptive explanations for foul events.

Despite these strides, a fully autonomous AI Referee remains elusive. Recent trends, such as the SoccerNet Challenges [4,10], predominantly frame officiating as a video classification task, mapping visual features directly to disciplinary labels based on statistical correlations. However, authentic refereeing is a complex legal adjudication process, not merely a perceptual one. Existing models [4,10,34] fail to logically derive verdicts by verifying factual preconditions and aligning them with specific regulatory clauses. This disconnect between visual perception and legal reasoning limits the reliability and explainability of current approaches. To bridge this gap, effective AI systems must move beyond pattern recognition to knowledge-driven reasoning. However, existing datasets lack the explicit alignment between model intuition and the strict textual framework of the *Laws of the Game* [33] required to develop and evaluate this capability. This necessity motivates the construction of **SoccerRefBench**, establishing the foundational resources detailed in Sect. 3

3 Dataset Construction

To bridge the critical gap between model intuition and legal adjudication in automated officiating, we introduce a comprehensive data framework designed for knowledge-driven reasoning. This section first outlines the motivation and overview of our proposed framework in Sect. 3.1. We then provide detailed descriptions of the data collection and curation processes for our multimodal benchmark, **SoccerRefBench**, in Sect. 3.2 and Sect. 3.3, respectively. Finally, we elaborate on the construction of our specialized domain repository, the **Ref-KnowledgeDB**, in Sect. 3.4, which serves as the foundation for the system's retrieval capabilities.

3.1 Motivation and Overview

Soccer refereeing is a highly specialized domain that requires precise interpretation of the rule and split-second decision-making. While existing benchmarks primarily focus on action recognition or general sports question-answering, they still lack evaluation standards specifically tailored for soccer refereeing, particularly in multimodal understanding and rule-based reasoning. To provide an evaluation platform for such a professional scenario, we introduce **SoccerRef-Bench**, a comprehensive multimodal benchmark designed to assess automated officiating according to professional refereeing standards, comprises two distinct modalities: (i) a textual subset assessing theoretical knowledge via standardized exams, and (ii) a video subset for evaluating practical judgment in controversial foul scenarios. To enable better reasoning and evidence retrieval in the automated officiating pipeline, we construct a searchable knowledge base **Ref-KnowledgeDB**, containing the official *Laws of the Game* [33] and historical precedents, thereby supporting knowledge-driven reasoning.

3.2 Data Collection

To construct a comprehensive evaluation benchmark, we aggregate data from authoritative refereeing examinations and large-scale video datasets. The overall data collection and aggregation pipeline is illustrated in Fig. 2.

3.2.1 Textual Data Collection. We collect a total of 1,218 multiple-choice questions covering diverse aspects of refereeing theory.

- **Chinese Referee Exams:** We select 118 high-quality questions from the Chinese Football Association (CFA) referee certification exams.
- **International Standards:** We collect 1,100 questions from publicly available referee certification exams conducted by the National Federation of State High School Associations (NFHS) and the Florida High School Athletic Association (FHSAA). To ensure temporal coverage and rule evolution adaptability, the dataset spans multiple years, including 2013, 2017, 2019, 2020, 2021, 2022, 2023, and 2025 for NFHS and 2016 for FHSAA.

3.2.2 Video Data Collection. For the visual component, we leverage the SoccerNet-MVFoul dataset [14], which provides multi-view video clips of foul incidents. We extract 600 representative samples that feature clear refereeing controversies.

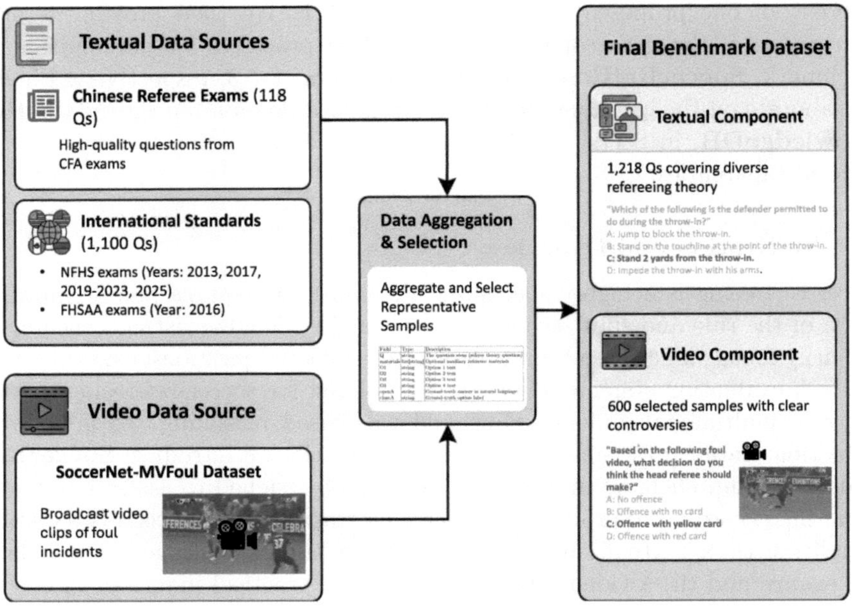

Fig. 2. Overview of the data collection pipeline for **SoccerRefBench**. The dataset integrates 1,218 textual theory questions from diverse international sources and 600 video-based judgment scenarios derived from the SoccerNet-MVFoul dataset.

3.3 Data Curation

To facilitate standardized and objective evaluation, we curate the collected raw data into a unified multiple-choice question format. Each entry in **SoccerRefBench** consists of a question stem, two to four candidate options, and exactly one correct ground-truth answer. This consistent closed-set QA structure across both textual and video modalities allows for precise accuracy metrics and direct comparison between different models.

For the textual component, data processing is mainly translation. For questions sourced from Chinese Referee Exams, we translated the content into English using LLM-assisted tools, followed by manual verification by domain experts to ensure terminological precision. For the National Federation of State High School Associations (NFHS) and Florida High School Athletic Association (FHSAA) exams, we retained the original official options.

For the video component, we transform the raw annotations from SoccerNet-MVFoul [14] into decision-making tasks. To align with the professional referee's disciplinary logic, we map the original ground-truth labels into four distinct severity levels: *No Offence*, *Normal Offence*, *Offence with Yellow Card*, and *Offence with Red Card*. For each video sample, the mapped ground truth serves as the correct option, while the remaining three severity levels are automatically assigned as distractors. This design compels the model to not merely recognize an action, but to adjudicate its severity against strict officiating standards.

3.4 Knowledge Base Construction

To support accurate decision-making in subsequent intelligent officiating, we construct a specialized domain repository named **RefKnowledgeDB**. This repository comprises two distinct vector databases designed to assist the automated pipeline in retrieval and reasoning.

3.4.1 Laws of the Game (LOTG) Knowledge Base ($\mathcal{K}_{rules}$). We construct the rule-based knowledge base using the latest edition of the IFAB Laws of the Game (2025/26) [33]. To preserve structural integrity and ensure precise citation, we parse the raw PDF documents and perform segmentation at the page level. Each page segment is enriched with metadata and encoded into a high-dimensional vector space using OpenAI's embedding model. This page-level granularity ensures that the retrieved context maintains the semantic coherence of specific regulations.

3.4.2 Classic Case Knowledge Base ($\mathcal{K}_{cases}$). To support high-level Case-Based Reasoning (CBR), we curate a specialized knowledge base comprising 184 historical incidents. These cases are primarily sourced from elite European leagues and the FIFA World Cup, capturing a wide spectrum of standard and controversial officiating scenarios. Each entry is structured in a JSON format that includes a detailed `Case Description`, the official `Decision`, and the perceived `Controversiality` level. This fused text is vectorized to form the retrieval index, while structured attributes are stored as metadata. This design enables the system to retrieve precedents based on semantic similarity across both scenario details and decision outcomes. For a comprehensive breakdown of the data format and source statistics, refer to Appendix B.

4 Methodology

We present **SoccerRef-Agents**, a multi-modal, multi-agent framework designed to mimic the cognitive decision-making process of professional football referees. Unlike traditional end-to-end models, our system decomposes the officiating task into perception, retrieval, legal interpretation, and final adjudication. In this section, we first formulate the problem (Sect. 4.1), show our multi-agent architecture(Sect. 4.2) and detail the agentic workflow for both textual and video-based scenarios (Sect. 4.3).

4.1 Problem Formulation

We define the refereeing task as a conditional generation problem that requires both a discrete decision and a legally grounded explanation. Given a query input q consisting of a textual description q_{txt} or in some cases, together with a video clip q_{vid}, the system aims to generate a final decision y and a corresponding explanation e. The decision y denotes the predicted outcome, and it represents the correct option for theoretical questions or the disciplinary action for video scenarios. Complementing this, e provides a comprehensive justification that synthesizes the specific input evidence with the Laws of the Game [33] and historical precedents. Based on the above definitions, the refereeing task can be formally expressed as follows:

$$(y, e) = \mathcal{F}(q; \mathcal{K}_{rules}, \mathcal{K}_{cases}),$$

where $\mathcal{F}$ represents the **SoccerRef-Agents** system, and $\mathcal{K}$ denotes the external knowledge bases as mentioned in Sect. 3.4.

4.2 Multi-agent Architecture

The core of our framework is a collaborative ecosystem comprising four specialized agents and one central decision-maker. Each agent is designed to handle a distinct aspect of the refereeing workflow, from perception to legal reasoning. To mitigate hallucinations and ensure legally reasoning, the agents are supported by two external vectorized knowledge bases that serve as long-term memory.

4.2.1 Agents. Each agent plays a complementary role, collectively emulating the collaborative decision-making process of a professional refereeing team:

- **Video Agent:** A Vision-Language Model (VLM) specialist responsible for parsing raw video frames into structured textual descriptions and providing initial option recommendations based on visual perception.
- **Rule Agent:** Responsible for interpreting the *Laws of the Game* [33]. It takes the retrieved rules and summarizes their applicability to the current scenario, ensuring decisions are grounded in the official statute.
- **Case Agent:** Specializes in historical analogy. It compares the current situation with retrieved classic cases to provide precedent-based insights, helping to resolve ambiguities through similar past judgments.
- **Context Agent:** Extracts and narrates the match importance (e.g., Derby, Final, League match) provided in the metadata text. This contextual information is crucial for judging subjective factors like "intent" and "game management."
- **Chief Referee Agent:** The final decision-maker. It aggregates the outputs from all subordinate agents (Video, Rule, Case, and Context) to synthesize a comprehensive rationale and derive the final verdict.

4.2.2 Knowledge Retrieval Mechanism. Among the aforementioned agents, the *Rule Agent* and *Case Agent* serve as the most direct and essential components for football rule-based decision-making. To support these two specific agents with precise domain knowledge, we implement a Retrieval-Augmented Generation (RAG) mechanism. This process retrieves the most relevant knowledge segments based on the semantic similarity between the query and the database entries.

To measure the semantic relevance, we utilize cosine similarity. The retrieval process extracts the top-K most relevant segments by maximizing this similarity score. Formally, given a query q' (which can be a text question or a generated video description) and a knowledge base $\mathcal{K}$ (either $\mathcal{K}_{rules}$ or $\mathcal{K}_{cases}$), the retrieval set $\mathcal{R}$ is defined as:

$$\mathcal{R}(q', \mathcal{K}) = \underset{k \in \mathcal{K}}{\text{TopK}} \left(\text{Sim}(\mathbf{E}(q'), \mathbf{E}(k)) \right) \quad (1)$$

where $\mathbf{E}(\cdot)$ is the embedding function mapping inputs to a high-dimensional vector space. The similarity function $\text{Sim}(\cdot, \cdot)$ is explicitly calculated as the dot product of the normalized vectors:

$$\text{Sim}(\mathbf{u}, \mathbf{v}) = \frac{\mathbf{u} \cdot \mathbf{v}}{\|\mathbf{u}\| \|\mathbf{v}\|} = \frac{\sum_{i=1}^{d} u_i v_i}{\sqrt{\sum_{i=1}^{d} u_i^2} \sqrt{\sum_{i=1}^{d} v_i^2}} \quad (2)$$

Here, $\mathbf{u} = \mathbf{E}(q')$ and $\mathbf{v} = \mathbf{E}(k)$ represent the embedding vectors of the query and the knowledge segment, respectively. The TopK operator selects the K segments with the highest similarity scores, which are then passed to the downstream agents for summarization and reasoning (Fig. 3).

4.3 Workflow and Reasoning Chains

Given the variations in the form and focus of the queries we receive, we build upon previous 5 agents to construct a collaborative multi-agent system, which is designed with two distinct reasoning pipelines based on the input modality.

4.3.1 Text-Mode Reasoning Pipeline. When the Router identifies the input as text, the workflow proceeds as follows: (i)*Retrieval:* The input text q_{txt} is used directly as the query to retrieve the top-3 relevant segments from both $\mathcal{K}_{rules}$ and $\mathcal{K}_{cases}$. (ii)*Specialist Analysis:* The *Rule Agent* generates a rule summary (S_{rule}) and a concise logic chain linking the text to the rule based on the retrieved laws. Simultaneously, the *Case Agent* generates a precedent summary (S_{case}) based on similar historical scenarios. (iii)*Final Adjudication:* The *Chief Referee Agent* receives the original text q_{txt}, S_{rule}, and S_{case}. It synthesizes this legal and historical context to select the correct option and generate an explanation.

$$S_{rule} = \mathcal{A}_{rule}(\mathcal{R}(q_{txt}, \mathcal{K}_{rules}))$$

$$S_{case} = \mathcal{A}_{case}(\mathcal{R}(q_{txt}, \mathcal{K}_{cases}))$$

$$(y, e) = \mathcal{A}_{chief}(q_{txt}, S_{rule}, S_{case})$$

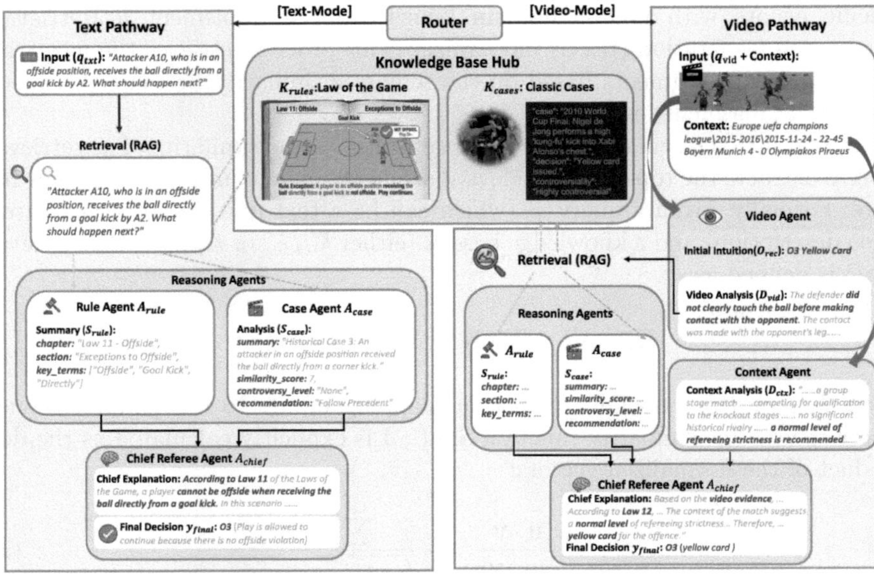

Fig. 3. Overview of the system's dual-pathway reasoning workflow. Depending on the input modality identified by the Router, the system executes either the Text-Mode or Video-Mode pipeline. The **Text-Mode Pipeline** directly utilizes the input query for retrieval. The **Video-Mode Pipeline** features a specialized Cross-Modal RAG mechanism, where the Video Agent converts visual information into a textual Video Analysis (D_{vid}) to bridge the semantic gap for retrieving laws and cases. Both pipelines culminate in the Chief Referee Agent, which synthesizes specialist summaries (S_{rule}, S_{case}) and comprehensive context to render final adjudication.

4.3.2 Video-Mode Reasoning Pipeline. When the Router identifies the input as video, the workflow proceeds as follows: (i) *Visual Perception:* The *Video Agent* processes the video q_{vid}. It outputs two key components: a preliminary recommendation (O_{rec}) and a detailed Video Analysis (D_{vid}), which describes the player actions, contact point, and intensity in natural language. (ii) *Contextualization:* The *Context Agent* processes the accompanying context text q_{ctx} to generate a match background description (D_{ctx}). (iii) *Cross-Modal Retrieval:* Crucially, we use the generated Video Analysis D_{vid} as the query embedding for the RAG module. This bridges the modality gap, allowing us to retrieve relevant rules and cases based on the visual narrative.The *Rule Agent* produces S_{rule} based on D_{vid} driven retrieval, and the *Case Agent* produces S_{case} based on D_{vid} driven retrieval. (iv) *Aggregation & Decision:* The *Chief Referee Agent* synthesizes the comprehensive information set: $\{O_{rec}, D_{vid}, D_{ctx}, S_{rule}, S_{case}\}$. This allows the Chief Referee to validate the *Video Agent*'s initial intuition against strict rules and precedents before making the final decision.

$$D_{vid}, O_{rec} = \mathcal{A}_{video}(q_{vid})$$
$$D_{ctx} = \mathcal{A}_{context}(q_{ctx})$$
$$S_{rule} = \mathcal{A}_{rule}(\mathcal{R}(D_{vid}, \mathcal{K}_{rules}))$$
$$S_{case} = \mathcal{A}_{case}(\mathcal{R}(D_{vid}, \mathcal{K}_{cases}))$$
$$(y, e) = \mathcal{A}_{chief}(O_{rec}, D_{vid}, D_{ctx}, S_{rule}, S_{case})$$

5 Experiments

Based on the multi-agent system we have constructed, we conducted extensive experiments to evaluate its performance. This section outlines the experimental protocols in Sect. 5.1, reports comprehensive quantitative comparisons against state-of-the-art MLLMs in Sect. 5.2 and Sect. 5.3, shows human evaluation in Sect. 5.4, and concludes with qualitative analysis in Sect. 5.5.

5.1 Experimental Settings

5.1.1 Baselines. We evaluate our **SoccerRef-Agents** against a comprehensive suite of state-of-the-art MLLMs on **SoccerRefBench**, covering both proprietary commercial APIs and open-source models. *(i) Commercial APIs:* We leading commercial APIs with top-tier performance on broad multimodal and reasoning tasks, including GPT-4o [23], Claude 4.5 Sonnet [1] and Gemini 2.5 Flash [11]. These API models are prompted with detailed system instructions but rely solely on their internal parametric knowledge (i.e., without external retrieval). *(ii) Open-Source Models:* We evaluate the Qwen3-VL series (8B and 32B) [32] as competitive public VLMs for both text and video understanding. Additionally, for the text-only task, we include DeepSeek-V3 [21] as a strong textual baseline.

5.1.2 Metrics. As for the evaluation on our proposed benchmark **SoccerRefBench**, we employ Accuracy (Acc) as the primary quantitative metric for both subsets. To further assess the interpretability and practical validity of the system's decisions, we introduce a human evaluation protocol. In this protocol, evaluations are conducted by individuals with professional refereeing experience. The details of this protocol are elaborated in Sect. 5.4.

5.2 Quantitative Results

We present the comparative results on **SoccerRefBench** in Table 1. Our observations are as follows: (i) The results on **SoccerRefBench** exhibit a broad performance spectrum, effectively differentiating the capabilities of various MLLMs. Accuracy scores span from 46.88% to 79.56% in the text domain and 23.50% to

Table 1. Main Results on **SoccerRefBench**. We compare **SoccerRef-Agents** with state-of-the-art commercial and open-source MLLMs. The best performance is highlighted in **bold**, and the second best is <u>underlined</u>. Note that DeepSeek-V3 [21] is a text-only model and is thus evaluated only on the Text subset.

Model	Text(%)	Video(%)	Overall(%)
Open-Source Models			
Qwen3-VL-8B [32]	46.88	23.50	39.16
Qwen3-VL-32B [32]	56.57	24.33	45.93
DeepSeek-V3 [21]	65.35	-	-
Commercial APIs			
Gemini 2.5 Flash [11]	69.38	26.33	55.17
Claude 4.5 Sonnet [1]	65.19	34.67	55.12
GPT-4o [23]	<u>77.83</u>	<u>37.67</u>	<u>64.58</u>
SoccerRef-Agents (Ours)	**79.56**	**40.17**	**66.56**

40.17% in the video domain. This significant variance underscores the complexity and diversity of our benchmark, confirming that it serves as a rigorous testing ground capable of distinguishing the performance gaps between standard open-source models, advanced commercial APIs, and specialized agentic systems. (ii) As shown in Table 1, **SoccerRef-Agents** achieves the highest accuracy across both modalities. In the text domain, our system reaches **79.56%**, surpassing the strongest baseline (GPT-4o [23]) by 1.73%. This indicates that even highly capable generalist models like GPT-4o struggle with the professional soccer referee theories and highly specific knowledge required for professional referee exams, whereas our RAG-enhanced *Rule Agent* effectively closes this gap. (iii) The video domain task proves to be extremely challenging for all models, with no baseline exceeding 38% accuracy. This highlights the intrinsic difficulty of distinguishing subtle foul grades solely from broadcast footage. Despite this, **SoccerRef-Agents** achieves state-of-the-art performance with **40.17%** accuracy, outperforming GPT-4o [23] (+2.5%) and significantly surpassing open-source video models like Qwen3-VL [32] (+15.8%). This performance gain validates our cross-modal design, where the system aligns visual descriptions with textual rules and historical knowledge to make more informed decisions.

5.3 Ablation Studies

To further investigate the individual contributions of our specialized knowledge bases and the synergy between the *Rule Agent* and *Case Agent*, we conduct ablation experiments on the **SoccerRefBench**. We evaluate three configurations: (i) **SoccerRef-Agents (Full)**, our complete multi-agent framework; (ii) **w/o Rule Agent**, where the system relies solely on historical precedents and internal knowledge; and (iii) **w/o Case Agent**, where the system only retrieves information from the *Laws of the Game* [33].

Table 2. Ablation Study of Knowledge Components. We report the Accuracy (%) on the Text (1,218 Qs), Video (600 Qs) subsets, and the weighted Overall performance.

Variant	Text	Video	Overall
w/o Rule Agent	78.90%	**42.50%**	**66.89%**
w/o Case Agent	**79.89%**	39.17%	66.45%
SoccerRef-Agents (Full)	79.56%	40.17%	66.56%

The results in Table 2 reveal a notable divergence in knowledge utilization across modalities. The text task exhibits rule-heavy characteristics, achieving peak accuracy (**79.89%**) when relying solely on the *Rule Agent*; here, historical cases act as noise that interferes with strictly literal rule interpretations. Conversely, the video task is inherently case-heavy, with the *w/o Rule Agent* variant reaching the highest accuracy (**42.50%**). This suggests that practical officiating requires the guide of precedents to navigate subjective visual scenarios where rigid rule-following may prove too restrictive. Although individual components yield marginal gains in specialized domains, our full **SoccerRef-Agents** framework provides the most robust balance across both modalities. Crucially, as shown in our human evaluation, integrating both the rule guideline and historical precedents is essential for generating the professionally justifiable and legally grounded explanations required for multi-modal refereeing.

5.4 Human Evaluation of Explanation Quality

Accuracy alone does not fully capture the utility of an AI referee; the reasoning process must be transparent, authoritative, and legally binding. Since current automatic metrics correlate poorly with logical validity in this specialized domain, we conduct a rigorous human evaluation campaign.

We focus our evaluation on comparing **SoccerRef-Agents** against the top-performing baseline, **GPT-4o** [23]. We randomly sample 100 textual questions and 50 video questions from our **SoccerRefBench**. We invite three certified referees authorized by the Chinese Football Association to act as expert annotators. To ensure objectivity, the evaluation is conducted in a blind setting where the source of each explanation is masked.Unlike general readability scores, our scoring rubric is strictly tailored to professional officiating standards. Experts rate each explanation on a 1–5 Likert scale whose definition can be checked in the appendix D.

The comparative evaluation results from three expert referees are detailed in Table 3. While GPT-4o [23] exhibits strong linguistic fluency, experts noted it frequently falters in rule adherence, inventing plausible-sounding but non-existent regulations. In contrast, our system effectively minimizes such domain-specific hallucinations. By explicitly citing the *Laws of the Game* [33] and anchoring reasoning in historical precedents, **SoccerRef-Agents** provides more trustworthy and legally grounded explanations, closely mirroring professional cognitive workflows.

Table 3. Human Evaluation Results. Three professional referees rated the explanation quality (1–5 scale). Columns denote average scores for Text (100 Qs), Video (50 Qs), and Overall weighted performance.

Model	Referee 1			Referee 2			Referee 3			Average		
	Text	Video	Overall	Text	Video	Overall	Text	Video	Overall	Text	Video	Overall
GPT-4o [23]	3.63	2.70	3.32	3.65	2.70	3.33	3.72	2.80	3.41	3.67	2.73	3.36
Ours	**3.76**	**2.76**	**3.43**	**4.09**	**3.24**	**3.81**	**3.96**	**3.18**	**3.70**	**3.94**	**3.06**	**3.65**

5.5 Qualitative Analysis

To demonstrate the interpretability and reasoning depth of **SoccerRef-Agents**, we present a visualization of the decision-making process in Fig. 4. Unlike black-box models that output a label without context, our system provides a transparent "glass-box" view of its logic through detailed `agent_traces`.

As illustrated in Fig. 4, our framework effectively handles diverse modalities. For theoretical questions, the system accurately retrieves specific chapters from the *Laws of the Game*. For instance, in the second column regarding a disqualified coach, the *Rule Agent* correctly pinpoints "Law 3 - The Players" and "Extra persons on the field of play". Simultaneously, the *Case Agent* retrieves a historical precedent with a high similarity score (9/10), reinforcing the *Chief Referee Agent*'s decision to "terminate the game" rather than merely delaying it. In complex visual scenarios, the *Video Agent* acts as the primary perceiver. In the third column, the agent explicitly notes that "the video frames do not clearly show any [contact]". This visual evidence drives the *Chief Referee Agent* to conclude "No Offence," aligning with the ground truth. Also, in the video questions, the *Context Agent* identifies the match such as "league match in the Bundesliga between Wolfsburg and Dortmund". These information provides match context for the *Chief Referee Agent* to confirm the standard of judgment. This granular visibility into the reasoning process confirms that **SoccerRef-Agents** does not merely memorize answers but actively constructs a legal argument, significantly enhancing trust in automated officiating. More results are provided in the Appendix E.

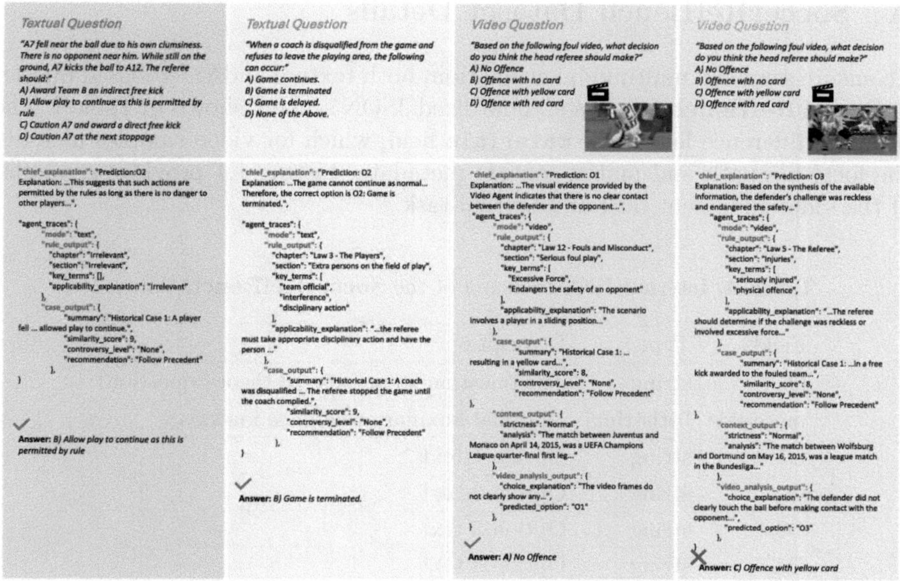

Fig. 4. Qualitative examples of **SoccerRef-Agents** on **SoccerRefBench**. The figure illustrates the step-by-step reasoning chains for both textual (left two columns) and video-based (right two columns) queries. Key intermediate outputs from the Rule Agent, Case Agent, and Video Agent are explicitly logged in `agent_traces`, providing legally grounded justifications for the final decision.

6 Conclusion

This paper presents a comprehensive framework for explainable and standardized automated soccer refereeing for multimodal scenarios. Concretely, we introduce **SoccerRefBench**, a unique multimodal benchmark bridging theoretical exams and practical video judgments, accompanied by a specialized vector knowledge base **RefKnowledgeDB** to ensure legal precision. To tackle the complexity of officiating logic, we establish **SoccerRef-Agents**, a novel multi-agent system that mimics the collaborative workflow of professional referee teams. By leveraging a cross-modal Retrieval-Augmented Generation (RAG) mechanism, our system effectively translates visual evidence into rule-based reasoning, bridging the gap between perception and adjudication. Extensive evaluations have demonstrated the superiority of our framework, showing that it not only achieves higher accuracy than general-purpose models but also provides transparent, citation-backed explanations. We believe this work establishes a new foundation for fair, transparent, and interpretable AI assistants in sports officiating.

A SoccerRefBench Dataset Details

To ensure seamless multimodal evaluation, both textual and video-based queries in **SoccerRefBench** follow a standardized JSON schema shown in Table 4. The primary difference lies in the `materials` field, which for video samples includes the local file path and match context metadata. Listing 1.1 provides examples of the video judgment task and textual task.

Table 4. Internal JSON Schema of the **SoccerRefBench** Dataset.

Field	Type	Description
Q	string	The question stem (referee theory question)
materials	list[string]	Optional auxiliary reference materials
O1	string	Option 1 text
O2	string	Option 2 text
O3	string	Option 3 text
O4	string	Option 4 text
openA	string	Ground-truth answer in natural language
closeA	string	Ground-truth option label

Listing 1.1. SoccerRefBench Dataset Example

```
{
    "Q": "Based on the following foul video, what decision do you think the head referee should make?",
    "materials": [
      {
        "path": "Dataset/video/SoccerNet/mvfouls/train/action_620/clip_1.mp4",
        "context": "europe_uefa-champions-league\\2014-2015\\2015-04-14 - 21-45 Juventus 1 - 0 Monaco"
      }
    ],
    "openA": "Offence with no card",
    "closeA":"O2",
    "O1": "No offence",
    "O2": "Offence with no card",
    "O3": "Offence with yellow card",
    "O4": "Offence with possible red card"
},
{
    "Q": "Player A1 kicks off to start the second half of the game. Player A1's kick goes directly into Team B's goal. The referee should:",
```

```
    "materials": [
      "none"
    ],
    "openA": "Award the goal and restart the match with a kickoff for Team B.",
    "closeA": "04",
    "01": "Disallow the goal and have Team A retake the kickoff.",
    "02": "Disallow the goal and have Team A take an indirect free kick from the halfway line.",
    "03": "Disallow the goal and award Team B a goal kick.",
    "04": "Award the goal and restart the match with a kickoff for Team B."
}
```

B Classic Case Knowledge Base Details

B.1 Raw Case Format

Before vectorization into the **RefKnowledgeDB**, historical cases are curated in a structured format capturing the incident, the official decision, and the perceived controversiality. Listing 1.2 showcases the raw entries.

Listing 1.2. Structured format of historical cases in the Classic Case Knowledge Base.

```
{
  "id": 4,
  "case": "2024 Premier League: Declan Rice receives a second yellow card for slightly kicking the ball away to delay the restart.",
  "decision": "Second yellow card and red card issued.",
  "controversiality": "Highly controversial"
},
{
    "id": 61,
    "case": "2012 UCL: John Terry knees Alexis Sanchez in the back during an off-the-ball incident.",
    "decision": "Red card issued.",
    "controversiality": "Non-controversial"
},
{
    "id": 179,
    "case": "2021 La Liga: Referee calls players back from the locker room to take a penalty after VAR review.",
    "decision": "Penalty awarded.",
    "controversiality": "Somewhat controversial"
}
```

B.2 Source Statistics

The cases are aggregated from authoritative tournament archives and officiating review panels. Table 5 summarizes the distribution of historical precedents.

Table 5. Distribution of sources for the Classic Case Database.

Source Authority	Number of Cases
FIFA World Cup	72
Premier League	40
UEFA Champions League	24
Bundesliga	19
La Liga	17
Euro Cup	12

C Multi-agent System Prompts

In this section, we provide the specialized system prompts for each agent in **SoccerRef-Agents**.

Rule Agent System Prompt

You are an expert AI Legal Analyst specializing in the IFAB Laws of the Game. Your task is to strictly analyze the provided rule excerpts and identify the exact clause that governs the user's scenario.

Rule Agent User Prompt

Context (Retrieved IFAB Laws): `{retrieved_rules}`
Scenario: "*{query_text}*"

Instructions:
- Analyze the specific Law, Section, and Bullet Point.
- Prioritize specific offenses (e.g., **Serious Foul Play**).
- Extract text verbatim if relevant.

Expected Output: JSON format with `direct_quote`, `key_terminology_match`, and `confidence` fields.

Context Agent User Prompt

Match Context: `{context_str}`

Instructions:
- Analyze the match importance (e.g., Derby, Final, League match), home/-away factors, and potential team rivalries.
- Determine the recommended refereeing strictness (Lenient, Normal, Strict).

Expected Output (JSON):
A JSON object containing:
- `strictness`: Recommended enforcement level.
- `analysis`: Brief justification based on match atmosphere and stakes.

Video Agent System Prompt

You are a professional AI Soccer Referee Assistant. The input contains video frames from a **live soccer match broadcast replay**. Output JSON only.

Video Agent User Prompt

Input Type: Broadcast Replay Video

Question: `{question_text}`

Options:
`{options_str}`

Instructions:
- Analyze the input video carefully.
- Select the ONE correct option ID.
- Provide a brief explanation in English.

Expected Output (JSON ONLY):
```
{
  "choice_explanation": "...",
  "predicted_option": "01"
}
```

Chief Referee Agent System Prompt

You are the Chief Referee Agent, the final decision-maker in a multi-agent soccer refereeing system. Your role is to synthesize evidence from specialized subordinate agents (Rule, Case, Context, and Video) to provide a definitive ruling on complex foul scenarios.

Chief Referee Agent User Prompt

=== **QUESTION DATA** ===
Question: {question_text}
Options: {options_text}
PS: 'A#' means player of team A with jersey number #, same for 'B#'.

=== **SUBORDINATE AGENT REPORTS** ===
[1] Reference Law:
{rule_str_placeholder} *%(Includes Text of Law, Match Logic, and Confidence)%*

[2] Reference Precedents:
{case_str_placeholder} *%(Includes Valid Precedent or No Precedent status)%*

[3] Reference Context (Video Mode Only):
{context_analysis}

[4] Visual Evidence (Video Agent):

- **Video Agent's Choice Explanation:** {desc}
- **Video Agent's Initial Intuition:** {pred}

=== **INSTRUCTIONS** ===
- Analyze the provided input text and subordinate reports carefully.
- Select the most correct ONE option ID.
- Provide a brief explanation in English.

OUTPUT FORMAT:
```
Prediction: [Option ID]
Explanation: [Reasoning]
```

D Details on Human Evaluation of Explanation Quality

We created an html webpage for the professional referees to score the quality of explanation output by the model

D.1 The Definition of Likert Scale

- **5 - Perfect:** Precisely identifies the foul or answers the theory question with correct legal citations. The causal logic is clear, and the terminology is professional.
- **4 - Good:** The verdict and key descriptions are correct. May contain minor terminological imprecisions or verbose explanations, but the core reasoning is valid.
- **3 - Fair:** The conclusion is correct, but the explanation contains slight hallucinations or misses rule support.

- **2 - Poor:** Cites incorrect rules or describes actions significantly inconsistent with the video evidence.
- **1 - Nonsense:** Contains severe hallucinations or chaotic logic that contradicts basic football common sense.

D.2 Human Evaluation Interface

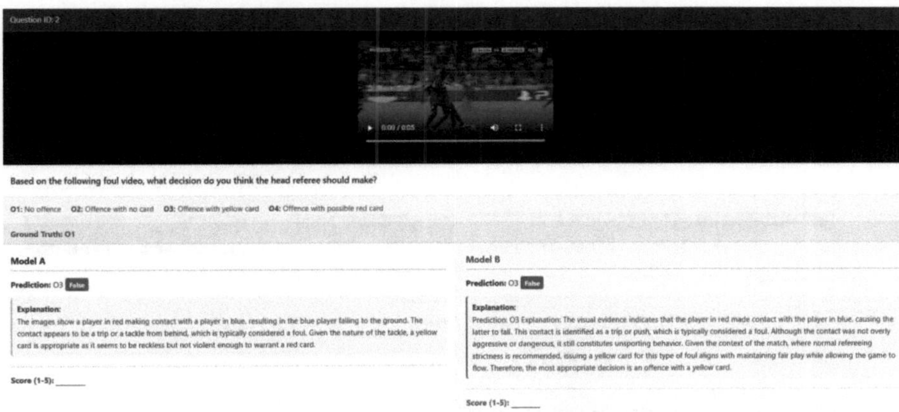

Fig. 5. Human Evaluation Interface.

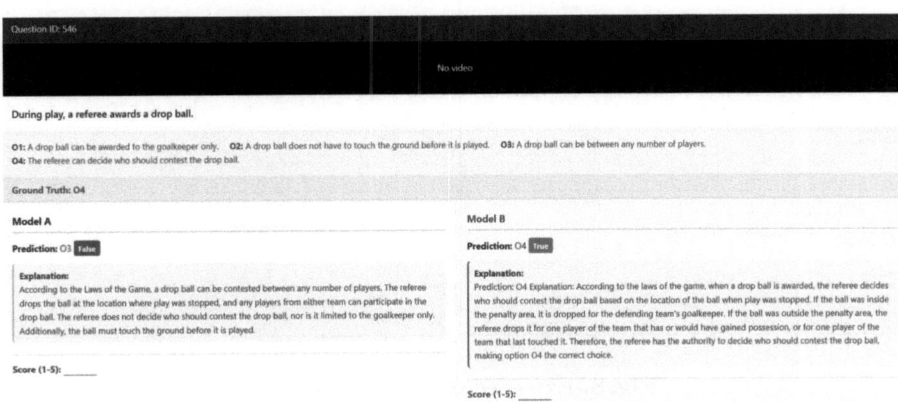

Fig. 6. Human Evaluation Interface.

E Additional Qualitative Results

Figure 7 and Fig. 8 present further examples of **SoccerRef-Agents**'s performance on **SoccerRefBench** (Fig. 5 and 6).

Fig. 7. Extended qualitative results.

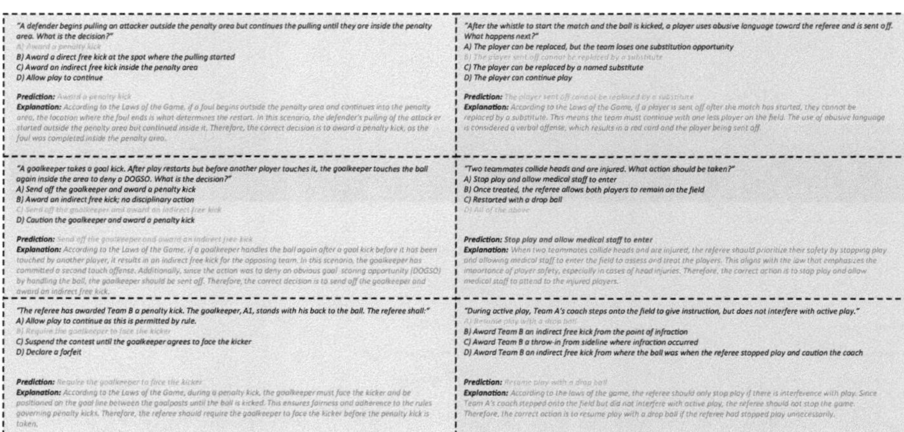

Fig. 8. Extended qualitative results.

References

1. Anthropic: Claude 4.5 sonnet. https://www.anthropic.com (2025)
2. Bai, L., Gedik, R., Egilmez, G.: What does it take to win or lose a soccer game? a machine learning approach to understand the impact of game and team statistics. J. Oper. Res. Society **74**(7), 1690–1711 (2023)
3. Bai, Z., et al.: Hallucination of multimodal large language models: A survey. (2024). arXiv preprint arXiv:2404.18930
4. Cioppa, A., et al.: Soccernet 2024 challenges results. ArXiv: 2409.10587 (2024). https://api.semanticscholar.org/CorpusID:272693834
5. Dong, B., Ni, M., Huang, Z., Yang, G., Zuo, W., Zhang, L.: Mirage: assessing hallucination in multimodal reasoning chains of MLLM (2025). arXiv preprint arXiv:2505.24238
6. Elmiligi, H., Saad, S.: Predicting the outcome of soccer matches using machine learning and statistical analysis. In: 2022 IEEE 12th Annual Computing and Communication Workshop and Conference (CCWC), pp. 1–8. IEEE (2022)
7. FIFA: Semi-automated offside technology. Inside FIFA (July 17 2023). https://inside.fifa.com/innovation/world-cup-2022/semi-automated-offside-technology. Accessed 13 Jan 2026
8. Fu, C., et al.: Video-MME: The first-ever comprehensive evaluation benchmark of multi-modal LLMs in video analysis. In: Proceedings of the Computer Vision and Pattern Recognition Conference, pp. 24108–24118 (2025)
9. Giancola, S., Amine, M., Dghaily, T., Ghanem, B.: Soccernet: a scalable dataset for action spotting in soccer videos. In: Proceedings of the IEEE Conference on Computer Vision and Pattern Recognition Workshops, pp. 1711–1721 (2018)
10. Giancola, S., et al.: Soccernet 2025 challenges results. ArXiv:2508.19182 (2025). https://api.semanticscholar.org/CorpusID:280870241
11. Google: Gemini 2.5 flash. https://deepmind.google (2025)
12. Gottschalk, C., Tewes, S., Niestroj, B., Jäger, C., Drees, J., Ernst, A.: Innovation in elite refereeing through ai technological support for dogso decisions. Int. J. Oper. Manage. **2**(3), 7–15 (2022)
13. He, X., et al.: Mmworld: Towards multi-discipline multi-faceted world model evaluation in videos. arXiv preprint arXiv:2406.08407 (2024)
14. Held, J., Cioppa, A., Giancola, S., Hamdi, A., Ghanem, B., Van Droogenbroeck, M.: Vars: Video assistant referee system for automated soccer decision making from multiple views. In: Proceedings of the IEEE/CVF Conference on Computer Vision and Pattern Recognition, pp. 5086–5097. (2023)
15. Held, J., Itani, H., Cioppa, A., Giancola, S., Ghanem, B., Van Droogenbroeck, M.: X-vars: Introducing explainability in football refereeing with multi-modal large language models. In: Proceedings of the IEEE/CVF Conference on Computer Vision and Pattern Recognition, pp. 3267–3279. (2024)
16. Kuang, J., et al.: Natural language understanding and inference with MLLM in visual question answering: A survey. ACM Comput. Surv. **57**(8), 1–36 (2025)
17. Kubayi, A., Larkin, P.: Match-related statistics differentiating winning and losing teams at the 2019 Africa cup of nations soccer championship. Front. Sports Active Living **4**, 807198 (2022)
18. Lee, G.J., Jung, J.J.: DNN-based multi-output model for predicting soccer team tactics. PeerJ Comput. Sci. **8**, e853 (2022)
19. Li, H., et al.: Sports-qa: A large-scale video question answering benchmark for complex and professional sports. arXiv preprint arXiv:2401.01505 (2024)

20. Li, Q., Chiu, T.C., Huang, H.W., Sun, M.T., Ku, W.S.: Videobadminton: a video dataset for badminton action recognition. In: 2024 IEEE International Conference on Big Data (BigData), pp. 1387–1392. IEEE (2024)
21. Liu, A., et al.: Deepseek-v3 technical report, (2024). arXiv preprint arXiv:2412.19437
22. Mkhallati, H., Cioppa, A., Giancola, S., Ghanem, B., Van Droogenbroeck, M.: Soccernet-caption: Dense video captioning for soccer broadcasts commentaries. In: Proceedings of the IEEE/CVF Conference on Computer Vision and Pattern Recognition, pp. 5074–5085. (2023)
23. OpenAI: Gpt-4o. https://openai.com (2024)
24. Plakias, S., Kokkotis, C., Giakas, G., Tsaopoulos, D., Moustakidis, S.: Can artificial intelligence revolutionize soccer tactical analysis? Trends in Sport Sci. **31**(3) (2024)
25. Qi, M., Wang, Y., Li, A., Luo, J.: Sports video captioning via attentive motion representation and group relationship modeling. IEEE Trans. Circuits Syst. Video Technol. **30**(8), 2617–2633 (2019)
26. Rao, J., Li, Z., Wu, H., Zhang, Y., Wang, Y., Xie, W.: Multi-agent system for comprehensive soccer understanding. In: Proceedings of the 33rd ACM International Conference on Multimedia, pp. 3654–3663. (2025)
27. Rao, J., Wu, H., Jiang, H., Zhang, Y., Wang, Y., Xie, W.: Towards universal soccer video understanding. In: Proceedings of the Computer Vision and Pattern Recognition Conference, pp. 8384–8394. (2025)
28. Rao, J., Wu, H., Liu, C., Wang, Y., Xie, W.: Matchtime: Towards automatic soccer game commentary generation (2024). arXiv preprint arXiv:2406.18530
29. Shao, D., Zhao, Y., Dai, B., Lin, D.: Finegym: a hierarchical video dataset for fine-grained action understanding. In: Proceedings of the IEEE/CVF Conference on Computer Vision and Pattern Recognition, pp. 2616–2625 (2020)
30. Somers, V., et al.: Soccernet game state reconstruction: End-to-end athlete tracking and identification on a minimap. In: Proceedings of the IEEE/CVF Conference on Computer Vision and Pattern Recognition, pp. 3293–3305 (2024)
31. Spitz, J., Wagemans, J., Memmert, D., Williams, A.M., Helsen, W.F.: Video assistant referees (var): The impact of technology on decision making in association football referees. J. Sports Sci. **39**(2), 147–153 (2021)
32. Team, Q.: Qwen3-vl. https://github.com/QwenLM/Qwen3-VL (2025)
33. The International Football Association Board: Laws of the Game 2025/26. The International Football Association Board, Zurich, Switzerland (2025). https://www.theifab.com, effective from 1st July 2025
34. Wang, J., Li, L.: A method for feature division of soccer foul actions based on salience image semantics. PLoS ONE **20**(6), e0322889 (2025)
35. Xia, H., et al.: Sportu: A comprehensive sports understanding benchmark for multimodal large language models, (2024). arXiv preprint arXiv:2410.08474
36. Xu, J., Rao, Y., Yu, X., Chen, G., Zhou, J., Lu, J.: Finediving: A fine-grained dataset for procedure-aware action quality assessment. In: Proceedings of the IEEE/CVF Conference on Computer Vision and Pattern Recognition, pp. 2949–2958 (2022)
37. Xu, J., Zhao, G., Yin, S., Zhou, W., Peng, Y.: Finesports: a multi-person hierarchical sports video dataset for fine-grained action understanding. In: Proceedings of the IEEE/CVF Conference on Computer Vision and Pattern Recognition, pp. 21773–21782 (2024)
38. You, L., et al.: Timesoccer: An end-to-end multimodal large language model for soccer commentary generation. In: Proceedings of the 33rd ACM International Conference on Multimedia, pp. 3418–3427 (2025)

39. Yuan, H., Ni, D., Wang, M.: Spatio-temporal dynamic inference network for group activity recognition. In: Proceedings of the IEEE/CVF International Conference on Computer Vision, pp. 7476–7485 (2021)
40. Zahan, S., Hassan, G.M., Mian, A.: Learning sparse temporal video mapping for action quality assessment in floor gymnastics. IEEE Trans. Instrum. Meas. **73**, 1–11 (2024)
41. Zhekambayeva, M., Yerekesheva, M., Ramashov, N., Seidakhmetov, Y., Kulambayev, B.: Designing an artificial intelligence-powered video assistant referee system for team sports using computer vision. Retos: nuevas tendencias en educación física, deporte y recreación (61), 1162–1170 (2024)
42. Zhou, J., et al.: MLVU: A comprehensive benchmark for multi-task long video understanding. arXiv e-prints pp. arXiv-2406 (2024)
43. Zhu, K., Wong, A., McPhee, J.: Fencenet: fine-grained footwork recognition in fencing. In: Proceedings of the IEEE/CVF Conference on Computer Vision and Pattern Recognition, pp. 3589–3598 (2022)

Design, Deployment, and Evaluation of an Open-Source College Football Championship Prediction Model

Charles Jeffrey Danoff[1] (✉) and Cecil Isaih Battiste[2]

[1] Mr. Danoff's Teaching Laboratory, LLC Post Office, Box 802738, Chicago, IL 60680, USA
contact@mr.danoff.org
[2] Fireball Findings, Atlanta, GA 30076, USA
isaih@fireballfindings.com

Abstract. This paper introduces a new open-source ranking model for college football. Historically, teams have been ranked by voters and this has led to numerous controversies and allegations of human bias. Additionally, many polls were designed last century and do not consider the new nuances of the College Football Playoff (CFP) era. Our model is trained only on playoff seasons and is purely driven by quantitative metrics. We explain our research framework and model architecture then share the results. Before the playoffs began our model successfully predicted the champion Indiana Hoosiers and had the runner-up Miami Hurricanes rated higher than the CFP Selection Committee.

Keywords: Football · Gridiron Football · Sports Polls · Predictive Analytics · American Football · College Football · Sports Analytics · Player-Ranking · Data Science · Multivariate Regression

1 Introduction

In the United States of America ranking men's college football (CFB) teams has been a contentious debate for over a century. It was easier in the early 1890s when "The Game" [1, 2] between Harvard and Yale was most important. However, soon afterward when there were over a hundred teams [3], it became more of a challenge as they cannot play each other each year since the regular season is only 12 games long.

Given these mathematical constraints, how could a national champion be reliably chosen? Historically, polls have been one approach [4]. They are public rankings designed to pick the top 25 teams before, during, and after the season. The best team was determined by voters each time. For most of CFB history, there was no championship or playoff. The top teams did not face one another in a tournament to determine the number one squad. The champion was a matter of opinion and ultimately decided by the polls.

Of course, human voters are fallible. Traditional polls are subjective, biased, and inconsistent. In years like 1915 instead of one national poll champion, there were four [5]. This often led to famous programs from popular conferences being at the top due to

Z. Liu and V. Misra (Eds.): ISACE 2026, LNCS 16610, pp. 428–441, 2026.
https://doi.org/10.1007/978-3-032-27272-0_27

big-name brand recognition. The Bowl Championship Series (BCS) [6, 7] was an attempt to remove human bias from the rankings, instead relying on a proprietary mathematical formula. It was used from 1998 to 2013, but those results still led to controversies [24]. Many fans were not fully comfortable with the idea of "a computer" deciding which two teams would be facing off in the national championship game instead of a playoff.

A famous example of an odd team out was the 2004 Auburn Tigers, who did not get a chance to compete for the national championship despite going undefeated and winning the traditionally powerful Southeastern Conference (SEC). The University of Southern California (USC) and the University of Oklahoma (OU) also went undefeated, but they started higher in the preseason polls relative to Auburn's initial ranking of #17. This kept them just out of reach for the Tigers.

The fact that Auburn never lost a game yet did not compete in the final game of the year seemed unfair to many. Due to the BCS model, situations like this could occur where there were only two musical chairs and three teams seeking a seat. The proposed solution was the current College Football Playoff (CFP) format.

Instead of the voters or computers immediately narrowing things down to one winner or two teams playing in a national championship game, the committee is tasked with selecting 12 teams who compete for the crown in a playoff. The original playoff consisted of four teams (2014–2023), with the expansion to 12 happening in 2024. Given how the CFB landscape has changed so drastically, we felt that a new type of ranking was necessary.

Put simply, our motivation was captured by co-author Isaih in 2024 [8] "SEC Bias and the overall discourse over CFB playoff rankings this year and last have driven me so nuts that I'm very tempted to come up with a new computer ranking system to replace the BCS by next year." That next year we made a quantitative ranking with the objective of predicting the likelihood that a given team will win the championship.

Our training data was constrained only to the CFP-era to preserve temporal validity. We do not use any poll rankings; it is purely based on interpretable numbers, hopefully free from regency and big-name brand bias of humans. The CFP era (2014–present) represents a structurally distinct decision environment. We do not care who is hypothetically the #1 team in abstract. We want to know who will emerge victorious from the playoff bracket.

Another issue is that many historical rankings lack transparency, reproducibility, and consistency. It is not clear who voted for which team nor is the methodology transparent. While the AP poll does publish its methodology and voters [9] the Coach's poll ballots are kept secret [10]. Other polls out there, like the BCS, are "proprietary" or "closed source" to borrow a term from software development. Fans cannot see the math nor adapt it to their own specifications. On the contrary, the code for our model is open. It contributes to the open-source sports analytics community. We want to give fans a poll they can easily understand and modify to suit their needs. There is a near-infinite amount of discussion and passion for the topic out there as many people across the country have a vested interest in CFB as fans want their team to have a fair shot at being crowned national champions. The game and the way teams are measured is ever evolving so we view our model as a step in the right direction to meet fans where they are at today and to give them a path towards more accurate analyses in the future.

This is an important facet of the novelty of our model. In addition, it is complemented by champion profile criteria derived from actual CFP winners. The games are over so we evaluate results of how our CFP-era–constrained training model fared during the 2025–26 season.

2 Research Design

To be clear, we are not researching football as is used in most countries or "soccer". Our focus is North American or "gridiron" football. If you are not familiar with the game, see our 2025 paper [11] for a brief explanation of rules and positions from a sports analytics perspective designed for an international audience. That paper describes the National Football League (NFL) while this one is focused on teams in the National Collegiate Athletic Association (NCAA) Division I Football Bowl Subdivision (FBS), also referred to as "college football" in general parlance.

A gap analysis of modern polls revealed a need for an objective, reproducible ranking system. Existing rankings are not optimized to work for CFP prediction, specifically. Most systems either rely on subjective inputs or ignore institutional regime shifts like the CFP. We sought to predict one thing: *Who will win the CFP and become national champion?*

This is a different goal than abstractly answering "Who is the best college football team?" as most traditional polls seemingly seek to find. Of course, we still considered using AP poll rankings as a predictor. Including them made the predictive model machine learning results "better" in terms of predictive accuracy, as shown in Subsect. 3.3, but we wanted ours to be "pure". Thus, we only chose metrics that were quantitative and free from human selector bias.

The research question guiding this study became: *What levels of Win Percentage (Win%), Simple Rating System (SRS), and Strength of Schedule (SOS) are associated with winning a championship in the CFP-era?*

We defined winning a championship as (y). A binary dependent variable where $y = 1$ indicates CFP champion, where $y = 0$ indicates non-champion. We had three independent variables:

- β_1 = Win% is the proportion of games won in season.
- β_2 = SOS, or Strength of Schedule, is a rating that "is denominated in points above/below average, where zero is average." [12] A high positive SOS means they faced a difficult schedule, where a negative SOS indicates a weak schedule.
- β_3 = SRS, or Simple Rating System, is "a rating that takes into account average point differential and SOS … it should be noted that margin of victory has been assigned a lower bound of 7 points and an upper bound of 24 points." [12] A higher SRS indicates a stronger team.

SRS and SOS are treated as distinct metrics. Our global model null hypothesis is that all coefficients in the model (Win Percentage, SRS, and SOS) are equal to zero. In other words, none of the three predictor variables have a statistically significant relationship with the response variable, y.

H_0: $\beta_1 = \beta_2 = \beta_3 = 0$ (all coefficients equal zero; predictors have no effect).

The global alternative hypothesis states that not every coefficient is simultaneously equal to zero.

H_a: Not all $\beta_i = 0$ (at least 1 predictor significantly affects championship probability).

The first single variable null hypothesis is that Win% is not a statistically significant predictor of championship probability when controlling for SRS and SOS.

$$H_{01} : \beta_1 = 0.$$

The first single variable alternative hypothesis is that Win% is a statistically significant predictor of championship probability when controlling for SRS and SOS.

$$H_{a^1} : \beta_1 \neq 0.$$

The second single variable null hypothesis tests whether SOS is associated with championship probability when controlling for Win% and SRS within the fitted model.

$$H_{02} : \beta_2 = 0.$$

$$H_{a^2} : \beta_2 \neq 0.$$

The final single variable null hypothesis tests whether SRS is a significant predictor, holding Win% and SOS constant.

$$H_{03} : \beta_3 = 0.$$

$$H_{a^3} : \beta_3 \neq 0.$$

To achieve our goal of making an open-source poll that successfully predicts the champion, we chose a hybrid approach. While we wanted a sound statistical foundation for our model, we prioritized machine learning (ML) results for predictability.

3 Deployment Methodology

Our software stack utilized Jupyter notebooks, Python code, and artificial intelligence (AI) large language models (LLMs). Specifically, we leveraged ChatGPT 5.1 from OpenAI, DeepSeek AI Version 3.2, Perplexity, Claude Sonnet 4.5, and Claud haiku 4.5 to assist with code generation, debugging, and methodological discussions.

For statistical testing of logistic regression we used the statsmodels python library. In the following subsections we detail our methodological approach from acquiring data, to architecting the model, determining championship criteria and then evaluating metrics.

3.1 Data Acquisition

We considered multiple sources, but decided upon the famous, wonderful Sports Reference, LLC college football [13] site as our primary source. It has over a century and a half of data from 1869 to 2025.

We created a custom web scraper in Python to acquire the data. It downloads from the URL www.sports-reference.com/cfb/schools/ each school's all-years cumulative overall win-loss record for regular season play and bowl games as well as its SOS and SRS data to derive a master list of schools.

This list is then traversed and the granular team-year data required for our analysis is extracted from www.sports-reference.com/cfb/schools/<school-name>/. You can find it in our GitHub repository [14]. It provides a csv file that we trimmed by excluding these three rows because the teams did not have SRS and SOS values:

- 1937 Virginia
- 2020 Connecticut
- 2020 Old Dominion

Rather than leveraging the full dataset, we decided to focus on the CFP era (2014–2024) as training inclusion criteria. Our training/validation split was 2014–2023 for training with 2024 held out. For our initial ex-ante 2025 predictions, we also use data through December 3, 2025 before the Big Ten and SEC conference championships.

During early exploratory work we posted on GitHub [14], we inadvertently allowed partial 2025 team-seasons into the CFP-era training set by filtering on Year $\geq$ 2014 without an upper bound. This yielded 1,566 team-seasons and 11 champions. For all results reported here, we corrected this by restricting the training window to completed CFP-era seasons only (2014–2024). This yields 1,430 team-seasons and 11 champions. The dependent variable for "Champion" was defined as:

Polls_AP Post = 1.
AND.
Polls_CFP Final = not null.

The AP Post was the final ranking after the season was completed. The CFP Final was the CFP ranking heading into the playoff tournament, and not null ensures only teams that played in the playoffs were included.

3.2 Statistical Tests

To conduct our statistical testing of hypotheses from Sect. 2 we performed a logistic regression using the Maximum Likelihood Estimation (MLE) method as detailed in Table 1 below:

Win% has a huge coefficient of 49.5 compared to the tiny coefficients for SRS and SOS. The Pseudo R-squared (McFadden) was 0.797 and Log-Likelihood was −13.09 (LLR p-value: 3.836e−22). Given Win% was significant at the 95% level, we rejected our global hypothesis that H_0: $\beta_1 = \beta_2 = \beta_3 = 0$ (all coefficients equal zero; predictors have no effect). Win% significantly affects championship probability.

Accordingly, we also reject our first single variable null hypothesis that Win% is not a statistically significant predictor. However, we are not rejecting our second and final single variable null hypotheses. Neither SRS nor SOS were significant. They are not helpful for inference to understand this statistical model, but our priority was predictive accuracy, thus we kept SOS and SRS in our machine learning model.

Table 1. Logit Regression Results

Variable Name	Coefficient	P-Value Significance of Coefficient	Standard Error
Intercept	−54.189	0.003	18.465
Win%	49.549	.012	19.829
SRS	0.172	0.940	0.183
SOS	0.581	0.108	0.362

3.3 Machine Learning Model Architecture

For ML modeling we chose logistic regression with balanced class weighting from the scikit learn python library. We used StandardScaler for feature normalization. The feature coefficients were:

- 2.492 = Win%
- 2.221 = SRS
- 0.899 = SOS

Win% was the most important feature, followed by SRS. SRS is approximately 89% as influential as Win% (2.221/2.492 = 0.891). SOS was only moderately important. We achieved 80% historical accuracy on 2014–23 champions for validation. The champions we missed were 2016 (predicted Alabama, actual Clemson) and 2017 (predicted Wisconsin, actual Alabama).

We also considered other features such as the highest AP Poll ranking a team achieved during the regular season, preseason AP ranking, and CFP ranking. Some combinations had better predictive power, i.e., better than 80% historical accuracy, but they relied on the external human polls. We wanted a model that was driven only by the numbers.

3.4 ML Model Evaluation Metrics

To evaluate the binary model we looked at the Receiver Operating Characteristic curve (ROC) and got 0.998. As you can see with the orange line in Fig. 1 below, nearly all of model falls in the "True Positive Rate".

To detect multicollinearity we calculated Variance Inflation Factor (VIF). By feature it was:

- 1.960 = SRS
- 1.654 = SOS
- 1.271 = Win%

The scores between 1 and 2 indicate "Mild to moderate correlation (usually fine)" [16] and given they are under 10 we did not take any corrective steps.

Noting the statistical tests in Subsect. 3.2 involved failing to reject two null hypotheses, to ensure the variables we kept were all adding value, we also did Stratified 5-Fold Cross-Validation. We got 100% recall for champions and consistent performance across all five folds. All three features have non-zero, stable coefficients with bootstrap Confidence Intervals (CIs) that exclude zero:

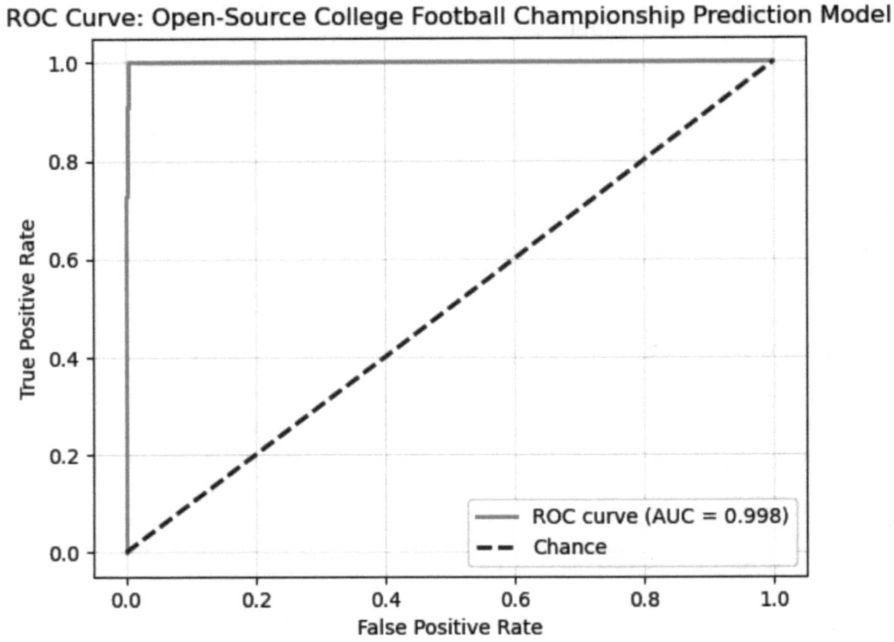

Fig. 1. ROC Curve for predictive model.

- 2.06 (CI $\approx$ 1.73–2.29) = Win%
- 2.13 (CI $\approx$ 1.91–2.41) = SRS
- 1.03 (CI $\approx$ 0.71–1.35) = SOS

To further assess whether all features provide value, we compared the full three-feature model (Win%, SRS, SOS) to single-feature baselines trained on 2014–2024 data. All models achieved perfect recall for champions in this period, but the full model achieved higher precision (0.16 vs 0.09) and F1 (0.28 vs 0.16) than a Win%-only model, and substantially higher precision–recall AUC (0.77 vs 0.65) despite similar ROC AUC (0.998 vs 0.996). SRS alone also performed competitively (F1 = 0.26), indicating that feature contributes meaningfully to championship signaling (Fig. 2).

3.5 Model Interpretability

The fitted logistic regression model produces a predicted probability of championship for each team-season. To help with interpretation we linearly rescaled to a 0–100 index for each school. These probabilities are referred to as the IC^2 score, where higher values indicate greater estimated championship likelihood. IC^2 refers to the names of co-authors and contributors.

3.6 Comparison to Pre-CFP Era

Having just eleven positive championship targets across 1,430 total team-seasons is not ideal for our model. It affects learned coefficients and generalizability as well as

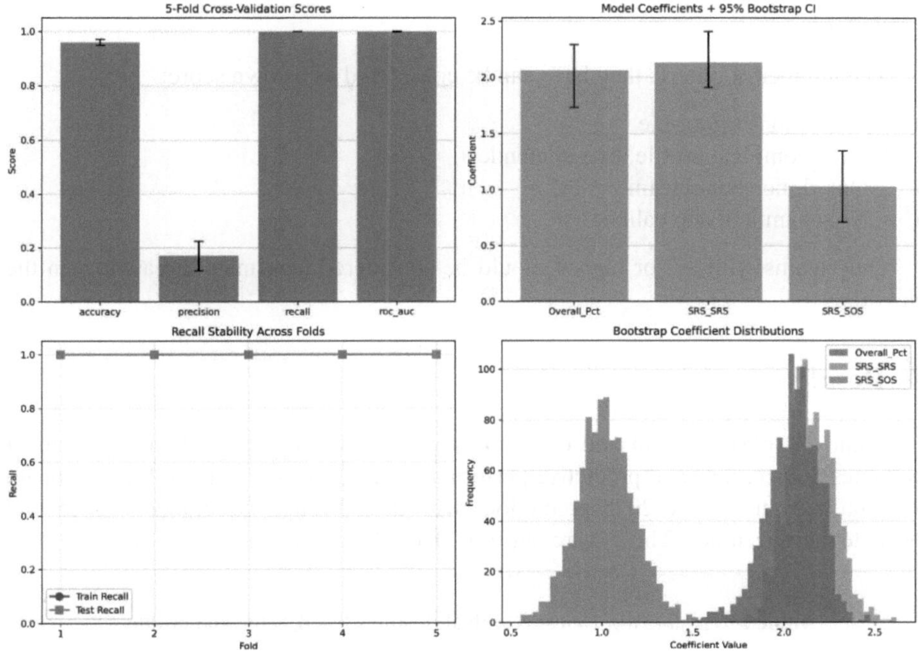

Fig. 2. Cross Fold Validation Data Visualizations

limiting statistical confidence in the model's superiority over simpler heuristics. We cannot change the fact the CFP-era is roughly twelve years old and we want to preserve CFP-era training exclusivity. However, as a check on our approach we also tested if certain elements of predictability were "timeless". The CFB world has changed so much over the years, so we decided not to include data from the nineteenth century nor most of the twentieth. We looked at 1980 to 2003, before the CFP era began which added 34 championship targets across 3,905 team seasons. The biggest change was that in this time range SOS was a significant predictor while it was not in the CFP-era. All the other results were similar to the CFP-era ones which adds to the validity our model.

3.7 Champion Profile Criteria

To complement our predictive model, we also identified three criteria for a champion. These can be used quickly to determine a team's chances of winning a championship. Prior champions in the CFP era have the following characteristics:

- Win% $\geq$ 0.875
- SRS $\geq$ 20.1
- SOS $\geq$ 5.2

And these are the averages of the champions:

- Win%: 0.958
- SRS: 24.4

- SOS: 6.6

The number of criteria they have can be considered as its own score:

- 3: Championship profile
- 2: Near-complete profile, true contender
- 1: One-dimensional team
- 0: Not championship caliber

Only teams with a 2 or higher should be considered legitimate threats to win the playoffs.

4 Results

This study is observational and does not attempt to make causal claims; instead, it evaluates associations and predictive performance using historical data. We will begin by detailing our ex-ante 2025 predictions with data through December 3, 2025 and evaluate their accuracy. These were our top 10 teams on that date (Table 2):

Table 2. Ex-ante top 10 teams with all features listed, score and profile.

Rank	IC^2 Score	Championship Profile
1. Ohio State	96.628	2
2. Indiana University	94.188	2
3. Texas Tech	82.267	2
4. Texas A&M	81.150	1
5. Notre Dame	79.661	2
6. Brigham Young University	79.264	2
7. Oregon University	79.161	1
8. University of Georgia	69.215	1
9. University of Miami	62.332	0
10. University of Mississippi	57.997	1

We had the eventual champion, Indiana, ranked second. Following our initial ex-ante run no team had a score of 3. Indiana, Ohio State, Notre Dame, BYU and Texas Tech each had 2 of the 3 criteria. Miami had zero at that time, indicating they had not presented championship caliber play at that point. That changed later on in the tournament as they showcased they were able to play at the highest-level beating Texas A&M and Ohio State who were each ranked higher than them on December 3rd. They also beat Mississippi who was ranked just below them then at tenth.

"IC^2 Score" indicates the likelihood they will win the championship. The biggest difference between our results and the committee was the strength of Notre Dame, which only increased as the weeks proceeded after beginning the season 0–2 against Miami and Texas A&M they won ten games straight to end at 10–2. Both of their losses came to strong teams that participated in the College Football Playoff. The damage from their loss to Miami was dampened as the Hurricanes kept winning. However, no amount of dampening would make any Notre Dame fan feel better as by the end of the season those two losses kept them out of the CFP. Notre Dame was a popular pick to make the CFP and analytics seemed to love them but they just missed the cut in the end due to human voting. We had Notre Dame as #5 in our ranking and that was validated by having them as #5 in the final one (Fig. 3).

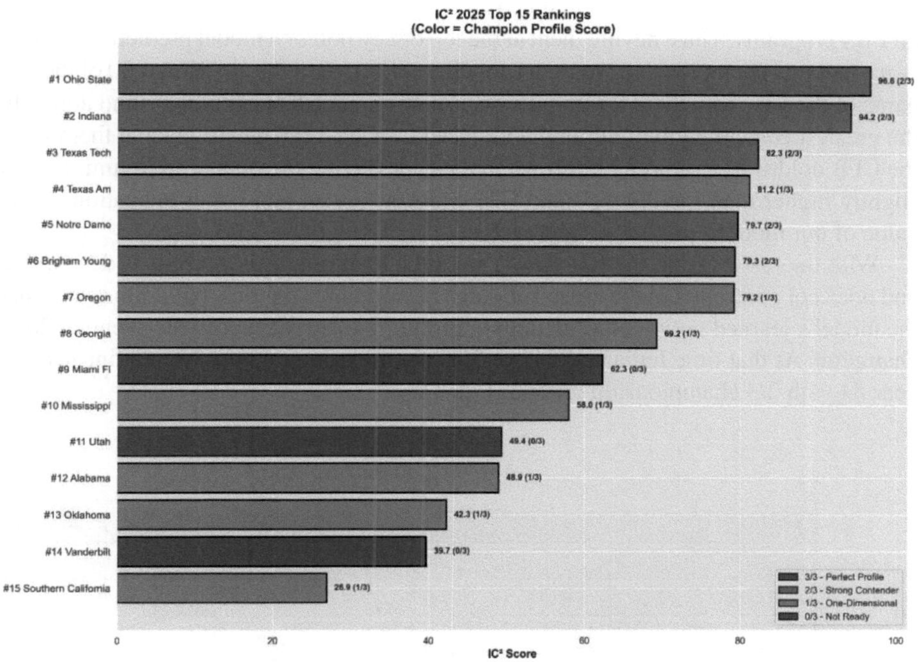

Fig. 3. Ex-ante top 15 bar chart with color coding for championship profile

At the same time Miami was #12 in the AP poll and Notre Dame was #9 in the week 15 rankings after the December 1st games [9]. Similarly, Miami was #12 in the CFP Committee Rankings on December 2nd [17] and Notre Dame was #10. Fans of the Fighting Irish had every reason to believe that they were going to make it to the playoffs but they were still left at the altar.

4.1 Predictions After Conference Championships

After Indiana beat Ohio State in the Big Ten Championship, we ran our model again on the updated results and had Indiana ranked first. Of course, almost everyone had that given Indiana was the only undefeated team between the Big Ten and SEC—the strongest conferences as measured by recent champions. The CFP committee followed suit, picking Indiana as the top seed for the playoffs.

So, heading into the playoff bracket Indiana had the highest score at 96.134 with a championship profile of 2. Miami had the 9th highest score at 61.338 with a championship profile of 0. Miami was the #10 seed in the playoff bracket [17] and the AP had them ranked #10 in their December 7 poll [9].

4.2 Final Model Rankings After the Season

Indiana won the championship, which was the outcome we predicted. Although this may not have been a farfetched prediction in this particular season, historically-speaking no team in college football has lost as much as the Hoosiers. Their 715 all-time losses leads all FBS programs. Thus, having them at the top of any poll or a model predicting them to win a national championship would be unbelievable up until the clock hit 0:00 of the last game of the year with them leading. It was a truly unprecedented outcome and arguably the greatest coaching job of all time with Head Coach Curt Cignetti leading them from the CFB doldrums to holding its crown in the end. Having the runner up Miami, ranked slightly higher than the AP Poll and CFP bracket was an additional indication of the value of our model's predictive approach.

With the results from the full season we did a final run. This analysis is descriptive and does not contribute to the cross-validated performance metrics, but it illustrates that the model's learned notion of a "champion profile" is consistent with the eventual 2025 champion. At that time Indiana did have 3/3 championship criteria. Miami finished the year #4 with 2/3 championship criteria (Fig. 4).

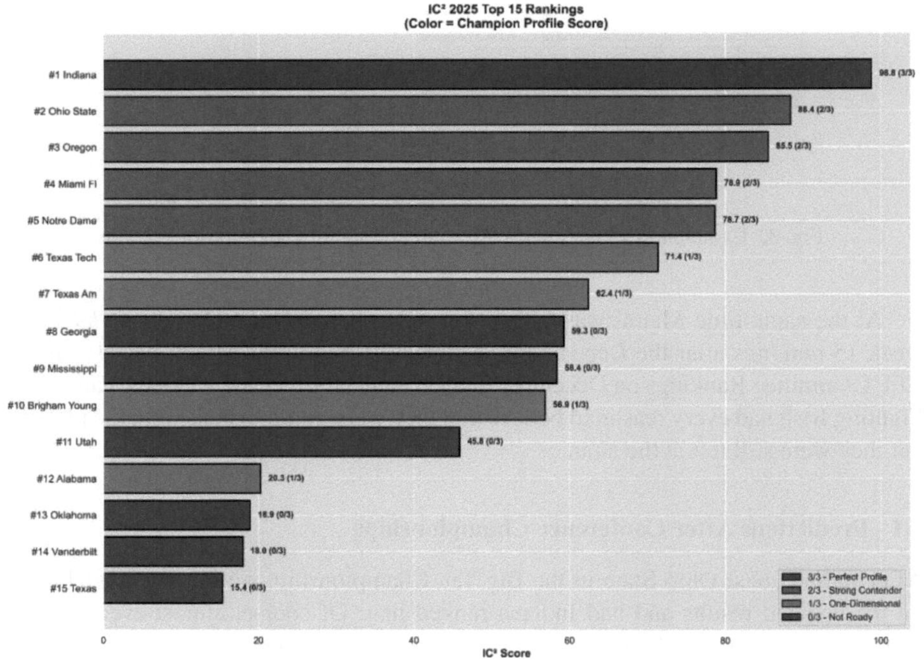

Fig. 4. Postseason top 15 bar chart with color coding for championship profile

5 Discussion

While we are excited about the initial results of our poll, we do feel it is important to acknowledge some limitations. The small number of features do help with interpretability, but they do not allow for capturing intangible factors like injuries and coaching changes. Additionally, the single-season test set (2024) has only $N = 1$ positive.

We plan to improve the model each year going forward to address some of these limitations. An example of a model improvement would be to control for the Blue Chip ratio as a way to capture more nuanced team recruiting and talent information [18, 19]. Many in the college football world believe that the high-school recruiting pipeline, and now making good use of the transfer portal are the biggest keys to winning. As they say, sometimes it is about the Xs and Os of the game (tactical performance) but sometimes it matters more about who has the better Jimmy's and Joe's—hence the importance of capturing the impact of the Blue-Chip ratio.

The infamous exclusion of Notre Dame has led to new rules for the 2026–27 season where Notre Dame is guaranteed a spot in the playoff if they are in the top-12 of the selection committee's CFP rankings by season's end. Conference champions of the SEC, Big Ten, ACC, and Big XII (the "Power 4" conferences) are also guaranteed playoff spots going forward [15]. Heading into the 2026 season we will consider adapting our model after the guaranteed spots have been filled to identify the at-large teams selected with a championship profile who may have a strong showing in the playoffs, like Miami in 2025.

We are hopeful the open-source license of our code encourages others to improve the model themselves as well. You can find the full data file and python code on GitHub [14]. We plan to continue refining it going forward to develop a community driven quantitative ranking. There are also other open-source college football projects such as this Python wrapper for the CFBD API [20]. We would like to explore leveraging this tool to improve our open-source model.

In addition, we want to improve upon the existing scraper we made for the Sports Reference website. Our goal is a simple, practical analytics environment focused on shared access, transparency, and speed. JupyterHub would provide a shared, common workspace then Streamlit could enable us to easily turn our finding and insights into simple, interactive apps. In the backend we would use a MySQL database on a cloud server.

Beyond improving our tools, we want to consider applying our model to women's college football. Flag football has been added to the emerging sports program [21] so this feels like an auspicious time to begin preparing IC^2-style, era-specific, interpretable models to support transparent rankings in this rapidly growing sport. We may be able to take advantage of the existing Women's 2025 IFAF Flag Football World Rankings [22].

6 Conclusion

It has seemingly become an annual autumn tradition to roast men's CFB polls. Whether it be whining that your team was unfairly ranked by The AP poll or how the CFP Selection Committee is biased towards big conferences. These frustrating results from human chosen rankings lead some to feel like ESPN reporter Bill Connelly has them "Extremely ready to go back to a BCS-like formula" [23].

Years after the BCS is gone, the desire to remove human bias to find the true "best" team in the country based purely on the numbers remains. Rather than teams of large/popular fanbases what some consider the top two conferences (the SEC and Big Ten) that seemingly get favorable treatment. Of course, the formula had its own controversies which is why we now have the CFP.

We offer our model as a BCS for those who began watching college football in the 12-team CFP-era and for those who would like to see the computer rankings come back in some form. There are other quantitative rankings out there, but many, like the Colley Matrix [25] were designed last century before there was a playoff. Our CFP-era specific training avoids historical bias and we have simple, interpretable features complemented by a champion profile that provides transparency.

The introductory version of this model we presented in this paper has 80% historical accuracy and predicted Indiana as the winner before the playoffs began. Additionally, it had the runner-up, Miami, higher rated than the AP Poll or CFP. We hope readers of this paper will join us to make the open-source model even better going forward.

Acknowledgments. We would like to thank the conference organizers for the opportunity to submit this paper. We also want to thank the open-source sports analytics community that has been one of the inspirations for this work, especially those active on Reddit and Twitter.

Disclosure of Interests. The authors have no competing interests.

References

1. Bergin, T.G.: The Game: The Harvard-Yale Football Rivalry, 1875–1983 (1984)
2. Wikipedia contributors: Harvard–Yale football rivalry. In Wikipedia, The Free Encyclopedia, 5 February 2026). https://en.wikipedia.org/w/index.php?title=Harvard%E2%80%93Yale_football_rivalry&oldid=1336670435. Accessed 16 February 2026
3. Wikipedia contributors: 1929 college football season. In Wikipedia, The Free Encyclopedia, 8 January 2026. https://en.wikipedia.org/w/index.php?title=1929_college_football_season&oldid=1331836018. Accessed 16 February 2026
4. 2009 NCAA Football Bowl Subdivision Records. http://fs.ncaa.org/Docs/stats/football_records/DI/2009/2009FBS.pdf
5. 2025 FOOTBALL BOWL SUBDIVISION RECORDS. https://s3.amazonaws.com/fs.ncaa.org/Docs/stats/football_records/FBS.pdf
6. Anderson Sports poll. http://www.andersonsports.com/football/ACF_frnk.html
7. Wikipedia contributors: Bowl Championship Series. In Wikipedia, The Free Encyclopedia, 29 December 2025. https://en.wikipedia.org/w/index.php?title=Bowl_Championship_Series&oldid=1330021077. Accessed 16 February 2026
8. Battiste, I. https://x.com/FireballFinds/status/1859242094570701154
9. AP Poll. https://apnews.com/article/how-ap-top-25-works-d4a80e192ecea1795711f023eb64b73d
10. Coach's Poll. https://sportsdata.usatoday.com/football/ncaaf/coaches-poll/2025/2025-09-02
11. Battiste, C.I., IV., Danoff, C.J., Hanes, C.: Lending a hand in bringing ballcarriers down: an extended study of individual defensive contributions in the national football league (NFL). SN Comput. Sci. **6**, 622 (2025). https://doi.org/10.1007/s42979-025-04161-4

12. College Football Stats Glossary. https://www.sports-reference.com/cfb/about/glossary.html#srs
13. Sports Reference College football. https://www.sports-reference.com/cfb/
14. https://github.com/danoff/IC2-Men-s-College-Football-Poll/blob/main/cbh_get_school_tables.py
15. https://apnews.com/article/cfp-college-football-playoff-expansion-bfb7c8a66f337c76591cbf68536593d6
16. https://www.geeksforgeeks.org/python/detecting-multicollinearity-with-vif-python/
17. https://collegefootballplayoff.com/sports/2025/11/4/wk-x-wk-rankings-2025.aspx
18. https://www.cbssports.com/college-football/news/blue-chip-ratio-2025-these-18-college-football-teams-can-actually-win-the-national-championship/
19. https://www.puntandrally.com/viewpowerratings.php?whichyear=2025&whatstat=bluechip
20. https://github.com/CFBD/cfbd-python
21. https://www.ncaa.org/news/2026/1/16/media-center-ncaa-adds-flag-football-to-emerging-sports-for-women-program.aspx
22. https://www.americanfootball.sport/ifaf-world-rankings/
23. Connely, B. https://www.espn.com/college-football/story/_/id/47201071/college-football-conference-championship-previews-ohio-state-alabama-georgia
24. Wikipedia contributors: Bowl Championship Series controversies. In Wikipedia, The Free Encyclopedia, 4 March 2026. https://en.wikipedia.org/w/index.php?title=Bowl_Championship_Series_controversies&oldid=1341738464. Accessed 30 March 2026
25. Colley, N.: Colley's Bias Free College Football Ranking Method: The Colley Matrix Explained Wesley. https://colleyrankings.com/matrate.pdf

Learning About Corner Kicks in Soccer by Analysis of Event Times Using a Frailty Model

Riley L. Isaacs(✉), X. Joan Hu, K. Ken Peng, and Tim B. Swartz

Simon Fraser University, Burnaby, BC, Canada
rli5@sfu.ca

Abstract. Corner kicks are an important event in soccer because they are often the result of strong attacking play and can be of keen interest to sports fans and bettors. Peng, Hu, and Swartz (2024, *Computational Statistics*) frame the commonly available corner kick data as right-censored event times, formulate the mixture feature of corner kick times caused by previous corner kicks, and explore patterns of corner kicks associated with several factors. This paper extends their modeling to accommodate the potential correlations between corner kicks by the same teams within the same games. We consider a frailty model for event times and apply the Monte Carlo Expectation Maximization (MCEM) algorithm to obtain the maximum likelihood estimates for the model parameters. We compare the proposed model with the model in Peng, Hu, and Swartz (2024) using likelihood ratio tests. The 2019 Chinese Super League (CSL) data are employed throughout the paper for motivation and illustration.

Keywords: Clustered Time to Event Data · Finite Mixture Model · MCEM Algorithm · Right Censoring

1 Introduction

Soccer corner kicks are awarded to the attacking team after the defending team puts the ball into touch across their own goal line. In elite soccer a very small percentage of corner kicks lead to goals, Casal et al. (2015) Yiannakos and Armatas (2006) found that more goals tend to be scored as a result of corner kicks than any other type of set piece. The stoppage in play allows both teams the opportunity to strategize, with the attacking team making decisions such as what depth and height to kick the ball, while the defending team decides which players or areas of the field to defend.

Corner kicks have a breadth of literature, including Casal et al. (2015) which investigates the efficacy of different types of corner kicks and investigates related variables. Liu et al. (2015) includes corner kicks as one of the performance variables when building team strength profiles. Maneiro et al. (2021)analyses the change in corner kick strategies over three consecutive World Cups.

Z. Liu and V. Misra (Eds.): ISACE 2026, LNCS 16610, pp. 442–455, 2026.
https://doi.org/10.1007/978-3-032-27272-0_28

This paper is a direct extension of Peng, Hu, Swartz (2024) which investigates the time elapsed since a starting point until a corner kick using event history analysis. Event history analysis is most commonly used in biomedical research, which faces many of the same challenges that occur in our analyses of corner kicks. Peng, Hu and Swartz (2024) addressed concerns regarding the right censoring of corner kicks. For a comprehensive summary on the methods commonly used to address right censoring in event time analysis, see Kalbfleisch and Prentice (2011). In the context of corner kicks right censoring occurs when a goal is scored, or the end of a half or game occurs. This stops play before the corner kick can be observed.

Peng, Hu and Swartz (2024) also addressed the fact that there is a non-ignorable probability of a corner kick almost immediately following another corner kick, typically as a result of a defensive deflection which goes out of bounds. This phenomenon means conventional time to event distributions are not reasonably suited to our corner kick problem. As in their initial paper we employ a mixture distribution to address the issue. McLachlan et al.(2019) reviews the theory and methodological developments of finite mixture models.

This paper extends the model of Peng, Hu and Swartz (2024) by exploring two different frailty models. These models are more general as they do not require the assumption that time to corner kicks are independent of each other. Frailty models are commonly used to model correlated event times in the life sciences, with Vaupel et al. (1979) introducing the notion of frailty to account for heterogeneity between groups when modelling mortality. It has also been used in reliability engineering as in Ghomghaleh et al. (2020) where a frailty model is shown to outperform the classical model for determining the remaining useful life of an excavator.

The 2019 Chinese Super League data includes the event history data for 233 games, which includes 2314 corner kicks. For the purpose of this analysis the corner kicks are split into Type 1 kicks which are corner kicks that are preceded by a starting event that is not a corner kick, and Type 2 kicks which are preceded by another corner kick.

Section 2 begins by introducing the structure of the data, and distinguishes the latent variables from those which are observed. Then the frailty model is introduced. Section 3 covers the special case that occurs when the latent frailty variables are gamma distributed and provides an MCEM algorithm that can be used to obtain maximum likelihood estimates. Section 4 describes our analysis of the 2019 Chinese Super League (CSL) data and a simulation study before we wrap up by discussing other methods for analyzing time to corner kick data.

2 Statistical Methodology

2.1 Data Formulation

For a set of event history data containing I teams we use i to denote the ith team, each of the I teams play J_i games with ij denoting the ith team's jth game. In the ith team's jth game there are n_{ij} events where they are either awarded a corner kick or a censoring event occurs such as a goal, or end of half. Each of the events where either a corner kick or censoring event occurs is assigned an index k. We let the random variables T_{ijk} and C_{ijk} represent the time to the corner kick from previous event and time to censoring event from the previous event, respectively. However we only observe $Y_{ijk} = min(T_{ijk}, C_{ijk})$ Additionally we assume non-informative censoring time. We also define an indicator of whether the corner kick is observed $\delta_{ijk} = I(Y_{ijk} = T_{ijk})$. Finally for each event we define Z_{ijk} to be a vector of covariates that may include whether or not the team is at home, and score differential at the time of the corner kick. We define $OD = \{y_{ijk}, z_{ijk}, \delta_{ijk} : i = 1, ..., I, j = 1, ..., J_i, k = 1, ..., n_{ij}\}$ to be the set of observed data.

As in Peng, Hu, Swartz (2024) we define Type 1 corner kicks to be a corner kick that occurs after play is started by any event that is not a corner kick. Type 2 corner kicks are corner kicks that occur after play is restarted by a corner kick. Type 2 corner kicks are broken down further into two categories, the first being Type 2 Short (Type 2-S) which is a corner kick that was generated directly by the preceding corner kick. There are also Type 2 Long corner kicks (Type 2-L) which are not generated directly by the previous corner kick and tend to have longer gap times. For every Y_{ijk} such that $\delta_{ijk} = 0$ we define the latent variable $\eta = I(Y_{ijk}|\text{CK is Type 2-L})$. This would be observable with tracking data, or even potentially with very detailed event history data. However, for the purpose of this paper we consider it to be unobservable. We define our first "full" set of data to be $FD1 = \{y_{ijk}, z_{ijk}, \delta_{ijk}, \eta_{ijk} : i = 1, ..., I, j = 1, ..., J_i, k = 1, ..., n_{ij}\}$. This is the data considered in Peng, Hu, Swartz (2024).

Let W_{ij} be a latent frailty random variable associated with the ith team's jth game. We define our second set of full data $FD2 = \{y_{ijk}, z_{ijk}, \delta_{ijk}, \eta_{ijk}, w_{ij} : i = 1, ..., I, j = 1, ..., J_i, k = 1, ..., n_{ij}\}$.

2.2 Statistical Model

In Peng, Hu, Swartz (2024) they specify two unique parametric proportional hazards models as follows. For Type 1 and Type 2-L kicks the hazard is

$$h_1^{(0)}(t|\boldsymbol{z}; \gamma_1, \lambda_1, \boldsymbol{\beta}) = \gamma_1 \lambda_1 (\lambda_1 t)^{(\gamma_1 - 1)} e^{\boldsymbol{z}'\boldsymbol{\beta}}. \quad (1)$$

The hazard function used for Type 2-S corner kicks is

$$h_2^{(0)}(t|\gamma_2, \lambda_2) = \gamma_2 \lambda_2 (\lambda_2 t)^{(\gamma_2 - 1)}. \quad (2)$$

This model is suited to data where all corner kicks are independent of one another. Analysis using this model requires that we assume independence of corner kicks. In reality, it is likely that a team's corner kicks within the same game are correlated due to their strategy, personnel, and form on a given day. Using a model that requires weaker assumptions about the correlation structure of the data would allow for valid inference provided the corner kicks are not all independent of each other. To avoid making the assumption that all corner kicks are independent we introduce the frailty random variable W_{ij} which acts multiplicatively on the hazard function for the ith team's Type 1 and Type 2-L corner kicks in their jth. Resulting in the following hazard functions:

$$h_1(t_{ijk}|\boldsymbol{z}_{ijk}, w_{ij}; \gamma_1, \lambda_1, \boldsymbol{\beta}) = w_{ij}\gamma_1\lambda_1(\lambda_1 t_{ijk})^{(\gamma_1-1)}e^{\boldsymbol{z}'_{ijk}\boldsymbol{\beta}}, \tag{3}$$

$$\text{and} \quad h_2(t_{ijk}|\gamma_2, \lambda_2) = \gamma_2\lambda_2(\lambda_2 t_{ijk})^{(\gamma_2-1)}. \tag{4}$$

Let $S_1(t|\boldsymbol{z}, w; \gamma_1, \lambda_1, \boldsymbol{\beta})$ and $S_2(t|\gamma_2, \lambda_2)$ be the unique survival functions determined by $h_1(t|\boldsymbol{z}, w; \gamma_1, \lambda_1, \boldsymbol{\beta})$ and $h_2(t|\gamma_2, \lambda_2)$ respectively.

Under this formulation if $w_{ij} \equiv 1$, our model $h_1(t_{ijk}|\boldsymbol{z}_{ijk}, w_{ij}; \gamma_1, \lambda_1, \boldsymbol{\beta})$ reduces to $h_1^{(0)}(t_{ijk}|\boldsymbol{z}_{ijk}; \gamma_1, \lambda_1, \boldsymbol{\beta})$. The proposed model may well be applicable to data where the timing of corner kicks taken by the same team within the same game are more similar to each other than other corner kicks. Meaning that if factors such as strategy, personnel and match day form do impact the timing of corner kicks this model will be more suitable than previous models.

2.3 Likelihood

For the kth observed time in the ith team's jth game, assume

$$P(\eta_{ijk} = 1|z_{ijk}; \alpha_0, \boldsymbol{\alpha}) = \pi(z_{ijk}; \alpha_0, \boldsymbol{\alpha}) = \frac{1}{1 + e^{-(\alpha_0 + \boldsymbol{z}'_{ijk}\boldsymbol{\alpha})}}. \tag{5}$$

We assume that all corner kick times not taken by the same team within the same game are independent, that the W_{ij} are independently sampled from a distribution with pdf $f_W(.)$, and that given W_{ij} all of the ith team's corner kicks in their jth game are independent. In the case of univariate frailty models the frailty distribution is often specified to be the gamma distribution, positive stable distribution, compound poisson distribution, or the log-normal distribution (Weike, 2003). Section two of Balan and Putter (2020)discusses some effects of the choice in frailty distribution.

The likelihood contribution of the ith team's jth game given data $FD2$ is

$$L_{ij}^{(1)}(\boldsymbol{\theta}) = f_W(w_{ij})\Pi_{k=1}^{n_{ij}} L_{ijk}^{(1)}(\boldsymbol{\theta})[\pi(z_{ijk}; \alpha_0, \alpha)^{\eta_{ijk}}(1 - \pi(z_{ijk}; \alpha_0, \alpha))^{1-\eta_{ijk}}]^{\delta_{ij,k-1}}, \tag{6}$$

where

$$\begin{aligned} L_{ijk}^{(1)}(\boldsymbol{\theta}) = {} & [(h_1(y_{ijk}|\mathbf{z_{ijk}}, w_{ij}; \boldsymbol{\theta}_1))^{\delta_{ijk}} S_1(y_{ijk}|\mathbf{z_{ijk}}, w_{ij}; \boldsymbol{\theta}_1)]^{1-\delta_{ij,k-1}} \\ & [((h_1(y_{ijk}|\mathbf{z_{ijk}}, w_{ij}; \boldsymbol{\theta}_1)^{\eta_{ijk}} h_2(y_{ijk}|\boldsymbol{\theta}_2)^{(1-\eta_{ijk})})^{\delta_{ijk}} \\ & (S_1(y_{ijk}|\mathbf{z_{ijk}}, w_{ij}; \boldsymbol{\theta}_1)^{\eta_{ijk}} S_2(y_{ijk}|\boldsymbol{\theta}_2)^{(1-\eta_{ijk})}))]^{\delta_{ij,k-1}}. \end{aligned}$$

The likelihood considering all games given data $FD2$ is

$$L^{(1)}(\boldsymbol{\theta}) = \Pi_{i=1}^{I}\Pi_{j=1}^{J_i} L_{ij}^{(1)}(\boldsymbol{\theta}). \tag{7}$$

In reality we do not observe $FD2$, and we only observe data OD. In general there is no marginal closed form of the likelihood function conditional only on OD. However, when all W_{ij} are independently sampled from a gamma distribution, there exists a closed form for the marginal likelihood given data $FD1$, this special case is discussed in detail in Sect. 4.

3 Computing Maximum Likelihood Estimates

$L^{(1)}(\boldsymbol{\theta})$ is conditional on $FD2$ which contains latent data making it impossible to analytically compute maximum likelihood estimates. Neath (2012)demonstrates that the Monte Carlo Expectation Maximization algorithm converges to the maximum of the observed data likelihood. This property makes MCEM a suitable choice for numerically computing the MLE.

Algorithm 1. MCEM Algorithm for General Frailty Distribution

Given the estimate at d iterations $\theta^{(d)}$, with $\theta^{(0)}$ for the initial value and an initial sample of $\eta_{ij1}^{(0)}, ..., \eta_{ijn_{ij}}^{(0)}$.

1: **Repeat**

1.1 MCE-step. Let $l^{(1)}(\theta) = log(L^{(1)}(\theta))$, approximate $Q(\theta, \theta^{(d)}) = E(l^{(1)}(\theta)|FD2; \theta^{(d)})$ using the sample mean $\tilde{Q}(\theta, \theta^{(d)}) = \frac{1}{M}\Sigma_{m=1}^{M} l^{(1)}(\theta)$ conditional on $\{(y_{ijk}, \delta_{ijk}, \boldsymbol{z_{ijk}}, \eta_{ijk}^{(m)}, w_{ij}^{(m)} : k = 0, ..., n_{ij}, j = 1, ..., J_i, i = 1, ..., I\}$. For $m = 1, ..., M$

a) Sample $w_{ij}^{(m)^{(d+1)}}$ from $f_W(w|\eta_{ij1}^{(m)^{(d)}}, ..., \eta_{ijn_{ij}}^{(m)^{(d)}}, OD; \boldsymbol{\theta}^{(d)})$

b) Sample $\eta_{ijk}^{(m)^{(d+1)}}$ from a $Bernoulli(P)$ distribution, where P is the conditional probability of a corner kick being Type 2-L given the observed time of the corner kick. $P = \frac{P_1}{P_1+P_2}$, where

$$P_1 = \pi(\mathbf{z}_{ijk}; \alpha_0^{(d)}, \boldsymbol{\alpha}^{(d)})(h_1(y_{ijk}|w_{ij}^{(m)^{(d+1)}}, \mathbf{z}_{ijk}; \boldsymbol{\theta}^{(d)}))^{\delta_{ijk}} S_1(y_{ijk}|w_{ij}^{(m)^{(d+1)}}, \mathbf{z}_{ijk}; \boldsymbol{\theta}^{(d)}),$$

$$and\ P_2 = (1 - \pi(\mathbf{z}_{ijk}; \alpha_0^{(d)}, \boldsymbol{\alpha}^{(d)}))(h_2(y_{ijk}|\boldsymbol{\theta}^{(d)}))^{\delta_{ijk}} S_2(y_{ijk}|\boldsymbol{\theta}^{(d)}).$$

Note η_{ijk} is not defined for Type 1 corner kicks ($\delta_{ij,k-1}$=0), in these instances there is no need to sample η_{ijk}.

1.2 M-step. Update the estimate of θ as $\theta^{(d+1)} = argmax_{\theta}\tilde{Q}(\theta, \theta^{(d)})$

2. **Until** the series $\{\theta^{(d)}, d = 1, 2, ...\}$ converges sufficiently. We consider the algorithm to converge when the change of 2-norm of $\theta^{(d+1)} - \theta^{(d)}$ is smaller than some tolerance.

3.1 Standard Errors

Luois (1982) provides a useful expression for the Hessian of the log posterior distribution for the EM algorithm. Using the data from the last step of the MCEM algorithm we numerically compute the following hessian matrix:

$$\frac{1}{M}\Sigma_{m=1}^{M} \frac{\partial^2 log(L^{(1)}(\boldsymbol{\theta}))}{\partial^2 \boldsymbol{\theta}} + \frac{1}{M}\Sigma_{m=1}^{M} (\frac{\partial log(L^{(1)}(\boldsymbol{\theta}))}{\partial \boldsymbol{\theta}})^2 - [\frac{1}{M}\Sigma_{m=1}^{M} \frac{\partial log(L^{(1)}(\boldsymbol{\theta}))}{\partial \boldsymbol{\theta}}]^2$$

The inverse of this matrix is the covariance matrix of which the diagonal entries provide standard errors for our parameter estimates.

3.2 Example of Frailty Distribution: Log-Normal

The log-normal distribution is a commonly used frailty distribution, it is not a member of the power variance family (PVF) which contains the gamma distribution and other frequently used frailty distributions (Balan and Putter, (2020). Constraining $E[w]$ to be 1 gives the following one-parameter Log-Normal distribution:

$$f_W(w) = \frac{exp(\frac{-(ln(w)+\frac{\sigma_w^2}{2})^2}{2\sigma_w^2})}{w\sigma_w\sqrt{2\pi}}.$$

We develop the following procedure for sampling from $f_W(w|FD1;\boldsymbol{\theta})$ which can be applied to part a) of the MCEM algorithm described earlier in this section. Using the fact that $f_W(w_{ij}|FD1;\boldsymbol{\theta}) \propto L_{ij}^{(1)}(\theta)$,

$$f_W(w_{ij}|FD1;\boldsymbol{\theta}) \propto r(w_{ij}) = exp(\frac{-(ln(w_{ij}) + \frac{\sigma_w^2}{2})^2}{2\sigma_w^2})w_{ij}^{\phi-1}e^{-w_{ij}\psi}$$

with $\phi = \Sigma_{k=1}^{n_{ij}}[\delta_{ijk}(1-\delta_{ijk-1}) + \eta_{ijk}\delta_{ijk}\delta_{ijk-1}]$ and $\psi = \Sigma_{k=1}^{n_{ij}}(\lambda_1 y_{ijk})^{\gamma_1}(1 - \delta_{ijk-1} + \eta_{ijk}\delta_{ijk})$.

We can use rejection sampling to sample frailty variables conditional on the data without needing to find the normalizing constant. The following is a rejection sampling protocol for this case.

Algorithm 2. Rejection Sampling Algorithm

1. If ϕ and ψ are both greater than zero sample u from a $Gamma(\phi, \psi)$ distribution and v from a uniform distribution on the interval $(0, 1)$. Else, sample u from a $Gamma(\phi+1, \psi+1)$ distribution and v from a $Unif(0, 1)$ distribution. Let $g(u)$ denote the pdf of the selected proxy distribution.
2. If $v < \frac{r(u)}{g(u)}$, let $w_{ij} = u$ and stop, else repeat. Doing this M times obtains a sample of size M from the conditional distribution of w_{ij}.

---

4 Special Case: Gamma Frailty

With the added assumption that all W_{ij} are independently sampled from a $Gamma(\frac{1}{\theta_w}, \frac{1}{\theta_w})$ distribution with pdf

$$f_W(w) = \frac{(\frac{1}{\theta_w})^{\frac{1}{\theta_w}}}{\Gamma(\frac{1}{\theta_w})}w_{ij}^{\frac{1}{\theta_w}-1}e^{-\frac{w_{ij}}{\theta_w}}, \quad (8)$$

it is possible to analytically integrate the frailty random variables out and obtain a marginal likelihood distribution conditional on $FD1$.

This distribution was chosen for its useful mathematical properties. It's mean is 1 meaning that the hazards for each team's game in our model vary around $h_1^{(0)}(t|\boldsymbol{z};\gamma_1,\lambda_1,\boldsymbol{\beta})$. The variance of this distribution is θ_w which is easily interpretable, it also means that as θ_w approaches zero, $f_W(w)$ approaches a point mass at 1. Intuitively this means the closer θ_w is to 0 the less hazard functions vary. Most importantly this distribution is selected because there exists a closed form for the marginal likelihood conditional on $FD1$.

The contribution of the ith team's jth game to the likelihood conditional on $FD1$ is

$$L_{ij}^{(2)}(\boldsymbol{\theta}) = \frac{(\frac{1}{\theta_w})^{1/\theta_w}}{\Gamma(1/\theta_w)} \frac{\Gamma(\alpha^{(2)})}{(\beta^{(2)})^{\alpha^{(2)}}} \Pi_{k=1}^{n_{ij}} L_{ijk}^{(2)}(\boldsymbol{\theta})[\pi(z_{ijk};\alpha_0,\alpha)^{\eta_{ijk}}(1-\pi(z_{ijk};\alpha_0,\alpha))^{1-\eta_{ijk}}]^{\delta_{ij,k-1}}, \tag{9}$$

where

$$\begin{aligned} L_{ijk}^{(2)}(\boldsymbol{\theta}) = {} & [(h_1(y_{ijk}|\mathbf{z_{ijk}};\gamma_1,\lambda_1,\boldsymbol{\beta}))^{\delta_{ijk}} S_1(y_{ijk}|\mathbf{z_{ijk}};\gamma_1,\lambda_1,\boldsymbol{\beta})]^{1-\delta_{ij,k-1}} \\ & [((h_1(y_{ijk}|\mathbf{z_{ijk}};\gamma_1,\lambda_1,\boldsymbol{\beta})^{\eta_{ijk}} h_2(y_{ijk}|\gamma_2,\lambda_2)^{(1-\eta_{ijk})})^{\delta_{ijk}} \\ & (S_1(y_{ijk}|\mathbf{z_{ijk}};\gamma_1,\lambda_1,\boldsymbol{\beta})^{\eta_{ijk}} S_2(y_{ijk}|\gamma_2,\lambda_2)^{(1-\eta_{ijk})}))]^{\delta_{ij,k-1}} \end{aligned}$$

and

$$\alpha^{(2)} = \frac{1}{\theta_w} + \Sigma_{k=1}^{n_{ij}} \delta_{ij,k}(1-\delta_{ij,k-1}+\eta_{ijk}\delta_{ij,k-1})$$

$$\beta^{(2)} = \frac{1}{\theta_w} + \Sigma_{k=1}^{n_{ij}} (\lambda_1 y_{ijk})^{\gamma_1} e^{\boldsymbol{z}_{ijk}\boldsymbol{\beta}}(1-\delta_{ij,k-1}+\eta_{ijk}\delta_{ij,k-1}).$$

This yields the following marginal likelihood:

$$L^{(2)}(\theta) = \Pi_{i=1}^{I}\Pi_{j=1}^{J_i} L_{ij}^{(2)}(\theta). \tag{10}$$

$L^{(2)}(\theta)$ is conditional on $FD1$ which still contains latent data making it impossible to obtain Maximum Likelihood Estimates by directly maximizing $L^{(2)}(\theta)$. The MLE can be obtained using $L^{(2)}(\theta)$ by implementing a slighty modified version of the MCEM algorithm outlined in Sect. 2.3.

4.1 Computing Maximum Likelihood Estimates (MLE)

By integrating out the frailty random variables we obtained $L^{(2)}(\theta)$ which is conditional on $FD1$. This allows us to simplify the MCEM algorithm and remove a step, because there is no longer the need to simulate the frailty random variables. The following is the simplified MCEM algorithm.

Algorithm 3. MCEM Algorithm for gamma Distributed Frailty Random Variables

Given the estimate at d iterations $\theta^{(d)}$, with $\theta^{(0)}$ for the initial value.

1: **Repeat**

1.1 MCE-step. Let $l^{(2)}(\theta) = log(L^{(2)}(\theta))$, approximate $Q(\theta, \theta^{(d)}) = E(l^{(2)}(\theta)|FD2; \theta^{(d)})$ using the sample mean $\tilde{Q}(\theta, \theta^{(d)}) = \frac{1}{M}\Sigma_{m=1}^{M} l^{(1)}(\theta)$ conditional on $\{(y_{ijk}, \delta_{ijk}, \boldsymbol{z_{ijk}}, \eta_{ijk}^{(m)} : k = 0, ..., n_{ij}, j = 1, ..., J_i, i = 1, ..., I\}$.

For $m = 1, ..., M$

sample η_{ijk} from a Bernoulli distribution with probability P, where P is the conditional probability of a corner kick being Type 2-L given the observed time of the corner kick. $P = \frac{P_1}{P_1+P_2}$, where

$$P_1 = \pi(\mathbf{z}_{ijk}; \alpha_0^{(d)}, \boldsymbol{\alpha}^{(d)})(h_1(y_{ijk}|w_{ij}, \mathbf{z}_{ijk}, \boldsymbol{\theta}^{(d)}))^{\delta_{ijk}} S_1(y_{ijk}|w_{ij}, \mathbf{z}_{ijk}, \boldsymbol{\theta}^{(d)})$$

$$and\ P_2 = (1 - \pi(\mathbf{z}_{ijk}; \alpha_0^{(d)}, \boldsymbol{\alpha}^{(d)}))(h_2(y_{ijk}|\boldsymbol{\theta}^{(d)}))^{\delta_{ijk}} S_2(y_{ijk}|\boldsymbol{\theta}^{(d)}).$$

Note η_{ijk} is not defined for Type 1 corner kicks ($\delta_{ij,k-1}$=0), in these instances there is no need to sample η_{ijk}.

1.2 M-step. Update the estimate of θ as $\theta^{(d+1)} = argmax_\theta \tilde{Q}(\theta, \theta^{(d)})$

2. **Until** the series $\{\theta^{(d)}, d = 1, 2, ...\}$ converges sufficiently. We consider the algorithm to converge when the change in the 2-norm of $\theta^{(d+1)} - \theta^{(d)}$ is less than a desired tolerance.

We employed the nlminb function to compute the maximum of the estimated-expected log-likelihood at each iteration of the MCEM algorithm. Various r functions can be used to generate the simulated data, we used the rbinom function to sample from the appropriate bernoulli distribution.

4.2 Standard Errors

Standard errors are similar to the general case however we replace $L^{(1)}((\theta))$ with the marginal likelihood function $L^{(2)}((\theta))$ resulting in the following hessian matrix:

$$\frac{1}{M}\Sigma_{m=1}^{M}\frac{\partial^2 log(L^{(2)}(\boldsymbol{\theta}))}{\partial^2\boldsymbol{\theta}} + \frac{1}{M}\Sigma_{m=1}^{M}(\frac{\partial log(L^{(2)}(\boldsymbol{\theta}))}{\partial\boldsymbol{\theta}})^2 - [\frac{1}{M}\Sigma_{m=1}^{M}\frac{\partial log(L^{(2)}(\boldsymbol{\theta}))}{\partial\boldsymbol{\theta}}]^2.$$

5 Data Analysis Using 2019 CSL Data

5.1 Analysis Using the Gamma Frailty Model

Peng, Hu, Swartz (2024) identified five covariates they believed may have an effect on the time to corner kick, and the probability that a Type 2 kick is Type 2-L. These five variables are definded as follows:

- $Z_1 = 1$ if the kick occurred in the first half, and $Z_1 = 0$ if the kick occurred in the second half.

- $Z_2 = 1$ if the corner kick is awarded to the home team, $Z_2 = 0$ if it is awarded to the away team.
- Z_3 is the score differential at the time of the kick, a positive value means the team is leading.
- Z_4 is the red card differential at the time the kick is awarded, a positive value means the team has more players on the pitch.
- Z_5 is the decimal odds (European odds) of the team that has been awarded the corner kick.

We began by fitting the model including all five of these covariates in the proportional hazard function for Type 1 and 2-L corner kicks as well as in the logistic regression model for Type 2-L probability.

Using the frailty model we found Z_2 (indicator of the team being at home) to have a significant positive effect on the hazard function. This aligns with common soccer knowledge that home teams tend to be awarded more corner kicks. We also found that Z_3 (score differential) has a significant negative effect on the hazard, which also aligns with common soccer knowledge. When a team is leading they are more concerned with maintaining their lead than they are scoring goals. In order to maintain better defensive structure and hold on to their lead teams will play more conservatively.

While Peng, Hu and Swartz (2024) found none of the covariate effects to significantly impact Type 2-L probability. We found three of the five covariates to have significant effects on Type 2-L probability. One possible explanation of this is that using the frailty model results in increased power in determining whether a covariate's effect on Type 2-L probability is significantly different from 0.

Table 1 displayed below contains the estimated parameters using the 2019 CSL data.

The indicator of home team, red card differential, and European betting odds were found to have significant effects on the Type 2-L probability of Type 2 corner kicks. This means under the new model three effects were found to be significant compared to none under the assumption that all corner kicks are independent. This potentially indicates that the frailty model is more powerful than the model in Peng, Hu, Swartz (2024). 94.4% of the simulated indicators of kick type from the final iteration of the MCEM algorithm were 1 (indicating a long gap time). This means that just over 1 in 20 corner kicks directly generates another corner.

We model all Type 2-S corner kicks as weibull random variables. When all covariates are 0 and the frailty random variable is exactly 1 Type 1 and 2-L corner kicks are weibull distributed. However, these corner kicks have drastically different event times. This is exemplified by the drastic difference in means. The Type 1 and 2-L weibull distribution under these strict conditions has a mean time to corner kick of 49.41 min. This is contrasted by the very short mean of the Type 2-S corner kicks that is only 36.93 s. Such a distinct difference suggests the necessity of a mixture distribution. We visualize this in Fig. 1 using the

Table 1. Bolded values indicate significance

Parameter	Estm	S.E.
In model for Type 1 and 2-L corner kicks:		
θ_w (variance of frailty RV)	**0.247**	**0.051**
λ_1 (rate)	**0.021**	**0.002**
γ_1 (shape)	**0.924**	**0.024**
β_1 (coef to Z_1)	-0.024	0.066
β_2 (coef to Z_2)	**0.172**	**0.082**
β_3 (coef to Z_3)	**-0.096**	**0.029**
β_4 (coef to Z_4)	-0.134	0.113
β_5 (coef to Z_5)	-0.019	0.015
In model for Type 2-S corner kicks:		
λ_2 (rate)	**1.463**	**0.062**
γ_2 (shape)	**3.542**	**0.379**
Logistic Regression Parameters:		
α_0 (intercept)	**1.638**	**0.086**
α_1 (coef to Z_1)	0.122	0.228
α_2 (coef to Z_2)	**0.296**	**0.118**
α_3 (coef to Z_3)	0.050	0.089
α_4 (coef to Z_4)	**-0.385**	**0.069**
α_5 (coef to Z_5)	**0.076**	**0.030**

estimated survival functions under these circumstances, which depict two very different survival functions.

The bold lines in the plots shown in Fig. 2 represent the home and away survival functions when the frailty random variable is exactly 1. Each plot contains an additional 50 faintly drawn lines which depict other survival functions at the same covariate levels but the frailty random variable is sampled from the $Gamma(\frac{1}{\theta_w}, \frac{1}{\theta_w})$ distribution. This demonstrates the heterogeneity of corner kicks that are not taken by the same team within the same game. Notice that the survival functions of the home team tend to be slightly lower than the away team's at the same time. This aligns with the common soccer knowledge that the home team tends to get more corners.

The third plot (Fig. 3) compares the survival functions estimated using the previous model with the survival functions estimated using the new model.

5.2 Model Comparison

To determine if the frailty model ia a significantly better fit than the model that assumes independence of all corner kicks we conduct a likelihood ratio test using the test statistic $\Lambda = -2[log(L^{(old)}(\theta)) - log(L^{(2)}(\theta))]$. The frailty model contains one additional parameter θ_w, so we assume Λ has χ^2 distribution with one degree of freedom. Obtaining the estimates using M=200 for the final iteration: $\tilde{Q}^{(old)}(\boldsymbol{\theta}_{old}, \hat{\boldsymbol{\theta}}_{old}) = -5407.3788$, and $\tilde{Q}^{(2)}(\boldsymbol{\theta}, \hat{\boldsymbol{\theta}}) = -5386.6376$ giving $\hat{\Lambda} = 41.4823$ that yields a p-value < 0.0001.

The Bayesian information criterion (BIC) for the model of Peng, Hu, and Swartz (2024) is 10869.78, while the BIC of the frailty model is 10828.30. A lower BIC is typically associated with striking a better balance between simplicity and model fit.

6 Discussion

In this paper we introduce a frailty model to address the correlation of a team's times to corner kicks within the same game. We then demonstrated that the new model provides a significantly improved fit to the 2019 CSL data than if independence among all corner kicks is assumed. Despite the analysis in this paper focusing on games played in the 2019 CSL season, we believe the insights into corner kicks may apply to other soccer games since the corner kick process is similar among professional leagues. For example, the average number of corner kicks per game is 9.93 with the CSL data, which is very close to the average in other seasons and other leagues. Future investigations using data across a range of leagues and years are needed to justify the generalisability of our findings.

This paper assumes that the corner kicks of the home and away team within the same game are independent of each other, which is a rather strong assumption. A multi-level frailty model may be employed to accommodate the potential correlation of corner kicks both at the team and game levels. We have started to conduct the research into this model that is better suited to reality.

Since 2000, sports betting has grown massively partly due to the accessibility of online gambling (Garcia, Perez, Suarez, (2025). The statistical analysis of soccer data allows the increasing number of sports bettors to make informed decisions. Extensive study of the goal scoring process in soccer using bivariate poisson processes already exists, as seen in Maher (1982), Dixon and Coles (1997), and Karlis and Ntzoufras (2003). These models can be applied to inform betting strategy on match results and total goals scored, both of which are popular wagers. The rise of sports betting has also given rise to boutique wagers, such as corner betting. One notable corner bet is an over/under bet on the number of corner kicks in a game or the over/under on the time elapsed until the first corner kick occurs. A natural extension of this paper is to use the outlined model to inform betting strategy and conduct market efficiency analysis similar to Palssen and Laurens (2023). Outside of betting, corner kicks seem to be an increasingly important aspect of the game. As of March 8th 18% of Premier League goals in the 2026 season have been generated by corner kicks, the largest proportion in a decade (Irfan, (2026). This is a 6% jump from the 2025 Premier League season indicating corner kicks are becoming an increasingly important aspect of the game.

While this paper directly provides a limited amount of coaching insight, it does align with common knowledge that taking a red card makes it more difficult to clear an opponents attack. One can also imagine inserting covariates that can be controlled by a coach into the model, for example an indicator of which formation was used. If certain formations decrease the expected time between corner kicks it can be viewed as increasing the strength of the team's attack.

7 Figures

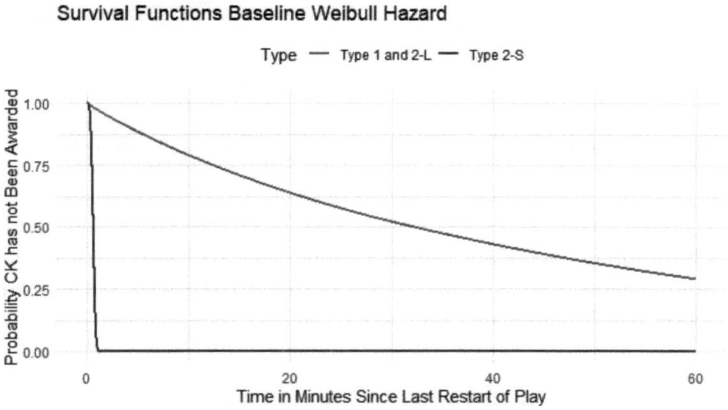

Fig. 1. The two survival functions plotted together when all covariate levels are fixed at zero.

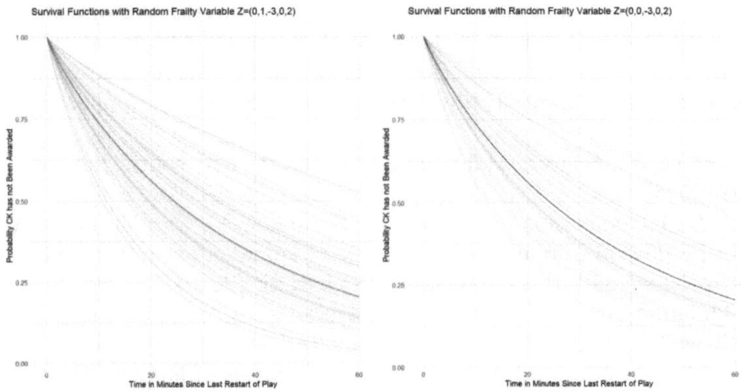

Fig. 2. Bolded line is the Type 1 and 2-L survival functions when the frailty variable is exactly 1 for two different combinations of covariates.

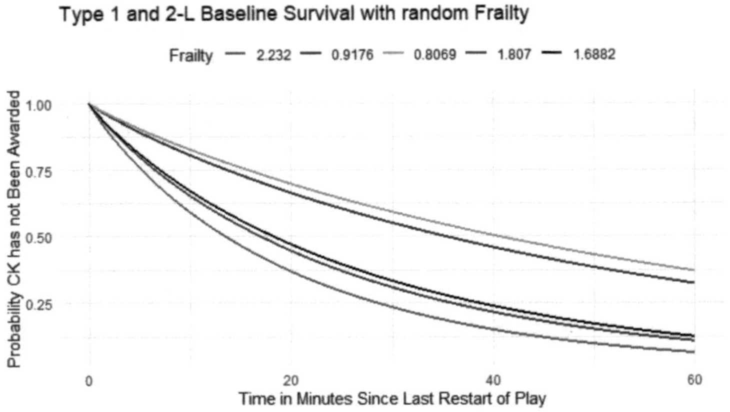

Fig. 3. The survival function for different frailty values when covariates are all fixed at zero.

Acknowledgements. We thank the two anonymous reviewers for their thoughtful comments and suggestions. This research was supported partly by an NSERC (the Natural Sciences and Engineering Council of Canada) Undergraduate Student Research Award.

Disclosure of Interests. The authors declare no competing interests.

References

Balan, T.A., Putter, H.: A tutorial on frailty models. Stat. Methods Med. Res. **29** (2020)

Casal, C.A., Maneiro, R., Arda, T., Losada, J.L., Rial, A.: Analysis of corner kick success in elite football. Int. J. Perform. Anal. Sport **15**, 430–451 (2015)

Dixon, M.J., Coles, S.G.: Modelling association football scores and inefficiencies in the football betting market. J. Royal Stat. Society: Series C (Applied Statistics) **46** (1997)

Garcia, J., Perez, L., Suarez, M.J.: Interest in sports and sports betting. J. Sports Econ. **26** (2025)

Ghomgaleh, A., Khaloukakaie, R., Ataei, M., Barabadi, A., Qarahasanlou, A.N., Rahmani, O.: Prediction of remaining useful life of komatsu excavator under reliability analysis in the weibull-frailty model. PLoS ONE **15** (2020)

Irfan, U.: The anatomy of a corner-kick: how set-pieces reshaped the premier league (2026). https://www.bbc.com/sport/football/articles/c24d84y67ydo

Kalbfleisch, J.D., Prentice, R.L.: The Statistical Analysis of Faulure Time Data, John Wiley and Sons (2011)

Karlis, D., Ntzoufras, I.: Analysis of sports data by using bivariate poisson models. J. Royal Stat. Society: Series D (The Statistician) **52** (2003)

Maher, M.J.: Modelling association football scores. Stat. Neerlandia **36** (1982)

Maneiro, R., Losada, J.L., Partell, M., Arda, A.: Observational analysis of corner kicks in high-level football: A mixed methods study. Sustainability **13**, (2021)

McLachlan, G.J., Lee, S.X., Rathnyake, S.I.: Finite mixture models. Ann. Rev. Stat. Appl. **6**, 355–378 (2019)

Neath, R.C.: On the convergence properties of the Monte Carlo EM algorithm (2012). arXiv:1206.4768 math.ST

Palsson, G., Laurens, M.: Forecasting football corner odds: Statistical modelling, betting strategies and assessing market efficiency. In: Master's Theses in Mathematical Sciences, (2023)

Peng, K., Hu, J., Swartz, T.: On the time of corner kicks in soccer: an analysis of event history data. Computational Statistics, pp. 31–17 (2024)

Vaupel, J.W., Manton, K.G., Stallard, E.: The impact of heterogeneity in individual frailty on the dynamics of mortality. Demography **16**, 439–454 (1979)

Weinke, A.: Frailty models, Max Planck Institute for Demographic Research (2003)

Yiannakos, A., Armatas, V.: Evaluation of the goal scoring patterns in European championship in Portugal 2004. Int. J. Perform. Anal. Sport **6**, 178–188 (2006)

Yiannakos, A., Armatas, V.: Performance profiles of football teams in the UEFA champions league considering situational efficiency. Int. J. Perform. Anal. Sport **15**, 371–390 (2015)

Forecasting High-Intensity Activity in Elite Gaelic Football: A Machine Learning Approach Using Wearable Sensor Data and Metabolic Work Ratio

Valerio Antonini[1(✉)], Mark Roantree[1,2], and Michael Scriney[1,2]

[1] School of Computing, Dublin City University, Dublin 9, D09 V209 Dublin, Ireland
valerio.antonini3@mail.dcu.ie, {mark.roantree,michael.scriney}@dcu.ie
[2] Insight SFI Research Centre for Data Analytics, School of Computing, Dublin City University, Dublin 9, Dublin, Ireland

Abstract. Elite Gaelic football demands rapid transitions between high-intensity efforts and recovery, yet accurately forecasting these changes in intensity remains a significant challenge for coaches and sport scientist. This study introduces a novel framework for forecasting intensity in elite football players by combining wearable sensor data with machine learning techniques. The Metabolic Work Ratio (MWR) is introduced as a new metric derived from metabolic power calculations, which captures the balance between high-intensity efforts and recovery within fixed time windows. Features derived from 3-min windows of wearable sensor data were extracted and used to train machine learning models to forecast transitions in MWR. Model interpretability was enhanced through SHAP analysis, identifying the magnitude and influence of the most impactful features. Our results demonstrate the feasibility of forecasting transitions between high-intensity and recovery phases, offering a proof-of-concept for data-driven methodologies that could support coaches and sport scientists in monitoring player workload and informing substitution decisions.

Keywords: Metabolic Power Forecasting · Wearable Sensor Data · Machine Learning in Sports Analytics

1 Introduction

Player performance analysis in sports has evolved significantly with advancements in technology and data analytics [14,30]. Traditional methods of evaluating athletes relied heavily on subjective assessments and basic statistical metrics, which often failed to capture the complex and dynamic nature of sports performance [31]. In recent years, the integration of wearable sensors and tracking systems has enabled the collection of detailed, high-frequency data on various physical and physiological parameters [13]. This development has enabled

Z. Liu and V. Misra (Eds.): ISACE 2026, LNCS 16610, pp. 456–472, 2026.
https://doi.org/10.1007/978-3-032-27272-0_29

machine learning to understand player performance better and create predictive models that can improve training and competition strategies [1,17,18].

Global Navigation Satellite System (GNSS) technology has traditionally been used to assess external load in soccer by measuring distance and time at specific speeds, with a focus on high-speed activity due to its importance in match performance [2]. However, traditional GNSS metrics underestimate the energy demands of team sports by ignoring the impact of accelerations and decelerations, which increase energy costs even at low speeds [26,29]. Research in soccer showed that the demands of soccer training are underestimated by traditional measurements of running speed alone, suggesting the use of estimations of metabolic power better inform the coach about the true demands of training sessions or games [15,27].

The metabolic power model is a theoretical approach designed to estimate the energy demands of accelerative and decelerative movements in team sports [11,29]. It operates on the principle that running with acceleration (deceleration) on flat terrain is energetically comparable to running uphill (downhill) at a constant speed, with the slope determined by the forward acceleration [29]. Given the well-established energy cost of uphill running, it is possible to translate the forward acceleration during sprint running into the equivalent up-slope and, obtain the corresponding energy cost [29]. This energy cost is combined with the instantaneous forward speed to compute the metabolic power [29]. This theoretical model has been applied to soccer to evaluate match performance in top-level players through video analysis and GNSS data, enabling the assessment of instantaneous metabolic power and redefining the concept of "high intensity" based on metabolic power rather than speed alone [15,26]. Metabolic power is defined as the required rate of ATP hydrolysis to perform the muscular work during running, representing the net metabolic demands incurred by locomotion [16]. It is calculated as the product of instantaneous energy cost (expressed in $J{\cdot}kg^1{\cdot}m^{-1}$) and speed ($m{\cdot}s^{-1}$), and is typically expressed in $W{\cdot}kg^{-1}$, indicating the amount of energy required per second per kilogram [28].

The formula to obtain the metabolic power MP used in this work has been indicated in [29]:

$$MP = EC \cdot v, \tag{1}$$

where v is the running speed ($m \cdot s^{-1}$), and EC the energy cost of accelerated running ($J \cdot kg^{-1} \cdot m^{-1}$). EC is obtained by:

$$EC = (155.4ES^5 - 30.4ES^4 - 43.3ES^3 + 46.3ES^2 + 19.5ES + 3.6)EM, \tag{2}$$

where

$$ES = tan(90 - arctan(\frac{g}{a_f})) \tag{3}$$

is the equivalent slope ($g \approx 9.81m^{-2}$ is the Earth's acceleration of gravity, and a_f the forward acceleration), and

$$EM = \sqrt{(1 + (\frac{a_f}{g})^2} \quad (4)$$

the equivalent mass reflecting the additional load imposed on the athlete due to acceleration [26].

Gaelic football is a high-demand intermittent sport characterized by repeated sprints and accelerations. Elite players cover 8160–9222 m per match, perform 166–184 accelerations, and cover 445–524 m at very high speeds (> 22 km/h) [6]. This stop-start nature necessitates accounting for accelerations, decelerations, and energy expenditure beyond velocity alone [32].

Using metabolic power in assessing aerobic fitness within elite Gaelic football players was validated in [21], giving researchers a greater understanding of player performance in real-world settings. The study highlights significant associations between metabolic power variables (among which high metabolic load distance) and objective measures of aerobic fitness, such as VO2max and velocity at VO2max (the maximum speed athletes can sustain while using their maximal oxygen uptake) [21]. The strong associations between average metabolic power, high metabolic load distance, and aerobic fitness suggest that these metrics offer a reliable method for monitoring aerobic fitness responses to training and gameplay in elite Gaelic football. With advancements in GNSS technology, practitioners can now monitor players' metabolic power in real-time during training and matches [21]. The study suggests weekly high metabolic power distance monitoring, which may be related to changes in the aerobic fitness characteristics of Gaelic football players [21].

Metabolic power variables have been explored in elite Gaelic football, revealing positional differences (midfielders highest) and temporal patterns (significant reductions as matches progress), emphasizing the dynamic nature of match demands [22].

Contribution. This study introduces the Metabolic Work Ratio (MWR), a novel metric that quantifies the balance between high-intensity efforts and recovery within fixed time windows by computing the ratio of active areas to recovery areas derived from metabolic power curves. Features derived from 3-min segments of wearable sensor data are extracted and used to train machine learning models to forecast MWR transitions in subsequent windows. This framework enables real-time workload monitoring and provides explainable, data-driven insights through SHAP analysis to support substitution strategies and workload management decisions. MWR builds on the well-established concept of work-to-rest ratio in intermittent sports research [6], operationalizing validated metabolic power estimates [21] into a dynamic ratio metric that captures the temporal alternation between exertion and recovery, a dimension not addressed by traditional cumulative indicators such as total distance or high-speed running distance.

2 Related Research

In their study, [12] used tracking data from 302 Dutch Eredivisie soccer matches (2018–2019) to predict players' physical performance in the game's early stages. By classifying underperformance as not meeting 100%, 95%, or 90% of a player's baseline, the approach provides precise predictions, with Random Forest and energy expenditure data proving the most accurate results.

In [25], researchers presented a machine learning method to predict running performance metrics of football players, such as distances covered during acceleration phases, high-intensity activities, and specific speed ranges, using biometric data from smart vests (e.g. energetic cost, metabolic power, anaerobic threshold, and maximum oxygen uptake). They identified Random Forest and Artificial Neural Networks as the most effective algorithms. These findings highlighted the value of biometric data for predicting player performance, supporting data-driven real-time match decisions.

Authors in [24] presented a machine learning framework for evaluating football players' performance, classifying them into active, normal, or weak categories based on various physical activity features collected during both training and match sessions. The active category represents players demonstrating high physical engagement, while the normal and weak categories represent average or lower physical output.

In [5], the authors investigated machine learning approaches for fatigue detection using IMU-derived sensor data from 19 athletes across repeated running sessions. Time and frequency domain features extracted from triaxial acceleration, angular velocity, and magnetic orientation were used to train machine learning models. The models achieved high predictive accuracy, with strong correlations between predicted fatigue and performance decline. While LSTM networks achieved higher results, Random Forest also performed competitively when supported by effective feature engineering.

Researchers in [23] analyzed physiological and kinematic data collected on elite professional male soccer players from the 2021–2022 soccer season to differentiate between training games and official matches using metabolic power (MP) and equivalent distance metrics (ED). Multiple supervised machine learning algorithms were applied to classify the data points into TGs or OFMs. The model performance showed high accuracy (89% to 98%), and strong discriminatory ability (AUC between 0.90 and 0.96). These results indicate that MP and ED are effective indicators for distinguishing training from official matches.

In their study [10], the authors developed a machine learning framework to monitor and predict performance attenuation in Gaelic football players by integrating physiological, anthropometric, and subjective markers. Data from 41 male athletes included neuromuscular, perceptual, biochemical, and anthropometric measures collected pre- and post-match to quantify individual performance decline. These attenuation scores served as predictive labels for models trained using oversampling methods to address class imbalance. Among the tested algorithms, Random Forest achieved the highest F1-score (0.75), highlighting strength, lower-body power, and speed/agility as key predictors.

While previous research has successfully used wearable sensor data and machine learning to predict player performance or classify activity states, these approaches often focus on traditional metrics such as running speed, total distance, or generic metabolic power, and rarely quantify the dynamic balance between high-intensity effort and recovery within short time windows, relying instead on cumulative or threshold-based metrics that do not capture the alternating nature of intermittent sport demands.

In contrast to the above, our framework introduces MWR to directly quantify the dynamic transition between high-intensity efforts and recovery, offering real-time, interpretable insights for workload monitoring in elite football.

3 Data

Data have been collected during 11 competitive Gaelic football intercounty games during the years 2019, 2020, and 2021. Players wore a STATSports Apex unit (Northern Ireland, UK), which incorporates a 10 Hz GNSS, a 100 Hz triaxial accelerometer, and a 100 Hz triaxial gyroscope. The validity of the STATSports Apex unit has been assessed by previous research [4]. The data were downloaded and analyzed using STATSports software (Apex version: 4.5.19).

4 Methodology

This section describes the steps to generate the final dataset starting from the raw data. The process is composed of the following steps:

Initial Data Loading and Processing. The study uses two types of sensors worn by the players: a 10 Hz GNSS sensor and a 100 Hz inertial measurement unit (IMU). The GNSS sensor captures positional data by recording latitude, longitude, and speed at 10 samples per second during play. Acceleration from GNSS data is computed as the rate of change of speed between consecutive time points. The IMU comprises a triaxial accelerometer and a triaxial gyroscope, each sampling at 100 Hz, providing 100 measurements per second along the x, y, and z axes. These data were aggregated at 1-second frequency by computing the average for speed, acceleration, and location (latitude and longitude), acceleration x, y, and z, and gyroscope x, y, and z in that second.

In this first step, the raw sensor data are processed to compute a set of per-second features:

- Metabolic Power. The formula to obtain metabolic power is described in Sect. 1. The metabolic power for each player in each second is computed and added as a new column to the original dataframe.
- Player Load and Gyroscope Load. Player load is obtained by using the following formula:

$$\text{PL} = \sqrt{(a_{x1} - a_{x-1})^2 + (a_{y1} - a_{y-1})^2 (a_{z1} - a_{z-1})^2} \tag{5}$$

PL is calculated as a variation of the vector magnitude, determined by taking the square root of the sum of the squared differences in acceleration over time across the three movement axes (x, y, and z) [7].
In the same way, the gyroscope load is computed [9]. Gyroscope load can be described as how fast the direction of the gyroscope's rotation changes between one moment and the next. It is measured by combining the rotation speeds around all three axes into a single value that shows the overall rate of directional change [9].
- Distance Metrics. Using the Haversine formula, minimum, maximum, and average distances to teammates are computed, providing insights into tactical positioning and collective movement patterns.
- Cumulative Workload Features. Four progressive workload metrics, describing the running activity of players since the beginning of the game, are calculated. Those metrics are: Cumulative High Speed Distance (distance covered above 5.5 m/s speed threshold), Acceleration count (number of accelerations exceeding $2\,\mathrm{m/s^2}$), Cumulative Metabolic Power, and Cumulative High Metabolic Load Distance (total distance covered above 20 W/kg threshold).

Time-Window Feature Engineering. In this step, the shape of the dataset is modified by aggregating data into 3-min time windows and extracting features that describe the player's activity. The choice of a 3-min sliding window is supported by findings in elite soccer research, where moving averages of 1, 3, and 5 min have been used effectively to capture peak running performance and workload fluctuations [3] and [19]. The input dataset is composed of the sequences of sensor (GNSS and IMU) data, metabolic power, distance, and cumulative metrics describing, for each player, 1 s of activity during games. By using sliding 3-min windows, a set of features, described in Table 1, is extracted from these variables.

Metabolic Work Ratio (MWR). MWR quantifies the balance between high-intensity work and recovery within each time window. MWR is computed through the following steps:

1. **Player-Specific Baseline**. Each player's average metabolic power $\bar{MP}$ is calculated across their entire training set:

$$\bar{MP} = \frac{1}{N_{train}} \sum_{i=1}^{N_{train}} MP_i \tag{6}$$

2. **State Segmentation**. For each 3-min window, metabolic power values are classified into active or recovery states:

$$\text{Action State}(t) = \begin{cases} 1 & \text{if } MP(t) > \bar{MP}_{\text{player}} \\ 0 & \text{if } MP(t) \leq \bar{MP}_{\text{player}} \end{cases} \tag{7}$$

State changes are detected using cumulative shifts to identify transitions (e.g., active → recovery → active).

Table 1. Features extracted from GNSS and IMU variables.

Variable	Features Extracted
Metabolic power	Average, Max, Cumulative metabolic power (total accumulated metabolic power from the start of the game up to the current window), High metabolic load distance (distance covered when metabolic power $\geq 20\ W \cdot kg^{-1}$), Cumulative high metabolic load distance, Percent time in zones (1: <10, 2: 10–20, 3: 20–35, 4: ≥35 $W \cdot kg^{-1}$), Trend (it fits a simple linear regression model to the sequence of values and returns the slope coefficient), Intensity drop (calculates the mean of the first and last quarters of the window, and returns the relative decrease as an index), Work-rest ratio (counts the total duration spent at high-intensity ($> 20\ W \cdot kg^{-1}$) versus resting).
Speed	Average, Max, Percent time standing/walking (≤2 m/s), jogging/running (2–5.5 m/s), high-speed running/sprinting (>5.5 m/s), Trend, Intensity drop, Distance covered, Cumulative distance
Acceleration	Average, Max, Number of accelerations (>2 m/s^2), Number of decelerations (<-2 m/s^2), Trend, Intensity drop, Mean acceleration jerk
Player Load	Average, Standard deviation, Count of peaks (>90th percentile)
Gyroscope Load	Average, Standard deviation, Count of peaks (>90th percentile)
Latitude & Longitude	Avg. distance to others, Avg. min/max distance to others, Closeness centrality score (nodes are the players and edges the distances)

3. **Segment Area Calculation.** For each contiguous segment of active/recovery states, the area between the metabolic power curve and the baseline is computed via trapezoidal integration:

$$\text{Area} = \int_{t_{\text{start}}}^{t_{\text{end}}} \left(MP(t) - \bar{MP}_{\text{player}}\right) dt \tag{8}$$

   - Active Area (AA). Sum of areas from all segments where $MP(t) > \bar{MP}(t)$:

$$\text{AA} = \sum_{\text{active segments}} \int_{t_{\text{start}}}^{t_{\text{end}}} \left(MP(t) - \bar{MP}_{\text{player}}\right) dt \tag{9}$$

   The AA is the sum of the area under the metabolic power curve during periods when the athlete's metabolic power is above their average metabolic power. This represents the high-intensity periods.

- Recovery Area (RA). Sum of absolute areas from all segments where $MP(t) \leq M\bar{P}(t)$:

$$\mathrm{RA} = \sum_{\text{negative segments}} \int_{t_{\text{start}}}^{t_{\text{end}}} \left(MP(t) - M\bar{P}_{\text{player}}\right) dt \tag{10}$$

  The RA is the sum of the area under the metabolic power curve during periods when the athlete's metabolic power is below their average metabolic power. This represents the recovery periods.

In Fig. 1, the Active and Recovery Areas are shown during 30 s of activity for a randomly selected player.

4. **MWR Computation**. The MWR for the window is calculated as:

$$\mathrm{MWR} = \frac{\mathrm{AA}}{|\mathrm{RA}|} = \frac{\sum_{\text{active}} \int_{t_{\text{start}}}^{t_{\text{end}}} \left(P(t) - \bar{P}_{\text{player}}\right) dt}{\sum_{\text{recovery}} \left| \int_{t_{\text{start}}}^{t_{\text{end}}} \left(P(t) - \bar{P}_{\text{player}}\right) dt \right|} \cdot t, \tag{11}$$

where t is the size in minutes of the time window. If no recovery occurs ($|\mathrm{RA}| = 0$), MWR is set to 0 to avoid division by zero. This formulation transforms raw metabolic power time series into a physiologically interpretable metric for workload monitoring in team sports. In summary, MWR quantifies the ratio of high-intensity work to recovery within a fixed-minute window, scaled by the window duration.

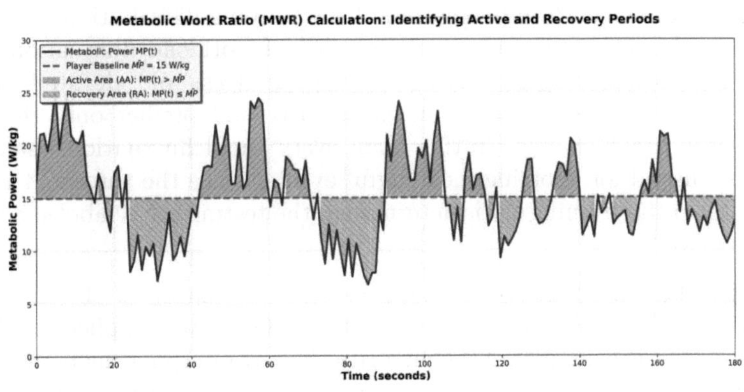

Fig. 1. Active and Recovery Areas obtained from the metabolic power trend and average metabolic power.

For each 3-min window, MWR provides an absolute measure of workload intensity. For forecasting purposes, the objective is to predict whether the upcoming window will represent an unusually high-intensity period for that player, identifying windows where workload demands significantly exceed the player's typical levels. To quantify these intensity deviations, the MWR_{change}

is introduced as a normalized measure that expresses how much the upcoming window's intensity differs from the player's individual baseline:

$$MWR_{change} = \frac{MWR_{t+1} - M\bar{W}R_{player}}{M\bar{W}R_{player}}, \tag{12}$$

where MWR_{t+1} is the metabolic work ratio calculated for the next 3-minute window, and $M\bar{W}R_{player}$ the player-specific average MWR computed across all training data.

This formulation has two critical purposes:

- Individualization: By normalizing against each player's training baseline rather than absolute thresholds, MWR_{change} accounts for individual differences. A MWR_{change} of $+0.50$ indicates the upcoming window will be 50% more intense than that player's average.
- Deviation Detection: Positive MWR_{change} values indicate the next window will have above-average intensity for that player, while negative values indicate below-average intensity.

The goal is to use features extracted from the current 3-min window (t), combined with cumulative workload metrics from the start of the match, to forecast MWR_{change} for the subsequent window (t+1).

3rd Quantile Labeling. Instead of predicting the exact value of MWR_{change}, the focus is on identifying significant workload transitions by labeling values above the 3rd quartile (75th percentile) of the training distribution as high-risk. This threshold captures the most critical 25% of workload fluctuations, which are often associated with increased physiological stress and elevated workload demand. Using the 3rd quantile lets us identify and predict only the largest and most important changes, rather than every small fluctuation, making our model more useful for spotting meaningful events. Once the threshold value for MWR_{change} in the training set is determined, the testing set is labeled according to this threshold.

Handling Class Imbalance. To address class imbalance in the dataset, the Synthetic Minority Oversampling Technique (SMOTE) was applied [8]. SMOTE generates synthetic examples of the minority class by interpolating between existing minority samples and their nearest neighbors, resulting in a more balanced class distribution for model training.

Model Prediction and Interpretation. To predict player metabolic power trends, several classifiers are employed, including Logistic Regression, Random Forest, Gradient Boosting, and XGBoost. Model selection is guided by performance metrics such as accuracy and F1-score. The results are compared using 3 different sets of features:

1. Standard: use features collected on the current time window in addition to some cumulative features since the beginning of the match.

2. Lag features 1: use features collected on the current time window, the same features collected in the previous time window, and some cumulative features since the beginning of the match.
3. Lag features 2: use features collected on the current time window, the same features collected in the previous 2 time windows, and some cumulative features since the beginning of the match.

The objective is to compare predictive results across varying time windows to determine the optimal temporal horizon for achieving high accuracy. This analysis aims to understand how a player's recent history affects changes in their metabolic power over time. For each game, SHAP values are computed [20]. These values are then averaged to obtain an importance score for each feature, along with the direction of its influence. This approach provides clear explanations of how different features and activity levels affect metabolic power trends.

Training and Testing Sets Definition. In the experiments, a single game was used in the testing set, while the remaining games were used for training. This setup simulates a real-world scenario where a team relies on past data to predict the workload in a new, ongoing game. After collecting the results for one test game, the testing game was changed, and the process was repeated. This procedure, known as Leave-One-Game-Out (LOGO) cross-validation, ensures that every available game is used as a test set once, simulating a realistic deployment scenario where past games inform predictions on unseen matches.

The calculation of MWR_{change} and the division into classes is repeated each time. Indeed, both the player-specific average MWR in the training set ($M\bar{W}R_{player}$), and the 3rd quantile of the distribution of MWR_{change} values change at each iteration as it changes the composition of the training set.

This methodology enables real-time intensity prediction while maintaining physiological interpretability through the MWR framework and player-specific adaptive thresholds.

5 Results

Players with fewer than three games were excluded to ensure reliability, as they represent small samples with variable playing times. For test sets, players with under five minutes were removed due to insufficient modeling data.

Once one game is selected as the testing game, the train and test sets are obtained by performing the steps described in Sect. 4. Then, MWR_{change} is computed, and its distribution in the training set is divided into classes using the 3rd quantile labeling. Finally, this threshold is used to divide the distribution of MWR_{change} in the testing set into classes.

5.1 Feature Set Evaluation

Table 2 summarizes the average accuracy and F1 scores achieved by the Gradient Boosting Machine model when trained on different sets of features. The

"Standard" feature set includes metrics extracted from the current time window and cumulative values since the start of the game (described in Sect. 4). The "Lag 1", and "Lag 2" feature sets augment the "Standard" features with data from one and two previous time windows. The results indicate that adding information from previous time windows does not increase the performance of the machine learning models: the F1 score for the "Standard" feature sets across the 11 games is the highest and the most stable (0.69 ± 0.05). The average accuracy does not vary significantly for the diverse feature set (0.71, 0.70, and 0.71), with "Standard" features obtaining more stable results (standard deviation equal to 0.04, 0.06 and 0.05; respectively). Therefore, we conclude that to accurately predict the metabolic power trend over the next 3 minutes of a game, it is most effective to consider the player's activity levels during the current 3 min, without unnecessarily increasing the temporal window. Some temporal information is still included in the cumulative features collected on some specific variables (Sect. 4), which return a history of the evolution of these variables since the beginning of the game.

Table 2. Comparison of predictive performance across different feature sets.

Features Set	Avg F1 Score	Avg Accuracy
Standard	0.69 ± 0.05	0.71 ± 0.04
Lag 1	0.68 ± 0.06	0.70 ± 0.05
Lag 2	0.68 ± 0.07	0.71 ± 0.05

The comparison of feature sets (Standard, Lag 1, Lag 2) in Table 2 also serves as an implicit evaluation of temporal context: augmenting the current window with one or two prior windows did not improve predictive performance, suggesting that the most relevant workload information is captured within the current 3-min window, supplemented by cumulative match-level features. While sequence-based models such as LSTM networks could provide a more expressive temporal baseline, the present study prioritized interpretability through SHAP analysis, which requires feature-based models to deliver actionable insights to coaches and practitioners. Exploring recurrent architectures as complementary approaches remains a direction for future work.

5.2 Model Comparison and Feature Importance

Figure 2 compares machine learning models using "Standard" features across 11 games. Tree-based ensemble methods prove most effective: Gradient Boosting (GB) achieves highest F1 scores in 6 games, Random Forest in 4. GB's performance varies (F1: 0.58–0.80), suggesting game-specific factors influence predictability. XGBoost shows intermediate performance. Overall, GB emerges as most robust (average F1: 0.67 ± 0.06), balancing predictive power and consistency. The superior performance of GB and RF highlights the importance of hierarchical feature interactions and non-linear decision boundaries in predicting metabolic workload transitions.

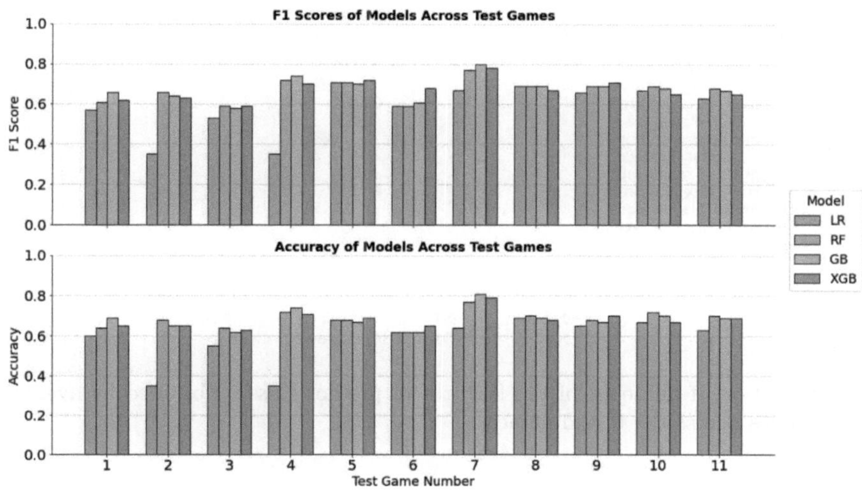

Fig. 2. Comparative analysis of four machine learning models (LR, RF, GB, XGB) across multiple test games: F1 scores (top) and accuracy (bottom).

The SHAP summary plot in Fig. 3 illustrates the mean feature contributions to the prediction of Class 1 (high MWR_{change}) across all games obtained using GB in combination with "Standard" features set. Cumulative_mp, cumulative_distance and cumulative_hmld are the most influential positive predictors, suggesting that higher values of these features increase the probability of a high MWR_{change} event in the next window. This may indicate that the level of activity increases in later stages of the game. Percent_time_zone4_mp has the strongest negative influence, indicating that higher time spent in the most intense metabolic power zones is associated with a reduced likelihood of Class 1 events in the next window. Similarly, max_speed, shows a negative contribution, suggesting how higher efforts in the current window are followed by recovery phases in the following window. Other features such as hsr or sprinting, num_accelerations, and std_player_load, also show meaningful negative contributions, whereas metrics like avg_avg_dist, avg_min_dist and avg_max_dist positively influence the model's prediction of class 1. The mix of positive and negative SHAP values among top features highlights the interplay between acute high-intensity exposure (which appears indicative of normal activity states) and cumulative workload (which elevates risk for significant workload changes). This pattern underscores how metrics on current window and historical metrics contribute significantly in predicting transitions in athlete load profiles.

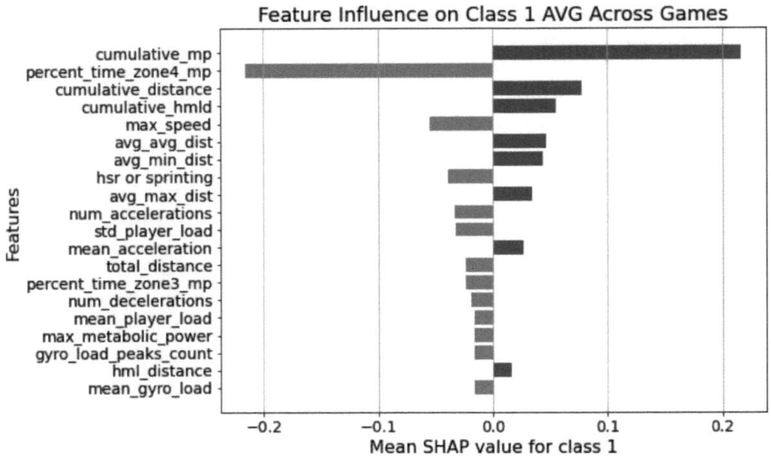

Fig. 3. Direction of influence of the features to predict class 1 obtained by averaging shapley values across the tested games.

5.3 Model Behaviour Analysis

Figure 4 shows conditional distributions of subsequent MWR classes. When current class is 0, 77.5% remain in class 0 (22.5% transition to class 1). When current class is 1, 69.2% transition to class 0 (30.8% persist in class 1). This indicates moderate persistence, with higher likelihood of remaining in lower workload states. The increased probability of transitioning from class 0 to class 1 (30.8%) suggests that high workload periods are often followed by a stability in intensity, potentially reflecting intensive game moments. Results depend on the 3-min window size.

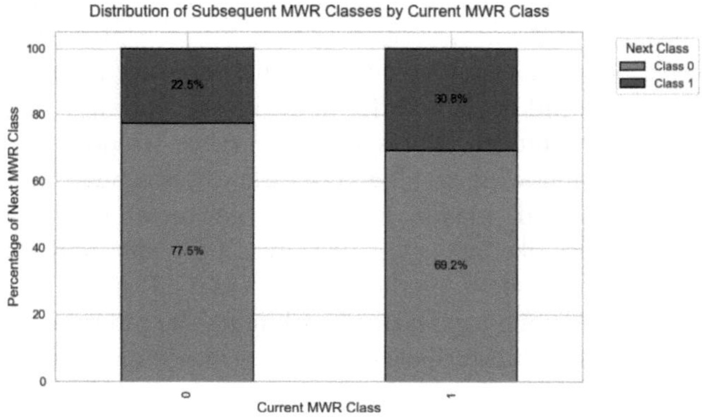

Fig. 4. Count of classes in the next time window based on the current class.

The boxplot in Fig. 5 shows the distribution of F1 scores across players, with colors indicating the number of games played. Several players, such as Players 15, 21, 23, 26, and 28 contributed a high volume of predictions. Others show few or short appearances on the field. High presence in the test set does not translate to higher or more stable F1 scores. For example, Players 3 and 18, despite their high activity, exhibited considerable variability in F1 scores. On the contrary, Players 16 and 24 combined high involvement with stable and elevated F1 performance. Some players with lower presence, such as Player 27 and 34, demonstrated consistently high F1 scores. These patterns indicate that both engagement level and prediction accuracy vary widely across participants, with no simple relationship between the two metrics.

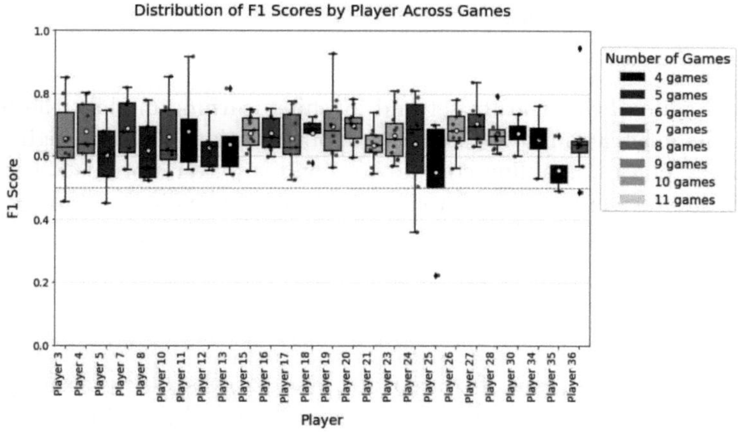

Fig. 5. Boxplots showing the distribution of F1 scores per player across games, with colors indicating the number of games played and individual points representing single-game performances.

Figure 6 illustrates the distribution of the model's weighted F1 scores across consecutive time windows in the first and second halves. In the first half, the F1 score starts at a moderate level and exhibits a generally upward trend, with some oscillations and local peaks, (540–720 and 1440–1620 windows). The model's performance stays relatively stable, and finishes the half with one of its highest values. The second half displays greater variability and more peaks, with F1 score reaching the highest and lowest values. After a drop in the middle of the half, the model's performance follows a growing trend towards the end of the half, with a drop in the last window. The model demonstrates robust predictive performance throughout the match, with a tendency for higher accuracy in the later stages of both halves. Interestingly, both halves follow the same pattern in the central part, with F1 scores reaching the same score in two consecutive windows (540–720) and (720–900).

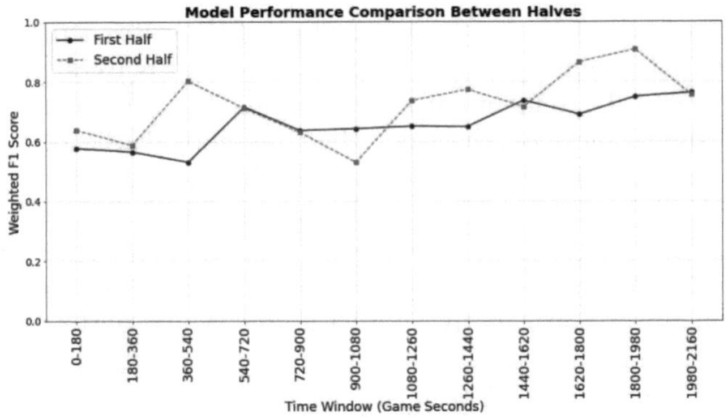

Fig. 6. F1 score of the predictive model across sequential time windows for the first and second half of the matches.

By leveraging a rich feature set and machine learning models, the proposed approach demonstrates reliable forecasting of transitions between high-intensity and recovery phases, enabling coaches to monitor player workload in real time and make data-driven decisions based on interpretable indicators that reflect the demands of match play.

6 Conclusion

This study presents a proof-of-concept for forecasting activity intensity in elite Gaelic football players using advanced sensor data and machine learning. The Metabolic Work Ratio (MWR), a novel metric based on metabolic power, quantifies the balance between high-intensity work and recovery. Data from 11 matches using GNSS and IMU sensors were processed to extract features describing activity levels, which trained models to predict MWR over subsequent 3-min windows. Results indicate promising predictive performance (average F1: 0.69 ± 0.05), enabling forecasting of high-intensity phases to support substitution strategies and workload management decisions. Several limitations should be acknowledged. First, data from a single elite county team across 11 matches constrains generalizability across teams, competition levels, and seasons; extending the framework to multiple teams remains a key direction for future research. Second, the fixed 3-min window, while supported by elite soccer research on moving average windows [3,19], may not capture brief sub-minute intensity spikes typical of intermittent team sports; future work should explore adaptive window configurations. Third, although MWR offers a novel perspective on workload dynamics, its physiological relevance requires further empirical validation beyond the theoretical grounding provided here. Finally, live deployment would require raw sensor data streams not typically available through standard commercial monitoring software, though this work demonstrates that accurate predictions are achievable when such data are accessible.

Acknowledgments. This work was supported by Science Foundation Ireland through the Insight Centre for Data Analytics (SFI/12/RC/2289_P2) and the SFI Centre for Research Training in Machine Learning (18/CRT/6183).

Disclosure of Interests. The authors have no competing interests to declare that are relevant to the content of this article.

References

1. Antonini, V., Mileo, A., Roantree, M.: Engineering features from raw sensor data to analyse player movements during competition. Sensors **24**(4) (2024)
2. Aughey, R.J.: Applications of gps technologies to field sports. Int. J. Sports Physiol. Perform. **6**(3), 295–310 (2011)
3. Augusto, D., Brito, J., Aquino, R.: Contextual variables affect peak running performance in elite soccer players: a brief report. Front. Sports Active Liv. **4** (2022)
4. Beato, M., Coratella, G., Stiff, A., Iacono, A.D.: The validity and between-unit variability of GNSs units (statsports apex 10 and 18 hz) for measuring distance and peak speed in team sports. Front. Physiol. **9**, 1288 (2018)
5. Biró, A., Cuesta-Vargas, A.I., Szilágyi, L.: AI-assisted fatigue and stamina control for performance sports on IMU-generated multivariate times series datasets. Sensors **24**(1), 132 (2024)
6. Boyle, E., Malone, S., Mangan, S., Doran, D.A., Collins, K.: Applied sport science of gaelic football. Sport Sci. Health **19**(1), 27–39 (2023)
7. Bredt, S.d.G.T., Chagas, M.H., Peixoto, G.H., Menzel, H.J., de Andrade, A.G.P.: Understanding player load: meanings and limitations. J. Hum. Kinetics **71**, 5 (2020)
8. Chawla, N.V., Bowyer, K.W., Hall, L.O., Kegelmeyer, W.P.: Smote: synthetic minority over-sampling technique. J. Artifi. Intell. Res. **16**, 321–357 (2002)
9. Chen, H., Schall, M.C., Fethke, N.B.: Gyroscope vector magnitude: a proposed method for measuring angular velocities. Appl. Ergon. **109**, 103981 (2023)
10. Cordeiro, M.C., Cathain, C.O., Daly, L., Kelly, D.T., Rodrigues, T.B.: A machine learning-based performance monitoring approach for athlete performance attenuation prediction (2025)
11. Di Prampero, P.E., Botter, A., Osgnach, C.: The energy cost of sprint running and the role of metabolic power in setting top performances. Eur. J. Appl. Physiol. **115**, 451–469 (2015)
12. Dijkhuis, T.B., Kempe, M., Lemmink, K.A.: Early prediction of physical performance in elite soccer matches—a machine learning approach to support substitutions. Entropy **23**(8), 952 (2021)
13. Draughon, G., et al.: Integration of wearable and ambient sensors towards characterization of physical effort. Mater. Res. Proc. **27**, 300–307 (2023)
14. El-Maghrabi, Y., Sharif, M.: Game changers or game predictors? big data analytics in sports for performance enhancement and fan engagement. J. Contemporary Healthc. Anal. **6**(6), 19–39 (2022)
15. Gaudino, P., Iaia, F., Alberti, G., Strudwick, A., Atkinson, G., Gregson, W.: Monitoring training in elite soccer players: systematic bias between running speed and metabolic power data. Int. J. Sports Med. **34**(11), 963–968 (2013)
16. Gray, A.J., Shorter, K., Cummins, C., Murphy, A., Waldron, M.: Modelling movement energetics using global positioning system devices in contact team sports: limitations and solutions. Sports Med. **48**, 1357–1368 (2018)

17. Hewitt, J.H., Karakuş, O.: A machine learning approach for player and position adjusted expected goals in football (soccer). Franklin Open **4**, 100034 (2023)
18. Jose, S., Maliackal, A.T., Sukumaran, A., Cyriac, J., Varkey, R.M.: Machine learning technique to analyze the health condition of athletes and predict their performance. In: 2023 International Conference on Circuit Power and Computing Technologies (ICCPCT), pp. 354–359. IEEE (2023)
19. Le Page, N., Link, D.: Load peak intensity in pre-season training sessions and official competitions in professional soccer. Int. J. Sports Sci. Coaching **20**(2), 669–678 (2025)
20. Lundberg, S.M., Lee, S.I.: A unified approach to interpreting model predictions. Adv. Neural Inf. Process. Syst. **30** (2017)
21. Malone, S., Shovlin, A., Collins, K., McRobert, A., Doran, D.: Is the metabolic power paradigm ecologically valid within elite gaelic football? Sport Sci. Health **17**, 551–561 (2021)
22. Malone, S., Solan, B., Collins, K., Doran, D.: The metabolic power and energetic demands of elite gaelic football match play. J. Sports Med. Phys. Fitness (2016)
23. Manzi, V., et al.: Exploring the interplay between metabolic power and equivalent distance in training games and official matches in soccer: a machine learning approach. Front. Physiol. **14**, 1230912 (2023)
24. Merzah, B.M., Croock, M.S., Rashid, A.N.: Intelligent classifiers for football player performance based on machine learning models. Int. J. Electric. Comput. Eng. Syst. **15**(2), 173–183 (2024)
25. Morciano, G., Zingoni, A., Calabrò, G.: Optimization and comparison of machine learning algorithms for the prediction of the performance of football players. Neural Comput. Appl. **36**(31), 19653–19666 (2024)
26. Osgnach, C., Poser, S., Bernardini, R., Rinaldo, R., Di Prampero, P.E., et al.: Energy cost and metabolic power in elite soccer: a new match analysis approach. Med. Sci. Sports Exerc. **42**(1), 170–178 (2010)
27. Pillitteri, G., et al.: Toward a new conceptual approach to "intensity" in soccer player's monitoring: a narrative review. J. Strength Condition. Res. **37**(9), 1896–1911 (2023)
28. Polglaze, T., Hoppe, M.W.: Metabolic power: a step in the right direction for team sports. Int. J. Sports Physiol. Perform. **14**(3), 407–411 (2019)
29. di Prampero, P.E., Fusi, S., Sepulcri, L., Morin, J.B., Belli, A., Antonutto, G.: Sprint running: a new energetic approach. J. Exp. Biol. **208**(14), 2809–2816 (2005)
30. Venugopal, S.: Big data-enhancement in sports: exploring the impact of technology integration. In: 2023 International Conference on Computer Communication and Informatics (ICCCI), pp. 1–3. IEEE (2023)
31. Windt, J., Hamilton, K., Cox, D.N., Zumbo, B.D., Sporer, B.C.: Capturing the "expert's eye': a perspective on developing a better understanding and implementation of subjective performance evaluations in team sports. J. Elite Sport Perform., 36710 (2022)
32. Young, D., Malone, S., Collins, K., Mourot, L., Beato, M., Coratella, G.: Metabolic power in hurling with respect to position and halves of match-play. PLoS ONE **14**(12), e0225947 (2019)

Short Papers

Addressing Last Mile Issues in Sports Analytics: A Case Study in Expected Goals in Soccer

Joe Gallagher, Daniel Dinsdale(✉), Arun Murali, Nils Mackay, Daniele Foroni, and Patrick Lucey

Stats Perform, 37 North Wharf Road, Paddington, London W2 1AF, UK
daniel.dinsdale@statsperform.com

Abstract. In this paper we discuss a "last mile" problem applied to sports analytics. Specifically, ensuring that models with high aggregate performance are reliable in rare edge case scenarios, which are often those that matter most to analysts and fans. We center this discussion around Expected Goals (xG), the most widely known predictive statistic in soccer. We show how combining statistical and sports domain expertise can be used to develop smarter features to condense the feature space, apply monotonic constraints to impose rationality on the learnt relationship between important geometric features, and use data augmentation to increase the exposure of the model to rare shot types. We develop a set of low-level evaluation criteria which show how model performance improves on rare shot archetypes and reacts more realistically to perturbations of input data, particularly concerning the geometric relationship between strikers and the goalkeeper, an important and highly sensitive feature in the model.

Keywords: Expected Goals · Sports Analytics · Machine Learning · Artificial Intelligence · Robustness · Sensitivity · Perturbation · Data Augmentation

1 Introduction

In sport, the moments that capture headlines are often those that defy expectation. For statistical modelling this is a problem: such moments are precisely those which most challenge these models. Notable instances include win probability models in late game scenarios with time-outs and clock management, where variable increment scoring (e.g., basketball and American football) amplifies sensitivity to rare events. Expected Goals (xG) in soccer is another example; a model which predicts the likelihood of a shot being converted into a goal at the moment the ball is struck. The majority of shots in soccer are somewhat similar: usually hit within the opposition box (63%) and with the goalkeeper in their 6-yard box (96%). If rarer edge cases are not explicitly considered during training and evaluation, the resulting models may exhibit high aggregate performance while remaining fragile in precisely the situations that matter most to practitioners and audiences. This mismatch between overall accuracy and situational reliability represents a classic "last mile" problem in applied sports analytics: the final step from a statistically sound model to one that is robust, trustworthy, and usable in real-world decision-making.

Z. Liu and V. Misra (Eds.): ISACE 2026, LNCS 16610, pp. 475–483, 2026.
https://doi.org/10.1007/978-3-032-27272-0_30

As richer datasets with more detailed shot descriptors have emerged from providers such as Opta, more advanced statistical models have been developed [1, 2]. Event-based xG is now dominated by machine learning, notably gradient-boosting approaches [3, 4] and recent advances in AI-assisted coding and modelling tools have significantly lowered the barrier to building such models. Given a structured dataset, it is now possible to automatically generate features, train and tune a model, and produce evaluation results within seconds. However, model complexity and automation cannot substitute for a deep understanding of the data generating process. Unless a specific modelling failure mode has been encountered before, it is unrealistic to expect a single automated pass to capture the full complexity of every data point, feature interaction, and domain-specific nuance - particularly in a sport as fluid and context-dependent as soccer. Practitioners must navigate trade-offs between aggregate performance and robustness, especially when models are deployed at scale and consumed by diverse downstream users. For models which utilize player and ball tracking data [5], which is becoming more common across many sports [6, 7], this problem of edge cases is exacerbated [8, 9].

In this paper we compare two event-based men's xG models, "V1" and "V2", near identical apart from seemingly small differences in geometric feature expression, feature selection, and data augmentation. We show how minimizing the loss of a model is not sufficient and examine how a slight reduction in overall loss metrics can be a worthwhile trade-off for improved generalizability in rarer shot scenarios, enhanced resilience to noise, and more common-sense intuition.

2 Initial V1 Model

2.1 High-Level Evaluation

We trained both models using XGBoost (eXtreme Gradient Boosting) [10] on an identical dataset of Opta events containing 1,002,309 shots from 29 competitions between 2018–2025. V1 consists of 23 features containing all seemingly relevant geometric features including engineered geometric simplifications such as goalkeeper angle to goal.

Standard evaluation metrics show V1 has good high-level performance (AUC-ROC: 0.837; PR: 0.479), is well calibrated (bias: -0.00137), and generates sensible predictions for the most common shot scenarios. However, digging deeper into individual predictions begins to unearth problems with this type of hands-off evaluation.

2.2 Shot Archetypes

Using soccer knowledge, we can stratify data points (shots) across archetypes depending on the properties of the shot, such as location, type (e.g. foot vs head), or context (e.g. goalkeeper out of position) and examine how well calibrated predictions are within these groups. We can subjectively define any number of archetypes according to common-sense criteria or objectively define via algorithms such as clustering.

Table 1 shows the bias of the model (sum of xG minus the sum of observed goals, expressed per 1000 shots). We can see V1 dramatically overestimates the likelihood of scoring from long range on an open goal, predicting 242 more goals per 1000 shots from such scenarios than are observed. V1 also overestimates (albeit less severely) headers on open goal, further suggesting that the model struggles with unusual goalkeeper positioning.

2.3 Permutation

Permutation of input data is a useful tool for validating models in terms of its commonsense and robustness to data perturbations. We can verify our model produces reasonable predictions, even in unusual shot scenarios, to ensure we maintain accuracy in the face of lower quality input data - common in live predictions when data is yet to receive its final quality assurance. Hence, we wish to trade off sensitivity to features and high accuracy on idealized input data, with robustness to unusual or noisy input data.

We analyze the robustness and sensitivity of our V1 model by permuting only the shot location (Fig. 1A) or goalkeeper location (Fig. 1B) and observing the effect on the predicted xG. This reveals a fundamental lack of understanding from the model in the relationship of the shot and goalkeeper coordinates. In Fig. 1B, the model correctly predicts lower xG when the goalkeeper is permuted in front of the shot. However, locations outside of the box, where the goalkeeper is not able to handle the ball, seem to be as effective at lowering xG as many locations in the box. Most worryingly, goalkeeper locations immediately behind the shot appear to increase xG most of all, yet not at locations further away such as the opposite flank of the pitch.

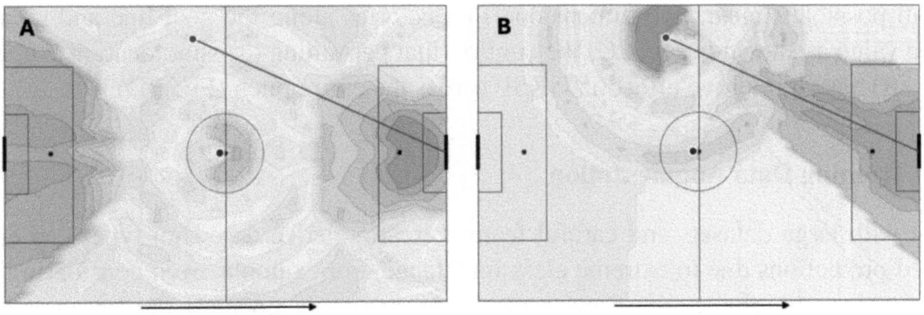

Fig. 1. Heatmap showing Expected Goals (xG) predictions for V1 model with either the shot location permuted (A) or the goalkeeper location permuted (B). The green dot shows the true shot location; the blue dot shows the true goalkeeper location. Red regions show higher xG predictions (i.e. better scoring opportunities) and blue regions lower xG.

3 V2 Model Improvements

3.1 Feature Engineering and Selection

We have shown how our V1 model has performed well overall but is struggling with edge cases. There are many common statistical approaches to reduce overfitting and produce more robust predictions. Regularization of models via loss penalties or careful prior specification in Bayesian models are very common [11]. Similarly, we could shift towards more interpretable and simple models such as regression-based approaches.

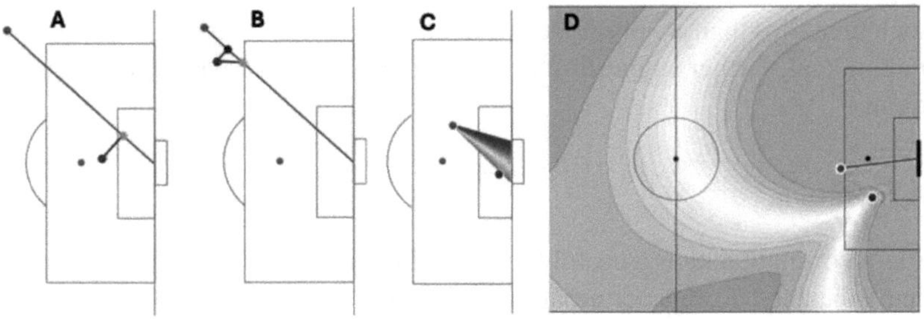

Fig. 2. Visual examples of the Goalkeeper (GK) distance to shot line of sight feature (shot location = green dot; GK location = blue dot). A) Nearest savable point is on shot trajectory line (cyan dot). B) The GK is outside of the box hence nearest savable point on projected shot trajectory is not nearest point (purple dot). C) GK save probabilities for shot locations at moment of a shot (red = high GKSP; blue = low GKSP). D) Heatmap of GKSP by permuted shot location.

For this work, we specifically address V1's poor handling of shooter-goalkeeper spatial relationship through feature engineering. We replace three goalkeeper distance to shot/goal and angle features with the introduction of a single goalkeeper save probability (GKSP) feature to regularize the model and help it maintain spatial common-sense. GKSP is based on (1) the goalkeeper's distance to the shot and (2) the distance to the nearest savable point on the shot trajectory (Fig. 2A,B). A Generalized Additive Model (GAM) is trained on these features using Goalkeeper Save as the target variable. As we want the observed shot trajectory to be unknown in an xG model, we calculate GKSP for all possible (linear, two-dimensional) trajectories along the goal line and take the mean value as shown in Fig. 2C. We confirm that permuting the shot location (i.e. as in Fig. 1B) has an intuitive effect on GKSP across the entire pitch (Fig. 2D).

3.2 Training Data Augmentation

Even with large datasets and careful feature creation, edge case shot types can cause biased predictions due to extreme class imbalance. For example, even considering low sample size, the challenging long range (>50 m) goalkeeper off the line archetype (Table 1; I) comprised only 0.02% of shots in our training set. We address this using data augmentation; specifically, adding noise to certain features whilst retaining the target value. To increase the model's exposure to our long-range open goal shot archetype, we took 15,000 shots >50 m from goal with the goalkeeper in an unsavable location (GKSP <0.01) and created 10 replicates of each shot with a random uniform noise of 0–5 m in both the x and y-coordinate. This increases the number of rare examples the model is exposed to, while maintaining the essence of the shot scenario.

3.3 Monotonic Constraints

Finally, we impose monotonic constraints to enforce unidirectional effects of certain features on predictions; for example, distance to the goal should inversely impact the chance of a goal being scored [4]. This is an example of imposing our prior knowledge to support model learning and prevent identifying ungeneralizable relationships.

4 V2 Model Performance

4.1 High-Level Evaluation

Basic evaluation shows the V2 model performs similarly to V1, although slightly worse on high-level metrics (AUC-ROC: 0.819; PR: 0.458; bias: 0.00153). We note the monotonic constraints on the GKSP feature account for most of this drop in performance.

4.2 Shot Archetypes

V1 performed poorly on unusual shot scenarios due to an inappropriate geometric understanding of the feature space and under-exposure to rarer edge cases. V2 vastly improves on this due to its common-sense understanding of shot geometry and the likelihood of a goalkeeper being in a location to intercept a shot. Although based on a small sample size, the positive bias in the long-range open goal archetype (Table 1; I) has been drastically reduced. The bias in open goal headers has also been reduced by half.

Table 1. Prediction bias (per 1000 shots) for the Expected Goals (xG) V1 and V2 models for 12 manually defined shot archetypes, alongside archetype label and sample size.

Archetype	*Label*	*Sample Size*	*V1 Bias p 1000*	*V2 Bias p 1000*
inside box (central)	A	76,957	−3.4	4.4
very close range	B	8,982	−10.8	10.7
close range (very wide)	C	1,671	−1.2	2.6
outside box (central)	D	132,397	−0.8	−0.3
corner of box	E	10,860	1.1	5.6
header	F	71,761	−0.8	0.6
one-on-one	G	6,226	−5.2	−0.7
very long range (GK in goal)	H	1,463	−5.7	−8.1
very long range (GK off line)	I	91	242.1	3.9
open goal (foot)	J	2,647	25.2	−5.4
open goal (head)	K	134	79.6	38.6
free kick	L	14,671	−4.3	1.3

Contextualize these biases using bootstrapping to compare with a background noise estimate in Fig. 3. From this, we judge all archetypes to be within acceptable limits. The worst archetype is now shots from the corner of the box (Table 1; E), but the estimate is both quantitatively small (we predict 5 more goals than observed for every 1000 shots) and at the margins of expected random noise.

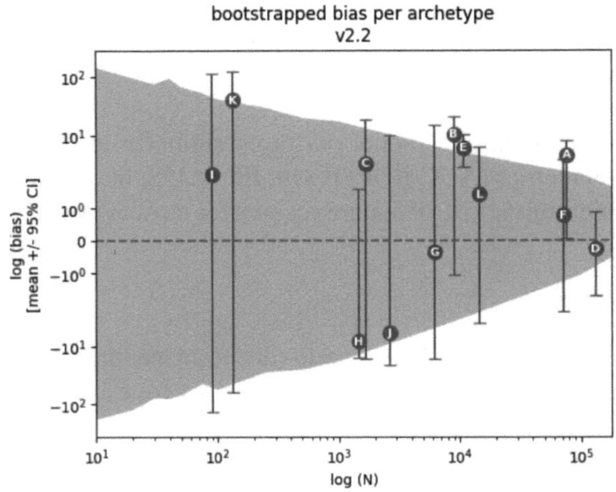

Fig. 3. Comparison of log sample size (x-axis) against the log bias (y-axis). Vertical lines show Bootstrapped bias (median ±95% CI) per 1000 shots (35% sample rate x 200 bootstraps) for each archetype label from Table 1. Blue ribbon shows bias (median ±95% CI) for 200 completely random shot samples of that sample size.

4.3 Permutation Plots

We repeat the spatial analysis of the shot from Fig. 1, this time examining how the V2 model predictions vary with permuted shot and goalkeeper positioning. We see a huge improvement in the understanding of shot and goalkeeper location dynamics, predominantly learned through the GKSP feature. Aside from a large reduction in predicted xG for this shot (V1: 0.61; V2: 0.37), we observe improved resilience as hypothetical edge cases based on unusual shot (Fig. 4A) and goalkeeper (Fig. 4B) locations look far more intuitive. Furthermore, the monotonic constraints imposed on the GKSP feature eliminate unwanted variation in xG across functionally identical scenarios where the goalkeeper is in an equally unsavable position.

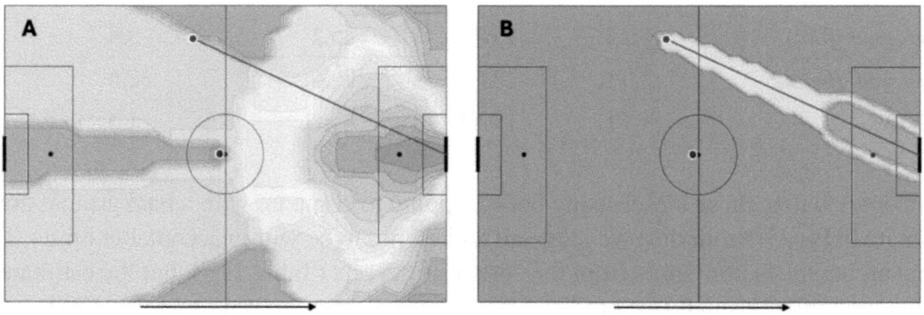

Fig. 4. A heatmap showing Expected Goals (xG) predictions for V2 model, with either shot location (A) or the goalkeeper location permuted (B). See Fig. 1 for further description.

5 Summary and Future Directions

Minimizing the loss of a model is not sufficient. Ensuring that your model generalizes appropriately and can deal with edge cases to produce reliable outputs is often the most important aspect of a model, particularly when used in an applied setting such as sports analytics.

As AI coding tools make it easier than ever to build sophisticated models, the role of the Data Scientist is increasingly shifting toward defining model requirements and ensuring the right balance between robustness, explainability, and performance for each application. In this regard, this paper has touched on a small selection of methods to identify edge cases, address performance and evaluate improvements with application to event-based xG in soccer. However, these tools are generalizable across all areas of sport analytics, where the skill of the modeler is in their ability to combine statistical and sports expertise to produce both accurate but also highly reliable predictions.

6. Appendix

6.1 Model Comparisons

Overview of V1 and V2 model comparison. Table 2 shows the features used in the V1 and V2 models. Little is changed except with regards to the goalkeeper featurization which has a large impact on the learning of shot versus goalkeeper location understanding. Figure 5 shows a basic overview of the V1 and V2 models which suggest a slight advantage to the V1 model.

Table 2. List of model features for V1 and V2 models.

Feature	*V1 Features*	*V2 Features*
GK distance to shot	X	
GK distance to goal	X	
GK angle to shot	X	
GK save probability		X
shot distance	X	X
shot angle to goal	X	X
pressure	X	X
clarity	X	X
body part = left foot	X	X
body part = head	X	X
body part = other	X	X
first touch	X	X
volley	X	X

(continued)

Table 2. (*continued*)

Feature	*V1 Features*	*V2 Features*
one-on-one	X	X
free kick shot	X	X
assist = pull back	X	X
assist = cross	X	X
assist = through ball	X	X
assist = lay off	X	X
assist = flick on	X	X
scenario = fast break	X	X
scenario = set play	X	X

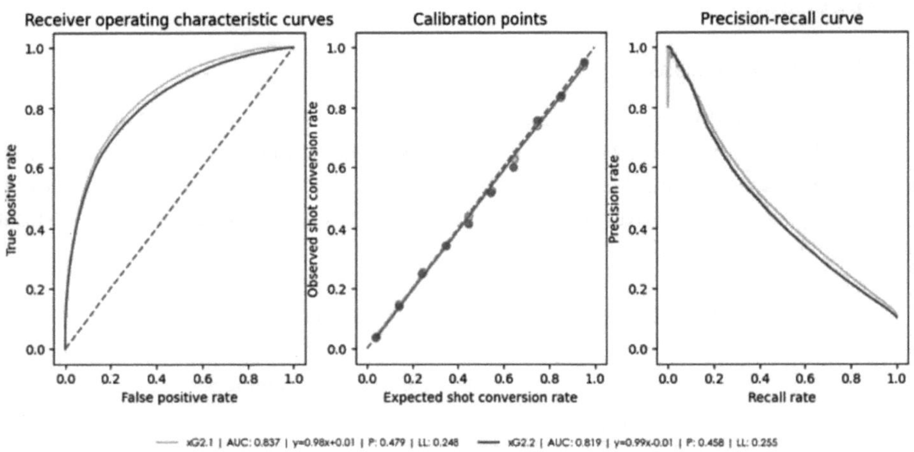

Fig. 5. ROC, Calibration and Precision-Recall curves for our Expected Goals (xG) V1 (light blue) and V2 (dark blue) models.

References

1. Assessing The Performance of Premier League Goalscorers. Accessed 26 Jan 2026
2. Robberechts, P., Davis, J.: How data availability affects the ability to learn good xG models. In: Machine Learning and Data Mining for Sports Analytics (2020)
3. What is Expected Goals (xG)? https://theanalyst.com/articles/what-is-expected-goals-xg. Accessed 26 Jan 2026
4. Upgrading Expected Goals. https://www.hudl.com/blog/upgrading-expected-goals. Accessed 26 Jan 2026
5. Anzer, G., Bauer, P.: A goal scoring probability model for shots based on synchronized positional and event data in football (soccer). Front. Sports Active Living (2021)
6. Mehrasa, N., Zhong, Y., Tung, F., Bornn, L., Mori, G.: Deep learning of player trajectory representations for team activity analysis. In: Proceedings of the MIT Sloan Sports Analytics Conference, Boston (2017)

7. Horton, M.: Learning feature representations from football tracking. In: Proceedings of the MIT Sloan Sports Analytics Conference, Boston (2020)
8. Hughes, H., et al.: Approaching in-venue quality tracking from broadcast video using generative AI. In: Proceedings of the MIT Sloan Sports Analytics Conference, Boston (2024)
9. Lucey, P., Bialkowski, A., Monfort, M., Carr, P., Matthews, I.: "Quality vs Quantity": improved shot prediction in soccer using strategic features from spatiotemporal data. In: Proceedings of the MIT Sloan Sports Analytics Conference, Boston (2015)
10. Chen, T.: XGBoost: A Scalable Tree Boosting System. Cornell University (2016)
11. Scholtes, A., Karakuş, O.: Bayes-xG: player and position correction on expected goals (xG) using Bayesian hierarchical approach. Front. Sports Active Living (2024)

Encoding Domain Expertise in Agents: Lessons from NFL Fantasy AI

Michael Butler[1(✉)], Henry Wang[1], Jake Lee[1], Kenton Blacutt[1], Dan Volk[1], Mike Band[2], and Diego Socolinsky[1]

[1] Amazon Web Services, Seattle, USA
mbutler@amazon.com
[2] National Football League, New York, USA

Abstract. Agentic AI systems can access vast data but struggle to apply domain expertise, namely the contextual understanding of how to use specialized information. This paper presents a practical framework for encoding such expertise, demonstrated with the National Football League (NFL) through NFL Fantasy AI, a production system delivering analyst-grade fantasy football advice, as assessed by NFL Pro analysts. We introduce a three-step encoding method: (1) analyst-sourced reasoning guidance, encoding analytical patterns as generalized guidance rather than enumerated rules; (2) category-level semantic framing, where experts describe data usage rather than definitions; and (3) LLM-optimized semantic interfaces, using model-to-model iteration for field naming and tool design. Deployed in eight weeks, the system achieved over 90% analyst agreement on response quality, sub-5-s response times, and zero policy violations across more than 10,000 production queries.

Keywords: National Football League · Next Gen Stats · Agentic Systems · Domain Expertise · Sports Analytics

1 Introduction

Fantasy football is the most popular category among the over 60 million fantasy sports players in North America [6], driving fan engagement [5] and generating subscription revenue [10] for the National Football League (NFL). The league recognized an opportunity to differentiate NFL Pro, its advanced analytics experience available through NFL+ Premium, by leveraging NFL Next Gen Stats (NGS), a real-time player and ball tracking system. This proprietary data represented untapped value, yet the challenge extended beyond data access: how could an AI system learn not just what the data means, but when and how do analysts use it to make expert recommendations?

Fantasy football analysts and language models can access the same data, yet only analysts know that a receiver's snap share matters more than yards-per-catch when evaluating floor versus ceiling (i.e., minimum expected output versus maximum upside). This gap between data access and contextual application defines the challenge of encoding domain expertise into agentic AI systems.

Z. Liu and V. Misra (Eds.): ISACE 2026, LNCS 16610, pp. 484–491, 2026.
https://doi.org/10.1007/978-3-032-27272-0_31

This paper presents a practical framework for encoding domain expertise into agentic AI systems under aggressive time constraints. Through NFL Fantasy AI, we demonstrate how semantic data dictionaries, analyst-sourced reasoning guidance, and Large Language Model (LLM)-driven data field and tool optimization transform raw statistics into contextual expert judgment, offering an alternative to traditional fine-tuning [8], Retrieval-Augmented Generation (RAG) [9], and knowledge graph approaches [11].

Deployed in eight weeks, the system achieved over 90% analyst agreement on recommendation quality. The framework proved transferable: analysts now use the system to draft content, and the architecture serves as a foundation for conversational access to NGS data beyond fantasy football.

2 Background and Related Work

Recent work establishes that LLMs can function as reasoning engines orchestrating external tools [12, 16, 18], with protocols like Model Context Protocol (MCP) [2] providing structured interfaces to external data. This shifts the central challenge from retrieval to application: can the model interpret results with domain-appropriate judgment?

Established approaches carry tradeoffs limiting their applicability to judgment-intensive tasks. Fine-tuning approaches, including parameter-efficient methods [8], require retraining as knowledge evolves and struggle to encode reasoning that depends on query intent. RAG [9] assumes retrieved passages contain sufficient interpretive context, yet expert judgment often resides in how information is weighed rather than what exists. Knowledge graphs [11] excel at entity relationships but do not naturally capture conditional reasoning such as "use this metric for floor, that metric for ceiling."

Sports analytics applications of LLMs have addressed system design [4], natural language querying [13], content retrieval [14], and media search [15]. These approaches address what data to retrieve, how to structure relationships, or how to adapt model weights. None addresses how an agent should interpret and apply domain data once retrieved. Our work targets this gap: we encode domain expertise into the agent's reasoning guidance and its semantic interface to data, teaching the agent not what statistics mean, but when and how analysts use them. The framing is prescriptive: not 'snap share measures percentage of offensive plays' but 'snap share indicates opportunity volume; use to assess workload floor and role stability, not scoring upside.'

3 Solution Overview

NFL Fantasy AI delivers analyst-grade fantasy advice through three architectural layers (Fig. 1): delivery infrastructure handling authentication and response streaming via Amazon EKS; agent orchestration using Strands Agents on Amazon Bedrock [1]; and a semantic data layer exposing NFL and third-party statistics through MCP servers [2].

We chose an agentic architecture over deterministic workflows because fantasy questions are inherently unpredictable. Player comparisons, trade evaluations, waiver recommendations, and matchup analyses arrive in any combination and sequence. The agent must dynamically determine which data to retrieve and how to synthesize it.

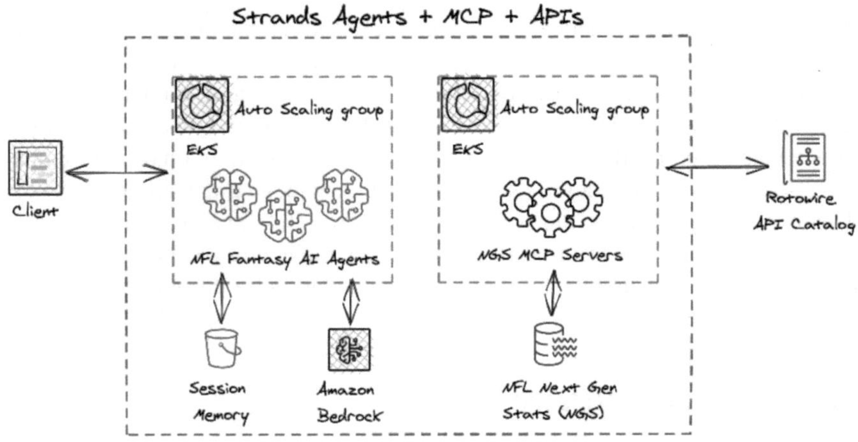

Fig. 1. NFL Fantasy AI solution architecture

The semantic data layer ingests NGS and third-party data (RotoWire injury reports, news, projections) through MCP, chosen over embedded tools for separation of concerns, independent scaling, and reusability. Critically, MCP's tool interface provided the surface area for encoding domain expertise, detailed in Sect. 4.

Production deployment required solving three additional engineering challenges: cost efficiency, resilience under peak load, and topic control. We achieved cost efficiency through three mechanisms: (1) semantic field curation and LLM-optimized tool docstrings; (2) strategic cache allocation for large MCP tool results; and (3) tool output structure optimized for deeply nested statistical data. Collectively, these reduced token consumption by 70%, doubled throughput, and cut inference costs by 45%. We achieved resilience through automatic fallback to secondary models under throttling conditions. Guardrails constrain the agent to fantasy football topics through layered defenses including prompt-based topic control and input/output classification, avoiding responses that could create brand or liability risk.

4 The Domain Expertise Encoding Framework

We developed a three-layer framework (Fig. 2) addressing the semantic gap between raw data and expert reasoning. Each layer encodes one aspect: reasoning guidance establishes how to think, category framing defines when to use data, and LLM optimization ensures the agent understands what the data means and how to obtain it efficiently.

4.1 Raw Domain Data

NGS data arrives via NFL-hosted API endpoints in JSON format. The NFL publishes API specifications listing available fields and data types, but not semantic definitions: field names `recRtPG` (receiving routes run per game) and `ptPct` (percentage of plays participated in) offer no interpretive guidance. We supplement NGS with RotoWire data (news, projections, depth charts) for situational context. The encoding framework described below addresses how we transformed undefined, abbreviated NGS fields into semantically accessible data.

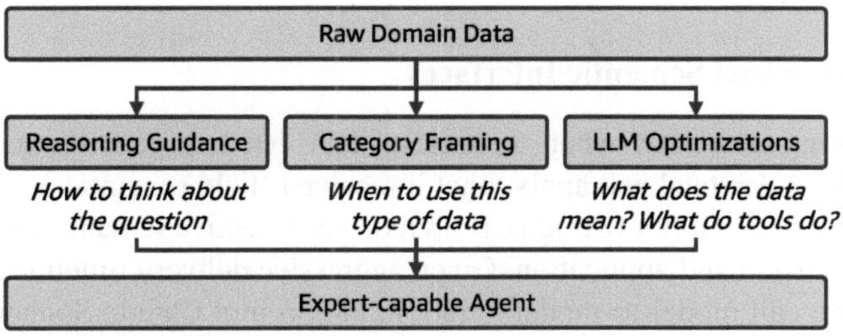

Fig. 2. The domain expertise encoding framework operates at three levels of abstraction: reasoning guidance, category framing, and LLM optimization of fields and tools.

4.2 Analyst-Sourced Reasoning Guidance

The first layer establishes the analytical approach guiding the agent's reasoning. Working with NFL Pro analysts, we articulated their reasoning process at a level of abstraction that generalizes across scenarios, capturing the structure of expert analysis [17]: what factors to consider, how to weigh competing evidence, how to frame recommendations, rather than enumerating specific rules. We embedded this guidance directly in the agent's system prompt, organized from analytical philosophy down to procedural steps. For example, we encoded temporal reasoning patterns, as seen in this excerpt:

"Fantasy Season (September to December): ALWAYS start with recent news... PRIORITIZE recent performance trends that may lead to future success... CONSIDER upcoming matchups in short-term prognostication."

At a procedural level, we encoded the sequence analysts follow, such as checking news and depth chart position before retrieving statistics (a backup's volume projection depends entirely on the starter's health status). This distinction (reasoning sequence, not conclusions) proved critical: overly specific rules (e.g., "recommend players with >15 targets per game") degraded performance on edge cases, while appropriately abstract guidance enabled robust generalization.

4.3 Category-Level Semantic Framing

When asked to document statistics, analysts instinctively described how to use them rather than defining them. Extending dataset documentation practices [7] beyond descriptive metadata, we formalized these insights into a semantic data dictionary organized around analytical categories rather than data structures.

Working with analysts, we developed 21 category descriptions covering player and team scenarios by position. For running backs, we describe participation: *"Snap share, touches, and route metrics that reveal weekly workload floor and role size; use to gauge sustainability and future volume"*, guiding the agent to retrieve participation data when assessing opportunity rather than past performance. For quarterbacks: *"Next Gen Stats efficiency and pressure metrics that reveal context behind traditional numbers"*, directing the agent toward advanced metrics when box scores require deeper interpretation.

4.4 LLM-Optimized Semantic Interfaces

Category framing addressed when to retrieve data, but two gaps remained: whether the agent could understand and apply what it received (field semantics), and whether it could efficiently obtain it (tool design). Both required effective semantic descriptions for LLM comprehension and application. Given aggressive delivery timelines, we adopted an approach we call model-to-model iteration: (1) prompt Claude Sonnet with source (field name, descriptor, tool docstring) and ask it to explain the element's analytical purpose; (2) identify failures where interpretation diverged from ground truth; (3) prompt Claude Opus with the actual purpose alongside Sonnet's misinterpretation, requesting compressed alternatives; (4) validate by re-testing Sonnet's comprehension. In practice, convergence typically required three iterations.

For field semantics, raw NGS field names like recRtPG carried no semantic signal. For example, recRouteParticipationPct ("percentage of receiving routes participated") became recRtPartPct ("route participation %"). Applied across hundreds of fields and combined with category-level framing, the LLM-optimized field descriptors yielded significant token reduction with equal or better comprehension.

For tool design, our original approach provided discrete tools for each use case (get_weekly_projections, get_season_projections, etc.), with well-documented parameters and usage examples. This produced substantial token overhead in the tool specification and a large number of tool calls to answer sample questions. Using the same protocol, we consolidated nine projection tools into a single get_projections tool [3] and compressed parameter names to their minimum LLM-effective form (positions to pos, players to plyrs). Notably, docstrings shifted from describing mechanical function to encoding analyst behavior. For example, a human-readable description like *"Team code(s) - filters player results and required for defense projections"* became *"team(s) - for matchup analysis, include both teams."* The resulting consolidation from 29 tools to 10 significantly reduced tool specification overhead, while the LLM-optimized parameter design reduced typical tool calls per query, as the agent could express nuanced intent in a single tool call.

5 Evaluation

5.1 Quality Assessment

Fantasy recommendations lack verifiable ground truth. Correct decisions depend on future outcomes. We evaluated whether agent reasoning aligned with expert standards through structured analyst review [19]. NFL Pro analysts authored 50 test questions spanning player comparisons, start/sit decisions, waiver pickups, trade evaluations, and matchup analyses. The agent processed each without human intervention. Analysts rated responses on three tiers: acceptable (substantively similar advice), acceptable with comments (directionally correct, requiring refinement), and unacceptable (different recommendations or flawed reasoning). After three evaluation rounds incorporating feedback, over 90% of responses received acceptable ratings. Evaluation was not blinded; analysts knew they were assessing AI-generated responses. Disagreements typically involved edge cases where reasonable analysts might differ, such as borderline start/sit decisions involving players with uncertain game-time injury status.

Additional validation emerged organically: the NFL Pro content team began using the agent to draft player insights, and in informal testing, analysts could not reliably distinguish AI-generated content from human-written content.

5.2 System Performance

The system achieved sub-5-s time to first token with complete responses under 30 s, stable across 10x traffic spikes on Sunday mornings. With over 10,000 production queries, guardrails prevented all off-topic and policy-violating responses.

5.3 Limitations

The encoding approach requires ongoing maintenance as domain knowledge evolves, demanding sustained expert collaboration. Analyst agreement measures reasoning alignment but cannot validate actual fantasy outcomes. For domains with stable patterns and large labeled datasets, fine-tuning may outperform runtime encoding [8]. We did not perform component-level ablation due to production timeline constraints. Production and proprietary constraints limit the implementation detail that can be disclosed.

5.4 Generalizability

Practitioners should assess whether: (1) queries are unpredictable or enumerable; (2) experts can articulate reasoning patterns, not just conclusions; (3) interpretation is context-dependent; (4) domain knowledge evolves frequently. When these conditions hold, our approach may offer a viable path to production-quality reasoning.

6 Conclusion

This paper presented a practical framework for encoding domain expertise into agentic AI systems, demonstrated through NFL Fantasy AI. By encoding expertise through analyst-sourced reasoning guidance, category-level framing, and LLM-optimized semantic interfaces, we achieved reasoning that NFL Pro analysts assessed as analyst-grade. The techniques may extend to other domains characterized by specialized terminology, contextual interpretation, and implicit expert reasoning.

Acknowledgments. The authors thank the NFL Next Gen Stats analytics team for their participation in evaluation and domain expertise sessions.

Disclosure of Interests. The system described in this paper was developed by Amazon Web Services (AWS) for the NFL and uses AWS commercial products.

References

1. Amazon Web Services: Amazon Bedrock User Guide. https://docs.aws.amazon.com/bedrock/latest/userguide/, Accessed 29 Jan 2026
2. Anthropic: Model Context Protocol Specification. https://modelcontextprotocol.io, Accessed 29 Jan 2026
3. Anthropic: Tool Use Best Practices. https://platform.claude.com/docs/en/agents-and-tools/tool-use/implement-tool-use, Accessed 29 Jan 2026
4. Davis, J., et al.: Methodology and evaluation in sports analytics: challenges, approaches, and lessons learned. Mach. Learn. **113**, 6977–7010 (2024). https://doi.org/10.1007/s10994-024-06585-0
5. Drayer, J., Shapiro, S.L., Dwyer, B., Morse, A.L., White, J.: The effects of fantasy football participation on NFL consumption: a qualitative analysis. Sport Manage. Rev. **13**(2), 129–141 (2010). https://doi.org/10.1016/j.smr.2009.02.001
6. Fantasy Sports & Gaming Association: Industry Demographics. https://thefsga.org/fantasy-sports-gaming-industry/, Accessed 29 Jan 2026
7. Gebru, T., et al.: Datasheets for datasets. Commun. ACM **64**(12), 86–92 (2021). https://doi.org/10.1145/3458723
8. Hu, E.J., et al.: LoRA: low-rank adaptation of large language models. In: Tenth International Conference on Learning Representations. OpenReview (2022). https://doi.org/10.48550/arXiv.2106.09685
9. Lewis, P., et al.: Retrieval-augmented generation for knowledge-intensive NLP tasks. In: Advances in Neural Information Processing Systems, **33** Curran Associates (2020). https://doi.org/10.48550/arXiv.2005.11401
10. Nesbit, T.M., King, K.A.: The impact of fantasy football participation on NFL attendance. Atl. Econ. J. **38**(1), 95–108 (2010). https://doi.org/10.1007/s11293-009-9202-x
11. Pan, S., Luo, L., Wang, Y., Chen, C., Wang, J., Wu, X.: Unifying large language models and knowledge graphs: a roadmap. IEEE TKDE (2024). https://doi.org/10.1109/TKDE.2024.3352100
12. Schick, T., et al.: Toolformer: language models can teach themselves to use tools. In: Advances in Neural Information Processing Systems, **36** Curran Associates (2023). https://doi.org/10.48550/arXiv.2302.04761
13. Schilling, A., et al.: Querying football matches for event data: towards using large language models. In: International Sports Analytics Conference and Exhibition, pp. 216–227. Springer (2024). https://doi.org/10.1007/978-3-031-69073-0_19
14. Strand, A.T., Gautam, S., Midoglu, C., Halvorsen, P.: SoccerRAG: Multimodal soccer information retrieval via natural queries. In: CBMI 2024, pp. 1–7. IEEE (2024). https://doi.org/10.48550/arXiv.2406.01273
15. Wang, H., Salekin, M.S., Lee, J., Claytor, R., Zhang, S., Chi, M.: Agentic generative AI for media content discovery at the National Football League. In: ISACE 2025. Springer (2025). https://doi.org/10.48550/arXiv.2510.07297
16. Wang, L., et al.: A survey on large language model based autonomous agents. Front. Comp. Sci. **18**(6), 186345 (2024). https://doi.org/10.1007/s11704-024-40231-1
17. Wei, J., et al.: Chain-of-thought prompting elicits reasoning in large language models. In: Advances in Neural Information Processing Systems, **35** Curran Associates (2022). https://doi.org/10.48550/arXiv.2201.11903

18. Yao, S., et al.: ReAct: synergizing reasoning and acting in language models. In: Eleventh International Conference on Learning Representations. OpenReview (2023). https://doi.org/10.48550/arXiv.2210.03629
19. Zheng, L., et al.: Judging LLM-as-a-judge with MT-bench and Chatbot arena. In: Advances in Neural Information Processing Systems, **36** Curran Associates (2023). https://doi.org/10.48550/arXiv.2306.05685

Author Index

Z. Liu and V. Misra (Eds.): ISACE 2026, LNCS 16610, pp. 493–494, 2026.
https://doi.org/10.1007/978-3-032-27272-0

MIX
Papier aus verantwortungsvollen Quellen
Paper from responsible sources
FSC® C105338

If you have any concerns about our products,
you can contact us on
ProductSafety@springernature.com

In case Publisher is established outside the EU,
the EU authorized representative is:
Springer Nature Customer Service Center GmbH
Europaplatz 3, 69115 Heidelberg, Germany

Printed by Libri Plureos GmbH
in Hamburg, Germany